Management ——Third Edition

Basic Elements of
Managing Organizations

Management
Third Edition

Basic Elements of Managing Organizations

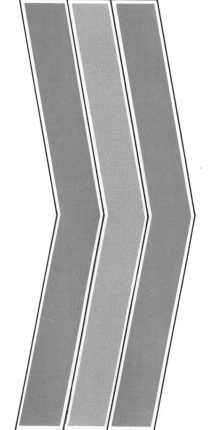

Ross A. Webber
Wharton School
University of Pennsylvania

Marilyn A. Morgan
McIntire School of Commerce
University of Virginia

Paul C. Browne
Wharton School
University of Pennsylvania

1985 Third Edition

RICHARD D. IRWIN, INC.   Homewood, Illinois   60430

© RICHARD D. IRWIN, INC., 1975, 1979, and 1985

ISBN 0-256-02841-9

Library of Congress Catalog Card No. 83–82468

Printed in the United States of America

1 2 3 4 5 6 7 8 9 0 K 2 1 0 9 8 7 6 5

Preface to the Teacher

That this book appears now in a third edition is evidence that numerous adopters have found its basic premises attractive. These premises were and continue to be:

People are the most important element in organizations.

The study of management is best approached from a basic understanding of human behavior and the influence process.

The history of management thought and its so-called schools is irrelevant to most students who are oriented toward future practice.

Most management jargon misleads rather than enlightens, so simple, common language is sufficient and desirable.

Students will pursue careers in a variety of institutions in addition to business, so these settings should be represented in the basic management course.

There are no universal management rules that apply always and everywhere, so students must develop a situational perspective on management practice.

An introduction to management should continually bridge the gap between theory and practice by offering numerous examples, cases, and student exercises.

Incorporating these judgments, this volume is a complete introduction to and survey of management. It is divided into eight parts, which examine the central elements of organizations and management.

Part One describes how the book is organized and introduces the students to the various ways of learning about organizations and management.

Part Two builds an understanding of individual needs and motivation along with the meaning or work and money to people.

Part Three demonstrates how informal groups emerge in organizations and how such groups make decisions when constituted into committees.

Part Four uses the knowledge about people and groups to survey managerial leadership and how it depends on influence which must fit the people, task, and situation involved.

Part Five thoroughly examines the core managerial functions of planning and controlling including strategic planning, specifying goals, and control through performance feedback.

Part Six discusses the design of organizational structures utilizing the classical organizational principles and newer dynamic guidelines for fitting organization, technology, and environment together.

Part Seven introduces the increasingly critical management functions of managing change and conflict.

Part Eight concludes with chapters on management careers and advice for handling problems such as role stress, frustration, black and female tokenism, and loyalty dilemmas.

Each chapter contains text, cartoons (one of the more popular features of earlier editions), review questions, and a section of notes and references on literature in the field. Each part ends with discussion questions, individual exercises for students to perform, and three cases for analysis.

The notes and references sections at the conclusion of each chapter were well received by instructors who adopted earlier editions. These sections include additional discussions of certain topics, descriptions of terms and concepts from the great contributors to management thought, and extensive quotations and citations. This feature lends flexibility to the book because less advanced students can use only the text while others are directed to the review questions, notes and references, discussion questions, and exercises.

The cases are set in a wide variety of institutions—including manufacturing, banking, insurance, hospitals, social work agencies, universities, and government. One half of the cases are new to this edition; most of the other half from the revised edition have been supplemented with new parts detailing more information, including subsequent events. Thus well over half the cases are "sequential cases" because the Instructor's Manual contains a "Part B" and sometimes a "Part C," which can be removed and reproduced for student use in comparing his or her recommendations with management's actions. This iterative process provides an exciting supplement to case learning.

Student response to earlier editions has been enthusiastic. From the beginning, adopters have written that students *read* the book. Students read the book because the topics are interesting and the prose simple; ideas are presented without confusing jargon, categorical hairsplitting, and needless name citations. The simplicity is deceptive, however, because the complex issues of modern management are well covered and extensive reference sections cite the relevant literature.

The most important addition to this volume is that two co-authors have joined the original author. Marilyn Morgan brings her experience in teaching, research, and practice to the behavioral topics including motivation, leadership, and career development. Paul Browne's experience is in management planning, policy, and control. Since writing the first edition, Ross Webber has benefited from continuing experience as a senior executive serving as Vice President of the University of Pennsylvania. This experience has been helpful in bridging the gap between theory and practice. Our joint effort has been to present an exciting text that is honest and thorough.

Ross A. Webber
Marilyn A. Morgan
Paul C. Browne

Contents

Management
Third Edition

Basic Elements of
Managing Organizations

Part One

Studying Management

CHAPTER 1 〉〉〉
A Preface for the Student

CHAPTER 2 〉〉〉
How We Know What We Know about Management

1

A Preface for the Student

Are you a squirrel or a human being? Well, of course you will reply that you are not a squirrel because you don't have four legs, large incisors, and a bushy tail. But physical attributes are not the critical difference. Rather, it is that you can transcend time.[1]* We may be the only creatures able to lift ourselves imaginatively above the flow of time, project ourselves into the future, and visualize "the future as history."[2] That is, we can conjure up a history that has not yet occurred—and then work to bring it to life. The squirrel gathering October's nuts is not really anticipating the winter cold but is responding to internal genetic instructions based on the sunlight's duration. As humans we have fewer genetic rules, so we must think about the future.

Picture an artist in your mind. She looks at nature and strives to translate its essence onto a canvas. Most painters don't reproduce what they see but filter it through a concept in their brain. This image of a future painting is then brought to present reality with paint and brush, creating a work of art that will live on into the future.

To be a manager is to behave much like the artist. You look at human needs and conceive of ways to satisfy them; then you apply resources to create an organization that will produce the desired goods and services. It is this working through an organization, however, that sharply distinguishes most artists from managers. Artists usually work alone; managers work with other people.

The process of managing is the human process of visualizing the future applied to a collection of individual humans in an organization. Human behavior, human decisions, human relations, and human dreams are at the core. The principles of management are not impersonal abstractions from economics, mathematics, mechanics, or geometry. Rather, we can hope to comprehend management only by understanding people.[3]

How This Book Is Organized

The organization of this book reflects the centrality of people in the process. That is, we start with individual motivation, then deal with people at work as individuals and then in groups. As groups grow in size, human relations and the leader's role become increasingly important so that the group as an organization can accomplish its objectives. The book's eight parts reflect this expansion from individual to group to organization:

Part One describes how the book is organized and reviews how we can learn about organizations and management.

Part Two builds an understanding of individual needs and motivation along with the meaning of work and money to various people.

Part Three demonstrates how informal groups emerge in organizations and how such groups make decisions when constituted into committees.

---

* Notes and references will be found at the end of this chapter.

Reprinted by permission: Tribune Company Syndicate, Inc.

FIGURE 1–1

Organization of the Book

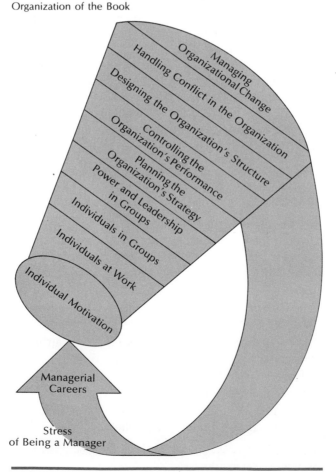

Part Four uses the knowledge about people to survey managerial leadership and how it depends on influence that must fit the people, task, and situation involved.

Part Five thoroughly examines the core managerial functions of planning and controlling, including strategic planning, specifying goals, and control through performance feedback.

Part Six discusses the design of organizational structures utilizing the classical organizational principles and the newer dynamic guidelines for fitting organization, technology, and environment together.

Part Seven introduces the increasingly critical management functions of managing change and conflict.

Part Eight concludes with chapters on management careers and advice for handling such problems as role stress, frustration, black and/or female tokenism, political insensitivity, and loyalty dilemmas.

Figure 1–1 summarizes these topics and shows how we make a complete circle from understanding the individual to considering the problems of the individual manager.

Each chapter contains text, cartoons, review questions, and a section of notes and references on literature in the field. These include additional discussions of certain topics, descriptions of terms and concepts from the great contributors to management thought, and extensive quotations and citations.

Each part ends with discussion questions, individual exercises for students to perform, and three cases for analysis. The cases are set in a wide variety of institutions, including manufacturing, banking, insurance, hospitals, social work agencies, universities, and government.[4]

Obviously, the authors believe that studying management can help you become an effective manager. However, we shall see that not everyone agrees! Therefore, let's look at managerial education and some skepticism about it.

How Managers Are Educated

Managers are increasingly well educated—or at least, they are going to school longer than did their predecessors.

A recent survey examined top-management succession.[5] Of the executives surveyed, 86 percent were college graduates; 33 percent of these held undergraduate

FIGURE 1–2

Education of Top Business Executives

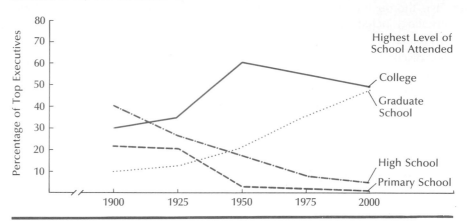

degrees in business; 27 percent in engineering, 13 percent in economics, 12 percent in social science, 11 percent in science and mathematics, and 4 percent in other fields. The trend appears to be toward engineering and science graduates.[6] Today, probably more than 90 percent of executives at the top of American corporations have attended college. Thirty years ago, as shown in Figure 1–2, this would have been less than 50 percent, and 80 years ago only 40 percent.[7] Only in Japan and the Soviet Union do college graduates now constitute a larger proportion of managers.[8] It is clear that a college degree is increasingly becoming essential. Those blue- and white-collar employees without college education in the pyramid are finding it more and more difficult to become supervisors and managers.[9]

Skepticism about Management Education

Not everyone agrees that college is helpful for learning to manage. In the stage show and movie *How to Succeed in Business without Really Trying,* the World Wide Wicket Corporation is near bankruptcy. Its new television show has been a fiasco; the public and competitors are laughing at the corporation's ineptitude; and a potential loss of millions of dollars looms. In the final scene of this imaginary tale, Wally Wumper, the self-educated, former window washer who is now the firm's owner, criticizes the stereotypic "old ivy" grad who is the company president. Voicing the time-honored American feeling of the self-made success toward the school-educated, of the practitioner toward the theoretician, Wally exclaims: "I should have expected this from a college man!"

Recently we encountered a similar attiude at a college reunion. We all exchanged the normal remarks on increasing girth, growing families, and career achievement. One former classmate was an amazingly successful entrepreneur with no exposure to business or economic courses. When he asked what we did, we explained that we taught management at a business school. His incredulous response was: "You teach management from *books?*" In defense, we gave him an argument on how intuitive management is no longer sufficient, that all practical people assume theories that they should examine, and that increasing complexity requires greater understanding of the determinants of managerial behavior. He remained unconvinced.

The suggestion of both Abe Burrow's fictional character and our real-life under-40 financial genius is that business success depends upon innate ability, common sense, and work experience, not on book knowledge, theory, and classroom discussion. There is some validity in the practical person's skepticism concerning the teaching of management.

Experience versus Training

Some classic statements of the advantages of experience over training have come from the Orient. An old Japanese text states: "Is it not true that one hundred years' training in a heavenly paradise does not compare with one day's work in the earthly world?" A 1,500-year-old Chinese manuscript observes: "Those who can manage the dykes and rivers are the same in all ages; they did not learn this business from Yu the Great, they learnt it from the waters. . . . Those who can think learnt from themselves and not from the Sages."[10]

No school, professor, or book can make you a manager. Only you can do this, and you can become a manager only by managing. Of course, you can learn skills that will be extremely helpful, particularly in such clearly defined areas as accounting, statistics, law, and finance. But these will not make you a manager; experience is the only teacher. Experience, however, is not a uniformly effective teacher. An old aphorism criticizes the person who has worked for 20 years but has only reexperienced the first year 20 times. Learning is not automatic.

One learns from experience only by testing that experience against tentative generalizations made for guidance in the future. What a school can do, and what this book intends to do, is to provide you with some insights and intellectual tools to be applied against your experience. Such application may help you to learn more fully and more quickly. Your instructor cannot make you into a manager, but he or she can help you to prepare yourself for that goal.

Practice versus Theory

Most of you are practical people; certainly most managers are. You are more concerned about doing things than thinking about them, more concerned with action than with contemplation. Most business students and managers are uneasy about theory. It is abstract and difficult, too unrelated to real problems, it seems, too "academic" and just plain "too theoretical." The word *theory* itself implies a criticism. Yet, we shall and must consider theory in a stimulating way, we hope. Theory is important because you and all men and women of action are also theorists. No matter how pragmatic you consider yourself, no matter how rooted in reality managers view themselves, you and they operate on theories. You all possess your own theories about motivation, authority, objectives, and change, among other concepts.[11]

We are not selling theories. We will not attempt to convince you that democratic management is better than authoritarian management or vice versa, or that centralization is better than decentralization or vice versa. Our intent in discussing theory is to expose you to others' views so that, as you confront your experience, you can

Tensions in Studying
Management
experience ⟷ training
practice ⟷ theory
art ⟷ science

clarify and develop *your own theories.* You will need them—and you will have them whether you know it or not.[12] You will be a better manager if you are aware of your assumptions and if you examine them periodically and modify them when necessary. Nothing is as practical as a good theory.

Art versus Science

Management encompasses both science and art. In designing and constructing plans and products, management must draw on technology and physical science, of course, and as much of this book will demonstrate, the behavioral sciences can also contribute to management.[13] Nonetheless, management is not all science. However much you hear about "scientific management" or "management science," in handling people and managing organizations it is necessary to draw on intuition and subjective judgment. The science portion of management is expanding; more and more decisions can be analyzed and programmed, particularly with mathematics. But although the artistic side of management may be declining in its proportion of the whole process, it will remain a central and critical portion of your future jobs.[14] In short:

Knowledge (science) without skill (art) is useless, or dangerous.

Skill (art) without knowledge (science) means stagnancy and inability to pass on learning.[15]

Like the physician, the manager is a practitioner. As the doctor draws on basic sciences of chemistry, biology, and physiology, the business executive draws on the sciences of mathematics, psychology, and sociology. The manager, again like the physician, does not find all answers in science. Science does not tell the manager everything he or she needs to know, and the manager cannot wait until it does so but must act *now.* Managers must go beyond what is known with certainty to what is only hazily perceived. Every practitioner draws on science and then makes an act of faith by leaping into the unknown, not blindly and incautiously, but leaping nonetheless.[16]

Increasing Difficulty of Management

Back in the early 1960s, a prominent educator-political leader observed that the youth of America were being innoculated with a certain "antivaccine" of leadership because schools gave them the impression that university officials, corporation executives, and politicians were corrupted by power, compromise, and status seeking.[17] The implied result was a bias against striving for leadership because to do so was somehow wrong. More recently, concern has been expressed about a crisis of management and flight from leadership.[18] This purportedly stems less from a moral distaste for the role than fear of its difficulty. And make no mistake about it: Management is becoming increasingly difficult in all kinds of institutions. Increased consciousness and greater participation in decision making have led to much greater conflict within organizations. These pressures impinge on the leaders and demand more sophisticated political skills than in the old days when the boss could just order subordinates to jump or else.

The Will to Manage

To be an effective manager thus requires modern interpersonal ability *and* old-fashioned willpower. Unfortunately, modern people seem unable to control themselves. Rapid communications make the world seem big and impersonal, and many events are reported over which individuals appear to exercise little or no control. Because schools teach something about how economics, psychology, and sociology explore the forces determining human behavior, many are quick to attribute others' behavior to "their background," an "inferiority complex," or a "traumatic experience." Or we blame our parents and their overprotectiveness for our inability to deal with the world's complexities. Some are very glib about this attitude, but much of the time it is a big cop-out.

We are not saying that humans are totally free. Behavioral science is helpful in explaining psychological and behavioral problems that affect a person's freedom of will. Nonetheless, neither are humans automatons. However influential the past and present environment, the individual is not completely determined. Leadership and management imply more than deterministic response to external factors; they also involve free choice and creative expression—in short, the acting out of the human will. To be an effective manager, one must possess a certain will to manage.[19] In addition, one must have the capacity to use what is helpful from science but the courage to act when everything is not known with certainty.

The Need for Managers

Many people today believe that large organizations are omnipotent, that they can always work their will and will automatically be successful without effort on the part of members.[20] Accompanying a dislike for big organizations is the assumption that they are machines which are guaranteed success by virtue of their size and momentum.

It would of course, take monumental mistakes to drive such a corporation as American Telephone and Telegraph to failure. Success seems so automatic that goofing off by the manager of the Northwest Chicago office, for example, could not do much harm. But not many years ago the same thing might have been said about the Pennsylvania Railroad. At one time it was the largest and most profitable corporation in the country; in time, it went bankrupt.

Yes, to the individual, organizations do appear omnipotent and independent of his or her own contribution. But, no, they are not automatic machines in which individual effort means nothing. We must have leader-managers who can recognize and live with this awareness, who can bridge the gap between individuals and organizations and demonstrate the importance of one to the other. The scope of the world's and America's problems is such that they will only be solved through large organizations. Managers in large public and private businesses, governments, and nonprofit institutions will play the central role in mobilizing and directing the human and material resources that are necessary to cure the conditions about which so many are concerned, young and old alike.

It is true that many governmental and business organizations seem to be out of control, pursuing their own interests at the expense of society, and many schools and hospitals seem to treat students and patients as if they existed for the institution, instead of the reverse. These ills exist, but this is no reason to reject organizations and shun the effort to manage them. Rather, we hope your course of study will provide you with the managerial tools to bring errant institutions under control, to make organizations work for people.

So you may or may not want to be a big business executive. You may or may not desire to climb the organizational ladder. Either choice is honorable. But we hope that you will want to be a leader in whatever organizations or institutions you find yourself and that you will be willing to assume the burdens of management in return for its rewards.

Notes and References on A Preface for the Student

1. R. Niebuhr, *The Nature and Destiny of Man* (New York: Charles Scribner's Sons, 1949).

2. R. Heilbroner, *The Future as History,* (New York: Harper & Row, 1960).

3. For a stirring affirmation of the continued centrality of people in organizations in the future, see W. H. Peterson, "The Future and the Futurists," *Harvard Business Review,* November–December 1967, pp. 168–85.

4. For an argument that management varies widely in different institutions, see M. D. Fottler, "Is Management Really Generic?" *Academy of Management Review* 6, no. 1 (1981), pp. 1–12.

5. F. A. Bond and A. W. Swinyard, "Report on Management Succession: Top Executive Positions" (Ann Arbor: Graduate School of Business Administration, University of Michigan, 1973). Of managers promoted to the post of chief executive officer in 1979, 98.9 percent were men; only 1.2 percent were minority. Twenty-five percent had MBA degrees; their average salary was $134,000, and they worked 57.5 hours per week. "The Organization Man, Continued," *Newsweek,* October 23, 1980.

6. B. S. Gilmer, "The Engineer: Business's New Elite," *Business Today,* Summer 1969, pp. 43–46.

7. On changing backgrounds and education of executives, see F. W. Taussig and C. S. Joslyn, *American Business Leaders: A Study in Social Origins and Social Stratification* (New York: Macmillan, 1932); W. Miller, ed., *Men in Business: Essays in the History of Entrepreneurship* (Cambridge, Mass.: Harvard University Press, 1942); M. Newcomer, *The Big Business Executive* (New York: Columbia University Press, 1955); W. L. Warner and J. C. Abegglen, *Big Business Leaders in America* (New York: Harper & Row, 1955); C. Wright Mills, *The Power Elite* (New York: Oxford University Press, 1956); and M. Newcomer, "The Big Business Executive—1965" *Scientific American,* 1965.

8. H. C. de Bettignies, "Managerial Background and Attitudes in a Comparative Perspective," in *Comparative Management,* ed. J. Boddewyn (New York: Graduate School of Business Administration, New York University, 1970).

9. K. Hooper, "The Growing Use of College Graduates as Foremen," *Management of Personnel Quarterly,* Summer 1967, pp. 2–12.

10. These sayings are quoted in J. T. Fraser, *The Voices of Time* (New York: Braziller, 1966), pp. 39 and 164. Business Schools are sometimes criticized for overemphasizing the theoretical. See "The Money Chase," *Time,* May 4, 1981, pp. 58–69.

11. C. R. Christensen of Harvard Business School observes, "Our theory is that management skills are largely self-discovered," adding that Harvard students are assumed to be bright enough to absorb theory from books and apply it in practice. He likens the teaching of management to the surgeon-cadaver type of medical instruction, conducted in an atmosphere in which students can make mistakes and learn without too much worry about immediate consequences. "The Executive Needs a Catholicity of Interest," *Business Week,* May 4, 1974, p. 54.

According to S. P. Robbins, conflict is the area where there is the most difference between what is taught as management theory and what actually exists in organizations. Therefore, power and conflict must be central topics in studying management—as they are in this book. See "Reconciling Management Theory with Management Practice," *Business Horizons,* February 1977, pp. 38–47.

On the difficulty of bringing theory and practice together, see W. J. Duncan, "Transferring Management Theory to Practice," *Academy of Management Journal,* December 1974, pp. 724–38; and H. Mintzberg, "The Manager's Job: Folklore and Fact," *Harvard Business Review,* July–August 1975, pp. 49–62.

R. J. House warns teachers that if they are solely concerned with practice and relevance, their students will become prisoners of the past and ill-suited to develop new ways of thinking when confronting future problems. "The Quest for Relevance in Management Education: Some Second Thoughts and Undesired Consequences," *Academy of Management Journal,* June 1975, pp. 323–33.

12. Douglas MacGregor, formerly a professor at M.I.T., wrote: "It is possible to have more or less adequate theoretical assumptions; it is not possible to reach a managerial action uninfluenced by assumptions, whether adequate or not." *The Human Side of Enterprise* (New York: McGraw-Hill, 1960), p. 7. Commenting on the influence of economic theory on pragmatic statesmen, the famous economist John Maynard Keynes wrote: "Practical men, who believe themselves to be quite exempt from any intellectual influence, are usually the slaves of some defunct economist. Madmen in authority, who hear voices in the air, are distilling their frenzy from some academic scribbler of a few years back." *The General Theory of Employment, Interest and Money* (New York: Harcourt Brace Jovanovich, 1936), p. 383.

13. The increase of behavioral content in basic management texts has been striking in the last decade. See C. Aronoff, "The Rise of the Behavioral Perspective in Selected General Management Textbooks," *Academy of Management Journal,* December 1975, pp. 753–68.

14. For an argument that management is an art and therefore business should train young managers just as artists are trained, see H. M. Boettinger, "Is Management Really an Art?" *Harvard Business Review,* January–February 1975, pp. 54–64.

15. This distinction between knowledge and skill is one that is identified with the Harvard Graduate School of Business Administration and its case orientation. See Edward Learned et al., *Business Policy: Text and Cases* (Homewood, Ill.' Richard D. Irwin, 1965); J. D. Glover and R. M. Hower, *The Administrator: Cases on Human Relations in Business,* 4th ed. (Homewood, Ill.: Richard D. Irwin, 1963), and A. R. Towl, *To Study Administration by Cases* (Boston: Harvard University Press, 1969).

16. D. A. Kolb observes, "Managerial education will not be improved by eliminating theoretical analysis or relevant case problems. Improvement will come through integration of the scholarly and practical learning styles." "Management and the Learning Process," *California Management Review,* Spring 1976, pp. 21–31. Several management schools are experimenting with ways of encouraging intuitive and creative approaches to management because of feelings that systematic and logical thinking can lead only so far. See "B-School Buzzword: Creativity," *Business Week,* August 8, 1977, p. 66.

For further discussion of the relation between behavioral science and management, see R. A. Webber, "Behavioral Science and Management: Why the Troubled Marriage?" *Proceedings of the Academy of Management 1970,* pp. 377–95; D. Hampton, C. Summer, and Ross A. Webber, *Organizational Behavior and the Practice of Management* (Glenview, Ill.: Scott, Foresman, 1968); F. J. Roethlisberger, "Contributions of the Behavioral Sciences to a General Theory of Management," paper presented to the Seminar on Management Theory and Research, U.C.L.A. Graduate School of Business Administration, November 1962; and F. Massarik and B. E. Krueger, "Through the Labyrinth: An Approach to Reading in Behavioral Science," *California Management Review,* December 1970, p. 70.

17. John Gardner wrote, "In the minds of some, leadership is associated with goals that are distasteful—power, profit, efficiency, and the like. But leadership, properly conceived, also serves the individual human goals that our society values so highly, and we shall not achieve those goals without it." "The Antileadership Vaccine," *Annual Report,* Carnegie Corporation of New York (1965).

18. J. B. Miner, "The Real Crunch in Managerial Manpower," *Harvard Business Review,* November–December 1973, pp. 146–58; W. G. Bennis, "Where Have All the Leaders Gone?" *The McKinsey Quarterly,* Autumn 1977, pp. 32–45.

19. For a discussion of will, see R. May, *Love and Will* (New York: W. W. Norton, 1969). Marvin Bower, a former senior partner of McKinsey and Company management consultants wrote a book titled, *The Will to Manage* (New York: McGraw–Hill, 1966).

20. Professor John Monro, former Dean of Harvard College, has observed that the difficulty with students turns on their expectations that institutions can work their will—whether that be educating or governing or anything else—irrespective of the individual effort invested. Whereas a generation ago survival was perceived by the young as a function of their diligence, students today are fooled by affluence and by a benign environment into believing that institutions will provide for them always. Interview by M. Frankel in the *New York Times,* July 24, 1972.

2

How We Know What We Know about Management

How do we know anything about management and organizations? Other than experience, are there any sources from which you can learn about management? Many exist, but unfortunately all of them suffer from certain weaknesses. We shall consider these sources roughly in the chronological order of their development: studying history, current observation, and systematic experimentation.[1]*

Studying History

The oldest approach to learning about management is to study how it was done in the past—from books, from listening to successful leaders, or from interviewing those currently on top about how they did it.

Management in Other Institutions

The writings of ancient, medieval, and modern historians, from Herodotus to Machiavelli to Schlesinger, have been culled for insights into administration for armies, churches, and kingdoms.[2] It is assumed that practice that has been successful in one institution will be applicable in another. It is also assumed that history has its uses, that the lessons of the past can offer guidelines to the present. Certainly, historical parallels can never be drawn without risk, but it is hoped that general lessons can be extracted, even from organizations long ago and far away. Studying how the Romans solved their control problems, over long distances and with inferior communication facilities, can have implications for the geographically dispersed corporation of today.

In some countries, this has been the only way to study management. In the Great Britian of the past, education for managerial leadership rested on immersing the young boy in the political and military history of his country.[3] Such great leaders as Wellington and Disraeli were examined, and such great events as Trafalgar and World War I were analyzed. This background, combined with the socialization process at the boarding schools wealthy young gentlemen attended, was thought to be the way to groom a future manager-leader who could lead in any setting or institution. His breeding, character, and training supposedly would convey confidence and leadership intuition.

We, and Great Britain, have less faith in the efficacy of this approach now, but it was remarkably successful for a long time. The study of history and other institutions *is* relevant to fledgling business or nonbusiness managers. The question nonetheless arises whether or not the experience of other institutions is applicable to a manager's present situation and a student's future organization. We have become increasingly skeptical of the universality of management and more aware of the differences between management under differing conditions. One style may be appropriate and effective in one setting but not in another. Therefore, simple application of a past hero's practice to your particular difficulty may be dangerous. Neither Dwight Eisenhower's nor George Patton's style may be helpful in your own business (because you have many competitors, not one enemy; because you have a militant union

---

* Notes and references will be found at the end of this chapter.

to deal with, not draftees; because you are short, fat, and shy and do not exude a command presence). What these illustrious generals did in World War II may even have had limited relevance for a captain in Vietnam. The wars were different, the enlisted personnel had different expectations, and the nation's support in the latter case was more questionable.

Extrapolation from the past and from other institutions is an old approach to management education. It still has some validity, and it is probably overly ignored by today's business students.[4] Nonetheless, its lessons usually carry only limited applicability to the present and to a particular organization. Time and setting do affect what is appropriate in management.

Problems in Learning from Other Institutions
- Is this past relevant to the present?
- Is the institutional experience transferable to another setting?
- Do you possess different personal attributes?

Practitioners Tell of Their Experience

Today's student cannot talk to Napoleon and Joan of Arc to learn their leadership secrets, but perhaps he or she can listen to a living manager who has been successful. In approaching business education, this is the solution of many schools; they hire a retired executive to tell the young aspirants how it is—or more exactly, how it was for the executive. This approach also has a long history. The earliest books specifically about managing business were written by practitioners.[5] Successful executives described what they did, based on common sense and intuition. The better practitioner-writers did more than just describe; they distilled the essence of their experience to suggest practices that seemed most critical and generally applicable. Eighty years ago, the president of a French mining concern described the basic functions of the manager: planning, controlling, directing, staffing.[6] Fifty years ago the president of New Jersey Bell Telephone analyzed the necessity for subordinates' acceptance of a superior's authority if the latter was to possess any real influence.[7] Twenty years ago, a longtime chief executive of General Motors discussed the need for top management to have independent communications about the activities of dispersed units in a large coporation (that is, the top managers should not rely exclusively on what their subordinates tell them).[8]

As logical and direct as this approach seems, it presents problems. Colleges that have hired retired executives as professors have not always been pleased. In the first place, many managers are not very articulate about what they have done as managers. They are so busy doing (and rightly so) that they have little time to think about how they are doing it. In addition, since they are achievement-oriented men and women, they are inclined to be neither introspective about their intentions nor analytical about their plans. Their talks and writings often are not helpful to students because they are superficial and overly rational. It frequently sounds as if the manager had had everything thought out in advance, events are so planned and controlled. Somehow the emotion, conflict, blood, sweat, and tears of real organizational life are drained from the practitioner's account. Consequently, students can be misled into learning the wrong lessons.[9]

Another problem with the older practitioner-teachers is the fact that they are older. Their experience looks backward to a fairly narrow past. They tell about things as they were 30 years ago when they were successfully climbing the ladder

Problems in Learning from Practitioners
- Are they aritculate and truthful?
- Are explanations superficial and overly rational?
- Is the past and limited experience relevant?
- Is the experience transferable to another setting?

"I can't say I've profited from my own mistakes. Mostly I've profited from others' mistakes."

From *The Wall Street Journal* with permission of Cartoon Features Syndicate.

in just a few organizations. Thus their insight may not be applicable to the present situation, and their organizations may not be similar to those of the students.

Practitioners have been writing about their experiences for many years. Because some of this material is valuable and interesting, this approach to learning about management is still with us; examples will be found throughout this volume. Unfortunately, much of the practitioner literature is oversimplified, overrationalized, and too dependent on a particular "common sense" that is neither universal nor common. Finally, many practitioners turned writer-lecturers are just plain boring.

Interviewers Ask Many Practitioners

Recognizing that practitioners frequently cannot articulate their particular experiences, an early improvement in management literature was derived from energetic interviewer-researchers who spoke with many managers in many organizations. Thus the sample size was vastly expanded and it is hoped, the writing was done by a talented communicator who could organize the various insights of successful managers. Drawing on the experiences of many individuals, the creative researchers attempted to distill varied experiences into more general conclusions. Indeed, the aim of these researchers, who are mainly professors in business schools, has been to develop a set of general "principles of management and organization."

More books about management have followed this approach than any other. For approximately 60 years, academicians have been drawing on their talks with practitioners in writing textbooks designed to train students and assist other practitioners.[10] In the 1930s a little book, *Papers on the Science of Administration,* summarized all of the general "principles" that then seemed to characterize researchers' descriptions of successful managerial practice.[11] It was believed that these were universal principles that applied to all organizations. Thus in 1946 when President Harry Truman appointed former President Herbert Hoover as chairman of a commission to examine administration in the U.S. government, the committee drew up a voluminous report (19 books now resting on library shelves, mostly unread) that compared the government against each of these principles. In general, the executive branch was found to be violating most of them.

That little book represented the high point in the study of management; we have been going downhill ever since! Not that we know less about management than we did then. Rather, we are less certain about what we know. We are less certain that the so-called principles are in fact principles; less certain that principles derived from past practices of successful executives (mainly in manufacturing companies) are applicable today in different kinds of business and organizations (or indeed in manufacturing concerns producing different kinds of sophisticated products with different types of people).

In short, like extrapolation from the past and learning directly from practitioners, this approach looks backward to a history and a distilled experience that may not be applicable to you in the future in your particular organizations. Nonetheless, we do not want to be too critical because the largest selling management books are still in this tradition. Students and managers do find them useful.[12] The best authors recognize the situational nature of their recommendations. Therefore, learning from practitioners as interpreted and organized by academic interviewers-researchers is still very important and is much used. You should be aware of its limitations, however.

Observing Current Organizations

Instead of looking at past successes, we can examine how current organizations and managers behave by actually observing them on the job. One approach is to work in a firm and record what you see. Another is to perform systematic field research by observing and interviewing as events unfold.

Participant-Observers Report

Anthropologists have studied the Samoans and Zunis by living among them for extended periods while systematically observing their customs and behavior.[13] So it has been with some organizational scholars.[14] A sociologist, for example, has become an automobile worker laboring alongside subjects, visiting in their homes, and hoisting beers and bowling with them in the evening. Drawing on training and organizing his insights around various conceptual ideas and theories, the sociologist was able to probe the reality of life on the line, rather than trusting to the selective memory of practitioners to tell them how they thought it was.[15]

This approach is exciting; it frequently seems to catch the joy, stress, and heartache of reality, in contrast to the abstract principles of some other approaches. Thus the theory that managers always pursue maximum profit is contradicted by the participant-observer's recognition that most harried managers don't even know how many of their decisions affect profits. Other things are more important to a department head, who is more concerned about meeting a quota, controlling rejects, and forestalling arguments than about profits per se. The department head assumes that success-

Problems in Learning from Interviews of Many Practitioners

• Were the practitioners truthful?

• Were they overly rational?

• Is the past experience relevant?

• Is their experience transferable to another setting?

fully dealing with these problems will increase profits but is not really sure. Similarly, a theory that blue-collar workers are primarily interested in money is contradicted by the participant-observer who quickly learns not to produce as much as he or she can under the incentive plan. Fellow employees are concerned about working themselves out of a job, getting the rate cut, and disrupting friendships on the job.

The main weakness of the participant-observer approach is that it usually offers a bottom-up view of the world. Most participant-observers have worked at low-level, blue-collar positions. The Ph.D. candidate or college teacher can obtain an assembly line job fairly easily but cannot become vice president of manufacturing so easily. Therefore, research and insights have dealt mainly with lower organizational levels. This has provided useful balance to the high-level concentration of previous approaches to management, which tended to present naive views of life lower down. Nonetheless, we suffer from a lack of participant-observer insights on managerial behavior. At this level, the work of some novelists and dramatists is helpful, but rare.[16]

Because of their individualized and subjective insights, participant-observer reports can be misleading. They describe reality, but only as perceived by one person. This person brings certain expectations and perceptual biases to his or her observations. Having been trained in a particular academic discipline, the person may be dangerously narrow in applying only the tools of that discipline and ignoring others. Thus a study of manufacturing workers by sociologists may catch the dynamics of social life and power relationships but fail to indicate that an economic recession occurred during their observation. Such an event would affect employees worried about their jobs, but research focusing on psychological or sociological variables may miss it.[17]

Finally, participant research is difficult to perform; it requires prior training and prolonged immersion in the organization. This means that a researcher will probably only study a few organizations in his or her career (perhaps only the one for the Ph.D. thesis). Thus such researchers tend to be younger people with only limited personal experience and with idealistic expectations. This gives them the advantage of fresh perspectives but reduces their ability to provide practical advice for managers.

Problems in Learning from Participant-Observers
- Is the bottom-up view distorted?
- Is the perception too narrow and subjective?
- Can we generalize from limited observation?
- Is the research difficult and limited?
- Is the experience transferable to another setting?

Systematic Field Research in Organizations

In the effort to bring some of the analytical rigor of the physical sciences to the study of management, systematic observation by trained observers was introduced. The researcher (an academic scholar, staff psychologist, or company personnel staff) does not depend solely on what people say; he or she also interviews peers, subordinates and superiors, managers and workers. Such interview research is similar to the good journalist who checks stories from a variety of sources to reduce bias and approach the truth. The insightful field researcher, however, can also analyze and comment, based upon specialized training and knowledge of theory.

An even more penetrating research scheme may include studying documents and administering questionnaires, which are less subject to intentional and unintentional distortion than interviews. Using questionnaires, the researchers can vastly increase the number of people from whom they gather data. This data can be organized, analyzed, and interpreted to transform it into meaningful information for managerial students, scholars, and practitioners.

Finally, and most desirably, researchers actually observe daily and hourly behavior. Their own perceptions of what transpired can be compared with others' recollections and interpretations. Systematic observation of actual communications (who talks to whom, who initiates, who responds, on what issues, and so forth) can be extremely helpful in understanding the actual process of management. The aim of the observer is to describe reality as truly as possible, to pick out the recurring patterns, and to analyze for associative or causative conditions—in short, to learn what causes what in order to predict.

In spite of the great advantages in probing reality that this approach possesses over practitioner reports and interviews, field observation has some important problems. First, as with participant observation, researchers bring certain perspectives to their observations. They cannot observe everything; reality is too confusing for this. Consequently, they tend to see things that fit their intellectual orientation toward psychology or sociology. Other elements of reality, such as economics and technology, may be slighted.[18]

Problems in Learning from Field Research

- Are the observations too narrow?
- Did unobserved events affect results?
- Have sufficient people and organizations been observed?
- Did the research change the organization?
- Are the findings transferable to another setting?

In addition, although field observers can observe a sizable number of people in one organization, this consumes much time. They are unlikely to study many organizations, even during an entire career. Thus the sample size may be smaller for field observers than for the researcher who merely interviews or collects questionnaires from many managers and organizations.

The biggest weakness of field observation, however, is that recurring relationships between factors (such as between worker productivity and manager leadership style) may be hidden by conditions that the researcher may not even know about. Some past unknown event may still generate such fear that people conform obediently when there is no apparent reason, or the mere presence of the researcher may change what he or she is trying to observe. If a professor talking with workers is the first person who has ever demonstrated any interest in their views, morale and performance may temporarily improve, and the research findings will be distorted.[19]

Systematic Experimentation

Field observers are somewhat passive. They endeavor systematically and reliably to record reality for later analysis. Sometimes this yields great insights, but too often the observers find that they have not gathered data that can be applied to structured hypotheses and conclusions, as in physical science. Therefore, like the physical scientists, they would like to experiment—either in organizations or in the laboratory.

Experiments in Organizations

An experiment reflects the scientist's intention to manipulate one factor while maintaining all other factors unchanged in order to observe what happens. For example, in the 18th century the first modern chemist observed a candle burning. He then covered the candle with an airtight glass container and saw that the flame was extinguished. By observing the changed result from this simple manipulation, the experimenter concluded that something in the atmosphere is necessary for combustion.

In a similar manner the experimenter attempts to change an organizational factor and observe what happens. Early experiments included modifying such physical work factors as lighting, rest periods, and ventilation and then measuring the change in productivity. More sophisticated field experiments have included efforts to change a company's managerial climate to authoritarian in some departments and participative in others and then compare productivity.[20]

The experimental approach is attractive to managerial scholars who dream of discovering highly predictable relationships similar to those in physics and chemistry. You will read about several important insights gained from such research. This approach is still with us, still developing, and still promising. Nonetheless, the field experimental approach has not produced the breadth of managerial knowledge hoped for. It has problems mainly because no scholar experimenting on a real business can dominate the experiment to the degree that the scientist can in the laboratory. First, while the experimenter endeavors to manipulate only one variable, other factors over which he or she has no control may change. Economic recession may occur, a competitor may announce a new product that hurts the experimental company, a union may strike, government legislation may hinder the company, or any number of events may occur in the firm's turbulent environment that will mask the effect of the researcher's manipulation.

In addition, as with observation, the mere presence of the researcher can have an unintended impact on people. They may behave differently just because the experimenter is there, and this distortion may be increased if employees know that an experiment is being conducted. The results may not mean much. A classic early research effort found that improved lighting was followed by increased worker productivity, but so was decreased lighting! The people apparently just enjoyed being the subjects of the experiment.

Finally, management and organizational research are not happy bedfellows.[21] Managers are concerned with performance and results, not scientific contributions. They are not hospitable to management research in general, particularly if there is any chance that experimentation would harm efficiency or profits. Management and science subscribe to different values. Consequently, the researcher may find managers interfering with work, changing factors that the researcher wants to remain unchanged, or even asking the researcher to quietly and quickly depart from the premises. For all these reasons, relatively few good organizational experiments have been conducted, and fewer have been reported.

Problems in Learning from Organizational Experiments
- Were the variables measured too restricted?
- Did unobserved factors affect the results?
- Did the research affect the results?
- Are the results transferable to another setting?

Experiments in the Laboratory

The final step in the effort to emulate physical science is the behavioral scientist's laboratory experimentation on human subjects. By this we do not mean a mad scientist conducting bizarre experiments on helpless, unwilling subjects, but a management scholar working with small voluntary groups (five is most common) in a normal classroom. The group may make decisions and endeavor to perform tasks presented to them. The experimenter can vary the tasks, modify the group composition, change the ways that the group can communicate, and revise the rewards. Since the groups are short lived (usually just a few hours), and since they are isolated in the classroom, few external conditions can affect them and distort the experiment. This research technique allows greater control, larger samples, and more thorough measurement because it is a simpler situation than a real company. The researcher can systematically vary one element and observe effects on behavior and performance that can threaten management.

Problems in Learning from
Laboratory Experiments

• Were the observations
  too restricted?

• Were the people typical?

• Was the situation
  artificial?

• Can the results be
  extrapolated to real
  organizations?

Experimental conditions make laboratory research attractive to management scholars, and much research has been conducted. We shall examine the research that is relevant. Nonetheless, laboratory research is not the final solution to learning about management and organizations. Like all other approaches, it has limitations. The chief drawback is its artificiality. Extending its results to real life is questionable. We have learned a great deal about how five-person teams make decisions, how simple and complex tasks require differing group communications, and how individuals and groups compare as decision makers. But we cannot be too certain that these findings, derived from temporary groups in a college classroom, really can tell us much about a group of executives in a specific corporation making decisions under pressure, when they must live with the results and with each other afterwards.[22]

The Gap between Managers and Management Research

As you read this book and other articles that may be assigned, and indeed as you continue your professional reading later on in your career, you will be exposed to managerial authors who come from all of these traditions and exhibit all these perspectives.[23] Do not, however, blindly accept the advice they offer, especially if they present rules for success. Rather, determine the basis of their writing: How did the writer come to this position? How did she or he obtain data? What is the writer's perspective? What are the writer's strengths and weaknesses?

The pursuit of reliable results leads some researchers to explore only trivial problems that have little importance to practitioners.[24] Impeccable methodology leads to reliable and replicable findings read by no one except a few academic colleagues.[25] In their training, behavioral scientists, organizational researchers, and management professors are often encouraged to study only limited, researchable problems; to state explicitly the theoretical background and hypotheses of their proposed study; to show clearly how they will measure each variable and what controls they mean to impose.[26] This makes sense in the effort to move away from the unreliable, subjective explorations of managers' intuitions and the doubtful principles that characterized earlier research. Unfortunately, the result is frequently trivial and uninteresting studies.[27] Thus some behavioral science has been described as "a mean and petty science pursued by people who take delight in counting the privies in Pittsburgh and discovering, with the most versatile of techniques, that people with high incomes spend more money than people with low incomes." In effect it resembles the deaf man in Tolstoy muttering answers to questions that no one has asked him.[28]

Neither is completely correct: not the behavioral scientist arguing that tight methodology and a restricted topic are necessary to promote slow, step-by-step development of organizational knowledge, nor the impatient manager or consultant who cannot wait but wants advice right now on big important issues.[29] These differing orientations of organizational scientist and managerial practitioner mean that neither understands a great deal about the other's work. Managers tend to be ignorant of even the more relevant and valid findings of organizational science.[30] And researchers tend to ignore the problems that managers believe to be important.

This gap is understandable, but unfortunate. It is essential that managers and researchers bridge the gap between them. As future managers, you should not ignore what behavioral science and managerial researchers have to say. You should not build your knowledge solely on nonscientific, intuitive, subjective, and normative statements that provide no supporting evidence. But neither can you ignore unreliable sources by focusing only on science. As a practitioner you will simply have to sift through what is offered, picking and choosing that which seems helpful, from whatever its origin.

Learning from Cases

A helpful approach to bridging the gap between theory and practice is to analyze cases and advance recommendations to managerial problems. This book will provide you with an opportunity to simulate actual experience by analyzing problems and making decisions. Learning from experience is both the oldest and newest way to learn how to manage. Experiential learning, however, is a little different from taking a job, working one's way upward, and becoming an executive. Experiential learning takes place through an educational process in and out of the classroom. Through cases and exercises, your instructor will involve you in analyzing situations, working with colleagues, and recommending solutions to real problems.[31] Although no money may be earned or lost in the venture (some schools are experimenting with this, however), you can participate in a simulated management process in which you will feel pressured to complete the task on time, interact with other students, and develop and defend your position before others. This approach can be very real in the sense that you and others become emotionally involved, and words fly thick, hot, and fast in class discussions.

Instructions for Case Analysis

Cases for analysis and solution are presented at the end of each part of this volume. These cases are taken from actual experiences of students, managers, and organizations. Most names and locations have been disguised to protect the innocent and the guilty. The cases are used to stimulate inquiry into the applicability of the concepts and theories presented in the book. The problems in the cases should lead you to a deeper appreciation of the theoretical material and its strengths and limitations in assisting the manager faced with real problems.

Using cases should sharpen your analytical skills. In preparing to study a case, you should immerse yourself in the world of facts, values, attitudes, and feelings depicted in this slice of life. Out of this confusion you must identify the problem(s) facing the manager in the case. To do this you must make a clear separation of symptom and cause. After the problem has been clearly identified as evidence of

Analyzing Cases
- Define problem.
- Analyze causes.
- Develop alternatives.
- Evaluate alternatives.
- Select alternative.
- Recommend plan for implementation.

inability to achieve certain organizational objectives and goals, you must identify the causes. Only on the basis of such a thorough analysis can you move on to the generation of alternative recommendations and the selection of your choice, putting the pieces of the situation back together in the context of the executive's goals and real-life constraints.

Your general approach to case analysis and reports should be as follows:

1. Define the Problem.   The problem is always a blocked managerial objective. What objective (profits, growth, cost control, predictability, change) is being undermined in the situation?

2. Analyze the Causes.   What factors are causing the problem of the blocked achievement of objectives (inadequate communications, poor motivation, indefinite plans, sloppy controls, interpersonal conflict, fear of change)? This should not be a search for villains, however, because individuals are seldom the sole causes of problems.

3. Develop Alternatives.   What action might be taken to remove the causes and solve the problem? Remember that these alternatives should deal with causes, not symptoms of the problem.

4. Evaluate Alternatives.   Evaluate the alternatives according to appropriate criteria:

How well does the alternative meet management's objectives?

How much time and organizational resources are required?

What are the costs?

Does the alternative conform to personal and organizational values for equitable and responsible behavior?

What is the probability of success?

5. Select Alternative (or combination).   What are the weak points of this alternative?

6. Recommend a Detailed Plan of Implementation.   Who should do what? When? How?

Not all the cases will require you to follow this entire format. Each case is followed by detailed questions, and your instructor will make specific assignments determining length and format of reply. The general approach above, however, can guide your thinking.

A Caution about Cases Analysis

You will enjoy working on those cases, but some cautions are in order. Analyzing cases and advancing recommendations is not a substitute for reading and discussing the theories and concepts presented in the various chapters. Cases and text should

Broom Hilda

Reprinted by permission: Tribune Company Syndicate Inc.

complement each other. The cases will offer an opportunity to apply some of the textual ideas, concepts, and theories to a real situation (at least a real situation described on paper).

This type of study will not be easy. Some of you will be frustrated by inability to fit the text to the case because transition from theory to practice is difficult for everyone. You may also be upset because you think you do not have enough facts. However, executives in their daily jobs seldom have all the relevant facts, but they must still make decisions. In the case situation also, with its limited information, a decision must be reached with the data at hand.

Finally, some of you will be concerned with the difficulty of knowing whether your report is right or wrong because the criteria for evaluation are subjective, not an easily stated percentage as in a mathematics test. It is an anxiety you must learn to live with, for it is also the manager's lot in real life. Simple answers exist only for simple jobs, and presumably you are aspiring for something higher. Just as in actual affairs of any manager, there is probably no one correct solution to any case, but there are incorrect solutions. You should be prepared with a well-thought-out justification for your recommendation.

The purpose of the cases is not to provide you with a list of right and wrong behavior. Rather, it is to give you insight into the world of management, to provide you with knowledge of what it was like for some actual managers, and finally to give you some modest practice in converting your theories into action. For learning to take place through the experience, you must commit yourself. You must be willing to be wrong in public. Only by taking positions and offering recommendations can you test yourself against your fellow classmates and your instructors.

SUMMARY

We have examined the various ways of studying and learning about management. No one can train you to be a manager. You must experience the process, but formal education can speed this learning and make it more effective. Management is and will remain a mixture of knowledge and skill, of science and art. Nonetheless, scientific knowledge can assist you in becoming a more effective practical manager.

You can learn about organizations and management in various ways:

1. From the historical experience of other institutions and organizations, particularly governments, armies, and churches.
2. From successful practitioners telling what they did.
3. From researchers who interview many successful and unsuccessful executives, organizing and distilling their insights.
4. From trained scholars who join real organizations and become participant-observers.
5. From systematic field research, including interviews, questionnaires, and direct observation of human behavior in organizations.
6. From experimenting with actual organizations to examine how changing one factor affects others.
7. From rigorous laboratory experiments on teams of people insulated from the distortions of the outside world.

No one of these approaches is perfect. All have advantages and disadvantages. As a future manager, you must draw on all the approaches to management, using what seems most helpful in your particular situation but always with awareness of the weakness and bias of your theory.

REVIEW QUESTIONS

1. Why can't training make you into a manager?
2. What are the major sources of knowledge about organizations and management?
3. What are the strengths and weaknesses of learning from the history of other institutions?
4. What are the strengths and weaknesses of learning from what practitioners say?
5. What are the strengths and weaknesses of learning from interviews with many successful practitioners?
6. What are the strengths and weaknesses of learning from participant-observers?
7. What are the strengths and weaknesses of learning from systematic field research in successful organizations?
8. What are the strengths and weaknesses of learning from experimentation in organizations?
9. What are the strengths and weaknesses of learning from experimentation in the laboratory?
10. Why is there a gap between managers and management research?
11. What are the steps in analyzing cases?
12. What is the relation between a problem and a cause?
13. What makes case analysis difficult and frustrating?

Notes and References on How We Know What We Know about Management

1. A general survey of studying organizations is found in G. Heald, ed., *Approaches to the Study of Organizational Behavioral Science* (Kennebunkport, Maine: Tavistock, 1970).

2. See, for example, R. L. A. Sterba, "The Organization and Management of the Temple Corporations in Ancient Mesopotamia," *Academy of Management Review,* July 1976, pp. 16–26. In a best-selling book, Anthony Jay wrote: "There are far more lessons, for those who care to read them, in the long annals of history than the few published case studies." *Management and Machiavelli* (New York: Holt, Rinehart & Winston, 1968), p. 28. Jay explores historical examples of modern managerial problems. See also R. P. Calhoon, "Niccolo Machiavelli and the Twentieth Century Administrator," *Academy of Management Journal* 12, no. 2 (1969), pp. 205–12.

3. On the education of British managers in the past, see D. Granick, *The European Executive* (Garden City, N.Y.: Doubleday Publishing, 1962), and various selections in R. A. Webber, *Culture and Management: Text and Readings in Comparative Management* (Homewood, Ill.: Richard D. Irwin, 1969). Of course proper management also depends on the cultural setting. See A. I. Kraut, "Some Recent Advances in Cross-National Management Research," *Academy of Management Journal,* September 1975, pp. 538–60.

4. G. D. Smith and L. E. Steadman, "Present Value of Corporate History," *Harvard Business Review,* November–December 1981, pp. 164–73. Not long ago, the chief executive officer of a prominent company scoffed at a business historian who was attempting to explain some possible applications of business history. "I don't want people wasting time on the past," he declared. "I'm trying to get them to pay attention to the future." "Then," replied the historian, "you can be replaced with an 18-year-old!"

5. For some discussion of early management thought, see E. Dale, *Management Theory and Practice* (New York: McGraw-Hill, 1965) and C. George, *The History of Management Thought* (Englewood Cliffs, N.J.: Prentice-Hall, 1968). Schools of Business have been creating "executive in residence" positions to give students exposure to practitioners. W. W. Wendel, "Desirable Job Title: Executive in Residence," *Harvard Business Review,* November–December, 1981, pp. 30–34.

6. The French mining executive was Henri Fayol. The book was *General and Industrial Management* (London: Pitman & Sons, 1949), first published in 1916.

7. The Bell Telephone executive was Chester Barnard—*The Functions of the Executive* (Cambridge, Mass.: Harvard University Press, 1938).

8. The former General Motors executive was Alfred P. Sloan—*My Years with General Motors* (Garden City, N.Y.: Doubleday Publishing, 1964). Some recent books by and about business leaders include: J. P. Getty, *As I See It* (Englewood Cliffs, N.J.: Prentice-Hall, 1976); S. Marcus, *Minding the Store: A Memoir* (Boston: Little, Brown, 1974); T. P. McCann, *An American Company: The Tragedy of United Fruit* (New York: Crown, 1976); M. Boas and S. Chain, *Big Mac: The Unauthorized Story of McDonald's* (New York: E. P. Dutton, 1976); A. Tobias, *Fire and Ice: The Story of Charles Revson, the Man Who Built the Revlon Empire* (New York: William Morrow, 1976).

9.   W. H. Gruber and J. S. Niles, "Research and Experience in Management," *Business Horizons* 16, no. 4 (1973), pp. 15–24.

10.   There are many books that summarize the views and practice of management. The best include: Peter F. Drucker, *The Practice of Management* (New York: Harper & Row, 1954); Harold D. Koontz and Cyril O'Donnell, *Principles of Management* (New York: McGraw-Hill; many editions dating from 1955); William H. Newman et al., *The Process of Management* (Englewood Cliffs, N.J.: Prentice-Hall; several editions dating from 1961).

11.   Luther Gulick, L. F. Urwick, and J. D. Mooney, *Papers on the Science of Administration* (New York: Columbia University, 1937). Lyndall Urwick summarized the contributions of the early management thinkers in *The Golden Book of Management* (London: N. Neame, 1956).

12.   For an interesting defense of the classical or traditional approach to management, see L. F. Urwick, "Why the So-called 'Classicists' Endure," *Management International Review* 11, no. 1 (1971), pp. 3–14. A review of the principles that are still taught is contained in J. E. Ross and R. G. Murdick, "What Are the Principles of 'Principles of Management'?" *Academy of Management Review,* January–February 1977, pp. 143–46.

13.   For a classic account of earlier anthropological studies, see Ruth Benedict, *Patterns of Culture* (Boston: Houghton Mifflin, 1934).

14.   As an example of participant observation, E. Chinoy wrote of his experience in *The Automobile Worker and the American Dream* (Garden City, N.Y.: Doubleday, 1955). Donald Roy described his experience as a machinist in "Banana Time—Job Satisfaction and Informal Interaction," *Human Organization* 18 (1960), pp. 158–69. A thorough review of the participant observer approach is contained in D. L. Phillips, *Knowledge from What? Theories and Methods in Social Research* (Skokie, Ill.: Rand McNally, 1971).

15.   See H. S. Becker and B. Greer, "Participant Observation and Interviewing: A Comparison," *Human Organization* 16, no. 1 (1957), pp. 28–25. On the difference between being an "insider" and being an "outsider" in an organization, see R. Evered and M. R. Louis, "Alternative Perspectives in the Organizational Sciences: Inquiry from the Inside and Inquiry from the Outside," *Academy of Management Review* 6, no. 3 (1981), pp. 385–95.

16.   Better known business novels by former executives include Sloan Wilson, *The Man in the Grey Flannel Suit* (New York: Simon & Schuster, 1955), and Cameron Hawley, *Executive Suite* (Boston: Houghton Mifflin, 1952). On the unique and important role of interpretive methods in the behavioral sciences, see S. Deetz, "An Understanding of Science and a Hermeneutic Science of Understanding," *The Journal of Communications,* 23 (1973), pp. 139–59.

17.   The best known early observer research is that of Elton Mayo, *The Social Problems of an Industrial Civilization* (Boston: Graduate School of Business, Harvard University, 1945). Also see F. J. Roethlisberger (with W. J. Dickson), *Management and the Worker* (Cambridge, Mass.: Harvard University Press, 1939).

18.   For a survey and critique of the narrow perspectives of industrial and organizational psychology, see H. Meltzer and W. Nord, "The Present Status of Industrial and Organizational Psychology," *Personnel Psychology* 26, no. 1 (1973), pp. 11–29. On the inadequacies of organizational sociology, see Chris Argyris, *The Applicability of Organizational Socilogy* (New York: Cambridge University Press, 1972). See also G. F. Wieland, "The Contributions of Organizational Sociology to the Practice of Management," *Academy of Management Journal* 17, no. 2 (1974), pp. 318–33. For examination of the relationship between research results and how the researcher wants thing to be, see G. Nettler, "Wanting and Knowing," in *American Behavioral Scientist* 17, no. 1 (1973), pp. 5–26.

19.   For advice on how to eliminate the distorting effect of the researcher, see Eugene Webb et al., *Unobtrusive Measures: Nonreactive Research in the Social Sciences* (Skokie, Ill.: Rand McNally, 1966).

20.   For a selection of organizational experiments, see W. M. Evan, ed., *Organizational Experiments: Laboratory and Field Research* (New York: Harper & Row, 1971). For approaches that less adversely affect the organization, see E. E. Lawler, "Adaptive Experiments: An Approach to Organizational Behavioral Research," *Academy of Management Review,* October 1977, pp. 576–85.

21.   For debate on whether experiments can or should be conducted on organizational strategy, see R. A. Cosier, "Dialectical Inquiry in Strategy Planning," *Academy of Management Review* 6 (1981), pp. 643–48; and I. I. Mitroff and R. O. Mason, "The Metaphysics of Policy and Planning: A Reply to Cosier," *Academy of Management Review* 6 (1981), pp. 649–51.

22.   For a plea for more realistic experiments, see R. L. Winkler and A. H. Murphy, "Experiments in the

Laboratory and the Real World," *Organizational Behavior and Human Performance* 10 (1973), pp. 252–70. H. Moskowitz argues against interpreting business behavior from nonbusiness subjects. He shows that managers are more rational decision makers, superior information processors, and greater risk-takers than students are. "Managers as Partners in Business Decision Research," *Academy of Management Journal* 14, no. 3 (1971), pp. 317–25. An optimistic assertion that we can still do much more with laboratory research is voiced by K. E. Weick, "Laboratory Experimentation with Organizations: A Reappraisal," *Academy of Mangement Review,* January 1977, pp. 123–37.

23. One result of the multiplicity of approaches to management is inconsistent and confusing terminology. For an evaluation of efforts to alleviate the terminology conflicts, see A. G. Bedeian, "A Historical Review of Efforts in the Area of Management Semantics," *Academy of Management Journal* 17, no. 1 (1974), pp. 101–4.

24. C. J. Grayson, Jr., argues that management science has grown so remote from and unmindful of the conditions of "live" management that it has abdicated its usability. "Management Science and Business Practice," *Harvard Business Review,* July–August 1973, pp. 41–49. C. C. Lundberg argues that this gap is at least partially caused by academicians attempting to get promoted; hence they do the "easier" and more theoretical work. "Hypothesis Creation in Organizational Behavior Research," *Academy of Management Review,* April 1976, pp. 5–12. H. Mintzberg argues that to be relevant, management science must be softer if it is to deal with policy issues. "Policy as a Field of Management Theory," Academy of Management Review, January 1977, pp. 88–102.

On the difficulty of bringing theory and practice together, see W. J. Duncan, "Transferring Managment Theory to Practice," *Academy of Management Journal,* December 1974, pp. 724–38.

For a thorough discussion of the relationship between reliability and validity, see D. Mechanic, "Some Considerations in the Methodology of Organizational Studies," in H. J. Leavitt, ed., *The Social Science of Organizations* (Englewood Cliffs, N.J.: Prentice-Hall, 1963).

25. A complaint also voiced about modern philosophy. R. Nozick, *Philosophical Explanations* (Cambridge, Mass.: Harvard University Press, 1982). See also, P. H. Birnbaum, "Integration and Specialization in Academic Research," *Academy of Management Journal* 24, no. 3 (1981), pp. 487–503.

26. One of the best surveys of social and behavioral science is by George C. Homans, *The Nature of Social Science* (New York: Harcourt Brace Jovanovich, 1967). Some helpful books on research include: H. M. Blalock, Jr., *An Introduction to Social Research* (Englewood Cliffs, N.J.: Prentice-Hall, 1970); H. M. Blalock and A. Blalock, eds., *Methodology in Social Science Research* (New York: McGraw-Hill, 1968); H. M. Blalock, Jr., *Causal Inferences in Nonexperimental Research* (Chapel Hill, N.C.: University of North Carolina Press, 1964); V. H. Vroom, ed., *Methods of Organizational Research* (Pittsburgh: University of Pittsburgh Press, 1967). Also see P. E. Connor, "Research in the Behavioral Sciences: A Review Essay," *Academy of Management Journal* 15, no. 2 (1972), p. 219.

27. A major compendium of behavioral science findings is Bernard Berelson and G. A. Steiner, *Human Behavior: An Inventory of Scientific Findings* (New York: Harcourt Jovanovich, 1964). They concluded:

> Indeed, as one reviews this set of findings, he may well be impressed by another omission perhaps more striking still. As one lives life or observes it around him (or within himself) or finds it in a work of art, he sees a richness that somehow has fallen through the present screen of the behavioral sciences. This book, for example, has rather little to say about central human concerns: nobility, moral courage, ethical torments, the delicate relation of father and son, or the marriage state, life's way of corrupting innocence, the rightness or wrongness of acts, evil, happiness, love and hate, death, even sex.—p. 666.

28. These observations on privies and Tolstoy were made by Mechanic in "Methodology of Organizational Studies."

29. Practitioners tend to superficial evaluation of behavior science research. In their quest for a sure-fire approach to solving problems, they are apt to accept or reject a finding without regard to outside factors that can influence the results. See F. G. Lippert, "Toward Flexibility in Application of Behavioral Science Research," *Academy of Management Journal* 14, no. 2 (1971), pp. 195–201. On the need for more "middle-range" as opposed to grand theories in organizational research, see C. C. Pinder and L. F. Moore, eds., *Middle Range Theory and the Study of Organizations* (Boston: Martinus Nijhoff, 1980).

30. The fact that practitioners are generally unfamiliar with the best behavioral research literature on management is documented in M. D. Dunnette and L. M. Brown, "Behavioral Science Research and the Conduct of Business," *Academy of Management Journal* 2, no. 11 (1968), pp. 177–88. That managers are familiar with some of this research but reject it is argued by J. A. Lee, "Behavioral Theory versus Reality," *Harvard Business Review,* March–April 1971, p. 20. See also: L. R. Sayles, "Whatever Happened to Management—Or, Why the Dull Stepchild?" *Business Horizons* 13, no. 2 (1970), pp. 25–34. This is a devastating critique of much management research. Also see M. J. Gannon and J. P. Noon, "Management's Critical Deficiency: Executives Unaware of Applicable Research," *Business Horizons* 14, no. 1 (1971), pp. 49–56.

31. R. Charam, "Classroom Techniques in Teaching by the Case Method," *Academy of Management Review,* July 1976, pp. 116–23. For a book utilizing exercises and games to teach through the experimental method, see D. A. Kolb, I. M. Rubin, J. M. McIntyre, *Organizational Psychology: An Experiential Approach* (Englewood Cliffs, N.J.: Prentice-Hall, 1974). See also M. Uretsky, "The Management Game: An Experiment in Reality," *Simulation and Games* 4, no. 2 (1973), pp. 221–40 and P. S. Greenlaw and F. P. Wyman, "The Teaching Effectiveness of Games in Collegiate Business Courses," *Simulation and Games* 4, no. 3 (1973), pp. 259–94.

Part Two

Individuals at Work

3

Individual Needs and Motivation

Years ago, a corporation president pointed out that the individual is always the strategic element in an organization.[1]* We now know that organizations are more than just collections of individuals for they possess *organizational* characteristics that go beyond the attributes of the individuals who compose them. Nonetheless, however much organizations change and management theory develops, human aspects will remain central. The essential requirements for future managers will continue to include knowledge about people. Accordingly, in this chapter we shall discuss individuals, their needs, and their motivation. Knowledge of needs and personality may be interesting to you as a person; but more important, as a prospective manager you must understand people in order to offer appropriate work and rewards and to influence others' behavior.

Conceptions of Human Nature

Humankind has been described from more perspectives than the proverbial elephant by the blind men. Many, many conceptions of human nature exist. Are we passive lumps quiet until activated by an external stimulus to which we respond with stress-reducing behavior? Are we dynamic energy bundles actively seeking outlets for destructive and creative drives? These general images have been major themes in ancient and modern psychological argument.

In one view, humans are seen as driven by biological instincts; in another by subconscious passions, fears, and memories. Another sees an organism to be trained to behave in predictable ways when a stimulus is presented, like a conditioned pigeon who pecks a red button when a bell is rung. But others conceive of us as uniquely human creatures striving to interact with the world and other people in order to satisfy a wide range of needs from physiological to spiritual, like the French workers who ate coq au vin while building Rheims Cathedral.

These differing conceptions of humankind fall roughly into three categories: (1) unconscious, (2) nonconscious, and (3) conscious.

Conceptions of Human Nature
* unconscious
  instincts
  subconscious
* nonconscious
  stimulus
  response
* conscious
  expectation
  decisions
  needs

The Unconscious Model

The unconscious approach argues that we are motivated by deep-seated instincts or forces rooted in the collective history of the species. Biological genetically inherited instincts or psychoanalytic phenomena have been offered as explanations for behavior.[2] Although these ideas are powerful, at this time they appear to be of limited usefulness for understanding the behavior of people in organizations. We shall refer to this approach only in the chapters on conflict and change.

The Nonconscious Model

The nonconscious, or behavioral, approach maintains that deep "instincts" or "needs" are irrelevant because they are not necessary to understand and predict behavior. Thus, the behavioralists state that we should focus on the link between

---

* Notes and references will be found at the end of this chapter.

behavior and consequences.[3] Consequences that are rewarding to the behavior will be repeated; the results are positively reinforcing. Consequences that are unpleasant will be adversive, and such negative reinforcements will be avoided. So all of us become conditioned to behave in certain ways by our experiences with positive and negative consequences. This is a powerful way of thinking about humankind and it is increasingly affecting managerial thought and action. We shall discuss the use of positive and negative reinforcements, especially in motivating people at work.

The Conscious Model

The conscious or cognitive approach is probably the most helpful theory because it seems most applicable to what managers do. No one image of men or women is correct or incorrect; all have elements of truth. All humans endeavor to avoid pain and enjoy pleasure. Sometimes external forces dominate and determine behavior, at other times behavior is self-generated, but at all times it is directed toward self-satisfaction. Therefore, we assume that human behavior has purposes, that it is not random or unconscious.[4] Most of the time, people more or less know what they are doing and why. In this chapter we shall examine how motivation depends on expectations of need satisfaction, what needs exist, and how needs may be structured.

Reprinted by permission of the Chicago Tribune–New York New Syndicate, Inc.

Managerial Assumptions about Workers

Managers usually assume that their employees are conscious in their behavior but are either lazy or hardworking. The first approach to understanding employees emphasizes the following characteristics:

1. The average employee has an inherent dislike of work and will avoid it if possible.
2. The average employee wishes to avoid responsibility.
3. The average employee has little ambition and wants job security above all.

This view suggests a more authoritarian approach to motivation by emphasizing managements' need to control, coerce, and threaten employees with punishment to get them to put forth adequate effort on the job.

The alternative assumption that employees are hardworking implies a more participative approach to motivation. This set of assumptions characterizes the average employee in the following manner:

1. The average employee is not lazy but wants to work hard at a challenging task.
2. External control and the threat of punishment are not necessary, since the average employee will exercise self-direction and control when working toward objectives for which the employee is committed.
3. The average employee is interested in accepting responsibility.
4. The average employee wants to display ingenuity and creativity.[5]

When operating under this set of assumptions about the nature of employees, the manager will develop a more participative approach to motivation. Delegating authority, expanding job responsibilities, and improving communication are likely activities.

Needs and Behavior

Behavior is directed to obtain wants that will satisfy needs, as indicated by the diagram of motivation in Figure 3–1.[6] We cannot see another's needs directly; we can only infer their existence from observing that people want various goods and conditions and act in order to obtain them. These wants can usually be described by the wanter; they are numerous, ranging from such material specifics as bread and chrome-plated baubles to such abstract states as security, love, prestige, and power. Although wants are apparently limitless, needs are not. They are relatively few, but these basic drives motivate behavior in quest of a much larger number of wants.

FIGURE 3–1

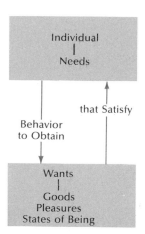

The Nature of Individual Needs

An unsatisfied need is the starting point in understanding human motivation. As shown in Figure 3–2, the unsatisfied need creates tension, which serves as a driving force to arouse the individual and suggests the choice of a specific behavioral act or pattern of acts to satisfy this need.

Locus of Control

People differ in their general belief that their need satisfaction depends on their own behavior. Locus of control is a concept suggesting a basic philosophic outlook

FIGURE 3–2

The Process of Motivation

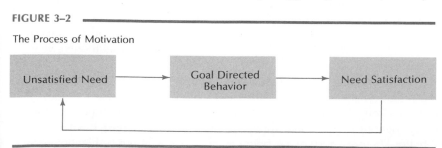

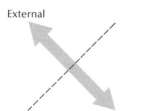

toward life.[7] It is a continuum with internal at one end and external at the other. (See Figure 3-3.)

Externally oriented people do not believe that what happens to them depends on what they do. The wants they obtain or the needs they satisfy seem to depend on the ubiquitous "others" out there who may be benevolent, malevolent, or uncaring. One is unlikely to exert much effort in pursuit of wants if he or she believes them to be entirely controlled by others or by pure chance. To be at the extreme external end of the locus of control continuum leads to motivational paralysis and helplessness. The world is likely to judge a person at this extreme to be insane.[8]

Internally oriented people believe that their need satisfaction depends on their own behavior. To be at the extreme internal end can also lead to insanity, however, because of one's burden in believing that *everything* that happens to him or her, all wants and needs satisfied, depends solely on oneself. Such a person can suffer from what psychiatry terms the *God complex* wherein the totally internally oriented person believes that only he or she is important, only their time is important, and all others must give way.[9] Fortunately, most of us are intermediate on the locus of control continuum, either mildly fatalistic and external or mildly optimistic and internal. We generally conclude that our own behavior determines most of our need satisfaction.[10]

The Structure of Needs

Since needs are inferences and not physical facts, we cannot prove their existence. Some, like hunger, are obvious, but others, like competence, are more subtle. Keeping this uncertainty in mind, we will discuss what seem to be the basic needs motivating human behavior.

Much debate has raged about how many needs exist. Suggestions range from as few as 3 to more than 20. One survey of people maintains that most are able to distinguish between only three kinds of needs:[11] (1) existence needs that relate to the biological necessities of life; (2) relatedness needs that deal with relations with other people; and (3) growth needs that express personal development. (See Figure 3-4.)

A slightly more complex model postulates five needs arranged in hierarchical fashion as in Figure 3-5: (1) physiological, (2) safety, (3) love, (4) esteem, and (5) self-actualization.[12] For a need to be lower on the hierarchy implies that it is prepotent. Physiological needs are placed at the bottom because satisfaction of those drives is essential for the maintenance of life; they are prepotent for motivating behavior. A person long without food would presumably be reduced to a sort of human piranha who thinks food, dreams food, and hunts food, without any other concern.[13] Such food-seeking monsters would not be interested in building monuments, wearing fine clothes, or even worshiping gods.

Happily, the hierarchical model suggests that as physical necessities are met (at least at a minimum level), new needs emerge to motivate behavior. Nonetheless, lower level needs must be satisfied before upper level needs become motivating. Before we can become concerned about social esteem, we must have sufficient food and shelter. Before most of us become concerned about achievement, we must have some affiliation, and so on. Still, only relative satisfaction is necessary.

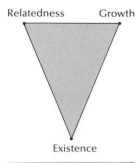

FIGURE 3-5

Basic Hierarchical Needs Model

Need Levels	Relevant Organizational Factors
Self-Actualization: Fulfilling oneself by maximizing the use of abilities	Job challenge Advancement opportunities Creativity
Esteem: Feeling of self-confidence Respect from others	Supervisory recognition Job title Responsibility Peer recognition
Social: Affiliation, friendship, affection, satisfying interactions with others	Compatible co-workers Employee-oriented supervision Professional friendships
Safety: Security, protection against danger, freedom from threat	Job security Fringe benefits Safe working conditions
Physiological: Hunger, thirst, shelter	Salary Heat and air conditioning Cafeteria

We do not know what the proportions are, but we can assume some percentage below 100 percent satisfaction of a lower need before the next higher need becomes motivating.[14] Of course, with physiological needs some minimal level is necessary to sustain life, but even here the necessary level of needs among affluent nations would be higher than the level in nations with lower standards of living. The essential point is that as lower level needs become relatively satisfied, they are less directly motivating for behavior. We are motivated mainly by the next level of unsatisfied need.

In the years since this hierarchical model was advanced, there has been substantial research on the nature and impact of these needs on human behavior.[15] Of special concern have been the upper levels of the hierarchy because *self-actualization* is difficult to define and too abstract a concept for many to understand. Originally, it conveyed a biological image: that one had an ultimate need to fully actualize one's potential, to become everything he or she was capable of becoming. It now appears that it is a more complex phenomenon, including elements of autonomy, power, competence, achievement, and creativity.

The Range of Needs

In this chapter, therefore, we shall assume the existence of a number of needs intermediate between the low and high estimates. Proceeding roughly up the hierarchy from the physiological needs, we will consider the following: existence needs (safety and security), relatedness needs (love, affiliation, social esteem, and power), and growth needs (self-esteem, competence, achievment, and creativity). This hierarchical model has not been proven, but it has been influential in shaping the thinking and behavior of many researchers and managers.[16] It is useful as a general framework for thinking about motivation.[17]

Basic and Physiological

Physiological needs are the most basic for the individual. This category consists of the basic needs of the human body (e.g., food, water, and shelter). Physiological needs dominate when all needs are unsatisfied, allowing no other needs to serve as the basis for motivation.

Safety and Security

Once individuals have achieved relative satisfaction of their physiological requirements, there emerges a new set of needs for safety or security. The person who has food and shelter may be concerned about securing the sources of these satisfactions. This is a very rational, prudent, and conscious security drive. There is also a more subtle, pervasive, and unconscious anxiety. This anxiety is most apparent in the child. At certain stages in their development, all children are upset by changes in the routine of daily life. They prefer a safe, orderly, predictable, organized world. Unexpected events are disturbing.

Need Categories
- achievement-creativity
- competence-self-esteem
- power-autonomy
- social esteem-prestige
- affiliation-love
- safety-security
- physiological

In American society, safety needs usually are met quite easily, but the fear experienced in urban areas today indicates the potential power (and political impact) of this need. Some people are guided predominantly by security motives throughout their lives, commencing long before they could make a rational analysis of the hazards of life. This attitude persists throughout their careers. The hazards they seek to protect themselves against are vague, pervasive, and fearsome, for these people have an underlying conviction that the environment is at best capricious and at worst malicious. Their overriding need, therefore, is to find some measure of safety, usually achieved by entering into relationships with gangs, groups, or organizations that seem able to guarantee them a reasonably unruffled life.

Many of us, and successful managers in particular, tend to snicker at security motives, as if they were somehow less mature or less respectable than the higher level drives for power and achievement. It is true that excessive security motivation prevents many people from fully utilizing their abilities, but everyone has some sort of security drive. Life is seldom so clear-cut or simple as to exclude influences that contribute to the need for security. A strong security motive is one that begins to manifest itself when only a modest amount of peril is present in the environment. Even a weak security drive could show its influence if the individual were placed under enough stress. Most of us, fortunately, are able to satisfy this need well enough to allow us to move on to other things.

Love and Affiliation

Most religions maintain that humans cannot live by bread alone. Even with secure sources of food and shelter, they are not satisfied; further needs emerge. The first is a need for social belonging, affection, membership, or affiliation. A complex need, affiliation ranges from simple enjoyment of a parent's "stroking" and the presence of other human beings (sociologists describe humans as social animals) to more complex desires for group affirmation of an individual's self-concept.[18] Thus affiliation can be either a means to an end or an end in itself.

Stress is implicit in most observations of this need. In an epic natural science research effort, for example, perhaps as much was suggested about humans as about chimpanzees, the subject of the study.[19] A film of the apes in their natural habitat shows a female chimp stranger entering the domain of an established tribe. Fear, anxiety, and longing are strikingly evident in her face; she wants to be accepted, perhaps because she needs the protection and companionship afforded by the group. A moving moment occurs when an old leader touches the newcomer's hand, signifying acceptance. Relief and gratitude are immediately evident.

The rewards of affiliation may be as great for humans. In a description of his prisoner-of-war experience, an American general indicated that he missed human companionship so much that he talked extensively to an enemy interrogator who acted warmly toward him.[20] Desire for companionship is implicit in all human relationships. Veteran soldiers comment on the tendency of new recruits to herd together for support when under stress, even though they know intellectually that grouping increases the danger. Loud music, decorated jeans, and current hairstyle reflect the teenagers' efforts to define themselves in terms of their companions. Thus self-image is derived from social image.[21]

Empirical research corroborates these observations. People under stress do tend to socialize.[22] When there is an apparent threat to an important belief, people are relieved to find their thinking is shared by many others, almost as if this agreement confirms the rightness and safety of their own ideas. The most important element in the pattern is the reassuring effect of sharing an opinion. More than just company is provided by affiliation. Socializing serves to make life seem a little more manageable, a little less inexplicable. Even if the others whom the individual seeks out cannot assist him or her, they are apparently still sought out, especially if they are under similar stress. If people are upset, they do not seek just any company indiscriminately; they prefer people who are in a similar predicament. Misery definitely loves company, particularly if the company has the same misery. Merely being in the presence of others, even unhappy others, seems to reduce unhappiness.

Even without stress, most people derive satisfaction from affiliation. They crave the active giving and receiving of sentiments, communications, and activities that characterize social life. We all experience a sense of security and warmth from being part of a community, whether it be our family, tribe, fraternity, school, or nation.

Social Esteem and Prestige

Most people need affiliation and membership. Yet once they have established mutual relationships, paradoxically, many individuals want to be a little different from others. Everyone wants to be equal, but as George Orwell put it in *Animal Farm,* some want to be more equal than others. With affiliation, a new need emerges—desire for social esteem and prestige, or social position differentiated from those of associates and peers.

Prestige is a set of unwritten rules about the kind of conduct others are expected to show in one's presence—what degree of respect, familiarity, or openness. These expectations may even be codified in books in some countries among some social classes and in government protocol. Americans, however, expect a breezy informality among almost all people. Here, desires for prestige are mainly satisfied not by how people behave toward you, but by how much they knowingly or secretly envy you.

The desire for social esteem is more a psychological than a behavioral phenomenon; "the grass is always greener" goes the cliché. Most of us, however, are happier when others think the grass is greener on our side of the street.

Foreign and domestic critics have satirized American status seeking, especially when it takes the form of conspicuous consumption. This is not a 20th-century American innovation; humankind has apparently always created social structures differentiating between the power and glory of individuals. People have evidently always sorted themselves out into chiefs and braves, nobles and peasants, executives and hourly workers, and they continue to do so.[23] The classless society has yet to appear; even communist societies acquire and propagate class systems.[24]

People seek prestige throughout their lives in countless ways, some subtle, others blatant, because there is a widespread need to have their relative importance clarified and to fix that importance at a level they feel they deserve. Hence prestige is a matter not of absolutes but of relatives—relative to what others have and relative to what one thinks one merits. This drive can be a potent motivator for people of both low and high absolute status.

Ego satisfaction is the positive goal of such a drive, avoidance of ridicule the negative. People like to be looked up to but fear being dismissed as inferior or irrelevant. Fear of ridicule is among the most potent of human motivations.[25]

Self-Esteem and Competence

Innumerable sources—philosophers, novelists, and parents—have suggested that social esteem is not sufficient. In the long run, we are told, what we think of ourselves is more important. Thus the need for self-esteem, competence, and the feeling that one is capable of meeting challenge emerges. We are now dealing with a complex phenomenon that perhaps lumps disparate needs into one package. The thrust of the set of needs referred to as self-esteem or competence, however, is clear: Individuals are more than just vehicles for instincts; they are also active observers and shapers of their environments.

One of the central motivations is learning to know what the world is like and how to get what one wants from it.[26] Even in young infants this competence motive can be seen in the form of random fingering of objects, poking around, and feeling whatever is in reach. Later it is evidenced in the joy of exploring, taking things apart, and sometimes putting them together again. The teacher hopes this drive is reflected in a desire to master a discipline and to expand intellectually. The competence need may also take another direction; self-esteem can be derived from competence in a wide variety of vocational and avocational activities. Whether an adult's competence need is strong or weak depends on the balance of successes and failures he or she has experienced in early and later encounters with the world. Success breeds future trials and future successes. Failure reduces the effort.

Most men and women want to feel they are doing something important, that their activities have social purpose. We want to feel that we are contributing members of society. There is ego satisfaction in awareness of the dependence and gratitude of others.

Power and Autonomy

Many years ago a contemporary of Freud's, Alfred Adler, stated that power is the best explanation for the behavior of exceptional people.[27] According to Adler, Freud was correct in suggesting that everyone has pleasure-seeking and life-sustaining drives similar to lower level needs. Adler maintained, however, that it was foolish to explain the towering good or evil persons of history by analyzing whether or not they had anal or oral sex hangups. For Adler, the central drive of such people was a need for power. Power can be a want that satisfies various needs. It can bring you safety if you can hire a private army; prestige if other people admire power; perhaps even a form of affiliation if you can compel slaves to do your bidding. The *need* for power is different, however. It is satisfied by the intrinsic process of influencing others by exercising power. Thus some people find it enjoyable to initiate for others' reaction, whether or not other needs are thereby satisfied.

The power need is measured by the individual's concern about control of the means for influencing other people.[28] Such concern may be inferred from emotional reaction to a dominance situation; for example, pleasure in winning or anger in losing an argument, statements about wanting to avoid weakness, concern with disputing a position, trying to put across a point, and giving a command. It is what drives the political leader to pursue the sensation of power or priviness to it, the feeling of being in on decisions that affect others' lives.[29]

As with social esteem, many of us have mixed feelings about the drive for power. The process of influencing and controlling other people can be intrinsically enjoyable. "Power and glory," wrote Bertrand Russell, "are chief among the infinite desires of man."[30] Friedrich Nietzsche declared, "All life desires above all is to express its power. Life is itself will to power. The impulse of survival is only an indirect consequence of this will."[31] Recently, a psychoanalyst has contended that violence springs from a person's having too little power rather than too much.[32] In contrast, others argue that "power corrupts" to take the theologian's view that the need for power reflects humanity's inherent weakness and basic sinfulness, for power emphasizes the / at the expense of the *Thou.*[33]

The inverse of personal power is freedom from the power of others. Freedom from arbitrary and unilateral authority, even from the benevolent despot, is a persistent theme in history. Indeed, the power drive has its roots in the helplessness of childhood when the child is dependent on and controlled by adults. The young person wants to gain power over these superiors in order to ensure that they will meet the childs' requirements. With maturity, he or she attempts to develop abilities to gain autonomy

**"Why don't you just fire somebody? That
always makes you feel better."**

from these power figures. The drive for autonomy reflects both fear of dependence
on others for satisfaction of physiological necessities and desire to fulfill higher needs.

Self-Actualization, Achievement, and Creativity

When esteem and power needs have been minimally satisfied, the highest level
of needs, the self-actualization needs, assume importance as motivators. When this
need state is operating, the individual seeks to maximize the use of abilities, skills,
and potential. The employee has a strong "desire to become more and more what
one is, to become everything one is capable of becoming."[34] Self-actualization needs
become dominant only after the satisfaction of all other needs. Furthermore, the
satisfaction of self-actualization needs increases rather than reduces, the strength
of these needs. Thus, this particular need state is limitless. Employees seeking to
satisfy self-actualization needs seek opportunities to use valued skills, develop new
skills, experience job challenge, and provide for advancement and growth.

What may be the apex of human needs at the top of the needs hierarchy are
the individual's drives for achievement and creativity. As with the competence need,
we are perhaps combining some distinct motives, but they all point in the same
direction: What a person can be, one must be. One should create and achieve
everything of which one is capable. Overcoming challenging, difficult, and novel
problems; creating new institutions and objects; developing one's attributes and
capabilities—all are sources of satisfaction.[35]

Achievement is a confusing term for this need because achievement means so many things and brings so many rewards. Teachers label a student a "high" or "low" achiever depending on the grades, but grades are not clearly related to achievement need.[36] Striving for good grades at a young age reflects the drives for security, affiliation, or social esteem more than for achievement. Like power, achievement can be a want that satisfies several needs. The need for achievement, however, is satisfied by the *process* of expending effort and experiencing successful completion. Thus it is a personal growth need rather than a social need.

To achieve means to carry to a termination, to bring into a perfected state or a successful conclusion, to obtain or gain as a result of exertion. The need for achievement is a drive to be engaged in activities that lend this satisfaction—to obtain as a result of exertion. In stories the need takes the form of how the hero, through persistent efforts, overcomes great obstacles and obtains the distant goal. The emphasis is less on the goods or honors than on successful achievement and satisfaction with the process itself. Great achievements, of course, may bring social prestige, power, security, perhaps even love. As satisfying as such things are, however, they do not reflect the need for achievement. People with high achievement needs may like status and money as much as others, but they are also concerned with the process of performing a task well, meeting high standards, overcoming difficult obstacles, and trying novel or creative methods. The achievement orientation is manifested in concern about effectively utilizing time for the accomplishment of tasks considered worthwhile and challenging.[37] People high in need for achievement express a basic attitude toward life: When challenged, they try harder and demand more of themselves. And external rewards are subordinate to internal feelings. It is the person with little need for achievement who expects a concrete reward for greater effort.[38] Although the high achiever certainly does not refuse tangible rewards, they are not the central thrust of motivation. Setting difficult but not impossible objectives and reaching them through personal effort provide delight and satisfaction.

You may feel that the list of needs is not complete. Where is altruism? Or where is sex? Remember that specific behavior can reflect multiple motivations; this characterizes both sex and altruism. Sex in our society is a vehicle for satisfying several needs, ranging from basic physcial pleasure to aspirations for love, prestige, and power. Having a steady boyfriend can be a source of security; having a beautiful girl friend can inspire envy in a boy's peers. The power of sex as a motivator is that it can be a want that satisfies multiple needs. Altruism relects needs for affiliation, status, power, and achievement. It is a growth drive as well as a manifestation of the social need.[39] We do not mean to imply that altrusim and sex are always Machiavellian or necessarily selfish. Both do express simple love and affiliation, but other needs are also involved.[40]

Need for Achievement
* self-standards
* challenge
* moderate risk
* novelty
* feedback desire
* internal locus of control
* time anxiety

Variations in Individual Needs

The need hierarchy is described as a flight of steps up which one moves a step at a time. Actually, the need structure is neither so unidirectional nor so fixed. Changing life conditions, such as losing a job, may suddenly confront one with the need to satisfy lower level needs for food, shelter, and security. Therefore, a time dimension must be added to the concept of the hierarchical ladder. Because we move up the ladder through time, the best image of need structure is less a hierarchical ladder than a set of spirals, one for each need. Such an image indicates that sometimes the need is motivating, sometimes not.

How Each Person Is Affected by Needs

Each need varies with each person as to how frequently and strongly it motivates behavior. For example, Sam Webster is concerned about security only infrequently. Perhaps once a month, he becomes anxious about his generally small bank account, his dependence on current income, and his give growing children; but he is generally quite secure, a person motivated by higher needs. He probably has a strong achievement need because be becomes frustrated if more than two or three days pass in which he cannot see that he has accomplished anything. He craves the feedback of task completion. But note that although he may be 'a fairly mature person who is generally motivated by inner-directed needs, he is sometimes concerned about security and sometimes motivated by what others will think of him.

The difference between people is the relative frequency of various drives. The self-actualizing person is more frequently motivated by competence and achievement needs; the other-directed person more frequently motivated by social and prestige needs; and the fearful more apt to be motivated by safety and security. Insecure people may be anxious about their economic state every day.[41] They frequently check the cash in their pockets, their bank account, and their job security. For others, anxiety lies in their human relationships: the wife who is so hung-up on her need for love that she demands continued reassurance from her husband that he loves her, that he is attracted to no other, and that he will not leave her; or the middle-aged man who obsessively seeks affection through temporary liaisons with younger women.

Consider the stereotypic artist consumed by her creative energies who forsakes worldly acclaim and even security in pursuing her particular muse.[42] She is motivated by a passion for frequent satisfaction of her need for achievement or creation, but it is unlikely that she has no lower level needs. Vincent van Gogh, an apparently archetypal inner-directed artist unmindful of the world's esteem, was in fact tormented by his alienation from people and the frustration of his social needs. Indeed, the more common model of the artist may be that of Pierre Auguste Renoir, who grew up in a protective family, remained married to a loving wife, gained social esteem, and pursued his creative genius as the dominant expression of a satisfying life.

It may be helpful to think of the need hierarchy as a photograph of your motivational state at a certain time, during which a single need may be motivating. Then think of a motion picutre of yourself moving through time. Sometimes you are mainly concerned about security, sometimes with love, prestige, power, or achievement. What motivates you at any given time will depend on your personality and your situation. A soldier in battle will be more concerned with personal safety or love for his buddies than with his competence and achievement needs. In an office in the Pentagon, however, a general may be driven by needs for esteem, power, and achievement.

Each person has a particular cycle of these needs—that is, how frequently and how strongly each need is felt. But almost all people possess all needs to some degree. The chemistry researcher with the Ph.D. may be mainly driven by desires for autonomy, competence, and achievement, but she also has needs for security and affiliation. The assembly-line worker may be concerned mostly with money and security, but he does have needs for esteem and competence. The drives are not all equal in frequency, duration, or intensity, but all people possess all needs to some extent.

How Culture Affects Needs

Just as individuals vary in their structure of needs, so do subcultural groups and whole societies. The average need structure may differ from country to country because different cultures teach different values and behavior.[43] Cultural factors influence child-rearing practices and the values and standards held by the family that are transmitted to the child. As we grow up, we learn the attitudes and assumptions about life that characterize the culture in which we were born. We are taught the traditions of our society, its religious concepts, ethical doctrines, and metaphysical assumptions. These may vary a great deal from place to place. Among the Zuni Indians, the person with a drive for power for achievement was considered odd, if not insane. Behavior was concentrated on fulfilling lower needs to provide physical well-being, love, and acceptance; higher level drives were not accepted by the society. In contrast, the Kwakiutl Indians of the Pacific Northwest demonstrated a fantastic drive for status and power, and social satisfaction and affiliation were much less valued. A brave who rejected the pursuit of prestige in favor of affiliation and love was thought to be strange, in the definition of their society—as well he might be by ambitious people in the United States today.[44]

Culture also affects needs in modern societies. When managers in many countries were surveyed, their needs were found to be quite similar, but with some interesting differences.[45] Considering the order of needs in the basic need hierarchy as physiological, security, social, esteem, autonomy, and self-actualization, the research eliminated the first need, since all people obviously must satisfy it. The study sought to find whether, as implied in the hierarchical model, the degree of satisfaction existing with each remaining need decreases as a manager proceeds up the hierarchy. For most people, the security need should be most satisfied, social next, and so on; self-actualization should be least satisfied.

The study found that this is true only in some countries. Figure 3–6 gives the satisfaction rankings assigned to these needs by several thousand managers in various clusters of countries (a cluster is composed of nations that tend to express similar views). As predicted by the hierarchical model of needs, managers in most countries rank self-actualization and autonomy as the least satisfied needs. They are at the top of the need hierarchy and would be the last to be satisfied. Managers in the United States and the United Kingdom rank satisfaction of the remaining needs in

FIGURE 3–6

Rankings of Need Satisfaction by Managers in Various Countries (no. 5 least satisfaction; no. 1, most satisfaction)

Need	Satisfaction Ranking Predicted by Model	U.S./U.K.	Latin Europe*	Nordic Europe†	Developing Nations‡	Japan
Self-actualization	5	5	5	5	5	3
Autonomy	4	4	4	4	4	2
Esteem	3	3	1	1	1	4
Social	2	2	3	2	3	5
Security	1	1	2	3	2	1

* Latin Europe: Spain, Italy, France, Belgium.
† Nordic Europe: Sweden, Norway, Denmark, West Germany.
‡ Developing countries: Chile, Argentina, India.
Source: Mason Haire, Edwin E. Ghiselli, and Lyman W. Porter, *Managerial Thinking* (New York: John Wiley & Sons, 1966).

the predicted order: Security is most satisfied, social next, and esteem in the middle. The ranks of these needs in the other nations vary. Thus the esteem need is relatively more satisfied in the other clusters, perhaps because satisfaction of this need is more important in these countries (such as in Italy), or because managers are from a wealthier social class with higher esteem, or just because their societies give greater prestige to managers.

The study also investigated differences among national attitudes by comparing the *importance* attributed by the managers to the various needs (see Figure 3–7). Managers in the United States and Italy rank security as relatively less important than the other managers do, especially those in India, Germany, and Spain. In these countries, the importance attributed to security probably reflects their history of economic, social, and political instability. Italians rank esteem as very important, and managers in all countries, especially Germany and India, rank satisfaction of the social need as less important than Americans do. In most nations it is more important to have prestige, honor, and respect than it is to be liked. In the United States, to be accepted and liked is apparently more desirable.

FIGURE 3–7

Rankings of Need Importance by Managers in Various Countries (no. 5, least important, no. 1, most important)

Need	U.S.	Italy	Germany	Sweden	Spain	India
Self-actualization	1	1	1	1	1	2
Autonomy	2	3	3	2	3	3
Esteem	5	2	4	5	5	4
Social	3	4	5	4	4	5
Security	4	5	2	3	2	1

Source: Mason Haire, Edwin E. Ghiselli, and Lyman W. Porter, *Managerial Thinking* (New York: John Wiley & Sons, 1966).

SUMMARY

Behavior is directed mainly at obtaining wants to satisfy needs. Wants are many, but needs are relatively limited. The strength of one's motivation to act depends upon: (1) our degree of confidence that our behavior will obtain the wanted goods, pleasures, or states of being, (2) our estimate of the probability that what is wanted will satisfy one or more of our needs, and (3) the value of the need(s) to be satisfied in comparison with other needs that might be pursued with our limited time and energy. The central assumption is that what one does makes a difference, that rewards depend upon behavior.

If you believe that rewards and satisfactions are based on chance or the whim of a malevolent force, your motivation is likely to be paralyzed.

On the need hierarchy, the most fundamental needs are physiological needs for food, warmth, oxygen, water, and so on. The drive for safety and security follows, and then for affiliation. As these needs are relatively satisfied, new needs emerge to motivate behavior. These include esteem, power, autonomy, competence, achievement, and creativity. Thus the range is from physical imperatives to creative desirables.

REVIEW QUESTIONS

1. What is the difference between a need and a want?
2. Upon what does motivational strength depend?
3. What is locus of control?
4. What is the difference between people oriented toward internal control and those oriented toward external control?
5. How do these different orientations affect motivation?
6. When confronted by mutually exclusive behavior choices, how do people generally choose?
7. What is the security need, and how is it reflected in behavior?
8. What is the affiliation need, and how is it reflected in behavior?
9. What is the esteem need, and how is it reflected in behavior?
10. What is the power need, and how is it reflected in behavior?
11. What is the difference between power and autonomy?
12. What is the need for competence, and how is it reflected in behavior?
13. What is the need for achievement, and how is it reflected in behavior?
14. What does the hierarchical need structure mean?
15. What does it mean for a need to be lower than another on the need structure?
16. How is each individual unique in his or her need structure?
17. How does culture affect people's need structures?
18. What does it mean if the need for esteem is below the need for affiliation on the needs hierarchy?

Notes and References on Individual Needs and Motivation

1. Chester I. Barnard, *The Functions of the Executive* (Cambridge, Mass.: Harvard University Press, 1938).

2. For a general overview and elaboration upon the nature of the individual, see E. Aronson, *The Social Animal,* 4th ed. (New York: Freeman, 1984).

For application of biological models of motivation to organizations, see D. Morris, *The Human Zoo* (New York: McGraw-Hill, 1969); L. Tiger and R. Fox, *The Imperial Animal* (New York: Holt, Rinehart & Winston, 1971); and A. G. Kefalas and W. W. Suojanen, "Organizational Behavior and the New Biology, *Academy of Management Journal,* September 1974, pp. 514–26.

For applications of Freudian-type psychology, see A. Zaleznik and D. Moment, *Interpersonal Dynamics* (New York: John Wiley & Sons, 1964); H. Levinson, *The Exceptional Executive* (Cambridge, Mass.: Harvard University Press, 1968); and H. Levinson, *Psychological Man* (Cambridge, Mass.: Levinson Institute, 1976).

3. On the behavioral approach and operant conditioning (linking desired behavior with a pleasurable reward), see B. F. Skinner, *Science and Human Behavior* (New York: Macmillan, 1953); W. K. Honig, ed., *Operant Behavior: Areas of Research and Application* (New York: Appleton-Century-Crofts, 1966); Albert Bandura, *Principles of Behavior Modification* (New York: Holt, Rinehart & Winston, 1969); and W. R. Nord, "Beyond the Teaching Machine: Operant Conditioning in Management," *Organizational Behavior and Human Performance,* vol. 4 (1969), pp. 375–401.

Nord argues that this approach has been underutilized, compared with Maslow's hierarchy of needs. He attributes this to the need hierarchy being considered more attractive than the mechanistic and animal orientation of operant conditioning but, he points out, there is more evidence for it than for the need approach. Actually, no conflict exists between operant conditioning and the need hierarchy: The conditioner-influencer can reward the subject-follower with wants that satisfy any of the needs, as long as the recipient finds them satisfying or pleasurable.

The behavioralists argue that it is behavior itself that is satisfying, and no underlying needs exist. A. Decoufle and N. Schwartz, "The Concept of Needs: A Survey of Illusions," *Futures* 6, no. 1 (1974), pp. 16–26. For an opinion that ignoring needs may render behavioral psychology nonsensical, see R. L. Burgess and R. L. Akers, "Are Operant Principles Tautological?" *The Psychological Record,* Summer 1967, pp. 305–12.

4. T. A. Ryan, *Intentional Behavior: An Approach to Human Motivation* (New York: Ronald Press, 1970). For a discussion of the "determined" versus "free" debate, see I. Chein, *The Science of Behavior and the Image of Man* (New York: Basic Books, 1972). B. F. Skinner suggests that we tend to admire people whose acts appear self-controlled and free (e.g., the person who sacrifices for another when he or she doesn't "have to"). In contrast, we denigrate or feel sorry for people who are compelled to do something. Skinner maintains that the distinction is meaningless, because he believes *all* behavior is compelled in the sense that it is a learned response to an internal or external stimulus. *Beyond Freedom and Dignity* (New York: Alfred Knopf, 1971). Chein responds by maintaining that behavioral psychologists tend to think others are determined, but they treat themselves as free.

5. Douglas McGregor, *The Human Side of Enterprise* (New York: McGraw-Hill, 1960).

6. L. Currie, "Wants, Needs, Well-Being and Economic Growth," *Journal of Economic Studies,* May 1975, pp. 47–59.

7. The "locus of control" literature is concerned with people's perceptions of internal or external control of their rewards. See J. B. Rotter, *Generalized Expectancies for Internal versus External Control of Reinforcement,* Psychological Monographs No 6.09, vol. 80, no. 1 (1966). A person may be classified as "external" because she or he believes (1) the world is difficult, (2) the world is unjust, (3) the world is governed by luck, or (4) the world is unresponsive. B. E. Collins, "Four Components of the Rotter Internal-External Scale," *Journal of Personality and Social Psychology* 29, no. 3 (1974), pp. 381–91.

8. M. Harrow and A. Ferrante, "Locus of Control in Psychiatric Patients," *Journal of Consulting and Clinical Psychology,* vol. 33 (1969), pp. 582–89. "Learned helplessness" is the phenomenon that results when a subject learns that release from pain or reward acquisition is independent of his or her behavior. S. F. Maier, M. P. Seligman, and R. L. Solomon, "Pavlovian Fear Conditioning and Learned Helplessness," in B. A. Campbell and R. M. Church, eds., *Punishment and Aversive Behavior* (New York: Appleton-Century-Crofts, 1969). In addition, people with internal control orientations tend to learn more effectively because they modify their own behavior on the basis of performance results. S. Wolk and J. DuCette, "Intentional Performance and Incidental Learning as a Function of Personality and Task Dimensions," *Journal of Personality and Social Psychology* 29, no. 1 (1974), pp. 90–101.

9. The "God complex" is described by Ernest Jones in *Essays in Applied Psychoanalysis* (London: Hogarth, 1951).

10. In a large-scale survey of its readers, *Psychology Today* reported four attitudes that appeared essential to happiness: "(1) emotional security, (2) lack of cynicism, (3) belief that life has meaning and that one's guiding values are right, and (4) feelings of control over the good things that happen as opposed to feeling that one is a pawn of events." P. Shaver and J. Freedman, "Your Pursuit of Happiness," *Psychology Today,* August 1976, p. 26 ff.

11. C. P. Alderfer, *Existence, Relatedness and Growth: Human Needs in Organizational Settings* (New York: Free Press, 1972).

12. Abraham Maslow, "A Theory of Human Motivation," *Psychological Review,* vol. 50 (1943), pp. 370–

96. See also A. Maslow, *Motivation and Personality* (New York: Harper & Row, 1954).

13. In the early 1800s many courageous pioneers sought a passage west across the American continent. One of these was the Donner party, which with ox-drawn wagons traversed the western plains and climbed the mountains that blocked their way. Some years ago, a diary of a member of this party was published. At the beginning of the journey, he described his companions as the salt of the earth—God-fearing, individualistic, but cooperative and socially concerned for one another's welfare. For many, however, the trip ended high in the Rocky Mountains. Marooned by enormous snowdrifts, they were unable to move forward or go back. As their supply of food was exhausted and they slowly froze on the wind-swept slopes, the party gradually deteriorated. They withdrew into themselves; concern shifted from the larger group to the immediate family and then to the individual. Finally there emerged the ultimate horror, cannibalism.

This tragedy is an unpleasant illustration of the hierarchy of human needs. To those still living, food became all-important and all-motivating. See H. Croy, *Wheels West* (New York: Hastings House, 1955) and George Keithley, *The Donner Party* (New York: Braziller, 1971). Another book that describes similar horrors of the strong preying upon the weak is George Harrison Salisbury, *The 900 Days: The Siege of Leningrad* (New York: Harper & Row, 1969).

For a classic literary example of starvation, see Knut Hamsum, *Hunger* (New York: Alfred A. Knopf, 1968; originally published in 1899). For a modern actual example, see P. P. Read, *Alive: The Story of the Andes Survivors* (Philadelphia: J. B. Lippincott, 1974).

14. It may not be the absolute strength of any need that motivates behavior, but the relative strengths within a person. That is, Frank may have both stronger affiliative and achievement needs than Bill, but Bill's achievement need may be so much stronger compared with his affiliative need. See M. R. Blood, "Intergroup Comparison of Intraperson Differences: Rewards from the Job," *Personnel Psychology* 26, no. 1 (1973), pp. 1–9.

15. For review of research on Maslow's need hierarchy, see D. T. Hall and K. E. Nougain," An Examination of Maslow's Need Hierarchy in an Organizational Setting," *Organization Behavior and Human Performance,* February 1968, pp. 12–35, and K. H. Chung, "A Markov Chain Model of Human Needs: An Extension of Maslow's Need Theory," *Journal of Academy of Management* 12, no. 2 (1969), pp. 223–34.

16. There is great difficulty in testing whether people distinguish between these needs, especially at work. Most studies suggest that satisfaction is mixed, perhaps into three clusters covering: (1) lower needs—security and social; (2) middle needs—esteem, power, and pay; and (3) higher needs—self-esteem, autonomy, and self-actualization. See L. K. Waters and D. Roach, "A Factor Analysis of Need Fulfillment Items Designed to Measure Maslow Need Categories," *Personnel Psychology* 26, no. 2 (1973), pp. 185–90; and R. Payne, "Factor Analysis of a Maslow-type Need Satisfaction Questionnaire," *Personnel Psychology* 23 (1970), pp. 251–68.

17. The failure to find unqualified support for Maslow's need categories in actual organizational settings may be because specific questions are not representative of needs, and concepts are more abstract than organizational conditions; Maslow's theory was not aimed at organizational settings. B. Schneider and C. P. Alderfer, "Three Studies of Measures of Need Satisfaction in Organizations," *Administrative Science Quarterly* 18, no. 4 (1973), pp. 489–504.

18. A. Montagu, *Touching: The Human Significance of Skin* (New York: Columbia University Press, 1971).

19. J. Goodall, "Chimpanzees of the Gombe Stream Reserve," in I. De Vore, ed., *Primate Behavior* (New York: Holt, Rinehart & Winston, 1965), pp. 425–73.

20. W. F. Dean, as told to W. L. Worden, *General Dean's Story* (New York: Viking Press, 1954). We apparently want to give as much as receive. See W. Gaylin, *Caring* (New York: Alfred A. Knopf, 1976).

21. Martin Buber writes: "The basis of man's life with man is two-fold, and it is one—the wish of everyman to be confirmed as what he is, even what he can become, by men; and the innate capacity in man to confirm his fellowmen in this way." "Distance and Relation," *Psychiatry* 20 (1957), p. 101.

22. S. Schachter, *The Psychology of Affiliation* (Palo Alto, Calif.: Stanford University Press, 1959); L. S. Wrightsman, "Effects of Waiting with Others on Changes in Level of Felt Anxiety," *Journal of Abnormal and Social Psychology* 61 (1960), pp. 216–22; Y. Teichman, "Predisposition for Anxiety and Affiliation," *Journal of Personality and Social Psychology* 29, no. 3 (1974).

23. S. W. Gellerman, *Motivation and Productivity* (New York: American Management Association, 1963), p. 151; G. D. Lenski, *Power and Privilege: A Theory of Stratification* (New York: McGraw-Hill, 1966).

24. Milovan Diljias, *New New Class* (New York: Praeger Publishers, 1957).

25. An anthropologist provides an interesting example of the desire to avoid ridicule and how education is seen as the answer:
A great chief from New Guinea attended a South Pacific conference and was laughed at by educated people from other islands. After introducing himself, his speech was short. "I come from the bush. I have no English. I cannot read or write. My tongue is thick. My head is a stone. In my country I am a big man, yet I stand before you as a child. I have been a leader in battle with bow and arrow and spear, but today I am a baby feeding at its mother's breast. Soon I will die and in a little while my son will come here in my place and sit among you and speak English and write his name and be a leader among you, and you will not laugh at him.

Mason Williams, *The Stone Age Island: New Guinea Today* (Garden City, N.Y.: Doubleday Publishing, 1964).

26. R. W. White, "Motivation Reconsidered: The Concept of Competence," *Psychological Review,* vol. 66 (1959), pp. 297–334; David C. McClelland, "Testing for Competence Rather than Intelligence," *American Psychologist* 28 (1973), pp. 1–14.

27. H. L. Ansbacher and R. R. Ansbacher, eds., *The Individual Psychology of Alfred Adler* (New York: Basic Books, 1956).

28. D. G. Winter, *The Power Motive* (New York: Free Press, 1973). P. S. Prescott writes:
In the long run (if not in the short), power and responsibility are more interesting than either sex or money . . . shows what happens to men of exceptional ability and fathomless ambition when they get caught up in the kind of executive cruncher that only an organization as influential as *The New York Times* provides.

Review of G. Talese, *The Kingdom and the Power* (New York: NAL/World, 1969), in *Look,* July 15, 1969, p. 16.

29. G. H. Quester wrote:
It may thus be the sensation of power or priviness to power that politicians are more constantly pursuing. To have tremendous impact, but all in the course of a single day, would be less satisfying than to have less aggregate impact, but spread out on a day-by-day series of digestible and perceivable doses. . . . The goal that explains party platforms, bureaucratic plans, advice given to the President in an international crisis, and

so on, may simply be priviness, sensing and knowing in full detail what actually explained a government decision, even when one's control or impact over that decision was not as great. To read an account of a policy decision in *The New York Times* the following morning, and to note where the *Times* has gotten the story wrong, must be one of life's great pleasures.

" 'Priviness' as the Central Goal of Politics," *Public Policy* 19, no. 4 (1971), pp. 595–610.

30. Bertrand R. Russell, *Power, A New Social Analysis* (New York: W. W. Norton, 1938), p. 12.

31. *The Will to Power,* trans. A. M. Ludovici, (London: Macmillan, 1929), p. 41.

32. Rollo May, *Power and Innocence: A Search for the Sources of Violence* (New York: W. W. Norton, 1972). It has even been suggested that excessive drinking is linked to those for whom personalized power is of particular concern; people drink to feel stronger. David C. McClelland et al., *The Drinking Man: Alcohol and Human Motivation* (New York: Free Press, 1972).

33. Lord Acton, *Essays on Freedom and Power* (New York: Noonday Press, 1943); Reinhold Niebuhr, *The Nature and Destiny of Man* (New York: Charles Scribner's Sons, 1949).

34. Abraham H. Maslow, *Motivation and Personality* (New York: Harper & Row, 1954) p. 92.

35. H. Heckhausen, *The Anatomy of Achievement Motivation* (New York: Academic Press, 1967).

36. Results of research on the relation between need for achievement and school performance are ambiguous, but, in general, less relationship is found with males than with females. This may be because achievement-oriented boys find school boring and do not especially value teacher or parental admiration. However, girls may tend to be less confident of their academic abilities and therefore find it more challenging. Of course, they also may be more obedient to teachers and parents. See T. Gjesme, "Sex Differences in the Connection between Need for Achievement and School Performance," *Journal of Applied Psychology* 58, no. 2 (1973), pp. 270–72, and D. Cole et al, "The Relation of Achievement Imagery Scores to Academic Performance," *Journal of Abnormal and Social Psychology* 65 (1962), pp. 208–11.

37. D. C. McClelland et al., *The Achievement Motive* (New York: Appleton-Century-Crofts, 1953).

38. D. C. McClelland, *The Achieving Society* (Princeton, N.J.: D. Van Nostrand, 1961). Recent support for McClelland's contention that achievement need is a central contributor to a nation's economic growth is given by K. B. Freeman, "The Significance of McClelland's Achievement Variable in the Aggregate Production Function," *Economic Development and Cultural Change,* July 1976, pp. 815–24.

39. On altruism, see J. H. Bryan and M. J. Test, "Models and Helping: Naturalistic Studies in Aiding Behavior," *Journal of Personality and Social Psychology* 6 (1967), pp. 400–7, and "Positive Forms of Social Behavior," special issue of *The Journal of Social Issues* 28, no. 3 (1972). A recent study suggests that people who risk injury to help others tend to be people familiar with violence and who enjoy the risk and attention. T. Huston, G. Geis, R. Thomas, and T. Garrett, "Good Samaritans as Crime Victims" in E. Viana, ed., *Crimes, Victims and Society,* (Leiden, Netherlands: Sijthoff, 1976).

40. What about religion and our spiritual yearning? We know that aspirations for immortality and closeness to God or gods are ancient, universal human traits. There also has been widespread debate over what they mean. Religious skeptics tend to see spirituality as a want that gives the illusion of satisfying fundamental needs. Thus Karl Marx labeled religion as "the opiate of the people"; Voltaire observed, "If God didn't exist, man would have to invent him"; and H. L. Mencken suggested, "Man created God in his own image." For the skeptic, religion fits into several levels in the need hierarchy: The ruling classes use religion as a vehicle for maintaining their preferential position; the followers find escape from the reality of an onerous world in the mumbo jumbo of religion; and for the people at the bottom of the social ladder, religion is a false search for security from the anxieties of daily life. Believers in religion, however, see human beings as possessing an inherent need to know, love, and worship God. For them, religion is very important and hence low on the need hierarchy; it is a prepotent need that must be satisfied before other needs will become motivating.

The biblical tale of Job suggests that we need God and might even prefer to give up all our needs (including life) in the worship of the Almighty. A modern version of this tale was presented some years ago in Archibald MacLeish's play *J. B.* A successful business owner, J. B. has a family, status, esteem, power, and achievement. In short, a wide variety of his lower and higher needs are satisfied, or he has an opportunity to satisfy them. Satan argues with God that J. B. will be reduced to the animal level, cursing God and seeking only physiological necessities if God will give Satan power over him. God does, and J. B. is put to the test: His business fails, his children are killed in an automobile accident, his wife leaves him, his home is destroyed, and he falls victim to a grievous disease. In the final act, J. B. grovels on the stage clad in rags, reduced to a pitiful state of deprivation. Nonetheless, he does not curse God; he still seeks higher values, even in the face of death. All of his higher needs have not been extinguished. Similarly, the diarist from the Donner party, referred to earlier, ends his entries with a notation that he expects to die shortly. Death came because he refused to participate in cannibalism. He had higher level needs which we was willing to pursue unto death.

J. B. and Job are fictional characters meant to suggest desirable human characteristics. The Judeo-Christian religion recognizes that most, if not all, of us are weak, and out of this weakness grows anxiety. In the New Testament we are enjoined not to be anxious—especially about our economic affairs.

> See how the lilies of the field grow; they neither toil nor spin, yet I say to you that not even Solomon in all his glory was arrayed like one of these. . . . But if God so clothes the grass of the field, which today is alive and tomorrow is thrown into the oven, how much more you, oh you of little faith! Therefore do not be anxious, saying "What shall we eat?" or "What shall we drink?" or "What shall we put on?" (The Gospel according to Matthew, Chapter 6:28–30.)

But humankind is anxious, always has been, and probably always will be. Our efforts to improve our standard of living and free ourselves form the vicissitudes of nature have been a persistent historical theme. Indeed, the Judeo-Christian tradition maintains that much of our economic effort is rooted in the basic anxiety of the human situation.

41.   Among people who grew up in poor families, those who received little love seem to later value money much more than those who received a lot of love as children. J. Horn, "Love: The Most Important Ingredient in Happiness," *Psychology Today,* July 1976, p. 98ff.

42.   Some years ago a meeting of psychoanalysts debated whether artist-geniuses were sane or insane in single-mindedly pursuing creativity. Some thought them neurotic, at least, in denying existence and relatedness needs. Others described them as the most rational and healthy of all, since they were self-actualizing. P. Hofmann, "Artists Defended on Mental Health," *The New York Times,* February 21, 1966. See also O. Rank, *Art and Artist: Creative Urge and Personality Development* (New York: Alfred A. Knopf, 1932).

43.   See R. A. LeVine, ed., *Culture and Personality: Contemporary Readings* (Hawthorne, N.Y.: Aldine Publishing, 1973), and "On Personality and Society," special issue of *American Journal of Sociology* 78, no. 2 (1972).

44.   Ruth Benedict, *Patterns of Culture* (Boston: Houghton Mifflin, 1934).

45.   Mason Haire, Edwin E. Ghiselli, and Lyman W. Porter, *Managerial Thinking* (New York: John Wiley & Sons, 1966). See also, S. Ronen and A. I. Kraut, "Similarities among Countries Based on Employee Work Values and Attitudes," *Columbia Journal of World Business,* Summer 1977, pp. 10–18.

4

Money, Work, and Human Needs

FIGURE 4–1

The Motivation to Work

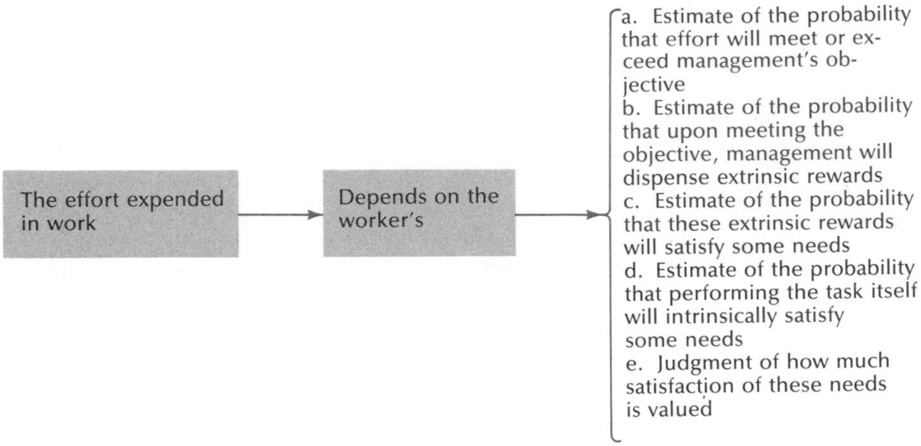

| The effort expended in work | → | Depends on the worker's | → | a. Estimate of the probability that effort will meet or exceed management's objective
 b. Estimate of the probability that upon meeting the objective, management will dispense extrinsic rewards
 c. Estimate of the probability that these extrinsic rewards will satisfy some needs
 d. Estimate of the probability that performing the task itself will intrinsically satisfy some needs
 e. Judgment of how much satisfaction of these needs is valued |

The motivation to work depends essentially on what the worker expects to get out of it.[1] Whether or not the employee will put much effort into work depends on the extrinsic rewards offered by management and on how intrinsically satisfying the task is to him or her—as Figure 4–1 illustrates.

The model is a helpful concept for beginning to understand the complexities of human behavior at work. It helps us to raise questions about the worker and work. Is it a simple, routine, and repetitive job that provides only money and perhaps security? Is it a complex and creative task that provides challenge and opportunity for achievement? Does the work make any difference to the worker? How can the task and rewards be designed to draw out the worker's efforts? These are the questions to be considered in this chapter.

Work and Survival

In examining the relationship between work and human nature, there is no more appropriate place to start than the Bible. The issue of work and its meaning is considered at the very beginning, in a passage dealing with the origins of life and humankind. Regardless of whether you believe that the Book of Genesis is literal, allegorical, metaphorical, or pure myth, it does deal with the fundamental issue of work, and its viewpoint has been pervasive. In the Garden of Eden, all the necessities of life are supplied; the physiological wants are met without effort or anxiety. It is Paradise. But Adam and Eve are said to have disobeyed certain divine laws, and God was angered. The Lord said to Adam:

> Because thou hast harkened to the voice of thy wife—and hast eaten of the tree wherefore I commanded thee that thou shouldst not eat, cursed is the earth with thy work; with labor and toil shalt thou eat thereof all the days of thy life.

In the sweat of thy face shalt thou eat bread till thou return to the earth out of which thou wast taken, for dust thou art and unto dust thou shalt return.[2]

What is the meaning of work in this passage? It implies clearly that work is a punishment and suggests further that work will be dirty, demeaning, and generally unpleasant, as befits the punishment that it is. And the reason for this work is to provide the physiological necessities of life. The meaning of the expulsion from Paradise is humankind's confrontation with its animal nature and its physiological needs—and its mortality.[3]

Work and Basic Needs

In addition to indicating that work is an unpleasant punishment necessary for survival, the biblical passage above implies that much of life is to be consumed in trying to satisfy our most basic needs; it is to be a brutal struggle for survival. Certainly for most of humankind, throughout most of history, in most societies, most of life has consisted of working to satisfy the lowest needs. In an industrialized country, such as the United States, this necessity to work means that most of us must find a job. Few are fortunate enough to be born to parents so situated that we do not have to earn money from a job in order to live.

From Washington Star Syndicate, Inc., "The Small Society."

Ever since Americans rejected the attractive but simplistic vision of a nation of independent yeoman farmers and chose instead the goal of a wealthy, complex, interdependent society, we have been moving to the cities and multiplying. Indeed, there is probably not enough arable land available for all of us to return to the Jeffersonian ideal. The possibilities for a Walden Pond type of independent existence are as dead as Thoreau. In short, we must work to earn the money to pay for the goods necessary to satisfy our physiological needs. Of course, we would also like to accumulate seniority and job security so that we can feel secure about the future. In the United States many jobs will meet these requirements, but this is a fairly recent development. For many people, having a job has been no guarantee that they could really live. The 19th and 20th centuries have provided many examples of concerted efforts by workers to improve their pay so they could meet their fundamental needs more comfortably. Even subsistence was at times in doubt.[4] We can be thankful that a job today generally provides sufficient pay for survival, at least.

Work and its financial rewards are obviously essential for most of us. Generally, we find a job and expend sufficient effort to keep it. Whether we exert greater effort beyond this minimum depends partially on our expectation that additional money (and associated promotions) will provide satisfaction of other needs.

Money and Basic Needs

Money is obviously most important for satisfying physiological and security needs. Whether used to purchase necessary goods, insurance policies, or preferred stock or deposited in the bank, money provides some feeling of security, especially if job tenure guarantees a predictable future flow. Given current crime rates in our cities, money may also be valued as a means of escape, of finding safety by moving into a different neighborhood or out to suburbia. For chronically insecure people, money can be the means for overcoming an unhappy childhood, a shield against disaster, and an enduring protective mother.[5]

Work and Social Satisfaction

The primary source of social satisfaction has been the family, but must the affiliation need also be recognized by employers as pertaining to work?

Work and Affiliation

Employers of the 19th and early 20th centuries saw no need for social satisfaction on the job. In office and shop, their posted policies frequently forbade "socializing," "idle gossip," or "conspiratorial meetings." Scientific management experts advised managers to treat people strictly as individuals and to offer individual piece-rate incentive pay to encourage each employee to produce to his or her maximum. Managers in the 1920s and 1930s were aware that many (if not most) workers limited their personal efforts in order to maintain their membership in an informal social structure.[6] At some point, for virtually everyone except the individualistic "rate-busters," the desire for communication, support, and friendship with associates on the job and during working hours becomes more important than the little bit of extra money that might be earned.

This relationship between work and affiliation satisfaction varies with the people involved, of course, but affiliative-oriented people are attracted to organizations in which they can communicate with others like themselves.[7] For young, unmarried, female clerical workers in an insurance company office, for example, physical conditions and management policy must be adjusted to recognize the affiliation need. Many of them may come to work mainly to fill the social gap that exists after high school graduation if they do not go to college or marry quickly. For ambitious, young saleswomen working on commissions, however, on-the-job satisfaction with fellow workers is much less relevant. Nonetheless, almost everyone socializes on the job, if task and technology allow it.[8]

In addition to maintenance of a family and provision for social relations with workers, Sigmund Freud suggested a third way a job can aid in the satisfaction of the affiliation need. Freud saw a job as forcing a person to set aside his or her own concerns and confront the world.[9] A job imposes discipline. It requires interpersonal communications that assist the individual to learn about the norms of society around us and to maintain a sense of reality, identity, and stability by continually testing our own views against societal norms. Not that these norms are always right, but the job and the contact with the world that the job requires enables a person to live in that world more easily and to find desired social satisfactions. In some ways, it provides a justification for existence.

Research on the mental health and attitudes of long-term unemployed males supports these suggestions.[10] These studies directly indicate the relevance of the job or a person's sense of membership in a society. Even though welfare and a variety of other governmental programs lessened fears and anxieties about the satisfaction of physiological and security needs, the unemployed men felt out of place. They were not members; they were not fulfilling the requirements of the head of the household. In many cases they became withdrawn and depressed, unable even to take satisfaction in the joys of their families. They were simply not confronting the world in the way that our society values.

A moving illustration of the purposiveness a job may provide is shown by the case of a Harlem sign painter who was retired at 93. After a lifetime of work and two days of retirement, William Washington Brooks went to the state unemployment office, not to apply for unemployment compensation or social security but to find a new job. When asked why, he responded: "A man, if he is a man, has got to work. A man with no work has part of his manhood taken away from him, and also his pride."[11]

From the opposite end of the economic scale, one of America's richest men took a job as a teacher against his family's wishes, after graduating from Harvard. He echoes Mr. Brooks' comments.

> I wouldn't change that experience one iota. I used to have more damn fun, great fun. I think it was the greatest experience I've had, because then I worked for somebody. This gives you a very different outlook on life than if you always order people around. It's unfortunate that many people I know never worked for anyone else and do nothing. These people are to be pitied. I could name a dozen of them I pity. I believe I'm the only member of my family who ever did work, who ever did take home a salary. But that's the greatest exeprience you can have.[12]

Money and Affiliation

Money may not be able to buy love and affiliation, but it helps. A family will play the major role in satisfying your social needs, but a job and income are still essential; you cannot live solely on love, nor can two live as cheaply as one (they probably require four times as much). Perhaps unfortunately, stable jobs and predictable funds are requisites for a stable and satisfying family life.[13]

Outside the family, although money may not buy friends, it can purchase hangers-on, groupies, and very friendly companions—as champion boxers and rock singers, for example, have discovered. It may also provide the opportunity to move in the social circles with which you want to associate (providing, of course, that you have the appropriate social veneer in knowing how to speak, eat, play, and so on). Moving to a posh neighborhood or joining the country club will not guaranteed friendships, but they may improve the chance for you and your children to meet the right people, especially if you are a status climber who identifies with wealthier people and has little desire to associate with your current peers.[14]

Work and Prestige

In reply to the question, "What do you do?" Americans generally respond with statements of association: "I'm associated with IBM," or "I'm with GE." Fifty years ago, the replies would have been, "I'm a machinist," or "I'm an accountant." The earlier responses were a legacy of the traditional European societies, where a person's craft has been a major determinant of social esteem, status, or prestige. However, craft in these countries was mainly determined by birth or family, which were the true status determinants. The United States has been less rigid in terms of social class. For example, attitudes toward status distinctions vary with geography and socioeconomic background—the criteria for social esteem in the Northeast or among the middle class is quite different from those in the Southwest or among the working class. But a person's association with a particular company of wide repute is a source of status. In the United States, the corporation as a source of social prestige has begun to obliterate the older tradition of status differentiation on the basis of vocation.

Work and Social Esteem

Position titles are perhaps the most pervasive means of giving social esteem on the job. Years ago Dale Carnegie, in the first edition of *How to Win Friends and Influence People,* described a janitor who felt rewarded when his title was changed to "custodial engineer" (so much so that he apparently did not complain about not getting a raise along with the title).[15] Today, at higher organizational levels, title escalation continues. More firms are calling division managers vice presidents and even presidents. The three-person "executive office" is growing in popularity, partly because this gives executive vice presidents the status they believe they deserve. "The value of the title is usually underestimated," contends the chairman of a company with 10 vice presidents among 200 employees. And a consultant argues that to a person who is not yet a vice president, the title may be worth 5 to 10 percent of his or her salary.[16]

Within the corporation, elaborated hierarchies of positions and their attendant status symbols and perquisites reflect the desire for status differentiation. Management ignores the necessity to correlate pay, title, and authority and status symbols at its peril. "A name on the door rates a Bigelow on the floor"—the advertising slogan for a rug manufacturer—has some validity; people expect title, pay, and status to be consistent. A large regional insurance office is a case in point. Two huge rooms stretch out like an airplane hangar, aisle after aisle. With clerks, secretaries, representatives, claimspersons, supervisors, and department heads all seated at seemingly identical desks, row after row, the scene resembles a bureaucratic nightmare in its mechanistic oppressiveness. Not surprisingly, management has difficulty with superior-subordinate relations, and particularly with supervisory morale. Giving out important-sounding titles (or even more money) would be inadequate to satisfy the desire for status on this job. One of the principal causes of dissatisfaction is the lack of physical manifestation of status differences, including individual manager offices to give quiet and privacy.

Money and Social Esteem

A magazine advertisement for an expensive scotch contained only these words: "Sometimes when a man has worked very hard and succeeded, he enjoys ordering things just because they're expensive." What is supposedly enjoyable? It is doubtful that the scotch is actually better than other brands. The implied satisfaction lies in a sense of esteem in being able to spend more. America has often been criticized by foreign and domestic moralists for this materialistic behavior. They may be correct, but it is not all bad. More than 200 years ago, an Englishman decried the efforts of rich businessleaders to obtain status and prestige by proclaiming, "Riches do not gain hearty respect; they only procure external attention." Nonetheless, in the United States, more than in most nations, money did bring prestige—if not in one generation, certainly in two. Through the "conspicuous consumption" of purchasing unnecessary or excessively expensive goods (such as buying a Cadillac Eldorado rather than a Chevrolet sedan), the American climbs the social ladder. This is an exaggeration, however, because even in America, prestige is affected by other factors—such as occupation, family reputation, education, and unfortunately, race, ethnicity, and religion.[17] However much we may criticize our materialism, it has reflected

"This is a crime of passion. I'm madly
in love with money."

democracy, opportunity, and an open society. Money's ability to bring social esteem has been an important contributor to our economic growth.

In recent years there has been much conjecture that middle-class young people are less interested in money than their parents are. As we mentioned in the preceding chapter, this could be because they have known relative security and affluence. They do not see money as such a vital necessity as do others who are less fortunate. But merely to say that young people are less interested in money is very misleading. In an informal survey, high school seniors indicated that they were not interested in becoming millionaires or working to amass a fortune.[18] Yet the average income that they expected to eventually achieve was over twice the income of the average American family! It takes substantial effort to reach this expected level, more than they probably expect. And they probably overestimate how well they will live with that income. If students are motivated to reach $40,000 per year (in today's dollars), it hardly suggests a decline in the importance of money.

Work and Higher Needs

In addition to serving as a source of satisfaction for physical demands, security, affiliation, and social esteem, the job also can help satisfy the more elusive concepts of competence, power, and achievement. A major contribution to self-esteem can come from competent performance of one's job. Indeed, many years ago this drive for self-esteem and competence was termed the *instinct for good workmanship.*[19] Management at the Maytag Company attributes the legendary reliability of its clothes washers to the work ethic of its employees. Located amidst cornfields in Newton, Iowa, the work force consists largely of people off the farms who, in the words of Maytag's president, "expect to *work* eight hours for eight hours' pay."[20] For some people the job can be a major satisfier of the drives for self-actualization. Running one's own business or managing an organization can provide the authority, prominence, challenge, and satisfying feedback craved by persons with high needs for power and achievement.[21] Work is a more central life interest, and they are concerned about career success.[22] A manifestation of the increased entrance of women into careers is reflected in a significant increase from the 1950s to the present of women who tie life success to job satisfaction.[23]

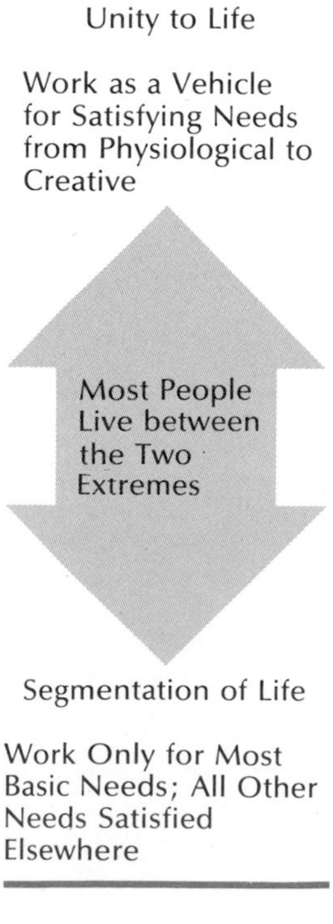

For such people, life possesses a kind of unity. (See Figure 4–2.) The labor they perform to gain life's necessities may also be done to express their higher level drives. The idealistic physician cures the sick, obtains the necessary victuals, pays for a Mercedes, and expresses creativity—all with the same activity. This perhaps accounts for the long hours professionals and executives work and their oft-quoted statements that they find recreation and fun in work, that their work is their life. This view of the centrality of work as an expression of human nature is illustrated by the romantic phrases in a little pamphlet formerly distributed to school children: "This is my work; my blessing, not my doom; of all who live, I am the one by whom this work can best be done in the right way." More recently, Pope Paul VI said that, "Work makes men noble and fosters brotherhood, humility, freedom, happiness and the spirit of adventure. . . . Work is thus the basis of modern social life."[24]

Nonetheless, for many (and probably most) men and women, their jobs do not

FIGURE 4–2

Unity to Life

Work as a Vehicle for Satisfying Needs from Physiological to Creative

Most People Live between the Two Extremes

Segmentation of Life

Work Only for Most Basic Needs; All Other Needs Satisfied Elsewhere

provide this kind of satisfaction—and it may be unreasonable to expect that they ever will. As jobs are related to the human need structure, it becomes clear that for some of us there is a unity (or at least substantial overlap) between labor and work, between activity to satisfy the lower needs and activity to satisfy higher needs. For most people, however, lower and higher needs are satisfied by entirely different activities. For example, work on automobile assembly lines is frequently cited as offering little satisfaction except money.[25] It is so busy, noisy, and machine controlled that workers can hardly socialize. A vice president of the United Automobile Workers conducted a membership survey to determine what union members wanted the leadership to demand of corporate management. His observation:

> Early retirement is far and away the major demand from rank and filers. It surprises me, but it's there. Early retirement comes through so clearly there's no question about priority. A guy puts in 20 years bucking that line and it's not so pleasant. Thus, the demand comes through. Money comes second.[26]

Minimizing time spent at work makes sense for a job with so few intrinsic satisfactions. Work a shorter week or retire early in order to have the time to satisfy all those needs that cannot be satisfied through work.[27] Segment your life sharply between time spent on and off the job.[28]

Money and Power

Money can also provide a feeling of power, and independent wealth can create a strong sense of autonomy. This was the source of Jefferson's contention that an independent income is essential in a political democracy. Think of what money can do for a young man of 18; for one thing, it can get him a car, which seems to promise freedom and escape from his parents: "I've got a hot-rod Ford and a two-dollar bill" is a line from an old song. A study shows that college students with high needs for power spend more money on prestige supplies—expensive liquor, quadraphonic sound systems, powerful motorcycles or automobiles—in other words, on things that will make them feel big, strong, powerful, and respected.

That young man's father probably sees a similar association between money and autonomy. One of the ambitions of many working Americans is to declare their independence by telling the boss to go to hell. Few of us have the courage to do this without having some money on hand or another promised job. As families move up in income above middle levels, their lifestyle changes less dramatically in material possessions than in attitudes and behavior. Contrary to the popular image, they do not necessarily purchase Continentals or build mansions. Those who achieve affluence apparently change most in two areas. First, they pay off their debts and are reluctant to incur new ones; freedom from financial obligations to others is one of the most profound satisfactions of high income. Second, they travel much more than other people, for travel seems to be a major vehicle for acting out the freedom that money offers.[29]

Money and Self-Esteem

The purchase of self-esteem is more ambiguous. Philosophers speak of the emptiness of prestige and material possessions unless one also has a personal sense of self-esteem. Nonetheless, many people seem to judge themselves in terms of what they earn. A recent television program demonstrated that people tend to respond to the question, "What do you do?" with the name of the organization for whom they work or with a statement like, "I earned $50,000 last year." A woman magazine editor, however, said "Ask me about sex life. Ask me my age. But don't ask my salary. I won't tell you. You'd stop taking me seriously because I earn so little. . . . Self-esteem is the reason. Money is our medium of exchange and many of us confuse it with real value and worth." In a competitive society, people may conclude that they are good if society pays them a substantial income. High pay becomes a measure of accomplishment, a sign of ability, your "score" in the game of life. In 1977, the highest paid business executive in the United States was the chairman of the Rapid-American Corporation who earned $915,866.[30] It neither reflected need nor his corporation's performance.

A student explored this motivation with the president of a food chain company. In reply to her question of why he worked, the president stated, "Well, for many reasons, but my house is important. When I pull into the driveway after a day's work and see that big, beautiful English Tudor mansion, I feel good. It makes it all worthwhile." Whether or not you accept this executive's sentiments, do not ignore the fact that it is not simply "keeping ahead of the Joneses" that motivates this man. He takes personal pleasure in what money has built; he feels satisfaction with himself.

Money and Achievement

The key to money's motivating power for higher-level needs is the person's ability to conceive of it as a means for future satisfaction and as a symbol of achievement instead of just a medium of exchange for obtaining immediate goods. When money is seen as a vehicle for long-run satisfactions, the job is considered more important. Colleges have little difficulty recruiting students for jobs, and summer positions are eagerly sought. Waiting on tables; hawking peanuts; and selling tickets, calenders, and birthday cakes are activities intended to earn money, not self-actualization. Of course students use some of the money they earn for short-run expenditures on food, clothes, dates, and fun, but the major reason for this work is to pay for school tuition and living expenses. They see a logical connection between present effort, money, and the long-run satisfactions that a college education will facilitate (and which perhaps will bring more money later). This may be an obvious thought process to you, but it does not exist everywhere and with everyone.

In some underdeveloped countries such as West Africa, business has experienced difficulty in attracting and holding native workers. They work a few weeks, collect and save their pay, and then return to their villages.[31] Some managers facilely conclude that these workers are lazy people with no ambition. Although it may be true that most West Africans do not feel the same compulsion to work as do many Americans, it is not true that they possess neither ambition nor higher-level needs. The problem is that they see their pay as related only to low-level needs. After earning and saving enough to support their basic necessities at their accustomed

Motivation for Money Depends upon

• whether or not it is perceived as means for long-run satisfaction

• whether or not it is perceived as means for obtaining wants that satisfy several needs.

• socioeconomic backgrounds

• strength of needs for autonomy, competence, and achievement.

• desire for intrinsically satisfying work

level, the natives return to their villages, the only place where they feel their needs for affiliation, esteem, and power can be satisfied. They neither expect nor conceive of a continually rising living standard requiring more and more money. Similarly, in Tahiti men have demonstrated little interest in working for money when they have to commit themselves to a fixed number of hours per day. Work is not valued, while free time is. They worked harder for money when they learned the satisfactions from purchasing goods and, more important, when payment shifted from time-based pay to payment immediately upon completion of the task. Under this plan, the natives will attempt to complete the task, collect their pay, and leave as early as possible. They like "fast money," not "slow money."[32]

The paradox of the poorest people in the poorest countries being the least responsive to money is widespread. Living on farms and in villages, they have always existed outside of a market and money economy. They must learn what money can do for them before they submit permanently to factory work and money's lure.

Even in the United States, money's meaning depends on a person's background. To those who have always been short of it, money can be relatively more important in the short run and less so in the long run. Poor children tend to perceive a quarter coin as physically larger than children of wealthier parents do.[33] In addition, poorer children tend to demonstrate less ability to delay gratification; they want the coin now rather than waiting for a greater payment later. Similarly, employees with more modest socioeconomic origins tend to be motivated by less money to perform a certain job than people from wealthier backgrounds are. A pay of $175 per week looks like big money to a poor high school junior; he may well be tempted to drop out of school and take such a job. A middle-class youth realizes that such pay and such a job probably offer little future, and certainly not the $40,000 a year he is thinking about.

How much money per year would it require to convince you to accept a certain job? It would depend on the job, of course, but suppose it were a totally boring, repetitive task devoid of any intrinsic interest. Suppose it was scrubbing the tile floor of an enormous office building with a toothbrush. This is a question which a group of young industrial engineers used to pose to themselves and others. What would your answer be? $10,000? $20,000? $50,000 per year? Your response will depend on your background, current needs, and personality, especially your need for achievement.[34] A person low in achievement drive is likely to be more motivated for money than the achievement-oriented person who is more concerned about the personal satisfaction the job offers. Paradoxically, then, for a relatively boring job, the higher achiever will want *more* money than a person with less need for achievement. The latter will work for less because he is not sacrificing satisfaction of his achievement need by taking the job. In contrast, the higher achiever apparently expects to be paid for his inability to satisfy this need.[35]

On jobs that are more intrinsically satisfying, achievement-oriented people tend to do their best, regardless of whether or not money is offered as reward. People with relatively low achievement needs, on the other hand, will work harder for increased financial rewards.[36] The major point is that the *more* money means to you for satisfying lower level needs, the *less* amount you will work for. The less money means to you for satisfying lower level needs and the more it is a vehicle for higher level needs, the more you will want for your work.

Money and Happiness

Among the inalienable rights enumerated in the Declaration of Independence are "life, liberty and the pursuit of happiness." Americans have been assiduously pursuing the elusive butterfly of happiness ever since, and money is part of this quest. Most of us were taught that "money won't buy happiness," and we believe it, but we also believe the "philosopher" Sophie Tucker, who observed, "I've been rich and I've been poor—but rich is better!"

Popular polls and systematic research do suggest that money and happiness are related. One poll shows a perfect correlation between income and personal statements of being very happy.[37] As average incomes have risen after World War II, the proportion of people describing themselves as "very happy" has consistently climbed. Americans today report themselves as far happier than in similar polls 25 years ago. In addition, those now earning over $15,000 per year are more likely to express this feeling than those earning $10,000–15,000, who in turn state they are happier than those earning $7,000–10,000, and so on. This polling was recently extended on a worldwide basis to industrialized and still-developing nations. It concluded that people in the less-developed countries enjoy less psychological and material well-being than do those in industrialized societies. The director of the research told the U.S. Senate Foreign Relations Committee, "Nearly half of the people of the world are engaged in an unending struggle for survival. Only in the advanced industrial states of the Western world can the inhabitants engage in anything akin to a 'pursuit of happiness.' . . . it was hoped that somewhere in the world a nation would be found whose people are poor but happy. We didn't find such a place."[38] Of course, the findings don't prove money brings happiness, but it does buy certain goods and conditions that provide opportunity to satisfy various needs.

From *The Wall Street Journal,* with permission of Cartoon Features Syndicate.

Nonetheless, there does seem to be an exception to this positive relationship between money and happiness: as Figure 4–3 indicates, reported happiness of college graduates appears to be unrelated to income. Although they are the happiest people in the lower income categories, they are the least happy group among those who earn the highest amounts of money. Possibly, college graduates' expectations exceed their accomplishments. Or perhaps they don't value money or economic security as highly as nongraduates do. They may think that having an important or exciting life is more valuable than having a rich or secure one. Consequently, they may care more about the psychological conditions of their jobs than the material ones.

Whatever it really is, happiness may stem from certain optimistic attitudes toward life that facilitate behavior that brings success. Happiness could in fact lead to money; some support for this relationship is found in research that demonstrates that higher income and better mental health seem to be associated. The poor tend to feel sicker physically and to be sicker mentally than the "well-to-do" (an apt phrase that combines income and mental state).[39] The popular stereotype of the harried, ulcerprone, nervous, wealthy male executive with a neurotic and hypochondriac wife is mainly false. To be sure, they are more likely to seek medical and psychiatric treatment, but in general the evidence indicates that it is the poor—trapped in substandard housing; dead-end, temporary, or nonexistent jobs; and no expectation of improvement—who experience more mental illness.

Thus money earned from a job can apply to the entire need hierarchy. Of course, money is not the sole source of need satisfaction. Socializing, discretion, responsibility, craftsmanship, and creativity are all work satisfactions. With higher needs for

FIGURE 4–3

Income and Happiness

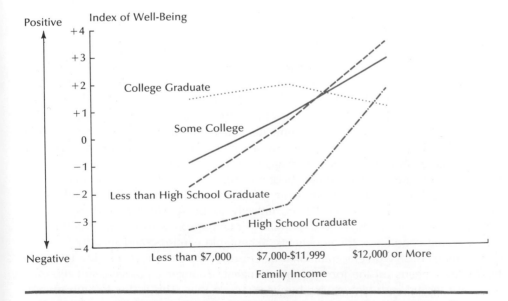

From P. Shaver and J. Freedman, "Your Pursuit of Happiness," *Psychology Today,* August 1976, p. 27.

competence and achievement, money is undoubtedly less important as a source of satisfaction than with physiological and security needs. Nonetheless, it seldom completely disappears, for it is a symbol that objectifies those things people value. The meaning of money as a symbol may change with a person's life history, for it is a neutral object each one interprets in terms of his or her needs. It may or may not be the root of all evil, but it certainly contributes to satisfaction of many needs. Its potential as a motivator is that it can be a want for multiple reasons. Management can utilize this potential.

Philosophies of Work

From the foregoing discussion, three major perspectives on work emerge:

Work as . . .
● punishment or
● intrinsically good or
● a means to satisfy needs

1. A job may be viewed as a punishment necessary to satisfy physiological and security requirements. Higher drives are to be pursued elsewhere, if at all. Work may even be seen as being commanded and therefore as inferiorizing and degrading. The truly successful person does not have to work.[40]

2. A job may be viewed as good in itself. "Work is noble," states the Talmud, "because it honors the workman." In the United States this has become the secularized Protestant ethic of Benjamin Franklin—and of Richard Nixon, who stated: "Labor is good in itself. A man or woman at work not only makes a contribution to his fellow man, but becomes a better person by virtue of the act of working."[41]

3. A job may be viewed as good only insofar as it is a means to at least partial satisfaction of a wide range of needs—for physical necessities, for social satisfaction and esteem, and, more important, for competence and achievement. In other words, work must have a purpose known to the worker.[42] As the French novelist Albert Camus put it, "Without work all life goes rotten. But when work is soulless, life stifles and dies."

It should be obvious that a manager cannot assume what work means to subordinates, nor that they all agree on its meaning, at least not above the necessity to obtain funds to satisfy basic needs. As an illustration of the differing expectations and desires that people demonstrate toward work, Figure 4–4 summarizes the views of several thousand employees in various kinds of positions. They ranked the four most important goals they hoped to achieve through their jobs, and these goals were then collected by the needs they appeal to.

The most dramatic evidence to emerge is that unskilled workers rank all four top goals corresponding to low needs on the hierarchy, and research professionals rank all four goals at high levels. Perhaps professionals take the fulfillment of lower level needs for granted; they forget about the importance of these needs. In contrast, unskilled workers are not likely to attain positions offering job challenge and autonomy, and the higher level needs are unlikely to be satisfied through their jobs; such needs are not considered important in comparison with lower level goals of nice working conditions, fringe benefits, acceptable earnings, and security.[43]

The blue-collar worker's traditional failure to complain about inability to satisfy higher level needs on the job may be changing. Younger employees are reported to be dissatisfied with high-paying but unattractive jobs. This is due to "job monotony," according to a UAW local president. "Five years ago, the union didn't even

FIGURE 4–4 ═══

Four Most Important Goals of Types of Employees

Goals Ranked in Need Hierarchy	Professionals in R&D	Managers	Technicians	Clerical Workers	Unskilled Workers
High—self-actualization and esteem needs:					
Challenge	1	1	3		
Training					
Autonomy	3	2			
Up-to-dateness	2	2			
Use of skills	4				
Middle—social needs:					
Cooperation		3/4		1	
Manager		3/4	4	2	
Friendly department				3	
Efficient department				4	
Low:					
Security			1		2
Earnings			2		3
Benefits					4
Physical conditions					1

Source: G. W. Hofstede, "The Colors of Collars," *Columbia Journal of World Business* 7, no. 5 (1972), pp. 72–79.

discuss it. But now they are, for younger, better educated workers are less compliant than their parents. For them, pay is not sufficient for life spent on the line. They are still a minority, but their pressure does concern management."[44] Concern has reached the point in some organizations where management has instituted programs to modify tasks so that they are more intrinsically satisfying.

SUMMARY

All who work do so because they expect to gain satisfaction from doing so. Most of us must work in order to earn the funds necessary to obtain goods basic to existence. But money can also take on a variety of other meanings and possibilities. It is an object on which we project our fears and dreams; it purchases basic satisfactions but can be symbolic of higher social and personal accomplishment. Just what it means to an individual will depend on his or her socioeconomic background and personal experience. Surely money loses some of its motivating power as we move up the need hierarchy and as we obtain more of it. Nonetheless, its motivating potential is great because money can be at least a partial vehicle for satisfying many needs among young and old.

REVIEW QUESTIONS

1. Upon what does the motivation to work depend?

2. What are the four estimates that a potential worker makes in deciding how much effort to expend?

3. What is the difference between extrinsic and intrinsic rewards for work?

4. What is the view of work expressed in the Garden of Eden story?

5. What is the relation between work and the physiological and security needs?

6. What is the relation between the nature of work and the affiliation need? How does it differ for various people?

7. What are the psychological problems for a person who is without a job for an extended time?

8. What is the relation of money to the need for affiliation?

9. What is the relation between work and the esteem need?

10. How do status symbols on the job contribute to need satisfaction?

11. What is the relation of money to social esteem? How does this vary with different communities and cultures?

12. What is the relation between work and competence and achievement needs? How does it differ for various people?

13. What is the relation of money to the need for power and autonomy?

14. What is the relation of money to self-esteem?

15. What is the relation of money to the achievement need?

16. Are people with high needs for achievement more or less motivated by money than those with lesser achievement needs? Why?

17. How can a job contribute to mental healthiness and happiness?

18. On what kinds of jobs would you expect employees strongly to desire early retirement?

19. What are the three major concepts of work?

20. Why do some people turn down an opportunity to earn more money under incentive systems?

Notes and References on Money, Work, and Human Needs

1. A thorough review of expectancy theory is found in L. Reinharth and M. A. Wahba, "Expectancy Theory as a Predictor of Work Motivation, Effort Expenditure, and Job Performance, *Academy of Management Journal,* September 1975, pp. 520–36. See also R. J. House, H. J. Shapiro, and M. A. Wahba, "Expectancy Theory as a Predictor of Work Behavior and Attitude: A Reevaluation of Empirical Evidence," *Decision Sciences* 5, no. 1 (1974), pp. 54–77, and R. E. Kopelman and P. H. Thompson, "Boundary Conditions for Expectancy Theory Predictions of Work Motivation and Job Performance," *Academy of Management Journal,* June 1976, pp. 327–58.

A problem with this theory is that people tend to be uncertain of valences and they sometimes act unpredictably. F. A. Starke and O. Behling, "A Test of Two Postulates Underlying Expectancy Theory," *Academy of Management Journal,* December 1975, pp. 703–14.

2. Genesis, 3:17 and 19.

3. Hannah Arendt, *The Human Condition* (Chicago: University of Chicago Press, 1958).

4. In discussing the demands of industrial workers in Manchester, Great Britain, in 1819, Thomas Caryle wrote:
These poor Manchester manual workers mean only, by day's wages for day's work, certain coins of money adequate to keep them living; in return for their work, such modicum of food, clothes and fuel as will enable them to continue their work itself! They as yet clamour for no more; the rest, still inarticulate, cannot yet shape itself into a demand at all, and only lies in them as a dumb wish; perhaps only, still more inarticulate, as a dumb, altogether unconscious want.

Past and Present, (London: Macmillan, 1927).

5. Women who work outside the home appear to do so essentially for money, not especially because they dislike housework or caring for children. The accompanying table indicates how women surveyed in 1956 and 1971 replied to the question "Why do you think women work?"

	1956	1971
Money only	54%	54%
Money and to be independent	4	3
Money and to get out of the house	14	16
Money and to keep busy	6	4
Money and find work interesting	3	5
Money and other reasons	6	77
Other than money	13	11

Most people seem to assume that money will be useful as a vehicle for satisfying needs. D. P. Schwab and L. D. Dyer, "The Motivational Impact of a Compensation System on Employee Performance," *Organizational Behavior and Human Performance* 9 (1973), pp. 215–25.

6. The classic early study showing work restriction is F. J. Roethlisberger and W. J. Dickson, *Management and the Worker* (Cambridge, Mass.: Harvard University Press, 1939).

7. R. O. Hansson and F. E. Fiedler, "Perceived Similarity, Personality and Attraction to Large Organizations," *Journal of Applied Psychology* 3, no. 3 (1973), pp. 258–66.

8. W. H. Form, "Technology and Social Behavior of Workers in Four Countries: A Sociotechnical Perspective," *American Sociological Review* 37 (1972), pp. 727–38.

9. Sigmund Freud, *Civilization and Its Discontents* (London: Hogarth Press, 1930; Garden City, N.Y.: Doubleday Publishing, 1958). A modern Freudian, Harry Levinson, wrote:
Work provides a means for reinforcing the conscience. Usually a person has to be at his job regularly at a

given time, and produce goods or services of a certain quality. The task itself makes demands on him for a level of performance, stimulating and reinforcing his internal desires to do well. . . . When people devote a significant amount of time to anything, implicitly they are assuming that it is important to do. They are justifying why they exist.

The Exceptional Executive (Cambridge, Mass.: Harvard University Press, 1968), p. 23.

Support for this view of work is found in research on scientists. The large proportion of the scientific community publishes very little, but even mediocre scientists write from time to time. They do this not because they really desire recognition nor believe their work is valuable, but almost as a religious act to show they are part of the scientific community. B. H. Gustin, "Charisma, Recognition and the Motivation of Scientists," *American Journal of Sociology* 78 (1973), p. 1119 ff.

10. Eli Ginzberg et al., *The Unemployed* (New York: Harper & Row, 1943).

11. Gay Talese, "A Sign Hanger, 93, Asks State to Help Him Start a New Career," *The New York Times,* June 17, 1963.

12. Skip Myslenski, "A Fan Philanthropic," *The Philadelphia Inquirer,* December 5, 1976.

13. S. Gellerman, *Motivation and Productivity,* chap. 4, "The Money Motive" (New York: American Management Association, 1963), and C. D. McDermid, "How Money Motivates People," in *Readings in Management,* ed. M. D. Richards and W. D. Nielander (Cincinnati: South-Western Publishing, 1962).

14. On money and love, Esther Vilar wrote:

Lacking money, or at least lacking the prospect of it, a man will have to do without a woman, and consequently without sex. Nevertheless, the relationship between the sexes involves a credit system; that is, women are prepared under certain circumstances (while the husband is still training for his profession) to earn their own money—more or less as a loan against future earnings—and to place their bodies at his disposal. In this case the interest rates are proportionately high. The profession for which the man is preparing during this time must promise an income lucrative enough to make the woman's investment worthwhile.

In general, it is axiomatic that a woman will be expensive in direct proportion to the attractiveness of her secondary sex characteristics. Hence, if one man meets another with an especially attractive wife, instead of being depressed he should consider how much money the woman is liable to cost her husand.

"Man Is Woman's Slave, and She Is Well Aware of It," *New York Times* Service, January 20, 1973. Obviously, many of us would disagree with this solely economic analysis of male-female relationships.

15. Dale Carnegie, *How to Win Friends and Influence People* (New York: Simon and Schuster, 1936).

16. Quotations on position titles from *The Wall Street Journal,* November 14, 1968, p. 1. Another manager is quoted as complaining about the trend: "The trouble is, you get status on top of status and jobs that sound identical but aren't at all comparable."

17. In an article on the "instant millionaires" produced by the New Jersey State lottery, sociologist Jerold Starr was quoted as follows:

The instant millionaire is catapulted out of the middle class, but he does not land in the upper class. Sociologists would term him "marginal." The class a person is part of is a combination of education, occupation and income. Usually, these three things go together— that is, if you are highly educated, you are likely to be paid well and hold a job in which you are likely to be with people much like yourself. We do not measure our status by what we own but who we associate with. You cannot buy your way into another class unless you have the education and general background to go with it.

T. L. Hine, "Instant Millionaire," *Philadelphia Inquirer,* March 21, 1971.

18. V. L. Warren, "Millionaires? Not Interested, Youths Insist," *New York Times,* May 3, 1968; N. Gilbert, "Teenagers Believe They'll Earn Top-Notch Salaries in Future," *Philadelphia Inquirer,* July 4, 1970. R. N. Taylor and M. Thompson report little difference on the basis of age in attitudes toward work. Money may be even more important to younger people. "Work Value Systems of Young Workers," *Academy of Management Journal,* December 1976, pp. 522–36.

19. Thorstein Veblen, "The Instinct of Workmanship," in M. Lerner, ed., *The Portable Veblen* (New York: Viking Press, 1961).

20. E. Faltermayer, "The Man Who Keeps Those Maytag Repairmen Lonely," *Fortune,* November 1977, p. 192 ff.

21. D. G. Winter, "Power Motivation in Thought and Action," Ph.D. thesis, Harvard University, 1967. Cited in David McClelland, "Money as a Motivator: Some Research Insights," *The McKinsey Quarterly,* Fall 1967, pp. 10–21. The manager who works for a firm tends to be slightly lower in need for power and achievement than self-employed entrepreneurs, but still higher than the general population. D. C. McClelland and D. G. Winter, *Motivating Economic Achievement* (New York: Free Press, 1969). Higher level managers tend to be more satisfied than lower level personnel, at least partially because they are the focus of more people and have greater prominence. L. E. Rice and T. R. Mitchell, "Structural Determinants of Individual Behavior in Organizations," *Administrative Science Quarterly* 18, no. 1 (1973), pp. 56–70.

22.   D. R. Goldman, "Managerial Mobility Motivations and Central Life Interests," *American Sociological Review* 38 (1973), pp. 119–26. In a research and development laboratory, the value inherent in performing an activity was found to be a much stronger predictor of work motivation than the expectancy that the activity would lead to valued outcomes. J. R. Turney, "Activity Outcome Expectancies and Intrinsic Activity Values as Predictors of Several Motivation Indexes for Technical Professionals," *Organizational Behavior and Human Performance* 11, no. 1 (1974), pp. 65–82.

For many comments on work, see Studs Terkel, *Working: People Talk about What They Do All Day and How They Feel about What They Do* (New York: Pantheon Books, 1974).

23.   M. J. Kavanagh and M. Halpern, "The Impact of Job Level and Sex Differences on the Relationship between Life and Job Satisfaction," *Academy of Management Journal,* March 1977, pp. 66–73.

24.   The Pope's comments were made at a May Day celebration and were quoted by United Press International, May 1, 1971. Eric Hoffer, the longshoreman-philosopher of San Francisco, takes a somewhat different position:

Readiness to work, so far from being natural and normal, is strange and unprecedented. That free men should be willing to work day after day, even after their vital needs are satisfied, and that work should be seen as a mark of righteousness and manly worth, is something that remains more or less incomprehensible to many people outside this country and western Europe (and clearly Japan).

Sociologists and psychologists have given many profound and erudite reasons for this fabulous readiness to work. These reasons are no doubt valid, but they are not the main ones. To me, the most significant fact is that there is a greater readiness to work in a society with a high standard of living than with a low one. The point is that we are more ready to strive for superfluities than for necessities.

To put it bluntly: the readiness for work springs from trivial and questionable motives. . . . A vigorous society is apparently a society made up of people who set their hearts on toys. The self-righteousness moralists decry such a society, yet it is well to keep in mind that to both children and artists, luxuries are more necessary than necessities. He who does not know that in human affairs the trivial is not the trivial has missed a chief clue to man's nature.

It is not true that a society needs a lofty purpose and a shining vision to achieve much. Both in the marketplace and on the battlefield, men who set their hearts on toys have often displayed unequalled initiative and drive.

"The Will to Work: Importance of Toys," *Philadelphia Inquirer,* June 23, 1968.

25.   E. Chinoy, *The Automobile Worker and The American Dream* (Garden City, N.Y.: Doubleday, 1955).

26.   Douglas Fraser, quoted in *Newsweek,* February 16, 1970. There is also increasing pressure for security. "A Hard Line on Life Time Security," *Business Week,* October 31, 1977, p. 33.

27.   In recent years substantial experimentation has taken place with shorter workweeks or different hours, in most cases a four-day, 40-hour week, which allows three-day weekends for whatever leisure activity is desired. In general, men respond more favorably to the system than women do, perhaps because the latter enjoy less leisure off the job. R. Poor, ed., *4 Days, 40 Hours* (Cambridge, Mass.: Bursk and Poor, 1970); *Flexible Working Hours* (London: Institute of Personnel Management, 1972); J. N. Hedges, "New Patterns of Working Time," *Monthly Labor Review* 96, no. 2 (1973), pp. 3–8; A. O. Elbing, H. Cadon, and J. R. M. Gordon, "Time for a Human Time-Table," *European Business,* Autumn 1973, pp. 46–55.

Employees seem to differ in their ability to utilize leisure time. Those who planned it were more favorable toward the four-day week one year after going on it than those who did not. Yet all had been equally positive when the reduced week was first implemented. W. R. Nord and R. Costigan, "Worker Adjustment to the Four-Day Week: A Longitudinal Study," *Journal of Applied Psychology* 58, no. 1 (1973), pp. 60–66.

28.   The growth of do-it-yourself hobbies among blue- and white-collar employees demonstrates the common desire to satisfy the competence drive and perhaps even the achievement motive through nonjob activities. Today's father may actually spend more time working than his 1890 great grandfather did—even though the workweek has declined more than 20 hours a week. When he came home from work, the 19th-century father, at least those relatively well off, simply rested, and that was it. The contemporary father paints the house, mows the lawn, fixes his automobile, and provides a variety of services for his family. Thus his total time working is greater than his grandfather's, and his avocational activity may be a major satisfier of needs for competence and achievement. Sebastian deGrazia, *Of Time, Work, and Leisure* (New York: Twentieth Century Fund, 1962).

29. J. Main, "Good Living Begins at $25,000 a Year," *Fortune,* May 1968, p. 158. Because of inflation, the figure cited in the title would probably be a good bit higher today.

30. A stinging criticism of "excessive top executive salaries apparently unrelated to performance" is given by J. C. Baker, "Are Corporate Executives Overpaid?" *Harvard Business Review,* July–August 1977, pp. 51–56.

31. M. Peil, in *The Ghanaian Factory Worker: Industrial Man in Africa* (New York: Cambridge University Press, 1972), observed:

  1. Ghanian factory workers resemble early industrial workers more than modern industrial workers in that their concern with pay is based on subsistence need rather than a demand for luxuries. *This means that they are still grossly underpaid.*

  2. Ghanaian workers differ from both the early industrial workers and modern workers in that they can return to their farms if they are not satisfied with industrial conditions. The implication is that they are basically *migrants,* while early industrial and modern workers were not. More important they are *target workers.*

  3. Ghanaian workers have never developed the sense of time considered necessary in urban industrial society. They still prefer to operate on "Ghanaian time," which is much more flexible than "European time."

  4. Most Ghanaian workers spend much time off the job with their relatives rather than with workmates. The implication is that they are still "encapsulated" in the network of their relatives.

  5. Ghanaian workers prefer to have large families.

32. B. Finney, "Money Work, Fast Money and Prize Money: Aspects of the Tahitian Labor Commitment," *Human Organization* 26, no. 4 (1967), pp. 195–99.

33. J. S. Bruner and C. C. Goodman, "Value and Need as Organizing Factors in Perception," *Journal of Abnormal and Social Psychology* 42 (1947), pp. 33–44.

34. The average response among the young engineers was $22,000 a year at a time they were averaging about $10,000 per year (in 1961). Inflation would more than double these figures.

35. David C. McClelland, *The Achieving Society* (New York: Van Nostrand Reinhold, 1961), p. 233.

36. McClelland experimented with school children of varying needs for achievement. In a competitive game:
  1. The boys with high achievement need performed better than those with low achievement need when no financial reward was offered.
  2. When money was offered as a prize, there was no difference in performance between the two types. In fact, the high achievers' performance declined a little, while the low achievers' improved.

The size of the reward offered does make a difference, however. Offered $2.50 for the best performance, a group of college students solved more arithmetic problems than when they were offered only $1.25—regardless of their level of achievement motivation. The "size" of reward is a relative matter, of course, according to one's own starting point and to what other people are getting. *The Achieving Society,* p. 233.

37. George Gallup, "Is America Becoming the Land of Happiness?" *Philadelphia Inquirer,* January 14, 1971.

38. This was the global survey on human needs and satisfaction conducted by the Gallup Poll of the American Institute for Public Opinion. "The Search for Poor, Happy People," *Psychology Today,* April 1977.

39. R. K. Faris and W. Dunham, *Mental Disorders in Urban Areas* (Chicago: University of Chicago Press, 1939); A. B. Hollingshead and R. C. Redlich, *Social Class and Mental Illness* (New York: John Wiley & Sons, 1958). Evidence suggests that unskilled workers are significantly more likely to suffer from personality disturbances and psychosomatic illnesses than are skilled workers and that these differences become manifest only after the individuals take up their work. See A. Kornhauser, "Mental Health of Factory Workers," *Human Organization* 21, no. 1 (1962), pp. 43–46, and S. V. Kasl and J. R. P. French, "The Effects of Occupational Status on Physical and Mental Health," *Journal of Social Issues* 18, no. 1 (1962), pp. 67–89. The poll on feelings of sickness was taken by Louis Harris for the Blue Cross Association. On every item, the poor felt worse. *New York Post,* November 20, 1968.

40. In an interesting book contrasting India and the United States, Louis Dumont cites the Indian's conception of work as "inferiorizing": "The Judeo-Christian tradition has it that creation is the 'work' of God; in Hinduism, it is the 'play' of the Gods." *Homo Hierarchicus* (Chicago: University of Chicago Press, 1970). On the viability of not working, see M. D. Dunnette, ed., *Work and Nonwork in the year 2001* (Monterey, Calif.: Brooks/Cole, 1973). He argues that not working is only debilitating when one does not have sufficient income for a minimally "comfortable" life. Americans on welfare, however, would prefer to work if they could. See L. Goodwin, *Do the Poor Want to Work? A Social Psychological Study of Work Orientations* (Washington, D.C.: Brookings Institution, 1972).

41. President Nixon's remarks on the virtues of work were delivered on Labor Day 1971, apparently to encourage greater productivity in American industry, an area where we have been losing our lead over other nations. Quoted in *Newsweek,* October 18, 1971, p. 31.

42. It is a moot point whether a sense of self-esteem and competence can be derived from work when there is no achievement. No matter how good one is at a task, if the work has no intrinsic meaning or makes no contribution to anyone, it may be torture. To work in the salt mines of Siberia was the worst of punishments, not because one could not do it well, but because it was meaningless. Army enlisted men know the futility of digging holes and then later filling them just to keep busy. In the Navy, this is similar to the seaman's having to paint bulkheads just because, like Mount Everest, they are there.

For defense of the work ethic and the belief that satisfying work is critical to a satisfying life, see *Work in America: Report of a Special Task Force to the Secretary of Health, Education and Welfare* (Cambridge, Mass.: MIT Press, 1973). See also R. E. Walton, "Quality of Life: What is It?" *Sloan Management Review* 15, no. 1 (1973), pp. 11–22.

43. J. M. Pennings, "Work-Value Systems of White Collar Workers," *Administrative Science Quarterly,* vol. 15, no. 4 (December 1970), pp. 397–405, and C. N. Weaver, "Job Preferences of White Collar and Blue Collar Workers," *Academy of Management Journal,* March 1975, pp. 167–75.

In general, people with lower status backgrounds give higher importance to extrinsic rewards. These views are developed early in life. M. W. McCall and E. E. Lawler, "High School Student's Perceptions of Work," *Academy of Management Journal,* March 1976, pp. 17–24.

44. Boredom Spells Trouble on the Line," *Life,* September 1, 1972, pp. 30–38.

5

Motivating People at Work

People join organizations to satisfy certain needs. They remain in organizations to satisfy these needs. We have just examined the importance of needs in determining individual behavior in organizational settings. The continued existence of an organization depends on its ability to motivate people to achieve personal and organizational goals. Need satisfaction is important, but only the beginning.

This chapter focuses on increasing your understanding of motivational processes in organizations. The major determinants of organizational behavior are discussed, and then several applications of motivational principles are explored.

Understanding Motivation in Organizations

Motivation and productivity are likely to be at the top of a manager's list of time-consuming problems. Since motivation is related directly to the effectiveness and success of an individual in an organization, it is a major concern of most managers.

Increased attention has been focused upon the ever-tightening constraints that are placed on the modern organization. All resources, including human resources, must be utilized appropriately if the organization is to improve its efficiency and effectiveness. Understanding individual motivation is a key to this improvement. The basic responsibility of a manager with respect to motivation is the following:[1]

1. Attracting and retaining competent employees.
2. Encouraging employees to perform the task for which they were hired.
3. Providing opportunities for employees to go beyond routine job performance and engage in creative and innovative behavior at work.

Our understanding of motivation must include the concepts of expectancy, equity, intrinsic and extrinsic rewards, and behavior modification. These four perspectives provide the basis of management's ability to understand, explain, and predict employee behavior.

The Concept of Expectancy

People are generally rational; that is, they behave in various ways because they expect to satisfy certain needs.[2] Their expectation is seldom certain but a matter of odds, chances, or probabilities. Whether a person performs a certain act (such as striving for an *A* in a course) depends on whether or not he or she believes the behavior has a good chance of satisfying some underlying need and whether or not the need is important.

The strength of the individual's motivation to behave is based on several questions one must answer for one's self.

Expectancy.   Will my behavior lead to obtaining the wanted goods, pleasures, or states of being? How likely is this? If I think the probability is small that I can obtain the want, I am less likely to try. I am more likely to try if the odds seem in my favor. I am also unwilling to try if I don't believe I have the necessary ability and more likely to try if I am confident.

Instrumentality.   Will the wanted goods or state of being bring pleasure (or avoid pain) by satisfying one or more of my needs? My motivation to behave to obtain the wants will be stronger if I believe the probability is high that the obtained want will be instrumental to satisfaction of a need.

Valence.   Is it worth the effort? How important is the need that will be satisfied, in comparison with my other needs and my limited energy?

Thus Rocky, for example, is unlikely to strive for high grades if his past efforts have yielded no success and he does not believe that he can achieve them, *or* if he doesn't get a kick out of an *A* because it does not satisfy any need, *or* if playing football and socializing are more valuable uses of his time. He may, however, work hard at sports because he knows he can play well *and* that success will lead to desired adulation and a possible professional contract, which might satisfy many of his needs. In contrast, you might grind for an *A* because you think you can do it; you enjoy pleasing your parents, beating others, or proving something to yourself; and your alternatives are not attractive, anyway.

We are not always as consciously rational and calculating as these questions suggest, but somehow we make the judgments. Through others' lessons and personal experience, we learn appropriate behavior to obtain desired wants, experience pleasure, and satisfy needs. With practice, we become more proficient so that the probabilities improve that our behavior will obtain our wants. When we cannot do two things simultaneously and we are confronted with mutually exclusive behavior choices, we tend to choose the one with the greatest expected satisfaction. This is roughly measured by probability of need satisfaction multiplied by the importance of the need. Thus sometimes we select the more likely alternative, even though it is less satisfying.

Hagar the Horrible by Dik Browne.

This expectancy model of motivation is powerful, but we need to recognize its weakness—weakness that reflects less on the theory than on human nature.[3] All behavior is just not predictable and consistent with expectancy, instrumentality, and valence. A major reason for this is that the model assumes individual maturity. But some immaturity characterizes us all. To a greater or lesser extent we lack the experience:

1. To make realistic confidence judgments about whether or not effort will lead to obtaining the desired wants; therefore we can vary between wild overconfidence or pessimism.

2. To judge whether or not obtaining the want will actually be instrumental for need satisfaction; in youth we tend to believe others who tell us something is to be desired because we haven't experienced it for ourselves.
3. To know the relative valence of our different needs; for example, just how much security do we need before achievement becomes more important?

Even quite mature people, however, sometimes act inconsistently because they are not truthful with themselves.[4] Consider cigarette smoking. Most people put high valence on good health and long life, and these people are familiar with the evidence that links smoking with cancer and lung and heart disease. Yet, many deny the link between behavior and result. They endeavor to alleviate the cognitive dissonance in their mind (that they enjoy smoking, but it is dangerous) by saying that it is not proven, that it is only statistical and won't include them, or that old Uncle Henry has smoked three packs a day for 50 years and is perfectly healthy. Do they really mean that the temporary kick of inhaling nicotine is more important than good health? Of course not, but they may never ask themselves that question. They reduce the dissonance by misperceiving the situation or denying some of their feelings or knowledge. Or they may just not think about the long run. Children tend to have short time-delay spans; they find it difficult to delay gratification because the future lacks much meaning to someone without much of a past. Immature persons act on the basis of immediate need without much anticipation of later, secondary consequences. So high insurance rates for youthful male drivers reflect not their ability (which is superior to older men) but their tendency to consider only the present thrill when tearing along the highway heedless of possibilities around the bend.

Sometimes behavior can become so habitual that we ignore more creative possibilities. If hungry, most of us would work hard to obtain meat to eat, but many Americans would starve without thinking of eating the insects that are consumed by other peoples. The Americans' behavior in satisfying hunger would be so conditioned that they would not conceive of alternatives. With time, we should learn to drop inappropriate behavior in favor of more effective actions that satisfy the underlying needs.

In spite of the model's weakness (or our own), however, this approach to human behavior is still extremely useful. See Figure 5–1.

Motivation and Equity

The basic premises of equity theory help us understand human behavior in work organizations. People do compare themselves with others. Explanations of this pro-

FIGURE 5–1

The Implications of the Expectancy Framework

The concept of EXPECTANCY suggests that
  managers should match jobs to employees.
The concept of INSTRUMENTALITY suggests that
  managers should match rewards to performance.
The concept of VALENCE suggests that
  managers should match rewards to employee needs.

cess of social comparison focus upon individuals' feelings of how fair they are being treated as compared to others.[5]

Inequity exists whenever employees feel that the outcomes received for their work inputs or contributions are disproportionate with the outcomes others receive for their inputs.[6] In the work situation, common inputs are education, previous job experience, and effort. Examples of outcomes are promotions, raises, recognition, and status.

The Equity Process

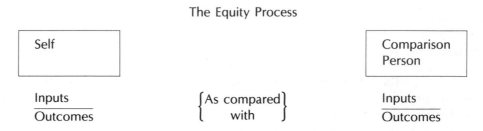

Feelings of inequity serve as motivating forces. When employees experience inequity, they feel tension and are aroused to remove the discomfort and restore a sense of equity. Most individuals will do something about it when they perceive inequity. Possible responses include the following:[7]

Change work inputs: Reduce job effort or increase absenteeism.

Change work outcomes: Work to increase possible outcomes.

Distort perceived inputs or outcomes: Decrease perceived effort, or increase status associated with the job.

Distort perceived inputs or outcomes of the comparison person(s).

Find a different comparison person.

Leave the organization.

Regardless of the specific action taken when inequity is perceived, the manager must view such situations as important because of their potential effect upon job satisfaction and performance. Careful communication with employees can help to avoid the negative consequences of this comparison process. Employees need to know: (1) the appraisal of the performance upon which rewards are being distributed, (2) the manager's evaluation of the rewards allocated, and (3) the comparison with other employees.

Intrinsic versus Extrinsic Rewards

The rewards employees receive for their job performance can be classified into two categories: intrinsic rewards and extrinsic rewards.[8] Intrinsic rewards are those rewards received by the individual as a direct result of task performance. They are often considered to be self-administered, since performing the job itself results in receiving the reward. Extrinsic rewards are positively valued job outcomes given to the individual by some other person in the work setting (see Figure 5–2).

The manager acts on behalf of the organization in the allocation of extrinsic

FIGURE 5–2 ━━━━━

Examples of Intrinsic and Extrinsic Rewards

Intrinsic Rewards	Extrinsic Rewards
Feeling of achievement	Pay
Autonomy	Time off
Challenge	Verbal praise
Task accomplishment	Promotion
Personal growth	Status symbols

rewards. In order to make sure that the use of such rewards promotes individual job performance and feelings of equity, they should be awarded contingent upon actual results. The use of the "pat on the back" can be just as effective as a monetary reward. Unfortunately, many managers overemphasize money and ignore many opportunities for the effective utilization of other extrinsic rewards.

The use of intrinsic rewards highlights the importance of good job design. The challenge to management is designing jobs for employees in such a way that intrinsic rewards become available after one exerts effort on assigned tasks. When a task is intrinsically motivating, employees are likely to exert high levels of energy to realize their potential and experience a sense of doing something worthwhile.[9] Some employees may perform with minimal extrinsic rewards if the job is intrinsically motivating.

Figure 5–3 presents a model of job design that explains how enrichment activities bring about positive results. Five critical job characteristics are identified: skill variety, autonomy, identification with a whole task or job, significance or importance of the task, and feedback. These job characteristics help to satisfy the employee's psychological needs and are more likely to result in job satisfaction and motivation.

FIGURE 5–3 ━━━━━

Job Characteristics that Enhance Intrinsic Motivation

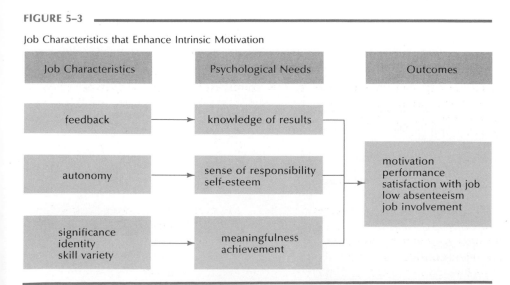

Adapted from R. J. Hackman and G. R. Oldham, *Work Redesign* (Reading, Mass.: Addison-Wesley Publishing, 1980), p. 77.

FIGURE 5–4

Reward Administration in Chinese Industrial Enterprises

Two types of incentives are currently used in China to reward workers for their labor and to motivate them to improve their performance. The government "applies the policy of combining moral encouragement with material reward, with the stress on the former, in order to heighten the citizens' socialist enthusiasm and creativeness in work"[10]

China's leaders, both past and present, have never questioned the superiority of nonmaterial incentives or moral encouragement. However, they have not been so naive as to assume that desire for material gain can be eliminated all at once.[11] Consequently, throughout the history of the PRC, particularly in periods of political stability and economic progress, one sees the dual use of material incentives and moral encouragement.

The principal forms of material incentives used are wages (based on time-work or piece work), subsidies, bonuses, other welfare benefits provided to workers, and directly linking the enterprise's or work unit's performance with the amount of profits to be retained for its own use.[12] This latter incentive ties in with the notions of competition and "democratic self-management" of enterprises.

Source: Rosalie L. Tung, "Patterns of Motivation in Chinese Industrial Enterprises," *Academy of Management Review,* July, 1981, pp. 481–89.

The manager's responsibility in reward administration is finding the appropriate balance between the use of extrinsic and intrinsic rewards. Both types of rewards are important in efforts to enhance employee performance. (See Figure 5–4.)

Organizational Behavior Modification. Managers influence the behavior of employees on a regular basis. (See Figure 5–5.) The basic principles of behavior modification and operant conditioning help managers to determine the most effective means of directing employee behavior and by so doing improve motivation and performance.[13]

FIGURE 5–5

Ways in Which the Manager Influences
Employee Behaviors

Strengthening Desirable Behaviors

   Positive Reinforcement
   Negative Reinforcement

Eliminating Undesirable Behaviors

   Extinction
   Punishment

Most human behaviors are learned behaviors, and we learn new behaviors throughout our lives. This process of learning new behaviors takes place in organizational settings as employees learn the appropriate values, skills, attitudes, and language of the organization. Of course, managers want productive, rather than unproductive, work behaviors to be learned by employees.

Reinforcement plays an important part in learning. New behaviors are learned and maintained because they are rewarded, and behaviors that are not rewarded will be discontinued. Managers do not have complete control over employee behaviors, but they can influence or shape these behaviors through reinforcement.[14]

Positive reinforcement increases the likelihood of a particular desired behavior. A reward that follows (is associated with) a behavior is called a positive reinforcer. For a reward to become a positive reinforcer, it must be contingent upon performance and be valued by the employee. Failure to meet either of these two conditions restricts the reward's use as a positive reinforcer.

Negative reinforcement, also referred to as avoidance learning, is based upon the employees desire to avoid undesirable outcomes. Employees learn to avoid unpleasant conditions by behaving in certain ways. A manager who has been reprimanding an employee every day about her performance is unlikely to reprimand when the employee correctly performs the task. The employee learns over time that the likelihood of being reprimanded or harassed is reduced when she demonstrates the appropriate job behavior.

Extinction refers to nonreinforcement as a means of eliminating undesired behavior. The frequency of a behavior that is not rewarded tends to decrease over time. Eventually the behavior will disappear. Thus the principle of extinction suggests that undesired behaviors in the work setting will decline as the result of a lack of positive reinforcement.

Punishment involves the use of unpleasant consequences and is used by organizations to discourage undesirable behaviors. When punishment is used as a means of eliminating behavior, adverse outcomes are administered as the result of unacceptable behavior. Punishment, or the threat of punishment, is used by managers because it usually produces the desirable effect. However, punishment is not effective in producing long-term changes in behavior, since the likelihood of undesirable behavior is reduced only when the punishing agent is present.

Managerial Applications of Motivation

Up to this point in the chapter, we have attempted to identify the basic frameworks used as the basis for understanding the dynamics of employee motivation in the workplace. The importance of this foundation is best appreciated by considering different applications of these ideas. In this section, we will examine several applications of basic motivational principles in organizations.

Before considering these motivation programs and activities, consider the basic managerial guidelines that can be drawn from the preceding discussion.

1. Managers need to recognize and deal with individual differences. Employees have different needs, expectations, and experiences which influence their job behaviors.

2. It is important that the manager establish a clear linkage between performance and rewards. Employees need to know what to do on the job and the resultant outcomes.

3. Both extrinsic rewards and intrinsic rewards have a positive effect on the motivation of employees.

4. The manager has the responsibility of expanding the motivating capabilities of the job. Job design techniques that expand opportunities for learning and growth can have positive effects upon employee motivation.

5. In general, the manager must realize the potential for actually "managing" motivational processes on the job. It takes a great deal of work to enhance motivation, but there is much within the control of management.

The examples of organizational applications of motivational frameworks are numerous. Managers are searching constantly for methods of improving motivation and productivity. In this section we will examine five specific applications—extrinsic rewards (e.g., money), positive reinforcement, intrinsic rewards through job redesign, quality control circles, and goal setting.

Management's Use of Extrinsic Rewards

Management's primary motivation technique has been and probably still is to offer extrinsic rewards for desired subordinate behavior and performance. Money is the most common extrinsic reward.

Management's Use of Money. Management has long assumed that the primary motivation for employees is money. In the early 19th century, during the fledgling Industrial Revolution, employers believed they should pay only subsistence wages, only enough to allow workers to obtain minimum food and shelter. This would ensure the preeminence of physiological and security needs. Because they would be unable to save, workers would begin to starve almost immediately if they were dismissed. The self-appointed moralists among management also claimed that the unenlightened workers would only waste extra money on frivolities, drink, and more children, anyway.

Scientific mangement and industrial engineering proponents in the early 20th century emphasized piece-rate incentives for production workers because they believed that everyone wanted more money, which would provide satisfaction off the job. A time-study engineer would measure a task and set a rate of pay for each unit turned out. Thus management might promise to pay a worker 50 cents per widget, so that a worker would earn $80 by producing 100 percent of what the engineer expected—20 per hour or 160 a work day (at 100 percent rate: $160 \times \$0.50 = \$80$). An employee who produced more would be paid more (at 110 percent rate: $176 \times \$0.50 = \$88$).

Workers and labor unions strongly fought incentive pay in the beginning because they feared an inhuman "speed up." Political passions even became involved, and incentive systems were banned from operations of the federal government. The arguments are muffled today, although feelings are still expressed on both sides of the issue. Some hold that production employees work harder when on incentives than when paid just for hours worked. Others maintain that the difference, if any, is not dramatic, and it costs management to measure the jobs and administer the standards. Laboratory research suggests that subjects perform better under piece rates that when on fixed pay for time. In actual work settings, widespread evidence exists that in fact most workers do not try to earn as much as they might when under incentives. Output restriction is common and long-standing. Managers usually perceive such behavior as being either antimanagement or irrational, but it may be neither.

Nonresponse to Incentive Pay.   There are several reasons a worker would turn down an opportunity to make more money.[15] One is that workers do not trust management; they may not believe that management will continue to pay the extra money if production is much above the 100 percent level expected. Suppose an engineer unintentionally sets a "loose" standard. This might mean that an employee would reach a day's expected production in only six hours. By working at the same rate for another two hours, the employee would earn more than 130 percent of the expected. Employees might like the additional money but may fear that earning this much would arouse management's concern. The industrial engineers might come around, ask questions, and set a tighter standard under which everyone would have to work harder to earn the same as before. Whether or not they have experienced this personally, many workers believe that management will cut loose standards, even if they have promised not to.

Another reason for nonresponse to incentive pay is that additional money is not valued. Many workers subscribe to a "pie view" of work, which maintains that there is only so much work to be performed. If one worker produces more, others will have less to do and may be fired. Managers usually scoff at this view, arguing that higher productivity would mean lower prices, greater sales, and hence more work. Rightly or wrongly, however, many employees still conclude that in the long run they will be more secure by restricting effort and current earnings.

In addition, most groups develop some conception of a "fair day's work." Not everyone concurs, but among managers, laborers, and students there is a tendency to define what should be done to ensure relative equality so that the average individual will not look bad. The sixth-grade teacher's pet who always completes the homework on time is disliked by many classmates, just as is the punch press operator who produces more than co-workers think proper. Many of us are unwilling to sacrifice the social satisfactions derived from our colleagues just to make more money.[16] Having more money to spend on music lessons for their children or mortgage payments for an expensive home may not appeal as much to some employees as to some owners, executives, and managers.[17]

Some workers may just want to do something else. In recent years some companies have been having trouble getting younger workers to put in overtime. The extra money at a time-and-a-half rate is apparently not enough to persuade them to put in extra time. They have needs to satisfy off the job. "At first everyone is eager for overtime work," one company executive observed, "but after a couple of months they really do not care too much about the extra money, and we find it increasingly

Reasons for Nonresponse to Incentive Pay
- Distrust of management.
- Security concerns.
- Social concerns.
- Preference for other activities.
- Can't see link between behavior, performance, and rewards.

difficult to get them to work overtime." They may want to pursue other activities after 5:00 P.M. and on Saturday. Nonetheless, union leaders argue that opposition to overtime is confined to a minority; most employees are still anxious to earn extra income—especially when economic conditions are poor and inflation is rampant.

Other workers do not believe performance leads to money: Performance on some jobs is not as easy to measure as is the production of widgets, for example, and it can be very difficult to tie financial rewards to actual performance. The widgets may be produced by a group rather than by an individual, and over a lengthy period rather than a short time. A computer, for example, is made by many people over several weeks. The specific contribution of any one person is impossible to isolate because it is so intermeshed with others' work. If management wants to offer incentive pay, it must be on a team basis under which all members would receive an equal percentage of their base wage. Such a system will work if the group is small and the time span is short. Nonetheless, if more than 10 or so people are involved and the task stretches over a week, an individual cannot associate

"I'm puzzled . . . you seem to be suffering from overwork, but nobody does that anymore."

From *The Wall Street Journal,* with permission of Cartoon Features Syndicate.

personal effort to pay. She or he may conclude that goofing off on Tuesday does not make much difference, since others do too.

For some jobs, output or performance is extremely difficult to judge, even for groups and departments. The performance of such staff specialists as engineers, researchers, accountants, personnel officers, and others is not reflected directly in widget production or even profits. We shall explore this problem more in Part 5 when we discuss planning and controlling, but evaluating some performance can be so subjective and unreliable that no one sees any connection between effort, performance, and pay. In such a situation, management usually rewards people with increased pay for seniority or loyalty, not performance.[18]

Making Rewards Effective.   Management cannot guarantee that offering increased money will motivate people to increased effort. It can, however, take steps to improve the likelihood.

For employees to respond affirmatively to a pay incentive plan, they must trust management (and believe that management will not cut the rewards if they do well), understand the plan, and see a close relationship between their performance and their pay.[19] Management must stand by its word, keep its promises, and not offer more than it can deliver. It should ensure that the highest performers are the most satisfied. This will make clear to others on what basis rewards are distributed. Employees should be able to observe that those who do better actually receive more than poor or average workers do.[20]

No one knows for sure how much more this should be.[21] Existing incentive plans have been criticized as paying too little; it is maintained that a 10 percent bonus for a week, month, or even year does not have sufficient impact.[22] Something much larger, at least 30 percent, is probalby necessary to substantially affect the recipient's lifestyle. Without such impact, the individual would not be very concerned about maintaining the increment through subsequent good performance. To pay such incentive earnings, however, requires management to make tough decisions differentiating between outstanding and average performers, because it would just be too expensive to pay large bonuses to everyone. Rather than upset nonrecipients, therefore, many organizations simply award 5 to 10 percent increases to everyone except the most incompetent. Such a policy does not motivate better performance; it simply encourages the average employee to remain with the organization.[23]

The key is that increased pay should follow improved performance, not just be awarded in the hope that people will automatically try harder if they are paid more. Suppose you are working as a short-order cook in a summer resort. Your pay is $3 per hour, not generous, but about what others are making in the area for similar work—and besides you can use the hotel golf course and swimming pool, and there are no restrictions on dating guests. It is a pretty good deal. If your employer decides to spontaneously raise your wages to $4 per hour, you will probably be pleased (and believe your deserve it). You may try to get the job again next summer, but you are extremely unlikely to work harder, cook your hamburgers faster, or keep the grill cleaner. Even if your increased satisfaction improved your performance slightly, it would probably only be temporary until your gratitude was obscured by the daily work demands and trivialities, like burning your fingers and running out

To Make Rewards Effective, Management Should . . .
- keep its promises.
- not offer more than it can deliver.
- ensure that people understand performance objectives and how rewards are linked to them.
- differentiate between levels of performance.
- distribute rewards promptly after performance, not before.

of buns. For you to really increase your effort for money would require you to believe that: (1) increased effort would lead to better performance; (2) your employer can determine the improved performance; (3) increased money will follow from this performance; (4) you would value the additional money because it would satisfy your needs; and (5) you would not have to unduly sacrifice satisfaction of other needs for security, affiliation, and so on.

Other Extrinsic Rewards.   Money is not the only reward, of course. Managers have long dispensed other extrinsic rewards, including promotions, titles, public and private praise, fringe benefits, and status symbols, such as office size and furnishings. In recent years interest in the use of nonfinancial rewards has grown fueled by efforts to apply behavioral theory.

As we saw in the preceding chapter, the key in behavior modification is to link a pleasant outcome with desired behavior. Thus management may dispense a reward that the employee perceives as valuable. There are three critical aspects of this process: (1) the reward, such as praise, must be contingent upon good performance; it should not be given out all the time to everyone regardless of results; (2) the reward must be dispensed quickly; and (3) the receiver must believe that the reward is instrumental to some need satisfaction.

The link between behavior, performance, and reward is not likely to be strong in the employee's eyes if too much time passes between behavior-results and the reward. Praising a person a week after the desired behavior is unlikely to have much impact. Promoting someone may retain its motivational effectiveness longer because most people see it as more valuable. Nonetheless, delaying a promotion for, say, more than two years is likely to sever a perceived link between performance and reward.

Publicity has recently been given to several organizations utilizing this behavioral approach to motivate performance by public praise and recognition. Kaiser Aluminum has been reported to give frequent and immediate small gifts, such as flashlights, T-shirts, and frisbees.[24] More dramatically, Mary Kay Cosmetics awards high-performing sales personnel with mink coats, diamonds, and pink Cadillacs.[25]

Recognizing good performance seems obvious to many managers, but it may well be that many organizations have become so bureaucratic and impersonal that no one pays attention to or takes time to express personal praise and gratitude. To a significant extent, in many firms most extrinsic rewards are not given for performance, but for loyalty and time. That is, employees are rewarded for seniority with promotions, larger offices, and better insurance plans. Rewards based on the calendar do motivate behavior, of course, but not especially performance. They motivate employees primarily to remain with the company, which may be valuable to management, but not necessarily performance relevant.

Management's Use of Positive Reinforcement

Positive Reinforcement programs are based on the assumption that individual behavior is a function of its consequences.[26] The principles of Organizational Behavior

FIGURE 5–6

Guidelines for Managing the Contingencies of Reinforcement

1. Don't give the same level of reward to all employees.
2. Failure to respond to behavior has reinforcing consequences.
3. Tell a person what behavior is likely to be reinforced or rewarded.
4. Tell a person what he or she is doing wrong.
5. Don't punish in front of others.
6. Make the consequences equal to the behavior.

Source: W. C. Hamner and E. P. Hamner, "Behavior Modification on the Bottom Line," *Organizational Dynamics,* Spring 1976, pp. 8–21.

Modification are used to channel and direct employee efforts. As we discussed earlier in the chapter, the basic principle of OB Mod is that desired behavior by the employee will be repeated if it is reinforced. In other words, reinforcing or rewarding a particular behavior increases the chance of the employee repeating that behavior.

One of the primary reasons managers fail to motivate employees is their failure to understand the contingencies of reinforcement. (See Figure 5–6.) Managers use rewards all the time to shape employee behaviors, but their efforts often produce minimal results because the methods used are inappropriate or inconsistent. Consider the fact that in many organizations special privileges, activities, and salary raises are allocated on the basis of length of service rather than performance level. In these situations employees are given rewards that are not necessarily conditional upon the behavior the manager seeks to promote. In short, managers can do more to better utilize the positive outcomes at their disposal.

Many organizations are establishing formal motivational programs that are based upon positive reinforcement techniques (see Figures 5–7 and 5–8).

FIGURE 5–7

Designing a Positive Reinforcement Program

1. Management defines and clearly specifies the behavioral aspects of acceptable performance (e.g., good absenteeism and tardiness record or completing tasks on schedule).
2. Conduct a performance audit to determine the extent to which employees are successfully meeting the behavioral performance criteria.
3. Determine specific behavioral goals for each employee.
4. Require that employees keep a record of their own work. This allows for ongoing, timely feedback on task accomplishment.
5. Examine the employees' records, as well as other performance indicators, and praise the positive aspects of their work performance.

Source: R. M. Steers, *Introduction to Organizational Behavior* (Glenview, Ill.: Scott, Foresman, 1981).

FIGURE 5–8

Positive Reinforcement Programs in Organizations

Organization	Types of Employees	Specific Goals	Frequency of Feedback	Reinforcers Used	Results
Michigan Bell— Operator Services	Employees at all levels in operator services	a. Decrease turnover and absenteeism. b. Increase productivity. c. Improve union-management relations.	a. Lower level— weekly and daily. b. Higher level— monthly and quarterly.	a. Praise and recognition. b. Opportunity to see oneself become better.	a. Attendance performance has improved by 50 percent. b. Productivity and efficiency has continued to be above standard in areas where positive reinforcement (PR) is used.
Connecticut General Life Insurance Co., Donald D. Illig, Director of Personnel	Clerical employees and first-line supervisors.	a. Decrease absenteeism. b. Decrease lateness.	Immediate.	a. Self-feedback. b. System-feedback. c. Earned time off.	Chronic absenteeism and lateness has been drastically reduced.
General Electric	Employees at all levels.	a. Meet EEO objectives. b. Decrease absenteeism and turnover. c. Improve training. d. Increase productivity.	Immediate—uses modeling and role playing as training tools to teach interpersonal exchanges and behavior requirements.	Social reinforcers (praise, rewards, and constructive feedback)	a. Cost savings can be directly attributed to the program. b. Productivity has increased. c. Worked extremely well in training minority groups and raising their self-esteem. d. Direct labor cost decreased.
City of Detroit Garbage Collectors	Garbage collectors	a. Reduction in paid workers-hour per ton b. Reduction on overtime c. 90 percent of routes completed by standard d. Effectiveness (quality)	Daily and quarterly based on formula negotiated by city and sanitation union.	Bonus (profit sharing) and praise	a. Citizen complaints declined significantly. b. City saved $1,654,000 first year after bonus paid. c. Worker bonus equalled $307,000 first year, or $350 annually per person.
B. F. Goodrich Chemical Co.	Manufacturing employees at all levels	a. Better meeting of schedules. b. Increase productivity.	Weekly.	Praise and recognition: Freedom to choose one's own activity.	Production has increased over 300 percent.

FIGURE 5–8 *(concluded)*

ACDC Electronics— Division of Emerson Electronics	All levels	a. 96 percent attendance b. 90 percent engineering specifications met. c. Daily production objectives met 95 percent of time. d. Cost reduced by 10 percent.	Daily and weekly feedback from foreman to company president.	Positive feedback.	a. Profit up 25 percent over forecast. b. $550,000 cost reduction on $10 million sales. c. Return of 1900 percent on investment including consultant fees. d. Turnaround time on repairs went from 30 to 10 days. e. Attendance is now 98.2 percent (from 93.5 percent.

Source: W. C. Hamner and E. P. Hamner, "Behavior Modification on the Bottom Line," *Organizational Dynamics,* Spring 1976, pp. 12–14.

The widespread success of these programs in improving performance and reducing costs has led to their overall acceptance in industry. Consider these two examples.[27] Positive reinforcement techniques were introduced in the accounting department of Collins Food International and led to a reduction in the accounts payable error rate from 8 percent to 0.2 percent. After developing such programs in several different areas, the 3M Company estimated that they saved $3.5 million in one year.

The uniqueness of PR programs rests in its combination of effective management techniques. The success of such motivational practices is explained by its use of job analysis, goal setting, accurate and timely feedback, and appropriate rewards tied to job performance. The principles of OB Mod are not difficult to understand. When properly applied, they constitute powerful managerial tools. Although there has been a great deal of success in this area, PR programs have been criticized in several ways (see Figure 5–9). In spite of these criticisms, PR should be accepted

FIGURE 5–9

Criticisms of PR Programs

PR programs ignore individual differences.

PR programs ignore prevailing work group norms.

PR programs ignore the fact that employees can be intrinsically motivated.

PR programs assume incorrectly that all behaviors must be externally reinforced in order to be learned.

PR programs are not new.

Source: R. M. Steers, *Introduction to Organizational Behavior* (Glenview, Ill.: Scott, Foresman, 1981).

as a very effective motivational technique. The empirical and organizational results are there—such techniques do improve performance.

Management's Use of Intrinsic Motivation

So far we have shown how work's extrinsic rewards, such as money, relate to human needs. The connection is strongest with physiological, safety, and security needs. People do work for more than money, however, they work also for the intrinsic satisfactions of performing a task, solving a problem, and achieving an objective. Now we shall discuss work's intrinsic rewards and current efforts to design jobs through enrichment and enlargement so that they can satisfy a wider range of human needs.

The process of modifying a job to appeal to higher level needs, and thereby to release latent employee energies, is variously termed *job enrichment, job expansion, job enlargement,* and *job loading.*[28] All essentially mean redesigning the task to improve both task efficiency and human satisfaction by building into people's jobs greater scope for personal achievement, recognition, more challenging and more responsible work, and opportunity for individual advancement and growth.[29] In short, the process provides the worker an opportunity to:

Perform interesting and difficult work.

Assume responsibility and exercise discretion and self-control, uninterrupted by overly frequent checks by higher management.

Achieve and practice creativity.

Obtain performance feedback based on clear standards of excellence.

Job Enrichment.   Assembly-line jobs are frequently thought to be among the most boring of tasks because they are narrowly specialized—one person attaching only right-front fenders, for example. The task is repetitive—it is right-front fenders all day long. It is also fairly easily learned in a day or so. The worker does not even control his or her own pace, but simply responds to the incessant demands of the line. Finally, there is no closure because the worker doesn't feel part of a complete task. The automobiles all look alike, and each disappears down the line. He or she can hardly identify with the cars in the yard awaiting shipment.

What the job enrichment attempts to do is to change the relationship between the worker and the job. At its simplest, it can call for parts of the job to be rearranged so that workers can have more variety. They could rotate among various existing tasks: right fenders, left fenders, windshields, wheels. This may be a little less frustrating, but multiplying boring and easily mastered tasks is not likely to be especially motivating. As a second approach, job enrichment could eliminate certain especially boring aspects of a job by automating them.

Vertical job loading is an aspect of job enrichment that entails redesigning jobs to give: (1) greater responsibility, (2) greater autonomy, (3) more closure, and (4) more immediate feedback to the individual or group. This might include transferring

"We don't 'fill jobs' in this corporation, young man!
We offer opportunities for the growth and enrichment
of the individual!"

Grin and Bear It by George Lichty. © Field Enterprises, Inc., 1978. Courtesy
of Field Newspaper Syndicate.

some of the superior's activities to subordinates. Horizontal job loading, another
aspect, might be applied by having workers perform some steps that precede and
follow them in the work flow. A single operator might fit on all four fenders, be
responsible for the car's entire front end, or do both rough and finished painting.

Feedback, closure, and a sense of wholeness might be the logical conclusion of
job loading. An automobile might be built from the ground up in one location by
one small crew. Mechanical lines would convey various parts to the work area,
but the crew would control their use. The task would be more complex, and the
completed product could be clearly seen and identified with.[30]

Sources of job enrichment are illustrated in Figure 5–10. The theory is that modifying jobs in these ways would make them more satisfying by restoring a long-absent
sense of craftsmanship. As high-level needs would be appealed to, greater commitment should be manifested. Thus technological change would lead to psychological
change, which would produce better performance.

Some Examples of Job Enrichment.   In an electronics company manufacturing
semiconductors, employees tended machines that sliced thin silicon wafers.[31] Their
work was highly programmed and controlled by the technology. The old and new
tasks were as follows:

Old Situation	Situation after Job Enrichment
Each employee rotated among all machines.	Each employee assigned to only two machines.
When machine failure occurred, operator called on maintenance group.	Each operator given training in maintenance; each conducts preventive and corrective maintenance on the two machines for which operator is responsible.
Operator changes the slicing blade (the most important component of the machine) following a rigid rule contained in a manual.	Operator given authority to decide when to replace blade, based on judgment.
Supervisor monitors operator and corrects unsatisfactory performance.	Performance feedback system developed that provides daily information on their work quality directly to operators.

FIGURE 5–10

Sources of Job Enrichment

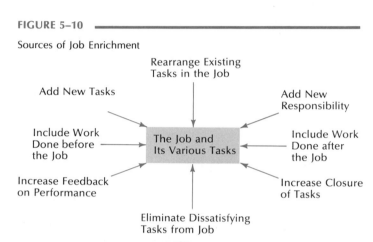

After these changes, product quality improved; the ratio of good output to input increased significantly. Machine maintenance costs declined, and employee attitudes improved substantially.

In another company, employees assembled power supplies on a highly fragmented assembly line. Units moved along a conveyor system in front of the operators who performed very narrow, specific, and repetitive tasks—such as adding a condenser, resistor, or tube. The task was much like an automobile assembly line.

Old Situation	Situation after Job Enrichment
Individual performs specialized task on units passing by.	Three- to five-person teams build entire unit.
Supervisor decides who should do what.	Team decides who should do what.
Inspectors and supervisor test output and correct performance.	Team conducts own quality audits.

After these changes, quality and quantity improved significantly. The teams demonstrated improved ability to adapt to schedule changes; the incidence of parts shortages declined; employee attitudes improved; and absenteeism declined.

The Limits of Job Enrichment.   In practice, job enrichment, enlargement, or loading has become something of a fad, something an up-to-date management wants to do, without much understanding.[32] It is possible to modify most jobs through various techniques. Even janitorial tasks can be improved by allowing the worker to schedule work, determine methods, and order materials. What is not so clear is whether or not this invariably leads to higher morale, better performance, and higher profits. Numerous reports have documented increased productivity and reduced costs from dramatic job changes, as in the preceding cases.[33] Few companies, however, are willing to make such dramatic changes, and failures in job enrichment have occurred.[34]

Job enrichment is not a cure-all for everything that ails management and employees. It is only applicable to settings where workers *are* and *feel* underutilized, and this condition is by no means universal.[35] In spite of widespread publicity given to job dissatisfaction, to blue-collar and white-collar "blues," complaints come from only a small minority of the work force. Most people do not judge their jobs to be degrading or even boring. For intellectuals to so judge them can be dangerous condescension, especially when the professors (and some union leaders) have never actually performed the jobs. Some polls even suggest that job satisfaction is generally high and has been increasing over the past 25 years.[36]

A manager cannot assume that work has the same meaning for everyone. Depending upon the overlay of the person's expectations and the job's realities, there are a number of possible ways workers will regard their jobs.[37]

A person with a truncated need structure who is influenced *only* by lower level needs will be motivated to obtain only money and possibly social satisfaction through the job. Whether the task offers opportunities for competence, for power, or for achievement is irrelevant. Indeed, the employee may become confused and upset if the job contains these opportunities and the manager attempts to appeal to these higher needs. The manager's effectiveness will depend upon how well authority is exercised over the means to satisfy the lowest needs, such as pay, working conditions, and hours.

A person with developed higher needs who has been taught or believes that a job is an unpleasant necessity and work a punishment will also be motivated to obtain only money and social satisfaction on the job. The money derived may be used to satisfy higher needs off the job. Whether the job or the manager offers opportunities for competence, power, or achievement is irrelevant. Manager effectiveness will depend upon how well the manager exercises authority over the means to satisfy the lowest needs.

Persons with developed higher needs who believe that a job is a legitimate outlet for these needs will be motivated to achieve competence, power, and achievement on the job. If the job or the manager provides no opportunity to fulfill these needs, the employees will probably respond with behavior detrimental both to themselves and to the organization. If the job or the manager provides opportunities for the fulfillment of such needs, the employees will respond with behavior constructive to themselves and the organization.[38]

Henry Ford's replacement of his carriage shop with an automobile assembly line was due to a technology that brought enormous productivity increases. It is not clear that we could abandon this approach to return to craftsmanlike techniques without enormous cost. Workers on the "new" old technology might be happier, but only if they went to the store and found goods to be no more expensive. Some of us may be willing to pay a certain cost for greater job satisfaction and an improved quality, if not a higher standard of living. At the moment we do not know for certain whether job enlargement, enrichment, or loading mean higher or lower costs.

In addition, more interesting tasks cannot be substituted for an unpleasant environment. Peole in interesting and challenging jobs are still likely to complain if fringe benefits, working conditions, and base pay are inadequate. Few people are so dedicated that they will stomach inferior hygiene provisions indefinitely; even committed professors complain about crowded offices and dirty washrooms. And some research suggests that people in organizations with very nice hygiene factors, such as working conditions, fringe benefits, and sympathetic superiors, may not care very much about job challenge.[39]

Management's Use of Quality Control Circles

In response to management's concern for motivation and productivity improvements and workers' increased concerns for improving the quality of their work life, many U.S. companies have adopted the Japanese technique referred to as quality control circles (QC circles). Union and management work together to remedy high production costs and improve the environment in which employees work.

The success of QC circles in Japan (see Figure 5–11) is explained by many in terms of particular cultural characteristics.[40] Organizational membership in Japan is characterized by lifetime employment, nonspecialized career paths, slow promotion

FIGURE 5–11

The Japanese Quality Circle

At Toyota Auto Body . . . a foreman described the procedure followed by the company, one that typifies circle activities:

> We think that the first step of analysis is to see whether or not the work is being implemented in accordance with the job standard. Usually, we grasp this phenomenon by plotting the cause-and-effect diagram with the relevant factors contributing to production being reviewed one by one. This is a time-consuming but effective method which involves extensive data gathering by each member of the circle.

Toyota began its circle program in 1964 and by 1976 had 760 circles, involving over 4000 workers, almost all of whom were blue-collar. The company won the Deming Prize in 1970. Employees could join more than one circle. The initial circle leaders had been foreman, but by 1969 ordinary workers were taking the place of the foremen. The size of the circles gradually decreased from the original size of 20.

Source: G. Munchus, "Employer-Employee Based Quality Circles in Japan: Human Resource Policy Implications for American Firms," *Academy of Management Review*, 8, no. 2 (1983), pp. 255–61.

FIGURE 5–12

Characteristics of Japanese Organizations

1. Lifetime employees have the time to learn how to be cooperative with each other.
2. Slow promotion puts a damper on employees' jockeying to get ahead—and thus checks a threat to intimacy. Infrequent evaluation avoids creating conditions of inequality and competitiveness. If one has not been formally evaluated, one cannot be labeled as better than or worse than others. Everyone is relatively equal, and equality breeds involvement.
3. Nonspecialized career paths keep employees generalists. They can't use their own expertise to solve problems but must cooperate to tap the skills of others.
4. Implicit control mechanisms are expressed in the corporate philosophy in terms of values that guide employees. Explicit rules and legions of overseers are not needed and thus do not stand in the way of employee interacting. No one need feel that a rule of a supervisor will prevent him from getting to know what other employees are doing.
5. Collective decision making of the bottom-to-top variety builds consensus, cooperation, and involvement.
6. Collective responsibility of groups rather than individuals spreads individual risks. The risk of cooperating with others is diminished, and thus cooperation is fostered.
7. A corporate commitment to satisfying the social as well as the economic needs of employees fosters an intimacy among personnel as they come to know each other as whole human beings rather than simply as workers.

Source: J. J. Sullivan, "A Critique of Theory Z," *Academy of Management Review* 8, no. 1 (1983), pp. 132–42.

and infrequent evaluation, implicit control mechanisms, collective decision making, collective responsibility, and a general concern for the employee's social as well as economic needs (see Figure 5–12).

One cannot argue with the success of QC circles in Japan. The question is whether or not this technique can be applied to American industry. Cultural differences may suggest limited application in the United States. QC circles are based largely on the idea of worker participation. American organizations can learn much about improving the level and type of participation offered to their employees. By studying the Japanese examples of QC circles, we might develop a better understanding of the relationship between participation and performance in the U.S. firms.

The American experience with QC circles as illustrated in Figure 5–13 suggests that there are several organizational conditions that contribute to the effective implementation of this performance improvement technique.[41] These conditions are summarized below.

Training. Training is an integral part of quality circles, since it is the key to how the leaders and members become problem solvers. Three levels of training are required: facilitators, leaders and circle members, and management. Training is

FIGURE 5–13

The American Experience with QC Circles

Industry	Results
Machine tool manufacturer	Cut accident costs: Year 1 $80,000 Year 2 $59,000 Year 3 $14,000
Metal fabricator	Increased shipments per employee by 15 percent without additional labor costs.
Electronic components manufacturer	Reduced reject rate on printed circuit boards from 9 percent to 4½ percent within nine months.
Bedding manufacturer	Increased output per employee hour by 8 percent.
Textile manufacturer	Increased monthly output by 14 percent.
Plastics company	Raised on-time shipments from 85 percent to 93 percent.

Source: W. Imberman, "Making Quality Circles Work," *Data Management*, November 1982, pp. 24–27.

required in the areas of QC concepts, QC process skills (communication, listening, time management, planning and scheduling), program design, and problem-solving techniques. Unless management is trained the QC circle effort will soon experience problems with lack of adequate management support. In addition, managers need to learn how to reinforce positively participative behaviors in their supervisors and circle leaders.

People Building.   There must be a sincere desire on the part of management to help employees grow and develop. If the QC circles are viewed as advantageous to management only, they are likely to be seen as another attempt at manipulation.

Voluntary.   Members should be completely free to participate. This offers visible proof to members that the program is for their benefit.

Management that Is Supportive.   Managers must assume a role of support but not domination. QC members need time, advice commitment, assistance in removing organizational blocks, and recognition for accomplishment.

The capacity of quality circles to stimulate communication, innovation, and an increased sense of worker responsibility is impressive. American industry is just beginning to "experiment" with this management technique. This method of improving motivation and productivity merits serious consideration.

Management's Use of Goal Setting

Managers have recognized that one of the most important elements in any motivation program is goal setting. Incorporating goals into the job itself results in specific task objectives for the individual employee. Goals themselves have strong motivational properties:[42]

1. Difficult goals will lead to higher performance than less difficult goals.
2. Specific goals will lead to higher performance than very general ones (e.g., "Do your best").
3. Goals will motivate people to higher performance only when they are accepted.

Organizational experiences with goal setting suggest that it is an effective means of improving worker motivation and performance. The effectiveness of this technique has been demonstrated in different types of organizations, for both managerial and nonmanagerial employees, and for extended periods of time.[43] Effective goals have six distinct characteristics (Figure 5–14): (1) goal specificity, (2) goal difficulty, (3) participation in goal setting, (4) feedback on goal effort, (5) peer competition for goal attainment, (6) goal acceptance.[44] Establishing goals with these characteristics will facilitate motivation and effective job performance.

FIGURE 5–14

What Makes a Good Goal

Goal Specificity.   Employees are more likely to perform at higher levels when they are given specific goals. The more specific the goal, the higher the performance, since role ambiguity and performance expectations are reduced.

Goal Difficulty.   More difficult goals lead to higher levels of effort and performance. This is particularly true for those with a high need for achievement, since increasing the difficulty of the goal increases the perceived challenge of the task.

Participation in Goal Setting.   Participation has the potential of increasing organizational efficiency and effectiveness as well as employee involvement and satisfaction.

Feedback on Goal Effort.   The amount of feedback on task-oriented behavior increases the motivational capabilities of goals. Feedback stimulates employees to exert greater effort and keeps job behavior on target.

Peer Competition for Goal Attainment.   A competitive situation sometimes enhances employee performance. The means of defining performance, the degree of task interdependence and the nature of the reward system are the determining factors.

Goal Acceptance.   Those goals that are set by employees are more likely to be understood and accepted than those goals imposed by management.

Source: R. M. Steers and L. W. Porter, "The Role of Task-Goal Attributes in Employee Performance," *Psychological Bulletin* 81 (1974), pp. 434–51.

SUMMARY

In this chapter, we first considered several different approaches to examining the important topic of motivation. After introducing the basic frameworks for understanding motivation and performance, several different organizational applications were presented: extrinsic rewards, positive reinforcement, intrinsic motivation, quality control circles, and goal setting.

When considered together, the topics in this chapter provide the basis for a powerful set of managerial tools. By fine-tuning motivational skills, the manager can be successful in understanding, predicting, and influencing performance in the organization. If used properly, these tools can help meet both individual and organizational objectives.

REVIEW QUESTIONS

1. Why is motivation a major concern of most managers?

2. With respect to motivation, what is the basic responsibility of a manager?

3. What does motivational strength depend upon?

4. What are the implications of the expectancy framework?

5. What does it mean when an employee is feeling a sense of inequity?

6. What are a few ways that employees respond to inequity?

7. How can a manager assist employees in preventing a feeling of inequity?

8. Define intrinsic rewards and extrinsic rewards. Give examples of each.

9. What can managers do to make certain employees are intrinsically rewarded?

10. How does reinforcement play a role in the manager-employee relationship?

11. What does *positive reinforcement* mean? What two conditions must be present for a reward to be a positive reinforcer?

12. What does *negative reinforcement* mean?

13. Define the two methods by which undesirable behavior may be eliminated.

14. Why is it that employees may be unresponsive to incentive pay?

15. What is a "pie view" of work?

16. What is the conception of a fair day's work?

17. Why does management sometimes reward seniority and loyalty rather than performance?

18. How can management increase the likelihood that money will motivate good performance?

19. What are the guidelines management can utilize regarding reinforcement?

20. What should be considered by management in designing a positive reinforcement program?

21. The success of positive reinforcement in industry can be explained in terms of several effective management techniques. What are they?

22. In what ways have positive reinforcement programs been criticized?

23. What opportunities does modifying a job for greater motivation attempt to provide?

24. What is job enrichment? What are the ways in which it is achieved?

25. What is vertical job loading?

26. What is horizontal job loading?

27. What is closure in a job?

28. Identify the essential characteristics for enhancing the motivational capabilities of the job.

29. What are some limits to job enrichment?

30. Define *quality circles.*

31. What are the organizational conditions contributing to the effective implementation of quality circles?

32. Define *goal setting.*

33. How do goals work as motivational tools?

34. Name a goal-setting technique used by many organizations.

35. What are the six characteristics necessary in order for goals to be effective in the work environment?

Notes and References on
Motivating People at Work

1. D. Katz and R. Kahn, *The Social Psychology of Organizations,* 2d ed. (New York: John Wiley & Sons, 1978).

2. The "expectancy" motivation model is built around three variables: valence of needs satisfied, want-need instrumentality, and effort-want expectancy. Valence refers to the perceived attractiveness of the needs that might be satisfied. Want-need instrumentality is defined as the perceived relationship between actual need satisfaction and obtaining the wanted goods, pleasures, or states of being. Effort-want expectancy refers to the perceived relationship between effort expended and obtaining what is wanted. In general, motivation strength = expectancy $\times$ instrumentality $\times$ valence. J. W. Atkinson, *Introduction to Motivation* (New York: Van Nostrand Reinhold, 1964); Victor Vroom, *Work and Motivation* (New York: John Wiley & Sons, 1964).

3. However, it is difficult to measure the elements in expectancy theory. F. L. Schmidt, "Implications of a Measurement Problem for Expectancy Theory Research," *Organizational Behavior and Human Performance* 10 (1973), pp. 243–51.

4. L. Festinger, *A Theory of Cognitive Dissonance* (Palo Alto, Calif.: Stanford University Press, 1957).

5. Social relationships are viewed as exchange processes where individuals make contributions and expect certain outcomes in return. The idea of equilibrium was first advanced by Chester Barnard, *The Functions of the Executive* (Cambridge, Mass.: Harvard University Press, 1938). He argued that people will join organizations and contribute their energies to the organization in exchange for the rewards they offer. This perspective is developed further in J. G. March and H. A. Simon, *Organizations* (New York: John Wiley & Sons, 1958).

6. The concept of equity was first introduced by J. S. Adams, "Injustice in Social Exchange" in *Advances in Experimental Social Psychology,* vol. 2, ed. L. Berkowitz (New York: Academic Press, 1965) and developed further by K. E. Weick, "The Concept of Equity in the Perception of Pay," *Administrative Science Quarterly* 11 (1966), pp. 414–39.

7. J. S. Adams, "Injustice in Social Exchange," in *Advances in Experimental Social Psychology,* ed. L. Berkowitz.

8. Several behavioral scientists have argued that intrinsic rewards are more important than extrinsic rewards. See, for example, F. Herzberg, *Work and the Nature of Man* (Cleveland: World Publishing, 1966). Although there is much controversy over which is more important, most behavioral scientists do believe that it is important to distinguish between intrinsic and extrinsic rewards.

9. For development of this idea, see W. T. Paul, K. B. Robertson, and F. Herzberg, "Job Enrichment Pays off," *Harvard Business Review,* March–April 1969, pp. 93–98; and J. R. Hackman and G. R. Oldham, "Motivation through the Design of Work: Test of a Theory," *Organizational Behavior and Human Performance* 16 (1976), pp. 250–79.

10. Article 10, *Constitution of the People's Republic of China* (Beijing: Foreign Languages Press, 1978).

11. T. K. Oh, "Theory Y in the People's Republic of China," *California Management Review* 19, no. 2 (1976), pp. 77–84; B. M. Richman, *Industrial Society in Communist China* (New York: Random House, 1969).

12. Z. Lin, "Initial Reform in China's Economic Structure," *Social Sciences in China* 3 (1980), pp. 17–194.

13. For a discussion of reinforcement, see E. L. Thorndike, *The Psychology of Learning* (New York: Teachers College, 1931); and C. L. Hull, *Essentials of Behavior* (New Haven: Yale University Press, 1951).

14. B. F. Skinner, *Contingencies of Reinforcement* (New York: Appleton-Century-Crofts, 1969).

15. For extensive discussion of this, see William F. Whyte, *Money and Motivation* (New York: Harper & Row, 1955); for response by managers, see Arch Patton, "Why Incentive Plans Fail," *Harvard Business Review,* May–June 1972, pp. 58–66.

For an interesting perspective on the relationship between incentives and performance, see E. E. Lawler, "Whatever Happened to Incentive Pay?" *New Management* 1, no. 4 (1984), pp. 37–41.

16. On comparatively simple clerical tasks, performance-based rewards for relatively independent workers were associated with higher performance than were equal rewards for interdependent workers who can talk to one another. Satisfaction, however, was lower with those on incentive pay. A. G. Weinstein and R. L. Holzbach, Jr., "Impact of Individual Differences, Reward Distribution and Task Structure on Productivity in a Simulated Work Environment," *Journal of Applied Psychology* 58, no. 3 (1973), pp. 296–301. See also M. London and G. R. Oldham, "Effects of Varying Goal Types and Incentive Systems on Performance and Satisfaction," *Academy of Management Journal,* December 1976, pp. 537–46.

17. A prominent management consultant cited the following incident:

Some years ago, the president of one of our clients badgered the chairman to increase his salary. As a result, our firm was retained to review the situation. It quickly became obvious to us that the President's $85,000 salary, which he wanted increased to $100,000, was high in terms of the size of the company and recent profit trends.

The chairman asked that we break the bad news as gently as possible to the president. So, at lunch one day, I started discoursing on the big bite that high taxes took out of any addition to top management's income.

"In fact," I said to the president, "if your salary were increased $15,000, for example, it would only add $2,700 to your spendable income." The president, who had been listening to my lecture with increasing irritation, exploded, "Hell, Arch, I *need* $2,700 in spendable income!"

Arch Patton, "Executive Compensation by 1970," *Harvard Business Review,* March–April 1964, pp. 137–46.

For a discussion of the impact of compensation on managerial motivation, see L. L. Cummings, "Compensation, Culture, and Motivation: A Systems Perspective," *Organizational Dynamics,* Winter 1984, pp. 33–44.

18. Arch Patton is sharply critical of pay practices in the federal government because: (1) merit increases average only 3 percent, (2) longevity increases are also 3 percent, (3) the only penalty for poor performance is withholding of longevity increase—and this is applied to less than 1 percent of the employees. "Does Federal Pay 'Demotivate' More than Motivate?" *Harvard Business Review,* January–February, 1974, p. 12 ff. See also J. M. Rosow, "Public-Sector Pay and Productivity," *Harvard Business Review,* January–February 1977, pp. 6–8.

19. These requirements for an effective incentive plan were discussed in C. Cammann and E. E. Lawler III, "Employee Reactions to a Pay Incentive Plan," *Journal of Applied Psychology* 58, no. 2 (1973), pp. 163–72. See also John Dearden, "How to Make Incentive Plans Work," *Harvard Business Review,* July–August 1972, pp. 117–24.

20. On the relation between performance and satisfaction, see Edward E. Lawler and Lyman W. Porter, "The Effect of Performance on Job Satisfaction," *Industrial Relations* 7 (1967), pp. 20–29. It has been suggested that:

merit pay
↓ ↑ ⟶ satisfaction
performance ⟋

if merit pay is based on measurable superior performance and if the increased reward is not too delayed. See C. N. Greene, "Causal Connections among Managers' Merit Pay, Job Satisfaction and Performance," *Journal of Applied Psychology* 58, no. 1 (1973), pp. 95–100; D. L. Cherrington, H. J. Reitz and W. E. Scott, "Effects of Contingent and Noncontingent Reward on the Relationship between Satisfaction and Task Performance," *Journal of Applied Psychology* 55 (1971), pp. 531–37; and S. M. Klein, "Pay Factors as Predictors to Satisfaction: A Comparison of Reinforcement, Equity and Expectancy," *Academy of Management Journal* 16, no. 4 (1973), pp. 598–610.

In an extensive examination of the role of pay, Edward E. Lawler observed the following relationships:

Pay not
tied to
performance
— Pay less important.
— Pay does not motivate.
— Pay satisfaction low.
— Absenteeism and turnover
among all employees.

Pay tied to
performance
— Pay is important.
— Pay motivates.
— Pay satisfaction high.
— Absenteeism and turnover
centered on poor
performance.

Pay and Organizational Effectiveness (New York: McGraw-Hill, 1971), p. 274.

21. R. L. Opsahl and M. D. Dunnette, "The Role of Financial Compensation in Industrial Motivation," *Psychological Bulletin* 66 (1966), pp. 94–118. See also, L. A. Krefting and T. A. Mahoney, "Determining the Size of a Meaningful Pay Increase," *Industrial Relations,* February 1977, pp. 83–93.

22. On the size of incentive bonuses, S. W. Gellerman wrote:

The increment must bring about a radical change in the individual's financial condition. The change must be more than one of degree; that, after all, could be expected to occur eventually anyway, at less hazard and at lower cost. It must be a change in order of magnitude. It must make possible things only dreamed of ordinarily. Unless the increment is princely, it is unlikely to excite the imagination or whet the appetite. It must do more than just raise income; it must change the individual's capital position. It must enable the traditional debtor to get out from under his debts; it must enable the man of no means to acquire at least some degree of real wealth. In short, the increment in income must change the individual's basic attitude toward money. That obviously requires a lot of money. Make no mistake about it; effective motivation with money is no piker's game.

"Motivating Men with Money," *Fortune,* March 1968, p. 145.

23. Giving extra money for loyalty or seniority is not irrational for management. To the extent that the added money makes the organization a more attractive place to work, people are less likely to quit or be absent. Hiring and training costs will be reduced and profits will be increased.

24. "Motivation Programme Is a Give-away," *International Management,* August 1977, p. 40 ff.

25. "Where Pink Cadillacs Come from," *Fortune,* September 1976, p. 28.

26. See E. L. Thorndike, *Animal Intelligence* (New York: Macmillan, 1911); J. B. Watson, *Behaviorism* (New York: Norton, 1924); and B. F. Skinner, *Contingencies of Reinforcement* (New York: Appleton-Century-Crofts, 1969).

27. Productivity gains from a pat on the back. *Business Week.* January 23, 1978, pp. 56–62.

28. Job enlargement appears to imply changes in the technical aspects of the job, and job enrichment requires changes in behavioral systems in an organization. The distinction is not made consistently, however. K. A. Chung and M. F. Ross, "Differences in Motivational Properties between Job Enlargement and Job Enrichment," *Academy of Management Review,* January 1977, pp. 113–22.

29. Job motivation and effort of achievement-oriented employees are associated with: (1) clear standards of excellence, (2) feedback on performance, (3) control over methods of task performance, (4) greater task difficulty, (5) availability of resources, (6) past success in similar tasks, and (7) self-confidence. Martin Patchen, *Participation, Achievement and Involvement on the Job* (Englewood Cliffs, N.J.: Prentice-Hall, 1970).

Frederick Herzberg summarizes the principles of job enlargement as follows: (1) Remove some controls while retaining accountability; (2) increase the accountability of individuals for their own work; (3) give a person a complete natural unit of work; (4) grant additional authority to an employee in the activity, (5) make periodic reports directly available to the workers rather than to the supervisor; (6) introduce new and more difficult tasks not previously handled; and (7) assign individuals specific tasks enabling them to become experts. "One More Time, How Do You Motivate Workers?" *Harvard Business Review,* January–February 1968, pp. 53–62. The recommendations in effect say that blue-collar jobs can be made more like managerial jobs, a point explicit in M. Scott Myers, "Every Man a Manager," *California Management Review* 10, no. 3 (1968), pp. 9–20; and Myers, *Every Employee a Manager* (New York: McGraw-Hill, 1970).

For an exploration of task-design issues from a social information processing perspective, see J. Thomas and R. Griffin, "The Social Information Processing Model of Task Design: A Review of the Literature," *Academy of Management Review* 8, no. 4 (1983), pp. 672–82.

30. For a description of job changes in an automobile company, see P. Gyllenhammer, "Volvo's Solution to the Blue-Collar Blues," *Business and Society/Innovation No. 7,* Autumn 1973, pp. 50–54; and "How Volvo Adapts Work to People," *Harvard Business Review,* July–August 1977, pp. 102–14. The steps include: (1) voluntary job rotation, (2) management-employee councils that hold discussion meetings, (3) small work groups that control their work process, and (4) employee-oriented facilities designed with employee advice. The president of Volvo reports that the program costs money and reduces turnover but does not say what it does for profits.

31. These examples from David R. Sirota, formerly a professor at the Wharton School, University of Pennsylvania. For examples of job enrichment at Texas Instruments, see W. J. Roche and N. L. MacKinnon, "Motivating People with Meaningful Work," *Harvard Business Review,* May–June 1970, pp. 97–110. For examples at American Telephone and Telegraph Company, see R. N. Ford, *Motivation through the Work Itself* (New York: American Management Association, 1969), and "Job Enrichment Lessons from A. T. & T.," *Harvard Business Review,* January–February 1973, pp. 96–106.

32. For a criticism that companies tend to blindly apply techniques like job enrichment to inappropriate situations, see D. Sirota and A. D. Wolfson, "Pragmatic Approach to People Problems," *Harvard Business Review,* January–February 1973, pp. 120–28.

33. See W. J. Paul, Jr.; K. B. Robertson; and F. Herzberg, "Job Enrichment Pays off," *Harvard Business Review,* March–April 1969, pp. 61–78.

34. A study of phone operators who experienced job expansion reported no increase in job motivation but a decrease in satisfaction because the expanded job allowed less time for socializing. E. E. Lawler III, J. R. Hackman, and S. Kaufman, "Effects of Job Redesign: A Field Experiment," *Journal of Applied Social Psychology* 3, no. 1 (1973), pp. 49–62.

European Business, Spring 1975, contains the following item.

Job enrichment schemes are popping up all over the world, but the active center is definitely Scandinavia. Other centers of experiment include the United States. *So what happened when a bunch of American auto workers went to work in a Swedish factory to test Swedish work reforms?*

The system has its drawbacks, they concluded.

The workers were six in number, and they hailed from the General Motors, Ford, and Chrysler engine factories. They ranged in age from 21 to 53 years old and in experience from eight months to 21 years. They were sent to a Saab engine plant at Södertälje, Sweden, under a Cornell University project funded by the Ford Foundation.

After four weeks on the job in the Saab factory, what were their feelings about Swedish job enrichment? They found the physical working environment better than at home. Roomier work space and the presence of safety officials everywhere made the plant seem safer than those in Detroit. It also appeared to them as better lit, cleaner, and cooler.

However, the plant's main feature—group work—triggered serious misgivings. Under the Swedish plan, workers are split into teams, and team members decide who will perform which task. Although the Americans welcomed this change from assembly-line work, they found the pace of work unexpectedly fast. Said one worker: "If I've got to bust my ass to be meaningful, forget it—I'd rather be monotonous."

The workers also had difficulty in adjusting to team work. Teams require an adaptation to other members' style of work. Some of the Americans preferred to be responsible only to themselves. They also had criticisms of the Swedish work system, *finding it too regimented and paternalistic.* Despite the attempts at worker participation in decision making, the Americans said they preferred the Detroit system where the union holds the power.

35. C. L. Hulin and M. R. Blood, "Job Enlargement, Individual Differences and Worker Responses," *Psychological Bulletin* 69 (1968), pp. 41–55. The seven largest and fastest growing occupations have apparently not been affected by job redesign: secretaries, retail sales clerks, teachers, restaurant workers, truck drivers and delivery people, bookkeepers and cashiers, and cleaning workers. S. A. Leviton and W. B. Johnston, "Job Design, Reform, Enrichment—Exploring the Limitations," *Monthly Labor Review* 96 (1973), pp. 35–41. M. Fein observes that job enrichment will not be entirely successful because the intrinsic nature of the job is secondary in importance to many blue-collar workers. Of primary concern to them are pay, job security, and the rules of his workplace. "Job Enrichment: A Reevaluation," *Sloan Management Review* 15, no. 2 (1974), pp. 69–88. For labor union views on the matter, see B. J. White, "Innovations in Job Design: The Union Perspective," *Journal of Contemporary Business* Spring 1977, pp. 23–33.

36. The data on job attitude trends are unclear. Some observers (and especially union leaders) deny that job dissatisfaction is widespread, and what does exist reflects only a minority of young workers who account for most absenteeism. The news media have exaggerated the issue, in this view. F. E. Armbruster, "A Vocal Minority of Dissatisfied Workers," *New York Times,* February 12, 1973.

H. R. Kaplan reports that in 1949, 69 percent of white workers were satisfied with the work they did, but this had increased to almost 90 percent by 1969. "Communications: How Do Workers View Work in America?" *Monthly Labor Review* 96 (1973), pp. 46–48. R. P. Quinn et al. report little change in attitudes in recent years. "Evaluating Working Conditions in America," *Monthly Labor Review* 96 (1973), pp. 32–42. A recent survey is in J. E. Thurman, "Job Satisfaction: An International Overview," *International Labour Review,* November–December 1977, pp. 249–68. See also D. W. Organ, "Inferences about Trends in Labor Force Satisfaction: A Causal-Correlational Analysis," *Academy of Management Journal,* December 1977, pp. 510–19.

37.   G. I. Susman, "Job Enlargement: Effects of Culture on Worker Responses," *Industrial Relations* 12, no. 1 (1973), pp. 21–38. J. J. Morse suggests that there should be a fit between job characteristics and workers' desires, but he also maintains that it already usually exists (at least in the places he studied). People with narrow and repetitive jobs generally perferred them. "A Contingency Look at Job Design," *California Management Review* 16, no. 1 (1973), p. 67 ff. J. M. Shepard examined automobile assemblers, maintenance personnel, and refinery control room operators. The strongest determinant of dissatisfaction was the objective task specialization; it was much more influential than the employee's expectations or desires. "Specialization, Autonomy and Job Satisfaction," *Industrial Relations* 12, no. 3 (1973), pp. 274–81. For an extensive review of the literature on the relation between people and jobs, see Chris Argyris, "Personality and Organization Revisited," *Administrative Science Quarterly* 18, no. 2 (1973), pp. 141–67.

38.   J. R. Hackman and E. E. Lawler III maintain that a job will be motivating and intrinsically satisfying only if it is high on all four core dimensions—autonomy, task identity (having a whole piece of work to do), variety, and feedback—and only people with desires for higher order need satisfaction will positively respond. "Employee Reactions to Job Characteristics," *Journal of Applied Psychology Monograph* 55 (1971), pp. 259–86. See also R. B. Dunham, "Reactions to Job Characteristics: Moderating Effects of the Organization," *Academy of Management Journal* March 1977, pp. 42–65.

39.   M. E. Gorson and R. D. Arvey, "The Relationship between Education and Satisfaction with Job Content," *Academy of Management Journal,* December 1975, pp. 888–92.

40.   W. Ouchi, *Theory Z* (Reading, Mass.: Addison-Wesley Publishing, 1981) contains an excellent review of Japanese management principles and their application to American organizations. In addition, see N. Hatvany and V. Pucik, "Japanese Management Practices and Productivity," *Organizational Dynamics* 9, no. 4 (1981), pp. 5–21.

For a detailed description of the usefulness of the Quality Circle concept in American industry, see R. Wood, F. Hull, and K. Azumi, "Evaluating Quality Circles: The American Application," *California Management Review* 26, no. 1 (1983), pp. 37–53.

41.   W. Thompson, "Is the Organization Ready for Quality Circles?" *Training and Development Journal,* December 1982, pp. 115–18.

42.   E. A. Locke, "Toward a Theory of Task Performance and Incentives," *Organizational Behavior and Human Performance* 3 (1968), pp. 157–89.

43.   To learn more about effects of goal-setting practices in organizations, see G. P. Latham and G. A. Yukl, "A Review of Research on the Application of Goal Setting in Organizations," *Academy of Management Journal,* December 1975, pp. 824–45.

44.   For an extensive review of this literature, see R. M. Steers and L. W. Porter, "The Role of Task-Goal Attributes in Employee Performance," *Psychological Bulletin* 81 (1974), pp. 434–51.

Discussion Questions and Exercises on Individuals at Work

Discussion Questions

1. Most religions maintain that humans do not live by bread alone, but the need hierarchy suggests that humans live by bread alone when there is no bread. What does this mean?

2. Why is the need for power so widely distrusted and condemned, when in fact many people have it?

3. In beginning the search for a new administrator, a group of faculty members said that they did not want anybody who "enjoyed exercising power." What do you think of their attitude?

4. Compare and contrast the needs for achievement and competence. Are they essentially the same, or different?

5. Are there other needs that you would add to the need hierarchy? Where? Why?

6. A study in one of the largest American corporations indicates that the two criteria "quality of college attended" and "rank in class" were the best predictors of future managerial success in that firm. If you were a recruiter for a large company, would you utilize these criteria? Why?

7. U.S. business managers report that autonomy and self-actualization are their least satisfied needs, and Japanese business managers report esteem and social needs as least satisfied. How do you explain these findings?

8. American business managers report that esteem is their least important need, but Italian managers rank it ahead of security, social, and autonomy needs. How would you explain this?

9. In the past, male managers tended to assume that women worked mainly to satisfy low-level needs, especially to earn money for clothes, to socialize, and to meet a husband. What do you think?

10. David McClelland has shown that up to about $25,000 per year (perhaps $50,000 in today's dollars), the higher managers' achievement needs, the higher their income. Above this level, however, managers seem to have lower achievement need (although still above average). (See the graph on page 110.) How would you explain this relationship?

11. The graduated federal income tax rises to high percentages at high incomes. A manager earning $20,000 would pay approximately $5,000; an executive earning $100,000 would pay approximately $50,000. Do you think such taxes hinder the organization's ability to attract and motivate outstanding people?

12. How do you reconcile the observation that high-achievement-oriented people are *less* motivated by money, but they want *more* money to perform a task that people with lower achievement need will do for less?

13. Why don't pension plans, health care facilities, and insurance benefits automatically contribute to greater effort and improved performance? How can such fringe benefits help the organization?

14. A large, regional over-the-road trucking firm hires only college graduates as drivers. After joining the Teamsters Union and completing a training program, they immediately earn more than twice as much as most other newly graduated employees. Most claim that they will drive for only a few years. Management likes them because they dress well, carry

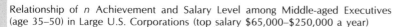

Relationship of *n* Achievement and Salary Level among Middle-aged Executives (age 35–50) in Large U.S. Corporations (top salary $65,000–$250,000 a year)

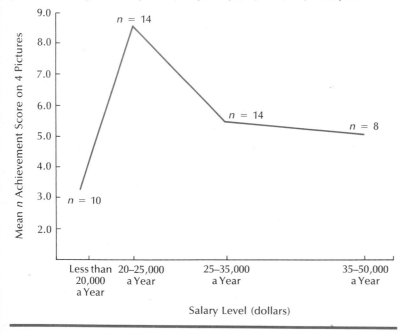

Source: David C. McClelland, *The Achieving Society* (New York: D. Van Nostrand Co., 1961).

attaché cases, and communicate well with customers. Do you think the drivers suffer from any status incongruency? Do you think they will remain in trucking? Do you think they will eventually present any problems to management?

15. We live in an era of what has been called "a revolution of rising expectations." How do you think prolonged economic slowdown would affect people, after years of expansion?

16. Labor unions are generally concerned with wages, benefits, and working conditions. How have unions contributed to an employee's higher level needs? How have they thwarted efforts to achieve higher level needs?

17. Few jobs were available for college graduates in the early 1980s. Some employers were even reluctant to hire college grads for clerical and maintenance positions. Why were these employers hesitant? What does our understanding of individual needs suggest about this situation?

18. In the early 1980s, the United States experienced high levels of unemployment. A great many auto workers and other long-term unemployed workers suffered enormously as benefits were exhausted. What impact do you suppose such long-term unemployment has on an individual?

19. In the early 1980s, the Ford Motor Company altered its Kentucky truck manufacturing plant to manufacture small trucks. It also changed its managerial philosophy at the plant. Workers were consulted on design and manufacturing issues. Truck-owning employees made practical design suggestions. Truck beds were now assembled from above, with the assembler standing on the floor next to fellow workers, rather than being isolated in a pit beneath the assembly line. Regular meetings occurred between management and workers. The truck that rolled off the assembly line incorporated over 2,000 employee suggestions. What impact will this change in managerial approach have on individual motivation? Why? What overall changes do you expect to occur?

Individual Exercises

1. Describe an event that suggests to you your transition from being mainly other directed to being mainly inner directed.

2. Compare your need structure with your perception of each of your parents'.

3. Maintain an informal record of how frequently you are aware of your needs for security, affiliation, esteem, power, autonomy, and achievement.

4. Take a class survey on how much income members would require to scrub a large tile floor with a toothbrush as a permanent job. Analyze the response.

5. Interview two people on why they work and which of their needs are satisfied or frustrated. Summarize and comment on their responses.

6. Examine the relationship between your needs and the rewards and satisfactions of any job you have held.

7. Is your attitude toward money different from that of your parents? How? Why?

8. If your state has a lottery, collect newspaper clippings on the winners. What do they say they will do with their winnings? What do people actually do? Analyze.

9. Do you think that your peers have unrealistic expectations about their future incomes? How will inflation affect their aspirations and satisfactions? How much money do you expect to make per year 20 years after graduation?

10. Describe how a sense of equity operates among your fellow students.

11. Describe and analyze a situation with which you are familiar where the sense of equity was offended.

Managerial Cases and Problems on Individuals at Work

Tom O'Brien: Father and Son

Tom O'Brien, Jr., a 28-year-old manager with the State Water Company, has come to talk with Dr. Willard Erdman, a neighbor who is a university professor.

O'BRIEN: My father is a Dartnell graduate. He just sort of assumed that I would go too—and I did. We were kind of an old-fashioned family, you know. I just did what my parents wanted me to. At least most of the time.

In college, however, I grew away from them. Oh, I still loved them, but one does have to declare one's independence sometime. It was the 1972 elections that really drove us apart. I mean, he was a lawyer and a big Republican politico. But how could he support Nixon? By the time of Watergate, we were hardly talking. Of course, my long hair, disreputable clothes, and lousy grades probably had something to do with it. I guess he also assumed that I would go on to law school.

ERDMAN: Why didn't you?

O'BRIEN: I couldn't stand to. To tell you the truth, lawyers strike me as being sort of prostitutes. I mean, they do what a client wants them to. They seem to have no integrity, no personal moral positions. The Watergate fiasco demonstrated that. I just didn't want to be a puppet for anyone. I mean if you can't reach your own judgments and act on them, what good are you?

ERDMAN: What did you major in in college?

O'BRIEN: I majored in English. It just seemed the most fun. From Blake to Vonnegut, I did enjoy the stuff. My marks weren't too good because I didn't want to write

the Mickey Mouse reports, but I could fly while reading poetry and listening to music. I never needed any dope. I must admit, I did play varsity hockey, not that I cared about winning, but I loved flying down the ice on the left wing, letting go with a hard slap shot and then seeing the red light indicate a goal. I really lived during those moments. I worked hard at staying in shape because those highs come only after hard work.

ERDMAN: What did you do after college?

O'BRIEN: Well, as I said, I decided against law school and never even told my father. Because I had no money (and owed the college), I needed a job. What I wanted was a job that wouldn't hassle me. One where I could be left alone pretty much, put in my time, and not worry about it at night.

I remembered my father's complaints about how lazy people in nonprofit institutions were, especially in the water company. So I went down there and took a job as a field representative. I would work in the field with a company car alone most of the time, gathering information and data from municipal officials and builders. Then I would write reports which I would just send via company mail to my boss. I never heard anything about them, except when I calculated something incorrectly.

ERDMAN: So what's the problem?

O'BRIEN: Well, in the beginning, it was just what I wanted. No boss breathing down my back, no office politicking, no late nights. Often I would knock off early to go swimming, play tennis, or drive somewhere for a rock concert.

But, after a while, I began to visit locations where

the company made installations, apparently in response to my earlier reports. A number of these installations were absurd, clearly inadequate, and unresponsive to the community's needs. To tell you the truth, I thought graft must have been involved between shady politicians, contractors, and the company. Later, I found out there was some graft, but it was mostly incompetence.

ERDMAN: What did you do?

O'BRIEN: I began to ask questions. To carry my reports to my boss, to ask him what happened with them, why certain decisions were made. At first he was noncommittal, but after a while he seemed very pleased. He began to call me into his office from time to time to talk about our problems.

I remember one situation two years ago. A developer was constructing a new tract of homes in a former orchard. The developer and the township officials were trying to get by with the cheapest water, drainage, and sewer systems possible. Their plans were clearly inadequate. When all those washers were operating and the kids were all taking baths, and if it was raining hard, the faucets would be dry while the tract drowned. Well, Steve (he was my boss) really felt strongly about it. He asked me to help him convince the officials to change the plan. At first I didn't want to be bothered, but I agreed to set up a series of meetings with officials and residents. The initial meetings were so discouraging that I just kind of got sucked in. Night after night, Steve and I phoned and visited residents to generate concern and pressure.

Well, it worked—and it rather felt like that red light flashing behind the goal cage. The plan was changed, the township voted a tax increase, and the contractor upgraded the installation.

Six months later, Steve was transferred and I was promoted to his job as regional supervisor. That job was a lot of work, but the shoddiness and incompetence of so many people was appalling. I hadn't been much of a field representative myself, but most of the others were terrible, goofing off, turning in inadequate figures, and not asking probing questions. They just weren't serving the people at all.

Well, I shaped things up. I spent a week on the road with each field representative, making calls and visits during the day, talking about their problems at night. Some quit, but most really seemed pleased to have me come out. And I solved some tough problems. As a result, my rates in my region have gone up only 5 percent, while in the state as a whole they have increased

11 percent. I really get a kick out of seeing the new field representatives take hold and ensuring quality installations constructed on time.

ERDMAN: Things seem to be going so well for you. What are you concerned about?

O'BRIEN: Last week I was offered a promotion to assistant vice president at the company headquarters in the state capital. It would mean a $10,000 increase and a fancy office. I'd be the youngest VP in the company, in charge of all 35 regional supervisors. Face it, I'm brighter than most of the duds with the water company. Most of them are only interested in security, retirement, and not taking a chance.

ERDMAN: Congratulations.

O'BRIEN: Dr. Erdman, you've got to realize that in my value system and in that of my friends at college, all of this means nothing. Or worse, it means I'm selling out to the establishment. I just don't know what I should do. Hell, I went to the water company so my work wouldn't interfere with my off-job life. Now, I'm spending half my time on the road, working 12 hours a day. I've been asked to run for the Democratic nomination for county freeholder. I like all this, but I don't know what it would be like in headquarters. I don't want to become like my father's stuffed-shirt clients. I don't want to play office politics all day. What do you think?

[Thomas O'Brien, Sr., now 54 years old, was later interviewed by Professor Erdman.]

ERDMAN: Tom, could you tell me something about what you're doing now?

O'BRIEN: Well, I'm trying to make ends meet. I've got two kids in college and two still in high school. Mainly I'm trying to build up my law practice again. You know it really suffered all those years I was serving in the state legislature and as county chairman. Then of course it all but ceased when I was serving in the governor's cabinet. I guess my drinking didn't help it much either.

ERDMAN: Your drinking?

O'BRIEN: Yes. I don't mind talking about it now because I've joined AA, but I was really on the stuff during my political days—all those receptions, cocktail parties, and rubber chicken dinners! Drinking just seems to go with the turf when you're away so much sleeping in motel rooms. I'm now into AA and serving as legal counsel for a couple of social assistance agencies concerned with drinking problems, especially among young people. This is the most enjoyable legal work I've done. It pays next to nothing but lots of good feelings.

ERDMAN: When did you enter politics?

O'BRIEN: I just sort of grew up with it. My father came over from Ireland as a boy many years ago, almost back in the days when signs said, "no dogs and Irishman allowed." He had nothing and worked as a construction laborer. And he was tough! He only hit me twice, but I can still feel that huge hand. Well, he would work hard and eventually owned his own construction company. We were poor in the beginning, but by the time I was graduating from high school he had the money to send me to college. He told me he wanted his own Ivy League lawyer because they were costing him so much dough in dealing with various city agencies. Luckily I was able to get in because I had good grades. Mom had always pushed me to do my homework and expected good grades. I either did well or got the deep freeze. Once I got a *D* in math and she didn't speak to me for three weeks. She relayed messages through my grandmother. Boy, did Mom get excited when I made the *A* honor role.

I got into politics because I specialized in construction and real estate law and you didn't accomplish much without political influence. I liked it. It's a great feeling to see a bill pass or a building constructed and know

that you made it happen. The state highway department didn't construct their central maintenance facility in this town by accident. And I guess I came to eventually dream of being senator or governor. It would have made the old man proud.

ERDMAN: Why did you give up politics?

O'BRIEN: Old age I guess. Evaporated dreams. No, I just had to change after I was ill. A scare like that really makes you think about things. My youngest two children are still at home, and I thought I should get to know them. Besides, you get tired of putting your career first, first, first. There are other things in life.

Questions on Tom O'Brien: Father and Son

1. Compare and contrast father and son.
2. What kind of a guy is O'Brien, Jr.?
3. What was he looking for in his work?
4. What did he find satisfying in his work?
5. Why do you think he is confused?
6. What advice would you give him?
7. What kind of a guy is O'Brien, Sr.?
8. What was he looking for from his work in the past? What is he looking for now?

Emery Air Freight Corporation (A)*

Emery Air Freight Corporation, the largest and most profitable air freight transportation company in the world, was founded in 1946, by John C. Emery, Sr. The company is a freight forwarder, or trucking carrier, consolidating cargo which goes to the airlines. Basically, Emery purchases "wholesale" cargo space from the airlines and retails this in small amounts. Emery provides pickup and delivery services in many cities around the world. It is the leader in an industry that has grown on an average of 20 percent per year in the late 1960s.

Most of the company's market is the small shipment customer. Therefore, when a Systems Performance Division was set up at Emery to determine the areas in which

the biggest potential profit payoffs exist, the area most closely scrutinized was the highly touted containerized shipment operation.

Because small shipments intended for the same destination fly at lower rates when shipped together in large, standard-size boxes called "bulk cargo containers," Emery had been increasing the use of these containers at an impressive rate each year. Managers responsible for the shipping dock were under the impression that bulk containers were already being used 90 percent of the time. But measurement of the actual usage—a measurement made by these same managers—showed that the figure was only 45 percent. The rest of the time shipments were being

---

© Marilyn A. Morgan, McIntire School of Commerce, University of Virginia.

* Parts B and C of this case are found in the *Instructor's Manual.*

sent out separately, i.e., as many small packages. Since Emery's largest single cost item is air freight—approximately $50 million per year—increased use of containers would cut costs substantially.

This discrepancy, between the perceived use of bulk containers and their actual use, gave the shipping division the jolt it needed to improve performance. But how could this best be accomplished?

This was the problem facing Edward J. Feeney, who was head of Systems Performance. What was causing this situation? Some of the people in his division believed that the employees on the shipping dock seemed indifferent about whether to use the containers even though the amount of time and effort they have to expend is the same for either method. Others thought, however, that most of the workers on the loading dock know how and when to use them but are only vaguely aware of the impact that container use has on company profits.

The Problem

How can the use of bulk containers for small shipments be increased?

Pay Raises at Happy Home Builders, Inc.*

Happy Home Builder's Inc. is a large single-family home contractor located in a major metropolitan area. Presently, Happy Home Builders, Inc. has six subdivisions under development with a construction superintendent in charge of each subdivision. Each has a crew of 10 persons which (s)he must supervise.

A year ago, the general manager (the superintendents' immediate supervisor) outlined the major responsibilities of the superintendent's job. Merit pay increases are based on how well the construction superintendent performs the following duties: (1) Contact the appropriate supplier allowing for the necessary lead time; (2) maintain the construction schedule outlined by the general manager minimizing overtime labor costs; (3) supervise a construction crew of 10 or fewer persons to make certain they perform their duties well and on time; (4) oversee all work performed and supplies delivered to make certain there are no defects or errors; and (5) return to the accounts payable clerk all suppliers' receipts noting on the invoice for which home the supplies were used.

A profile of each superintendent is as follows:

Albert Anslow is married and has four children, and his wife is unemployed. He completed two years at the local community college. Before joining Happy Homes three years ago as a superintendent, Albert worked as a superintendent for nine years with another construction firm. He usually gives the suppliers ample time to deliver. As a result of pushing his crew hard and expecting top-notch performance, he is usually ahead of construction schedule. His crew has exhibited a great deal of respect for him. There is a problem with the accounts payable clerk in that Albert often fails to note on the supplier's invoice for which home(s) the supplies were used. Home buyers rarely report a defect in workmanship and seem to be pleased with the finished product. Albert is enthusiastic about his job and is anxious to please management. He is very knowledgeable about his work and can handle any construction problem that may occur. Presently, Albert's salary is $400 per week.

Betty Boynton currently draws a salary of $350 weekly. She is single. Before joining the organization a year ago, Betty had just received a B.S. degree in structural engineering. She usually orders her supplies in time and is rarely behind the construction schedule. Betty is extremely well informed about her work and has submitted a few ideas to the firm that have proved profitable. Her supervisory skills are acceptable; yet, the crew often claims that she has a new way of doing some things which serves to confuse the crew members. Betty has an excellent attitude about her job. Recently, Betty was offered a job with another construction firm which promises to pay her a weekly salary of $450. The general manager feels Betty will not leave the firm if the offer can be matched.

Clarence Clatterbaugh never graduated from high school. Fifteen years ago he joined Happy Homes as a crew member. He has been a superintendent for six years. Currently, Clarence draws a weekly salary of $400. He is a nice man and has a very easygoing manner. Frequently, his crew members fail to show up, requiring the remaining members to work overtime in order to complete the job on time. On many occasions, work did fall behind sched-

* © Marilyn A. Morgan and Angela F. Koogler, McIntire School of Commerce, University of Virginia.

ule. The crew members feel Clarence is terrific to work for and that he is very fair with them. Home buyers have never complained about workmanship and are extremely pleased with their new home. Clarence is not the "go getter" that some of the other superintendents are, but he usually is reliable. He is very knowledgeable about his work and never incurrs problems that he cannot solve. The accounts payable clerk has often commented on how meticulous Clarence is regarding the suppliers' receipts. Clarence is married and has one son in college.

Diana Delegro currently receives a salary of $375 per week. She is married and has two children. Diana completed two years at a community college before joining the firm as a superintendent five years ago. By and large, management feels that Diana has performed her job satisfactorily. That is, each construction phase is usually completed on schedule, the suppliers are contacted at the appropriate time, and her supervisory skills are average. Diana's crew members have indicated that she is a competent supervisor, and the accounts payable clerk has stated that Diana usually submits suppliers' invoices detailing the necessary information. There have been many complaints from home buyers regarding poor workmanship, indicating that Diana is not thorough when inspecting work that has been completed. Diana has a good attitude about her job and appears to be fairly well informed about her work.

Edward Eagleton has been a superintendent for 10 years at Happy Homes. He graduated from high school, is married, and has three daughters in college. Edward is very civic-oriented, and having lived in this city all of his life, he knows many people. As a result, Edward has been responsible for many people buying a "Happy Home," helped the firm get quick approval from city hall regarding new zoning laws, and remedied any problems incurred with the building inspector. In this respect, he would be difficult to replace. As a superintendent, Edward has frequently been late contacting the suppliers and, consequently, the construction schedules have fallen behind. The members of Edward's crew have stated that he is a fairly good supervisor. On the average, management feels

he supervises his crew fairly well. All reports from the home buyers indicate that there are few defects or errors in the workmanship. The accounts payable clerk has complained that Edward fails to submit the receipts from suppliers. When the receipts are submitted, they are usually incomplete. Management feels that Edward's attitude and job knowledge are acceptable. Currently, his weekly salary is $450.

Francis Fortney is divorced, has one child, and has been a superintendent at Happy Homes for three years. She joined the firm after completing two years at the community college and working as a superintendent for eight years with another construction firm. Presently, her salary is $375 per week. Francis is extremely well informed about her job, and her attitude is average. She usually gives the suppliers sufficient lead time and rarely falls behind the construction schedule. She has exhibited adequate supervisory skills and her crew members have never indicated there were any problems. The accounts payable clerk is frequently tracking down Francis for her receipts, and often it is found that Francis has misplaced them. Homeowners have consistently complained that appliances do not work, indicating that Francis does not conduct a thorough walk-through inspection before the owners move in.

1. Make an individual decision about the percentage raise you would give to each of the construction superintendents. Your results should be justified by a rationale or decision rule.
2. Work in groups of four to eight persons. Share your raise decisions with the other members of your group. As a group, decide on a set of raises. Discuss this case only with members of your own group.
3. Appoint a group spokesperson who can report the following information to the class:
    a. The raises recommended by your group.
    b. The rationale through which each person's raise was determined.

Part Three

Groups at Work

6

Group Development and Structure

Near the end of the tragic riot at Columbia University in 1968, the police dragged a small number of demonstrators out of the president's office, which they had been occupying. Amidst the kicking, screaming, and swearing, one young student in the grip of an officer exclaimed, "God, how exciting. That's the first time I've ever felt part of anything in my life!" Her words are testimony to the satisfaction that people find in informal groups and with collective action.[1]*

In this chapter we shall discuss the emergence of social relationships and informal organizations out of the formal technical system designed by management. We will see that groups offer individuals identification and emotional support, assistance in meeting objectives, and protection. In addition, we shall describe informal structure in terms of status, leadership, and cohesion. Once a social structure develops, it takes on a life of its own. The group pursues objectives that contribute to individual goals but may also limit members' autonomy. In this chapter therefore, we shall also examine the behavior of some groups and see how they exercise discipline in demanding conformity from members. Then we shall consider the kinds of problems and opportunities that informal organization poses for management.

The Emergence of Informal Groups

Groups in organizations develop over time. Newly formed groups show quite different behavior patterns than do mature ones. Small groups are formed and move through several stages of development.[2] Behavioral scientists have identified several different ways of considering these stages. For our purposes, we will consider these three aspects of development: forming, structuring, and performing.

During each of these stages there are particular issues with which group members must deal. Knowing which stage of development a group is in is important because it helps to determine which style of leadership is most effective for moving the group toward accomplishment of its goals. These stages overlap, and groups require different lengths of time for development, so it is often difficult for a manager to assess the particular stage to which a group has matured. Figure 6–1 presents a summary of the issues that are important in each stage.

Theoretically, management is only concerned with the formal aspects of organization: the duties, behavior, and communications of people. If there is any concern with feelings or sentiments, it is usually an unstated hope that everyone will cooperate and remain emotionally neutral. Management assigns certain duties to individuals as their jobs. In carrying out these activities, they interact or communicate with others. Theoretically, this is all the manager need be concerned with—whether they perform the duties effectively and efficiently, communicating as necessary. But there is more to organizational relationships than this. Unplanned sentiments will emerge because people dislike or like (and rarely are neutral about) the people with whom they work. These sentiments encourage them to elaborate their communications and activities with others in a variety of unplanned and informal patterns.[3] The pattern of emergent informal activity can be illustrated as in Figure 6–2.

Whenever management brings people together in an office or workplace and

---

* Notes and references will be found at the end of this chapter.

FIGURE 6–1

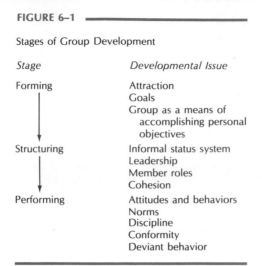

Stages of Group Development

Stage	Developmental Issue
Forming	Attraction
	Goals
	Group as a means of accomplishing personal objectives
Structuring	Informal status system
	Leadership
	Member roles
	Cohesion
Performing	Attitudes and behaviors
	Norms
	Discipline
	Conformity
	Deviant behavior

expects them to work together, elaboration occurs inevitably. Out of the technical or formal system of work, a second system emerges. Employees form friendships, which grow into groups, which take on a life of their own. Their sentiments lead to the various informal activities, such as showing a new employee how to do the job, taping equipment safety buttons, scheduling the work, covering for each other on the time clock, and restricting production. Such informal activities reinforce positive feelings so that a group becomes something more than a mere collection of individuals. As the group develops customary ways of doing things, its stable characteristics denote that the group has become an informal organization.[4]

Thus membership in a group is related to technology and work flow; the social system grows out of the technical system. For a group to develop, the people have to be located fairly close together and must have an opportunity to communicate. People who share similar occupations and who can talk to one another are more likely to discover or develop mutual interests and sentiments and to become attached to one another in some informal structure.

FIGURE 6–2

Emergence of Informal Organization

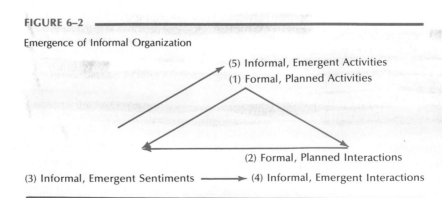

What Groups Offer Individuals

Humans join groups most fundamentally for companionship, to satisfy the affiliation need discussed in Chapter 3. Most people crave the giving and receiving of recognition and the exchange of sentiments that compose community spirit. To gain this feeling, they must simplify their worlds because they cannot be close to everyone they encounter. It is impossible to communicate with all of them, and no one could maintain so many simultaneous relationships. Although family and friends are the major sources of group satisfactions, we do not leave this social desire at home when we go to work.

People who have no opportunity for social contact at work tend to find their work unsatisfying. This dissatisfaction may lead to low productivity, high turnover, and absenteeism. In a textile plant, employees who worked in isolated jobs were highly dissatisfied and consistently failed to meet production standards.[5] When the company permitted these workers to take rest periods as a group, production and satisfaction increased. The opportunity to interact (and joke) with others doing similar work can make any job more pleasant.[6]

Groups Offer Individuals
- affiliation
- identification
- emotional support
- assistance
- protection

Identification and Emotional Support

Emotional support from a group is especially valued when people are under stress. Veteran soldiers warn young recruits about their tendency to crowd together for support when under attack—even though the new soldiers know this increases rather than decreases the danger for them. Yet, the group may inspire the frightened individual to courageous action. Joe Marm, a second lieutenant on duty in South Vietnam, grabbed two side arms and a pile of grenades, ran up a hill alone, and destroyed a machine-gun nest, killing eight Vietcong. Recommended for the Congressional Medal of Honor, Marm said he had made the attack for this reason: "What would the fellows have thought of me if I had been afraid to do it?"[7] Similarly, studies of soldiers in World War II indicate that men who were closely tied to cohesive groups were more responsible in carrying out their duties, more confident of being able to perform well as soliders, less fearful in battle, and less likely to capitulate or surrender under stress.[8] These studies also indicated that a soldier's willingness to show bravery and make sacrifices was correlated not with loyalty to country or understanding of the war issues, but with loyalty to the immediate group. In other words, men who performed heroic acts were motivated largely by the desire not to let their buddies down.

Life in the business organization is not so dangerous, but group support can be just as necessary to the individual—especially to the low-skilled worker who, as one person, is relatively unimportant to management. Informal work groups at low levels serve as a vehicle for expressing independence from management and help bind blue-collar workers to the formal organization. These informal groups can produce continuity between the workers' outside life and their participation in a job to which they may have very limited allegiance.[9]

Most people find it very difficult to exist in situations that exclude social support. In both the Korean and Vietnam conflicts, American prisoners of war tended to talk to their captors more than the official policy specified: name, rank, and serial number.[10] After prolonged solitary confinement and existence on skimpy rations slipped under a door, many prisoners experienced an overwhelming compulsion to talk when taken to an interrogator, even though they knew him to be the enemy. This behavior does not mean that compromise and collaboration are inevitable just because humans crave affection; the process is more subtle. The prisoner of war, for example, is no longer sure what is right and what is wrong. Isolated from human companionship and communication, the prisoner loses touch with the essential support for ethical behavior which is social corroboration of individual conscience.

Even the development of individual conscience is heavily influenced by social contact, because self-identification is greatly affected by others. This is clear with some teenagers who try to be everything their friends say they should be. Wornout clothing and Neanderthal hair styles at one period or preppie outfits and short haircuts at another may reflect the young person's efforts to define self in terms of companions. Thus self-image derives from social image.[11]

The definition of self through others can take on bizarre forms. "Absolute abstinence from sexual activity," the prime requisite for joining the Esoteric Fraternity of California, hardly suggests that such a group would be successful, but this informal organization has existed continuously for almost 100 years, during which it has published books and pamphlets that remain in demand.[12] Of course, it never included more than a dozen members and now numbers only two brothers, both over 90. Yet it survived because for those few who joined, it provided acceptance, support, and the certainty that the kingdom of God would be established on earth "when man gives up the sex act." The Communist Party has managed to enroll more members than the Esoteric Fraternity with a similar appeal to some: The rule of Marx will be established when people give up their pursuit of private property and gain. A party member might derive strength and identity from his or her supposed part in the vanguard of the Revolution of the Proletariat and as an agent of historical destiny.

Assistance in Meeting Objectives

The group can assist in solving very specific problems and protect the individual from mistakes. A new salesclerk may not be sure how to handle a complicated problem of returned merchandise. A lab technician may be hesitant about asking a supervisor to repeat instructions, yet be afraid of ruining the experiment without additional information. In each case the employee turns to fellow workers for assistance because most prefer this source of help. Inexperienced people consistently prefer getting assistance from fellow employees rather than their managers. Indeed, this ability to provide assistance is a source of substantial prestige for the giver.[13]

In a wartime prison camp, a strong group can assist the individual prisoner to define the basis of ethical behavior. In the shop and office, likewise, the group can help the individual to define desirable and undesirable behavior. How much time should be taken for a coffee break? Is it all right to talk to fellow employees while the boss is in the room? Must all copy be shown to the advertising manager? Even when there are established rules, a question remains: Is everyone expected to live by the letter of the law? Most employees do not want to violate the generally accepted rules of the game; at the same time, they do not want to conform to restrictive rules that everyone else ignores. They want to know the "right thing" to do. The group fills an important function by providing its members with a kind of guide to correct behavior—correctness not in terms of written polices, but in terms of what is actually acceptable. In your summer work experience, the group may have taught you how to operate the punch press more easily by taping the safety buttons, how to schedule your work, and how to leave work early. In return, you might have fetched coffee and cokes.

Protection

Secure middle-class people tend to forget that a fundamental function of the family is to protect its members from a hostile world. In the urban ghetto, the family's difficulty in accomplishing its mission sometimes leads to family deterioration and the joining of street gangs by the children. The gang is a source of companionship, identification, and social support, of course; but more basically it may be necessary for survival. Thus jackets with words like "The Cool Men" function like "Cherry Hill High School Cougars" but even more so. "The Cool Men" are warning others to leave their brothers alone.

Co-workers in the punching department may perform a similar function. They protect each other from being caught and punished by management for their illicit activities, such as bypassing the safety buttons and covering up for each other. Behavior among government officials and business managers is not dissimilar. Members of a clearly identified group will attempt to protect themselves from the probes

"The motion has been made and seconded that we obey the law."

From *The Wall Street Journal,* with permission of Cartoon Features Syndicate.

of newspaper reporters, investigators, or consumers, even when they sincerely believe they are doing nothing wrong. Some groups who become very loyal and trusting toward one another also become suspicious of all outsiders. Groups define boundaries, which can become defensive barriers.

The Structure of Groups and Informal Organization

Most people desire affiliation and group membership. Yet once they have established mutual relationships, many people also want to be better than their companions. With affiliation, social differentiation and status systems emerge.

Informal Status Systems

Even within small informal groups, subtle status differences can be seen. The type of membership and status that a person enjoys within a work group depends upon factors the person brings to the organization as well as factors derived from the job.[14]

Status Derived from Nonjob Factors. Many young people who decry status seeking by their parents may be responding less to their parents' behavior than to their own world. Concern about status and elaborate informal status structures characterize most school life. In response to the question of what ensured status in their school, two 12-year-olds responded as follows:

A girl: Being cool, wearing the right clothes, and being able to cut up your friends without hurting their feelings too much.

A boy: Being tough so you can push guys around, sticking together, and being good in sports.

Nonjob Sources of Informal Status
- personal characteristics
- skill
- age
- sex
- ethnicity; race
- education

Personal attributes and behavior are sources of status in informal organizations, as being good in sports was a status symbol in high school. Among student groups, higher status tends to be associated with physical size, appearance and dress, self-confidence and self-assurance, sociability, and intelligence.[15] The importance of these factors in determining status changes from place to place, however. The middle-class culture of the 12-year-old female in the example above seems to value verbal cleverness highly. Such might not be the case with girls from different socioeconomic backgrounds that put a high value on homemaking skills. Similarly, with the boys, other groups might value antiauthority bravado highly. The point is that almost *any* physical attribute or behavior may be admired and thus be a source of informal status.

Similarly, what employees bring to the workplace influences their status on the job. This quality pertains to who and what a person is, not what he or she does. Among the nonjob qualities that confer status are education, age, sex, and ethnic background.[16] In general, higher status is attributed to older males with more education and the "right" ethnicity (which can vary from location to location depending on whether the majority more highly values Irish-Americans, Polish-Americans, blacks, white Anglo-Saxon Protestants, or whatever).[17]

Status Derived from On-the-Job Factors.   The job also influences the status system. In fact, when management creates an organization, it consciously creates a status system, based primarily on pay and authority. Titles, job descriptions, evaluation programs, pay systems, and work measurement practices all influence the informal social structure.

Job Title.   Obviously a superintendent is more important than a general supervisor, and a general supervisor outranks a supervisor. Engineers outrank technicians; secretaries are above stenographers. In almost every organization, job titles are subtly graded according to levels of status, and the status of each individual depends in part on the job he or she holds.

Pay.   Pay is one of the most important determinants of status. Higher pay means higher status, and even a difference of a few cents per hour can have a significant effect on a job's status. How one is paid also helps to determine status. Being salaried on a monthly payroll may be less convenient, but it carries more prestige than a weekly or daily wage.

Work Schedules.   The freedom to choose one's hours, or being excused from punching the time clock, is a mark of distinction. Working a day schedule is usually thought of as a higher status job than shift work.

Mobility.   Generally, a job that allows a person to move around freely interacting and communicating with many different people is assigned higher prestige than one that allows no autonomy or discretion over movements. This mobility is also related to autonomy or freedom from close management supervision, a status factor generally yielding higher prestige in the informal social structure.

Symbols of Office.   There is a vast range of physical factors that are desirable in themselves but that also serve as symbols for higher status. These include such things as: In which company lunchrooms can you eat? Can you leave the building for morning coffee? Do you have a reserved parking space? What kind of clothing do you wear in the office? What kind of office do you have—furniture, telephone, carpeting, and so on?

Seniority.   The number of years on the job is often related to age but is even more important in most work groups. Greater seniority is a source of status up to the point when old age undermines the individual's position.

In short, people on the job structure themselves in various relationships that integrate on-job and off-job status factors. An informal social structure will be created; employees will admire certain people and consider certain jobs attractive; they might even plan their careers around movement through these positions. The highest status positions will tend to be occupied by people high in both external and internal status factors. This informal status system may approximate the formal structure of the company, but it will probably deviate in a number of ways, as we shall illustrate later.

On-Job Sources of Informal Status
- title; position
- pay
- work schedule
- mobility
- symbols
- seniority

Group Member Roles and Behavior

Every group member is partially responsible for contributing to effective group process. Two broad sets of activities are essential to maintain an effective group—task and maintenance activities.[18] Task roles and activities are related to the accom-

FIGURE 6–3

Sample Group Task and Maintenance Activities

Task Activities	Maintenance Activities
Initiating	Encouraging
Giving information	Harmonizing
Seeking information	Expediting
Elaborating	Setting standards
Coordinating	Observing process
Summarizing	Providing feedback

plishment of the group objectives. Maintenance roles and activities focus on maintaining the health and well-being of the group as an ongoing social system.

Although a formal leader, chairperson, or supervisor assumes these roles and often performs the appropriate activities, the effectiveness of a group depends upon members' willingness to contribute to these activities. Task and maintenance activities are skills. Each member should work to develop these skills and thereby assist the group in performing these functions.

Group Leadership

The group leader is usually the person who combines the most status factors from off and on the job: the "right" sex, age, seniority, skill, physical attributes, ethnic background, and enough mobility to maintain his or her leadership position. In one manufacturing department, Sid is the informal leader because he has been there 10 years, is an excellent operator (one of the sources of his status is that Sid can produce what management expects in only five hours—leaving two hours in which to goof off ostentatiously), and is the best bowler in the department.

The super person who can fulfill both task and maintenance roles is rare, so two or more people are often involved. First there is the task leader who pushes the group to fulfill its mission—to win the game, prepare for the rumble with a contending gang, or stand up against management's pressure for more output. At times the task leader pushes the informal group in much the same way a formal manager does, but in so doing the leader may threaten the group's closeness so that social ties are loosened.

To maintain these social ties and keep the group viable is a mission of social leadership. The social leader is frequently the "best liked" person in the group, the one who smooths relationships, relaxes tension by cracking a joke, counsels the disappointed, and strengthens the groups social-emotional ties. In some families Father is the task leader, always setting high standards and pushing. In contrast, Mother may be the social facilitator, emitting love, understanding, and acceptance. Many families split parental roles like this, but reverse roles for mother and father are common. In Bill's boyhood gang, he was the task leader, but the social leader was "Crazy Frank," who would pull stunts like loosening his belt so that his pants fell down when he carried the ball. Frank knew a thousand corny jokes and exhibited a warm interest in and enjoyment of people, who liked him in return. In the manufacturing department, one of the oldest employees seemed to be the social leader. He brought the cards for the luncheon poker game and usually set up the bowling dates.

Group Cohesion

The success of informal groups in all their objectives depends to an important extent upon the internal strength or cohesion of the group. Part of the difficulty in the prisoner of war camps was inadequate group cohesion. When stable values and standards of behavior do not develop, group members cannot work together in mutual dependency. Cohesion is both cause and consequence: It aids the pursuit of group objectives, and at the same time it can be strengthened by the sharing of concentrated effort. The sources of cohesion are many and varied, as the following summary suggests:[19]

Homogeneity.   One of the most cohesive work groups we ever observed was composed entirely of an ethnic or national group called the West of Englanders. All of the six to seven people in the group had come from the Land's End section of England many years before, and they maintained their sense of identification—perhaps because they were very much an ethnic minority among Italians and Poles. The ethnic tie was so strong that this group was one of the few to contain both male and female members (this combination usually weakens cohesion). These production workers held stable values and assistance expectations; they controlled production (at a fairly high level) and were remarkably successful in getting management to respond to them.

Groups whose members have different interests and backgrounds are often less effective in promoting their interests. When, for example, people with sharp differences in rates of pay and job duties work near each other, the resulting group is seldom cohesive. The group may often be characterized by conflicting cliques that hinder common action.

Even when group members do similar work, competition will often hinder cohesion—unless the group can agree to regulate the competition. At a large automobile dealer, the bottom three sellers among 25 salespersons are fired every month, regardless of their sales. Under these circumstances, the salespersons do not develop a cohesive group. Where expulsion depends upon absolute rather than relative performance, however, a basically homogeneous group with good cohesion will assist the poor performer in improving output.

Stability.   Stable membership contributes to higher cohesion. With time the members come to know each other, learn the values and expectations of the group, and learn how to behave. This was one of the problems in the prisoner of war camps; where the barracks groups were systematically broken up, no cohesive groups could develop.

Communication.   To be a group, people must be able to talk with one another. Only in this way can their similarities and common interests be developed, their

Sources of Group Cohesion
- homogeneity
- shared goals
- stable membership
- communication
- isolation
- small size
- outside pressure
- high status

values and standards established, and joint action initiated. Groups in which the members can communicate easily with one another are more likely to be cohesive. Internal group unity can be thwarted in such areas as noisy steel mills, long assembly lines, or even quiet offices where "gossiping" is frowned upon and there is no privacy for conversation.[20]

Isolation. Physical isolation from other groups tends to build cohesiveness. Contrast the school spirit of a college isolated in the country with the nonchalance that characterizes students in large urban universities. Miners have demonstrated, in countless lengthy strikes, that workers isolated from the rest of the community will stick together more stubbornly than those who are socially integrated with it.

Even simple physical boundaries on a group may be essential for cohesion. If a group cannot identify its members and clearly differentiate itself, cohesion will be low. In long assembly lines, it is difficult to distinguish logical groups. A large insurance company has a one-story office building that resembles nothing so much as an airplane hanger. Several hundred clerical and supervisory personnel work together in one large area with no physical boundaries between people. In such circumstances it is difficult for cohesive groups to emerge.

Small Size. This insurance office also illustrates that too many people hinder the development of cohesive groups. Larger groups hinder communication, reduce homogeneity, and encourage breaking up into small cliques.[21] Small departments, therefore, tend to knit more closely than large ones do. Loyalty, as in the military, is a product of frequent face-to-face contacts; it is easier to have close relationships with all members of a small group than a large one.

Outside Pressure. Because members of groups tend to herd together under stress, continuous outside pressure from management may produce high cohesion. Under organizational stress, lateral and peer communications tend to increase, while vertical communications decrease. Personal differences are minimized when threatened by a common danger—or a tough supervisor. And this closeness may remain after the threat is relieved. Perhaps the most closely knit army veterans of World War II are those of the 11th Armored Division, which was so badly mauled by the Germans in the Battle of the Bulge. They still publish a newsletter, meet frequently, hold annual conventions, and maintain high camaraderie in spite of great differences among the members in economic and social achievement since the war.

A tough management policy toward personnel may well encourage the formation of strong informal groups as a protective and retaliatory device. On the other hand, a more sophisticated and manipulative manager who systematically promotes internal competition, transfers people, and prevents communication will hinder the development of group cohesion.

Status of the Group. People often prefer to identify with high-status groups and are more likely to feel loyalty toward a high-status group than a low-status one. The factors conferring status upon a group as a whole are very much the same as those giving status to the individual within the informal organization. They include special skills, monopoly control over certain functions, responsibility and autonomy, opportunities for promotion out of the area, preferred physical location and working conditions, and influence in organization affairs.

Although it is true that high-status groups tend to have higher cohesion, it is not clear whether status per se is the cause of high cohesion or that the factors conferring status (such as seniority, ease in communication, autonomy, and freedom from close supervision) simply allow cohesion to develop.

Attitude and Behavior Expectations

At several universities, undergraduate students voted against adoption of academic honor systems that would have abolished faculty proctoring of examinations. Considering the widespread and well-publicized activities in support of greater student participation in university administration, these rejections seem contradictory. The explanation lies with the proposals voted upon. They placed individual responsibility on the student not to cheat, but also required the student to take some action if he or she observed someone else cheating. At one northeastern university the required action was a report either to a faculty committee or to a student group. The students rejected this proposal because it conflicted with an underlying student norm—one should not "fink" on classmates. Indeed, in Air Force Academy cheating scandals, the parents of several cadets suspended for not reporting code infractions were vociferous in support of this norm as applying to American society as a whole: One should not be punished for not reporting a crime if one didn't commit it.[22]

After the first defeat at the university referred to above, the honor system was amended to make the report to the faculty optional, but students were required to tell cheaters they had been observed. Students did not have to take further action, although they did have that option. Again, the proposal was defeated. The undergraduates were apparently unwilling to approve any system that required them to exercise any control over their peers. The idea contradicted the student conception of proper behavior.

Informal groups thus develop attitudinal norms and standards of behavior.[23] That is, people who interact frequently in groups tend to think and act alike; continuous association leads to shared values and norms.[24] These expectations grow out of needs to maintain the group, remove sources of stress, and promote cooperation.

The following characteristics of group norms in work settings serve as a guide for understanding their importance in group dynamics.[25]

1. Norms are structural characteristics of groups that summarize and simplify group influence processes. They highlight those processes within the group that are intended to regulate and regularize group member behavior.
2. Norms apply only to behavior—not to private thoughts and feelings. In other words, member behaviors, not attitudes and beliefs, are the focus of consideration.
3. Norms are developed only for behaviors that are viewed as important by most group members.
4. Norms usually develop gradually, but the process can be shortened if members

so desire. Norms develop as members learn what behaviors are in fact important for the group to control.

5. Not all norms apply to everyone. Some norms, for example, do not apply to high-status members who have more freedom to deviate.

Of special importance are group attitudes toward assistance and work effort. One of the reasons for the development of informal groups is mutual assistance, and most groups value and expect cooperation and helpfulness among regular members of the group—hints on how to machine parts, assistance on difficult jobs, warning against management inspection, assistance in camouflaging mistakes, and a whole host of informal practices. In order to maintain standing in a group and receive its benefits, this aid must be given.

If the basic attitude of the group toward the company is positive, informal expectations can greatly assist management. If the group is fundamentally interested in getting the job done, the workers will fill the gaps and work out the ambiguities in management assignments. They will be willing to shift with the varying demands of the job in order to assist hard-pressed colleagues without specific management direction. Even under the best conditions, however, a strong informal organization opposes some of management's desires. And when the basic attitudes toward management are adverse, the group's behavioral expectations can be directed against management's desires in a variety of ingenious ways that managers and workers develop to compensate for perceived inadequacies in the formal system of rewards. As we saw in Chapter 5 on work's extrinsic rewards, many groups restrict effort and output in order to protect long-term interests.

How Some Students Behave in Groups

Groups tend to behave in fairly consistent and predictable ways. To illustrate, we shall consider some student groups first, then some characteristic worker groups. Data collected on the perceptions and behavior of many management students have made certain patterns evident.[26] When students are assigned to groups to prepare team reports on cases, the behavioral expectations that emerge are as follows:

All group members are expected to be at meetings on time, to have read the case before the meeting, and to work equally hard.

Time is at premium. Group members are expected to work hard for a certain length of time, but no more. For most groups, the highest grade that can be earned in the allotted time is desired, but few groups will expend more time just to obtain a higher grade.

In general, the actual write-up of the reports is rotated among all the group members so that each person carries this most onerous burden.

Many of these student groups contain one minority group member who differs from the majority in sex, race, or nationality. Most group members in management classes are white American males; the minority group members include American females, black American males, and English, French, Japanese, and other nationality males.

It has been observed that in general:

The group leader will be from the majority.

American females tend not to strive for group leadership when in the minority, to be rejected when they do so, and to adhere scrupulously to group norms—such as punctuality, preparation, and willingness to type the final draft.

Black American and French males tend to reject and be rejected by the majority white Americans because they do not adhere to the group norms. Some just withdraw from the group entirely if their attempts to lead are rebuffed.

English males tend to strive for group leadership, indeed to replace the group by performing the work themselves—for example, suggesting that they will completely analyze the case and write the report alone if the others will simply accept the grade. The English male is sometimes successful in so dominating the group because he saves the majority Americans' time and effort and is perceived as being exceptionally competent in the English language.

Japanese males tend to be frustrated by their experience with the majority because they perceive the Americans as not caring very much, as setting low standards and not trying. In turn, the Americans tend to perceive the Japanese as not having much to contribute (perhaps because of language problems). In some sad instances, the Americans even cut the Japanese out of the group by not informing them of the meetings, perhaps because the Japanese would threaten their objective of writing a report as quickly as possible.

These findings on minority member behavior in groups are only tentative and suggestive. The point is that different kinds of people respond differently to working in groups, and most individuals find it difficult to be minority members.

"It's not just that I think war is too important to be left to generals. I think it's too important to be left to men."

From *The Wall Street Journal,* with permission of Cartoon Features Syndicate.

Characteristic Work Groups

Based on acceptance of and cooperation with management decisions or the frequency and nature of the challenge issued by the group to management, there are four kinds of groups: (1) apathetic, (2) erratic, (3) strategic, and (4) conservative.[27]

Apathetic groups are least likely to exert concerted pressure on management. They manifest low cohesiveness and widely distributed leadership. They are frequently composed of low-skilled workers, such as migrant laborers on farms, who are easily replaced. They cannot afford to offend management in any way.

Erratic groups behave inconsistently toward management. There seems to be no relation between the seriousness of their grievances and the intensity of their protest. The activities they indulge in are not contrived to solve their problems but seem to be emotional reactions to frustration. These groups tend to seek individual, autocratic leaders who are likely to be active in the organizing phase of union growth but are shunted aside when more reasonable and stable union-management relations are required. They frequently are interdependent, semiskilled workers such as on an assembly line, where a complaint is likely to affect everyone.

Strategic groups are shrewdly calculating pressure groups that continually object to unfavorable management decisions and seek loopholes in existing policies and contract clauses that would be to their benefit. They demand constant attention to their problems and can reinforce their demands by group action. Groups so classified are highly cohesive. The leadership consists of a small core of highly active and influential group members, each of whom specializes in such functions as dealing with management, dealing with union, maintaining internal unity, or taking the lead in voicing dissatisfaction.

Conservative groups are a secure, powerful elite, relatively independent of union activities. Their jobs usually involve critical skills. They are self-consciously assured, successful, and usually stable in their external relations with management as well as in their internal affairs. Skilled machinists and craftsers, such as pattern makers, are often conservative.

This typology of group behavior need not be restricted to blue-collar workers; it can be extended to office employees and even professionals. For example, urban school teachers can be described by the following model. Grammar school teachers groups are generally apathetic and have engaged in little active union organizing or agitation. In the past, many were women with lesser stakes in the job, perhaps seeing it merely as supplementary income or as a vehicle for expressing their desires to contribute to society. In either case, concrete steps to improve socioeconomic conditions are not seen as desirable. Nor, in fact, do these teachers probably have the power and cohesion to undertake such action successfully.

The junior high school teachers are an erratic group. This is the most difficult teaching level in urban systems. Many of the delinquency problems such as truancy, lack of control, and violence occur among these pupils. By senior high school, many of the most difficult pupils have left or have been expelled. Some junior high school teachers have been the organizing force in the development of independent labor unions to improve the lot of teachers (and perhaps the quality of education). Many, however, are just caretakers, and rather apathetic about the whole situation.

The high school teachers are a strategic group—especially in the competitive-admission high schools. Their power has given them certain privileges in pay and working conditions, so they have not been very active in the union movement, preferring to favor the professional association.

Group Discipline and Member Conformity

Whether or not the members of the group act upon their common values and expectations depends upon the individual's desire to be a member of the group and the group's ability to enforce its desires.[28] The more eager an individual is to be a member, the more one will conform to the group's norms of behavior, and the easier it will be to enforce group rules.[29]

" 'Oops!' has no place in the vocabulary of a surgeon."
From *The Wall Street Journal,* with permission of Cartoon Features Syndicate.

Among informal social groups, popularity is associated with respect for the group's norms. Deviates are rejected; conformers are popular.[30] The more closely individuals conform to the accepted norms of the group, the better liked they will be; the better liked they are, the closer they will conform; the less they conform, the more disliked they will be. People like to be liked, so they tend to engage in actions that will maintain or increase the esteem received from those around them. This means that there is always a tendency to go along with the group—a tendency that will be ultimately realized unless there are strong countervailing influences.

In Groups . . .
• regulars conform to norms and are accepted but leaders may have more freedom
• isolates don't conform to norms and are rejected but they may conform to other reference groups

Withdrawal of the group's contribution to the individual is the primary method of enforcement. The group strongly influences the behavior of its members by providing them with support, reinforcement, security, encouragement, and protection for their "proper" behavior, and by punishing them for deviations through the use of ridicule, hostility, and threat of expulsion. When an individual is genuinely attached to a group and is in close and continuous contact with it, his or her behavior and beliefs are extremely resistant to change. In such circumstances, the group can exercise firm control over the individual.

If an independent soul refuses to abide by group values and standards, initial group reaction may simply be gentle ribbing or good-natured sarcasm. If these fail to alter the individual's behavior, more serious reasoning and persuasion follow, sometimes escalating to heated argument. Simultaneously some of the social benefits derived from group membership, such as assistance and socializing, may be reduced. The member's status in the group is thereby reduced. If the member still does not conform, overt coercion or complete ostracism may be used, depending upon the importance of the issue and the moral standards of the group. Nonetheless, if errant individuals do not drive satisfaction or benefits from the group, if they have alternative sources of satisfaction, or if they just don't give a damn, the group's ability to enforce its norms and standards will be weakened.[31]

Regulars and Conformity

Different individuals have differing relationships with the informal organization and its norms and standards. Regulars are those who conform most closely to all informal group expectations, perhaps because they need the group more and obtain more satisfactions from it. A majority of people may be regulars in fairly cohesive work groups. In one study of production workers, 60 percent were classified as regulars on the basis of their behavior; they restricted production to the informal norm.[32] Most of the regulars were from the dominant ethnic background, were sons of working-class, labor union fathers, had grown up in the city, were Catholic, voted Democratic, lived in similar neighborhoods, and were socially active and friendly off the job.

Informal group leaders are usually high-status regulars. As group members, they generally must conform to norms. Indeed, compliance to the group norms is necessary to the achievement of high status. Sid can't leave his punch press early every day and expect the group to cover for him, even though his fellow workers look up to him. The group norm is that each individual can leave early and have someone punch his time card only once a month. Nonetheless, by virtue of his informal leadership, Sid has accumulated credits which allow him to deviate from the group's expectations a little more than others can before sanctions are applied.[33] He might well be able to leave early twice a month. And more important, by virtue of these credits and his status, the informal leader may be able to induce the group to amend its norms. Sid might be able, for example, to gain the group's agreement to increase its output if management convinced him that the department's survival depended on improved productivity.

Isolates and Reference Groups

Isolates hold themselves aloof from the work group. The term *isolate* suggests that such uncommon people are entirely independent, detached from the group's attractions, and free to pursue their own personal interests. In fact, the isolate may not be free at all but rather marching to a different drummer, some specific or indefinite group with which he or she identifies. From this reference group the isolate derives values and behavioral norms that she or he may attempt to follow.[34] Somehow, following these perceived norms (however distorted the perception) and living up to the values of others perceived as one's betters is satisfying. The study of production workers referred to above showed that the 10 percent who were considered "rate-busting" isolates averaged over 150 percent of the group production norm. They tended to consider themselves middle class, to vote Republican, to live in different neighborhoods, and to be from rural backgrounds, Similarly, a study of retail salespersons indicated that the highest performers identified with wealthier groups, even to purchasing more expensive homes than they could afford.[35]

The distant reference group unknowingly influences the would-be member much as the group regular conforms to the expectations of immediate associates. Of course there is a difference. The regular gets frequent feedback from the group that they accept and reward said regular for conformity. The problem for the isolate who identifies with a distant reference group *is* distance. The reference group may not be physically close enough to reward the individual with friendship and support; in fact, the group may not even know of the isolate's existence. Continued identification under these conditions requires an enormous amount of fortitude and persistence.

Society is ambivalent about isolates who demonstrate courage in stubbornly refusing to give in to immediate associates who tend to condemn such a worker as untrustworthy, a scab, a fink, or worse. Yet when we can identify with the reference groups of such people, we laud them as heroes or saints. Probably on no other area are people more inconsistent. We admire the truly religious people who reject the materialism and irrelevancy of contemporary society, but most of us do not want them around because they make us uncomfortable.

Deviants

Many informal organizations contain a small third category of people: the deviants. Deviants usually include a mixture of people on the fringes of the group, for a variety of reasons. They include people who cannot reach the group's minimum performance goals because of inexperience, lack of skill, and physical handicaps of age or injury. The regulars accept the low performance because they understand it is not a threat to the group; management will not be on their necks because of the deviants' low productivity.

Deviants also include persons who have earned low status by their on- and off-job attributes. Temporary, young employees, such as students, or people with the "wrong" ethnic or racial characteristics may be on the group's fringe. Such an individual will be included in the regular's horseplay and may even partake of some of the group's aid and benefits. A younger brother who idolizes his older sibling is in this category. Because of his dogged willingness to stand the jokes and taunts of the gang and his eagerness to run errands, he is allowed to hang out with the group.

SUMMARY

The rich fabric of emergent relationships in informal organization and small groups has been considered. Groups in organizations develop over time. This development entails movement through three stages: forming, structuring, and performing. The mature, fully functioning group shows quite different behavior patterns than the newly formed group. Several different tasks and activities are of importance within each stage.

Groups offer some individuals substantial benefits: social satisfaction, identification, emotional support, assistance in meeting objectives, and protection. Informal structure emerges from the formal organization as activities, interactions, and sentiments are elaborated into a status system. An individual's status in the informal system depends on the personal attributes brought to the job and the on-job factors, such as pay, title, seniority, skill, and working conditions he or she faces.

The responsibilities of members in a group include the performance of task and maintenance roles. Task activities relate to the accomplishment of group objectives. Maintenance roles focus on the functioning of the group as a group.

Leaders of informal organizations are high-status group members who fulfill dual leadership roles of fostering group tasks and maintaining social relations.

The success of this informal leadership in conjunction with group characteristics like homogeneity, isolation, and response to outside pressure determines the degree of group strength or cohesion that will exist.

Emergent groups develop expectations about proper attitudes and behavior to which members are expected to conform. Of special importance to management are restrictions on effort and output that groups impose on members.

We have examined how some student groups behave, particularly their expectations about equal effort and minimizing time demands. When student group members are also minority group members, certain student categories may tend to behave in certain ways: to slavishly conform, to not conform, to withdraw, to dominate the group.

Work groups tend to fall into limited behavioral categories: apathetic groups dominated by management; erratic groups, whose behavior is difficult to predict and causes management problems; strategic groups, which are always fighting management for better conditions; and conservative groups, which enjoy high status and favorable positions because of their importance to management.

Nonconformance to group norms results in group sanctions to force the recalcitrant member into line.

Regulars tend to conform, isolates do not. Hence the latter are rejected and isolated and cannot participate in the advantages of informal life. Some nonconformists are actually conforming to the dictates of distant reference groups. Others always reject all group pressures and hence are actually not free of the group. Finally, independents make their own decisions about behavior, sometimes conforming, sometimes not.

REVIEW QUESTIONS

1. What stages of development do groups move through?

2. What are the major issues within each developmental stage?

3. What form of organization emerges from management's formal pattern of planned activities and interactions?

4. What do groups offer individuals?

5. Why are groups especially helpful to an individual under stress?

6. How can groups help in self-identification and self-control?

7. How can groups help an individual to achieve his or her objectives?

8. How can a work group provide its members with some independence from management?

9. What is the informal status system?

10. What nonjob factors influence a person's informal status?

11. What on-the-job factors influence a person's informal status?

12. What are task roles and activities in groups?

13. What are maintenance roles and activities in groups?

14. Who are the leaders in informal organizations?

15. What is the difference between a "task leader" and a "social leader" in the informal organization?

16. What is group cohesion?

13. What factors strengthen group cohesion?

18. What factors weaken group cohesion?

19. What kinds of attitudinal and behavioral expectations do groups develop?

20. What seem to be common expectations in student task teams?

21. How do student teams tend to treat minority group members?

22. What are the various kinds of characteristic work groups?

23. What is an apathetic work group? Why?

24. What is an erratic work group? Why?

25. What is a strategic work group? Why?

26. What is a conservative work group? Why?

27. What factors influence whether or not an individual will conform to the group's expectations?

28. How does a group enforce its expectations against nonconformers?

29. What is the difference between nonconformity and independence?

30. What does *counterdependent* mean?

31. Why do independents sometimes conform?

32. What is the difference between group regulars and isolates?

33. Who tend to be the group leaders?

34. What is the relation of a group leader to the group's norms?

35. What are reference groups?

36. Why is society ambivalent about isolates and nonconformers?

37. What are group deviants?

Notes and References on Group Development and Structure

1. B. G. Myerhoff, "The Revolution as a Trip: Symbol and Paradox," *Annals* 395 (1971), pp. 105–16. Bernard Berelson and G. A. Steiner wrote, "What is distinctly human comes from the primary fact that man lives his life in groups with other people." *Human Behavior: An Inventory of Scientific Findings* (New York: Harcourt Brace Jovanovich, 1964), p. 325.

2. Different schemes describing the stages of group development include the following: B. W. Tuckman, "Developmental Sequence in Small Groups," *Psychological Bulletin* 64 (1965), pp. 384–99; J. S. Heinen and E. Jacobson, "A Model of Task Group Development in Complex Organizations and a Process of Supplementation," *Academy of Management Review* 1 (1976), pp. 98–111; B. Bass, *Organizational Psychology* (Boston: Allyn & Bacon, 1965).

3. George C. Homans, *The Human Group* (New York: Harcourt Brace Jovanovich, 1950); W. F. Whyte, "An Interaction Approach to the Theory of Organization," in Mason Haire, ed., *Modern Organization Theory* (New York: John Wiley & Sons, 1959), pp. 155–83; G. H. Graham, "Interpersonal Attraction as a Basis of Informal Organization," *Academy of Management Journal* 14, no. 4 (1971), pp. 483–95; R. T. Keller, "A Look at the Sociotechnical System," *California Management Review* 15, no. 1 (1972), pp. 86–91.

4. Leonard R. Sayles and George Strauss described this development as follows:

> Employees form friendship groups based on their contact and common interest—and these groups arise out of the life of the organization. Once these groups have been established, however, they develop a life of their own that is almost completely separate from the work process from which it arose. This is a dynamic, self-generating process. Brought together by the formal organization, employees interact with one another. Increasing interaction builds favorable sentiments toward fellow group members. In turn, these sentiments become the foundation for an increased variety of activities, many not specified by the job description: special lunch arrangements, trading of job duties, fights with those outside the group, gambling on paycheck numbers. And these increased opportunities for interaction build stronger bonds of identification. Then the group becomes something more than a mere collection of people. It develops a customary way of doing things—a set of stable characteristics that are hard to change. It becomes an organization in itself.

Human Behavior in Organizations (Englewood Cliffs, N.J.: Prentice-Hall, 1966), p. 89. For nonmanagers, especially, the group may be more important to the individual than the organization is. T. Rotondi, Jr., "Organizational Identification and Group Involvement," *Academy of Management Journal,* (December 1975, pp. 892–96.

5. Elton Mayo, *The Human Problems of an Industrial Civilization* (Boston: Graduate School of Business Administration, Harvard University, 1946).

6. T. Burling, E. Lentz, and R. Wilson, *The Give and Take in Hospitals* (New York: G. P. Putnam's Sons, 1956); D. Roy, "Banana Time: Job Satisfaction and Informal Interaction," *Human Organization* 18 (1960), pp. 158–68.

7. Quoted in *The New York Times,* November 17, 1966.

8. E. A. Shils, "Primary Groups in the American Army," in Robert K. Merton and Paul F. Lazarsfeld, eds.,

Continuities in Social Research: Studies in the Scope and Method of the American Soldier (New York: Free Press, 1950), pp. 16–39.

9. F. E. Katz, "Explaining Informal Groups in Complex Organizations," *Administrative Science Quarterly* 10, no. 2 (1965), pp. 204–21. Informal satisfactions, however, cannot completely replace or make up for inadequate formal rewards. See W. E. Reif, R. M. Monczka, and J. W. Newstrom, "Perceptions of Formal and the Informal Organizations," *Academy of Management Journal* 16, no. 3 (1973), pp. 389–403.

10. On Korean prisoners of war, see W. F. Dean, *General Dean's Story* (New York: Viking Press, 1954); E. Schein, "The Chinese Indoctrination Program for Prisoners of War," *Psychiatry* 19 (1956), pp. 149–72; and E. Kinkead. *In Every War but One* (New York: W. W. Norton, 1959).

11. M. Rosenberg, *Society and the Adolescent Self-Image* (Princeton, N.J.: Princeton University Press, 1965).

12. C. Hillinger, "The Last of the Esoteric Fraternity," *International Herald Tribune,* April 27, 1971.

13. Peter M. Blau, "Patterns of Interaction among a Group of Officials in a Government Agency," *Human Relations* 7 (1954), pp. 337–48; and Blau, *The Dynamics of Bureaucracy* (Chicago: University of Chicago Press, 1955).

14. A survey of status systems is found in A. Mazur, "A Cross-Species Comparison of Status in Small Established Groups," *American Sociological Review* 38, no. 5 (1973), pp. 513–30.

15. Ralph M. Stogdill, "Personal Factors Associated with Leadership: A Survey of the Literature," *Journal of Psychology* 25 (1948), pp. 35–71; G. Maclay and H. Knipe, *The Dominant Man: The Pecking Order in Human Society* (New York: Delacorte, 1972); C. N. Alexander, "Status Perceptions," *American Sociological Review,* (December 1972), pp. 767–73.

16. J. Berger, B. P. Cohen, and M. Zelditch, Jr., "Status Characteristics and Social Interaction," *American Sociological Review* 37, no. 3 (1972), pp. 241–55.

17. Abraham Zaleznik, C. R. Christensen, and F. J. Roethlisberger, *The Motivation, Productivity and Satisfaction of Workers: A Prediction Study* (Boston: Graduate School of Business Administration, Harvard University, 1958).

18. This discussion is based on K. D. Sheats and P. Sheats, "Functional Roles of Group Members," *Journal*

of Social Issues (1948), pp. 41–49; E. H. Schein, *Process Consultation: Its Role in Organization Development* (Reading, Mass.: Addison-Wesley Publishing, 1969), pp. 39–41; and R. Likert, *New Patterns of Management* (New York: McGraw-Hill), 1961, pp. 166–69.

19. See Leonard R. Sayles, *The Behavior of Industrial Work Groups* (New York: John Wiley & Sons, 1958).

20. Robert Blauner found that the assembly line increases worker desire for informal groups while simultaneously restricting the chance of their actually developing. *Alienation and Freedom* (Chicago: University of Chicago Press, 1964). Also see M. Krain, "Communication as a Process of Dyadic Organization and Development," *The Journal of Communication,* December 1973, pp. 392–408.

21. N. Tichy, "An Analysis of Clique Formation and Structure in Organizations," *Administrative Science Quarterly* 18, no. 2 (1973), pp. 194–208.

22. On cheating problems at the Air Force Academy, see "Fall from Honor: Exam Cheating Scandal," *Newsweek,* February 1, 1965; and "Scandal in Colorado Springs," *Time,* March 3, 1967.

23. J. W. Thibaut and H. E. Kelley, "On Norms," in *The Social Psychology of Groups* (New York: John Wiley & Sons, 1959), pp. 127–35.

For a detailed description of how group norms are developed, see D. C. Feldman, "The Development and Enforcement of Group Norms," *Academy of Management Review* 9, no. 1 (1984), pp. 47–53.

24. George C. Homans wrote:
Interaction between persons leads to sentiments of liking, which express themselves in new activities, and these in turn further interaction. . . . the more frequently persons interact with one another, the stronger the sentiments of friendship for one another are apt to be. . . . the more frequently persons interact, the more alike in some respects both their activities and sentiments tend to become.

The Human Group (New York: Harcourt Brace & Jovanovich, 1950), pp. 119, 120, 133.

25. J. R. Hackman, "Group Influence on Individuals," in M. D. Dunnette, ed., Handbook of Industrial and Organizational Psychology (Skokie, Ill. Rand McNally, 1976).

26. Ross A. Webber, "Majority and Minority Perceptions and Behavior in Cross-Cultural Teams," *Human Relations* 27, no. 9 (1974), pp. 873–90.

27. Leonard R. Sayles, *The Behavior of Industrial Work Groups* (New York: John Wiley & Sons), 1958.

28. For a survey of relations between groups and individuals, see Dorwin Cartwright and Ronald Lippitt, "Group Dynamics and the Individual," *International Journal of Group Psychotherapy,* January 1957, pp. 86–102. A major problem in communes seems to be the conflict between the group as a goal and a source of solutions to individual problems versus individuals "doing their own thing" and finding help outside. L. D. Brown and J. C. Brown, "The Struggle for an Alternative: A Case Study of a Commune," *Human Organization* 32, no. 3 (1973), pp. 257–66.

29. It has been noted that "If a person wants to stay in a group, he will be susceptible to influences from the group, and he will be willing to conform to the rules which the group sets up." Leon Festinger, S. Schachter, and K. Back, *Social Pressures in Informal Groups* (New York: Harper & Row, 1950), p. 91.

30. Michael Argyle, *The Scientific Study of Social Behavior* (London: Methuen, 1957).

31. George C. Homans wrote:

Men give social approval as a generalized reinforcement to others that have given them activity they value, and so make it more likely that the others will go on giving the activity. One of the kinds of activity some men find valuable is that their own behavior and that of others they are associated with in a group should be similar in conforming to a norm. . . . People that find conformity valuable reward conformers with social approval, but withhold approval from those that will not conform, or even express positive dislike for nonconformists as having denied them a reward they had a right to expect. . . . Some members of a group conform for the norm's sake and some for the approval's sake, but both will come to say that they do it for the norm. The more a member values an activity incompatible with conformity . . . and the more valuable are his sources of social approval other than the conformers in his group, the less likely he is to conform.

Social Behavior: Its Elemental Forms (New York: Harcourt Brace Jovanovich, 1961), p. 129.

32. Melville Dalton, cited in W. F. Whyte, *Money and Motivation* (New York: Harper & Row, 1955).

33. This "idiosyncratic theory of leadership" is from E. P. Hollander, *Leaders, Groups and Influence* (Oxford: Oxford University Press, 1964).

34. On reference groups, see H. H. Hyman and E. Singer, eds., *Readings in Reference Group Theory and Research* (New York: Free Press, 1968); M. Rosenberg, "Which Significant Others?" *American Behavioral Scientist* 16, no. 6 (1973), pp. 829–60.

35. C. J. French, "Correlates of Success in Retail Selling," *American Journal of Sociology* 66, no. 2 (1960), pp. 128–34.

7

Group Decision Making

Formal groups such as committees constitute a central feature of participative leadership—especially for assistance in problem solving and decision making. In this chapter we shall consider under what conditions these groups are desirable and how groups compare with individuals in the performance of certain tasks.

Comparing Individual and Group Performance

"A camel is a racehorse designed by a committee," according to one of many popular sayings on the inadequacies of groups as decision makers. Nevertheless, committees continue to be designated as a vehicle for making decisions because they offer advantages in breadth of experience, varied knowledge, absorption of antagonism, and mutual support.

Compared to Individuals, Groups Tend to Be . . .

- slower than most
- less accurate than the best
- more accurate than most

To compare aspects of individual versus group performance, numerous exercises have been conducted with managers and students. It has been found, for example, that five-person groups take longer than the average individual working alone (50 percent longer), but more than three fourths of the groups produce better performance (an average of 30 percent better).[1]* Most groups, however, are worse than the best individual in the group.

These findings suggest that a group structure may be an advantage where being correct or avoiding mistakes is of greater importance than speed.[2] Under these conditions, the group does seem to improve on the performance of most people.[3] Comparison of individual and group performance can be summarized as follows:

The best individuals are usually better than groups as to accuracy, speed, and efficiency.

The average individual is faster than most groups, but makes more errors.

Groups are more accurate but slower than most individuals.

Age and position level also seem to affect group performance. One research project examined the performance of groups composed of members of various ages: high-level general executives averaging 47, 40-year-old middle managers, 32-year-old young managers, and graduate and undergraduate business students about 25 and 20 years old, respectively.[4] When these people worked as individuals, there were no significant differences in task performance among the different categories. Yet, lower level young people are more effective in utilizing group decision making than older, higher level managers. The difference between group performance and average individual performance decreases with increasing age and level of the group members. Younger groups improve more on individual performance. In fact, college students constitute the only groups that frequently have higher group scores than their best individual. Among all others, the best individual is usually better than the group.

So younger people seem to be more effective in utilizing groups for decision making than older and higher level managers. Time and age seem to weaken ability to work jointly with others—or perhaps the younger students have come through an educational system which has placed great emphasis on group activity.[5] The reasons might also include younger peoples' lesser sensitivity to status, more personal

---

* Notes and references will be found at the end of this chapter.

flexibility, greater willingness to express opinions, and more "team spirit." Nonetheless, all groups offer advantages and disadvantages with respect to most individuals—more correct answers, fewer errors, but slower.

Factors Affecting Group Performance

Groups are superior to individuals on problems for which the collective judgment of a group is superior to the judgment of most individuals working alone. The group (1) provides an error-correcting mechanism because discussion improves individual judgments, (2) furnishes social support to group members, and (3) fosters competition among members for mutual respect.[6] Nonetheless, these advantages exist only under certain task conditions that are conducive to group decision making.[7]

When the problem has a definite and identifiable solution.

When the initial judgements of the individuals in the group are not homogeneous, so that a range of possible solutions is available to the group for its consideration.

When the task requires that each member make a judgment about the same matter.

When rewards and punishments are given to the group as a whole rather than to individuals within the group.

When the information or skills needed for the solution are additive.

When the task can be subdivided.

When the task includes "traps" that single individuals might miss.

In addition to the nature of the task, certain social conditions will affect group performance. Favorable social conditions facilitating group decision making are as follows:[8]

When there is little expression of personal, self-oriented needs.

When whatever self-needs are expressed tend to be satisfied during the course of the meeting.

When there is a generally pleasant atmosphere and the participants recognize the need for unified action.

When the participants feel warm and friendly toward one another in a personal way.

When the group's problem-solving activity is understandable, orderly, and focused on one issue at a time.

When the chairman aids the group in penetrating its agenda problems.

In general, both the group's effectiveness and member satisfaction are increased when the members see their personal goals as being advanced by the group's success. When members push their own needs, both satisfaction and effectiveness decline.

The Effect of a Dominant Individual

The fact that the person who can dominate the group may be most satisfied causes problems with group problem solving. Personality, organizational position

Dominant Individual Tends
to . . .
- inhibit discussion
- short-cut diagnosis
- hinder disagreement
- reduce creativity
- curtail contributions of
  some members

or personal status may make one individual so dominant in the group that the group's effectiveness is jeopardized.[9] For example, in mixed business groups, the presence of the senior executive tends to inhibit problem diagnosis and discussion. Lower status members are sometimes reluctant to disagree or even to participate. This speeds the decision-making process, of course, because the leader can push the group along to the answer stage, but the advantage of group participation in problem analysis will be lost.[10] Awareness of this phenomenon may explain why long-time General Motors Chairman Alfred Sloan used to establish committees with himself as chairman but then would not attend early group meetings.[11] By his absence, it appears, he wanted to facilitate open and candid discussion in the analytical stage of the problem-solving process. Only when progress toward a solution was deemed desirable and possible did he participate.

A high-status person, such as a certified expert, may continue to dominate a group after its attention has shifted to a problem outside his or her area of expertise.[12] An experience in one class dramatically demonstrated this distortion. Five-person teams were participating in a vocabulary-type exercise. Since one team was short an individual, a psychology professor was drafted to complete the team. On the first set of words, the students continually deferred to the professor's judgment—even when some were skeptical. They deferred because he was of higher status

Drawing by Levin; © 1978 The New Yorker Magazine, Inc.

and they knew he had impressive academic credentials. Just by chance, however, he also happened to have a rather poor vocabulary. The group did badly. When the students gradually became aware of his inadequacies, they rejected him as leader.[13]

Under the pressures of hierarchical or status difference, some group members may conform merely for social approval. Further, conformity and agreement may set in so early that all opinions are not considered, and group members may become so dependent on other persons for knowledge and information that they cannot make contributions on their own. Any of these developments would hinder group performance.

Impersonal Group Decision Making

Concern over these negative aspects of individual dominance of face-to-face groups has led to the development of more impersonal group decision procedures.[14] The Delphi technique represents one of the most promising efforts to eliminate personal factors (other than knowledge) from group problem solving by (1) keeping group membership anonymous, or (2) disclosing members but keeping specific communications anonymous, or (3) allowing only written communications.[15] Each member takes a position. The central thrust of these positions (usually two-thirds distribution) is communicated to all members. On the second round each can modify her or his position or not—but the member must give specific written reasons for departing from the central range of the other responses. This impersonal iterative process is continued for several rounds as the group moves toward a central, common position. Many decisions by such separated groups are superior to those by face-to-face groups.[16]

Groups and Risk Taking

The idea that groups may be more willing to take risks than individuals is still a matter of controversy. Many people, especially business managers, have argued that group decision making inhibits daring and risk taking and promotes the conservative course when a choice must be made between more or less risky actions. A group's apparent ability to reduce errors suggests the conservative stance. Nonetheless, laboratory experiments indicate the opposite effect: Group decisions following discussion tend to be riskier than individual decisions.[17] Perhaps the individual can hide his or her responsibility better in the group, or perhaps resonance from other group members overcomes uncertainty and builds courage (or facilitates self-delusion); but in the experimental setting with ad hoc groups created by the researchers, the risk orientation is quite consistent.[18]

Actually groups do not invariably promote risky decisions. Rather, they reinforce the prevailing cultural or climatic attitude.[19] If the individual attitudes are on the conservative side of a neutral point, subsequent group discussion moves the decision toward more decisive conservatism.[20] Similarly, if the average attitute is slightly in favor of risk taking, group discussion tends to produce a "risk shift." This shift is particularly pronounced because most people tend to think that they personally are less conservative and more risk oriented than "average" others. Consequently, they may be quite surprised to see that those others are not as conservative as expected. This leads to a shifting of personal positions in the direction of risk.

Obviously, one must be cautious about extrapolating to real life from laboratory research performed mainly with undergraduates—especially on the subject of risk. Groups of college students temporarily together in an afternoon class are very different from teams of executives who have a future in working together and established status relationships that influence their deliberation.[21] Such traditional or real-life groups may handle risk differently.

Groupthink: The Push for Consensus

Sometimes the pressure to reach group consensus actually prevents an effective decision.[22] Although groups are used to produce divergent ideas and perspectives, sometimes members are forced to think in a uniform direction. This push for "group-think" causes the realistic appraisal of alternatives to be driven out by the concern for the seeking of concurrence.

Groupthink is actually a side effect of cohesion. The development of group norms (e.g., avoiding unpleasant disagreements and strong desires to hold the group together) which serve to improve morale overshadow critical thinking. Over time, members of highly cohesive groups lose their willingness and ability critically to evaluate the ideas and suggestions of others in the group. Figure 7–1 presents the symptoms of the groupthink phenomenon.

The leader of a group can do much to avoid the problems suggested by groupthink:

1. Assign the role of critical evaluator to each group member; encourage a sharing of objections.
2. Avoid, as a leader, seeming partial to one course of action.
3. Create subgroups operating under different leaders and working on the same problem.
4. Have group members discuss issues with subordinates and report back on their reactions.
5. Invite outside experts to observe group activities and react to group processes and decisions.
6. Assign one member to play a devil's advocate role at each meeting.
7. Write alternative scenarios for the intentions of competing groups.
8. Hold "second-chance" meetings after consensus is apparently achieved on key issues.

Problem Solving Alone and with Others

The choice between group and individual decision making is not really an either/ or proposition. It depends upon the stage that has been reached within the decision process.

FIGURE 7–1

Symptoms of Groups Pushing Too Quickly for Consensus

1. *Invulnerability*—Most or all the group members develop an *illusion* of invulnerability that leads them to ignore obvious dangers or important constituencies. This leads them to become overly optimistic and to take enormous risks.

2. *Rationale*—Just as group members believe themselves to be invulnerable, they collectively construct rationalizations to discount warnings or any other sources of information that run contrary to their thinking. Thus, sources of any negative information are discredited in group deliberation.

3. *Morality*—Members of the group begin to believe unquestioningly in the inherent morality of the group's position. This belief inclines the group to cast their position in absolute moralistic language. Opposing views simultaneously are thought of as inherently evil. In addition, such thinking leads group members to ignore the ethical or moral consequences of their actions.

4. *Stereotypes*—Groupthink leads group members to engage in stereotyped perceptions of other people and groups. Opposing leaders, for example, are cast as evil, satanic types, or dunces who could not possibly understand reasonable positions. Such stereotyping effectively blocks any reasonable negotiations between differing groups.

5. *Pressure*—Members suffering from groupthink apply pressure to any members who express opinions that threaten group consensus. They are branded as obstructionist. If any member doubts the group's illusion of invulnerability, rationale, morality, or stereotypes, he or she will be branded as subverting the welfare of the group and may even be banished from the group. Thus, there is great pressure to conform and avoid rocking the boat.

6. *Self-censorship*—Parties to high-level deliberations sometimes ruefully regret, after a debacle, not having spoken up and expressed doubts or positions. Most group members suffering from groupthink err on the side of keeping quiet in group deliberations and avoiding issues that are likely to upset the group. This is seen as a response to the perceived pressure to conform.

7. *Unanimity*—Self-censorship leads to the illusion of unanimity of opinion within the group. The false assumption is that anyone who remains silent in the discussion is in full agreement with the group's decision. The illusion of unanimity leads members to be complacent in the group's decision and to fail to properly consider all alternatives.

8. *Mindguards*—Finally, members affected by groupthink appoint themselves as 'mindguards'—people who have the self-appointed duty to protect the leader and other key group members from adverse information that might shake the complacency of the group. As an example, consider the instance of Attorney General Robert Kennedy warning Arthur Schlesinger not to share his doubts about the Bay of Pigs invasion with the president, because the president's mind was already made up.

Source: A. D. Szilagyi and M. J. Wallace, *Organizational Behavior and Performance* (Santa Monica, Calif.: Goodyear Publishing, 1980), pp. 418–19.

The Decision–Making Process

The conditions for ideally rational decision making can be summarized as follows:

1. An individual is confronted with a number of different, specified alternative courses of action.
2. To each of these alternatives is attached a set of associated consequences.
3. The individual has criteria that permit him or her to rank all sets of consequences according to preference and to choose that alternative that has the preferred consequences.[23]

Given these conditions or prerequisites, the process of decision making includes:

Steps in Decision Making
- perception of problem
- diagnosis
- definition of problem
- generation of solutions
- selection
- implementation

1. Diagnose.   Identify and clarify the problem as to its nature and causes. Give the requirements for a satisfactory solution, and indicate limits within which the solution must function.

2. Find Alternative Solutions.   Alternatives will range from doing nothing to finding a way around the difficulty, removing the difficulty, or even modifying the objective. Unless there is a good answer among the alternatives considered, the final decision is doomed to failure.

3. Analyze and Compare Alternatives.   Compare alternatives as to advantages and disadvantages. Ensure that the alternatives under which a choice is to be made are really the ones that should be under consideration.

4. Select the Alternative to Be Followed.   In the process of finding and comparing alternatives, particular effort should be made to identify all significant consequences of each choice.[24]

Limits on Rational Decisions

Many factors interfere with perfect rationality in decision making. Perceptual distortions, psychological biases, fear, and anxiety all play a role. No factor is more central in forcing a departure from the ideal model than is time. "Time is money" is a cliché that encourages the manager to bypass perfect rationality in order to get on with the task.[25] This is not necessarily bad; indeed it may be irrational to be perfectly rational.[26] Nonetheless, time does distort the process, and it is important to know something about how it does so in order to compensate for this tendency.

Lack of Awareness of Problems and Alternatives.   The rational model of decision making assumes that the decision maker: (1) is aware of the problem, (2) is aware that he or she must make a decision, (3) has a set of alternatives, and (4) possesses a criterion for making the decision. But these are major assumptions. Problems do not spring forth with identifying flags, and frequently the manager does not know that there is a problem—it is not "felt." If the managers are pressed for time and basically the business is operating satisfactorily, they do not use present time to search for future problems.[27] Time is seldom taken to search systematically for or consider alternatives unless the present course is causing stress. Creativity, however, contributes little unless it is preceded by continuous saturation and search. Furthermore, search is essential to avoid crisis decision making, with the distortions that this implies.

The ideally rational decision-making model also assumes that the decision maker has collected *all* possible alternatives and decides after examining all of them. Obviously, this is impossible, and time is a major element in this impossibility. The manager can seldom take the time to determine all or even most possibilities but draws up a partial list based on personal experience, the experience of associates, and articles and advertisements in the media. It is hoped that some creative ideas emerge.[28] Frequently, evaluation is not postponed until all alternatives are listed; the manager evaluates as he or she goes along, developing alternatives. The search for alternatives may cease as soon as a satisfactory choice is found, even though all the possibilities have not been exhausted and a better solution might be ahead somewhere.[29] Of necessity, time limits search and directs it toward a satisfactory rather than optimal answer. Thus time limits rationality.

Pressure to Act Prematurely. The achievement-oriented manager assumes that in any situation there must be something to do. This pressure to act pushes him or her to choose an alternative too quickly. Of course, one alternative could be to do nothing, but the mere investment of time in the decision-making process creates a movement for using that investment—and such use is more apparent in a decision for change. In other words, time may oppose initiation of search, but once initiated, time pressures for the choice of some change. The Bay of Pigs fiasco in the early days of the Kennedy administration illustrates this phenomenon: The decision-making process had a momentum that eliminated the alternative of no action and pushed toward choice among the poor alternatives promising action.[30]

In work with executives, we have repeatedly observed their inclination to shortcut the decision-making process by combining causes with problem definition. For example, in a case discussed with numerous groups, a vice president has constructed a new assembly line to which he has assigned a rather passive and reluctant engineer as supervisor. The new production unit is not producing at the desired rate. When discussing this problem, time and again managers start with the conclusion that the supervisor's weakness is the vice president's problem. This may or may not be so, but it dangerously distorts further thought about the matter. The supervisor is not *the problem;* the problem is the growing back-log of orders and customer cancellations (with resulting loss of profits) growing out of lagging production. The weak supervisor may be a cause of the inadequate production, but he is not the problem. This is a very important distinction. Defining the supervisor as the problem will tend to focus subsequent thought on how to change him or get rid of him. Seeing him as merely a cause will at least allow thinking to explore what other causative factors may be involved (such as faulty selection of operators, inadequate training, and equipment problems).

Confusing Problems and Causes. In the deliberations about communist Cuba in the early 1960s, government officials tended to define the problem as Castro.[31]

Therefore, solutions were oriented around how to get rid of him, since he seemed immune to our exhortation to change his ways. But Fidel was not the problem. He was a cause, but only one of several having historical roots well before he became a factor. The problem was the threat of Cuba's geography and form of government to the United States. How might the land be used against American interests (a point that became all too evident later in the missile crisis), and how could Cuban agents foment terror and revolution in Latin America (as Che Guevara attempted to do)?[32] These were the problems, not Castro. If Cuba could have been isolated from the rest of the world, its land denied to others, its agents confined, Castro's presence would have been irrelevant to the United States. Perhaps this was not the answer, of course, but defining Fidel as the problem was misleading and dangerous. Time pressure encourages the decision maker to confuse problems, causes, and solutions. The decision maker needs to fight it.

In the broad sense, we tend to place action ahead of diagnosis and to reward speed, but the experienced decision maker may move a little more slowly as wisdom is gained. President Harry S. Truman was widely admired as a decisive decision maker. If anything, he made decisions too easily without sufficient diagnosis; but he never shrank from the decision, and he rarely worried about past decisions. He said that he went to sleep as soon as his head touched the pillow. In his memoirs, Truman's Secretary of State Dean Acheson observes that Truman gradually slowed down his decision making, put off the tendency to jump immediately into action, and expanded the period of diagnosis; yet he retained the ability to make the decision by a deadline. Acheson advances many sarcastic observations on the tendency of later Presidents not to decide but to struggle "to keep their options open." To Acheson, this was merely indecision.[33]

More systematic research with scientists indicates that the creative person works slowly and cautiously while analyzing problems and gathering data. Once the basic data are obtained and the point of synthesis and decision is almost reached, the

"I suppose we can take comfort in the fact the experts
don't know what's going on, either."

individual works rapidly. The less creative person spends less time in analyzing the problem but more time in attempting to synthesize the material.[34]

The Group in the Decision Process

The contribution of the group to decisions varies with the phases in the process; that is, orientation, evaluation, and control.[35]

1. Orientation.   In this particular phase each member of the group has some relevant facts about the problem to be solved. In addition, however, each member is partly ignorant and uncertain about the problem-solving situation. Thus orientation entails the distribution of information among the members. Interactions specifically involve asking for and giving information.

2. Evaluation.   In this phase, members will attempt to harmonize differences in opinions and interests with the purpose of reaching a solution. Interactions involve expressing feelings, giving opinions, and developing an analysis.

3. Control.   Directional interactions occur at this stage to pressure members into line and toward a group decision. Ideas, suggestions, and possible alternatives are weighed and ranked in terms of the group's task.

The reaction of group participants can be negative or positive. Negative reactions are disagreements, tension, and antagonisms. Generally, in each phase, both negative and positive reactions may occur. However, as the problem-solving process moves toward the control phase, negative reactions tend to increase. Once preliminary success is experienced with a solution, the positive reactions tend to increase.

A clue to how this works is offered by the following incident: A group was working on an exercise problem, which went well until they reached the solution stage. At this point, a young woman (an extremely bright Phi Beta Kappa graduate) jumped up exclaiming, "I can't stand this anymore!" With that, she bolted from the room. To everyone's surprise, she returned quickly with a correct solution. She explained that she left when she had enough information; the group's questions and talk were a hindrance after this. The noise and confusion interfered with her thought.

What happens is that the group is helpful in diagnosis: analyzing the problem, the objective, and the limits upon the solution. This is apparent in the pattern of questions; they are asked in batches, with one person's question triggering off three or four from others. Then a silence follows, then another cluster of questions, and so on. Everyone feels free to utilize the information necessary to analze the problem, but discussion interferes with the detailed formulation of a solution. In short, a group may be helpful in the analytical stage of decision making (perhaps three fourths of the total time to make the decision), but a hindrance to final evaluation and selection.

Assets and Liabilities in Group Decision Making

As we have suggested, the forces operating in a group may be classified as assets, liabilities, or either assets or liabilities. The category depends on the skills of the members, especially those of the leader.[36] The requirement for achieving a level of proficiency in group performance hinges on the development of a style of leadership that maximizes the group's assets and minimizes its liabilities.

Group Assets

The principal assets of group structure in decision making are the following:

1. There exists more knowledge in a group than in any of its individual members; therefore, the sum total of knowledge and information is greater in group processes.
2. Group members present a greater number of approaches to a problem. This aids those who may get into a thinking rut.
3. Participation in group problem solving increases acceptance by group members and eliminates the problem of persuasion.
4. When those who must implement the decision participate in making it, they have a better comprehension of the decision. They not only understand the solution but are aware of the alternatives that have been considered and rejected.

Group Liabilities

The forces operating within groups that can be classified as liabilities include the following:

1. Social pressure from group members leads to conformity, regardless of the objective quality of the solution. Reaching agreement is confused with finding the right answer.
2. Problem solving has a variety of potential solutions. Each solution receives both critical and supportive comments from members of the group. If the number of negative and positive comments for each solution are algebraically summed, each may be given a value. The first solution that receives a certain positive value tends to be adopted by the group, regardless of its quality. Higher quality solutions introduced after the critical value for one of the solutions has been reached have little chance of achieving real consideration.
3. A dominant individual may negate the group and convert the process to individual decision making.
4. "Winning" each point can come to be each group member's objective, to the detriment of the collective performance.

Factors that Can Serve as Assets or Liabilities

Some group characteristics can be considered either assets or liabilities. These include the following:

1. Discussions that lead to disagreement can either create hard feelings among members or lead to a resolution of conflict and hence to an innovative solution.

The skill of a leader is determined by his or her ability to create a climate for disagreement that will permit innovation without risking hard feelings.

2. Disagreement in discussion can take many forms. It is up to the leader whether a discussion drifts toward conflicting interests or mutual interests are located. Cooperative problem solving can only occur after the mutual interests have been established, and these can be identified by the discussion leader.

3. Decisions in groups take much longer to arrive at than decisions by individuals. When decisions that require quick solutions are decided by a group process, this hurts the effectiveness of such decisions. Longer time in making decisions means fuller discussions and better solutions to the problems but can be an inefficient time use, as well as fatiguing and boring.

4. The group can become caught up in its own deliberations, so pleased with its internal relations that it gets out of touch with the outside world—an event sometimes labeled "groupthink." The group may even become so enamored of its proposals that critics are denigrated and dismissed as irrational. A current university curriculum reform committee composed of faculty and students is working well. The members are beginning to like and respect one another. Their mutual sentiments and social enjoyment are encouraging them to invest more time in the formal task. Three 7:30 breakfast meetings have been held! This is conducive to group effectiveness, but it can be dangerous. The majority may get so wrapped up in each other and their task that they are out of touch with the people they are representing. The radical proposals of the committee majority may be impractical and will be opposed by the majority of faculty and students, who are not caught up in the group's mutually reinforcing deliberations. As a result of this process and their isolation, committees composed of rational members can recommend some wild proposals.

5. In reaching a solution to the problem, some members of a group must change their opinions. In group situations, however, who changes can be an asset or a liability. For example, if persons with the most constructive views are induced to change, the end product suffers, whereas if persons with the least constructive points of view change, the end product is upgraded. The leader can influence who changes and thereby influence the quality of the decision. However, the leader must be careful not to dominate the group and influence the decision alone.

SUMMARY

There are important differences in decision making by individuals and groups. Groups offer advantages on certain kinds of problems when conditions are favorable, mainly on specific problems with clear-cut answers when open communication is facilitated because status and hierarchical distinctions are absent or not important. Training, experience, age, and personality also affect group effectiveness, but groups tend to make fewer errors, to be willing to take higher risks, and to improve on the performance of average individuals—but not on that of the best group members.

Whether the advantages of group decision making justify the additional time required depends on three critical factors: (1) whether speed is essential (as when a military unit is under attack or a prospective customer is threatening to terminate negotiations); (2) whether an incorrect decision can be tolerated (as it cannot be when making important defense decisions in Washington, D.C., or automotive styling decisions in Detroit); and (3) whether the organization has an exceptional individual who would be hindered by the group (as the United States had with President Lincoln or as a few corporations have had with entrepreneurial founders).

REVIEW QUESTIONS

1. On what dimensions are groups superior to individuals in problem solving?

2. On what dimensions are individuals superior to groups?

3. How does the age of group members appear to affect group performance as compared with individual performance?

4. Under what task and social conditions do groups seem to be superior to individuals?

5. For groups to be effective, what must be the relationship between group objectives and individual member goals?

6. How does an overly dominant individual affect group performance?

7. Why do some members dominate the group effort?

8. Under what conditions may individual dominance improve group performance?

9. What is the Delphi technique? What is its objective?

10. How does impersonal decision making attempt to counter the dangers in individual dominance?

11. Why are groups thought to be more risk taking than individuals?

12. In what way are groups not necessarily always more risk taking?

13. What are the steps in rational decision making?

14. What composes the diagnosis of a problem?

15. What factors limit rational decision making?

16. Why are managers sometimes not aware of problems?

17. How and why are alternatives limited in decision making?

18. How do decision makers satisfice rather than optimize?

19. How and why does pressure to act affect decision making?

20. How do decision makers confuse problems and causes?

21. What seems to be the difference between "more creative" and "less creative" people in their approaches to decision making?

22. In what phases of the decision-making process are groups most helpful?

23. In what phase of the decision-making process are groups least helpful, if not a hindrance?

24. What are the assets in group decision making?

25. What are the liabilities in group decision making?

26. What factors can be assets *or* liabilities? How does this depend on the group leader?

Notes and References on Group Decision Making

1. Ross A. Webber, "The Relation of Group Performance to the Age of Members in Homogeneous Groups," *Academy of Management Journal* 17, no. 3 (1974), pp. 570–74. The findings are shown in the accompanying table.

	Individual $n_1 = 240$	Group $n_2 = 48$
Mean time to complete vocabulary test	4.5 min.	6.8 min.
Mean score (number correct out of 25 questions)	13.2	17.5
Mean errors (number incorrect)	11.8	7.5
Mean efficiency (number right per minute)	3.0	2.6

2. This was pointed out more than 40 years ago. M. E. Shaw, "A Comparison of Individuals and Small Groups in the Rational Solution of Complex Problems," *American Journal of Psychology* 44 (1932), pp. 491–504.

3. I. Lorge et al., "A Survey of Studies Contrasting the Quality of Group Performance and Individual Performance, 1920–1957," *Psychological Bulletin* 55 (1958), pp. 337–72.

4. Webber, "Relation of Group Performance to Age of Members." The results appear in the table on page 158.

5. One study indicates that older groups tend to communicate more, so it is possible that they might be more effective on more complex problems. H. W. Smith, "Some Developmental Interpersonal Dynamics through Childhood," *American Sociological Review*, October 1973, pp. 543–52.

6. Peter M. Blau and W. Richard Scott, *Formal Organizations* (San Francisco: Chandler Publishing, 1963).

7. Bernard Berelson and G. A. Steiner, *Human Behavior* (New York: Harcourt Brace Jovanovich, 1964), p. 355.

8. B. Collins and H. Guetzkow, *A Social Psychology of Group Processes for Decision Making* (New York: John Wiley & Sons, 1964).

9. W. T. Smelser, "Dominance as a Factor in Achievement and Perception in Cooperative Problem-Solving Interactions," *Journal of Abnormal and Social Psychology* 62 (1961), pp. 535–42. M. Malder shows that members tend to shift attitudes in the direction of the more powerful members. "Power Equalization through Participation?" *Administrative Science Quarterly* 16, no. 1 (1971), pp. 31–39.

10. N. R. F. Maier and L. R. Hoffman, "Acceptance and Quality of Solutions as Related to Leaders' Attitudes toward Disagreement in Group Problem Solving," *Journal of Applied Behavioral Science* 1 (1965), pp. 373–86. Freedom to disagree is important to group performance and member satisfaction. Member control balanced equally among all members is associated with both much disagreement and much effectiveness. E. L. Levine, "Problems of Organizational Control in Microcosm: Group Performance and Group Member Satisfaction as a Function of Differences in Control Structure," *Journal of Applied Psychology* 58, no. 2 (1973), pp. 186–96.

11. A. P. Sloan, Jr., *My Years with General Motors* (Garden City, N.Y.: Doubleday Publishing, 1964).

12 W. Doyle, "Effects of Achieved Status of Leader on Productivity of Groups," *Administrative Science Quarterly* 16, no. 1 (1971), pp. 40–50. Status differences based

Relation of Group Performance to Age of Members

Subjects	Mean Score (no. correct)	Mean Time (min.)	Mean Group Effectiveness (group score minus mean of individuals in group)	Mean Group Excellence (group score minus best individual score in group)
Executives mean age 47				
40 individuals	13.4	4.0		
8 groups	15.8	9.0	+1.8	−1.4
Middle managers mean age 40				
55 individuals	13.3	4.2		
11 groups	15.1	6.2	+1.7	−2.9
Young managers mean age 32				
90 individuals	13.2	4.2		
18 groups	15.3	5.3	+2.3	−3.1
M.B.A. students mean age 25				
90 individuals	14.3	4.7		
18 groups	16.3	6.0	+3.7	0
B.S. students mean age 20				
40 individuals	11.5	5.5		
8 groups	17.5	6.0	+3.5	+1.5

on expert power tend to impede group creativity, according to P. A. Collaros and L. R. Anderson, "Effects of Perceived Expertness upon Creativity of Members of Brainstorming Groups," *Journal of Applied Psychology* 53 (1969), pp. 159–63. Mixed-status groups may be less productive, less efficient, and less inclined to take risks. E. M. Bridges, W. J. Doyle, and D. J. Mahan, "Effects of Hierarchical Differentiation on Group Productivity, Efficiency and Risk-Taking," *Administrative Science Quarterly* 13 (1968), pp. 305–39.

13. Of course, where the expert actually knows the most about the task under consideration, his or her dominance can help the group. W. A. Frederickson and G. Kizziar, "Accurate, Deceptive, and No Prior Feedback about Decisionmaking Acumen as an Influencer of Group Decision Making," *Journal of Applied Social Psychology* 3, no. 3 (1973), pp. 232–39.

14. A. Van de Ven and A. L. Delbecq, "Nominal versus Interacting Group Processes for Committee Decision-Making Effectiveness," *Academy of Management Journal* 14, no. 2 (1971), pp. 203–12.

15. N. C. Dalkey, "The Delphi Method: An Experimental Study of Group Opinion," Memorandum RM 5888–PR, The Rand Corporation, June 1969.

16. J. Hall, "Decisions, Decisions, Decisions," *Psychology Today,* November 1971, pp. 51 ff.

17. D. J. Bem, M. A. Wallach, and N. Kogan, "Group Decision Making under Risk of Aversive Consequences," *Journal of Personality and Social Psychology* 1 (1965), pp. 453–60.

18. M. A. Wallach, N. Kogan, and D. J. Bem, "Diffusion of Responsibility and Level of Risk Taking in Groups," *Journal of Abnormal and Social Psychology* 68 (1964), pp. 263–74.

19. D. G. Marquis, "Individual and Group Decisions Involving Risk," *Industrial Management Review,* Spring 1968, pp. 69–75.

20. E. B. Ebbesen and R. J. Bowers, "Proportion of Risky to Conservative Arguments in a Group Discussion and Choice Shift," *Journal of Personality and Social Psychology* 29, no. 3 (1974), pp. 316–27; E. A. Cecil, L. L. Cummings, and J. M. Chertkoff, "Group Composition and Choice Shift: Implications for Administration," *Academy of Management Journal* 16, no. 3 (1973), pp. 412–22; A. Vinokur and E. Burnstein, "Effects of Partially Shared Persuasive Arguments on Group Induced Shifts," *Journal of Personality and Social Psychology* 29, no. 3 (1974), pp. 305–15.

21. A. Y. Lewin and W. L. Weber, "Risk Taking in Ad Hoc and Traditional Groups," paper presented to Institute of Management Science, September 8, 1966.

22. I. L. Janis, "Groupthink," *Psychology Today,* November 1971; and *Victims of Groupthink* (Boston: Houghton Mifflin, 1972).

23. For a comprehensive discussion of managerial decision making, see D. W. Miller and M. K. Starr, *Executive Decision and Operations Research* (Englewood Cliffs, N.J.: Prentice-Hall, 1960), and I. L. Janis and L. Mann, *Decision Making* (New York: Free Press, 1977). See also R. W. Pollay, "The Structure of Executive Decisions and Decision Times," *Administrative Science Quarterly,* December 1970; S. Beer, *Brain of the Firm* (New York: Penguin Books, 1973); and J. L. McKenney and P. G. W. Keen, "How Managers' Minds Work," *Harvard Business Review,* May–June 1974, pp. 79–90.

For an assessment of our current state of knowledge on group decision making, see R. A. Guzzo, *Improving Group Decision Making in Organizations* (New York: Academic Press, 1982).

24. A. O. Elbing, *Behavioral Decisions in Organizations* (Glenview, Ill.: Scott, Foresman, 1970). H. I. Ansoff defines the steps in managerial problem solving as follows: (1) problem recognition and identification, (2) diagnosis, (3) analysis and generation of alternatives, (4) strategic decision, (5) program analysis and step-by-step plan, (6) program decision, (7) communication and leadership of plan, (8) measurement of results, (9) assessment of trends, and (10) prospects for the future. "Managerial Problem-Solving," *Journal of Business Policy* 2, no. 1 (1971), pp. 3–20.

25. On time and money, see C. H. Jones, "The Money Value of Time," *Harvard Business Review,* July–August 1968, pp. 94–101, and P. L. Watson, *The Value of Time: Behavioral Models of Modal Choice* (Lexington, Mass.: Lexington Books, 1974).

26. See S. Kadar, "Rationality and Irrationality in Business Leadership," *Journal of Business Policy* 2, no. 2 (1972), pp. 39–44. See also C. R. Peterson, ed., "Cascaded Inference," special issue of *Organizational Behavior and Human Performance* 10, no. 3 (1973).

27. On the tendency to neglect the important search activity that is the first phase of decision making, see J. G. March and H. A. Simon, *Organizations* (New York: John Wiley & Sons, 1958).

28. The most expensive aspect of problem solving tends to be the collection of information necessary for analysis and alternative generation. See H. J. Watson, "A New Approach to Valuing Information," *Managerial Planning* 22, no. 3 (1973), p. 18 ff.

29. S. G. Winter, "Satisficing, Selection and the Innovating Remnant," *The Quarterly Journal of Economics,* May 1971, pp. 237–61.

30. For details on the Bay of Pigs decision, see Theodore Sorenson, *Kennedy* (New York: Harper & Row, 1965) and Arthur M. Schlesinger, Jr., *A Thousand Days* (Boston: Houghton Mifflin, 1965). Writing about a later and more effectively managed crisis (the Cuban missile confrontation), Robert Kennedy said:

> often thought afterward of some of the things we learned from this confrontation [on Soviet rockets in Cuba]. The time that was available to the President and his advisers to work secretly, quietly, privately, developing a course of action and recommendations for the President, was essential. If our deliberations had been publicized, if we had had to make a decision in 24 hours, I believe the course that we ultimately would have taken would have been quite different and filled with far greater risks. The fact that we were able to talk, debate, argue, disagree, and then debate some more was essential in choosing the ultimate course. Such time is not always present, although, perhaps surprisingly, on most occasions of great crisis it is; but when it is, it should be utilized.

Thirteen Days: A Memoir of the Cuban Missile Crisis, (New York: W. W. Norton, 1969), p. 111.

31. The concentration on Castro as the problem in Cuba is especially evident in the oral history transcripts in the John F. Kennedy Memorial Library. Reports on conversations between Senator George Smathers of Florida and President Kennedy indicate consideration of the implications of assassinating Castro as a solution. Henry Raymont, "Oral-History Fills out Record of JFK Years," *Denver Post,* August 23, 1970.

32. For more on the Cuban Missile crisis, see G. T. Allison, "Conceptual Models and the Cuban Missile Crisis," *American Political Science Review* 14 (1969), pp. 689–718; and Allison, *Essence of Decision* (Boston: Little, Brown, 1971).

33. For Truman on himself, see Harry S. Truman, *Memoirs* (Garden City, N.Y.: Doubleday Publishing), vol. 1, *Year of Decisions* (1955) and vol. 2, *Years of Trial* and Hope (1956). Of President Truman, Dean Acheson wrote:

> His judgment developed with the exercise of it. At first, he was inclined to be hasty as though pushed out by the pressure of responsibility, and—perhaps also—by concern that deliberateness might seem to be indecisiveness. But he learned fast and soon would ask, "How long have we got to work this out?' He would take what time was available for study and then decide. . . . No one can decide and act who is beset by second thoughts, self-doubt, and that most enfeebling of emotions, regret. With the President, a decision made was done with and he went on to another. He learned from his mistakes (although he seldom admitted them), and did not waste time bemoaning them. . . . Not in any sense self-deprecating, his approach was sturdy and confident, but without any trace of pretentiousness. He held his own ideas in abeyance until he had heard and weighed the ideas of others, alert and eager to gain additional knowledge and new insights. He was not afraid of the competition of others' ideas; he welcomed it. Free of the greatest vice in a leader, his ego never came between him and his job.

Present at the Creation: My Years in the State Department (New York: W. W. Norton, 1969), pp. 731–33.

34.   On creativity and problem solving, Bernard Berelson and G. A. Steiner wrote:

> In a problem-solving situation, the more creative man works slowly and cautiously while he is analyzing his problem and gathering his data. Once he obtains the basic data and approaches the point of synthesis, he works rapidly. The less creative man spends less time in analyzing the problem but more time in attempting to synthesize his material.

Human Behavior, (New York: Harcourt Brace Jovanovich, 1964) p. 227. See also M. I. Stein and S. J. Heinze, Creativity and the Individual (New York: Free Press, 1960).

35.   R. F. Bales and F. L. Strodtbeck, "Phases in Group Problem Solving," Journal of Abnormal and Social Psychology 46 (1951), pp. 485–95.

36.   These are summarized by N. R. F. Maier in "Assets and Liabilities in Group Problem Solving: The Need for an Integrative Function," Psychological Review 74, no. 4 (1967), pp. 239–49.

8

Managing Groups and Committees

Like it or not, managers must deal with informal organizations and work groups.[1] If managers attempt to treat everyone as individuals, as they might prefer, they would unwittingly create more problems. In dealing with informal organizations managers should:

1. Recognize that all organizations are sociotechnical systems, that out of required technical and structural behavior imposed on employees, an unplanned, informal organizational life centered around work groups will emerge.
2. Attempt to influence the informal system when taking action.
3. Keep formal activities from unnecessarily threatening the informal organization. That is, they should not inadvertently transgress the informal system.
4. Draw on the informal system to contribute to formal objectives by integrating its objectives and interests with those of the formal organization.

Problems with Informal Groups

Unfortunately, in dealing with the informal organization, management frequently encounters three overlapping problems: (1) conflict between formal and informal status systems, (2) employees' offended sense of distributive justice, and (3) status incongruity.

Conflict between Formal and Informal Status

A common fault of management is insensitivity to the social side of the sociotechnical system.[2] They design and modify the formal organization without anticipating the impact on the social life of the job. Difficulty is sometimes created for management when formal organizational structure conflicts with an informal status system—that is, when management evaluation of jobs and positions does not correspond to group evaluation. For example, Figure 8–1 illustrates the formal and informal status of jobs in the Rose City Chemical Plant before and after a technological change.

The job of handler required a semiskilled manual operator to sort raw and finished materials. Working conditions were good, the area was clean and well lighted, but the job required relatively little training and skill. The pay rate was $4 per hour.

FIGURE 8–1

Conflicting Formal and Informal Job Status at Rose City Chemical Plant

Formal Status System before Change		Informal Status System before and after Change	Formal Status System after Change	
Assistant supervisor	salary	Assistant supervisor	Assistant supervisor	salary
Head operator of continuous processing	$6.00/hr.	Head operator of continuous processing	Tank room operator	$6.50/hr.
Tank room operator	$5.00/hr.	Tank room operator	Head operator of continuous processing	$6.00/hr.
Handler	$4.00/hr.	Handler	Handler	$4.00/hr.

The next higher position, tank room operator, was responsible for a batch chemical process that used eight large tanks in another room in the same building. The operator had to add chemicals, control flows, and make various tests. The job was a promotion from handler; it paid $5 an hour and required greater skill and experience, including some fairly sophisticated knowledge of chemical tests. In addition, the tank room operator had greater autonomy and responsibility. However, the working conditions were atrocious. Since various digestive processes using organic enzymes were percolating in open vats, the area was like the inside of a stomach. The smell, heat, and humidity all detracted from the desirability of the job.

The most desirable job in the department was as head operator of continuous-processing equipment. The "white coverall" head operator received $6 an hour for manipulating a console and making some important decisions regarding chemical flows, times, temperatures, and so forth. The head operator performed very little manual work; the work area was clean, well lighted, and much cooler than the tank room.

For years, the informal social structure and the formal organizational hierarchy were similar. Management and the employees agreed on which jobs were more desirable. The wage rates reflected both management and group judgments of job status. Each worker saw his career as progressing up through these positions—from handler to tank room operator to head operator. In general, the more senior people were head operators, the next in seniority were tank operators, and newer people were handlers.

One day the harmony ended. Because of technological developments in another department, it was necessary to redesign some of the operations in the tank room, increasing the responsibilities of the tank room operator and calling for greater skill and technical sophistication. Even greater decision-making discretion and autonomy were given to the tank room operator. The wage and salary administrator reevaluated the job, and pay was increased to $6.50 an hour—$0.50 an hour more than the head operator received. However, working conditions were not improved. The tank room was still dirty, smelly, and unpleasant. The formal status structure now went from handler to head operator to tank room operator. Unfortunately, the work group refused to modify its own hierarchy. The pay increase for the tank room operator was not enough to give that job higher status than the head operator's position. The men could not see the high point of their careers as moving to the tank room. They still wanted to progress from handler to tank room operator to head operator—and were willing to take a cut in pay to move to the last job.

The technical change at Rose City Chemical not only upset the status system; it also offended the workers' sense of distributive justice.

Status Incongruity

An employee is also likely to feel offended when there is inconsistency or incongruity between nonjob and on-job status factors—that is, between the attributes he or she brings to the job (such as age, sex, ethnicity, or education) and the rewards expected from it (pay, intrinsic satisfaction, working conditions, privileges, formal status, or informal prestige).[3] For example, consider the problems of blacks in business.

Formal Status—On-Job
Status Factors:
- pay
- title
- position
- task
- mobility
- conditions

Informal Status—Nonjob
Status Factors:
- age
- skill
- sex
- education
- ethnicity
- race
- personality

Their effort to climb to higher positions leads some whites to perceive a status incongruity, however illegitimate the perception. Some whites still assign low personal status to blacks. Historically, this has been consistent with the jobs they have filled—low skilled, low paying, dirty, and monotonous. Then there was consistency between off-job and on-job status factors. At present, however, one of the most in-demand persons in American society is the black MBA graduate. How far he or she will climb in business is still undetermined, but the black college graduate's movement into positions of relative importance, high on internal status (in such factors as pay, skill, authority, and office furnishings), means status incongruity, in the opinion of some whites. Because some white men think they bring higher personal status factors to the job, they may be upset when they have lower job status.

Some companies who desire to hire and promote blacks attempt to maintain the white's perception of status congruity by either rewarding the blacks (or other minority member) less or requiring greater contributions on their part. Southern tobacco companies apparently have had some success in putting black supervisors over white workers at relatively low levels. To be a black implies low personal status, but the blacks appointed are brighter, harder working, and better educated than the whites working under them. White males are less offended by a black (or female) receiving equal rewards if it is patently obvious that the latter is superior. Of course, blacks and white females are increasingly offended by this inequity. Status congruity is preserved for the white males, but it is intentionally violated for others. If they feel inferior and really believe they have less to offer, they may not care, or they may not have complained in the past because they needed the work. Obviously, these days are ending. Blacks and white females are awakening to the injustice of *their* status incongruence. The solution is the elimination of race and sex as sources of status relevant to work, but we are dealing with informal factors here that come from outside the organization.

Because the wage and salary staff at the Rose City Chemical Plant refused to increase the head operator's rate, the junior workers in the tank room were making more money than more senior operators—thus creating status incongruity. The only way management was able to solve this problem was to make extensive physical modifications in the tank room to improve working conditions. These changes made conditions in the tank room roughly similar to those for the head operator, which in turn raised the informal status of the tank room operator's job. In other words, management was able to solve the problem only by modifying the status factors to make informal and formal status systems congruent.

A manager's ability to hire, transfer, and promote people is hindered to the extent that they are upset by incongruent status comparisons. We are not implying that management need be afraid to act for fear of the stress of status incongruity. What we do say is that the manager should be aware of possible causes and consequences of such status comparisons when he or she takes actions that affect the informal status system within the organization.

Disadvantages and Advantages of Informal Groups

It is important for managers to realize that there are both disadvantages *and* advantages to informal groups. They may create problems for management.

1. Their informal expectations may conflict with management objectives, especially when groups restrict production.

2. Their pressures for member conformity may block ambition, frustrate satisfaction of higher level needs, and block contributions from the more capable people. Fearing group sanctions, they may not work as hard to distinguish themselves.

3. Their very existence lends a certain inertia and resistance to change. It is not that employees are categorically opposed to change. Rather, all social systems take on vested interests in the existing status structure. The group and informal organization would collapse unless it was satisfying, so its very success makes it resistant to ambiguous management changes that may undercut it.

These are, of course, all problems of which management must be cognizant. But emergent groups and informal organization can also offer advantages to management.

1. They lend stability to the formal organization by increasing the work satisfaction of some employees. Absenteeism and turnover may even be less than they might because groups can tie the individual to the organization.

2. They exercise discipline in ways that management would find hard to duplicate. Although the group may allow a certain amount of formal rule violation, they usually limit this and discipline members who violate management regulations too frequently or flagrantly.

3. Flexibility and training may even be provided. The informal organization can fill in the bureaucratic gaps by teaching people how to really perform the job. This can ease the burden of first-line supervision.

4. The group and informal leaders can be a vehicle for redressing grievances (even in the absence of a union). Acting as a representative of less outspoken members, high-status leaders can communicate concerns to management of which they may not even be aware.

Disadvantages of Informal Organization
- conflicting objectives
- restriction of effort
- blocking of ambition
- inertia
- resistance to change

Advantages of Informal Organization
- lend stability
- increase morale
- discipline
- mutual assistance
- provide leadership
- redress grievances

Managing Formal Groups

What we know about informal organization and formal committees can serve as a basis for guidelines on how management can utilize committees effectively.

Uses of Committees

Committees can be used by management for four general purposes:

1. Exchanging views and information, with understanding as the primary objective.
2. Generating ideas and a list of alternative actions to be implemented by individual managers.
3. Recommending a single course of action.
4. Solving a problem and making a decision that binds all members.

Committees can perform all these functions, but the first two are probably the easiest. As we have seen, groups have difficulty in actually reaching decisions because they are more effective in analyzing problems than in synthesizing answers. It is very important to define the committee's purpose clearly and state its authority in writing when the committee is constituted.[4] In doing so, management must decide which of the four general purposes the particular committee is to serve. Is it to:

1. Submit just a problem diagnosis?
2. Prepare a list of possible solutions with pros and cons?
3. Recommend just one action?
4. Implement the proposal? Does it have the authority to do so?

When Committees Are Desirable

In general, committees should be used only when they can perform a specific function better than an individual can. They should not be used as substitutes for hazy organizational structure or as a crutch for weak managers—although they are frequently used as both, thus adding to the ill repute in which many managers hold groups. Committees can be effective under the following conditions:[5]

1. When a manger's subordinates as a group have more experience on a specific problem than the superior does. This is not a rare situation in modern organizations with many specialities. Such committees usually dispense advice to the superior on complex policy matters, especially in new areas, such as entering a new market, launching a new product, or responding to social demands for more responsibility.

2. When power over a vital organizational activity should not be vested in a single individual. Such power may require more knowledge than one person possesses, or the issue may be so vital that no one could bring a totally unbiased view to the issue. Or it may just be difficult to find an individual who could stand the pressure alone. University boards of trustees, insurance company investment teams, and automobile corporation finance committees all are committees designed to spread authority, ease the burden, and avoid mistakes.

3. When a committee is necessary to share responsibility for difficult and unpopular

---

FIGURE 8–2 ▬▬▬▬▬▬▬▬▬▬▬▬▬▬▬▬▬▬▬▬▬▬▬▬▬▬▬▬▬▬▬▬

Determining the Appropriateness of Participative Decision Making

It is appropriate to be more participative when:

- The quality of the decision is important.
- Subordinate acceptance of the decision is critical for its effective implementation.
- The manager trusts subordinates to focus on organizational rather than personal goals.
- Conflict among subordinates is minimal.

It is appropriate to be less participative when:

- The manager has all the necessary information to make a high-quality decision.
- The immediate problem is well structured or where there is a common solution that has been applied in similar situations in the past.
- Time is limited and immediate action is required.

Source: V. H. Vroom and P. Yetton, *Leadership and Decision Making* (Pittsburgh: University of Pittsburgh Press, 1973).

decisions. Where decisions are likely to draw substantial criticism from organizational members, so that courage is required of the decision makers, committees can diffuse the responsibility for the decisions.

4. When they are of the right size. The size of a committee is frequently beyond the chairperson's control because political considerations may dictate that various interest groups be represented. Where it is possible to control size, however, research suggests that groups of five to seven persons are most desirable.[6] Committees larger than seven make it too difficult to keep everyone in mind; less than five members leads to superficial discussion without sufficient controversy.

What the Committee Chairperson Should Do

In most committees a chairperson is necessary. Task-oriented groups want strong directions on how the group should proceed. Unless the chair is a "take charge" person, he or she tends to be rejected.[7]

Group performance is probably best when the chair can combine the task and social leadership roles. One unable to do both should retain the task leadership and allow someone else to play the social role.[8]

The committee chairperson should exercise strong leadership but should not dominate the group's decision. This is a key point—and a difficult one. To gain maximum advantage from group problem solving, a leader should play a role quite different from that of the members. He or she should distinguish between problem solving and persuasion, emphasizing the former and avoiding the latter.[9] The following can be identified as problem-solving and persuasion activities.

Problem-Solving Activities (emphasize)	Persuasion Activities (avoid)
Searching for ideas	Selling opinions
Exchanging opinions	Defending a predetermined position
Listening	Refuting and criticizing
Group participation, involvement, and interest	Two-person interaction

The chair should structure the group's deliberations, circulate written agendas in advance, and exert pressure to keep members working. However, the chair should not attempt to impose a personal position. One doing so is likely to succeed by virtue of power and higher status, but lower status members, especially subordinates, may withdraw or become "yes people," and in effect there will be no group or committee. In short, the chair should not dominate with her or his contributions. Instead said person must concentrate on the group process, listen in order to understand rather than to refute, assume responsibility for accurate communication between members, be sensitive to unexpressed feelings, protect minority points of view, keep the discussion moving, and develop skills in summarizing. The chair should attempt to involve people of all status levels in the deliberations and to find creativity in as many places as possible. Here are some guidelines for committee chairpersons:[10]

"Barton, do you have something you want to share with
the rest of us?"

From *The Wall Street Journal,* with permission of Cartoon Features Syndicate.

Never compete with group members; give all members' ideas precedence over
 your own.

Listen to all the group members without premature judgment.

Permit no one to be put on the defensive

Use every member of the group.

Keep the energy level high by demonstrating alertness, interest, and intensity.

Keep the members informed about where they are and what is expected of them.

Remember that you are not permanent.

Managerial Attitudes on Group Decision Making

Cross-cultural research has probed managerial views on the desirability of subordinate
participation and group decision making.[11] Figure 8–3 summarizes these views as
reported by managers in a variety of national cultures and U.S. organizations.

The most negative views were expressed by managers in Italy and less developed
countries (India, Chile, and Argentina). The foreign shoe company managers were
primarily executives in Africa and Asia, all of whom seemed to believe that their
subordinates had nothing to offer, perhaps because of their low education, undevel-
oped skills, and poverty.

American business managers were less favorable toward group decision making
and participation than were the Japanese.[12] The American cultural philosophy and
managerial system emphasize individuals and their personal responsibility to make
decisions. "Groupthink" is distrusted by many individualistic Americans and even
called socialistic by some. Yet, some research suggests that it is the formal participa-

FIGURE 8–3

Differing Managerial Attitudes about Participation

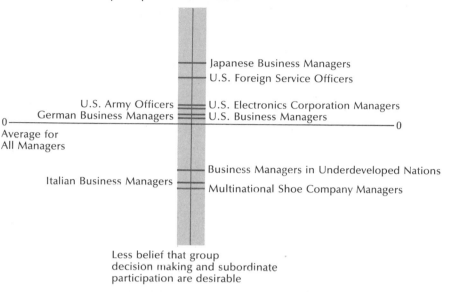

More belief that group
decision making and subordinate
participation are desirable

Japanese Business Managers
U.S. Foreign Service Officers

U.S. Army Officers — U.S. Electronics Corporation Managers
German Business Managers — U.S. Business Managers

0 — 0
Average for
All Managers

Business Managers in Underdeveloped Nations
Italian Business Managers — Multinational Shoe Company Managers

Less belief that group
decision making and subordinate
participation are desirable

Source: Based on data in Mason Haire, Edwin E. Ghiselli, and Lyman W. Porter, *Managerial Thinking* (New York: John Wiley & Sons, 1966). Supplemented by additional data.

tion of subordinates that is distrusted by American managers, not informal involvement.[13] For example, U.S. practice has been compared with that of Yugoslavia, Israel, and Italy. Figure 8–4 shows that Yugoslavian organizations have formal rules requiring subordinate participation in decision making, yet informal consultation between superiors and subordinates is so rare that actual participation seems minimal. Italy has no formal participation system and no informal participation either. The gap between most managers and workers is enormous. Israeli Kibbutzim have both

FIGURE 8–4

Formal and Informal Subordinate Participation

		Formal System of Participation?	
		No	Yes
Informal Participation?	No	Italy	Yugoslavia
	Yes	U.S.	Israel

formal mechanisms for subordinate participation and informal consultation to a high degree. Actual informal communication between American managers and workers is closer to the Israeli example than Yugoslavia or Italy.

Japanese business managers are the most positive toward group decision making and participation. Participation is thought to have great advantages, particularly in developing widespread commitment to group decisions. Japanese groups apparently take a long time to make decisions, but implementation is rapid because all opposition has been overcome prior to the final choice.[14] American groups may find that when their more rapid decisions are put into operation, they are subject to passive resistance and active sabotage from group members who are not convinced.

The Japanese participatory style is rooted in their history and culture, as American individualism is in ours, but the Japanese place much less stress on *individual* performance. By hiring the very top college graduates, Japanese businesses hope to ensure that only good managers will exist. These managers are trained well and promoted slowly. Traditionally individual performance records are not maintained, and merit reviews are not given because it is the team that is important, not the individual.[15]

One American sample seems almost as positive about participation as the Japanese. Foreign Service officers of the U.S. Department of State perceive substantial advantages in group decisions. Some American business managers to whom this data have been presented have observed that this only verifies what they have always thought about the "fuzzy thinking" of the State Department. But consider the task and structure of the Foreign Service: The typical embassy is composed of an ambassador, a deputy, and various professional experts in political, military, and economic affairs. The ambassador may be a political appointee who is not very competent in many of these areas. He or she is dependent on the Foreign Service subordinates, and they in turn are dependent on each other in order to formulate reports and recommendations that integrate their various areas.[16]

In addition, and perhaps more important, Foreign Service officers want to avoid mistakes. Given the leading and vulnerable position of the United States, even small judgmental errors may have major adverse impact on American interests and indeed on world peace. Decisions in Santo Domingo are not isolated; they could expand to affect relations with Cuba, Latin America, and the world. As we have seen, the possibility of reducing errors is one of the great advantages of groups.

This desire to avoid mistakes may also reflect a personal desire to protect one's career, to avoid black marks on individual records by not exposing positions. Groups make authority and accountability more diffuse so that the individual can attempt to hide in the group. But here the Foreign Service task plays a role. Unlike a business manager, who can point to profits, productivity, low costs, or other quantitative proof of his or her good performance, the Foreign Service officer finds it difficult to demonstrate good work.[17] The officer's task is so nebulous that success is frequently indicated by something *not* happening: no riots, no burning of U.S. Information Agency libraries, no citizens arrested. It may seem that no news is goods news— and any news is bad. In this kind of setting, one tries to avoid accumulating any bad marks, to keep one's record clear, to see that if one can't accumulate brownie points, one can at least avoid black marks. Participation and group process can facilitate this.

SUMMARY

Managers should understand informal organization for two reasons: (1) so that they do not inadvertently transgress the informal system producing reactive behavior that blocks formal objectives and (2) in order to integrate the formal and emergent systems for better performance. Of particular concern to management are problems of offended equity when people do not perceive equality and balance between their contributions/costs and rewards/receipts to and from the organization. Improper reward distribution, status incongruency, and conflicting formal and informal status systems sometimes result. We are not saying that management must always accommodate informal groups and shift formal organization, policy, and procedures to satisfy them. Managers may attempt to change the norms of the informal group. To do this successfully, however, requires understanding of informal group dynamics.

Managers should recognize that informal groups and organizations will always emerge from the formal structure and task; that all organizations are technical and social systems. This may complicate the manager's life and create problems, but it can also improve organizational effectiveness and be beneficial to management by contributing predictability, stability, flexibility, and morale.

Management may attempt to draw formally on the advantages of groups by creating committees to exchange information, analyze problems, or reach decisions. Clear definition of the committee's function and authority is essential in order to benefit from the situation when committees are desirable: when the group possesses more experience and expertise than an individual; when a variety of different, unbiased views are valuable; when power should not be concentrated in an individual; or when responsibility should be shared.

Strong task leadership in pushing the group through an agenda is generally desirable, but chairpersons should not attempt to dominate the group or impose their own views. If they have power and status, they may succeed, but this will undercut the committee and destroy the advantages of the group process.

These various managers also express differing views on subordinate participation and group decision making. Japanese business managers are most favorable toward this, and those managers in underdeveloped counties are much more skeptical about what their subordinates have to offer. American business managers take an intermediate view, and U.S. Foreign Service officers are more favorable toward participation, perhaps as a reflection of their tasks and situations.

REVIEW QUESTIONS

1. How can the formal and informal status systems conflict?

2. Why should such conflict concern management?

3. What is status incongruity? Why should this concern management?

4. Why and how should managers be aware of emergent informal organization?

5. What problems can the informal organization create for management?

6. What are the possible advantages to management of the informal organization?

7. For what general purposes can committees be used?

8. How should purpose be defined? When are committees desirable?

9. How can a group be harmonious but get out of touch with realities in the organization?

10. How can a committee chairperson exercise strong leaderhsip without overly dominating the committee?

11. How can a chairperson differentiate between problem-solving activities and persuasive activities?

12. What are the guidelines for a committee chairperson?

13. Which nation's business managers seem to be most in favor of group participation? Why?

14. Which nation's business managers seem to be least in favor of group participation? Why?

15. Why may U.S. Foreign Service officers be so favorable toward group participation and decision making?

Notes and References on Managing Groups and Committees

1. Most fundamentally, management must deal with groups because they have power. David Mechanic, "Sources of Power of Lower Participants in Complex Organizations," *Administrative Science Quarterly* 7, no. 3 (1962), pp. 349–64.

2. A. O. Elbing, "The Danger of Applying a 'Technical' Mind to Human Decisions," *European Business,* Spring 1973, pp. 48–53.

3. J. S. Adams, "Inequity in Social Exchange," in Leonard Berkowitz, ed., *Advances in Experimental Social Psychology,* vol. 2 (New York: Academic Press, 1965), pp. 267–300; P. S. Goodman and A. Friedman, "An Examination of Adams' Theory of Inequity," *Administrative Science Quarterly* 16 (1971), pp. 271–88.

4. R. A. Golde, "Are Your Meetings Like This One?" *Harvard Business Review,* January–February 1972, pp. 68–77.

5. Cyril O'Donnell, "Ground Rules for Using Committees," *Management Review,* October 1961, pp. 63–67.

6. A. C. Filley, "Committee Management: Guidelines from Social Science Research," *California Management Review* 13, no. 1 (1970), pp. 13–21; and G. E. Manners, Jr., "Another Look at Group Size, Group Problem Solving, and Member Consensus," *Academy of Management Journal,* December 1975, pp. 715–24.

7. L. Schlesinger, J. M. Jackson, and J. Butman, "Leader-Member Interaction in Management Committees," *Journal of Abnormal and Social Psychology* 61, no. 3 (1960), pp. 360–64. See also V. H. Vroom and P. W. Yetton, *Leadership and Decision Making* (Pittsburgh: University of Pittsburgh, 1973), and V. H. Vroom and A. G. Yago, "Decision Making as a Social Process: Normative and Descriptive Models of Leader Behavior," *Decision Sciences* 5 (1974), pp. 160–86.

8. E. G. Borgotta, A. S. Couch, and R. F. Bales, "Some Findings Relevant to the Great Man Theory of Leadership," *American Sociological Review* 19 (1954), pp. 755–59.

9. G. M. Prince, "How to Be a Better Meeting Chairman," *Harvard Business Review,* January–February 1969, pp. 98–108.

10. Ibid.

11. Mason Haire, Edwin E. Ghiselli, and Lyman W. Porter, *Managerial Thinking* (New York: John Wiley & Sons, 1966).

12. A questionnaire survey of attitudes on democratic practices (such as employee balloting on policy issues) is reported in D. W. Ewing, "Who Wants Corporate Democracy?" *Harvard Business Review,* September–October 1971, p. 12 ff. Not surprisingly, democratic practices are more favored by younger managers, but Ewing feels that support is growing at all levels.

13. A. S. Tannenbaum, *Hierarchy in Organizations* (San Francisco: Jossey-Bass, 1975).

14. P. Hesseling and E. E. Konnen, "Culture and Subculture in a Decision-Making Exercise," *Human Relations* 22 (1969), pp. 31–51.

15. On Japanese management, see: T. F. M. Adams and N. Kobayski, *The World of Japanese Business* (Tokyo and Palo Alto: Kodonsha, 1969); M. Y. Yoshino, *Japan's Managerial System* (Cambridge, Mass.: MIT Press, 1968); G. V. England and R. Koike, "Personal Value Systems of Japanese Managers," *Journal of Cross-Cultural Psychology* 1 (1970), pp. 21–40.

16. Upon leaving public office, former Attorney General and Undersecretary of State Nicholas Katzenbach commented that State Department decisions, unlike those reached at the Justice Department, required consultation with numerous other agencies of the government. He said this made decision making at State more difficult. W. Hoge, "Departing Katzenbach Sums It All Up," *New York Post,* November 20, 1968.

17. As former Secretary of State, Dean Rusk pointed out that the State Department often does not get credit for its triumphs. Its mistakes show; a lot of its successes do not. If State succeeds in getting a foreign government to adopt a certain policy, it can't very well announce the fact in public. S. Grover, "Diplomatic Dissent," *The Wall Street Journal,* November 12, 1969. On State Department careers, see C. E. Bohlen, *Memoirs* (Boston: Little, Brown, 1967 and 1972), and G. F. Kennan, *Witness to History* (New York: W. W. Norton, 1973).

Discussion Questions and Exercises on Groups at Work

Discussion Questions

1. For many years, Europeans have commented on the group orientation of Americans. In comparison with more tradition-directed countries, we seem to be more other directed. For example, a study of parents faced with a decision about rules for their children indicated that German parents would apply family and church teachings. In contrast, American parents were much more likely to consult their friends and neighbors with similar aged children. How would you explain this?

2. How does an informal organization influence the behavior of its members? Why do members allow themselves to be influenced?

3. How is individual productivity related to the informal organization and status structure?

4. Research suggests that absenteeism is not correlated with an employee's attitudes toward the company or superior but is related to the attitudes toward fellow workers. How would you explain this?

5. "The primary question is often not whether a group will form and provide some social satisfactions for its members, but whether these satisfactions will be derived from relationships built around task accomplishments or whether the time and energy invested in obtaining these satisfactions are drained off into nontask-related and ritualistic activities." What does this mean?

6. For years managers and industrial engineers have been critical of work groups for "irrationally" foregoing opportunities to make more money on incentive jobs by restricting production. How might such output restriction actually be rational?

7. "The formal organization could not effectively operate without the informal social groups that make up its infrastructure." What does this mean?

8. In spite of repeated efforts to organize them, most engineers have refused to join labor unions. Many might even agree that strong collective action would help them as a body, but they do not want to join. How would you explain this?

9. Perhaps the most group-oriented phase of life is the early teen years. For example, the decision to smoke is more influenced by peers than by parents. Discuss why.

10. All channel network research among American college students, business executives, and dropout young people suggests at least one common phenomenon: The first person who says he or she should be the decision maker is usually rejected. How would you explain this?

11. Why might many groups be willing to reach more risky decisions than individuals would be?

12. Would you prefer a president of the United States to be oriented toward individual or group decision making? Why?

13. One of the greatest burdens of being a professor is participation in committee meetings. Much time is involved in group discussion, drafting recommendations, and making decisions. Why do you think colleges and universities have so many committees?

14. In a comparative study of managerial attitudes, American and German business managers were

skeptical of group participation in decision making. Managers in underdeveloped countries were strongly opposed. In contrast, Japanese business managers and U.S. Foreign Service officers are much more favorable toward group decision making. How would you explain these contrasting views?

Individual Exercises

1. Make a list of the informal ethical code or behavioral rules that exist in your college, fraternity, or dormitory. How are they enforced? Do the same for any job you have held.

2. Describe and analyze a situation where someone experienced status incongruity.

3. Describe and analyze the status system in any group of which you are a member or which you have observed (fraternity, team, club, job, etc.).

4. Describe and analyze a situation where you (or someone you have observed) was subject to group pressure to conform. How was discipline enforced? Did it work? Why?

5. Describe any groups with which you are familiar that can be characterized as apathetic, erratic, strategic, or conservative with respect to an authority structure.

6. Choose a group to which you belong, perhaps your Management class or project group. Describe this group's development in terms of Figure 6–1. In what stage of development is this group? Describe the group's maturation in terms of the issues or activities addressed within each developmental stage.

7. Retrospectively analyze your decision about attending college. *(a)* What were your objectives and problems? *(b)* What alternatives existed, and how did you generate them? *(c)* What were the limits on your selection and the criteria by which alternatives were evaluated? *(d)* Did you make a rational decision? In what way were you not perfectly rational?

8. Examine a group to which you belong (now or in the past) for symptoms of the groupthink phenomenon.

Managerial Cases and Problems on Groups at Work

Critical Work Characteristics: A National Assessment*

Listed below are several items describing various aspects of a job. First you will work with this information on your own, and then you will be asked to work in groups of four to five persons.

Individual Procedure

Personal Ranking. As you think about your own career, how important is each aspect of the job to you? Rank order from 1 (most important) to 12 (least important). Enter the rankings in the table on page 178 in the column labeled Personal Preference.

National Ranking. Think about the American work force, particularly managers and professionals. How important is each aspect of the job to this group? Rank order from 1 to 12. Enter the rankings in the column labeled Individual Ranking.

Group Procedure

1. As a team, rank the importance of the 12 items for the American work force. The group should work to reach consensus on each item. Do not vote! Enter the group's results in the column labeled Group Ranking.
2. The instructor will read to you the rankings that resulted from a national survey. Enter these ranks in the column labeled National Survey.
3. The instructor will tell you how to fill in the remaining columns.

Discussion Questions

1. Who was most influential in your group? Why? How did (s)he influence others?
2. How do you feel about your own level of influence on the group? What would you do differently next time?
3. How accurate were you? High accuracy, high influence? High accuracy, low influence? Low accuracy, high influence? Low accuracy, low influence?
4. How accurate was your group? Did the group do better than most individuals in your group?
5. How different are your personal preferences from the national survey results?

---

* Based on P. A. Renwick, E. E. Lawler, and the *Psychology Today* staff, "What You Really Want from Your Job," *Psychology Today,* May 1978.

How Important Is Each of the Following Aspects of a Job?

	Personal Preference	Individual Ranking	Group Ranking	National Survey	Influence	Individual Accuracy	Group Accuracy
Amount of praise you get for job well done							
The friendliness of people you work with							
Amount of pay you get							
The amount of freedom you have on your job							
Opportunity to develop your skills and abilities							
Chances to do something that makes you feel good about yourself							
The respect you receive from people you work with							
The amount of job security you have							
Chances for getting a promotion							
Physical surroundings of your job							
Chances to accomplish something worthwhile							
Your chances for taking part in making decisions							
TOTALS							

The Case of the Dope Department (A)*

It wasn't called the Dope Department because it possessed narcotic or hallucinogenic qualities in atmosphere or product. The name came from the odor of ether that permeated the building, an odor much like the airplane dope used in constructing balsa and paper models. The department's product consisted of about 20 different kinds of viscous liquid compounds used by another department to manufacture transparent film to be left clear, or coated with photographic emulsion or iron oxide.

Before the Change

The department was located in an old four-story building, as in Exhibit 1. The work flow was as follows:

1. Twenty kinds of powder arrived daily in 50-pound paper bags. In addition, storage tanks of liquid would be filled weekly from tank trucks.

2. Two or three dope helpers would jointly unload pallets of bags into the storage area, using a lift truck.
3. Several times a shift, the helpers would bring the bagged material up the elevator to the third floor, where it would be temporarily stored along the walls.
4. Mixing batches was under the direction of the group leader and was rather like baking a cake. Following a prescribed formula, the group leader, mixers, and helpers operated valves to feed in the proper solvent and manually dumped in the proper weight and mixture of solid material. The glob would be mixed by giant egg beaters and heated according to the recipe.
5. When the batch was completed, it was pumped to a finished product storage tank or the second floor.
6. After completing each batch, the crew would thoroughly clean the work area of dust and empty bags, because cleanliness was extremely important to the finished product.

---

* Part (B) to this case is contained in the Instructor's Manual.

EXHIBIT 1

Elevation View of Dope Department before Change

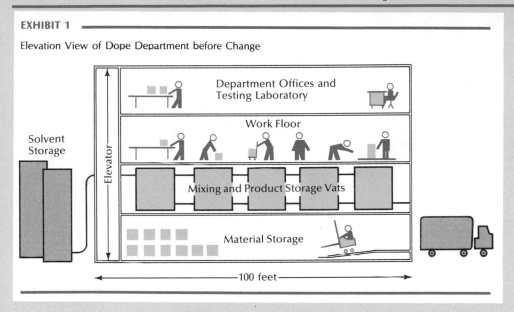

EXHIBIT 2

Organization Chart of Dope Department before Change

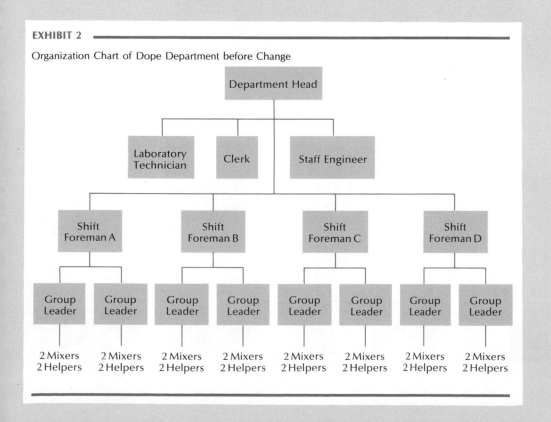

To accomplish this work, the department was structured as in Exhibit 2.

The helpers were usually young men 18 to 25 years of age; the mixers 25 to 40, and the group leaders and foremen, 40 to 60. Foremen were on salary; group leaders, mixers and helpers on hourly pay.

To produce 20 million pounds of product per year, the department operated 24 hours a day, 7 days a week. Four crews rotated shifts: for example, shift foreman A and his two group leaders and crews would work two weeks on the day shift, 8:00 A.M. to 4:00 P.M.; then two weeks on the evening shift, 4:00 P.M. to midnight; then two weeks on the night shift, midnight to 8:00 A.M. There were two days off between shift changes.

During a typical shift, a group leader and his crew would complete two or three batches. A batch would frequently be started on one shift and completed by the next shift crew. There was slightly less work on the evening and night shifts because no deliveries were made, but these crews engaged in a little more cleaning. The shift foreman would give instructions to the two group leaders at the beginning of each shift as to the status of batches in process, batches to be mixed, what deliveries were expected, and what cleaning was to be done. Periodically throughout the shift, the foreman would collect samples in small bottles which he would leave at the laboratory technicians' desk for testing.

The management and office staff (department head, staff engineer, lab technician, and department clerk) only worked on the day shift, although if an emergency arose on the other shifts, the foreman might call.

All in all, the department was a pleasant place in which to work. The work floor was a little warm but well lighted, quiet, and clean. Substantial banter and horseplay occurred when the crew was not actually loading batches, particularly on the nonday shifts. The men had a dartboard in the work area on which the target was that month's *Playboy* centerfold. Competition was fierce and loud. Frequently a crew would go bowling right after work, even at 1:00 A.M., for the community's alleys were open 24 hours a day. Department turnover and absenteeism were low. Most employees spent their entire career with the company, many in one department. The corporation was large, paternalistic, well paying, and offered attractive fringe benefits, including a large, virtually automatic bonus for all. Then came the change. . . .

The New System

To improve productivity, The Dope Department was completely redesigned, the technology changed from batches to continuous processing. The basic building was retained, but substantially modified as in Exhibit 3. The modified work flow is as follows:

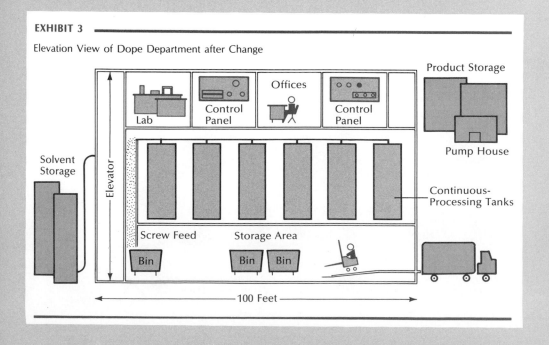

EXHIBIT 3

Elevation View of Dope Department after Change

1. Most solid raw materials were delivered via trucks in large aluminum bins holding 500 pounds.
2. One handler (formerly helper) is on duty at all times in the first floor to receive raw materials and to dump the bins into the semiautomatic screw feeder.
3. The head operator (former group leader) directs the mixing operations from his control panel on the fourth floor, located along one wall across from the department offices. The mixing is virtually an automatic operation once the solid material has been sent up the screw feed; a tape program opens and closes the necessary valves to add solvent, heat, mixing, and so on. Sitting at a table before his panel, the head operator monitors the process to see that everything is operating properly within specified temperatures and pressure.

This technical change allowed the department to reduce its personnel greatly. The new structure is illustrated in Exhibit 4.

One new position was created, that of a pump operator who is located in a small separate shack about 300 feet from the main building. He operates pumps and valves that move the finished product among various storage tanks.

Under the new system, production was increased to 25 million pounds per year. All remaining employees received a 15 percent increase in pay. Former personnel not retained in the Dope Department were transferred to other departments in the company. No one was dismissed.

Questions on the Case of the Dope Department (A)

1. Why was the Dope Department formerly perceived as such a desirable place to work?

2. How do you think the technical change affected the social system? In terms of the exchange between employer and employees, how did the contributions/costs and benefits/rewards change for the (a) helper turned handler? (b) mixer turned pump operator? and (c) group leader turned head operator?

3. Do you think absenteeism and turnover were affected?

4. What did management gain from the technical change?

5. Do you think management lost anything?

6. What could management have done differently?

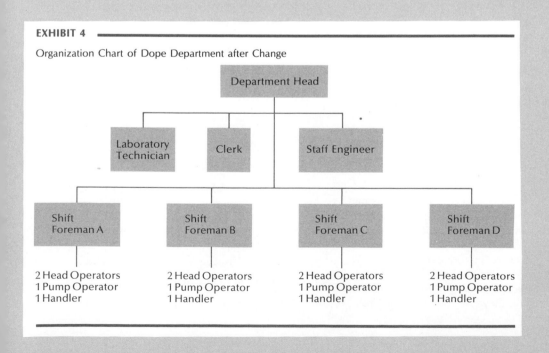

EXHIBIT 4

Organization Chart of Dope Department after Change

Maureen Daly and the Computer Center

Maureen Daly is manager of Data Processing in a medium-size company. She supervises a department consisting of two group supervisors, six computer operators, and six programmers. All but two programmers and one operator are men. Maureen has filled all these positions since she came to work for the Periscope Company nine years ago as a programmer. She had always been interested in numbers and mathematics which she learned early from her mother who taught math in a junior high school. Her father was also a teacher, of electricity and electronics. Maureen grew up with high aspirations and confidence in her abilities. She majored in mathematics in college and then earned an M.S. in computer science. She has also completed all her course work for a Ph.D., but hasn't written a dissertation yet.

After attending a management development program and listening to Professor William Eastman talk about managerial leadership, she requested a private meeting with Eastman.

DALY: Professor Eastman, I enjoyed your talk on leadership last week although I didn't like your bias in favor of autocratic management. It seemed old-fashioned and insensitive.

EASTMAN: I didn't mean to be biased. I thought I used the term *authoritarian,* not *autocratic* and I hoped to suggest that an authoritarian style is appropriate and perhaps even essential in certain circumstances.

DALY: Well, maybe, but I think most young managers today know that they can't just make decisions unilaterally and order subordinates around. People don't like to be dictated to; they want to feel that they are involved in the way their area operates. To have that sense of involvement they should participate in departmental decisions.

EASTMAN: Is that the way you run your department?

DALY: Yes. Every morning I have a meeting with my two supervisors and the three senior operators and programmers to discuss what has to be done that day and what problems exist. We strive to reach concensus on each issue before going on. In addition, once a week I hold a meeting with the junior programmers and operators to discuss how things are going. I encourage them to contact me directly if they have any personal prob-

lems. I call all of them by their first names and most of them call me Maureen. I think we all get along very well.

EASTMAN: Well, what's your problem?

DALY: None really, I guess . . . but. . . .

EASTMAN: But?

DALY: Two weeks ago I had an annual merit review and I am still distressed by what the vice president told me.

EASTMAN: What did he say?

DALY: He said that I didn't have control of my department; that things are drifting; that one of the supervisors and a senior programmer had gone to him to complain about the time wasted in meetings deciding where to locate the coffee machine and about my supposed inability to make decisions. He also told me that there had been complaints about horseplay on the evening shift involving a water pistol fight I never heard anything about. Worst of all, he said I have limited promotion potential because I'm not a strong enough manager.

EASTMAN: What do you think about all this?

DALY: That's what I wanted to ask you! I don't know what to think. I try to treat my people as adults, respect their opinions and invite their participation, and motivate them to set their own performance standards, but they seem to behave like children, some of them anyway, and my senior people go around my back to complain. Perhaps you're right after all.

EASTMAN: About what?

DALY: That managers really should be autocrats.

EASTMAN: That's not what I said!

Questions on Maureen Daly and the Computer Center

1. What appears to be Daly's leadership style? How would you rate her on the leadership dimensions?

2. What seems to be her problem? Why?

3. What should Professor Eastman do? Why?

4. What advice would you offer Daly? Why?

Part Four

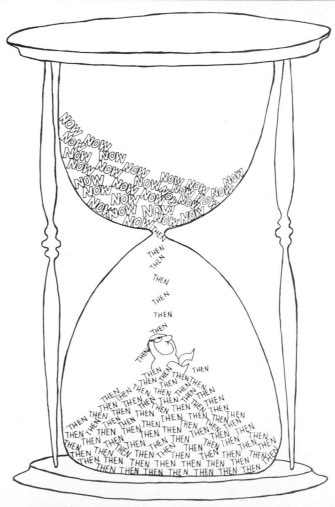

Reprinted by permission of Sperry Corporation.

Managerial Leadership

9

Sources of Power and Influence

Back in the early 1970s a group of professors and students were meeting as a search committee to find a new university dean. After discussing the position's responsibilities, one of the faculty members intoned, "We don't want a person who really enjoys exercising power." Most of the group nodded in agreement—visions of Lyndon Johnson and Richard Nixon probably dancing in their heads. But, what nonsense! To appoint as a manager a person who *dislikes* power? When power is absolutely central to effective and efficient management? No wonder colleges and universities are often poorly administered.

There is no way around it; power and influence are central to the manager's job. Therefore, in this chapter we shall discuss influence, the reasons one person would follow another, and the bases of the influencer-leader's power. This will lay the foundation for the debate over leadership style covered in the next chapter.

Power, Authority, and Influence

Three concepts that will be mentioned frequently are influence, power, and authority. In spite of (or because of) the widespread use of these terms, no consistent and universally accepted definitions exist.[1]* We shall use them as follows:

Influence is indicated by a follower's modification of behavior or attitudes in response to the leader's behavior.

Power includes the personal or positional attributes that are the bases of the influencer-leader's potential influence.

Authority is only one of several power bases—that which is given to the leader by organizational officials.

The Bases of Power

When someone successfully influences another, we infer that the influencer possesses power. Thus, influence implies power, and power is necessary for influence. (See Figure 9–1.) However, power is not just the brute force of coercing the reluctant follower; rather it takes several forms.[2]

Coercive power is based on a follower's perception that the influencer has the ability to punish—and that the punishment will be unpleasant or frustrating of some need.

Reward power is based on a follower's perception that the influencer has the capacity to reward and that the reward will be pleasant or satisfying of some need.

Legitimate power is based upon the follower's internalized values, which convince her or him that the influencer has a legitimate right to influence and that the follower is bound to accept. This is at the core of a traditional influence system, in which leadership positions are endowed with formal authority.

FIGURE 9–1

Power and Influence

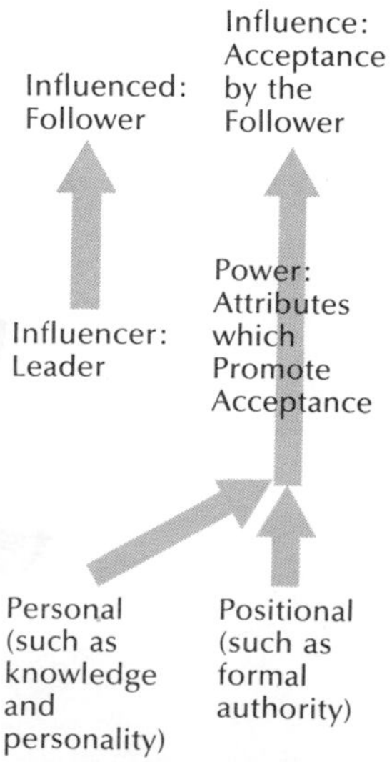

Influence: Acceptance by the Follower

Influenced: Follower

Power: Attributes which Promote Acceptance

Influencer: Leader

Personal (such as knowledge and personality)

Positional (such as formal authority)

---

* Notes and references will be found at the end of this chapter.

Referent power is based on the follower's desire to identify with a charismatic leader to follow out of blind faith. The identification can be maintained if the follower behaves as the leader indicates.

Expert power is based on the follower's perception that the leader has special knowledge or expertise that can be useful in satisfying one of the follower's needs.

Representative power is delegated upward to a leader by a group with an implied agreement to follow as long as the leader consults the followers and generally leads in the direction they want to go.

Bases of Power
- coercive
- reward
- legitimate
- referent
- expert
- representative

These power bases underly the various forms of influence through appeal to the follower's needs.

Influence as Appeal to Needs

In order to influence anyone, you must appeal to one or more of the needs discussed in Chapter 3. If you are holding a loaded gun to my head and you communicate a willingness to fire, the chances are that I will do what you ask. The odds are stacked in your favor. But certainly history demonstrates many similar situations in which people have chosen *not* to obey. The implication is clear: The influence process depends upon the follower as much as or more than it depends upon the leader. It is a decision by the follower whether or not to respond that determines whether or not the process is to succeed. Perhaps the follower does not have much choice, and perhaps the choice is not always consciously considered, but it is still said person's decision whether or not to go along. Therefore, in considering influence we must also consider the process of "followership," the reasons a person would allow himself or herself to be influenced.[3]

Roughly paralleling the needs hierarchy is a continuum of influence processes summarized in Figure 9–2. The basis of this continuum is six fundamental reasons people respond: fear-hope, tradition, blind faith, rational faith, rational agreement, and joint determination.

FIGURE 9–2

Influence and Leadership Styles

Follower's Need Hierarchy	Influence Process	Leadership Style	Leader's Power Basis
Competence, achievement	Self-determination	Abdicative	
Power, autonomy	Joint determination	Participative	Representative
Esteem, prestige	Rational agreement	Peruasive	Expert
Social, affiliation	Rational faith		Referent
	Blind faith		Legitimate
Safety, security	Tradition	Authoritarian	Reward
Physiological	Fear-hope	Autocratic	Coercive

Reprinted by permission of the Chicago Tribune-New York News Syndicate.

Influence through Fear or Hope

Influence through fear or hope drawing on coercive or reward power can work if logically and consistently applied. Nonetheless, it is not certain that they *will* work in a particular situation with specific people. We are dealing with odds, not certainty. Whether an influence process will motivate a person to behave in the desired way depends on the individual's perception and judgment as to whether effort will lead to the reward offered (or lack of punishment promised), *and* whether this reward will satisfy a fundamental need. Thus the motivation model discussed in Part Two can be modified to include the influence process (see Figures 9–3 and 9–4).[4]

As indicated in the figure, the follower's motivation and effort depend upon the follower's:

a. Estimate of the probability that effort will meet the influencer's objective.
b. Estimate of the probability that upon meeting the objective, the influencer will dispense rewards or withhold punishment.
c. Estimate of the probability that the rewards will satisfy some of his or her needs.
d. Value placed upon satisfaction of her or his needs.

FIGURE 9–3

Influence Model Based on Coercive and Reward Power

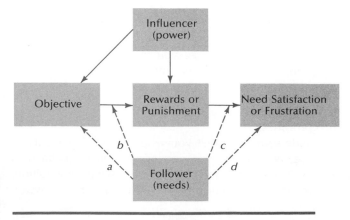

FIGURE 9–4

Influence through Fear and Hope

Appeals to
Follower's
Physiological,
Safety, and
Security Needs

↑

Influence
through Fear-Hope

↑

Draws on
Autocratic/Authoritarian
Leader's
Coercive or Reward
Power

The follower's motivation and effort will be great if he or she highly values need satisfaction, *and* thinks the influencer's rewards will be instrumental in satisfying these needs, *and* thinks that efforts will meet the influencer's objectives so that he or she will be rewarded. Breaking the system at any point undermines the influencer's influence.[5]

Conditions Undermining Influence

Suppose your parents attempted to influence your study efforts by promising you some reward for straight *A*s on your report card. You might or might not be influenced to try. Under the following conditions you would not be influenced to do so:

1. You believe that no amount of effort on your part would produce straight *A*s. Perhaps you think the instructors don't like you, or that you don't have the time to devote to the effort, or even that you are just too dumb. Under these conditions, your parents' attempt to influence you would break down in the first step; you just would not make the effort.

2. You do not believe your parents. If you don't really think that they would punish you or reward you for not meeting or achieving their objective, you would not be influenced. In this example you would probably believe them, but many parents do issue unrealistic threats "to knock your block off" or "you'll never ever watch television again" that they cannot possibly apply. Consequently, many parents do lose their credibility with their children.

Credibility is very important to the influencer; his or her threats and promises must be believed. When organized crime entered the loan sharking business, its credibility was one of its biggest assets. The borrowers were influenced to pay back the loan on time because they believed the lender's threats that they absolutely would be punished—no escape was possible.

3. You do not value your parents' reward or are not afraid of punishment. Before you would be influenced, your parent would have to be able to satisfy or frustrate some of your needs. If all your parents promised as a reward was their admiration, and if this does not mean much to you, their influence would be lessened.

Conditions Facilitating Influence

There are other conditions that would encourage you to strive for the desired grades. Under the following conditions, your parents might be able to influence you:

1. You believe you have some chance of making straight *A*s.
2. You believe your parents' promises.
3. Your parents' sanctions include something that you would find either satisfying or frustrating. If they promised you a new car, you might well be inclined to try to reach their objectives. If they threatened to cease paying your tuition, you might also be so influenced, unless you do not care about school anyway

or if you thought you could raise the funds yourself. In general, promise of reward is more effective than the threat of punishment.[6]

On the job, subordinates are likely to work hard if the path from their efforts to their goals is clear—if they think that they can meet their superior's desired productivity and if they are quite certain that the money, promotion, or other rewards offered will be granted and that said rewards will satisfy some of their needs, such as security or esteem. But if job rewards are viewed as unrelated to productivity, because they depend upon seniority or economic conditions, the subordinates are not likely to work above the minimum level necessary to keep the job. They may even believe that higher productivity will lessen their security. Or, if the subordinate's really important needs are for competence and achievement, that person is unlikely to put forth much effort in a routine job if all the superior offers in exchange for high productivity is money. Finally, if the subordinate distrusts the superior's promise of rewards or does not believe his or her threats, the influencer has no influence.

This general influence model clearly defines a central leadership problem: *to formulate, communicate and ensure that the followers understand the path-goal relationships.*[7] The followers must understand the goals, the criteria for evaluating performance, the sanctions promised and their meaning for them. The leader must design the system so that goal achievement leads to the follower's personal reward and need satisfaction. Otherwise, he or she will be no leader, no influence will result, and there will be no followers.

The Problem of Using Fear

Across the span of human history and in many societies even today, fear is one of the most common influence systems.[8] Fear of being hurt physically or psychologically has long characterized families, tribes, armies, and kingdoms. In business organizations, fear often takes the form of anxiety about losing a job and income.

Under influence by fear, it makes no difference whether subordinates understand the reasons for directives or agree with them. Agreement or disagreement is irrelevant. All that the influencer cares about is whether subordinates understand what they are supposed to do. Coercion will lay less heavily on subordinates if they understand and agree with the directives, but their understanding and agreement would not fundamentally alter the situation. (See Figure 9–5.)

A British government minister recently made a speech in which he bemoaned the apparent decline of fear as a motivator in British industry. He felt that somehow Britons do not work hard enough because they do not fear loss of their jobs. Perhaps social legislation and governmental guarantees against starvation have reduced the ability of the British employer to utilize fear. Much of the same thing is probably also true in the United States. Fear as a motivator at work declines during full employment when other jobs are available but increases with economic recession. Of course the elimination of fear has been a prime purpose of government and labor unions for many years. Nonetheless, managers may wish they could use fear because it is so simple and straightforward. They would not have to play amateur psychologist;

they could simply assume that everyone needs a job to satisfy basic needs, and they could then manage appropriately.

The use of fear as a managerial tool may be inverted in modern organizations. Some paternalistic companies have made conscious efforts to eliminate the use of fear in management's relations with blue-collar and clerical workers, while facilitating fear of ridicule and dismissal as a primary motivator of managerial personnel.[9] Because of high pay and organizational prestige, middle managers may be particularly subject to fear. In addition, they have no union to represent their interests, and usually no due process appeal procedures.

In spite of its attractiveness to leaders, fear as a device has one great handicap: it is expensive. The leader must monitor followers closely to see that they are doing what they are told and that they are not departing from their instructions. If noncompliance is detected, in order to maintain the follower's fear, the leader must punish. This process of policing and punishing can be quite costly. Hitler's Minister of Economics, Albert Speer, observes in his memoirs that he made a mistake in using slave labor in some Nazi manufacturing plants.[10] Of course he was imprisoned for 20 years on this charge, but he indicates that his conclusion is supported on economic grounds. A study of a slave-labor bomb manufacturing plant shows what can be accomplished by resistant workers even under conditions that are entirely oriented around fear.[11] They hindered production by withholding the simplest judgments and persistently asking for detailed instructions on what to do next. In addition, they were able to sabotage production by improperly fitting the fuses. The sabotage was evident only when the weapon was dropped; duds were numerous. Their insubordination was impossible for the guards to detect unless they stood directly over individual workers. Therefore, in order to influence the slaves to behave as desired, it became necessary to increase their probability of being caught—and this required more guards. The plant soon had almost as many guards as slaves. In such a situation, it is more sensible to eliminate the slaves and assign guards to the work. Then management must feed only half as many persons.

Most applications of fear suffer from this expense of monitoring performance and applying sanctions because it is essential that the influencer maintain credibility that transgressions will be detected and punished.[12] The crime syndicate loan shark must convey to clients the mixed message of absolute honesty and commitment to the contract—in both directions. The potential deadbeat must know with certainty that retribution will follow. So in law enforcement, high probability of detection and certain moderate punishment are greater deterrences to crime than are low probability of detection and uncertain severe punishment.[13] The problem is that detection is more expensive than punishment.

The Advantage of Using Hope

Emphasizing the positive reward for desired behavior is at the base of modern behavioral psychology and much ancient leadership practice. (See Figure 9–6.)[14] As we saw in Chapter 5, this may take varied forms in addition to money. The major arguments in favor of rewards over punishment are:

The leader can clearly define the desired behavior, not just the undesired. The fear approach implies that the follower has only two courses of action—what the leader desires and what he or she abhors. In fact, other alternatives may exist that the leader doesn't anticipate. The follower may choose one of these in hope of retaining some autonomy and still escaping punishment.

Research suggests that fear of punishment often galvanizes more effort, but the hope of rewards leads to greater follower understanding and satisfaction with what is expected.[15] So under fear, a subordinate may work hard, but at the wrong task.[16] Under hope, he or she is more likely to do what is desired and is happier doing it. The key is the influencer-leader must know precisely what he or she wants the follower to do—and be able to determine when it is done.

FIGURE 9–6

Hope as Influencer

Influence through Tradition

Tradition probably has been the most common influence mechanism in human history. (See Figure 9–7.) The king is obeyed because he is the king, or because he is a representative of God, or, as in ancient Egypt, because he *is* god, or at least because the people think so. As St. Paul put it: "Let everyone submit himself to the ruling authorities, for there exists no authority not ordained by God."[17] Response is quasi-automatic, almost unconscious, the kind of habitual obedience that is the intent of close-order drill learned during the first weeks in military training. Tradition may start out as mainly fear, but the response becomes institutionalized and internalized into the class structure and the ideology of the society. One responds out of respect for one's betters or because there is some natural social order that is customary and believed "right." Adolph Eichmann, the notorious Nazi, obeyed because it was his job and because his culture had trained him to respond to authoritarian directives without question.[18]

Responding to traditional authority is not simply habit, of course. In the U.S. Marines, tradition draws on the follower's internalized sense of responsibility to all those who fought at Tripoli, on Tarawa, or in Vietnam; the young recruit is part of them, and he would feel guilty if he did not do his duty and obey. Thus the great advantage of a tradition-based influence system is that it offers positive motivation instead of the negative orientation of fear. It says, in effect, respect authority, be obedient, and do what you're told—and if you do, you will be rewarded with acceptance into the community. Such acceptance may bring profoundly warm and satisfying feelings of security and affiliation.

The submergence of self into the group for short periods of time—during games, while singing in a choir, marching in a protest demonstration, even at times in military drill—is attractive to most people. A traditional, ascriptive society may extend this to all existence. It can offer the greatest degree of certainty that is possible in human society because it specifies who has authority, defines each person's obligations, and relieves most people of much onerous decision making. In effect, a tradition-based system can perpetuate childhood, a state attractive to many.[19] For such people, the influence mechanism is not even perceived as imposed; it is absorbed

FIGURE 9–7

Influence through Tradition

Follower Internalizes Leader's Values

↑

Appeals to Follower's Safety, Security, and Affiliative Needs

↑

Influence through Tradition

↑

Draws on Authoritarian Leader's Reward and Legitimate Power

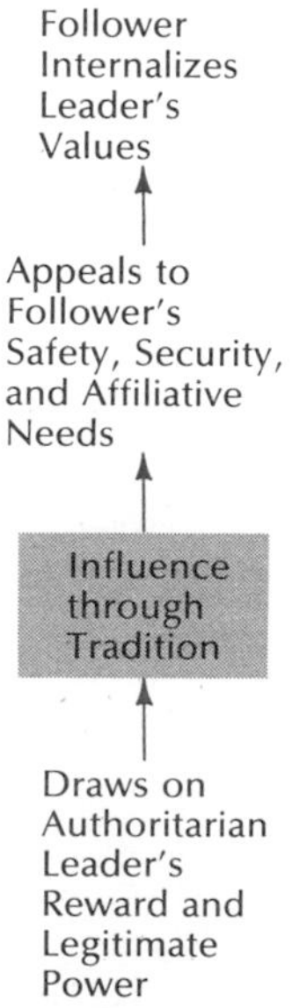

and integrated into their personalities so thoroughly that they feel they are exercising free choice. Influence and control are highest when they are least apparent.

Tradition as the basis for obedience was commonly assumed in 19th-century management literature, when a firm's management structure was closely allied with the class structure of the society.[20] It was assumed that "inferiors" should and would respond to "betters." At first, those higher up were assigned certain obligations for the well-being of people lower down, but this ethic was gradually dropped, to be replaced by a philosophy of survival of the "fittest" in which success in climbing the social and organizational ladder was rewarded with decreased social responsibility. Yet the assumption of obedience remained: Inferiors should respond to their superiors. The manager should create esprit de corps, but fundamentally the subordinates should respond because that is their place. Under this influence system, as with fear, it makes no difference whether or not the follower understands the reason for the directive or agrees with it, and he or she certainly has not participated in formulating the directive.

Although we Americans like to think of ourselves as egalitarian, we do have many superior-subordinate relationships that attempt to program obedience: parent-child, teacher-student, employer-employee. (See Figure 9–8.) All have in common some traditional feeling that within certain limits the subordinate will respond to the superior's suggestions. Nicolai Lenin observed at the beginning of Communist rule in the Soviet Union in 1918 that the Russian economy was built upon fear and that this had grave defects. What the new Russia required, according to Lenin, was "Soviet Americanism." What Lenin meant by this was that American workers tended to do what they were told at work and to labor consistently without being policed.[21] In 1938, the president of a large American corporation observed that the average workers in this country expected to do what they were told, within certain limits—what was termed a *zone of indifference.*[22] The limits of that zone have probably narrowed in the past 40 years, however. We are less willing to respond automatically to authority and do what we are told than we once were.

FIGURE 9–8

How Do First-Level Managers Exercise Influence?

The use of influence has shifted from administrative and technical competence to competence in interpersonal and group relations. First-level managers can:

Use positive reinforcement in the form of incentive schemes, job redesign, and awareness of psychological needs, including peer group acceptance and pride.

Try negative reinforcement—both the traditional type (write up, fire, suspend) and more indirect means (job reassignment, job redesign, forced overtime).

Delegate the resolution of a sticky problem to a shop steward or another union official.

Appeal to workers for support on the basis of having gone out on a limb for them or having given over some prerogative to them in the past.

Appeal to workers on the basis of understanding their position, since many first-level supervisors once stood in their shoes.

Appeal to workers on the basis of previously agreed-on goals and plans for achieving them.

Source: W. E. Sasser and F. S. Leonard, "Let First-Level Supervisors Do Their Job," *Harvard Business Review,* March–April 1980, pp. 113–21.

Reprinted by permission of the Chicago Tribune-New York News Syndicate.

A decline in respect for authority in American society may be reflected in decline in response to an authority figure just because he or she is an authority figure.[23]

Note that in the traditional system the follower responds to the leader's position. In the army the officer is identified by uniform and insignia. The soldier obeys the order, regardless of the personal characteristics of the officer issuing the directive, because he or she respects the position of the officer. Whether the officer is tall or short, fat or thin, black or white, man or woman is irrelevant; the follower responds to the position, not the person. This impersonality of influence and its associated stability and predictability constitute the great advantages of tradition as a means of influence.

Influence through Blind Faith

Influence on the basis of blind faith reflects a kind of Alexander the Great or Napoleon syndrome. We respond to the great leader who has "charisma."[24] To the ancients, charisma was a gift of God, a gift of grace, or magical powers that were given to a few favored humans. Only fools would not respond to the charismatic leader. But what is the charismatic leader to us today? Haven't we outgrown the ignorance and superstition of earlier blind followers? Or has the source of power shifted from magic to psychology? (See Figure 9-9.)

People tend to respond to the leader who has characteristics they admire, to the person who is a super model of what they would like to be. Perhaps most fundamentally, they respond out of strong emotional attachment, even love for the leader in whom they have blind faith. The relationship is personal rather than general, for charisma is not simply an attribute of the leader but the fit between his or her characteristics and the follower's needs. Lawrence of Arabia possessed charisma for the Arabs in World War I, but his dramatic, stylistic behavior offered no appeal to postwar Britons who did not support him in his political bid.[25] In contrast, Winston Churchill's brand of charisma was not felt until the country faced extinction; then his personal attributes matched the people's concerns. These characteristics became less relevant to voters with the end of the European war in 1945, when his government was quickly voted out of power.

Seventy years ago management literature indicated that one was born either a

FIGURE 9-9

Influence through Blind Faith

Follower Identifies with Leader

↑

Appeals to Follower's Affiliative and Esteem Needs

↑

Influence through Blind Faith

↑

Draws on Authoritarian Leader's Referent Power

manager or a follower. Either one had natural leadership abilities, or one did not. We have less belief in this argument today because charismatic natural leaders seem all too rare. They do exist in business, but we cannot depend on their being in abundant supply; business and government require more managers than charisma can supply. We now believe that many people can develop into effective managers through education and experience. Indeed, in highly structured bureaucracies, personal charisma might even be a handicap in getting ahead. Nonetheless, business still seems to want some attributes associated with "natural leadership" and "command presence"—witness a finding at one university that corporations hired men over six feet tall for $1,000 per year more than they hired graduates under that magic height![26]

Fear, Tradition, and Blind Faith as Authoritarian Leadership

Whenever the attempt to influence is based on fear, tradition, or blind faith and draws on coercive, reward, legitimate, or referent power, the influence process is essentially authoritarian. The leader tells the followers to do something; the followers respond because they fear being punished, they want the reward, they feel a responsibility to obey, or they love the leader and believe in his or her abilities. In all four instances the process is essentially a one-way authoritarian communication to which followers respond without questioning whether or not specific directives are appropriate to the task. They neither understand the reasons for the order nor agree with it.

Influence through faith is more limited than the other authoritarian forms, however. The charismatic leaders' powers are partially dependent on performance. If they and their followers experience a series of failures, the leaders' charisma and referent power will fade.

Charismatic leaders influence people through personality, not position. Therefore, these leaders endeavor to bring themselves in direct interaction with many people throughout the organization. They bypass various levels of management because they want to tie people to themselves, not to lieutenants. Franklin D. Roosevelt was often criticized as being a poor manager because his assignment of duties was sloppy and he evidenced little respect for the structure of government. He would personally contact people throughout the system and give them projects, unknown to their peers or superiors.[27] He cultivated individual, personalized relationships, not organizational, impersonal positions. General Robert Johnson, of Johnson & Johnson demonstrated quite similar behavior. He would descend by helicopter on his plants unannounced, bypass the resident manager in charge, and move directly to individuals at various levels, whom he cultivated personally. Such behavior can be upsetting to organizationally minded people, but it can create a sense of identification with the top and willingness to sacrifice for the company that can be very powerful.

The Predisposition to Obey

We have implied that the followers' response to the authoritarian leader's power is generally rational in that it reflects the followers' belief that obedience serves their interest in avoiding pain, sustaining life, remaining a member, and so on. Another theory maintains that fear, tradition, and blind faith all draw upon a nonrational power phenomenon.[28] Many people are characterized by a predisposition to submission. Whether this is instinctual or learned behavior is not clear. Is it derived from the ancient experience of the species, going back to the primeval dominance of the tyrant ape, or does it reflect contemporary child-rearing patterns?[29] The essential argument, however, is that most people make an automatic, unconscious, and hypnoticlike response to dominators just because they are dominant. Certain rituals, symbols, and tones of voice reinforce the dominator and cue inhibiting forces, which supposedly block out parts of rational thought that might interfere with automatic responses. Support for this view is found in disturbing research in which a majority of people administered what they thought to be extremely painful electrical shocks to a stranger merely because a scientist said it was part of an experiment.[30] Their rationality, judgment, humanity, and ethical sense seemed overwhelmed in the face of expert power.

Influence through Rational Faith

If we could count the number of influence incidents in modern organizations, especially among managers and professionals, the most common influence process probably would be rational faith.[31] The followers respond because they believe the leader knows what she or he is talking about, based upon some evidence of knowledge and ability. (See Figure 9–10.) This is similar to our relationship with a physician. We can reach a somewhat rational judgment that the physician is qualified from the diplomas, license, and certificates on the office wall. It is even possible to learn about the quality of a physician's medical school and hospital residency. We can ask friends about their experience with him or her. In general, then, we can make a rather rational decision that the physician is knowledgeable and wants to serve us. Nonetheless, however rational the decision about the person, the response to specific suggestions is pretty much on faith. We cannot even read the doctor's handwriting on the prescription form, much less know precisely how the prescribed medicine will help us. In most cases we must just accept it.

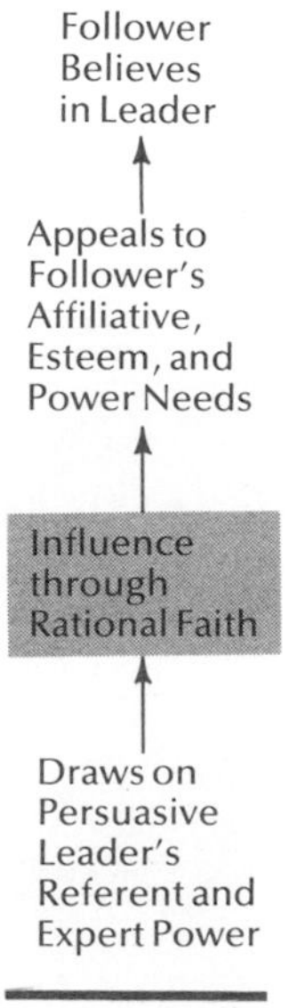

For a business example of this process, consider the following incident: A young staff specialist is hired to provide expertise to a number of production managers. Initially, the only influence process available to the specialist is persuasion—gaining the rational agreement of the managers. To be effective the specialist prepares elaborate, clear presentations, even rehearsing with a colleague to anticipate any questions. By data, logic, and argument, the specialist attempts to gain the agreement of superiors. After a year of this kind of relationship, one day she goes to talk with one of the managers. An hour has been reserved for the presentation. She arrives and begins her pitch. After a couple of minutes, however, the busy manager interrupts: "I'm just too busy to go over this. *We'll do whatever you want to do.*"

The manager is being rational but is also acting on faith. The rationality is based on prior experience with the specialist; the staff members track record is good. Past advice has helped the production department, so the manager makes the rational judgment that the young specialist is competent and concerned. Nonetheless, in

FIGURE 9–10

Influence through Rational Faith

Follower Believes in Leader

↑

Appeals to Follower's Affiliative, Esteem, and Power Needs

↑

Influence through Rational Faith

↑

Draws on Persuasive Leader's Referent and Expert Power

accepting the latest proposal without detailed examination, the manager is acting on faith that it is as good as previous ones have been.

Influence through Persuasion

FIGURE 9–11

Influence through
Persuasion and
Agreement

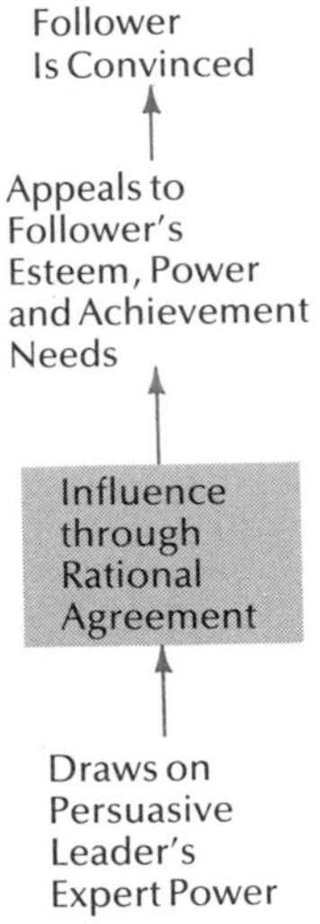

Follower
Is Convinced

↑

Appeals to
Follower's
Esteem, Power
and Achievement
Needs

↑

Influence
through
Rational
Agreement

↑

Draws on
Persuasive
Leader's
Expert Power

A follower may obey because he or she understands the reason the action is necessary and agrees that it is the proper thing to do. (See Figure 9–11.) The leader has been persuasive, able to explain rationally why an activity must be performed. Obviously, this process consumes more time than any of the influence means discussed so far. The explanations imply substantial discussion and even two-day conversations in contrast to the one-way broadcasts characterizing fear, tradition, and faith.

In trying to convince or persuade the follower, a leader is paying a compliment to the follower, saying in effect, "I think you have the ability and the knowledge to understand what I am asking, and I respect you enough to take the time to explain." Thus the follower may feel that she is being treated in a somewhat more adult manner; at least her needs for esteem and competence are appealed to.

Much of the time, a charismatic leader will draw on referent and expert power to persuade followers rather than ordering them. As a result, the followers will tend to feel that they share in the leader's power rather than being dominated by it. Success reinforces power, and people respond out of rational and blind faith. Winston Churchill motivated his people because he persuasively articulated the challenge facing the nation and successfully built on their faith and respect for him.

Conditions for Effective Persuasion

Not many possess Churchill's personality, but persuasive leadership may be the only option for a potential influencer who has no other power but his or her own expertise. Armed with knowledge, the influencer attempts to convince others to follow the advice. Research suggests that persuasion will be more effective under the following conditions:[32]

1. If the influencer has high credibility based on perceived expertise and trustworthiness.[33]
2. If the influencer initially expresses some views that are also held by the audience or potential followers.
3. If the information is perceived as privileged for a few, when large numbers want to hear it.[34]
4. If the influencer's personal appearance and characteristics please or at least do not offend the audience.
5. If the followers have recently responded on a smaller but similar matter.[35]
6. If one side of the argument is presented when the audience is generally friendly or when the influencer's position is the only one that will be presented.
7. If both sides of the argument are presented when the audience starts out disagreeing or when it is probable that they will hear the other side from someone else.

8. Up to an indefinite limit, the more extreme the change the influencer asks for, the more actual change he or she is likely to get.

9. When opposite views are presented one after another, the one presented last will probably be more effective.

10. There will probably be more opinion change in the desired direction if the influencer explicitly states conclusions rather than letting the audience draw its own. If the audience is quite intelligent, however, their implicit conclusion drawing is likely to be better.

11. Appeal to fear will frequently work if the influencer advances explicit, plausible recommendations for action. But, if she or he makes no such recommendations, the appeal to fear may be rejected.

12. Audience participation through group discussion and decision making helps to overcome resistance. Having members of the audience state the espoused views is likely to increase their adoption of them.[36]

13. The support of just one of two others can overcome the majority's initial resistance if the minority is consistent in expressing certainty.

The Shift from Persuasion to Blind Faith

There are no consistent findings on whether emotional or rational appeals are more effective. It depends on the kind of audience and its state at the time. In general, however, people are more easily persuaded when their self-esteem is low. If the persuader accumulates success, however, his or her influence may shift from rational agreement to rational faith. The widespread existence of this influence style even at high management levels is well illustrated by the words of President Harry S. Truman:

> And people talk about the powers of a President, all the powers that a Chief Executive has, and what he can do. Let me tell you something—from experience!
>
> The President may have a great many powers given to him in the Constitution and may have certain powers under certain laws which are given to him by the Congress of the United States; but the principal power that the President has is to bring people in and try to persuade them to do what they ought to do without persuasion. That's what I spend most of my time doing. That's what the powers of the President amount to.[37]

SUMMARY

Influence is the central dimension in managerial leadership. In general, individuals can be influenced when they believe that their needs will be fulfilled by their response. Influence through fear, tradition, or blind faith is essentially authoritarian leadership, which has been effective and common in the past. It requires the leader to possess either coercive, reward, legitimate, or referent power. Rational faith and rational agreement draw on the leader's referent and expert power so that he or she can exercise persuasive leadership. Joint determination and participative leadership shift the focus from the leader's to the follower's power and goals, to draw on their higher level needs.

Note that we have not said that any one basis of influence or power is better than another. Fear, tradition, and faith have the great advantage of being quick; the follower should respond immediately to a curt directive. Nonetheless they have drawbacks:

1. Fear is offensive to many, and it can be expensive to maintain the police mechanism that is necessary.
2. Tradition may suffer because of declining respect for positional authority.
3. Faith suffers from the drawback that people who can generate this emotional response are rare.

Influencing through attaining the follower's rational agreement has attractions; but it is time-consuming, and the leader is not always sure of having the right reasons or being able to explain it in a rational way. The leader may simply feel that something must be done, and this feeling is difficult to convey. Participation in decision making is also very

time-consuming, and what is attractive to one follower is not always attractive to everyone. Some people will not want to take the time to participate in solving what they see as the leader's problems.

Influence is a problematic process, not a matter of certainty. No manager can be certain that he or she will succeed in influencing others' behavior. Whether a particular leadership style will be effective depends upon the follower's estimate of several probabilities, which may be expressed by the following questions:

1. Can I do what the leader desires?
2. Will the influencer reward or punish me?
3. Will this satisfy or frustrate any of my needs?
4. How important are these needs in comparison to other alternatives?

All influence processes are logical and may be effective if potential followers perceive their behavior as reaching goals that satisfy fundamental needs. Actual leadership effectiveness will depend on the mesh between the style, people, and situation—a matter to be examined in the remaining chapters of this part.

REVIEW QUESTIONS

1. What are the bases of an influencer-leader's power?
2. What is coercive power?
3. What is reward power?
4. What are the basic elements in the general influence model using coercive and reward power?
5. What probability estimates does a prospective follower make when responding to an influencer?
6. What conditions undermine influence utilizing coercive and reward power?
7. What conditions facilitate influence utilizing coercive and reward power?
8. What is the path-goal relationship? Why should a manager make it clear?
9. What is legitimate power?
10. What is referent power?
11. What is expert power?
12. Why is it necessary to understand the follower in order to understand leadership?
13. What are the major reasons a follower follows?
14. Why is fear so attractive to managers as an influence technique?
15. What are the managerial drawbacks of fear?
16. What is tradition as a basis of influence?
17. What is the advantage of tradition over fear?
18. What is the relation between tradition as an influence mechanism and a culture's respect for authority?

19. What is blind faith as a basis of influence?

20. What is charisma, and how does a person get it?

21. What is the major difference between traditional and blind faith leadership?

22. What is rational faith as a basis for influence? What is rational? What is faith?

23. What is rational agreement as a basis for influence?

24. What factors increase an influencer's persuasiveness?

Notes and References on Sources of Power and Influence

1. According to Amitai Etzioni, "Power is an actor's ability to induce or influence another actor to carry out his directives or any other norms he supports. . . . A person may be said to have power to the extent that he influences the behavior of others in accordance with his own intentions." *Comparative Analysis of Complex Organizations* (New York: Free Press, 1961). W. J. Goode argues that the term *power* is too ambiguous. He distinguishes between four influence systems: force, prestige, wealth, and love. "The Place of Force in Human Society," *American Sociological Review* 37, no. 5 (1972), pp. 507–19.

For a sense of the confusion about such terms as *authority, power,* and *influence,* see R. L. Peabody, *Organizational Authority* (New York: Atherton Press, 1964); C. J. Friedrich, ed., *Authority* (Cambridge, Mass.: Harvard University Press, 1958); R. Martin, *The Sociology of Power* (London: Routledge & Kegan Paul, 1977).

2. J. R. P. French and B. H. Raven, "The Bases of Social Power," from Dorwin Cartwright, ed., *Studies in Social Power* (Ann Arbor: University of Michigan Press, 1959).

In a study of a manufacturing firm, the various power bases ranged in order from least effective to most effective as follows:

most effective	Referent power
↑	Expert power
	Reward power
↓	Coercive power
least effective	Legitimate power

K. R. Student, "Supervisory Influence and Work Group Performance," *Journal of Applied Psychology* 52 (1968), pp. 188–94.

Etzioni distinguishes between three kinds of involvement of people in organizations: (1) alienative involvement, where fear and dislike of the influence are strong; (2) moral involvement, where intensive and emotional commitment stems from internalization of values and identification with the leaders; and (3) calculative involvement, where people conform only when it is in their interest. *Comparative Analysis of Complex Organizations.*

Rensis Likert distinguishes between four systems of management: (1) authoritative, (2) benevolent authoritative, (3) consultative, and (4) participative group. *New Patterns of Management* (New York: McGraw-Hill, 1961), and *The Human Organization* (New York: McGraw-Hill, 1967).

For a thorough discussion of this and other issues related to power, see J. Pfeffer, *Power in Organizations* (Marshfield, Mass.: Pitman, 1982).

For other books on power and influence, see Peter M. Blau, *Exchange and Power in Social Life* (New York: John Wiley & Sons, 1964); J. T. Tedeschi, ed., *Social Influence Processes* (Hawthorne, N.Y.: Aldine Publishing, 1972); L. Wheeler, *Interpersonal Influence* (Boston: Allyn & Bacon, 1974), and P. G. Swingle, *The Management of Power* (New York: John Wiley & Sons, 1976).

See also, V. E. Schein, "Individual Power and Political Behaviors in Organizations: An Inadequately Explored Reality," *Academy of Management Journal,* January 1977, pp. 64–72. A technique of inventorying a leader's power is given in J. A. Lee, "Leader Power for Managing Change," *Academy of Management Review,* January 1977, pp. 73–80.

3. It is the follower's perception of the relationship that is critical. Likert observes, "An individual's reaction to any situation is always a function not of the absolute character of the intervention, but of his perception of it. It is how he sees things that counts, not objective reality." "A Motivational Approach to the Modified Theory of Organization and Management," in Mason Haire, Jr., ed., *Modern Organization Theory* (New York: John Wiley & Sons, 1959), p. 161.

4. The probabilistic influence model is a combination of Atkinson's and Vroom's motivation models. It is usually called "expectancy" or "instrumentality" theory. The basic idea is that:

$$\frac{\text{Motivation}}{\text{or effort}} = \frac{\text{Reward expectation} \times}{\text{Instrumentality} \times \text{Valence}}$$

where instrumentality is the relationship between the reward and need satisfaction, and valence is the relative importance of the need. See J. W. Atkinson, *An Introduction to Motivation* (New York: Van Nostrand Reinhold, 1964), and V. Vroom, *Work and Motivation* (New York: John Wiley & Sons, 1964). For various explanations and tests of expectancy theory, see Jay Galbraith and L. L. Cummings, "An Empirical Investigation of the Motivational Determinants of Task Performance: Interactive Effects between Instrumentality-Valence and Motivation-Ability," *Organizational Behavior and Human Performance* 2, no. 3 (1967), pp. 327–57; George Graen, "Instrumentality Theory of Work Motivation: Some Experimental Results and Suggested Modifications," *Journal of Applied Psychology Monograph,* April 1969, Part 2; R. D. Arvey, "Task Performance as a Function of Perceived Effort-Performance-Reward Contingencies," *Organizational Behavior and Human Performance* 8 (1972), pp. 423–33; H. G. Heneman III and D. P. Schwab, "An Evaluation of Research on Expectancy Theory Predictions of Employee Performance," *Psychological Bulletin* 78 (1972), pp. 1–9; H. P. Dachler and W. H. Mobley, "Construct Validation of an Instrumentality-Expectancy-Task-Goal Model of Work Motivation: Some Theoretical Boundary Conditions," *Journal of Applied Psychology* 58, no. 3 (1973), pp. 397–418; and E. E. Lawler III and J. L. Suttle, "Expectancy Theory and Job Behavior," *Organizational Behavior and Human Performance* 9 (1973), pp. 482–503.

Expectancy theory assumes human rationality. Some maintain, however, that people cannot compare alternatives very well, that estimates of probability are not independent of desirability (we tend to attribute higher probability to things we want to happen), and that we do not optimize, we satisfice. O. Behling and F. A. Starke, "The Postulates of Expectancy Theory," *Academy of Management Journal,* September 1973), pp. 373–88.

F. Petrock and V. Gamboa show that this expectancy theory is very close to operant conditioning even though they originate in different schools of behavioral science. "Expectancy Theory and Operant Conditioning: A Conceptual Comparison," in W. R. Nord, ed., *Concepts and Controversy in Organizational Behavior* (Pacific Palisades, Calif.: Goodyear Publishing, 1976), pp. 175–87.

5. D. E. Berlyne and K. B. Madsen, eds., *Pleasure, Reward, Preference* (New York: Academic Press, 1973).

6. J. Z. Rubin and R. J. Lewicki, "A Three-Factor Experimental Analysis of Promises and Threats," *Journal of Applied Social Psychology* 3, no. 3 (1973), pp. 240–57.

7. On the concept of "path-goal," see R. J. House, "A Path-Goal Theory of Leader Effectiveness," *Administrative Science Quarterly* 16, no. 3 (1971), pp. 321–38; and B. S. Georgopoulos, G. M. Mahoney, and N. W. Jones, "A Path-Goal Approach to Productivity," *Journal of Applied Psychology* 41 (1957), pp. 345–53.

8. A study of discipline in the same industry in the 1830s and 1970s suggests little change in the use of fear. C. Gersuny, "A Devil in Petticoats and Just Cause: Patterns of Punishment in Two New England Textile Factories," *Business History Review,* Summer 1976, pp. 131–52.

9. W. H. Rogers discusses the use of fear in *Think: A History of IBM and the Watsons* (New York: Stein & Day, 1969).

A study of the advertising industry suggests that management's sensitivity to fear depends upon age and career stage. Little fear exists at low levels because pay is relatively poor and changing jobs is an accepted practice. Being dismissed is not a serious blot on a young account executive's record. However, when managers and professionals reach 30 to 45 years old, a period of rising earnings and expenses, they become anxious and receptive to motivation through fear. They are locked in because it is unlikely that they could move to new positions with equal pay and because their lifestyles are dependent on substantial income. In time, some manage to save enough so that the power of fear declines. An executive who lasts in advertising until age 45 or so probably has accumulated sufficient capital to be able to work elsewhere for less money. In the past, some dismissed or disillusioned older advertising professionals went into teaching. The modest salary, along with their substantial savings, enabled them to maintain their homes in suburbia without too much sacrifice. Such financial and job mobility is, of course, affected by general economic conditions and position opportunities. J. Bensman, *Money and Sense* (New York: Macmillan, 1967).

Perhaps the most dramatic reversal in the use of fear

took place in the U.S. Army. The "new" army attempted to improve life for enlisted personnel, preparatory to converting to an all-volunteer basis. The use of threats and punishments by officers was discouraged. Yet, in Vietnam, in the late 1960s and early 1970s, enlisted men in substantial numbers utilized fear as a control mechanism to keep their *superiors* in line. Threats of violence and some actual "fraggings" (rolling an activated hand grenade under the officer's bunk) all but reversed the balance of power and fear in the field. An army judge argued that once intimidated by even the threat of fragging, an officer is useless to the military because the officer can no longer carry out the orders essential to the function of a field force. Through intimidation and scare stories, fragging is influential to the point that virtually all officers had to take into account the possibility of retaliation before issuing an order to their men. S. Linden, "The Demoralization of an Army," *Saturday Review,* January 8, 1972, p. 12 ff.

10.   Albert Speer, *Inside the Third Reich* (New York: Macmillan, 1970). R. K. Aufhauser maintains that the on-the-job management of slaves in the Old South anticipated and was essentially the same as later "scientific management." Routine tasks and coercion were supposedly similar. "Slavery and Scientific Management," *The Journal of Economic History* 33, no. 4 (1973), pp. 811–24.

11.   E. Kogan, *Der SS Staat* (Bermann-Fischer, 1947) cited in R. Bendix, *Work and Authority in Industry* (New York: John Wiley & Sons, 1956).

12.   J. Horai and J. T. Tedeschi, "Effects of Credibility and Magnitude and Punishment on Compliance to Threats," *Journal of Personality and Social Psychology* 12 (1969), pp. 164–69; S. A. Kaplowitz, "An Experimental Test of a Rationalistic Theory of Deterrence," *Journal of Conflict Resolution* 17, no. 3 (1973), pp. 535–72.

13.   B. A. Campbell and R. M. Church, eds., *Punishment and Aversive Behavior* (New York: Appleton-Century-Crofts, 1969).

14.   H. Wiard, "Why Manage Behavior? A Case for Positive Reinforcement," *Human Resource Management,* Summer 1972, pp. 15–20.

15.   R. T. Keller and A. D. Szilagyi, "Employee Reactions to Leader Reward Behavior," *Academy of Management Journal,* December 1976, pp. 619–26.

16.   S. Kerr, "On the Folly of Rewarding A, While Hoping for B," *Academy of Management Review,* December 1975, pp. 769–83.

17.   Romans 13:1.

18.   H. Arendt, *Eichmann in Jerusalem* (New York: Viking Press, 1963).

19.   Erich Fromm, *Escape from Freedom* (New York: Farrar Rinehart, 1941).

20.   Henri Fayol, *General and Industrial Management* (London: Pitman & Sons, 1949), and Vroom, *Work and Motivation.*

21.   Bendix, *Work and Authority in Modern Industry;* I. R. Levine, *The New Worker in Soviet Russia* (New York: Macmillan, 1973); and V. Andele, *Management Power in the Soviet Union* (Lexington, Mass.: Lexington Books, 1976).

22.   Chester I. Barnard, *The Functions of the Executive* (Cambridge, Mass.: Harvard University Press, 1938).

23.   Louis Harris. A poll comparing public respect for the leadership of major American institutions in 1966 and 1971 demonstrated significant declines in just five years. *Philadelphia Inquirer,* October 25, 1971. In the United States it appears that intellectuals are in conflict with tradition. S. N. Eisenstadt, "Intellectuals and Traditions," *Daedalus* 101 (1972), pp. 1–19.

24.   Max Weber described charisma in *The Theory of Social and Economic Organization* (New York: Free Press, 1964). See also E. F. Borgatta et al., "Some Findings Relevant to a Great Man Theory of Leadership," *American Sociological Review* 29 (1954), pp. 755–59; D. Bryne, *The Attraction Paradigm* (New York: Academic Press, 1971); and T. L. Hudson, ed., *Perspectives on Interpersonal Attraction* (New York: Academic Press, 1973).

25.   On Lawrence of Arabia, see J. E. Mack, *A Prince of Our Disorder: The Life of T. E. Lawrence* (Boston: Little, Brown, 1976). Lawrence was famous for heroism, but people who knew him remember him mainly for his kindness, generosity and ability to spread cheer.

26.   A half-humorous, half-cynical description of how to obtain power is contained in M. Korda, *Power* (New York: Random House, 1976). A more serious discussion of something similar is contained in J. P. Kotter, "Power, Dependence, and Effective Management," *Harvard Business Review,* July–August 1977, pp. 125–36.

27.   Arthur Schlesinger, Jr., *The Coming of the New Deal* (Boston: Houghton Mifflin, 1959).

28.   N. S. Timasheff, "The Power Phenomenon," *American Sociological Review,* August 1938, pp. 499–509.

29.   Desmond Morris, *The Naked Ape* (New York:

McGraw-Hill, 1966); Erik H. Erikson, *Childhood and Society* (New York: W. W. Norton, 1950).

30. Stanley Milgram, *Obedience to Authority* (New York: Harper & Row, 1974).

31. Trends in authority patterns and the growing importance of "willingness to serve" as a basis of authority are discussed in R. Albanese, "Criteria for Evaluating Authority Patterns," *Academy of Management Journal,* March 1973, pp. 102–11.

For a different perspective on the use of influence in management, see D. Kipnis, S. M. Schmidt, C. Swaffin-Smith, and I. Wilkinson, "Patterns of Managerial Influence: Shotgun Managers, Tacticians, and Bystanders," *Organizational Dynamics,* Winter 1984, pp. 58–67.

32. Research on persuasion is summarized by P. G. Zimbardo and E. B. Ebbesen, *Influencing Attitudes and Changing Behavior* (Reading, Mass.: Addison-Wesley, 1969). See also G. R. Miller and M. Burgoon, *New Techniques of Persuasion* (New York: Harper & Row, 1973), and R. L. Applebaum and K. W. E. Anatol, *Strategies for Persuasive Communication* (Columbus, Ohio: Charles E. Merrill Publishing, 1974).

33. For many years there has been a belief in the "sleeper effect," by which the audience conceivably would in time forget the poor credibility of a distrusted persuader and eventually come to believe the message, after initial rejection of it. This has recently been quite strongly disproved for most people. See N. Capon and J. Hulbert "The Sleeper Effect: An Awakening," *The Public Opinion Quarterly* 37, no. 3 (1973), pp. 339–58 and P. M. Gillig and A. G. Greenwald, "Is It Time to Lay the Sleeper Effect to Rest?" *Journal of Personality and Social Psychology* 29, no. 1 (1974), pp. 132–39.

34. H. L. Fromkin and T. C. Brock, "A Commodity Theory Analysis of Persuasion," *Representatives Research in Social Psychology* 2 (1971), pp. 653–54.

35. J. L. Freedman and S. C. Fraser, "Compliance without Pressure: The Foot-in-the-Door Technique," *Journal of Personality and Social Psychology* 4 (1966), pp. 195–202; P. Pliner et al., "Compliance without Pressure: Some Further Data on the Foot-in-the-Door Technique," *Journal of Experimental Social Psychology* 10 (1974), pp. 17–22.

36. R. N. Widgery and G. R. Miller, "Attitude Change Following Counterattitudinal Advocacy: Support for the Adverse Consequences Interpretation of Dissonance Theory," *The Journal of Communication,* September 1973, pp. 306–14.

37. Quoted in Clinton Rossiter, *The American Presidency* (New York: Harcourt Brace Jovanovich, 1956). See also L. W. Koenig, *The Chief Executive,* 3d ed. (New York: Harcourt Brace Jovanovich, 1975).

10

Leadership Styles

If a scientist places a pigeon in a cage with a feeding mechanism activated by a red button, the hungry bird will peck in various places in the cage. When the bird accidentally pecks a red button, the scientist reinforces the behavior by giving a piece of corn. When the pigeon pecks the red button again, he again receives corn, and so on. Soon the pigeon will peck the button repeatedly. The scientist is training and controlling the pigeon, but the pigeon is also controlling the researcher. All the bird has to do is peck a button, and the scientist gives him food. In this operation, what is cause and what is effect?[1]*

Reprinted by permission: Tribune Company Syndicate, Inc.

The Interdependence of Leader and Follower

Thus influence is reciprocal.[2] To control, one must be controlled to some extent; that is, the influencer must be influenced. The fear-dispensing dictator *must* punish insubordination or lose all credibility—others' belief that the dictator will respond to the offense.[3] Similarly, a tradition-based system will collapse unless it provides its loyal, obedient supporters with warmth and security. Charismatic leaders expecting blind faith must respond to certain follower demands. Basically, they must give of themselves; they must allow their followers to see them, hear them, touch them. Every influence mechanism and every leader thus implies two-way influence, some mutual control.[4]

This mutuality has an important implication: influence is expandable. It is not a fixed pie that can only be divided; it is not a zero-sum game requiring a manager to lose influence when a subordinate gains. Both may gain increased influence as they mutually benefit from a relationship. Influence downward may be enhanced rather than reduced by upward influence.[5] Both managers and workers in more effective organizations perceive themselves as possessing greater influence. The greater the total influence everyone has in the system, the greater seems to be the total system effectiveness.[6]

---

* Notes and references will be found at the end of this chapter.

FIGURE 10–1

Influence through Representation

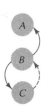

B's influence on C seems to be greater if C perceives B as having influence over A.

Influence through Representation and Joint Determination

The vehicle for generating this greater influence is mainly through joint determination and participative leadership drawing on expert and representative power. (See Figures 10–1 and 10–2.) A follower who has participated in determining what is to be done will probably understand the decision and agree that a certain course of action is necessary and proper. In this participation the follower's higher level needs are involved. He or she exercises some power and has an opportunity to be heard and exercise abilities. Voluntary implementation should result from this participation and determination.

Participative leadership moves beyond the leader's power to recognize the follower's power. Their expertise is solicited and combined with the leader's so that decisions are jointly reached. It is hoped that their higher level needs are energized through the joint-determination process.

Most practicing managers are not enthusiastic about participative leadership because it is difficult to apply and they fear losing power. In addition, this influence style can be very time-consuming. Nonetheless, strong arguments have been advanced against older authoritarian styles (sometimes referred to as Theory X) in favor of more participative approaches (Theory Y).[7]

The Debate between Authoritarian and Participative Leadership

FIGURE 10–2

Influence through Joint Determination

Follower
Believes
in Process

↑

Appeals to
Follower's
Power, Competence,
and Achievement
Needs

↑

Influence
through
Joint
Determination

↑

Draws on
Participative
Leader's and
Follower's Expert
Power
and Representative
Power

To facilitate comparison of the various points, they are arranged in parallel as follows:

Arguments for Authoritarian Appeal to Lower Level Needs

1. Authoritarian is the most predictable and effective style because everyone has physiological, safety, and security needs that most can satisfy only through money earned from a job.

2. Much work is unpleasant and many people are lazy. More or less, these conditions will always prevail, so authoritarian leadership is essential. Otherwise, most people will do as little as possible.

3. Authoritarian leadership is efficient because it is speedy; the superior simply tells the subordinate what to do, so no time is wasted in discussion. Too much concern for employees will only cripple managers, rendering them incapable of making tough decisions.[8]

Arguments for Participative Appeal to Higher Level Needs

1. All people may possess lower needs, but they are not necessarily dependent on any one job to satisfy them. They may have skills that are in such demand that they have alternatives available, some of which may satisfy both lower and higher needs. Increasingly, mobile employees will move to these jobs.

2. Most people are not inherently lazy. The expenditure of physical and mental effort in work is as natural as play or rest. We are energetic and are excited by challenging and satisfying tasks. Frustrating work can be modified to release talent and drive; the job can be a vehicle for satisfying competence and achievement needs.

3. Nondirective leadership can lead to more creative and effective performance because people invest more of themselves in the task. They will exercise self-direction and self-control in the service to which they are committed. When people participate in defining organizational objectives and the system by which their performance is evaluated, they understand better and are more committed.[9]

4. Authoritarian leadership is easier for most managers. They do not have to analyze the various needs of their subordinates because they assume a simple model of human nature—that people have low-level needs and must keep their jobs to satisfy them. This assumption of subordinate uniformity of physiological and security needs makes this style especially effective for a large number of people. In addition, most managers' personalities are better suited to being "mature autocrats" rather than democratic leaders.[10]

5. Authoritarian leadership is honest and straightforward: the superior (a) defines the desired behavior, (b) states the rewards and punishments, (c) judges the subordinates' performance and dispenses the sanctions, (d) does not meddle with subordinates' personality, analyze their motives, or judge their lives. This frank approach is attractive to many who distrust the indirection of other leadership styles.

6. Most subordinates expect superiors to be authoritarian; that is the way they have been raised and educated. A superior's departure from this expectation may be interpreted as weakness, and subordinates may walk all over the superior.

4. An increasing general educational level means that more people understand human complexities and desires for satisfaction of higher level needs. The average manager or worker possesses more education than in the days when authoritarian leadership styles were developed; they are simply obsolete. As a result, many people are underutilized.

5. Participative leadership is more honest because the superior respects the subordinates and there is fuller communication about what each expects of the other.[11]

6. Subordinates increasingly want to influence the terms of this relationship. Children are not so automatically obedient because child-rearing and educational patterns have changed to encourage increased participation, responsibility, independence, and self-control.

Note that both sides in this debate accept the idea that the ultimate aim of the organization is effective and efficient performance. They differ on the means to achieve it. The authoritarians believe that strong management control and appeal to lower level needs is more effective. The advocates of the nondirective, participative style believe that appeal to higher needs will draw more from people.

This philosophical debate is interesting but inconclusive. Both sides seem partially right. To test the arguments requires empirical research, which has been widely conducted over the past 30 years.

Research on Leaders, Morale, and Performance

Research on managers in all kinds of positions indicates that there is no consistent difference in behavior between those who are more effective and those who are less so.[12] What makes managers behave as they do on the job? What makes one successful and another unsuccessful? What characteristics or behaviors make it more likely that an individual will become a leader? If placed in a formal position of leadership. What characteristics make it more or less likely that a person will be effective?

Personal Traits

There seem to be traits or personal charcterics that make it more likely that one will assume a position of leadership.[13] The leader tends to have more dominant characteristics in the following areas than the average member of the group:

Intelligence.

Scholarship.

Dependability in exercising responsibility.

Social participation.

Cooperativeness.

Adaptability.

Sociability.

Initiative.

Persistence.

Knowing how to get things done.

Insight into situations.

The qualities, characteristics and skills required in a leader are determined to a large extent by the demands of the situation in which one is to function as a leader.

The "great man" (or woman) theory of leadership is popularly recognized, but systematic research has not discovered any ideal leader or manager personality.[14] Successful managers come in many guises, and there are no consistent personality differences between those judged effective or ineffective. The point is that successful leadership depends less on the leader's personality than it does on the situation. In addition, there is no one "best" leadership style that is effective in all situations. What has evolved is a contingency theory of leadership, which states that effective managerial style is contingent upon the fit between the factors affecting leadership. These factors and their interrelationships are illustrated in Figure 10–3.

This chapter may be the most difficult in the book because the subject is so complex. Much research has been conducted, and results are often inconsistent—so much so that some scholars believe the field is in crisis.[15] It is not even firmly established that leaders directly affect the performance of the group they lead! Yet,

FIGURE 10–3

Contingency Theory of Leadership

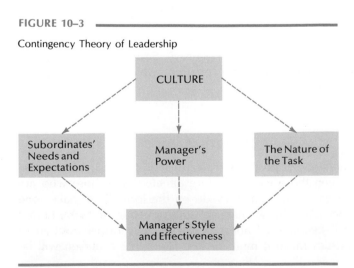

most of us somehow believe that leadership is important, that it is a central force in organizational life, and that to be truly effective a manager must also be a leader. Therefore, we shall discuss *(a)* the relationship between subordinate expectations, morale, performance, and leadership style; *(b)* the relationship between task and style; and *(c)* the impact of culture.

A Test of Leadership Styles

The arguments for participative leadership suggest that:

Managerial leadership style	affects	Subordinate morale	affects	Subordinate and organizational performance

Supposedly, nondirective leadership and greater subordinate participation would lead to higher morale, greater personal investment in the organization, and more effective performance.[16] This has been tested in several ways, such as the following experiment conducted in a large corporation.

Four parallel divisions performing similar work but geographically separated were selected for this experiment.[17] Each was organized in the same way, used the same technology, and had similar employees. None of the department managers knew that an experiment was under way. All they knew was that company executives had selected them for some training.

Managers in Divisions A and B were given a part-time training program for six months in what the trainers called hierarchical management. The intent was to teach the managers how to control the departments more closely by drawing decision making upward. The program was roughly designed to train effective authoritarian managers, and the style parallels the authoritarian style outlined above.

Managers in Divisions C and D were trained in participative management: how to delegate, how to involve subordinates in group decision making, how to communicate and motivate. This style was less directive and more appealing to subordinates' middle-and higher level social, power, autonomy, and competence needs.

One afternoon a week the various managers attended a training program at which professors talked to them. Nonmanagerial employees were not involved in the training. Since the divisions were located in different parts of the country, personnel of one division did not know what was going on in the other units.

The researchers measured productivity and employee morale at the end of the training sessions and again one year later. The results of the experiment are shown in Figure 10–4. Productivity increased under both systems, but more under the authoritarian style. In Divisions A and B, the improved productivity was achieved primarily through redesigning the work flow, increasing specialization, better definition of what management expected, and transferring excessive employees. There was some reduction of goofing off because of closer supervision, but most of the productivity increase came from working differently, not harder.

FIGURE 10–4

Productivity and Morale under Hierarchical and Participative Management

	Hierarchical or Authoritarian		Participative	
	Division A	Division B	Division C	Division D
Productivity	▲ 25%		▲ 20%	

Morale:

Absenteeism	▲ increased	▼ decreased
Turnover	▲ increased	▼ decreased
Attitudes	▼ deteriorated	▲ improved

Productivity also increased in the participative divisions for a variety of reasons: group meetings and suggestions for reorganizing the work, more effort, less absenteeism, and fewer departures of people.

Morale, as measured by three different indices, declined in the hierarchical divisions and increased in the participative ones.

The results give strong support for neither the authoritarian nor the participative style. Both seem to work, but the former does so at the cost of lowered morale. Yet, this lowered morale did not seem to affect performance adversely; management still enjoyed a productivity advantage in the hierarchically controlled divisions.

The researchers reportedly wanted to go on for another year to see how productivity and morale would look then. They thought that the engineers and office methods specialists had squeezed out all the waste that they could. Divisions A and B would have been faced with stable work methods and unhappy employees, so that they then might fall behind Divisions C and D, in which interested and committed people were endeavoring to improve performance. Unfortunately, company management said no and the experiment ceased. Perhaps the executives could not make up their minds between the two styles; perhaps the authoritarian style offended their

Horrible Hagar

sense of propriety, or the increased turnover frightened them; or perhaps the advantages of the participative style were not sufficient to underwrite the training costs that would have been required even to attempt to convert the general leadership style in the company.

This research has been debated for some time because it did not answer the question of where management should be on the needs-influence-leadership continuum. The authoritarians saw it as proving that morale is irrelevant, that centralized management can produce efficiently even when people are unhappy. This position has added strength in this case because company management refused to allow managers in Divisions A and B to punish by firing or to reward anyone with increased pay. Even though these two mainstays of authoritarian management could not be used, the authoritarian divisions still improved more than the participative ones did.

Those who favor participative management appealing to higher needs argue that this style was at a disadvantage in this research. The tasks were clerical, low-skilled, and repetitive—filing, changing forms, and typing letters. There was limited opportunity to make them more exciting. In addition, the employees were mainly young, unmarried females in their first jobs. To male managers, these "girls" presumably are accustomed to following orders, and are neither career oriented nor ambitious. It is believed that they view a job as just a place to earn a little money, pass the time and socialize. Yet, in spite of this unpromising situation, the participative divisions did substantially improve productivity and morale. The question is how much more effective might this approach be in other settings.

Summary of Relationships

Similar research on the relationship between leadership, morale, and performance has been conducted in many different organizations. In general, it has been found that:

Participative leadership style (especially superior's consultation of subordinates and expressed confidence in them) tends to be associated with high morale.[18]

High morale is associated with less turnover, less unexcused absenteeism, and fewer accidents.[19]

There is no consistent and reliable association between morale and productivity; higher job satisfaction does not directly lead to better performance.[20]

Hence no consistent relationship exists between leadership style and performance. Neither authoritarian nor participative influence appears generally superior to the other.[21]

Slightly more often than not, higher morale *is* associated with higher productivity among blue-collar and white-collar employees, but numerous instances have been found where low morale and high productivity coexist. Apparently the conditions that determine a person's job satisfaction and job performance are not identical. Three situations commonly exist:

1. Low Morale and Low Productivity. Where management does not care much, does not sufficiently define and structure the situation, and does not push employees for performance, workers tend to have low morale—probably because they are anxious about the future in an organization with such managerial attitudes. Several studies indicate that subordinates prefer democratic or even authoritarian leadership to abdicative laissez-faire.[22] Employees just do not try under the latter condition.

2. High Morale and Moderate Productivity. Where management exerts greater pressure for performance and sets higher standards, employee morale is higher and performance is better.

3. Low Morale and High Productivity. Where management pressure for performance and concern about productivity is so great that automatic and semiautomatic equipment is installed, productivity is determined by the technology more than by the people operating it. The pace of the assembly line and the automatic controls in chemical processing, for example, determine productivity, not the operator's effort or attitudes.[23] In fact, they may work least when the equipment is operating best. All that is necessary is that the employees be willing to come into work and do their jobs.

A fourth condition is rarer but may be occurring more frequently: abysmal morale and poor productivity under great management pressure for performance. Where productivity is mainly determined by technology, employee morale may be so bad that employees stay home or sabotage the process. Such a state may exist where the job is utterly boring but the workers would rather not quit because the money or benefits are desired or because they do not have many alternatives. They may retaliate by welding soda bottles inside automobile door panels, "forgetting" to lubricate machine bearings, or "accidentally" erasing computer tape programs. Figure 10–5 summarizes these general findings on morale and productivity.[24]

FIGURE 10–5

Possible Relationship between Productivity, Morale, and Management's Pressure for Performance

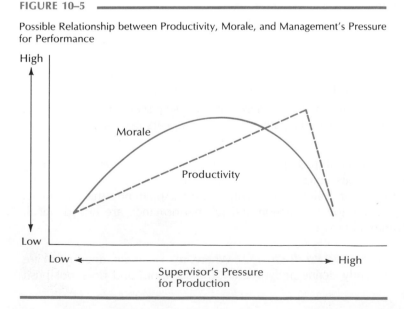

You should now recognize that morale is *not* a good predictor of performance. A manager's efforts to obtain high subordinate morale will not make people work any harder or produce any more. In fact, some researchers suggest that morale does not precede performance; it follows it—that is, good performance leads to high morale if management rewards the performance, like this:

Good performance -------------------> Management rewards -------------------> Employee morale

Put another way: (1) Job satisfaction depends on rewards, (2) rewards depend on performance, and (3) so satisfaction depends on performance, not vice versa.[25]

A Multidimensional Approach to Leadership

You should now be able to see that the distinction between ends of the needs-influence-leadership continuum is too simple. Effective leadership is not just being either hard or soft; it can require a manager to be both.

Two Dimensions of Leadership

This perspective on leadership distinguishes between two facets of the process:[26]

1. Initiating structure and pressure for performance—the degree to which the leader builds psychological structure for followers by assigning particular tasks, specifying procedures, clarifying expectations, and scheduling work to be done.

2. Consideration and representativeness—the degree to which the leader creates a supportive environment of psychological support, warmth, and helpfulness by being friendly and approachable, looking out for subordinates' welfare, going to bat for them, and representing their interests upward.

Either one of these in the absence of the other tends to be associated with poorer performance, but in positive combination they are highly effective.[27] In short, with relatively low-level employees:

Low managerial pressure + Low representativeness ----------> } Lower subordinate performance

High managerial pressure + Low representativeness ----------> } Lower subordinate performance

Low managerial pressure + High representativeness ----------> } Lower subordinate performance

But . . .

High pressure + High representativeness ----------> } Higher subordinate performance

Subordinates' satisfaction with a superior's initiating structure pressure or consideration-representativeness varies with their skills and jobs. Lower level plant and office employees highly value their boss's representativeness, and their morale tends

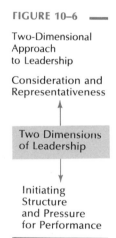

FIGURE 10–6

Two-Dimensional Approach to Leadership

Consideration and Representativeness

↑

Two Dimensions of Leadership

↓

Initiating Structure and Pressure for Performance

FIGURE 10–7

Satisfaction of Lower Level Employees in Response to Superior's "Consideration"

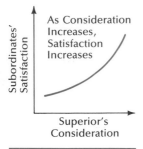

FIGURE 10–8

Satisfaction of Lower Level Employees in Response to Superior's "Pressure"

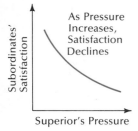

to be greater with increased consideration as Figure 10–7 illustrates.[28] Perhaps this is because their jobs are not intrinsically satisfying.

As Figure 10–8 shows, however, such employees tend to resent a superior's initiating structure and exerting pressure. This may be because their tasks are quite simple and routine. The work is so obvious that additional leader pressure is considered unnecessary. Morale may decline under increasing pressure; but when management also shows high consideration, morale will still be higher than under similar pressure with less supervisory consideration (see Figure 10–9).

Higher level, more skilled employees, such as engineers and scientists performing more complex tasks, respond differently.[29] Leader consideration is less important to them because their jobs contain more intrinsic satisfaction. Consequently, Figure 10–10 indicates that their satisfaction seems unrelated to supervisory consideration. Nonetheless, Figure 10–11 shows that such people respond positively to the manager's initiating structure. The superior's definition of objectives, procedure specification, scheduling, and pressure may clarify an ambiguous situation. Higher level employees can more clearly see the path-goal relationship between what must be done to achieve objectives, receive rewards, and satisfy needs.[30]

In positions demanding great creativity, tentative research suggests that neither the leader's consideration nor pressure is important. Thus college professors' productivity appears to be unrelated to their superiors' styles. Output is mainly dependent on the professor's internal drive, not on his or her department head or the dean.[31] In general, it appears that the less structured is a task, the less important is leadership consideration or pressure.

These research findings have led to a change of thinking among many theorists who have suggested that managers can be both hard and soft, simultaneously task

FIGURE 10–9

Satisfaction of Lower Level Employees in Response to Superior's Consideration and Pressure

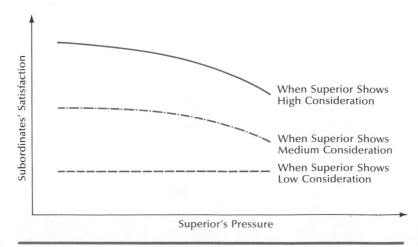

oriented *and* people concerned.[32] A popular utilization of this concept has been to describe managers on a two-dimensional managerial grid of task and people orientations, rated on a scale of 1 to 9, as in Figure 10–12.[33]

On the managerial grid, a 1,1 manager is a nothing—he or she is abdicative; a 1,9 is a country club type, concerned only with people and morale, not with performance; a 9,1 is a task-dominated slave driver and autocrat. The desired paragon is the 9,9 manager, who is greatly concerned with both people and task.

The managerial grid is a promising concept, and training programs have been instituted to encourage managers to move toward the 7,7, 8,8, and 9,9 positions. Nonetheless, it is by no means established that most effective managers are at 9,9

FIGURE 10–10

Satisfaction of Higher Level Employees in Response to Superior's "Consideration"

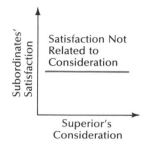

FIGURE 10–12

The Managerial Grid®

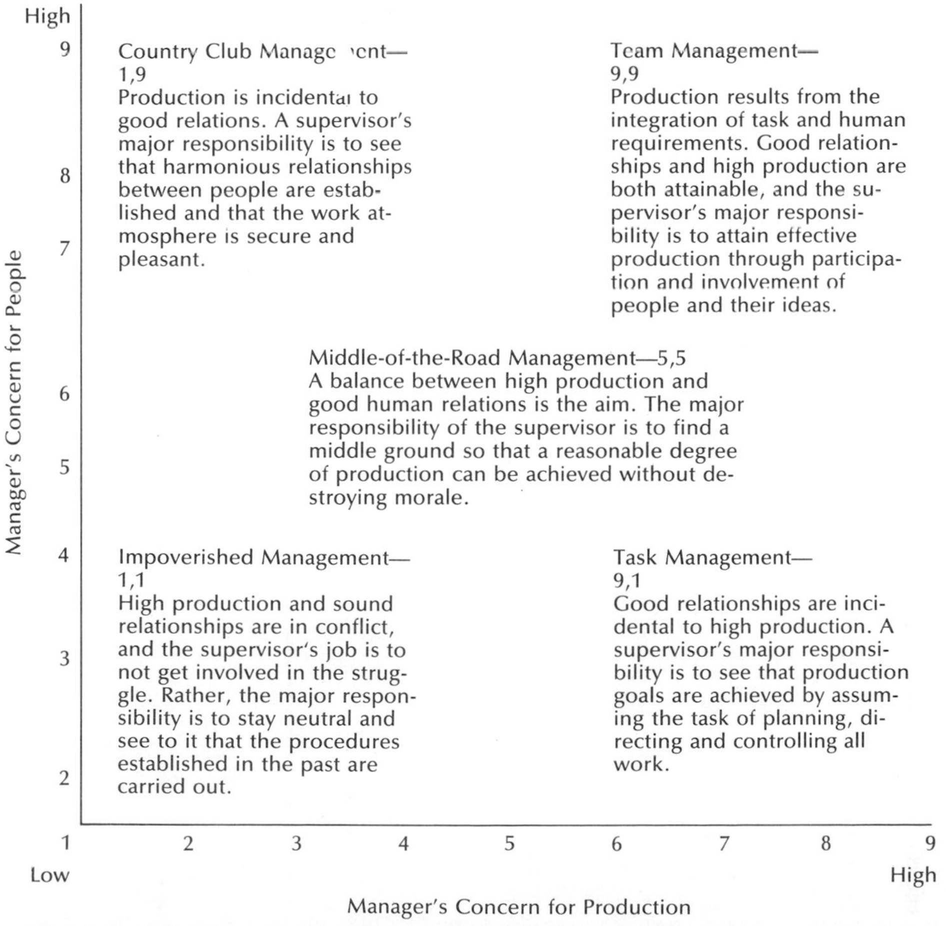

High

9 — Country Club Management—1,9
Production is incidental to good relations. A supervisor's major responsibility is to see that harmonious relationships between people are established and that the work atmosphere is secure and pleasant.

Team Management—9,9
Production results from the integration of task and human requirements. Good relationships and high production are both attainable, and the supervisor's major responsibility is to attain effective production through participation and involvement of people and their ideas.

Middle-of-the-Road Management—5,5
A balance between high production and good human relations is the aim. The major responsibility of the supervisor is to find a middle ground so that a reasonable degree of production can be achieved without destroying morale.

Impoverished Management—1,1
High production and sound relationships are in conflict, and the supervisor's job is to not get involved in the struggle. Rather, the major responsibility is to stay neutral and see to it that the procedures established in the past are carried out.

Task Management—9,1
Good relationships are incidental to high production. A supervisor's major responsibility is to see that production goals are achieved by assuming the task of planning, directing and controlling all work.

Manager's Concern for People (vertical axis, 1–9)

Low   Manager's Concern for Production   High

(horizontal axis: 1 2 3 4 5 6 7 8 9)

FIGURE 10–11

Satisfaction of Higher Level Employees in Response to Superior's "Initiating Structure"

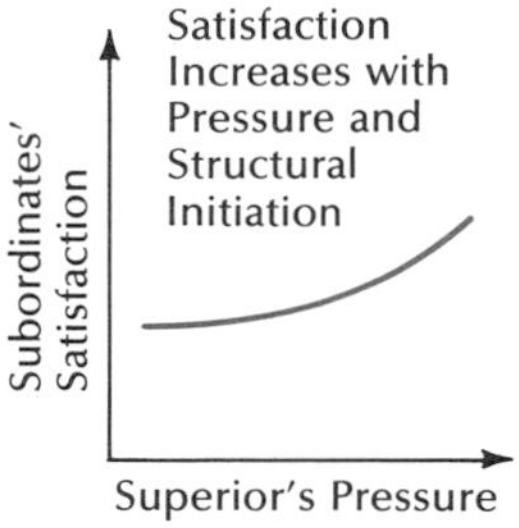

Satisfaction Increases with Pressure and Structural Initiation

Subordinates' Satisfaction

Superior's Pressure

Source: Robert R. Blake and Jane S. Mouton, *The Managerial Grid®* (Houston: Gulf Publishing, 1964).

FIGURE 10–13

Effects of the Four-Dimensional Leadership Approach

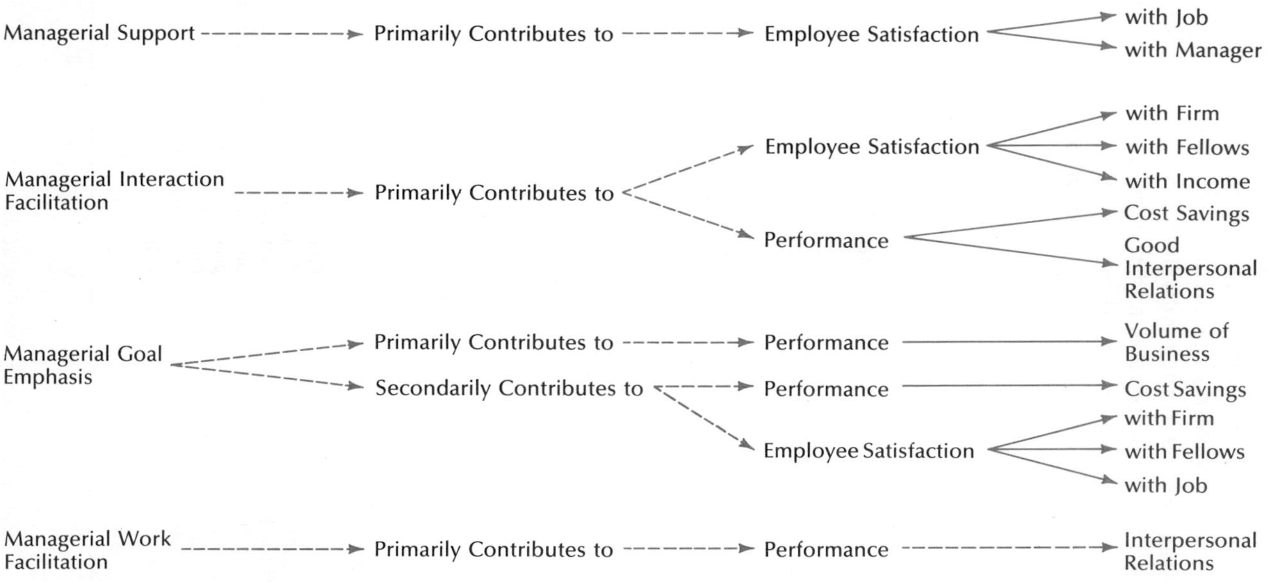

Managerial Support -------→ Primarily Contributes to -------→ Employee Satisfaction
→ with Job
→ with Manager

Managerial Interaction Facilitation -------→ Primarily Contributes to
→ Employee Satisfaction
  → with Firm
  → with Fellows
  → with Income
  → Cost Savings
→ Performance
  → Good Interpersonal Relations

Managerial Goal Emphasis -------→ Primarily Contributes to -------→ Performance
→ Volume of Business

Secondarily Contributes to -------→ Performance
→ Cost Savings

-------→ Employee Satisfaction
  → with Firm
  → with Fellows
  → with Job

Managerial Work Facilitation -------→ Primarily Contributes to -------→ Performance
→ Interpersonal Relations

(this is extremely doubtful) or that it would be desirable for all managers to move in this direction.

Four Dimensions of Leadership

The two dimensions of structure-pressure-task orientation and consideration-representativeness-people orientation may be too simple to explain entirely as complex a phenomenon as leadership, however. Furthermore, performance and satisfaction are not unitary concepts. Satisfaction with what? With the organization? With the job? Performance of what? Cost reductions? Customer relations? Sales? Different leadership dimensions may contribute differently to the various performance and satisfaction measures.

It has been suggested, therefore, that there are four leadership dimensions:[34]

1. Support.   Leader behavior that enhances the followers' feelings of personal worth and importance is called support.

2. Interaction Facilitation.   Leader behavior that encourages followers to develop close, mutually satisfying relations with one another is interaction facilitation.

3. Goal Emphasis.   Leader behavior that stimulates enthusiasm for achieving excellent performance is goal emphasis.

4. Work Facilitation.   Leader behavior that clarifies and directs the work—obtaining resources, planning, scheduling, defining tasks, and coordinating is work facilitation.

Research suggests that these different leadership dimensions have different effects on performance and satisfaction. These findings are by no means certain nor complete, but it appears that the effect of each of these dimensions is as shown in Figure 10–13.

Subordinates' Expectations and Leadership

Since the most important aspect of influence is its acceptance by subordinates (as we argued in Chapter 9), it follows that a leadership style is affected by subordinates. If they refuse to accept a leader-manager, he or she must either change style or depart. Of course, subordinates are not always entirely in command; they may be so desperate for jobs, for example, that they will accept anything and anyone. Nevertheless, the decision is theirs.

In the debate over proper leadership style, we have shown that some academicians and industrial humanists call for management appeal to the higher level needs for autonomy, competence, and achievement. Other academicians and some practitioners respond that these reformers make a false assumption: They analyze themselves and their higher level drives and erroneously conclude that all employees are like them in desiring responsibility, discretion, challenge, and creative opportunity.[35] But in reality not everyone has developed higher level needs, or if they have, they do

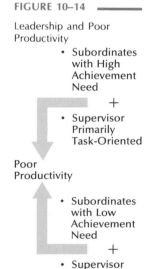

FIGURE 10–14

Leadership and Poor Productivity

- Subordinates with High Achievement Need

    +

- Supervisor Primarily Task-Oriented

Poor Productivity

- Subordinates with Low Achievement Need

    +

- Supervisor Primarily People-Oriented

FIGURE 10–15

Leadership and High
Productivity

FIGURE 10–15

Leadership and High
Productivity

- Subordinates
  with High
  Achievement
  Need

- Supervisor
  Primarily
  People-
  Oriented <u>or</u>
  Balanced
  People- and
  Task-
  Orientation

High
Productivity

- Subordinates
  with Low
  Achievement
  Need

- Supervisor
  Primarily
  Task-Oriented
  <u>or</u> Balanced
  People- and
  Task-
  Orientation

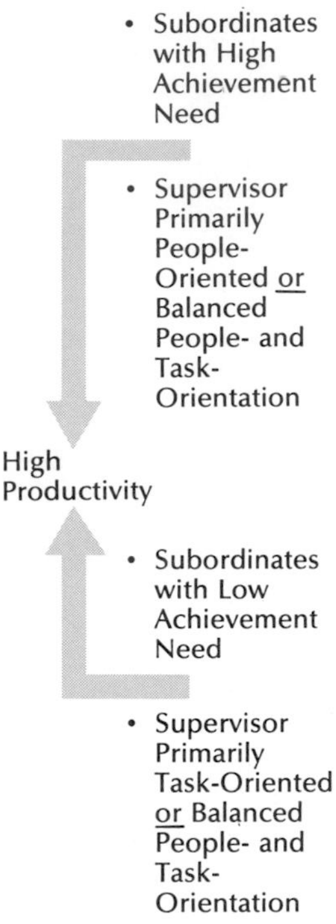

not necessarily consider work to be an appropriate place to satisfy them. The *most* satisfied subordinates in one study were those with authoritarian personalities who worked for a directive boss.[36]

Many companies in the past 25 years have instituted human relations training programs designed to modify supervisory style to make managers less overbearing and more sensitive to the needs and desires of their subordinates. All too often, such programs for leaders and supervisory personnel did no good or even hurt the organization. Not only did the training and philosophy run against the experience and personalities of the supervisors, but many workers distrusted management's intentions.[37] They perceived the attempt to depart from straightforward authoritarianism as manipulative—a plot to get them to work harder, to produce more without additional income. In more difficult settings of longstanding management and worker antagonism, supervisors' efforts to be kinder, more understanding, and "more people oriented" may be perceived as "weakness," which could cause things to get completely out of control. Where workers have been historically dissatisfied, with little interest in their work, productivity may *decline* if a change is made to participative management.[38] (See Figures 10–14 and 10–15.)

One experiment of leadership styles with workers of high and low needs for achievement indicated the following relationships.[39]

The poorest productivity was associated with the combination of low-achievement-need workers and a primarily maintenance-consideration-representation supervisor. The supervisor's people orientation could not seem to get these people to do much.

Poor productivity was also associated with high-achievement-need workers and a primarily production-pressure-task supervisor. This supervisor's task orientation was perhaps seen as unnecessary and offensive.

High productivity was associated with high-achievement-need workers and a primarily people-oriented supervisor *or* a balanced people- and task-oriented supervisor. High-achievement-need workers seem to provide their own motivation if the supervisor builds a good human relations climate.

High productivity was also associated with low-achievement-need workers and primarily task-oriented supervisor *or* a balanced task- and people-oriented supervisor. Low-achievement-need workers do not seem to produce unless pushed.

Clearly, there must be a fit between a leader-manager's style and the personalities and expectations of subordinate followers. In the next chapter we shall see that no manager is entirely free to choose any leadership style he or she desires because it must fit the task and technology involved.[40] There is no one best style for everyone and everywhere.

SUMMARY

Persuasive arguments exist for influencing through authoritarian appeal to physiological and security needs: It is speedier, easier, more universal, more predictable, more realistic in recognizing human laziness, more honest and straightforward, and more suited to most managers' personalities and subordinates' expectation. Nonetheless, a strong case can also be made for participative appeal to power, autonomy, competence, and achievement needs: Today's more educated and mobile employees have more alternatives, can apply latent energies and excitement to challenging work, will offer creativity when committed to work, and increasingly demand more participation, responsibility, and self-control.

Research on leadership indicates that participative leadership tends to result in higher morale and that this morale is associated with less turnover and absenteeism. Nonetheless, no consistent and strong relationship exists between worker morale and productivity. Higher morale does not always lead to higher performance, and higher performance may be achieved under authoritarian leadership, regardless of whether employees like it or not.

Better performance is especially likely when managerial behavior encompasses two dimensions: (1) initiating structure—pressure for performance plus (2) consideration-representativeness toward and for subordinates. The most desired managers are those who demonstrate high and balanced orientations toward both task and people in such a way as to clarify the path-goal between behavior and need satisfaction for everyone. Subordinates know what is to be done, what the rewards will be, and how these will satisfy their needs. Such leaders seem to recognize that influence is not one way downward, that they will have greater influence to the extent that their subordinates perceive themselves and their boss as being able to exert influence upward.

Subordinates' expectations also influence a manager's behavior. They are educated and habituated to certain styles related to their expectations about work. A superior's appeal to autonomy, competence, and achievement needs will be fruitless if subordinates do not possess these needs or have neither desire nor expectation of satisfying them through work. They may well distrust a participative superior whom they perceive as manipulating them to more effort for no greater rewards. Of course, other subordinates may want to satisfy higher level needs through nondirective leadership and shared power.

REVIEW QUESTIONS

1. What is the theoretical advantage of self-determination as a basis for influence?

2. How is an authoritarian leadership style thought to be predictable?

3. What assumptions about human nature does the authoritarian style make?

4. What is apparently efficient about the authoritarian style?

5. Why is the authoritarian style probably easier for most managers?

6. What assumptions about human nature are made in a more participative style?

7. Why might participative approaches lead to more effective performance?

8. Why is there no one best leadership style or leader personality?

9. What are the major factors that influence a manager's style?

10. What is a contingency theory of leadership?

11. In the test of leadership styles, what happened to productivity in the hierarchical departments? How?

12. What happened to morale in the hierarchical departments? Why?

13. What happened to productivity in the participative departments? How?

14. What happened to morale in the participative departments? Why?

15. What were the different interpretations of the test?

16. What behavior does morale seem to be associated with? What behavior is not associated with morale?

17. What is the general relationship between management "pressure, morale, and productivity?"

18. How can low morale and high productivity exist at the same time?

19. What is meant by management's initiating structure and pressure for performance?

20. What is management's consideration and representativeness?

21. How are management pressure, representativeness, and subordinate performance related?

22. How are managerial pressure, consideration, and subordinate satisfaction related for *low-level* employees?

23. How are managerial pressure, representativeness, and subordinate satisfaction related for *high-level* employees?

24. What are the elements in the Managerial Grid®? What is task management? Country club management? Impoverished management? Team management?

25. What are the dimensions in a four-dimensional approach to leadership?

26. What is managerial support?

27. What is managerial interaction facilitation?

28. What is managerial goal emphasis?

29. What is managerial work facilitation?

30. How do subordinates' expectations affect leadership style?

31. In the experimental situation on achievement need, how was poor productivity associated with subordinates' achievement need and supervisor's style?

32. How was high productivity associated with subordinates' achievement need and supervisor's style?

Notes and References on Leadership Styles

1. O. Aldia, "Of Pigeons and Men," in R. Ulrich, T. Stachnik, and J. Mabry, eds., *Control of Human Behavior* (Glenview, Ill.: Scott, Foresman, 1966), pp. 218–21.

2. T. R. Mitchell, *People in Organizations* (New York: McGraw-Hill, 1978).

3. Horai and Tedeschi, "Effects of Credibility and Magnitude and Punishment," R. B. Mogy and D. G. Pruitt, "Effects of a Threatener's Enforcement Costs on Threat Credibility and Compliance," *Journal of Personality and Social Psychology* 29, no. 2 (1974), pp. 173–80. It is suggested that: (1) the greater the credibility of the threat source, the more compliant the subject, and (2) the credibility of the threat source is determined by (a) the cost to the source of carrying out the threat and (b) the subject's knowledge or lack of knowledge of the source's behavior after other threats.

4. A former assistant secretary of state writes of his awareness of the two sides of control in his first days in office:

> The taste of power, or whatever it was that I tasted the first day, went to my head too, but not quite as I had been warned it would. I had come into the office with projects and plans, and I was caught in an irresistible movement of power, meetings, ceremonies, crisis, trivialities. There were uncleared paragraphs and cleared ones, and people waiting for me to tell them what my plans were, and people doing things that had nothing to do with my plans. I had moved into the middle of a flow of business that I hadn't started and wouldn't be able to stop. There were people in place to handle this flow, and established machinery in operation to help me deal with it. The entire system was at my disposal. In a word, I had power. And power had me.

C. Frankel, *High on Foggy Bottom* (New York: Harper & Row, 1969).

5. D. C. Pelz, "Influence: A Key to Effective Leadership in the First-Line Supervisor," *Personnel* 29 (1952), pp. 209–21; A. S. Tannenbaum, "Control in Organizations: Individual Adjustment and Organizational Performance," *Administrative Science Quarterly* 7, no 2 (1962), pp. 236–57.

6. On the relation between participation and sense of influence, see V. Ries, "Influence Structure in Yugoslav Enterprise," *Industrial Relations* 9 (1970), pp. 148–66; J. T. McMahon and G. W. Perritt, "The Control Structure of Organizations: An Empiricial Examination," *Academy of Management Journal* 14, no. 3 (1971), pp. 327–40; M. Rosner et al., "Worker Participation and Influence in Five Countries," *Industrial Relations* 12, no. 2 (1973), pp. 200–12; and B. Drake and T. Mitchell, "The Effects of Vertical and Horizontal Power on Individual Motivation and Satisfaction," *Academy of Management Journal,* December 1977, pp. 573–91.

7. Douglas McGregor summarizes the assumptions of the authoritarian approach regarding the individual under the label of Theory X.

> The average human being has an inherent dislike of work and will avoid it if he can.

> Because of this human characteristic of dislike of work, most people must be coerced, controlled, directed, or threatened with punishment to get them to put forth adequate effort toward the achievement of organizational objectives.

The average human being prefers to be directed, wishes to avoid responsibility, has relatively little ambition, and wants security above all.

In the same work, McGregor summarizes the assumptions of the participative approach regarding the individual under the label of Theory Y.

The expenditure of physical and mental effort in work is as natural as play or rest.

External control and the threat of punishment are not the only means for bringing about effort toward organizational objectives. Man will exercise self-direction and self-control in the service of objectives to which he is committed.

Commitment to objectives is a function of the rewards associated with their achievement.

The average human being learns, under proper conditions, not only to accept but to seek responsibility.

The capacity to exercise a relatively high degree of imagination, ingenuity, and creativity in the solution of organizational problems is widely, not narrowly, distributed in the population.

Under the condition of modern industrial life, the intellectual potentialities of the average human being are only partially utilized.

The Human Side of Enterprise (New York: McGraw-Hill, 1960).

8. M. P. McNair argues that concern about people and "human relations" has become excessive, that managers are losing their business effectiveness. "Thinking Ahead: What Price Human Relations?" *Harvard Business Review,* March–April 1957, p. 15.

For a strong argument that corporate executives should be judged solely on economic performance and not on the emotional well-being of their employees, see William Gomberg, "The Trouble with Democratic Management," *Trans-Action,* July–August 1966.

9. T. R. Mitchell believes participation increases individual effort because: (1) the greater communication makes objectives clearer, (2) rewards are more likely to be those that people value, (3) social influence on behavior is increased, and (4) self-control over behavior is improved. All of this suggests that the individual increases his or her probability estimate of achieving the objectives and receiving satisfying rewards. "Motivation and Participation: An Integration," *Academy of Management Journal,* December 1973, pp. 670–78. Also see: A. Lowin, "Participation in Decision Making: A Model, Literature Critique, and Prescriptions for Research," *Organizational*

Behavior and Human Performance 3 (1968), pp. 68–106; D. G. Searfoss and R. M. Monczka, "Perceived Participation in the Budget Process and Motivation to Achieve the Budget," *Academy of Management Journal,* December 1973, pp. 541–54; R. D. Pritchard and M. I. Curtis, "The Influence of Goal Setting and Financial Incentives on Task Performance," *Organizational Behavior and Human Performance* 10 (1973), pp. 175–83; L. L. Cummings, "A Field Experimental Study of the Effects of Two Performance Appraisal Systems," *Personnel Psychology* 26, no. 4 (1973), pp. 489–502; C. R. Forrest, L. L. Cummings, and A. C. Johnson, "Organizational Participation: A Critique and Model," *Academy of Management Review,* October 1977, pp. 586–601.

10. One psychologist argues that most managers are incapable of exercising participative leadership because of their strong personalities; they lapse into manipulation. Therefore, authoritarian leadership is more honest. E. E. Jennings, "Business Needs Mature Autocrats," *Nation's Business* (Washington, D.C., Chamber of Commerce of the United States), September 1958, p. 34 ff.

11. Rensis Likert, *The Human Organization: Its Management and Value* (New York: McGraw-Hill, 1967). Likert identifies his System IV as the best management style. In this style, there is:

1. Complete confidence and trust between superiors and subordinates.

2. Freedom of subordinates to discuss job with superiors.

3. Participation of subordinates in generation of new ideas.

4. Participation and involvement in setting goals.

5. Subordinate responsibility for organizational goals.

6. Much communication.

7. Acceptance of downward communication by subordinates.

8. Accuracy in upward communications.

9. Friendly interpersonal relations.

10. Much cooperative teamwork.

11. Use of linking pin in assigning people to decision-making groups.

12. Identical formal and informal organization.

13. Use of control data for problem solving, not punishment.

For one perspective on the importance of participative management, see M. Sashkin, "Participative Management Is an Ethical Imperative," *Organizational Dynamics,* Spring 1984, pp. 4–22.

12. Ross A. Webber, "Managerial Behavior, Personality and Organizational Structure," Ph.D. thesis, Columbia University, 1966.

13. R. M. Stogdill, *Handbook of Leadership* (New York: Free Press, 1974).

14. J. Pfeffer, "The Ambiguity of Leadership," *Academy of Management Journal,* January 1977, pp. 104–12.

Various suggestions and tentative insights have been offered on the relationship between managers' personalities and job behavior. Some of them are discussed below.

Surveys suggest that people who occupy leadership positions tend to exceed the average in the following respects: (1) intelligence, (2) scholarship, (3) dependability, (4) activity and social participation, (5) sociability, (6) initiative, (7) persistence, (8) independence, (9) less defensiveness, and (10) greater willingness to admit mistakes. R. M. Stogdill, "Personal Factors Associated with Leadership," *Journal of Psychology* 25 (1948), pp. 35–71. For various surveys of personality and management, see T. W. Harrell, *Managers' Performance and Personality* (Cincinnati: South-Western Publishing, 1961); K. Rogers, *Managers: Personality and Performance* (London: Tavistock, 1963); T. W. Harrell, "The Personality of High-Earning MBA's in Big Business," *Personnel Psychology* 22 (1969), pp. 457–63; and "The Personality of MBA's Who Reach General Management Early," *Personnel Psychology* 26, no. 1 (1973), pp. 127–34.

Many managers are characterized by higher-than-average needs for power and achievement. They enjoy exercising influence over other people and solving challenging, novel problems providing individual feedback. Many marketing, sales, and top-line executives particularly possess these qualities. People very high in needs for power and autonomy are especially attracted to small business. On managers and achievement needs, see David C. McClelland, *The Achieving Society* (New York: Van Nostrand Reinhold, 1961). On power needs, see D. G. Winter, *The Power Motive* (New York: Free Press, 1973). On entrepreneurs, see J. A. Hornaday and C. S. Bunker, "The Nature of the Entrepreneur," *Personnel Psychology* 23 (1970), pp. 47–54.

Managers vary in their "tolerance for ambiguity." People low in this tolerance tend to overly categorize people and situations into stereotypes. This makes the world seem less uncertain and more under control. Such people are sometimes described as having "authoritarian" personalities because they are attracted to the clarity and certain structure of authoritarianism. On the job they may attempt to maintain greater centralization and closer control over subordinate activities. As a result, they may experience difficulty in unstructured situations. See T. W. Adorno et al., *The Authoritarian Personality: Studies in Prejudice* (New York: Harper & Row, 1950); E. Frenkel-Brunswik, "Intolerance of Ambiguity as an Educational and Perceptual Personality Variable," *Journal of Personality* 18 (1949), pp. 108–43; and J. A. Ilardo, "Ambiguity Tolerance and Disordered Communication," *Journal of Communication,* December 1973, pp. 371–91.

High executives in large corporations may be especially low in affiliative needs; they have been described as "impersonal" in maintaining distance between themselves and work associates. This presumably allows them to be more coolly rational in making decisions about people and more mobile in changing positions and locations. W. E. Henry, "Psychodynamics of the Executive Role," *American Journal of Sociology* 54 (1949), pp. 286–91.

Managers with rather passive personalities who prefer to talk little paradoxically tend to be directive on the job and to spend more time checking and directing their subordinates. They tend to spend less time responding to others, more time on communications that they initiate. Dynamic, high-initiative, and talkative managers (the closest to the Madison Avenue stereotype) tend to be responsive and nondirective. They tend to spend less time giving orders and more time responding and talking to people who initiate conversations with them. Webber, "Managerial Behavior, Personality and Organizational Structure."

More speculatively, it has been suggested that executives just below the top tend to be characterized as having excessive drive, ambition, and a greater sense of urgency— to be fighting time itself. Those at the very top seem to be more relaxed (and have less heart disease than their immediate subordinates). Harry Levinson, *Executive Stress* (New York: Harper & Row, 1970).

The tentativeness of the findings on managerial personality and behavior underlies the illegitimacy of much of the personality testing that is conducted in organizations. Such testing has been under attack in recent years because of its intrusion into personal privacy and possible unethical manipulation. More fundamentally, use of such testing is apparently declining because it does not work. The typical firm gives the tests to its high-level executives, draws up a desired profile from the results, and hires young managers who best fit the profiles. When some of these hirees start climbing the ladder in later years the testers congratulate themselves, but this is self-fulfilling prophecy. If management selects only people of similar personalities, some of them are bound to reach the top. This is no proof, however, that entirely different personalities might not have been equally or more successful. See John P. Campbell et al., *Managerial Behavior, Performance, and Effectiveness* (New York: McGraw-Hill, 1970).

15. C. N. Greene, "Disenchantment with Leadership Research: Some Causes, Recommendations, and Alternative Directions," and R. J. House, "A 1976 Theory of Charismatic Leadership," both in J. G. Hunt and L. L. Larson, eds., *Leadership: The Cutting Edge* (Carbondale, Ill.: Southern Illinois University Press, 1977). For a review of leadership research, see R. M. Stogdill, *Handbook of Leadership: A Survey of Theory and Research* (New York: Free Press, 1974). See also M. Biesesi, "Strategies for Successful Leadership in Changing Times," *Sloan Management Review,* Fall 1983, pp. 61–64.

16. D. W. Organ, "A Reappraisal and Reinterpretation of the Satisfaction-Causes-Performance Hypothesis," *Academy of Management Review,* January 1977, pp. 46–52.

17. This experiment is an old one, but it nicely illustrates the problems in comparing leadership styles. Reported by Rensis Likert, in "Measuring Organizational Performance," *Management Record* 18, no. 4 (1956), pp. 128–31. Also see N. C. Morse and E. Reimer, "The Experimental Change of a Major Organizational Variable," *Journal of Abnormal and Social Psychology* 5 (1966), pp. 120–29; D. Katz, N. Maccoby, and N. C. Morse, *Productivity, Supervision and Morale in an Office Situation* (Detroit: Dorel Press, 1950).

18. Participation and good job attitudes tend to be associated regardless of individual values. J. K. White and R. A. Ruh, "Effects of Personal Values on the Relationship between Participation and Job Attitudes," *Administrative Science Quarterly,* December 1973, pp. 506–14.

A subordinate's satisfaction with a superior reflects both the superior's expressed confidence in the subordinate and the superior's consultation of the subordinate. However, the former seems more important; the quality of participative management is more important than the volume. R. E. Miles and J. B. Ritchie, "Participative Management: Quality versus Quantity," *California Management Review,* Summer 1971, pp. 48–56.

B. G. Fiman found that supervisors perceived by their subordinates as being participative or following "Theory Y" did have more subordinates who were more satisfied but whose performance was not higher than others on similar routine clerical tasks. "An Investigation of the Relationships among Supervisory Attitudes, Behaviors and Outputs: An Examination of McGregor's Theory Y," *Personnel Psychology* 26, no. 1 (1973), pp. 95–105.

19. I. C. Ross and A. Zander, "Need Satisfaction and Employee Turnover," *Personnel Psychology,* Autumn 1957, p. 327. Low turnover is not necessarily an indicator of high morale or performance. Dissatisfied people stay because of inertia or because they cannot leave; they may be tied to the community because of family reasons or because they have no other options. V. S. Flowers and C. L. Hughes, "Why Employees Stay," *Harvard Business Review,* July –August 1973, pp. 49–60.

In general, the greater the participation and the smaller the community size, the greater the sense of job involvement and the lower the turnover. A. L. Siegel and R. A. Ruh, "Job Involvement, Participation in Decision Making, Personal Background and Job Behavior," *Organizational Behavior and Human Performance* 9 (1973), pp. 318–27. Nonetheless, managers and professionals higher in need for achievement tend to change jobs more frequently. G. H. Hines, "Achievement Motivation, Occupations and Labor Turnover," *Journal of Applied Psychology* 58, no. 3 (1973), pp. 313–17.

20. Victor Vroom surveyed more than 20 studies of job satisfaction and performance. He calculated a slight positive correlation between job satisfaction and job performance of +.14. Most of these studies were of blue-collar and clerical employees. Studies of managers and professionals indicated a stronger correlation between their satisfaction and performance. *Work and Motivation* (New York: John Wiley & Sons, 1964).

Another study indicates that among blue-collar operators, job productivity is most correlated with satisfaction of the security need (+.17) and the social need (+.16). Correlation with higher needs for esteem, autonomy, and self-actualization is very low. D. G. Kuhn, J. W. Slocum, Jr., and R. B. Chase, "Does Job Performance Affect Job Satisfaction?" *Personnel Journal,* June 1971, p. 455. For an early study of these matters, see A. H. Brayfield and W. H. Crockett, "Employee Attitudes and Employee Performance," *Psychological Bulletin* September 1955, pp. 396–424.

21. After reviewing the history of his research on productivity and job satisfaction, R. L. Kahn observes that he abandoned the use of satisfaction or morale as a variable intervening between supervisory or organizational characteristics on the one hand and productivity on the other. "Productivity and Job Satisfaction," *Personnel Psychology* 13, no. 3 (1960), pp. 275–87. Frank Friedlander observes that even if participation in decision making did serve to motivate an individual, this in itself is no assurance that the change will be reflected in improved performance. "Motivation to Work and Organizational Performance," *Journal of Applied Psychology* 50, no. 2 (1966), pp. 143–52.

22. A study of engineers and technicians indicates that they prefer a manager who clarifies structure and shows consideration. They dislike laissez-faire leadership. R. J. House, A. C. Filley, and S. Keer, "Relation of Leader Consideration and Initiating Structure to Research and Development Subordinate Satisfaction," *Administrative Science Quarterly* 16, no. 1 (1971), pp. 19–30.

23. Attitudes do not predict behavior or performance where the task predominates and the worker has no autonomy. J. B. Herman, "Are Situational Contingencies Limiting Job Attitude—Job Performance Relationships?" *Organizational Behavior and Human Performance* 10 (1973), pp. 208–24.

24. Figure 10–5 is not drawn to scale, but it suggests relationships discussed by Robert Dubin, "Supervision and Productivity: Empirical Findings and Theoretical Considerations," in Dubin et al., eds., *Leadership and Productivity* (San Francisco: Chandler, 1965).

25. For discussion of how performance may precede morale, see E. E. Lawler III and L. W. Porter, "The Effect of Performance on Job Satisfaction," *Industrial Relations* 7, no. 1 (1967), pp. 20–29; and R. A. Sutermeister, "Employee Performance and Employee Need Satisfaction: Which Comes First?" *California Management Review* 13, no. 4 (1971), pp. 43–47.

It may even be that influence style follows performance—managers may be more participative with and responsive to subordinates with better performance and more favorable job attitudes. See A. Lowin and J. R. Craig, "The Influence of Performance on Managerial Style: An Experimental Object-Lesson in the Ambiguity of Correlational Data," *Organizational Behavior and Human Performance* 3 (1968), pp. 440–58; and G. F. Farris and F. G. Lim, "Effects of Performance on Leadership, Cohesiveness, Influence, Satisfaction and Subsequent Performance," *Journal of Applied Psychology* 53 (1969), pp. 490–97.

26. R. M. Stogdill and A. E. Coons, *Leader Behavior: Its Description and Measurement* (Columbus: Ohio State University Press, 1957); A. K. Korman, " 'Consideration,' 'Initiating Structure,' and Organizational Criteria: A Review," *Personnel Psychology* 19 (1966).

27. Martin Patchen, "Supervisory Methods and Group Performance Norms," *Administrative Science Quarterly* 7, no. 3 (1962), pp. 275–93. Other researchers aren't so sure that the two dimensions are so separate. L. L. Larson, J. G. Hunt, R. N. Osborn, "The Great Hi-Hi Leader Behavior Myth," *Academy of Management Journal*, December 1976, pp. 628–41.

28. Figures 10–6, 10–7, 10–8, 10–9, and 10–10 on employee satisfaction are not drawn to scale but suggest relationships discussed in E. A. Fleishman and E. F. Harris, "Patterns of Leadership Behavior Related to Employee Grievances and Turnover," *Personnel Psychology* 15 (1962), pp. 43–56.

29. R. J. House, L. A. Wigdor, and K. Schulz, "Leader Behavior, Psychological Participation, Employee Satisfaction and Performance: An Extension of Prior Investigations and a Motivation Theory Interpretation," in W. M. Frey, ed., *Proceedings Seventh Annual Conference of Eastern Academy of Management* (Amherst: University of Massachusetts Press, 1970), pp. 179–95.

When the dimensions of consideration and initiating structure were applied to college teachers, it was found that:

Undergraduates valued consideration, and this was the main factor in their evaluation of instructors.

For instructors high in consideration, high structural initiation did not detract from student evaluation.

Graduate students emphasized consideration less and initiating structure more than undergraduates.

B. Lahat-Mandelbaum and D. Kipnis, "Leader Behavior Dimensions Related to Students' Evaluation of Teaching Effectiveness," *Journal of Applied Psychology* 58, no. 2 (1973), pp. 250–53.

Among undergraduates, it appears that satisfaction with a course and the grade achieved are higher when the pressure to perform is high. In an easier course, there was less correlation between satisfaction and grade. R. B. Ewen, "Pressure for Production, Task Difficulty and the Correlation between Job Satisfaction and Job Performance," *Journal of Applied Psychology* 58, no. 3 (1973), pp. 378–80.

A study of new-hired, hard-core unemployed black women indicates that supervisory consideration was positively associated with job success, and supervisory pressure was negatively related. It was concluded that attempts to be successful with the hard-core unemployed should not only encourage supervisory styles that are initially supportive but should refrain from imposing structure on a culture that may be unaccustomed to external, rigid demands on behavior. R. W. Beatty, "Supervisory Behavior Related to Job Success of Hard-Core Unemployed over a Two-Year Period," *Journal of Applied Psychology* 59, no. 1 (1974), pp. 38–42.

30. R. J. House, "A Path-Goal Theory of Leader Effectiveness," *Administrative Science Quarterly* 16, no. 3 (1971), pp. 321–38. The path-goal model of behavior assumes a "rational" connection between judgment of effort and result. But, as we saw in Chapter 3, some people believe that they play little role in results, that random outside events and people affect success and failure. Such people may not perceive any connection between results and their effort. J. F. Gavin, "Self-Esteem as a Moderator of the Relationship between Expectancies and Job Performance," *Journal of Applied Psychology* 58, no. 1 (1973), pp. 83–88.

See also H. K. Downey, J. E. Sheridan, and J. W. Slocum, "Analysis of Relationships among Leader Behavior, Subordinate Job Performance, and Satisfaction: A Path-Goal Approach," *Academy of Management Journal,* June 1975, pp. 253–62.

31. S. Coltrin and W. F. Glueck, "The Effect of Leadership Roles on the Satisfaction and Productivity of University Research Professors," *Academy of Management Journal,* March 1977, pp. 101–16.

32. Task orientation and social interaction orientation are not mutually exclusive. One can be high in both. J. J. Ray, "Task Orientation and Interaction Orientation Scales," *Personnel Psychology* 26, no. 1 (1973), pp. 61–73.

33. On the Managerial Grid®, see R. R. Blake and J. S. Moulton, *The Managerial Grid®* (Houston: Gulf Publishing, 1964). For a test of your own leadership style, see P. Hersey and K. H. Blanchard, "So You Want to Know Your Leadership Style?" *Training and Development Journal* 28, no. 2 (1974), pp. 22–37.

34. D. G. Bowers and S. E. Seashore, "Predicting Organizational Effectiveness with a Four-Factor Theory of Leadership," *Administrative Science Quarterly* 11, no. 2 (1966), pp. 238–63.

35. Henry Tosi "A Reexamination of Personality as a Determinant of the Effects of Participation," *Personnel Psychology* 23 (1970), pp. 91–99.

36. Authoritarian personality subordinates were most satisfied under a directive superior, but even low-authoritarian personality subordinates were displeased with a superior who left them completely alone. Tosi concludes that some structure is essential in all situations. "The Effect of the Interaction of Leader Behavior and Subordinate Authoritarianism," *Personnel Psychology* 26, no. 3 (1973), pp. 339–50. Also see K. M. Bartol, "Male versus Female Leaders: The Effect of Leader Need for Dominance on Follower Satisfaction," *Academy of Management Journal* 17, no. 2 (1974), pp. 225–33.

37. R. J. House, "Leadership Training: Some Dysfunctional Consequences," *Administrative Science Quarterly* 12, no. 4 (1968), pp. 556–71; F. E. Fiedler, "The Effects of Leadership Training and Experience: A Contingency Model Interpretation," *Administrative Science Quarterly* 17, no. 4 (1972), pp. 453–70.

38. R. M. Powell and J. L. Schlacter, "Participative Management: A Panacea?" *Academy of Management Journal* 14, no. 2 (1971), pp. 165–73. Obviously, the authors do not think it is.

39. J. Misumi and F. Seki, "Effects of Achievement Motivation on the Effectiveness of Leadership Patterns," *Administrative Science Quarterly* 16, no. 1 (1971), pp. 51–59.

40. Robert Tannenbaum and W. W. Schmidt, "How to Choose a Leadership Pattern," in R. Tannenbaum, I. R. Wechsler, and F. Massarik, *Leadership and Organization* (New York: McGraw-Hill, 1961). The title is misleading because no manager enjoys completely free choice of leadership style.

11

Contingency Leadership

When one of the authors was a young Ensign in the United States Navy, I was frightened of the career officer who was the ship's Executive Officer (second in command). He seemed so mean. I concluded that it was his personality. But when the next Executive Officer was just as tough, I began to wonder. By the appearance of the third intimidating Executive Officer, I had come to recognize that it wasn't the men's unpleasant personalities, it was the requirements of the post. The Executive Officer simply must be a disciplinarian, the person who says "no" so that the Commanding Officer can captain the ship. Thus, the style is mostly dictated by the job itself.

Of all the factors influencing managerial behavior, the nature of the task is strongest. More than anything else, task and technology affect how a manager leads his or her subordinates.

Managerial Behavior and the Nature of the Task

We can illustrate the impact of task most dramatically by considering laboratory experiments on communication networks and managerial behavior in different positions and in different settings.

Communication and Leadership in Networks

In network research, the researcher experiments with five-person groups in a room where the interconnections between subjects can be manipulated. The team members do not know what network they are in because each sits in a closed booth from which he or she can see no one. The booths have either slots in the wall for written messages or telephone lines to communicate with other members. The wheel, circle, and all-channel networks illustrated in Figure 11–1 are three of the arrangements tested.[1] *

FIGURE 11–1

Types of Communication Networks

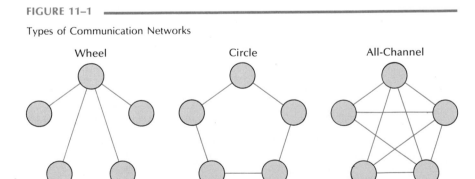

Wheel   Circle   All-Channel

Source: Harold Guetzkow and Herbert A. Simon, "The Impact of Certain Communication Nets upon Organization and Performance in Task-Oriented Groups," *Management Science,* April–July, 1955, pp. 233–50.

* Notes and references will be found at the end of this chapter.

In a group structured as a wheel, the person at the hub can communicate with all of the people at the spokes. The latter, however, can communicate only with the hub. Regardless of the personality of the individual located at the hub, after numerous repetitions of the solution of simple problems by the group, he or she will emerge as the decision maker or leader. A "natural leader" at one of the spoke positions may attempt to lead, but in all groups tested, the spokes came to recognize that the hub must be the decision maker, because the individual at the hub can get all the necessary information more easily than anyone else can. In a simple problem, such as identifying a symbol or color of marble common to all five participants, the hub collects the information from all others, compares it, decides, and simply informs the others of the answer. Since the hub occupies a critical communication link, she or he becomes the manager.

In an all-channel group, everyone can communicate with everyone else. Yet, in a series of repetitious and simple problems, most of the all-channel members find it inefficient to operate on this basis, so they transform themselves into a wheel network. Voluntarily, they restrict their communication links. In most groups some individual emerges as the occupant of the critical communication point at the hub. The others communicate only with that person. The process is facilitated if one individual is clearly a leader in terms of analytical ability and articulateness. Nonetheless, even where the members of the group are balanced as to personality and prestige, the all-channel net tends to convert itself to the wheel. In short, centralized management emerges because of the difficulty and inefficiency of transmitting all information to every member of the organization.

The third network tested, the circle, is slower than either of the others, apparently because it is difficult for a leadership structure to emerge in such an arrangement. All positions are equal; none has more access to information, as did the hub in the wheel, and no individual can communicate with everyone to establish leadership, as in the all-channel network.[2]

The more central a person is in the network, the more satisfied he or she is likely to be.[3] Centrality means receiving and sending more communications and thus being better able to solve the problems. Centrality is also satisfying because the person in that position knows more about what is going on. Such centrality rapidly develops in the wheel net, where there is little room for spontaneity. A hierarchy emerges that conforms to the formal demands of the system in which the central person at the hub sends and receives information from all. Thus on simple, repetitive problems, centrality assists development of problem-solving procedures that complete the tasks faster, with fewer errors, and fewer communications.

The advantages of centralization depend upon the nature of the task, however.[4] For example, if mottled-colored agates are substituted for solid-color marbles, the groups have troubles; finding the common marble is then very difficult for the wheel. The hub individual is overwhelmed because the perception and communication problems are just too great. That individual collects all the marble descriptions— but no two are alike! One person describes a marble as "yellow-green," but another categorizes the same marble as "aqua." Circle and all-channel nets also have difficulty but more are able to find solutions because of their feedback advantages. By not

FIGURE 11–2

Nets and Task

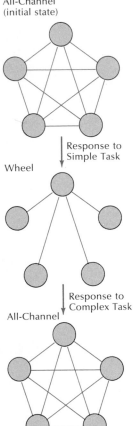

All-Channel
(initial state)

Response to
Simple Task

Wheel

Response to
Complex Task

All-Channel

restricting their communications as they did with simple problems, a freer exchange of perceptions is possible—"You remember that marble, Mike. It's what Diane was telling you about last time," and so on.

Task requirements therefore tend to determine network leadership, and groups adapt as necessary. (See Figure 11–2.) In one experiment, all-channel groups first worked in sequence eight simple, routine problems and then a series of four very difficult problems involving inference.[5] Most of the groups centralized (formed wheel networks) for the easier problems; speed increased, errors decreased, and the groups showed higher satisfaction. When a more difficult problem was given to the same groups, however, the heavy pressure on the central position led to quick decentralization (return to the all-channel net) by every group. In short, simple repetitive tasks tend to be solved by authoritarian means, and more complex and ambiguous tasks are more likely to be handled by participative means.

Behavior in Various Managerial Positions

Managers occupy a wide variety of positions, each with its own particular demands and responsibilities. As a result, managerial posts differ as to the hours required, the behavior desired, and the capacity of incumbents to control their own behavior.[6] There are no generally accepted definitions of different managerial positions, but we can consider one survey as an example.[7] The positions considered in this survey do not apply everywhere, of course; they are illustrative only. In descending order in the organizational hierarchy, the positions surveyed were: (1) general executives, (2) functional control managers, (3) sales managers, (4) service managers, and (5) operating supervisors.[8]

Two dimensions of the behavior of these managers are especially illustrative for

FIGURE 11–3

Time Spent in Response Behavior

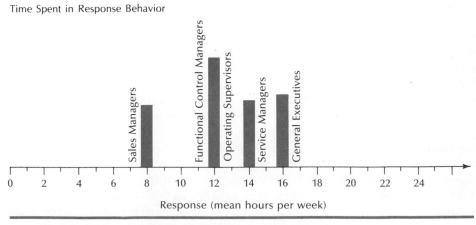

Source: R. A. Webber, *Time and Management* (New York: Van Nostrand Reinhold, 1972).

understanding the differences in positions: (1) responding to various people and (2) directing subordinates.

1. *Response behavior.* This dimension sums up the demands made upon the manager to respond to others. It includes time talking with people who call or come to the manager. (See Figure 11–3).
2. *Directive behavior.* The authoritarian dimension of management is suggested by time devoted to checking, auditing, giving orders, and directing the activities of others. (See Figure 11–4).

The difference in the behavior demonstrated by managers in the various positions was not random; it reflected differences in the demands imposed on each position. All positions do not allow the same autonomy or discretionary control over one's own behavior. In control over use of time, the positions surveyed ranked as follows:[9]

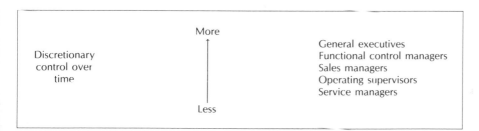

For example, service managers occupy the most programmed managerial position—they demonstrate the least variability in behavior. The job's requirements are so explicit and demanding that relatively little discretion is left to the incumbent.

FIGURE 11–4

Time Spent in Directive Behavior

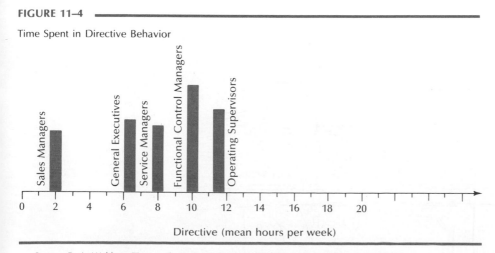

Source: R. A. Webber, *Time and Management* (New York: Van Nostrand Reinhold, 1972).

Many requests, directives, and demands come to the service manager. In a typical situation, the service manager has a door, a phone, sometimes a teletype, perhaps even an old-fashioned pneumatic tube. A person walks in the door, the phone rings, a message is printed out. All request the service manager to provide something—parts, repairs, tests, drawings, trucks. To most of these communications, the service manager responds by categorizing the request and issuing it to a subordinate. This manager's job is primarily responding to others' demands, so the organizationally determined imperatives of the position are great.

In contrast, high-level general executives have great discretion in controlling their own behavior. Behavior varies more widely among these managers than for any other position because the demands are ambiguous. Explicit short-range demands are relatively rare—for example, these officials apparently make fewer decisions (although more important and more difficult) than service managers or operating supervisors.

Note that we do not imply that either participative or authoritarian leadership is better. A supportive style is indicated by more time spent in responding to subordinates with advice and discussion and less time spent in checking on their performance and issuing directives. Authoritarian leadership is associated with more directing and checking, less responding. Contrasting styles reflect positional demands and the autonomy that is allowed. Because general executives have the most discretionary control over behavior, they tend to be participative in encouraging others to contact them, while refraining from directing. In contrast, operating supervisors and service managers have less discretion because job demands are explicit and constant; such managers are likely to be authoritarian. Thus, highly structured managerial positions with many explicit demands tend to manifest authoritarian leadership. The key variable is time: the time span required to obtain feedback on performance and the time span between performance reviews.[10] The shorter these time spans, the more structured the position and the less discretionary the behavior.

From *The Wall Street Journal,* with permission of Cartoon Features Syndicate.

Behavior in Different Settings

Similar findings were realized in a study of organization and leadership styles in four companies in two industries: container manufacturing plants and research and development laboratories.[11] These two settings are about as different as possible. Can manufacturing is repetitious and highly mechanized. Rolls of steel or aluminum are fed to machinery that cuts, shapes, coats the metal with plastic, and prints the label. The machinery determines productivity as long as people keep it running. Although the technology is sophisticated, the manager's task is relatively simple: Keep the equipment on line and the people working. It should be similar to the experience of the wheel network with the solid-color marbles. In contrast, research and development is more ambiguous and dependent on individual and team creativity. It should be similar to the experiment with the mottled-colored marbles and the all-channel network.

Two pairs of the two organizations were compared: a profitable, effective container manufacturer versus a less successful container company, and an innovative, prestigious, new-product laboratory versus a less successful research facility. The results were as follows:

The effective container manufacturer was characterized by centralized management decision making and a basically authoritarian climate. Worker morale was apparently good; at least the working conditions and benefits were considered acceptable.

The less successful container manufacturer was characterized by decentralized decision making and a more participative climate. Morale was lower than in the more authoritarian, more effective plant.

The effective research and development laboratory was characterized by decentralized decision making and a participatory climate. Researcher motivation and morale was generally high.

The less successful research and development lab was characterized by a factory-like climate with centralized decision making and authoritarian control. Researcher morale and motivation were generally low.

This distinction of behavior by company activity extends to parts of organizations as well. In hospitals, the leadership climate on surgical floors is markedly different than it is on medical floors.[12] The patients and tasks are different. In surgery, the mission is usually clear: to perform a certain operation and assist recovery. Authority is centralized in one person who must be able to make rapid decisions to which others respond quickly. Communications are mainly unidirectional downward. Everyone else, including residents, interns, and nurses, is low in status compared with the chief surgeon.

In contrast, medical teams are in a different situation. Their task is more ambiguous and much slower: diagnosis and development of treatment plans and hourly care of the patient. What is to be done for the patient is more subtle and less predictable than in surgery. Communications are much more likely to be two-way, up and down between physician in charge and others who are closer to the patient. Decision making is more of a joint endeavor because the doctor is more dependent on resident personnel.

FIGURE 11–5

Comparison of Leadership Styles and Task Structure

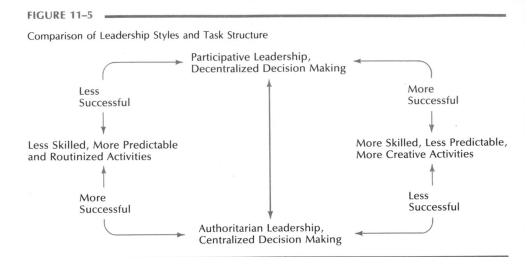

The relationship of participative and authoritarian leadership styles to different types of activities are compared in Figure 11–5.

Situational Leadership

Fitting together the situational factors affecting managerial behavior in the contingency theory of leadership is complex. However, we can describe the situation along three major dimensions:[13]

1. Leader's position power: What formal power to reward and punish followers does the leader possess? The greater the power, the greater the ability to influence.
2. Leader-follower relations: How much do followers or subordinates like and respect their superior as a person? To the extent that they like the superior, his or her ability to influence them is increased.
3. Task structure: How narrowly can the task be defined for issuing directions? Is it a programmable, repetitive task or an ambiguous, unstructured activity requiring creative input from the followers?

Eight common combinations of these dimensions can be defined. These situations are listed in Figure 11–6 in order of "favorableness" to the leader. Favorableness is judged by the influence possessed by the leader; the more influence possessed, the more favorable the situation for the leader.

Where Task-Oriented Leadership Works

Evidence exists that the task-oriented, authoritarian leader seems to work best when in *very favorable* and *very unfavorable* situations.[14] Where the leader is liked and respected, possesses great formal power, and the task is simply structured,

FIGURE 11–6

Effective Leadership in Various Situations

Favorableness of Situation	Effective Leader is . . .	Situation	Leader-Follower Relations	Task Structure	Position Power
Favorable for Leader					
	Task oriented, authoritarian	1	good	structured	high
		2	good	structured	low
		3	good	unstructured	high
	People oriented, permissive, considerate	4	good	unstructured	low
		5	poor	structured	high
		6	poor	structured	low
	Task oriented, authoritarian	7	poor	unstructured	high
		8	poor	unstructured	low
Unfavorable for Leader					

the situation (No. 1) is so favorable that response to the authoritarian style seems automatic, quick, and effective. Such might be the response to a quality testing manager who directed a group of semiskilled people on fairly routine tasks. It would also characterize the successful football coach driving a team to shape up.

Where the leader is disliked, he or she has little power, and the task is ambiguous, the situation (No. 8) is so unfavorable that the leader has little choice: Only the task-oriented manager seems to work. A more people-oriented, participative manager will probably be just brushed aside by "followers." This has been the case with unpopular managers supervising scientists and engineers in innovative industries. It also characterized the plight of some young U.S. Army infantry officers in Vietnam. Although they appeared to have power, actually many were so inexperienced and dependent on their subordinates in a very confusing battle situation that they were in danger of losing all influence.

Where People-Oriented Leadership Works

In contrast, intermediate favorable-unfavorable situations tend to be best handled by a more people-oriented, participative, permissive, and considerate approach.[15] Where the leader is liked but has little formal power and the task is unstructured, involvement of followers is necessary. Many college department heads find themselves in this situation (No. 4). The intermediate favorable-unfavorable situation also might apply to an administrative assistant to the president. One who is liked by everyone as a sensitive young "comer" but who performs an unstructured job with low positional and personal power might follow a more people-oriented, participative style.

This contingency model with its eight situational categories is by no means the definitive aid to understanding what leadership style is appropriate. New ideas will undoubtedly be advanced, but the model makes what will remain important points:

1. Sometimes a manager can and must exercise task-oriented and authoritarian leadership regardless of subordinates' desires *and* regardless of his or her own preference. At such times a manager must bite the bullet, make authoritative decisions, issue directives, and ensure compliance.

2. Sometimes a manager can and must exercise people-oriented and participative leadership, regardless of his or her own preference. At such times, a manager must invite subordinates to participate, join in their discussions, and ratify their decisions.

The manager's problem, of course, is knowing what situation he or she is in. This requires both skill and experience.

Increasing the Likelihood of Leader Effectiveness

The effectiveness of a leader, is expected to increase when there is a fit between style, traits, behaviors, and the situation. In other words, the situation determines the appropriateness of a particular leadership style.

We have indicated that a manager can choose between three sets of leadership behaviors. Directive behavior is more "boss centered" and emphasizes initiating structure and pressures for performance. Supportive leadership is centered around employees and emphasizes considerate leader behaviors. Participative leader behavior is often referred to as group or team-oriented behavior, since the manager emphasizes both initiating structure and consideration but also shares the responsibility for task performance and maintenance functions with the group. When is each approach more appropriate?

Directive Leadership.   The following conditions suggest the appropriateness of a more directive approach to leadership:[16]

1. Efforts to provide a more structured situation are appreciated by employees when the job is so unstructured that task ambiguity creates frustration and tension.
2. In those situations in which subordinates need information and technical support from the manager, more directive behavior is seen as coaching and facilitates task accomplishment.
3. Employees with high dependency needs respond well to a directive approach.
4. A manager with strong position power can often use a directive style quite effectively.
5. Many employees have an expectation of a very directive leadership style.

Supportive Leadership.   Possible situations indicating the appropriateness of a supportive style are listed below:[17]

1. Some jobs require a high degree of interaction among employees. A supportive leadership style can facilitate this interaction by creating a more cooperative climate.
2. Highly structured, routine tasks deny employees intrinsic outcomes. Supportive leader behaviors can serve to offset this negative feature.
3. A supportive style is effective with employees who have high social and affiliation needs.

Participative Leadership.   Those conditions suggesting a more participative approach to leadership are listed below:[18]

1. A high degree of interaction and dependence among employees suggests the use of a participative style to facilitate the frequency and quality of interactions.
2. When understanding and acceptance of a decision are important, a participative approach is required.
3. Participative leader behavior can be used when the tasks are intrinsically motivating.
4. If employees have the appropriate knowledge, information and experience to make informed choices and contributions, a participative style is useful.
5. Employees whose goals are compatible with organizational and group objectives respond well to participative behaviors.
6. Participative leadership is appropriate with individuals who have a strong need for achievement and autonomy.

Culture and Management

At the most general level, managerial behavior is affected by the culture in which each manager operates. Culture influences managerial philosophy and practice mainly through motivation. The idea that management works through people, however tautological, is vital for managers in a culture that differs from their own. Culture affects people, their needs, wants, and aspirations, all of which the manager must tap.[19] Not only does the culture in which the manager operates influence leadership style, but as noted in Chapter 3, culture influences the individual's need hierarchy, and hence it influences the motivation of managers and workers alike. Motivation in turn affects managerial attitudes and assumptions.[20]

In one study of managerial thinking, an attitudinal questionnaire was completed by thousands of managers in many countries.[21] The questions were divided into several areas, three of which will be considered here:

1. The capacity versus incapacity of the average person for leadership and initiative.
2. The desirability of management's sharing information and objectives with subordinates versus giving them only narrow and specific directives.
3. The desirability of subordinates' controlling their own performance (self-control) versus control by management (external control).

Figure 11–7 illustrates the findings about the attitudes of managers in different cultures regarding these three areas, based on standard scores. The horizontal line 0–0 represents the average of all respondents in all countries. Points above the line are greater than average; points below the line are less. The attitudes of U.S., Japanese, and German business managers and managers in underdeveloped nations are contrasted with the expressed attitudes of business students in the United States.

FIGURE 11–7

Managerial Attitudes in Different Cultures

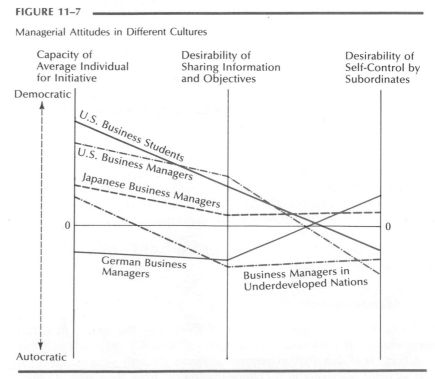

Source: Based on data in Mason Haire, Edwin E. Ghiselli, and Lyman W. Porter, *Managerial Thinking* (New York: John Wiley & Sons, 1966), supplemented with additional data.

Managerial Attitudes in Industrialized Nations

Among all business managers studied in the industrialized nations, those in the United States demonstrated the most optimistic or democratic assumption about the capacity and initiative of the average employee. Similarly, they expressed the most agreement with the desirability of sharing information about organization objectives rather than issuing narrow, detailed directives. In comparison with others, however, U.S. managers expressed themselves as downright authoritarian on control style; they feel that management must exercise close control and that money is the primary mechanism in doing so. In short, U.S. business managers espouse a more idealistic philosophy about human nature and managerial communications than most foreign managers do, but they are more skeptical about whether they should share any authority with subordinate groups or allow them much self-control. The fact that the response of American business students is quite similar to that of the American business managers surveyed suggests cultural continuity.[22]

The German business managers surveyed seemed most different from the U.S. managers. They manifested an elite-oriented view about the average individual's capacity for initiative and were skeptical about sharing information. Like many European managers, they are unlikely to communicate the basis of top decisions to lower managers.[23] Yet, in comparison with others, they seem to believe in self-control instead of close managerial control. Other research supports this; German business generally has not constructed the elaborate staffs, budgetary controls, and performance review systems that are characteristic of American management.[24]

The question is not whether any national pattern is better than any other. With Japan and Germany making a real race with the United States in business competition, it is apparent that the managerial attitudes in all three countries will work. The more relevant question is whether any pattern is suited to the situation of the managers involved. For example, the German–U.S. difference reflects many factors, one of them being the attitudes toward authority, which have their roots in the child-rearing patterns and the social support given to authority figures in each culture.

In 1959, a survey of German and American mothers examined the attributes they considered desirable in their children.[25] They were asked to rank 10 favorable attributes in order of desirability, including such characteristics as sociability, creativity, obedience, popularity, and self-reliance. German mothers ranked obedience first as the most desired attribute. American mothers ranked obedience last, judging it to be desirable but not as much so as social compatibility, respect for others' rights, and self-confidence, among others. A current survey might indicate improvement in the importance of obedience as a reaction to perceived overpermissiveness, but its low ranking is consistent with traditional American attitudes toward authority.[26]

As far back as colonial times, foreign observers noted the antiauthority climate in America: children were disrespectful to parents, buildings were torn down not long after completion, and a secular religion of progress seemed to rule the land. In part this attitude can be explained by our youth as a nation and our intention to forge a new history rather than continuing the English past. It was also fostered by our distrust of centralized power and government; the shortage of labor, which provided opportunity; and the ready availability of land. In the early years of U.S.

history, a son did not have to live indefinitely under his father's hand, waiting to inherit the farm. He could and did leave, for a job in the city or his own piece of land. The myth of the frontier had enough reality to shape attitudes toward authority in the developing nation.

German culture, in contrast, has set a higher premium on childhood and adulthood obedience. Given their cultural attitudes toward authority, German managers have been able to issue a directive and assume that it will be carried out, without close monitoring of their subordinates. In the United States, we have been optimistic about individual capacity but skeptical about behavior of subordinates (and children) when we are not watching. Consequently, we are inclined to monitor more closely and to utilize economic incentives or sanctions as a mechanism to ensure compliance.

These situations are not static, of course. In Germany one of the older major corporations is the Siemens Company, the tenth largest electrical goods manufacturer in the world. In the past 15 years its world position has been declining, largely because of lagging product innovation in competition with the Japanese. The company analyzed its problem to be overrigidity and inadequate communications, particularly upward in the organization. The customary procedure had been for top management to make decisions and pass directives down the line. Consequently, lower levels were ignorant about the organization's problems and objectives and could offer little help except obedience to orders. Encouragement of frank criticism and consideration of suggestions have provided the central thrust of Siemens's reform efforts (as exemplified by the chief executive's observations that "previously, anybody who dared criticize the company would have been shot," and "there are fewer Prince Albert coats on Siemens executives now").

Siemens has apparently made progress in freeing up the organization, but their altered assumptions about individual capacity and the desirability of communication also seem to have produced changes in management's control system. Siemens is now installing much more elaborate planning, control, and budgeting systems, paralleling American management practices. Rather than assuming the good intentions and obedience of subordinates, they are beginning to monitor behavior more closely and to strengthen management control.[27]

Thus, although the German pattern may have worked in their culture in the past, it may also have been detrimental to creativity, innovation, and organizational flexibility. The U.S. business pattern has worked in American culture, but at some cost in efficiency—particularly in expenditures for staff departments that have been substantially higher per 1,000 production workers than in almost all other industrialized countries.[28]

Managerial Attitudes in Underdeveloped Nations

Figure 11–7 indicates that elitist and autocratic attitudes were expressed by managers in underdeveloped nations. They were the most negative on communicating anything but narrow instructions, on the possibility of subordinate participation, and on control. More than any other managers, they seem to communicate only specific instructions and to control subordinate behavior closely.

Other research indicates that American chief executives think that successful managers are interested in subordinates' ideas, while Latin American and Asian managers express much less agreement with this idea.[29] They see giving exact directions to subordinates as much more important. Managers in underdeveloped countries seem to feel that subordinates have little ability and little to offer other than muscle, and they are not to be trusted. Given the relatively few educated people and traditional social structures in many underdeveloped countries, those assumptions are probably valid, but they do reflect a cultural perspective.[30] For example, American managers in India perceive their Indian subordinates as being more competent and trustworthy than Indian managers perceive their native subordinates, whom they tend to characterize as incompetent and untrustworthy. Consistently, American organizations in less developed nations are judged to demonstrate more democratic leadership styles than local companies.[31]

Non-American managers in underdeveloped countries of which they are not natives seem to echo imperialism's old philosophy. Many feel that autocratic strength is essential; any departure from strong central control and the exercise of sanctions might be interpreted as weakness, opening the situation to dangerous questions and threatening subordinate actions.

The apparently more democratic American managerial views are not necessarily better or appropriate in other countries, however. Some studies show that in direct competition with American multinational firms, locally owned and managed Latin American companies perform better.[32] One experiment with participative management indicated that whereas this style led to increased productivity, employee cooperation, and satisfaction in the United States, the same style applied in Norway had no effect on performance.[33] Workers did not view their participation as legitimate.

Managerial Attitudes in Different Institutions

Managerial attitudes vary not only among different national cultures, but also among various institutions within a culture. Figure 11–8 summarizes the attitudes of managers in three U.S. institutions—an electronics corporation, the army, and the nursing profession. Personnel completed the same questionnaire as in the international study.[34]

American managers in the electronics corporation surveyed expressed views roughly similar to those expressed by the larger sample of American business managers. The position on the three issues taken by U.S. Army officers and civilian hospital nursing supervisors roughly fell between those of business managers in the United States and Germany. In comparison with other Americans, these professionals are less optimistic about the capacity of the average individual and less favorable to sharing information and objectives with subordinates, although they are higher than the German managers in both areas. In their belief in self-control by subordinates, they are closer to the German managers than to the U.S. managers. The reasons for these attitudes might include the following factors:

1. The degree of respect and support for authority has undoubtedly been higher in the military than it has in American society in general. Therefore, military managers could make certain assumptions about obedience without as great a need for close monitoring.[35]

FIGURE 11–8

Managerial Attitudes in Various Organizations

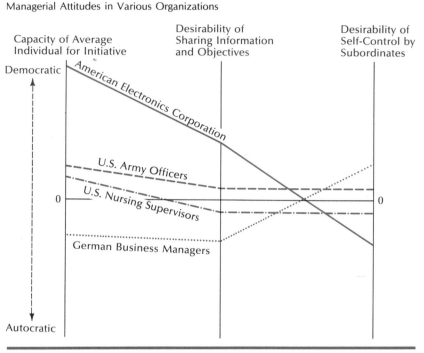

2. The cultures of hospitals and the nursing profession would seem to be similar in their traditional emphasis on authority and obedience. Undoubtedly this was related in the past to the power of the male physician over female nurses, but today's female nursing supervisors also subscribe to this philosophy in their attitudes about subordinates.[36] Although more assertive styles are appearing, especially among university-trained registered nurses, the orientation toward passive acceptance of authoritarianism has long been part of the training in hospital schools of nursing.[37]

3. Business managers frequently suggest that lack of close control and underutilization of financial leverage are characteristic of a nonprofit orientation. Differing missions and fairly abundant availability of funds in the past for both the army and for health care may have retarded the development of the budgetary control mechanisms that develop in business organizations.

4. The tasks of Army officers and nursing supervisors may support their attitude profiles. Authoritarian management is associated with: (1) need for great reaction speed (as when under attack); (2) need for predictable and standard action (so that it fits in with the behavior of others); (3) repetition of relatively simple tasks; and (4) involuntary tasks—especially where risk is involved.

5. Finally, the profiles of these two institutions may suit the majority of the employees or subordinates they manage. All managers are constrained by the expectations of their subordinates. If they have relatively few exceptions of satisfying any needs

on the job, an authoritarian style is encouraged. The ambition, education, and skill of their subordinates may reinforce the attitudes of military officers and nursing supervisors.

SUMMARY

Managers never completely control their own leadership behavior. It is affected by the demands of the position and by the task, among other factors. Research and experimentation in laboratories and in real organizations suggest that repetitive, routinized, relatively simple, and programmable tasks tend to be handled by centralized decision making and authoritarian control. Ambiguous, unpredictable, and complex tasks tend to be handled by more decentralized decision making and participation.

Different managerial positions, from operating supervisors to general executives, tend to be characterized by differing task and time demands that lead to behavior consistent with the above observations: authoritarian control in positions under explicit task and time demands; more nondirective behavior in higher level positions with less explicit demands allowing more discretionary control over behavior.

Contingency theory suggests that task-oriented authoritarian leadership is most effective in situations that are either very favorable or very unfavorable to the manager. A favorable situation is one in which the leader's power is great, relations with subordinates are good, and the task is highly structured. An unfavorable situation is one in which the manager's power is weak, relations are poor, and the task is unstructured and unpredictable. Situations of intermediate favorableness are better handled through more people-oriented, considerate, and concerned leadership.

National culture exercises a pervasive influence on behavior, values, and expectations. In comparison with managers in other countries, American business managers are the most democratic in their views on the capacity of average individuals and the desirability of sharing information and organizational objectives with subordinates. Nonetheless, they believe relatively more strongly that management should monitor and control subordinate behavior closely. In contrast, German business managers demonstrate autocratic attitudes about people and sharing information but apparently assume that subordinates will automatically obey explicit directives. Their performance does not have to be monitored closely; they can control themselves.

Managers in underdeveloped countries demonstrate elitist views: that good managers should give narrow directives and control subordinates closely. U.S. Army officers and civilian hospital nursing supervisors exhibit attitudes intermediate between those of American and German business managers. Their cultures seem to share aspects of both democracy and authoritarianism.

REVIEW QUESTIONS

1. What are wheel, circle, and all-channel communication networks?

2. How does the wheel network solve repetitive simple problems?

3. In the wheel network, who emerges as the decision maker on simple tasks? Why?

4. How does the all-channel network solve repetitive simple problems?

5. In the all-channel network, who emerges as the decision maker on simple tasks. Why?

6. What happens to the wheel and all-channel performance when the problem is transferred from simple to complex?

7. Why do high-level general executives spend relatively little time giving directives, as compared with operating supervisors?

8. Why do sales managers spend so little time responding to others, compared with general executives?

9. How do positions vary in the degree of discretionary control over behavior that the manager enjoys? Why?

10. Why do general executives have great discretionary control, and service managers possess much less?

11. What was the management style in the successful mass-production container plant? How did this compare to the less successful container plant?

12. What was the management style in the successful research and development laboratory as compared with the less effective laboratory?

13. In the contingency theory, what is the favorableness and unfavorableness of the situation to the leader?

14. What situations are best handled by a task-oriented, authoritarian style?

15. What situations are best handled by a people-oriented, permissive style?

16. How does culture affect attitudes toward work and management?

17. What nation's business managers seem to make the most optimistic assumptions about the average employee? Which ones are the least optimistic?

18. What nation's business managers seem to believe most in the desirability of close control through rewards? Which ones believe most in employee self-control?

19. What factors might explain the difference between the attitudes of German and American business managers?

20. How is the U.S. managers' preference for close control expressed in management practice? Does this seem inconsistent with their views on the capacity of the average individual?

21. Why do managers in underdeveloped nations manifest such autocratic views?

22. How do the attitudes of U.S. Army officers and civilian nursing supervisors compare with those of American and German business managers? Why?

Notes and References on Contingency Leadership

1. Harold Guetzkow and Herbert A. Simon, "The Impact of Certain Communication Nets upon Organization and Performance in Task-Oriented Groups," *Management Science* 1, nos. 3 and 4 (1955), pp. 233–50.

2. In the research of Guetzkow and Simon, all 15 wheel groups had a person at the hub make decisions, and they reached their optimal speed by the 8th of 20 trials. Of the 20 all-channel nets, 16 converted basically to wheels and achieved speeds as fast as original wheels by the 17th to 20th trials. Of the 21 circle nets, a variety of structures emerged, but only 4 converted to three-level hierarchies and reached speeds almost as fast as the wheels; the other circles ended up using 60 percent more time.

3. Alex Bavelas, "Communication Patterns in Task-Oriented Groups," *Journal of Acoustical Society of America* 22 (1950), pp. 725–30.

4. Harold J. Leavitt, "Communication Nets in Groups," in *Managerial Psychology,* 2d ed. (Chicago: University of Chicago Press, 1964). See also G. Heise and G. Miller, "Problem Solving by Small Groups Using Various Communication Nets," *Journal of Abnormal and Social Psychology* 46 (1951), pp. 327–35; G. H. Lewis, "Organization in Communication Networks," *Comparative Group Studies* 2 (1971), pp. 149–60; and P. Mears, "Structuring Communication in a Working Group," *Journal of Communication* 24, no. 1 (1974), pp. 71–79.

5. C. Faucheux and K. D. Mackenzie, "Task Dependency of Organizational Centrality: Its Behavioral Consequences," *Journal of Experimental Sociology and Psychology* 2, no. 4 (1966), pp. 361–75; M. E. Shaw and J. M. Blum, "Effects of Leadership Style upon Group Performance as a Function of Task Structure," *Journal of Personality and Social Psychology* 3 (1966), pp. 238–42.

On the tendency of groups to continue old problem-solving patterns when the task changes, see A. M. Cohen, "Changing Small-Group Communication Networks," *Administrative Science Quarterly* 6, no. 4 (1962), pp. 443–62. However, experiments indicate that leaders can change their style as the task changes. W. A. Hill and D. Hughes, "Variations in Leader Behavior as a Function of Task Type," *Organizational Behavior and Human Performance* 11 (1974), pp. 83–96.

6. One fact seems to characterize almost all managers: They work long hours. According to data from the household surveys of the Bureau of Labor statistics, managers put in more time than any other nonfarm occupational group. The list runs: (1) managers, officials, and proprietors, 47.0 hours per week; (2) crafters and first-line supervisors, 40.9 hours; (3) professional and technical workers, 39.6 hours; (4) operatives, 39.6 hours; (5) sales workers, 36.6 hours; (6) clerical workers, 35.6 hours; (7) laborers, 34.4 hours, and (8) private household workers, 22.0 hours per week. Other research indicates that the average manager spends approximately 43 hours per week at the office. To this must be added seven hours per week at home doing paperwork and business, another five hours on business entertaining, and perhaps five hours on commuting (which is probably low)—a grand total of some 60 hours per week. Data on hours worked per week from Bureau of Labor Statistics, *Employment and Earnings* 17, no. 11 (May 1971).

For a rich description of the leadership process at several different levels of management, see M. Maccoby, *The Leader* (New York: Simon and Schuster, 1981).

7. Ross A. Webber, *Time and Management* (New York: Van Nostrand Reinhold, 1972). For other behavioral definitions of positions, see: Leonard R. Sayles, *Managerial Behavior* (New York: McGraw-Hill, 1964), and Rosemary Stewart, "A Behavioral Classification of Managerial Jobs," *Omega: The International Journal of Management Science* 1, no. 3 (1973), pp. 297–304.

8. Sample sizes in the Webber survey were: general executives, 11; functional control managers, 10; sales managers, 8; service managers, 7; and operating supervisors, 10.

9. Variation in managerial behavior may be greatest at the top levels because these executives are above bureaucratic controls, according to John Child, "Strategies of Control and Organizational Behavior," *Administrative Science Quarterly* 18, no. 1 (1973), pp. 1–17. Also see Rosemary Stewart, "The Manager's Job: Discretion versus Demand," *Organizational Dynamics* 2, no. 3 (1974), p. 67 ff.

10. F. A. Heller found authoritarian decision making associated with unimportant and very time-pressured decisions; production was most centralized, general management less so. "Leadership, Decision Making and Contingency Theory," *Industrial Relations* 12, no. 2 (1973), pp. 183–99. On discretionary time spans, see Eliott Jacques, *Measurement of Responsibility* (New York: John Wiley & Sons, 1972).

W. A. Hill reports that most managers are perceived by their subordinates as demonstrating several leadership styles at different times. Therefore, he concludes, managers are flexible. It is doubtful that all are, however. See W. A. Hill, "Leadership Style: Rigid or Flexible," *Organizational Behavior and Human Performance,* 9 (1973), pp. 35–47.

11. J. J. Morse and J. W. Lorsch, "Beyond Theory Y," *Harvard Business Review,* May–June 1970, pp. 61–68.

12. R. L. Coser, "Authority and Decision Making in a Hospital: A Comparative Analysis," *American Sociological Review,* February 1958, pp. 56–63.

The very training of surgeons tends to strengthen authoritarian views. John Eisenberg, Deborah Kitz, and Ross A. Webber, "Development of Attitudes about Sharing Decision Making—A Comparison of Medical and Surgical Residents," *Journal of Health and Social Behavior,* March 1983), pp. 85–90.

13. On the contingency theory of management, see Fred E. Fiedler, "A Contingency Model of Leadership Effectiveness," *Advances in Experimental Social Psychology,* vol. 1 (New York: Academic Press, 1964), pp. 149–90; and Fiedler, *A Theory of Leadership Effectiveness* (New York: McGraw-Hill, 1967).

A review of the research is contained in T. R. Mitchell et al., "The Contingency Model: Criticism and Suggestions," *Academy of Management Journal,* September 1970, pp. 253–67. For mixed results on tests of the model, see F. E. Fiedler, "Validation and Extension of the Contingency Model of Leadership Effectiveness: A Review of Empirical Findings, *Psychological Bulletin* 76 (1971), pp. 128–48; George Graen et al., "Contingency Model of Leadership Effectiveness: Antecedent and Evidential Results," *Psychological Bulletin* 74 (1970), pp. 285–96; George Graen, J. Orris, and K. Alvares, "Contingency Theory of Leadership Effectiveness: Some Experimental Results," *Journal of Applied Psychology* 55 (1971), pp. 196–201; and A. K. Korman, "On the Development of Contingency Theories of Leadership: Some Methodological Considerations and a Possible Alternative," *Journal of Applied Psychology* 58, no. 3 (1973), pp. 384–87.

For a devasting criticism of Fiedler's contingency model, see C. A. Schriesheim and S. Kerr, "Theories and Measures of Leadership: A Critical Appraisal of Current and Future Directions," in J. G. Hunt and L. A. Larson, eds., *Leadership: The Cutting Edge* (Carbondale, Ill.: Southern Illinois University Press, 1977).

14. L. K. Michaelsen has reported that in a very unfavorable situation, supervisors directed most of their behavior toward the achievement of their primary goals; whereas in a very favorable situation, they concentrated more on the achievement of secondary goals. Groups supervised by task-oriented leaders were more effective in situations of either high or low favorability, and groups supervised by interpersonal relations-oriented leaders were more effective in situations of intermediate favorability. "Leader Orientation, Leader Behavior, Group Effectiveness and Situational Favorability: An Empirical Extension of the Contingency Model," *Organizational Behavior and Human Performance* 9 (1973), pp. 226–45.

15. The manager in an intermediate favorable situation may have a difficult time diagnosing the situation. Intelligence may help here to a greater extent than in the very favorable or unfavorable situations. See L. S. Csoka, "A Relationship between Leader Intelligence and Leader Rated Effectiveness," *Journal of Applied Psychology* 59, no. 1 (1974), pp. 43–47, and L. L. Larson and K. M. Rowland, "Leadership Style and Cognitive Complexity," *Academy of Management Journal,* March 1974, pp. 37–45.

For a thorough discussion of the leadership style required in the decade ahead, see D. L. Bradford and A. R. Cohen, *Managing for Excellence* (New York: John Wiley & Sons, 1984).

16. See S. Kerr, C. A. Schriescheim, C. J. Murphy, and R. M. Stogdill, "Toward a Contingency Theory of Leadership Based upon the Consideration and Initiating Structure Literature," *Organizational Behavior and Human Performance* 12 (1974), pp. 62–82; and R. J. House and T. R. Mitchell, "Path-Goal Theory of Leadership," *Journal of Contemporary Business* 5 (1974), pp. 81–97.

17. T. W. Johnson, "The Path-Goal Theory of Leadership: A Partial Test and Suggested Refinement," *Academy of Management Journal* 18 (1975), pp. 242–52; and House and Mitchell, "Path-Goal Theory."

18. T. R. Mitchell, "Motivation and Participation: An Integration," *Academy of Management Journal* 16 (1973), pp. 670–79; and House and Mitchell, "Path-Goal Theory."

For a general discussion of the keys to effective leadership, see M. W. McCall, *Leadership and the Professional* (Greensboro, N.C.: Center for Creative Leadership, 1982).

19. J. A. Lee, "Cultural Analysis in Overseas Operations," *Harvard Business Review,* March–April 1966, pp. 106–14.

To develop an appreciation for leadership orientations and issues in other cultures, see J. G. Hunt (ed.), *Leaders and Managers: International Perspectives on Managerial Behavior and Leadership* (Elmsford, NY: Pergamon Press, 1984).

20. Years ago, scholars and practitioners tended to think that the principles of management were universal, that they applied everywhere. Increasingly, we have come to recognize that American management does not work everywhere and is not universal. See R. F. Gonzales and C. McMillan, "The Universality of American Management," *Academy of Management Journal* 4 (1961), pp. 34–41; W. Oberg, "Cross-Cultural Perspectives on Management Principles," *Academy of Management Journal* 6 (1963), pp. 129–43. Also see A. F. Negandhi and B. D. Estafen, "A Research Model to Determine the Applicability of American Management Know-How in Differing Cultures and/or Environments," *Academy of Management Journal,* December 1965, pp. 309–18; Harold D. Koontz, "A Model for Analyzing the Universality and Transferability of Management," *Academy of Management Journal,* December 1969, pp. 415–30; G. F. Farris and D. A. Butterfield, "Are Current Theories of Leadership Culture Bound?" in E. A. Fleishman and J. G. Hunt, eds., *Current Developments in the Study of Leadership* (Carbondale, Ill.: Southern Illinois University Press, 1973); and A. Pizam and A. Reichel, "Cultural Determinants of Managerial Behavior," *Management International Review* 17, no. 2 (1977), pp. 65–72.

21. Mason Haire, Edwin E. Ghiselli, and Lyman W. Porter, *Managerial Thinking,* New York: John Wiley & Sons, 1966).

For surveys of cross-cultural management research, see Ross A. Webber, *Culture and Management: Text and Readings in Comparative Management* (Homewood, Ill.: Richard D. Irwin, 1969); and G. V. Barrett and B. M. Bass, "Comparative Surveys of Managerial Attitudes and Behavior," in J. Jean Boddewyn, ed., *Comparative Management: Teaching, Training and Research* (New York: New York University Press, 1970).

22. For a view that modern American management is still basically authoritarian and that managers treat others as objects, see Harry Levinson, *The Great Jackass Fallacy* (Boston: Graduate School of Business Administration, Harvard University, 1973). One survey indicates that business students are more Machiavellian and more willing to use coercion than managers. R. J. Burke, "Effects of Organizational Experience on Managerial Attitudes and Beliefs: A Better Press for Managers," *Journal of Business Research* 1, no. 1 (1973), pp. 21–30.

23. Otto Nowotny, "American versus European Management Philosophy," *Harvard Business Review,* March–April 1964, pp. 101–8. A study of French management documented the emphasis on authority, close management, and assumption of executive omnipotence. Decentralization was viewed as management failure. G. Trepo, "Management Style à la Française," *European Business,* Autumn 1973, pp. 71–79.

24. F. Harbison and C. Myers, *Management in the Industrial World* (New York: McGraw-Hill, 1959). The German style places great emphasis on long-run financial stability; short-run profits are less important. Prudence, close control, and centralization are paramount—J. D. Daniels and J. Arpan, "Comparative Home Country Influences on Management Practices Abroad," *Academy of Management Journal* 15, no. 3 (1972), pp. 305–15.

25. Survey reported in *Newsweek,* September 23, 1968. See also R. D. Meade and J. O. Whittaker, "A Cross-Cultural Study of Authoritarianism," *Journal of Social Psychology* 72 (1967), pp. 3–7.

26. Another study offers insights into attitudes in the

United States as compared with those in the Soviet Union. It probed teenagers' willingness to engage in antisocial or antiauthority behavior (such as cheating on examinations, breaking street lights, and stealing public property), under three conditions: (1) when teachers or parents were to be told of the act, (2) when only their friends were to be told, and (3) when no one but themselves was to know.

Russian girls indicated virtually no willingness to engage in antiauthority behavior under any circumstances—even on an anonymous test. In the United States, results indicated girls are much less likely to engage in such behavior than are boys. Soviet boys were willing to perform these acts if no one was to know, much less if teachers and parents were to be told, and *least* if friends were to know. Soviet culture, reinforced by fear or tradition, holds such behavior in low regard. This is apparently not the case in the United States, where boys were willing to engage in *the most* antiauthority behavior when their friends were to know—*even more than if no one were to know.* Apparently, the bravado associated with such behavior brings admiration and prestige. Uri Bronfenbrenner, *Two Worlds of Childhood* (New York: Russell Sage Foundation, 1970). Also see G. F. Jensen, "Parents, Peers and Delinquent Action," *American Journal of Sociology* 78, no. 3 (1973), pp. 562–75.

27. "Siemens Manufactures a New Sense of Purpose," *International Management,* February 1971, p. 11 ff.

28. See R. Bendix, *Work and Authority in Industry* (New York: John Wiley & Sons, 1956).

29. R. B. Peterson, "Chief Executives' Attitudes: A Cross-Cultural Analysis," *Industrial Relations* 10, no. 2 (1971), pp. 194–210; and Peterson, "A Cross-Cultural Perspective of Supervisory Values," *Academy of Management Journal* 15, no. 1 (1972), pp. 105–17.

30. The amount of education common in a country may be the single largest influence on managerial attitudes. Musbaw Ajiferuke and J. Jean Boddewyn, "Socioeconomic Indicators in Comparative Management," *Administrative Science Quarterly* 15, no. 4 (1970), pp. 453–62. See also R. Farmer and B. Richman, *Comparative Management and Economic Progress* (Homewood, Ill.: Richard D. Irwin, 1965).

31. A. R. Negandhi and S. B. Prasad, *Comparative Management* (New York: Appleton-Century-Crofts, 1970). However, a study of successful U.S. managers transferred to Europe and Latin America indicates a shift of management style from employee to task orientation and from the participative to the authoritarian approach; they changed their opinions of subordinates. G. G. Alpander, "Drift to Authoritarianism: The Changing Managerial Styles of the U.S. Executive Overseas," *Journal of International Business Studies* 4, no. 2 (1973), pp. 1–14.

32. R. W. Wright, "Organizational Ambiente: Management and Environment in Chile," *Academy of Management Journal,* March 1971, pp. 65–74. See also A. R. Negandhi and B. C. Reimann, "A Contingency Theory of Organization Re-examined in the Context of a Developing Country," *Academy of Management Journal* 15, no. 2 (1972), pp. 137–46.

33. J. R. P. French, J. Israel, and D. As, "An Experiment on Participation in a Norwegian Factory," *Human Relations* 13 (1960), pp. 3–19. In contrast, in New Zealand, receptivity to participation is much greater. G. H. Hines, "Sociocultural Influences on Employee Expectancy and Participative Management," *Academy of Management Journal* 17, no. 2 (1974), pp. 334–39.

34. Haire, Ghiselli, and Porter, *Managerial Thinking.*

35. R. G. Gard, "Leadership in the Military," *Perspectives in Defense Management,* Spring 1973, pp. 49–56. Paradoxically, the authoritarianism of enlisted men seems to decline while in the service. One interpretation is that the experienced deprivation increases their sensitivity, respect, and tolerance for fellow citizens. K. Roghmann and W. Sodeur, "The Impact of Military Service on Authoritarian Attitudes," *American Journal of Sociology* 78, no. 2 (1972), pp. 418–30.

36. V. Wilson, "An Analysis of Femininity in Nursing," *American Behavioral Scientists* 15, no. 2 (1971), pp. 213–20. Nurses seem to perform best and to be most satisfied where supervision demonstrates a high task structure orientation, along with high consideration. L. Gruenfeld and S. Kassum, "Supervisory Style and Organizational Effectiveness in a Pediatric Hospital," *Personnel Psychology* 26, no. 4 (1973), pp. 531–44.

37. D. A. Ordrack, "Socialization in Professional Schools," *Administrative Science Quarterly,* March 1975, pp. 97–103.

Discussion Questions and Exercises on Managerial Leadership

Discussion Questions

1. If you drop an empty cigarette pack on a street in Bern, Switzerland, some citizen is likely to tell you to pick it up. If you drive down a Zurich street in the wrong direction in the middle of the night, someone will probably record your license plate number and report you to the police. In general, the Swiss observe their laws strictly. What does the influence model suggest about this?

2. Do you think fear, tradition, and blind faith are declining as influence systems in American political and economic life?

3. Why would any influence system work, theoretically?

4. A very successful regional sales manager for a national company states that he has every one of his sales representatives call him twice a day at appointed times when they are on the road. When asked why, he replied, "Well, first of all to keep them on the job, but mostly because salespersons get lonely out there. Most of them are insecure and anxious people; I want to buck them up twice a day, to show them someone cares." How would you analyze this manager's style?

5. Advocates of more participative management are sometimes rejected as unrealistic (and uneconomic) dreamers by more authoritarian managers. The participative advocates in turn argue that the authoritarians are simply afraid to change their style. What do you think of this?

6. A successful company president responded to a discussion of influence by observing, "I never met a person I couldn't motivate by either money or sex." What do you think of his view?

7. Most incoming students at the Wharton Graduate Division, University of Pennsylvania, seem to think that high morale leads to high productivity in industry. Nonetheless, 20 years of research indicates only a low correlation between these factors. Why do students' expectations apparently differ from the results of empirical research?

8. "Many a man is entirely incapable of assuming responsibility. He is a success as the led, but not as the leader. He lacks the courage or willingness to assume responsibility and the ability of handling others. He was born a salaried man, and a salaried man he had better remain." This is a statement in *The Boy, How to Help Him Succeed* by N. C. Fowler, published in 1902. What do you think of this view?

9. A battery company has operated a plant in the Northeast for many years. Until World War II, the company imported Filipinos to perform manufacturing operations that used sulfuric acid and lead components (apparently because they thought Filipinos had a natural resistance to lead poisoning). The workers stayed in the United States until they had saved some money, or until they became ill, and then returned to their home islands. Management generally treated

these people in a highly authoritarian manner, spelling out tasks and procedures in detail and supervising closely. In spite of this control, manufacturing was inefficient—little things were not done, cooperation was lacking, and effort was minimal. In addition, none of the workers seemed interested in filling supervisory positions.

Since World War II, the plant has changed greatly. The company relies much less on its coercive authority. What might have been the factors that explained the old style and the reasons for a change?

10. A study in South America indicated that where required capital funds were modest, Latin American-owned and managed firms were more authoritarian and more profitable than American-owned and managed companies in the same country. How would you explain this?

11. Why do you think the medical profession and health care institutions have generally been authoritarian in style?

12. Research suggests that large universities are more democratic in degree of faculty participation than small colleges, in which the administration tends to dominate. How would you explain this? Which situation do you think students would prefer?

Individual Exercises

1. Describe a person who has charisma *for you*. What attributes do you admire? How does he or she behave?

2. Describe an influence situation in which you have been involved, and analyze how it fits the probabilistic influence model in Figure 9–3.

3. Under which leadership style would you prefer to work? Why? Under what circumstances might you change your view?

4. Describe and analyze the relation between morale and performance in two organizations with which you are familiar (camp, summer job, team, etc.).

5. Describe and analyze the relation between managerial pressure and representativeness for any two superiors for whom you have worked.

6. Suppose you were a division manager who had three supervisors reporting to you: Supervisor A possesses a strong need for achievement; B is high in the power need; and C is very status and affiliative oriented. How would you vary your style in relation to each?

7. Suppose you were hired as a manager of 16 drill press operators in a plant. Your predecessor was a classic autocrat. Your own inclination is toward participative leadership. What problems might you face?

8. Describe and analyze a situation in which your peers' and subordinates' expectations affected your leadership style (on a job, in a team or fraternity, etc.).

Managerial Cases and Problems on Managerial Leadership

Frank Perriman's Appointment (A)*

Indefatigable Mutual Insurance is a large national company with more than 10,000 employees in the 50 states and Canada. Its basic organization has been as shown in Exhibit 1. Each divisional vice president has access to the president if so desired, but most actual communications between the field and home office are with the functional vice presidents, who set policy and monitor performance in their respective functional areas. The two senior vice presidents have acted as staff to the president in their areas of expertise—one in actuarial and statistical matters, the other in investments and finance. In general, Indefatigable Insurance has been a highly centralized, regionally dispersed organization.

Frank Perriman has had exceptional and striking success at Indefatigable. After experience primarily in sales, Frank was appointed vice president of the Middle Division at age 35—the youngest such appointment in the company's history. One annual report contained an individual picture of Frank (the only divisional vice president so honored) with a caption describing him as an example of what could happen to young people at Indefatigable. In general, however, most company executives were fairly old.

After eight years as division vice president, in June Frank was promoted to senior vice president (thus making three senior vice presidents) and transferred to the home office. The president sent the notifications shown in Exhibits 2 and 3.

At times Frank thought he had no problem. After all, he had been given a significant promotion. Nonetheless,

* Part (B) to this case is contained in the *Instructor's Manual.*

he was concerned because he feared resentment from others and was unclear what the president wanted. Frank had recently attended an executive program where they had discussed a case entitled "The Dashman Company," which told about a new vice president who utterly failed to exert any impact on the organization (see Exhibit 4). Accordingly, he decided to see Professor Eagleson, who had conducted various management training programs for the firm.

During the conversation, Eagleson pointed out that there was disparity in the managerial styles of the various division vice presidents. For example, when conducting a training program for managers in the Northern Division, he had the divisional functional managers draw an organization chart. This chart is illustrated in Exhibit 5. When sitting in the Northern Division's vice president's office one day, a divisional functional manager had come in with a problem about how to treat a certain policyholder. The vice president had asked the manager to read the relevant home office regulation on the matter and then directed the functional manager to adhere exactly to the home office rule.

By chance, Professor Eagleson had once been sitting in Perriman's office when a similar event occurred. After listening to the divisional manager and reading the home office regulation, Perriman had advised the manager that the regulation didn't exactly apply, so they were free to handle the matter as they deemed best. If headquarters would later complain to the manager, Perriman promised to say the action was his responsibility. When the Middle Division divisional managers had drawn the organization

EXHIBIT 1

Organization Chart

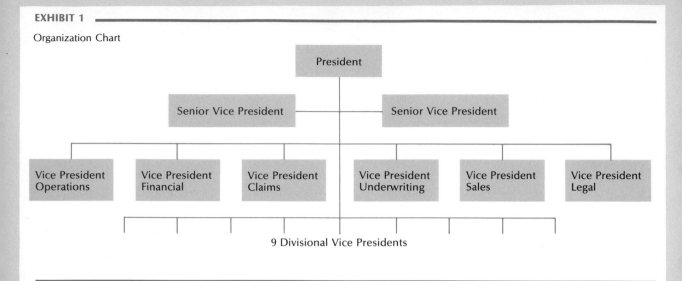

EXHIBIT 2

Organization Bulletin

HOME OFFICE ADMINISTRATION
June 29

ORGANIZATION BULLETIN—GENERAL No. 349

Effective August 1, Mr. Frank Perriman, Vice President and Division Manager, Middle Division, will transfer to the President's staff at the home office.

Perriman will be responsible to the President for achieving division performance in accordance with company policies and objectives.

Mr. Perriman will assist Division Managers in obtaining well-coordinated efforts by all departments and will establish and use measurements of results for each Division.

Divisional Vice Presidents will report to and be responsible to Mr. Perriman.

Thomas Achison
President

EXHIBIT 3

Organization Bulletin

HOME OFFICE ADMINISTRATION
July 14

ORGANIZATION BULLETIN—General No. 351

Effective July 14, the Board of Directors made the following election: Mr. Frank Perriman—Senior Vice President.

Thomas Achison
President

EXHIBIT 4

Dashman Company[1]

The Dashman Company was a large concern making many types of equipment for the armed forces of the United States. It had over 20 plants, located in the central part of the country, whose purchasing procedures had never been completely coordinated. In fact, the head office of the company had encouraged each of the plant managers to operate with their staffs as separate independent units in most matters. Late in 1940, when it began to appear that the company would face increasing difficulty in securing certain essential raw materials, Mr. Manson, the company's president, appointed an experienced purchasing executive, Mr. Post, as vice president in charge of purchasing, a position especially created for him. Mr. Manson gave Mr. Post wide latitude in organizing his job, and he assigned Mr. Larson as Mr. Post's assistant. Mr. Larson had served the company in a variety of capacities for many years, and knew most of the plant executives personally. Mr. Post's appointment was announced through the formal channels usual in the company, including a notice in the house organ published by the company.

One of Mr. Post's first decisions was to begin immediately to centralize the company's purchasing procedure. As a first step he decided that he would require each of the executives who handled purchasing in the individual plants to clear with the head office all purchase contracts which they made in excess of $10,000. He felt that if the head office was to do any coordinating in a way that would be helpful to each plant and to the company as a whole, he must be notified that the contracts were being prepared at least a week before they were to be signed. He talked his proposal over with Mr. Manson, who presented it to his board of directors. They approved the plan.

Although the company made purchases throughout the year, the beginning of its peak buying season was only three weeks away at the time this new plan was adopted. Mr. Post prepared a letter to be sent to the 20 purchasing executives of the company. The letter follows:

Dear _____ :
    The board of directors of our company has recently authorized a change in our purchasing procedures. Hereafter, each of the purchasing executives in the several plants of the company will notify the vice president in charge of purchasing of all contracts in excess of $10,000 they are negotiating at least a week in advance of the date on which they are to be signed.
    I am sure that you will understand and that this step is necessary to coordinate the purchasing requirements of the company in these times when we are facing increasing difficulty in securing essential supplies. This procedure should give us in the central office the information we need to see that each plant secures the optimum supply of materials. In this way the interests of each plant and of the company as a whole will best be served.

Yours very truly,

Mr. Post showed the letter to Mr. Larson and invited his comments. Mr. Larson thought the letter an excellent one but suggested that, since Mr. Post had not met more than a few of the purchasing executives, he might like to visit all of them and take the matter up with each of them personally. Mr. Post dismissed the idea at once because, as he said, he had so many things to do at the head office that he could not get away for a trip. Consequently he had the letters sent out over his signature.

During the two following weeks replies came in from all except a few plants. Although a few executives wrote at greater length, the following reply was typical:

Dear Mr. Post:
    Your recent communication in regard to notifying the head office a week in advance of our intention to sign contracts has been received. This suggestion seems a most practical one. We want to assure you that you can count on our cooperation.

Yours very truly,

During the next six weeks the head office received no notices from any plant that contracts were being negotiated. Executives in other departments who made frequent trips to the plants reported that the plants were busy, and the usual routines for that time of year were being followed.

---

[1] All names have been disguised.

Case material of the Harvard Graduate School of Business Administration is prepared as a basis for class discussion. Cases are not designed to present illustrations of either correct or incorrect handling of administrative problems.

Copyright, 1947, by the President and Fellows of Harvard College.

---

chart in their training session, it was as in Exhibit 6. In general, Eagleson felt that the Northern Division's vice president's behavior was more typical of the division vice presidents than Perriman's.

When Perriman asked Eagleson what he thought the president expected of the new position, the professor said

he wasn't sure. Nonetheless, he mentioned that when he had recently seen the president about company training programs, the executive had expressed concern about his age, next year's 100th anniversary celebration of the firm, and about the company's expense position. He had remarked on the way to lunch that the only thing wrong

EXHIBIT 5

Partial Organization Chart as Drawn by Northern Division Regional Functional Managers

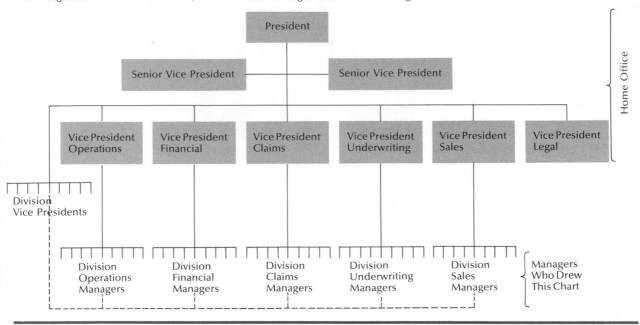

EXHIBIT 6

Partial Organization Chart as Drawn by Middle Division Regional Functional Managers

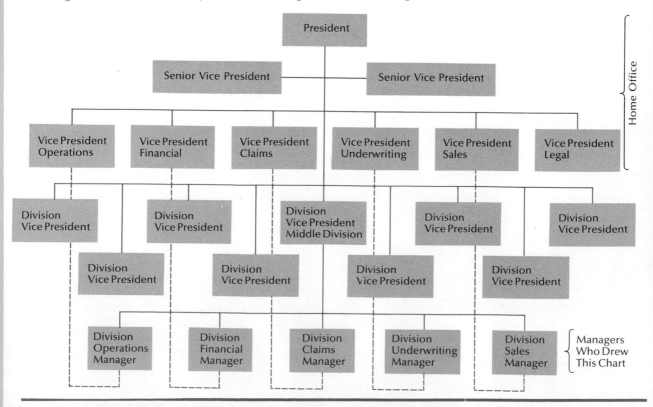

with the company was that the field personnel "just didn't follow home office rules." The president indicated that the company was losing money on automobile insurance policies especially because sales was selling to less desirable risks—contrary to the company's long-standing strategy of preferred risks. Perhaps, the president concluded, the field staff should be reduced and sales curtailed.

Pondering these points, Perriman wondered if one of his first steps as senior vice president should be to pick a fight with one of the home office functional vice presidents in order to impress the division vice presidents with his willingness to battle on their behalf.

Questions on Frank Perriman's Appointment (A)

1. Discuss any problems Perriman might have in establishing authority and influence in his new post.

2. What factors should aid Perriman?

3. What do you think the divisional vice presidents will think of this appointment? Why?

4. What do you think the functional vice presidents will think of this appointment? Why?

5. How do you think Achison should have proceeded?

6. How do you interpret the differences in the organization charts as drawn by the division functional managers in the Northern Division as compared with the Middle Division?

7. What does the president's remarks to Professor Eagleson suggest about his intentions for Perriman as the new senior vice president?

8. What recommendations would you offer Perriman now? Why?

Webster Arsenal (A)*

Webster Arsenal has been one of the U.S. Army's rifle and pistol manufacturing facilities since before the Civil War. Located in central Indiana, it is the largest industrial employer in the area, even though it employs only 800 persons.

The commanding officer and arsenal director is Colonel Sheridan Grant, a career army officer. Grant has been at Webster for two years and expects to remain until his retirement in two more years because he has been passed over for promotion to general. His associate director is a civilian, William Johnson, who has spent his entire career at Webster since leaving the military 20 years earlier. Johnson was promoted to associate director last year because he had a good record as a tough production manager and was then the most senior executive. Most of the additional personnel are civilians who are members of the civil service. A few army people occupy guard, clerical, and research positions, but their duties are essentially the same as the civilians with whom they work. The associate director is charged with responsibility for most day-to-day operations.

Although the arsenal is a nonprofit institution, it does have performance criteria set by the Department of the

Army in Washington, D.C. Essentially these include the following:

1. Remaining within budget.
2. Meeting production quotas with necessary reliability and quality.
3. Reducing costs on standard items.
4. Maintaining equipment in working order.
5. Maintaining personnel at peak efficiency.
6. Upgrading personnel skills through training.

Most of the production and testing equipment is old because the army has not provided sufficient funds for maintenance or replacement. Washington officials have chosen to spend money on more glamorous, sophisticated, and innovative weapons systems than the simple rifles and hand guns manufactured at Webster. As an apparent result of these equipment problems, the arsenal has experienced great difficulty in meeting its objectives. Prior to approximately eight months ago, the facility usually failed to achieve objectives only one or two months a year, but now they have failed four months in a row. A special problem has been inaccurate rifling (cutting the spiral grooves inside the gun barrel), which has required 30 to 40 percent reworking every month.

Colonel Grant is not a typical army officer, or at least he does not fit the stereotype. The best physical description

---

* Part (B) to this case is contained in the *Instructor's Manual.*

of him is that he is everyone's image of the kindly father—or grandfather—because his hair is all gray at 51. Grant expresses great faith in people.

> I have been in the Army for almost 30 years and the number of outright shirkers and goldbrickers I have encountered can be counted on my fingers. Most men will give you honest effort if you treat them fairly, show a strong personal interest, keep them informed, and let them participate in decisions so they can affect some aspects of their work.
>
> In addition, an officer or manager should keep his objectives in view and demonstrate a sense of perspective. I never conduct inspections to demonstrate that I'm a tough S.O.B., only to assist people in improving performance. No room has to be perfectly clean, none of that white-glove stuff, just clean enough so as not to affect product quality. In fact, my inspections here aren't really inspections at all, more like informal chats from time to time.

When William Johnson was promoted to associate director, Colonel Grant talked with him about his leadership philosophy. Johnson thought his views were fine, but he said he felt production workers needed a firm hand or performance would deteriorate.

Johnson set to work with an energy belying his years to correct the deficiencies he observed. New cleaning and inspection schedules were instituted, and a new gleam became evident in the plant. The floors and machinery definitely improved in appearance. Several training course instructors spoke to Johnson about employee complaints that their supervisors were not allowing them to attend the training courses held on company time, but Johnson replied that the place would have to be put in shipshape order first. Then he would see that the men were allowed to attend class again (although he did wonder how much training could be accomplished in the classroom).

Several supervisors complained to the colonel during this period about how tough things had become in recent months, but Grant reassured them that things would improve when budgetary pressures let up. Meanwhile, they should give their best efforts because he, the arsenal, the fighting men, and the nation were dependent on them. At one point, Grant considered talking to Johnson about the complaints but declined to do so because he believed that a subordinate should have freedom to perform a task delegated to him.

The department head in rifling is Frank Widner, the youngest supervisor in the arsenal. A mechanical engineer from the state university, Widner had spent three years in the army as an infantry officer, with two years in Vietnam. He had been awarded a purple heart and a bronze star for bravery in action. Widner wears his hair as long as he thinks he can get away with and sports a fine mustache. His appearance is in sharp contrast to most of the short-haired, middle-aged employees he supervises. Yet he is close to his subordinates; he plays with them on a departmental softball team and hoists a few beers several evenings a week.

Widner is having trouble, no doubt about it. Quality has been declining, and he does not seem to be able to do anything about it. His men say that this is due to the old equipment, which breaks down most every day. Frequently, the maintenance gang (which is in a separate department) doesn't have the time or can't fix it, so Widner has been repairing it himself. He really is a wizard mechanic, but he finds himself spending most of his time repairing equipment himself while his men watch.

Widner and Johnson have some conflicts. Widner can put up with the older man's wisecracking about his hair, but he resents Johnson's criticism of his department. In response to Johnson's pressures to keep the department area clean, Widner has assigned two disgruntled operators as cleaners and asked the others to join in when they are waiting for their equipment to be repaired or whenever they can.

The simmering feud between Johnson and Widner exploded yesterday afternoon when Widner had his shirt off and was lying under the rifling drill replacing a stripped gear. When Johnson came in, the following conversation took place:

JOHNSON: Widner, where the hell are you?

WIDNER: Over here, under the machine, O.K.?

JOHNSON: Get your ass up here. Those goldbrickers of yours are sitting in the courtyard drinking cokes. Break time ended 10 minutes ago. Damn it, you can't even keep your area clean, much less meet your production goals. What the hell are you doing about it?

WIDNER: Nothing! They've worked hard today; they'll be back as soon as the break is over. Besides, there's not much for them to do because of this lousy equipment. When are you going to fight for some money to replace it? That's what you should be doing, not pussyfooting around here looking for dust particles. Go xxxx yourself.

JOHNSON: O.K. wise guy, that's it. I'm going to see what the colonel thinks about this. Maybe you will be out in the park strumming a guitar with your hippie friends tomorrow.

Johnson immediately went to see the colonel.

JOHNSON: Colonel, you've got to can Widner. His men are running wild, and he just told me to xxxx myself. He's insubordinate. I want him out.

GRANT: Hold on, tell me calmly what happened. Frank seems like a nice young man. I'm sure there must be some simple misunderstanding.

JOHNSON: Like hell. He's no leader, and I think he's chicken. He does the work while his men stand around. He's afraid of them and too buddy-buddy. Unless you do something, I'm going to file a formal complaint with Washington.

GRANT: Let me talk to Frank first. Then I'll get back to you.

JOHNSON: O.K., but I've run out of patience.

Questions on Webster Arsenal (A)

1. What are the problems at Webster Arsenal?

2. What are the causes of these problems?

3. Analyze the leadership styles of Grant, Johnson, and Widner.

4. Analyze the tasks confronting Grant, Johnson, and Widner. How do their styles fit their tasks?

5. What should Grant say to Widner?

6. What recommendations would you offer Grant?

Bases of Power: A Self-Assessment Activity

Procedure

1. Complete the questionnaires on the "best boss" and the "worst boss."

2. The instructor will tell you how to score and interpret the results.

3. Share your results with other members of your group or class. For what type of leader do you want to work?

Bases of Power Questionnaire*

BEST BOSS

Please think of the *best* boss for whom you have ever worked. Consider the following statements as they pertain to this person. Please mark each statement in the appropriate blank with one of the following values: STRONGLY AGREE = 5; AGREE = 4; NEUTRAL = 3; DISAGREE = 2; STRONGLY DISAGREE = 1.

1. _____ I respect him/her personally, and want to act in a way that merits his/her respect and admiration.

2. _____ I respect his/her competence about things in which he/she has more experience than I.

3. _____ He/she can give special help to those who cooperate with him/her.

4. _____ He/she can apply pressure on those who do not cooperate with him/her.

5. _____ He/she has a legitimate right, considering his/her position, to expect that his/her suggestions will be carried out.

6. _____ I defer to his/her judgment in areas in which he/she is more familiar than I.

7. _____ He/she can make things difficult for me if I fail to follow his/her advice.

8. _____ Because of his/her job title and rank, I am obligated to follow his/her suggestions.

9. _____ I can personally benefit by cooperating with him/her.

10. _____ Following his/her advice results in better decisions.

11. _____ I cooperate with him/her because I have high regard for him/her as an individual.

12. _____ He/she can penalize those who do not follow his/her suggestions.

13. _____ I feel I have to cooperate with him/her.

14. _____ I cooperate with him/her because I wish to be identified with him/her.

15. _____ Cooperating with him/her can positively impact on my performance.

* Questionnaire developed by J. D. Hunger from an article titled "Influence and Information: An Exploratory Investigation of the Boundary Role Person's Basis of Power," by Robert Spekman, *Academy of Management Journal,* March 1979.

Bases of Power Questionnaire*

WORST BOSS

Please think of the *worst* boss for whom you have ever worked. Consider the following statements as they pertain to this person. Please mark each statement in the appropriate blank with one of the following values: STRONGLY AGREE = 5; AGREE = 4; NEUTRAL = 3; DISAGREE = 2; STRONGLY DISAGREE = 1.

1. _____ I respect him/her personally and want to act in a way that merits his/her respect and admiration.

2. _____ I respect his/her competence about things in which he/she has more experience than I.

3. _____ He/she can give special help to those who cooperate with him/her.

4. _____ He/she can apply pressure on those who do not cooperate with him/her.

5. _____ He/she has a legitimate right, considering his/her position, to expect that his/her suggestions will be carried out.

6. _____ I defer to his/her judgement in areas in which he/she is more familiar than I.

7. _____ He/she can make things difficult for me if I fail to follow his/her advice.

8. _____ Because of his/her job title and rank I am obligated to follow his/her suggestions.

9. _____ I can personally benefit by cooperating with him/her.

10. _____ Following his/her advice results in better decisions.

11. _____ I cooperate with him/her because I have high regard for him/her as an individual.

12. _____ He/she can penalize those who do not follow his/her suggestions.

13. _____ I fell I have to cooperate with him/her.

14. _____ I cooperate with him/her because I wish to be identified with him/her.

15. _____ Cooperating with him/her can positively impact on my performance.

---

* Questionnaire developed by J. D. Hunger from an article titled "Influence and Information: An Exploratory Investigation of the Boundary Role Person's Basis of Power," by Robert Spekman, *Academy of Management Journal*, March 1979.

Part Five

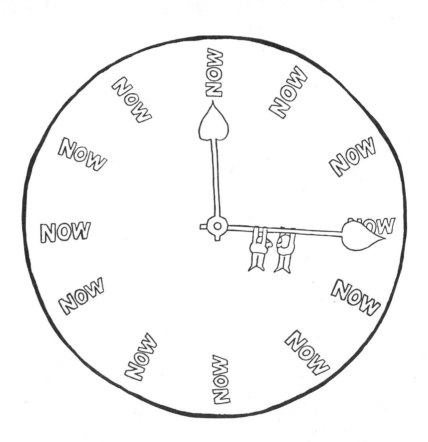

Planning and Controlling

12

Strategic Planning

Almost with the first appearance of homo sapiens, concern for the future was manifested in handcrafted tools, burial arrangements, and cave art. Ancient people took time out of the present to prepare physically and psychologically for the future. This ability to draw upon past experience in the present to plan for the future has conferred upon humans an advantage that, in the struggle for existence against other species, has proven superior to their foes' greater muscular strength, swiftness of action, or ferocity. Unlike animals, which are subject to their predetermined or accidental relations to time, we are granted the possibility, limited though it is, of conditioning the order of our time. Thus we have the possibility to relate freely to both our past and our future, and by means of these relations to mediate present activity in the interest of that future. This is time's great promise.[1]*

The prehistoric cave dweller's attitude toward time was not dissimilar to that of managers today. They understand that to affect the future, something must be done in the present. All human organizations, from families to social clubs to public institutions, are expressions of our recognition of time's passing, coupled with a desire for permanence. The corporation is a particularly clear example of our efforts to overcome time, to ensure a future, and to exploit it. Time is not the same for the corporation as it is for the entrepreneur; it is as a marble edifice to a sand castle. If effectively structured and administered, the company can outlive the founders.

These may be beautiful thoughts, but they are tough to act upon. All managers are faced with the nagging reality of their jobs—pressure to concentrate on the present, ignore the past, and let tomorrow take care of itself. Managers who are so taken in, however, are not exercising human leadership to its fullest potential. Behaviorally and psychologically, management should be oriented toward the future, carving time out of the present in the service of tomorrow—like those cave painters. "The ideal executive," maintains one corporation chairperson "should have a feel for the future, not only from the standpoint of where his own business is going, but where his competitors are going, what other industries are doing, and what the country is likely to do."

In this chapter we shall first survey the general nature of planning—definitions, need for planning, time spans, hierarchical relationships, and phases of the process. Then strategic planning will be discussed, including the scope of strategic choice, and the importance of understanding the environment as well as internal resources and capacities.

The What and Why of Planning

In A. A. Milne's childhood classic *Winnie the Pooh,* Christopher Robin tells his group of stuffed-animal friends that before they can search for the North Pole they ought to get organized. Pooh asks what getting organized means, and Christopher replies, "Organizing is what you do before you do something, so that when you do it, it's not all mixed up." Of course, what the juvenile sage is describing is not

---

* Notes and references will be found at the end of this chapter.

organizing, but planning—the traditional management function for handling the future.[2]

Definitions of Planning

The definitions of planning are many: thinking about what you want and how you are going to accomplish it; determining in advance what is to be done; preparing for the future by making decisions now. Planning represents management's attempt to anticipate the future and guard itself against the threat of change, which humans are urgently aware of because of their time sense.[3] Planning is our effort to visualize "the future as history" by determining how we would want the future to appear if we could jump ahead in time and look backward.[4] "The purpose of planning," according to one executive, "is not to show how precisely we can predict the future, but rather to uncover the things we must do today in order to have a future."

Increasing Needs for Planning

When a certain Marxist economist visited the Unites States and talked to the press, he commented on how strange American business was. It seemed to him that our managers were always complaining about the dangers of a planned economy, yet American businesses do more planning than anyone else in the world. The socialist economist suggested that more time, effort, and money are expended on economic planning in the United States than in the Soviet Union. The planning may be more decentralized here (and too short range in perspective), but we do live in a planned economy, as is essential in a vast industrialized, interdependent system.[5]

The imperatives of modern technology have exercised a profound influence on the requirements for planning.[6] Continuing, narrowing specialization has made tasks more complex and lengthy. An increasing span of time separates the beginning from the completion of the task; lead times have grown enormously. The Spanish Armada that threatened England in 1588 consisted of 120 ships built from scratch in *one* year. A comparative fleet today would require some 20 years to construct. The supersonic aircraft was not flown until more than 10 years of development.[7]

More Planning Required because of . . .
- more complex technology
- narrower specialization
- longer lead times
- larger investments
- greater uncertainty
- larger size
- more systematic competitors

To initiate, promote, and complete large endeavors requires time and money. Management attempts to remain flexible and in position to cancel the program at minimum loss, but eventually it must commit itself to completing the task. Planning is critical at this point, for managers must attempt to foresee what can happen that might affect the program and to develop contingency responses to maintain progress. Thus planners have the central mission of minimizing uncertainty and its consequences.

In addition, increasing company complexity and the interdependence of its parts mean that decisions in various functions–such as marketing, finance, and production—cannot be made separately. Greater product and service diversification increases the volume of decisions proportionately. High-level planning must try to view the organization as a total system and ensure that objectives and goals in the various areas are compatible.[8]

Reprinted by permission of the Chicago Tribune–New York News Syndicate, Inc.

Years of expansion in the 1950s and 1960s led to the growth of enormous organizations, which can be dangerously resistant to change. Top-level executives may want to gain greater control over their sprawling enterprises, and centralized planning is one way of doing this.[9]

As the practice of systematic planning spreads throughout the many organizations in our economy, it becomes more difficult to maintain a successful competitive position. Managers are driven to more effective planning because their competitors are also becoming better planners.[10]

To be sure, some firms in rapidly growing markets fulfill their growth and profit objectives without a clearly defined strategy. It may be possible to simply "muddle through" without long-range strategic planning if management is alert and flexible enough to institute incremental changes when necessary.[11] Such a short-run reactive strategy may succeed if supplemented with good short-range goals and controls (to be discussed in later chapters). Some research does suggest that there are organizations that follow this path successfully,[12] but other research indicates that long-range effectiveness can be enhanced by a more active strategy for dealing with the world through formal planning.[13] The relative average pretax profit position of firms with formal and informal planning from 1960 to 1970 are suggested in Figure 12–1.

Time Spans of Plans

In labeling plans, most managers have been influenced by the financial orientation of banks, which consider that a loan for over five years is long range, one to five years is intermediate, and less than one year is short range. This is not a helpful scheme. Whether a plan is long or short range depends upon its impact on the business and whether or not decisions in the plan can be modified.[14] A more appropriate approach to categorizing plans considers the factors that management can manipulate. First, in long-range planning management can determine the structure and strategy of the organization. In other words, long-range planning may involve a fundamental redirection of the concern's ends and means. Second, in intermediate-range planning, management must accept the general structure and strategy of the organization but can manipulate the quantity of inputs, outputs, people, material, and capital. Third, in short-range planning, structure, strategy, and quantities are fixed, but management can manipulate the application of resources and technology

FIGURE 12–1

General Interrelation of Profits and Planning

Source: Adapted from D. W. Karger, "Integrated Formal Long-Range Planning and How to Do It," *Long-Range Planning* 6, no. 4 (1973), pp. 31–34.

FIGURE 12–2

Functions of Plans with Various Time Spans

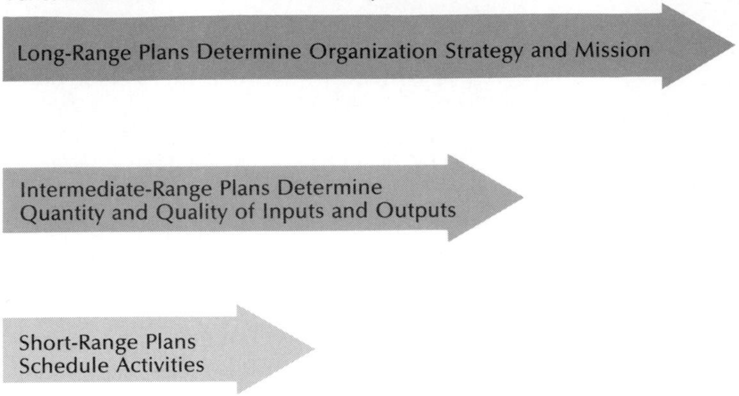

Long-Range Plans Determine Organization Strategy and Mission

Intermediate-Range Plans Determine
Quantity and Quality of Inputs and Outputs

Short-Range Plans
Schedule Activities

in scheduling specific activities. The functions of long-range, intermediate-range, and short-range plans are shown in Figure 12–2.

The actual time spans in each of these definitions can vary widely. In the automobile industry, long-range plans would cover 10 years or more, intermediate-range plans varying quantity and quality might be somewhere between 1 and 2 years, and short-range plans might cover two to four weeks. In contrast, long-range plans for a small garment manufacturer doing business in a rented loft can extend no more than six months to a year because it is so dependent on the styles and ideas generated by customers and designers elsewhere. Such a company's intermediate-range plans would run two or three months, and short-run plans would be daily. Therefore the difference between long- and short-range plans depends on the organization's technology and product. All three time ranges are necessary, however. Even though its horizon is closer in time, the clothing company needs its six-months long-range planning as much as General Motors needs its 10-year perspective.

The Hierarchy of Plans

Planning can be visualized in terms of a hierarchy related to the organizational hierarchy in the sense that as we go down this hierarchy, we move from top to bottom in the organization in terms of who performs the planning. We also increase specificity and detail and decrease the plan's time span. This relation is illustrated in Figure 12–3.

Theoretically, such a hierarchy of plans means that if every unit understands its unit goals and reaches them successfully, then the entire company's specific goals and continuing objectives will be achieved. Whether this happy state is reached, however, depends on how well the objectives and goals have been defined and parceled out. The managerial task is enormously simplified if objectives are properly defined and allocated. Then each lower manager will have a specific unit goal he

FIGURE 12–3

Relation of the Hierarchy of Plans to the Organizational Hierarchy

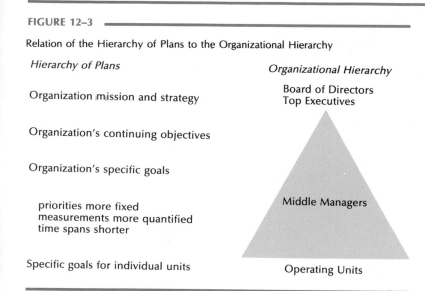

Hierarchy of Plans

Organization mission and strategy

Organization's continuing objectives

Organization's specific goals

priorities more fixed
measurements more quantified
time spans shorter

Specific goals for individual units

Organizational Hierarchy

Board of Directors
Top Executives

Middle Managers

Operating Units

or she understands, that is within the managers ability, and for which he or she is responsible. The manager knows how it is to be measured and when the deadline is.

The hierarchy of plans successively narrows the problems and alternatives confronting each layer of management. From the realm of all possible areas of actions in the world, the corporate definition and strategy accepts some and rejects others. The continuing objectives eliminate more and the specific goals even more, so that the activities eventually become focused.[15]

Even if managers' goals and problems are narrower at the middle and lower levels, their ability to achieve and handle them is helped by knowledge of organizational strategy and ability to link one's unit's goals to the overall objectives. Indeed, subordinates' perceptions of the manager as an effective leader improve with their understanding of how the manager and they fit into the organization's planning and control process.[16]

The Phases of the Planning Process

Plans in organizations are rarely born overnight, nor are they easily translated into action. There are several phases through which the process generally evolves. In small organizations these may not be easy to discern. In larger, diversified corporations, however, they are often quite visible. Figure 12–4 provides a simple view of these phases and how they relate to the hierarchy of plans.[17]

Early in the process, senior corporate managers articulate a set of general strategic guidelines for the corporation as a whole, which they then communicate to managers in charge of discrete segments of the organization's business activities. These units are often established around particular markets, products, or technologies.[18] General

FIGURE 12–4

Iterative Loops in the Strategic Planning Process

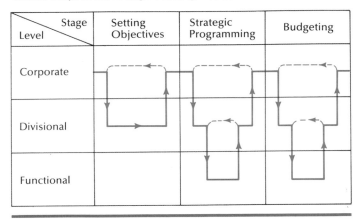

Electric pioneered with this type of planning focus. It calls units at this level strategic business units, or SBUs. The nomenclature has become widespread.

Tank McNamara

Each business unit manager, based on familiarity with the unit's markets and its internal resources and strengths, recommends to top management a general strategy for her or his unit. Corporate management balances the aggregation of all such proposals to ascertain that jointly they can produce the corporation's overall desired outcomes.

The next stage involves the development of specific strategic programs through which each business unit will carry out the general plan it has negotiated with corporate management. At this stage functional managers are informed of the key strategic challenges facing the unit and invited to propose detailed plans for meeting them. Business unit management must see to it that there is sufficient cross-functional integration at this point to assure a coherent unit plan. The integration must deal with the important interdependences among the various functions.

Out of these programs come rough estimates of sales and profit levels, anticipated market share, investment requirements, research and development costs, personnel commitments, and operating schedules. A summary of these is presented to senior management. At the corporate level once again the summation of all strategic programs is examined to see that the programs can satisfy corporate needs and do not exceed overall corporate resources. Often, negotiations are conducted between the corporate and the business levels to work out adjustments.

In the final phase of the process, approved strategic programs serve as the basis for elaborating short-term schedules and specific resource allocations in detailed budgets. These are developed at the functional unit level and then aggregated to form a business unit budget and plan of operations for the coming year. Budget proposals are then presented to top management for review, revision, and approval. Soon thereafter the process starts again.

The Need for Dreams

Planning as a decision process is widely discussed, but this is not the most important aspect of planning. The key to planning is the determination of desires, and the critical aspect is knowing where you want to be and how you want the future to turn out.

Though a sense of the ideal, a concept of where the organization should go and what it should become, is central to planning, it is lacking in many managers who have woefully underdeveloped imaginations about the future. What is needed is some "wishful thinking," a definition of the ideal picture of where management wants to be and when it wants to get there. These aspirations have little likelihood of complete fulfillment, and they probably will change with time. Nonetheless, some sort of wishful projection is essential if planning is to be more than ad hoc responses to present conditions.[19]

Such dreams should be more than a list of unrelated aspirations; the ideas should be integrated into a cohesive scenario that has a threefold purpose. The first purpose is to provide a conception of what the organization should be like as a whole, and ideally. Without this, even small correctional measures cannot be evaluated effectively. Even worse, lack of imagination (rather than an excess of it) leads to mistakes and missed opportunities. Without a self-determined sense of the ideal, management tends to play follow the leader after the latest fad, whether it be Theory Y, operations research, or management by objectives—all worthy ideas, but useless to the organization that has no sense of its desired future.

The second purpose of wishful projection is to provide a guide for planning systematically for transition of the existing organization into what is desired. Without this, management will proceed only in a piecemeal manner, responding to current pressures rather than to long-run needs. It is part of management's predicament that it can often do least to change situations that are close to it and about which it knows the most, but it may have greater influence over future situations of which it knows relatively little.

Third, and probably most important, wishful planning may excite and fire the imaginations of participating managers. As a prominent consultant puts it: "Planning should excite managers to the point where they strain sufficiently at the leash of tradition and custom to break with them. I know of no better way to bring them to such a point than to involve them in the idealized design process."[20]

Creating Strategies for Competitive Performance

The wishful plan may have quantitative components regarding sales, market share, profit, and so on, but a more important aspect is a qualitative scenario of the kind of institution management wants to create and the activity in which it wants to be involved.[21] In short, what kind of business would the company most like to be? Why is it in this business? What does it intend to do? Most important, what public needs, desires, or values can it satisfy?[22]

The Scope of Strategic Choice

The questions to be asked in defining the scope of an organization's strategy fall into four categories:[23]

1. Services to be provided: What products or services will the firm sell or provide to what customers?[24]
2. Basic ways these services will be produced: What will the company make, by what processes, and what will it buy from what sources?
3. Sequencing and timing of major steps: What moves will be made early, and what can be deferred?
4. Targets to be met: What are the criteria for success, and what levels of achievement are desired?

Such basic questions lie at the foundation of all institutions—business or other, profit seeking or charitable. These are the kinds of questions that should concern top management, because continued success will depend upon appropriate definitions of the organization's nature and purpose. Some specific questions for use in formulating planning strategy are suggested in Figure 12–5.

Corporate Strategy. At the corporate level the key choices have to do with the scope diversification.[25] Does the firm wish to remain in one line of business or enter several markets? If it is in several markets, are they related in some way? Perhaps it is by technology—as in the case of the Corning Glass Works, which has expanded into various markets related to the use of glass and ceramics, or maybe by customer base and distribution channels—as in the case of Procter & Gamble, which has emphasized consumer packaged goods. Or are they unrelated? Consider for example the case of International Telephone and Telegraph, which has built telecommunications equipment, operated hotels, produced and sold food, and developed and exploited natural resources.

Other considerations for corporate management include the rate of change in the diversification pattern and whether to emphasize growth by internal development

FIGURE 12–5

Questions for Formulating Strategy

1. Record current strategy:
   a. What is the current strategy?
   b. What kind of business does management want to operate (considering such management values as desired return on investment, growth rate, share of market, stability, flexibility, character of the business, and climate)?
   c. What kind of business does management feel it ought to operate (considering management's concepts of social responsibility and obligations to stockholders, employees, community, competitors, customers, suppliers, government, and the like)?
2. Identify problems with the current strategy:
   a. Are trends discernible in the environment that may become threats and/or missed opportunities if the current strategy is continued?
   b. Is the company having difficulty implementing the current strategy?
   c. Is the attempt to carry out the current strategy disclosing significant weaknesses and/or unutilized strengths in the company?
   d. Are there other concerns with respect to the validity of the current strategy?
   e. Is the current strategy no longer valid?
3. Discover the core of the strategy problem:
   a. Does the current strategy require greater competence and/or resources than the company possesses?
   b. Does it fail to exploit adequately the company's distinctive competence?
   c. Does it lack sufficient competitive advantage?
   d. Will it fail to exploit opportunities and/or meet threats in the environment, now or in the future?
   e. Are the various elements of the strategy internally inconsistent?
   f. Are there other considerations with respect to the core of the strategy problem?
   g. What, then, is the real core of the strategy problem?
4. Formulate alternative new strategies:
   a. What possible alternatives exist for solving the strategy problem?
   b. To what extent do the company's competence and resources limit the number of alternatives that should be considered?
   c. To what extent do management's perferences limit the alternatives?
   d. To what extent does management's sense of social responsibility limit the alternatives?
   e. What strategic alternatives are acceptable?
5. Evaluate alternative new strategies:
   a. Which alternative *best* solves the strategy problem?
   b. Which alternative offers the *best* match with the company's competence and resources?
   c. Which alternative offers the *greatest* competitive advantage?
   d. Which alternative *best* satisfies management's preferences?
   e. Which alternative *best* meets management's sense of social responsibility?
   f. Which alternative *minimizes* the creation of new problems?
6. Choose a new strategy:
   a. What is the *relative significance* of each of the preceding considerations?
   b. What should the new strategy be?

Source: F. F. Gilmore, "Formulating Strategy in Smaller Companies," *Harvard Business Review,* May–June 1971, p. 8.

or by acquisitions.[26] Beyond the diversification issues, corporate management must be concerned with the pattern of resource allocation among business units. Where should it cut back, and where should it invest? The resources to be allocated are not only dollars, but also technical and managerial talent.

Business Strategy. The focus at the business-unit level is different. It revolves around the question of how to become and remain a successful competitor in each market. For the nondiversified corporation, this challenge blends in with the others faced at the corporate level.

Two different approaches for formulating business strategies have been suggested: outside-inside and inside-outside. Successful strategies almost always balance the two. It is necessary to find a position in the competitive arena that responds to customer needs, takes advantage of internal strengths, and exploits the relative weaknesses of competitors.[27]

Outside-Inside Approach to Strategy: Understanding the Environment

The dream of the entrepreneur who starts a new business is to discover an unfulfilled public need, a latent demand that people are just waiting to express for a not-yet-invented product or service. If the firm can develop such a product, it will be in the strongest market position. In this case, the firm's strategy will have been shaped by the outside environment.

In some cases the demand is apparent, but the product or service is not. The oral contraceptive is an example; every pharmaceutical firm knew such a pill would sell, but they did not know how to make it. Management's response to such a clearly discernible potential need is technological research and development.[28]

Usually, however, the demand is more latent; people have not really thought about what new product or service they want. They don't know what they're missing. In this situation, management's central strategy becomes "to create a customer." Skimobiles were not in great demand until companies began manufacturing, advertising, and selling them; but a substantial number of people readjusted their wants and expenditures to include skimobiles when they became available.

Making latent demands manifest is a more risky venture than responding to a preexisting but unsupplied market. Identifying latent wants requires intuition and some faith.[29] Most of all, it requires sensitivity to conditions and trends in the world outside the organization.[30] This sensitivity should be followed up by questions management asks itself, such as the following: If there is a population trend from concentrated urban centers to dispersed suburban areas, what demands might this create? (More personal modes of transportation—subcompact cars, motorcycles, bicycles?) If working hours are declining, what will people demand during increased leisure hours? (Camping equipment? Neighborhood pools? Tennis courts?). If the U.S. birthrate is declining and the proportion of older people is increasing, what will this mean? (An increase in medical services? Health care products? Home entertainment facilities?)

Competitors also respond to customer needs. A successful strategy, must therefore be built with an appreciation for the structure of the competitive arena and the strategies being pursued by various competitors. In some industries there are only three or four large producers, as was the case in the automobile industry in the United States until the late 1960s. In other settings there are many small participants with none dominating the market place. This is the case in the car-washing business in many large metropolitan areas. Often an industry is characterized by clusters of businesses—a few large ones, perhaps leading the way in product development,

FIGURE 12–6

Key Environmental Variables Affecting Demand

1. Economic: the basic demand patterns—past, present, and forecast—for products currently being produced; forecast demand potential for newly conceived products; competition—resources committed by competing firms to product/market areas in which the firm has a present or potential interest.
2. Social: social-psychological impact of present and potential products and services; social value systems and their impact on the definition of priorities in the allocation of national resources and individual income; patterns of social relationships and their impact on present and potential economic markets.
3. Technological: speed and direction of development of related technologies and the potential impact of this development on present and potential products and production technologies.
4. Governmental: legislation and administrative policy and their impact on present and potential organizational commitments and actions.

Source: W. D. Guth, "Formulating Organizational Objectives and Strategy: A Systematic Approach," *Journal of Business Policy* 2, no. 1 (1971), pp. 24–31.

pricing, and advertising, and a large number of smaller ones, serving specialized or local niches in the market. A good example can be seen in the soft drink industry.[31]

In essence, the outside-inside approach to strategic planning requires managers to monitor the organization's environment continuously in order to uncover latent demands for goods and services to which they can respond (see Figure 12–6). Managers look for unfulfilled needs that they might convert into wants they can satisfy. The key seems to be for management to move with the environment rather than attempting to push the world into some shape it thinks it ought to be in.

Inside-Outside Approach to Strategy: Understanding the Company

The inside-outside approach is not a mutually exclusive alternative to the outside-inside approach to planning strategy. It is a complement and a necessity if the already successful firm is to remain so. Management begins to apply this approach by asking itself what the company's particular skills and differential advantages are. What does the company offer? What is unique about it?

Essential to defining the company's purposes and adapting to changing external conditions is identifying what the company really is. For example, through the years Minnesota Mining and Manufacturing Company has evolved into the 3M Company; it went from sandpaper to roofing materials, to transparent tape, to magnetic tape, to photocopying, to reflective signs. These products are in widely different markets with different competitive conditions, but all are based upon a single technical skill—how to apply a closely controlled layer of material on a flexible base. It is a skill with wide application, and 3M is undoubtedly still looking for new ones.

Other organizations have developed service departments for their internal uses and then discovered that they possessed a capability wanted by the outside world. For example, Chilton Publishing Company developed a behavioral science research department and a computer center to support its business magazine publishing and marketing business. Its skills in research and computing became so advanced that these services are now sold to other firms, and income is thus generated to supplement the publishing business. Similarly, Du Pont's instrument division grew from internal services; Westinghouse sells management development advice; and some milk delivery firms are competing for package delivery with the U.S. Postal Service.

The aim of the inside-outside approach is to define the organization's mission in as broad terms as possible but to stay within the limits of its capabilities. As a senior IBM executive puts it:

> We want to be in the problem-solving business—this is our mission. Our business is not to make computers. It is to help solve administrative, scientific and even human problems. If your mission is broad enough, you do not find one day that a competitor's new product has outmoded all your equipment.[32]

Since Xerox wants to avoid confinement to the copy business, its management sees it as meeting the demand for more information and knowledge through supplying automated office systems.[33] Clearly, the future includes growing competition between Xerox and IBM because each is expanding its own strategic definition.

In these examples management examined what capabilities it possessed and how they might be expanded to new applications or generalized to serve others. In short, the organization determined what it had that others could use.

Determining Feasible Strategies

Inside-outside or outside-inside strategic planning fits together three classes of variables: (1) potential market needs or wants, (2) environmental opportunities and constraints, and (3) the organization's skills and resources. Management's feasible strategies are derived from the overlap of these factors (see Figure 12–7). For example, Denny's Inc., a California-based chain of full-menu coffee shops has been expanding into the eastern United States.[34] The chairperson believes (1) that the attractiveness of fast-food, limited menu, drive-in-type restaurants will decline with growing customer sophistication and (2) that Denny's, with its over 100-item menu, will be better able to serve these customers than the eastern limited-menu places can, even if they expand their offerings. The effectiveness of this strategy will depend on whether this assessment of the environment and the firm's capabilities is correct.

One of the difficulties in teaching strategic planning is that we must frankly recognize that it is not firmly established by systematic research that strategy really exists! To be sure, we can examine an organization's history and usually see a pattern suggesting that management had a coherent strategy.[35] But often those managers did not in fact explicitly debate or plan the strategy that emerges over time. Thus strategy may be viewed as intended or unintended; the strategy maker may *formulate* his or her strategy through a conscious process before making specific decisions; or strategy may *form* gradually as decisions are made one by one.

This ambiguity presents a dilemma for management education because logic suggests that a planned strategy would be more desirable. This is one of the areas of management in which stylistic intuition seems to play a large role.[36] For example, the president of a prestigious Ivy League university once pushed for eliminating its successful school of allied medical occupations even though it was well thought

FIGURE 12–7

Strategic Analysis

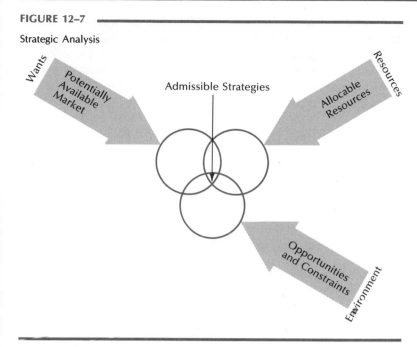

Source: D. R. Ziemer and P. D. Maycock, "A Framework for Strategic Analysis," *Long-Range Planning* 6, no. 2 (1973), pp. 6–17.

of and was turning a profit. Apparently, he didn't feel that it was appropriate for the university's image to be training physical therapists and masseurs. Was it a good decision? This is difficult to judge because it depends in the long run on whether or not the purer research image contributes more to the institution's health.

In spite of the uncertainty, however, strategy in the future will probably be increasingly *planned*.

SUMMARY

Planning is management's vehicle for confronting the future by making present decisions. Formal planning has grown in importance for many organizations because of increased technological complexity, financial and competitive risk, time lags, size, and the management-decision burden.

Long-range planning, to 10 or 20 years in the future, rests on dreams and a sense of what management would like the organization to become. These dreams are converted into a strategy based on a definition of the organization arrived at by seeking answers to questions about products and services to be provided, basic ways they will be produced, the sequence of steps to be taken, and the objectives to be met.

In large, diversified firms, corporate strategy fo

cuses on the choice of businesses in which to engage and the allocation of financial, technical, and management resources among the various businesses. At the business-unit level strategy focuses on becoming and remaining competitive in a given market, industry, or service. The planning process typically involves corporate, business, and functional managers interactively in three phases: objective setting, strategic programming, and budgeting.

An outside-inside approach to strategy begins with a search for unfulfilled wants or latent demands in the external environment. The inside-outside approach builds on the organization's unique skills that can be offered to the world—or at least to part of it. The intent is to define a broad mission that will not be subject to rapid obsolesence.

Dreams and strategies will be idle exercises unless they are converted into continuing objectives and specific goals with priorities for accomplishment. The next chapter takes up continuing objectives.

REVIEW QUESTIONS

1. Why is it increasingly important to engage in strategic planning?

2. What seems to be the general relationship between planning and business success?

3. What is the difference between long-range, intermediate-range, and short-range planning?

4. What is the hierarchy of plans?

5. How does the hierarchy of plans narrow the range of managerial choices?

6. What are the phases of planning in a typical large, diversified firm?

7. How do these phases relate to smaller, less complex organizations?

8. Why are the interactions between levels of management important in developing strategic plans?

9. What is a wishful projection, and how does it relate to planning?

10. What are the major questions to be asked when defining the essential strategy of an organization?

11. What is the difference between corporate strategy and business strategy?

12. What is the outside-inside approach to strategy?

13. What does it mean to create a customer?

14. What are the key environmental factors of which management should be aware?

15. Why is the behavior of competitors important to the business strategist?

16. What is the inside-outside approach to strategy?

17. Feasible strategies for management reflect the intersection of what three variables?

Notes and References on Strategic Planning

1. Friedrich Nietzsche described man as "the only animal who can make promises." The best survey of human nature and its relation to time is Reinhold Niebuhr, *The Nature and Destiny of Man* (New York: Charles Scribner's Sons, 1949). See also Ross A. Webber, *Time and Management,* (New York: Van Nostrand Reinhold, 1972).

2. J. K. Craver, "The Effect of the Future on Today's Decisions," *Long-Range Planning* 6, no. 2 (1973), pp. 29–34.

3. This has been noted by S. G. F. Brandon:
In a true sense, all the planning that must precede each human enterprise represents an attempt to anticipate future contingencies and win some form of security against the menace of temporal change of which man's time sense makes him so urgently aware. But the advantages which this time sense thus confers in material benefits are offset by what may be described as a profound sense of spiritual insecurity which also stems from consciousness of time.

"Time and the Destiny of Man," in J. T. Fraser, ed., *The Voices of Time* (New York: Braziller, 1966), p. 144.

4. See Robert Heilbroner, *The Future as History,* (New York: Harper & Row, 1960). See C. Eden, "Modeling the Influence of Decision Makers on the Future," *Futures,* August 1977, p. 272 ff.; and R. D. Evered, "Interest in the Future," *Futures,* April 1977, pp. 285–300.
A survey of the many books on planning is contained in R. J. Mockler, "Theory and Practice of Planning," *Harvard Business Review,* March–April 1970, p. 148 ff. The most comprehensive treatment of planning is probably G. A. Steiner, *Top Management Planning* (New York: Macmillan, 1969). Three good smaller books are K. Andrews, *The Concept of Corporate Strategy* (Homewood, Ill.: Dow Jones-Irwin, 1971), E. K. Warren, *Long-Range Planning: The Executive Viewpont* (Englewood Cliffs, N.J.: Prentice-Hall, 1966; and R. L. Ackoff, *A Concept of Corporate Planning* (New York: Wiley-Interscience, 1970). Two newer books are: F. T. Haner, *Business Policy: Planning and Strategy* (Cambridge, Mass.: Winthrop, 1976); and B. Taylor and J. R. Sparks, *Corporate Strategy and Planning* (New York: John Wiley & Sons, 1977).

5. The attractiveness of national planning by the government has declined in recent years, probably because of reduced faith in what a national government can do. See T. Alexander, "The Deceptive Allure of National Planning," *Fortune,* March 1977, p. 148 ff. See also B. Schwarz, "Long-Range Planning in the Public Sector," *Futures,* April 1977, pp. 115–27. J. L. Badaracco, Jr. and D. B. Yoffie, " 'Industrial Policy': It Can't Happen Here," *Harvard Business Review,* Nov.–Dec. 1983.

6. M. A. Maidique and Peter Patch, "Corporate Strategy and Technological Policy," in M. L. Tuschman and W. L. Moore, eds., *Readings in the Management of Innovation* (Marshfield, Mass.: Pitman Publishing, 1982).

7. For an extended discussion of technology and planning, see John K. Galbraith, *The New Industrial State* (Boston: Houghton Mifflin, 1967).

8. S. R. Katsky, "Relationship of Organizational Size to Complexity and Coordination," *Administrative Science Quarterly* 15, no. 4 (1970), pp. 428–38. Katsky suggests that:
1. Firms with little functional differentiation are coordinated personally by line managers.
2. Firms with a middle range of functional differentiation utilize specialized staffs for coordination.
3. Organizations with much functional differentiation tend to coordinate through impersonal rules.

9. G. A. Steiner lists the trends in planning as follows:
   1. A major new factor in planning will be the increasing injection of social values and goals into the decision-making process.
   2. There is a growing convergence between business and government planning which will become of growing concern in corporate planning.
   3. Planning systems will change to accommodate the participation of more people in an enterprise.
   4. Planning will expand in importance relative to other functions.
   5. It follows that more companies will undertake formal corporate planning.
   6. Corporate planners will get closer to chief executives, and there will be some tendency for the growth in numbers of planners who are the peers of the chief executive officer.
   7. Planning staffs will expand and tend to split from the top planner when he gets close to the chief executive.
   8. Computerized models and simulations will be increasingly used in the planning process and will grow rapidly in use at the topmost strategic planning level.
   9. Cost-benefit analysis will increase significantly to replace in some degree or at least supplement traditional return-on-investment type of analysis in the planning process.
   10. Planning will embrace new types of forecasts.
   11. The personality characteristics and intellectual requirements of the typical corporate planner will undergo gradual change.
   12. Planners will teach managers how to plan and help them do it.

"Tomorrow's Corporate Planning and Planners," *Managerial Planning* 20, no. 5 (1972), pp. 1–7. See also C. E. Summer, "The Future Role of the Corporate Planner," *California Management Review* 3, no. 2 (1961), pp. 17–31.
There is a recent trend in many large organizations to emphasize the central role of line managers in strategic planning, with staff planners taking on more of a support role.

10. The rise in the use of systematic planning among U.S. corporations is mirrored in the appearance of a growing number of consulting firms specializing in strategic analysis and of large-sample models of the strategic dimensions of important industrial sectors. One such model, developed by General Electric and the Strategic Planning Institute of Cambridge, Mass., is called PIMS (profit impact of marketing strategies). See Carl Anderson and Frank Paine, "PIMS: A Reexamination," *Academy of Management Review,* July 1978, pp. 602–12.

11. On operating without long-range plans, see C. E. Lindblom, "The Science of 'Muddling Through,'" *Public Administration Review* 19 (1959), pp. 79–88; Lindblom and D. Braybrooke, *A Strategy of Decision* (New York: Free Press, 1963); and Lindblom, *The Policymaking Process* (Englewood Cliffs, N.J.: Prentice-Hall, 1968). This topic and conscious planning are discussed in Henry Mintzberg, "Strategy Making in Three Modes," *California Management Review* 16, no. 2 (1973), pp. 44–53. See also M. Marks, "Organizational Adjustment to Uncertainty," *The Journal of Management Studies,* February 1977, pp. 1–7.

12. S. C. Wheelwright reports that (1) the proactive "synoptic" procedure led to consideration of a much wider range of alternative strategies than did the responsive "incremental" procedure; (2) the incremental resulted in better agreement among the planners on the strategy and objectives (and also more commitment) than the synoptic; (3) as evaluated by both planners and judges, the incremental procedure generally led to better strategies than did the synoptic procedure. "An Experimental Analysis of Strategic Planning Procedures," *Journal of Business Policy* 3, no. 3 (1973), pp. 61–74.
In James Brian Quinn, "Strategic Goals: Process and Politics," *Sloan Management Review,* Fall 1977, pp. 21–37, the author argues that "incremental 'muddling'" in many instances represents "purposeful, politically astute, and effective management practice" (p. 21).

13. On the advantages of planning, see S. Thune and R. House, "Where Long-Range Planning Pays Off," *Business Horizons,* August 1970, pp. 81–87; D. M. Herold, "Long-Range Planning and Organizational Performance: A Cross-Validation Study," *Academy of Management Journal,* March 1972, pp. 91–103; S. Schoeffler, R. D. Buzzell, and D. F. Heany, "Impact of Strategic Planning on Profit Performance," *Harvard Business Review,* March–April 1974, pp. 137–45; and C. W. Roney, "The Two Purposes of Business Planning," *Managerial Planning,* November–December 1976, pp. 1 ff. Also see Philippe Haspeslagh, "Portfolio Planning: Uses and Limits," *Harvard Business Review,* January–February 1982, pp. 58–73.

14. W. Alderson, "Perspectives on the Planning Process," *Academy of Management Journal* 2, no. 3 (1959), pp. 181–96.

15. P. H. Grinyer, "Some Dangerous Axioms of Corporate Planning," *Journal of Business Policy* 3, no. 1 (1973), pp. 3–9.

16. C. A. Reimnitz, "Testing a Planning and Control Model in Non-Profit Organizations," *Academy of Management Journal,* March 1972, pp. 77–87.

17. See R. F. Vancil and P. Lorange, "Strategic Planning in Diversified Companies," *Harvard Business Review,* January–February 1975, pp. 81–90.

18. See E. R. Biggadike, "The Contributions of Marketing to Strategic Management," *Academy of Management Review* 6, no. 4 (1981), pp. 621–32.

19. The concept of the "wishful projection" is from R. L. Ackoff, *A Concept of Corporate Planning* (New York: Wiley-Interscience, 1970). See also H. I. Ansoff, "Strategy as a Tool for Coping with Change," *Journal of Business Policy* 1, no. 4 (1971), pp. 3–7. "The Concept of Strategic Management," *Journal of Business Policy* 2, no. 4 (1972), pp. 2–15, and C. A. R. MacNulty, "Scenario Development for Corporate Planning," *Futures,* April 1977, p. 128 ff.

M. B. McCaskey emphasizes that planning is not exclusively tied to setting goals. It should include identifying areas of activity and preferred styles of acting—especially when the organization's environment is unstable and its activities are unpredictable. "A Contingency Approach to Planning: Planning with Goals and Planning without Goals," *Academy of Management Journal* 17, no. 2 (1974), pp. 281–91.

20. Ackoff, *A Concept of Corporate Planning.* For a summary of research on strategy, see C. W. Hofer, "Research on Strategic Planning: A Survey of Past Studies and Suggestions for Future Efforts," *Journal of Economics and Business,* Summer 1976, p. 261 ff.

Ansoff aruges that strategic thinking should permeate the management process, not be confined to planning. I. Ansoff, ed., *From Strategic Planning to Strategic Management* (New York: John Wiley & Sons, 1975). See M. A. Libien, "Product Design Is Everybody's Business," *Managerial Planning,* January–February 1977, pp. 30–33.

21. K. J. Cohen and R. M. Cyert describe the major steps as (1) formulation of goals, (2) analysis of the environment, (3) assigning quantitative values to goals, (4) the microprocess of strategy formulation, (5) the gap analysis, (6) strategic search, (7) selecting the portfolio of strategic alternatives, (8) implementation of the strategic program, and (9) measurement, feedback, and control. "Strategy: Formulation, Implementation and Monitoring," *Journal of Business* 46, no. 3 (1973), pp. 349–67. See also W. F. Glueck, "Organizational Planning and Strategic Planning," *Journal of Business Policy* 3, no. 1 (1973), pp. 48–59; S. P. Sethi and J. Hogle, "A Conceptual and Operational Framework for Developing the Long-Range Planning Process," *Journal of International Business Studies* 4, no. 2 (1973), pp. 31–50; and F. R. Sagasti, "A Conceptual 'Systems' Framework for the Study of Planning Theory," *Technological Forecasting and Social Change* 5 (1973), pp. 379–93.

22. Peter Drucker argues that "effective" management has little to do with "efficiency" but deals with satisfying public needs, desires, and values, which may not be "economic" at all. *Management: Tasks, Responsibilities, Practices* (New York: Harper & Row, 1974). He gives many examples of people he considers effective managers.

23. W. H. Newman, "Selecting Company Strategy," *Journal of Business Policy* 2, no. 2 (1972), pp. 60–71.

24. M. T. Cunningham, "Product Planning: the Essence of Corporate Strategy," *Journal of Business Policy* 2, no. 4 (1972), p. 47.

25. The classic work on diversification is Albert Chandler, *Strategy and Structure* (Cambridge, Mass.: MIT Press, 1962.) See also Richard Rumelt, *Strategy, Structure and Economic Performance* (Boston, Division of Research, Harvard Business School, 1974).

26. E. R. Biggadike, "The Risky Business of Diversification," *Harvard Business Review,* May–June 1979.

27. A popular recent book on this subject is Kenichi Ohmae, *The Mind of the Strategist* (New York: McGraw-Hill, 1982).

28. Examples of outside-inside planning are given in M. L. Kastens, "Outside-In Planning," *Managerial Planning* 22, no. 5 (1974), p. 1 ff.

29. H. W. J. Rittel and M. W. Webber, "Dilemmas in a General Theory of Planning," *Policy Sciences* 4 (1973), pp. 155–69. The authors maintain that the search for scientific bases for policy will fail because policy problems cannot be definitely described, and there are no "solutions" in the sense of objective answers. Also see M. Anshen and W. D. Guth, "Strategies for Research in Policy Formulation," *Journal of Business,* 46, no. 4 (1973), pp. 499–511.

30. A General Electric company planner maintains that business planning must be (1) more farseeing (at least a 10-year forecast), (2) more complex (including the "soft" side of social and cultural developments as well as economic and technological ones), and (3) more adaptive. I. H. Wilson, "Futures Forecasting for Strategic Planning at General Electric," *Long-Range Planning* 6, no. 2 (1973), pp. 39–42. See also J. C. Chambers, S. K. Mullick and D. D. Smith, "How to Choose the Right Forecasting Technique," *Harvard Business Review,* July–August 1971, pp. 45–74, and S. Makridakis and S. Wheelwright, "Integrating Forecasting and Planning," *Long-Range Planning* 6, no. 3 (1973), pp. 53–63.

31. Michael Porter, *Competitive Strategies* (New York: Free Press, 1980).

32. Jacques Maisonrouge, then president of IBM World Trade Corporation, quoted in *Harvard Business Review,* January–February 1972, p. 45. This strategic definition has reduced IBM's willingness to purchase unrelated businesses. One result is that it has accumulated more cash than can be applied to the problem-solving business.

"IBM's Cash Problem: Too Much to Handle," *Business Week,* December 5, 1977, p. 62.

33. "Why Xerox's Money Machine Slows Down," *Business Week,* April 5, 1976, p. 60 ff.

34. "Denny's Taken Its Menu East," *Business Week,* September 19, 1977, p. 111 ff.

35. H. Mintzberg, "Strategy Formulation as an Historical Process," *International Studies of Management and Organization,* Summer 1977, pp. 28–39; and George David Smith and Lawrence E. Steadman, "Present Value of Corporate History," *Harvard Business Review,* November–December 1981, pp. 164–72.

36. J. P. Edwards, "Strategy Formulation as a Stylistic Process," *International Studies of Management and Organization,* Summer 1977, p. 13 ff.

13

From Plans to Action: Setting Objectives and Goals

The Multiple Objectives of Management
    Continuing Objectives for Businesses
    Continuing Objectives for All Organizations

Setting Priorities
    Pragmatic Focus
    Strategic Focus
    Life-Cycle Focus

Setting Specific Goals
    For Every Objective, a Goal
    Less Measurable Goals

Summary

Review Questions

Notes and References

The foregoing chapter dealt at length with the process of strategic planning. This chapter focuses on the content of plans: objectives, priorities, and specific goals. In order to move from wishing to acting, it is necessary to become specific. Effective strategies are based on a coherent set of underlying continuing objectives that give an organization its character. These are the objectives that are the long-run, ongoing concerns of the organization at the present time and for at least the next five years, probably for the next 10 years, and perhaps forever. When these objectives are articulated by management and communicated to the organization's members, they serve as a vehicle for mobilizing and focusing energy and effort.

The Multiple Objectives of Management

The continuing objectives that should be of concern to managers can be organized into two categories: those that pertain to all businesses and those that pertain to organizations in general.

Continuing Objectives for Businesses

Years ago Peter Drucker pointed out what leaders in well-managed businesses have always known: Managers should have multiple objectives in addition to profits.[1]* Here is his list.

Profitability.   Profitability is often measured by gross or net profits after all expenses have been deducted from income. More often, and more validly, it is measured as net return on the funds invested in the business—net profit divided by total money invested in the firm. Certainly profit is a legitimate and honest objective, but there is debate about whether management does or should maximize profits.

In the 18th-century, Adam Smith model of capitalism, the motivation of the owner-manager was assumed to be profit maximization. In 20th-century America, Henry Ford argued that profits were a means, not an end. He indicated that the major objective of Ford Motor Company was to provide inexpensive transportation to the public: "If one does this, one can hardly get away from profits." Other observers have replied that this is utter nonsense, that a firm's major objective must be profit maximization, or it will fall behind in the competitive race. More enlightened modern executives have suggested that profits will be maximized in the long run only if due regard is given to public image, good citizenship, employee welfare, management development and other objectives.

Behaviorialists have suggested that the discussion over whether or not management attempts to maximize profit is irrelevant because maximization is impossible.[2] This argument proceeds on several levels, as suggested below:

1. "Maximization" is an absolute mathematical concept that implies a rigorous manipulation of a wide variety of variables. Until the advent of computers in business, this was impossible. Even with computers, it may be impractical.

---

* Notes and references will be found at the end of this chapter.

2. Humans are not maximizing creatures. In no area of human life do we attempt to maximize in the mathematical sense. Rather, we tend to be satisficers. That is, we pick out a sensible objective and select an alternative that comes reasonably close, without undue concern about irrational maximization.

3. Practically, it is impossible for most managers to maximize profits. Below the top executive level, managers cannot determine the impact of their multitudinous decisions on even short-run profits, much less the long run. Therefore, most managers develop certain ground rules about controlling costs, finding acceptable prices, repairing what is absolutely necessary, and so on.

Most managers are concerned about profits and do attempt to increase them, but this is only one of several motivations affecting their daily decisions. These include staying within budgets, reducing costs, increasing the number of subordinates, increasing the money and equipment over which they have discretionary authority, increasing their own income, and generally expanding organizational slack, which is the excess resources they control.

Market Standing.   A firm should set objectives on where it wants to be relative to competitors. This might be market share compared with the competition or a market niche wherein the company enjoys a competitive advantage.

According to some observers, one of the major problems of many basic industries, such as steel and chemicals, has been overconcern with earnings and short-run cash flow.[3] Managers in these industries should be more willing to sacrifice short-range profits to gaining market share. In this view, market share is critical because once you gain it, it tends not to shift back. That is, market share may be difficult to obtain, but it is also relatively difficult to lose.

By market share we may mean a percentage of the whole market or a secure niche in the market. Because of IBM's strong position, Burroughs chose not to compete directly for overall market share but pushed instead for slow growth in limited areas.[4] Burroughs faired much better than larger firms (such as RCA and GE) who attacked IBM at its strength. Both RCA and GE eventually gave up. A similar example of a different market share objective can be found in the highly competitive pocket-calculator industry.[5] Texas Instruments, Inc. placed high importance on market share and employed a pricing system based on high sales volume for a limited product line. From experience TI believed production costs would decline as output rose because of economies of scale and organizational learning. In sharp contrast the Hewlett-Packard Company gave high priority to identification. In an industry wherein price cutting was rampant, H-P was able to thrive by offering high-price products for a select segment of the market. It equipped its calculators with special features and then offered them at an average price higher than their competitors. To stay in the market with this strategy, however, H-P had to vary its product line continually and offer new models as the competition rushed in to undercut its price. The innovation objective was thus critical.

Productivity.   Productivity is a ratio, like efficiency, rather than a measure of gross output. The ratio relates output of goods and services to input of such resources as labor hours, materials, and invested capital. Especially during times of economic contraction or severe cost inflation (or worse yet, both together), efforts to improve productivity are critical for remaining competitive.

Service.   To maintain market position and profitability, service objectives are essential to point out desired timely and appropriate quality responses to customers and clients.

State of Resources.   State of resources is a maintenance objective reflecting management's responsibility to protect its equipment, buildings, inventory, and capital funds. This concept can be extended also to the area of human resources.[6]

Innovation.   The objective of innovation defines the need for development and delivery of new products or services in order to maintain market position.

"J.D., I've devised a plan that would make mincemeat out of our competitors. Just how far will you authorize me to sink?"

Drawing by Frascino; © 1978, The New Yorker Magazine, Inc.

Social Contribution—Public Responsibility.   Although in the United States we believe in an inherent right of any individual or group to form a business, no such organization has a right to continue unless society deems it valuable. Thus the objective of social contribution is concerned with the firm's impact on the environment, the quality of life, and social justice.

Continuing Objectives for All Organizations

The business objectives described above emphasize results, but we need also to recognize systematic or process objectives that apply to business and all other organizations.[7] The distinction between these two categories is somewhat arbitrary, however, because one shades into the other. Nonetheless, if time and attention are not allocated to the process objectives, the results will not be achieved for very long.

Identification.   Clarity of purpose cannot be assumed. Attention must be devoted to achieving consensus and commitment to organizational objectives among members of the organization. This requires top managers to act as internal salespeople selling the idea of the organization to its own people. During his long tenure as chief executive officer at General Motors, Alfred Sloan spent almost half his time from 1920 to 1950 traveling around the company articulating his conception of the company and its strategy.[8] Similarly, Joseph Wilson gave emphasis to this identification objective when he was building the modern Xerox Corporation in the late 1950s and early 1960s.

Integration.   No organization can exist unless its members perceive some overlap between their own personal objectives and the firm's. This may mean only exchanging their time for the organization's money, but it generally implies a feeling that at least such needs as security, affiliation, and esteem are served by contributing to the organization. Thus management should be concerned about integrating individual needs and organizational objectives. Sloan instituted a top-level bonus committee, which acted more as a visibility committee guaranteeing to hundreds of GM executives that someone at the top was interested in them; that they would not be lost in a huge bureaucracy. In spite of its enormous size, General Motors was able to create a sense of integration between individual and organization among its managers.

Social Influence.   To facilitate problem solving and goal achievement, all organizations must distribute power and authority. We used to assume that power flowed from the top down in hierarchical fashion. But this can no longer be taken for granted because of increased burdens on the top levels and changed expectations at lower levels. Therefore power distribution should be as planned as other aspects of management.

Collaboration.   No matter how well managed, all organizations composed of human beings will experience internal conflict. Rather than bemoaning this as a sign of management's failure or personnel irrationality, management should see it as another area in which to set objectives. That is, management should institute means of managing conflict and means of measuring their performance in doing so.

Adaptation.   Again, no matter how well-managed and well-planned, all organizations confront time and changes in the environment. Competitors introduce new

Continuing Objectives for All Organizations

Identification: achieving clarity, consensus, and commitment to organizational objectives.

Integration: integrating individual needs and organizational objectives.

Social influence: distributing power and authority.

Collaboration: producing mechanisms for the control of conflict.

Adaptation: responding appropriately to changes induced by the environment.

Revitalization: dealing with growth and decay.

technology, market tastes change and new laws are passed which threaten the institution's viability. Accordingly, management needs to set objectives for monitoring the external world and responding appropriately internally.

Revitalization.   Revitalization is the most ambiguous objective, for it suggests the desirability of change for the sake of change—even though the organization is not experiencing difficulty and nothing has dramatically altered in the outside world that demands adaptation. Management should be concerned with developing personnel vitality and creativity in order to be ready for proactive impact on the environment, rather than reactive response.

Notice that these continuing objectives have no priorities, numbers, or time limits. They simply define in qualitative terms the values that characterize the organization.[9] Most organizations do not have a written statement embracing all of their continuing objectives. Rather, these objectives exist in the combined minds of various executives and come into play only when specific goals are being formulated.

Figure 13–1 is the statement of continuing objectives for a large health- and personal-care products corporation. Many people are skeptical about such written statements (especially when profits are mentioned last) and see them as merely public relations gimmicks designed to advertise the companies and their products. Although such cynicism may be justified at times, we cannot assume that the sole continuing business objective is profit, for strategic success demands a much richer model of the organization and its purposes.

Setting Priorities

Because resources of money, materials, labor, and time are limited, everything cannot be done at once. Where there are more problems than resources, priority decisions are necessary. These decisions may be made as a result of situational pressures, or at the discretion of the manager. If situational demands are allowed to predominate, important tasks may well be ignored.

Setting priorities allows management to concentrate by considering problems sequentially rather than simultaneously. Effective executives may concentrate in three ways.[10]

1. They build on their strengths and those of their colleagues. This means concentrating on those activities they do best.
2. They concentrate on outward contribution. Results guide their efforts rather than just work. They begin by asking themselves what results are desired rather than first thinking of the tools or techniques of the task.
3. They concentrate on the few major areas wherein superior performance will produce outstanding results.

The specific criteria used to determine what matters are to be dealt with can have a dramatic influence on an organization's ability to pursue its strategy.

FIGURE 13–1

Statement of Continuing Objectives

Our Credo

WE BELIEVE THAT OUR FIRST RESPONSIBILITY IS TO THE DOCTORS, NURSES, HOSPITALS,
MOTHERS, AND ALL OTHERS WHO USE OUR PRODUCTS.
OUR PRODUCTS MUST ALWAYS BE OF THE HIGHEST QUALITY.
WE MUST CONSTANTLY STRIVE TO REDUCE THE COST OF THESE PRODUCTS.
OUR ORDERS MUST BE PROMPTLY AND ACCURATELY FILLED.
OUR DEALERS MUST MAKE A FAIR PROFIT.

OUR SECOND RESPONSIBILITY IS TO THOSE WHO WORK WITH US —
THE MEN AND WOMEN IN OUR PLANTS AND OFFICES.
THEY MUST HAVE A SENSE OF SECURITY IN THEIR JOBS.
WAGES MUST BE FAIR AND ADEQUATE,
MANAGEMENT JUST, HOURS REASONABLE, AND WORKING CONDITIONS CLEAN AND ORDERLY.
EMPLOYEES SHOULD HAVE AN ORGANIZED SYSTEM FOR SUGGESTIONS AND COMPLAINTS.
SUPERVISORS AND DEPARTMENT HEADS MUST BE QUALIFIED AND FAIR MINDED.
THERE MUST BE OPPORTUNITY FOR ADVANCEMENT — FOR THOSE QUALIFIED
AND EACH PERSON MUST BE CONSIDERED AN INDIVIDUAL
STANDING ON HIS OWN DIGNITY AND MERIT

OUR THIRD RESPONSIBILITY IS TO OUR MANAGEMENT.
OUR EXECUTIVES MUST BE PERSONS OF TALENT, EDUCATION, EXPERIENCE AND ABILITY.
THEY MUST BE PERSONS OF COMMON SENSE AND FULL UNDERSTANDING.

OUR FOURTH RESPONSIBILITY IS TO THE COMMUNITIES IN WHICH WE LIVE.
WE MUST BE A GOOD CITIZEN — SUPPORT GOOD WORKS AND CHARITY,
AND BEAR OUR FAIR SHARE OF TAXES.
WE MUST MAINTAIN IN GOOD ORDER THE PROPERTY WE ARE PRIVILEGED TO USE.
WE MUST PARTICIPATE IN PROMOTION OF CIVIC IMPROVEMENT,
HEALTH, EDUCATION AND GOOD GOVERNMENT,
AND ACQUAINT THE COMMUNITY WITH OUR ACTIVITIES.

OUR FIFTH AND LAST RESPONSIBILITY IS TO OUR STOCKHOLDERS.
BUSINESS MUST MAKE A SOUND PROFIT.
RESERVES MUST BE CREATED, RESEARCH MUST BE CARRIED ON,
ADVENTUROUS PROGRAMS DEVELOPED, AND MISTAKES PAID FOR.
ADVERSE TIMES MUST BE PROVIDED FOR, ADEQUATE TAXES PAID, NEW MACHINES PURCHASED,
NEW PLANTS BUILT, NEW PRODUCTS LAUNCHED, AND NEW SALES PLANS DEVELOPED.
WE MUST EXPERIMENT WITH NEW IDEAS.
WHEN THESE THINGS HAVE BEEN DONE THE STOCKHOLDER SHOULD RECEIVE A FAIR RETURN.
WE ARE DETERMINED WITH THE HELP OF GOD'S GRACE,
TO FULFILL THESE OBLIGATIONS TO THE BEST OF OUR ABILITY.

Reprinted by permission of Johnson & Johnson. Copyright Johnson & Johnson 1979.

Pragmatic Focus

Most managers find it difficult to be as rational or methodical as suggested above. In contrasting his former work as a professor with his job in government, Henry Kissinger stated the essential dilemma: "Before, I could always deal with a problem in what I thought was a reasonable way. I could work at something until I thought I understood it. Here, I've had to put problems in order of priority and hope that the low priority ones won't hit us before we get to them."[11] A former chair of New Jersey Standard Oil defines the problem similarly:

> QUESTION: Have you found in your years in business that there is a best time to think and plan your day?

> ANSWER: No, I don't think so. As a matter of fact, in our business, we might plan this way, but the plan won't last very long. You can walk in the office at 9:00 in the morning, and at 9:15 something you didn't have any idea about will rise in the way of a pretty important problem or crisis. So what you do is you give priority to the things on the basis of your judgment of what has the highest priority.[12]

Order of Arrival.   There are tremendous pressures directing the attention of managers away from issues central to attaining strategic objectives. Some of these are cultural. Perhaps more than members of any other culture, Americans do first things first. Arrival time here is a criterion for obtaining a seat at the theater, restaurant, or on a bus; in many countries, age, sex or status are more relevant criteria than first come, first served. Priority due to order of arrival is very democratic of course, but it is a poor method of management. Lesser matters will outnumber and submerge more important ones if all are handled in order of occurrence.

Urgency.   As suggested by the quote from Henry Kissinger, urgency can overwhelm strategic importance. An organization's multiple objectives can be arrayed along a continuum of most dominant to most deferrable. Most dominant are those to which everyday demands will dictate attention. Deferrable objectives are those that can safely be ignored for short periods of time.

For example, the executive team of a private power company determined the list of objectives shown in Figure 13–2. This list was developed only after several hours of free discussion among the management group. The group's initial list had seemed more idealistic. At the outset the managers, who were all engineers by training, stressed integration and innovation. Later discussion, however, was centered on capacity, time, reliability, and cost. They agreed that most meeting time was concerned with these matters, and relatively little on-the-job time was devoted to integration and innovation.

One executive finally concluded that the engineering and research division really did not want innovation after all, but required adaptation and adoption of ideas developed elsewhere. The more important objectives were perceived by management as less urgent and hence deferrable.

Notice how high in importance these utility executives ranked identification. One might think that since it was a stable organization, the power company would have

FIGURE 13–2

Objectives Determined for an Engineering and Research Division

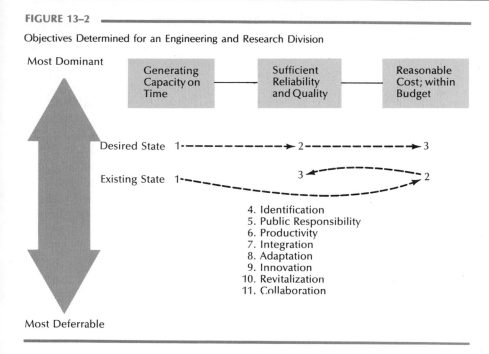

long since settled its identification issue. Yet this organization had several glaring contradictions. The first floor of the building was a retail store operated by the marketing department that sold electrical utilities—ranges, refrigerators, air conditioners, heating units. Yet on the top floor, top management was worrying about how it could possibly meet the region's energy needs the following summer when the temperature was expected to reach 95°F. In pricing there was a similar inconsistency. There was a policy of discounts to large users, even though national interst might be served better by (1) giving discounts to those who reduced their consumption and (2) penalizing consumers with expanding accounts! The managers believed that the firm should be confronting these issues.

A sense of urgency stems from proximity of a task deadline and fear of not meeting it. Managers tend to give great weight to urgency, especially when faced with many jobs that can be accomplished quickly. The temptation to work on these jobs is seductive. When President Dwight Eisenhower tried to arrange his affairs so that only the truly important and urgent matters came across his desk, he reportedly discovered that the two seldom went together. He found that the really important matters were seldom urgent, and the most urgent matters were seldom important.[13]

Regardless of whether fear is self-centered or other-concerned, it tends to be a short-run criterion. At times fear will and should dominate—as when a military unit is under attack, a riot is imminent, or bankruptcy looms. In such situations the present must take precedence over the future. Yet if urgency predominates for very long as the criterion for assigning priorities to objectives, failure can be expected.

Such pragmatic responses to the everyday pressures of life in organizations often bleed away the resources needed to pursue strategic purposes. Special effort is needed to overcome them.

Strategic Focus

In order to direct attention to important strategic issues, management must ask itself: Are we allocating time and resources in accordance with our defined priorities? Are we allocating sufficient time and resources to more deferrable, but still important objectives? The second question is particularly important because setting priorities is actually more critical for deferrable objectives. Time will probably be allocated to the more dominant objectives because of urgency; managers will be unable to avoid them. However, process-oriented, more deferrable objectives must also have attention, or strategic performance will eventually be eroded. The primary benefit of the lengthy discussion in the Engineering and Research Division was to pinpoint just what objectives were being slighted.

A definitive answer to the question of how much time should be devoted to each objective is impossible because situations differ, and little research exists that details time allocation for managers under differing conditions. A recent survey suggests, however, that top-level executives, at least, are becoming increasingly engaged in innovation, integration, and revitalization. This is the main conclusion from extensive interviews in large corporations. Comments by four executives were as follows:

> I spend a substantial portion of my time in selecting and moving people. We expect to expand our rotational system and this will take more of my time.
>
> Certainly 15 percent, I think, of the time of most of the higher executives is spent on development of people, planning for their future development.
>
> It's my number one job. I spend more time on selection and development of personnel than on any other activity.
>
> Top executives seem to have a consensus that more of their time will be devoted to coordinating research and development, developing and implementing new products.[14]

Regardless of the specific percentage of time spent on each objective, the point is that time must be allocated to more deferrable objectives if the organization is to survive in the long run. A well-established technique for ensuring that time is utilized in this way is to separate functions among people so that some managers (usually called line managers) concentrate on the more dominant objectives and other personnel (called staff) consider the deferrable ones. Such a distinction is better than nothing because a less pressured staff does spend more time on deferrable activities than line managers might. Nonetheless, the integration of deferrable objectives into each managerial position is desirable because this facilitates their actual implementation.

Some firms have created parallel mechanisms to help line managers maintain a dual focus—on longer term strategic issues and more pressing operating issues. At General Electric, for example, SBU managers are responsible simultaneously for operating and strategic outcomes identified in the planning process. Their performance evaluation includes aspects of both dimensions. Texas Instruments introduced the use of two budgets. One was the operating budget with financial and market share goals for the current year. The other was the strategic budget with resources to be spent this year on items that would build for the future of the business.

Life-Cycle Focus

Another way of concentrating effort and resources on issues critical to the organization's healthy development is to recognize that its fundamental needs at any one time depend on the stage of growth and maturation it has reached. Just as people have certain developmental stages in their lives, firms face common sets of crises they must surmount in the organizational stages of founding, youth, and maturity.[15] Each of these stages has certain critical concerns and key issues, as outlined in Figure 13–3.

Birth as Developmental Stage.   The critical concerns at the birth stage are creation and survival. The entrepreneurial planner's key issues are what to risk and what to sacrifice—such as money, security, aspirations, and even personal life. For example, a recent business graduate has uniquely combined college academic and social experience by inventing a disposable valve for tapping beer kegs. Most kegs use a metal valve that sells for about $15 and is good for about 10 kegs if it is not lost or damaged (many are, however, long before they are worn out). His wood and plastic valve would sell for about $1.50. His critical early decisions were: whether or not to sell his idea to a large company; whether or not to try to start his own business; whether or not to accept a full-time job and work part-time in his own business; and how much and who would invest in his business. And finally, how long to keep at the new business before taking a job. He decided to borrow from his family and invest one year full-time in developing his product.

If the critical issues of creation and survival are resolved effectively, a new system comes into being and becomes viable by accepting realities, thus learning from experience. The unhappy alternative is that the entrepreneur's idea remains abstract or inadequately developed, so the organization fails to adjust to its environment and either dies or requires continuing sacrifice.

Birth Concerns
- risk?
- sacrifice?

At birth the planning knowledge and skill required are clearly perceived short-range objectives in the mind of the top manager who is able to translate the knowledge into self-action and directives.

Birth Needs
- short-range objectives
- self-action
- directives

Youth as Developmental Stage.   Once an organization comes into existence, critical concerns about stability and reputation are confronted. Stability depends upon the ability of the young organization's management to organize, to impose discipline and rational delegation. Reputation depends on willingness to evaluate management's own performance objectively. Unless these key issues are addressed, the organization will merely react to crises, drifting instead of being directed. It will probably encounter continuing difficulty in attracting good personnel and customers.

Two graduate management students encountered these concerns in a small boat-building business they had initiated while in college. They began by constructing small fiberglass rowboats in the garage of a relative's summer shore house. They

Youth Concerns
- stability
- reputation

FIGURE 13-3

Concerns and Consequences in Organizational Development Stages

Develop-mental Stage	Critical Concerns	Key Issues	Consequences if Concerns Are Not Met	Result if the Issue Is Resolved		Planning Knowledge Needed	Personal Skills Needed
				Correctly	Incorrectly		
Birth	To create a new organization.	What to risk (money? security? present job?).	Frustration and inaction.	New corporate system comes into being and begins operating.	Idea remains abstract; company is undercapitalized and cannot adequately develop product or service.	Clearly perceived short-range objective in mind of top person.	Ability to transmit knowledge into action by self and into orders to others.
	To survive as a viable system.	What to sacrifice (home life? company aspirations?).	Death of organization; subsidy by others.	Organization accepts realities, learns from experience, becomes viable.	Organization fails to adjust to realities of its environment and either dies or remains marginal, demanding continuing sacrifice.	The short-range objectives that need to be communicated.	Communications know-how, ability to adjust to changing conditions.
Youth	To gain stability.	How to organize (how willing to impose discipline and delegation?).	Reactive, crisis-dominated organization; opportunistic rather than self-directing attitudes and policies.	Organization develops efficiency and strength but retains flexibility.	Organization overextends itself and returns to survival stage, or it establishes stabilizing patterns which block future flexibility.	How top person can predict relevant factors and make long-range plans.	Ability to transmit planning knowledge into communicable objectives.

Maturity						
To gain reputation and develop pride.	How to review and evaluate (how willing to examine ourselves?).	Difficulty in attracting good personnel and clients; inappropriate, overly aggressive and distorted image building.	Organization's reputation reinforces efforts to improve quality of goods and service.	Organization places more effort on image creation than on quality product, or it builds an image which misrepresents its true capability.	Planning know-how and understanding of goals on part of whole executive team.	Facility at allowing others a voice in decision making, obtaining commitments from them, and communicating objectives to customers.
To achieve uniqueness and adaptability.	Whether and how to change (modify our definition of the firm?).	Unnecessarily defensive or competitive attitudes; diffusion of energy; loss of most creative personnel.	Organization changes to take fuller advantage of its unique capability and provide opportunities for its personnel.	Organization develops too narrow a specialty to ensure secure future, fails to discover its uniqueness, and spreads its efforts into inappropriate areas.	Understanding on part of top management of how others should set their own objectives and of how to manage subunits of the organization.	Ability to teach others to plan; proficiency in integrating plans of subunit into objectives and resource of organization.
To contribute to society.	Whether and how to share.	Possible lack of public respect and acceptance; punitive legislation.	Organization gains public respect and appreciation for itself as an institution contributing to society.	Organization may be accused of "public be damned" attitude.	General management understanding of the larger objectives of organization and of society.	Ability to apply own organization and resources to the problems of the larger community.

Source: G. L. Lippitt and W. H. Schmidt, "Crisis in a Developing Organization," *Harvard Business Review*, November–December 1967, p. 103.

performed all the construction and marketing by themselves with remarkable success. They could literally sell everything they made because their price was so low (virtually zero overhead) and quality so high (they built them by hand). To deal with the burden, however, in time they hired several cousins and friends to work in the shop. This was satisfactory as long as one of the two partners was present working alongside the others.

When September arrived, however, they began to face problems when the partners entered graduate school and attempted to supervise construction only one or two days a week. Quality declined, and they became aware that even relatives will party on the job when not being supervised. Stronger discipline, closer supervision, sharper delegation of accountability, and better quality control procedures were essential. The solution to these problems raised one of the birth issues again, namely, who was to sacrifice by dropping out of graduate school in order to manage the business?

To deal with the youth issues of stability and reputation, the required planning knowledge is the interaction between short run and long run, between internal organizational conditions and external developments. This means an ability to transcend the present and communicate overall strategy to others while giving them some sense of participation in the process.

Many entrepreneurs who create a business or creatively combine existing businesses have difficulty in converting from the critical concerns of birth to those of youth. Some are impatient with the discipline needed to organize rationally; others are too personally driven to be objective about evaluating themselves or the actual performance of their "baby." Consequently, they are often replaced by more professional managers. William Durant created the General Motors Corporation out of existing firms—Buick, Oakland, and Chevrolet—by imaginative acquisition and financial manipulation. Nonetheless, he was such a poor administrator that when an endangered GM raised funds by selling stock to the Du Pont Company, the latter insisted that Durant be replaced by a more professional manager—Alfred Sloan, an engineering graduate of MIT, who was president of the Hyatt Roller Bearing Company.

Maturity as Developmental Stage.   From creation to stability to change is the general trend of concerns. Managerial success often leads to new issues of uniqueness and adaptability. In what way should the organization change, for change is inevitable if the firm is not to stagnate and become dangerously vulnerable to competitors' initiatives. If these issues are effectively handled, however, the organization takes advantage of its unique people and competencies. If not, it is likely to remain too narrowly specialized, oblivious to opportunities to apply its attributes in growth fields. Important skills needed to do this include understanding how the organization fits into the larger society and the ability to teach other managers to take this larger view without excessive reliance on the top levels.

From a small percentage of the automobile business in the early 1920s, General Motors rapidly expanded to pass Ford Motor Company in the 1930s at least partly because Henry Ford, Sr., became too locked into his strategy of a simple, no frills car for the masses. He simply didn't change quickly enough to offer hardtops, colors, models, and luxury extras that GM did. Even worse, Ford lost its most creative

Youth Needs
- objective evaluation of own performance
- discipline and delegation

Maturity Concerns
- uniqueness
- adaptability

Maturity Needs
- understanding of external trends
- education of subordinate managers

personnel, which led to its almost being denuded of effective managers by the 1940s when the elder Ford passed on.

An organization's evolution is paralleled by a series of discrete changes in planning as illustrated in Figure 13–4.[16] Although not as smooth or mechanical as the following description implies, firms seem to change their stance toward planning through a series of transformations.

Phase I: Entrepreneurial Stage.   Managers in phase I utilize little planning. They are more fire fighters under constant pressure, responding half in panic to problems arrayed against them. Since at this stage organizations are typically small, they may feel no need to plan—especially if growth is satisfactory. About the only planning-like activity is financial budgeting performed by the controller or accountants under pressure of banks and other creditors.

Phase II: The Administrative Gap Stage.   The gap stems from success, which requires increased management control. Management begins to recognize that some managerial tasks are no longer being completed. To overcome the constant scrambling, this phase is oriented to developing formal planning—especially for more effective daily control. The time horizon is still a relatively short one or two years, but management begins to be more involved in planning, rather than leaving it to the accountants.

Phase III: The Expectation Gap Stage.   Things are less hectic in this stage if phase II has been handled well. Management is now concerned about maintaining the system for reasonable growth. Nonetheless, in most instances growth is slower and management's expectations exceed the reality. Management may believe that the company now has the capacity to grow more rapidly. In the transition from phase I to phase II, the organization's opportunities seemed to be running ahead faster than management's ability to control the development. Now in the phase II to phase III transition, management's expectations run ahead more quickly than the firm—probably because the organization's products or services have matured or new competition has emerged.

Recognizing these developments, management will generally implement systematic means of collecting and utilizing external data in its planning. The new focus becomes monitoring the firm's environment and expanding the time horizon. Diversifying products and markets becomes of growing interest here (and more so in the next phase). In an effort to foster continued growth and to reduce variance in sales and profits, management attempts to reduce its reliance on its major line of business. In a sample of 100 firms selected randomly from the 500 largest American industrial corporations, the proportion whose major single business accounted for less than 70 percent of total corporate sales had increased from approximately 30 percent in 1949 to almost 65 percent in 1969.[17] In short, fewer firms are dependent on a single product.

Phase IV: The Strategic Development Stage.   Senior managers in phase IV become developers looking for means to expand and diversify a steady, stable business. Excessive variability becomes the enemy and predictability perhaps the most

FIGURE 13–4

Phases of Planning
I   Entrepreneurial Stage
II Administrative Gap Stage
III Expectation Gap Stage
IV Strategic Development Stage

I   Entrepreneurial Stage
    • fire fighting
    • response
    • accounting

II Administrative Gap Stage
    • formal planning for control
    • short-range
    • management involvement

III Expectation Gap Stage
    • reasonable growth
    • monitor external world
    • longer time horizon
    • diversification

desired performance attribute. In this phase many firms dramatically expand effort to institute a fully comprehensive, formal long-range planning system. If successful, they are better able to maintain desired moderate growth.

Of course, not all firms pass predictably through these phases, nor are all managers alert to the need for strategy and planning system changes. Indeed, research indicates that predictability may be so desired that management will accept a stagnating or even deteriorating situation as long as its doesn't reach a crisis.

IV Strategic Development
    Stage
    ● expansion
    ● diversification
    ● formal long-range
      planning

Setting Specific Goals

The list of continuing objectives for business and other organizations ignored the competition among them. Because we applied no priorities and set no deadlines for the various objectives, it was possible to discuss them without considering how they operate together. It may be impossible, for example, to expand profits and market share simultaneously. Improving productivity and curbing pollution may be mutually self-defeating.[18] When the organization sets goals to be accomplished in a specific time period—next week, month, year, or decade—it encounters conflict among the continuing objectives.

The central difference between continuing objectives and specific goals is that the latter have time limits and measurements: profits should be up $100,000 in the next year; productivity up 10 percent in six months; market share increased by 5 percent in five years; capacity expanded by 300,000 tons in two years. For every specific goal, there should be a deadline for accomplishment and a criterion to measure performance.[19]

HAGAR THE HORRIBLE

Hagar the Horrible by Dik Browne.

For Every Objective, a Goal

Most desirably, every specific goal would be measurable on a bipolar scale (such as good/bad, accept/reject, go/no go) or in numbers (pounds, gallons, kilowatts, customers, percentages, and dollars).

For each continuing objective, there would be a specific goal for the next relevant time period and a specific indicator by which achievement is to be measured. Some examples of continuing objectives and their specific goals and performance indicators are listed below.

Continuing Objective	Specific Goal for Coming Year	Performance Indicator
1. Provide a fair return on investment.	Provide a 15 percent rate of return; up 5 percent from last year.	Net profits for year as a percentage of net invested capital ($125 million).
2. Ensure an important share of the market.	a. Retain 75 percent of old customers	a. Percentage of people whose last purchase was from us who replace item with new purchase from us.
	b. Capture 25 percent of first-time purchasers	b. Percentage of people purchasing item for first time who purchase from us.
3. Manufacture goods efficiently.	Improve productivity by 5 percent	a. Number parts produced per week divided by the total hours of labor utilized per week.
		b. Installation of new punching machine by August 1.

Less Measurable Goals

If a continuing objective has no parallel specific goal for the next appropriate time period, managers are unlikely to devote much attention to it. Their energies will be focused on the specific goals by which their performance is being evaluated. Simply stating that high employee morale is a continuing objective is unlikely to influence the behavior of managers who are also concerned about the net rate of return on investment, market share, and productivity. Even stating that the manager's goal is to improve morale by 15 percent in the next year will have little impact if no indicator is defined or no measurement is taken. To motivate the manager to attempt to improve morale would require more specificty, as in the following example:

Continuing Objective	Specific Goal	Performance Indicator
Encourage high employee morale.	Improve morale by 15 percent.	a. Turnover reduced by 15 percent. $$\frac{\text{Number people resigning job in year}}{\text{Number people employed on average during year}}$$
		b. Average index of morale on Professor Jones's morale test increased by 15 percent.

The performance indicator should in fact measure the specific goal and hence its contribution to the relevant continuing objective. On the more easily quantifiable objectives, such as profitability and productivity, this relationship is clear. On more subjective objectives, such as morale, however, the relationship between indicators and continuing objectives is more uncertain: Turnover statistics or a score on a test may not really measure morale.

Unfortunately, not all of the continuing objectives can be converted into quantifiable specific goals. How does one quantify public responsibility? Being a good citizen? Achievement of identification, collaboration, or revitalization? Because such objectives are difficult to measure in quantitative form, management must often settle for qualitative statements that suggest what behavior most probably indicates objective achievement. For example, contributing to the United Fund and to private colleges may add to meeting social responsibility; not breaking laws may mean good citizenship; perhaps conflict is being managed well if strikes are few; or hiring new managers may produce revitalization. These are plausible conclusions, but proving

"We must consider the health of the community, we must consider our image and we must consider the fine of $25,000 a day."

them with numbers is difficult or impossible.[20] Here are some statements of relevant behavior that serve as performance indicators for less measurable objectives.

Continuing Objective	Specific Goal for Coming Year	Performance Indicator
1. Develop middle management for executive responsibilities.	a. Develop a merit review system for middle managers.	a. Report submitted to VP by December 1.
	b. Send 10 managers to university executive programs.	b. Number of managers sent by January 1.
2. Be a good corporate citizen.	Reduce air pollution at plant by 15 percent.	By January 1 pollution output should be 125 lbs./hr. (or less) measured at stack by electro-static test.
3. Provide a safe and satisfying workplace for employees.	a. Eliminate dangerous conditions in Plant B by automating the loading operation.	a. Installation of the new loader should be 50 percent complete by end of year. Deadline is in 18 months.
	b. Reduce injuries by 10 percent.	b. $\dfrac{\text{Employee-days lost to injuries}}{\text{Total employee-days available for year}}$

Many efforts are currently under way to develop "social auditing" methods to monitor how the organization is performing on these more difficult to measure objectives and goals.[21]

SUMMARY

Top management defines the general nature of the organization and its relation to the world. It points out the general direction in which the enterprise would like to move and the dreams it wants to bring into reality. To make the dreams and strategy more meaningful to others, continuing objectives should be determined and communicated. These objectives are multiple. In addition to profits, they include market standing, productivity, social contribution, innovation, state of resources, service, identity, integration, collaboration, adaptation, and revitalization.

Priorities may be based on order of arrival, urgency, or contribution to objectives, but the latter is most appropriate where possible. Objectives can be ranged in order of importance from most dominant to most deferrable. The tendency is for current operating concerns to squeeze out important strategic issues. It is important that some resources be allocated systematically, even to the most deferrable objectives.

Strategy and objectives should be framed in the light of the organization's developmental stage and the key issues it then faces: birth (what to risk and sacrifice), and youth (how to organize and evaluate), or maturity (how to change and share).

Continuing objectives are converted into specific goals by: (1) setting time limits for each objective, (2) defining the specific performance indicators by which each goal is to be measured, and (3) ranking the objectives in order of priority for the next relevant time period. For each continuing objective, there should therefore be a specific goal and a performance indicator by which achievement is to be measured.

Specific goals are allocated to each organizational unit, and they become the unit's specific goal: the most precise and detailed statement of expected performance for the next time interval. These specific unit goals may take the form of performance standards for individuals and groups and budgets for departments and divisions.

REVIEW QUESTIONS

1. What is the difference between the process and the content of planning?

2. What are the continuing objectives for business? How are these primarily "ends" objectives?

3. What are the continuing objectives for all organizations? How are these "means" objectives?

4. Why is profit maximization an unsatisfactory objective?

5. Why must priorities be set among the various continuing objectives?

6. What are the criteria for setting priorities?

7. What is the drawback in using order of arrival as a criterion?

8. What is the drawback in using urgency as a criterion?

9. Why does one priority list of continuing objectives not apply to all organizations?

10. What is the difference between "most dominant" and "most deferrable" objectives?

11. Why must time be allocated to deferrable objectives?

12. What are the stages of organizational development?

13. What is an organization's critical concern at its birth?

14. What are an organization's critical concerns and key issues during its youth?

15. What are an organization's critical concerns and key issues when approaching maturity?

16. What are the major differences between continuing objectives and specific goals?

17. What should be the relationship between continuing objectives, specific goals, and performance indicators?

18. How should the goals for less measurable objectives be stated?

Notes and References on Setting Objectives and Goals

1. Peter F. Drucker, *The Practice of Management* (New York: Harper & Row, 1954).

2. See R. Cyert and J. March, *A Behavioral Theory of the Firm* (Englewood Cliffs, N.J.: Prentice-Hall, 1963). W. K. Hall noted:

> Few, if any, alternatives are explicitly considered in selecting a project for funding. Instead, individual projects are sequentially sponsored upward through the review process where they are either eventually selected or rejected. The process of sponsorship is governed by managerial commitment to a project. While the economics of the project has some influence on the level of commitment, it is dominated by the individual managers' assessments of the "benefits of being right versus the costs of being wrong."

"Strategic Planning, Product Innovation and the Theory of the Firm," *Journal of Business Policy* 3, no. 3 (1973), pp. 19–27. For economic theories of the firm, see F. Matchlup, "Theories of the Firm: Marginalist, Behavioral and Managerial," *American Economic Review* 57, no. 1 (1967), pp. 1–33.

3. D. E. Schendel and G. R. Patton, "Corporate Stagnation and Turnaround," *Journal of Economics and Business,* Summer 1976, pp. 236–41.

4. B. Uttal, "How Ray MacDonald's Growth Theory Created I.B.M.'s Toughest Competitor," *Fortune,* January 1977, p. 94 ff.

5. "Flexible Pricing," *Business Week,* December 12, 1977, p. 78 ff.

6. For a general review of the issue of the strategic management of human resources, see the papers from a symposium on Strategic Planning and Human Resource Management published in *Human Resource Management* 22, Spring/Summer, 1983.

7. W. G. Bennis, *Organizational Development* (Reading, Mass.: Addison-Wesley Publishing, 1969).

8. A. Sloan, *My Years at General Motors* (Garden City, N.Y.: Doubleday Publishing, 1964).

9. For a discussion of value objectives as opposed to performance objectives, see J. E. Ramsey, "A Framework for the Interaction of Corporate Value Objectives, Corporate Performance Objectives and Corporate Strategy," *Journal of Economics and Business,* Summer 1976, pp. 171–80.

10. Peter F. Drucker, *The Effective Executive* (New York: Harper & Row, 1967), p. 103.

11. Kissinger interview with Associated Press correspondent Saul Pott, August 23, 1970.

12. M. J. Rathbone, quoted in *Lessons of Leadership,* by the editors of *Nation's Business* (Garden City, N.Y.: Doubleday Publishing, 1966), p. 4.

13. President Eisenhower's conclusion about trivial and important matters is described in J. Engstrom and A. Mackenzie, *Managing Your Time* (Grand Rapids, Mich.: Zondervan, 1967), p. 68.

14. P. E. Holden, C. A. Pederson, and G. E. Germance, *Top Management* (New York: McGraw-Hill, 1968).

15. This discussion drawn from G. L. Lippitt and W. H. Schmidt, "Crisis in a Developing Organization," *Harvard Business Review,* November–December 1967, p. 101 ff. On these issues see also J. R. Kimberley and R. H. Miles, *The Organizational Life Cycle* (San Francisco: Jossey-Bass Publishers, 1980).

16. C. Gilmour and G. Sheehan, "The Effect of Crisis on Organizational Planning," *Journal of General Management,* Winter 1976–77, pp. 50–59.

17. R. P. Rumelt, *Strategy, Structure and Economic Performance of the Fortune 500,* (Cambridge, Mass.: Harvard Business School, 1974).

18. For examples of the overstressing of certain objectives, see W. E. Fruhan, Jr., "Pyrrhic Victories in Fights for Market Share," *Harvard Business Review,* September–October 1972, pp. 100–107; and J. T. Hackett, "Drawbacks of Continuing Corporate Growth," *Harvard Business Review,* January–February 1974, p. 6 ff.

19. G. P. Latham and G. A. Yukl, "A Review of Research on the Application of Goal Setting in Organizations," *Academy of Management Review,* December 1975, pp. 824–45. See also R. L. Morasky, "Defining Goals—A Systems Approach," *Long-Range Planning,* April 1977, pp. 85–89.

20. K. R. Andrews argues that managers will make more "moral" decisions only when specific goals are applied to social responsibility issues. "Can the Best Corporations Be Made Moral?" *Harvard Business Review,* May–June 1973, pp. 57–64.

To put this idea into effect, the First Pennsylvania Bank developed a Social Scorecard, which sets specific, numerical goals in hiring and promoting minority groups, lending them money, and buying from them. The president stated that the program is working because bank officials knew they would be held to account for their social performance as well as their profit performance:

> That's the whole point. Our stance is that they are of equal importance. A lot of our people are not committed. A lot of them think this is for the birds. . . . Why are they doing it? To get their paychecks. It's as simple as that. If you want your meat and potatoes, you've got to do it.

J. R. Slevin, "Inside the Economy," *Philadelphia Inquirer,* January 22, 1974.

21. R. A. Bauer and D. H. Fenn, Jr., "What Is a Corporate Social Audit?" *Harvard Business Review,* January–February 1973, pp. 37–48. M. Epstein, E. Flamholtz, and J. J. McDonough, "Corporate Social Accounting in the United States of America: State of the Art and Future Prospects," *Accounting, Organizations and Society* 1, no. 1 (1976), pp. 23–42; E. Marques, "Human Resource Accounting: Some Questions and Reflections," *Accounting, Organizations and Society* 1, no. 2–3 (1976), pp. 175–78; and J. E. Post and M. J. Epstein, "Information Systems for Social Reporting," *Academy of Management Review,* January 1977, pp. 81–87.

14

From Action to Results: Controlling Performance

Once a firm has identified its desired outcomes in terms of strategic objectives and has translated these into specific goals and action programs, there remains the challenge of transforming them into concrete results. This must be done through the actions of the organization's members. In Part 6, Structuring Organizational Systems, we will explore in detail the means by which management strives to shape and channel patterns of behavior in the organization. This chapter makes the transition from planning to controlling performance.

The central idea of control is to undertake measures that can keep actions on the track until desired outcomes are attained.[1]* The two principal means of achieving control are through performance feedback and through policies and procedures.[2]

Control through Performance Feedback

Feedback control picks up at the end of the planning process when the specific goals of an individual, department, or organization become the expected performance against which management will evaluate actual results.[3] The steps in control are as follows:

1. Communicating specific goals.
2. Measuring actual performance.
3. Reporting the actual performance to appropriate people.
4. Comparing actual performance with specific goals.
5. Deciding to do nothing, to correct behavior, or to modify goals.

Feedback control is one of the most widespread phenomena of nature, as well as of modern science and technology. Time-lapse photography, which speeds up the passage of days and weeks, suggests dramatically that plants "think." They move in the direction of light or water. What actually is happening is that the plant's sensors detect more light in one direction than in another. So it is in all feedback-control systems. The system has its objectives or needs: It must take in external resources, it must process these resources to convert them into products for internal use and external delivery; it must monitor how it is doing to detect dangerous divergences. Such systems guide all living organisms as well as the temperatures in our homes, automation on the assembly line, and navigation in space.[4]

Figure 14–1 illustrates the interaction between the elements of a feedback-control system. In a business, the goal setter might be top management; the controller, a middle manager; the information processor, a staff assistant (such as a cost engineer, or accountant, or even a computer); the sensor, another accountant or quality control technician. These relationships would parallel the organizational hierarchy, in which each level of management is goal setter for the next lower level, which acts as controller for itself and goal setter for the next lower level. Thus in United Basic Chemical Corporation, the board of directors is goal setter for the president, who is goal setter for the Cleaning Division manager, who is goal setter for the Detergent Manufacturing Department head.

Note that the arrows associated with the sensor go in both directions—in and

---

* Notes and references will be found at the end of this chapter.

FIGURE 14–1

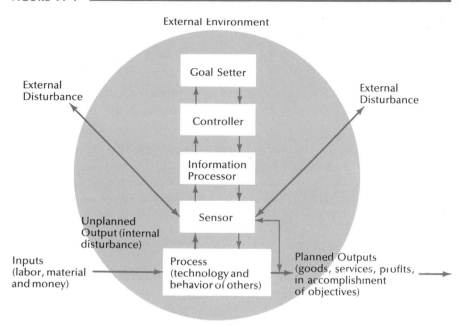

out. This suggests that effective managers and staff personnel acting as sensors are not passive but active. They do not just wait until results and disturbances come to their attention but actively probe the internal and external environments for unplanned-for conditions. In short, they are active intelligence gatherers.

The inputs in a business feedback control system are labor, materials, and money. The output is the product or services of the firm. Disturbing influences could originate from inside or outside the firm. From inside, they could be unplanned outputs: morale problems, equipment breakdowns, absenteeism, resignations, and deaths. From the external environment, disturbances could come from union activities, government regulations, a competitor's actions, technological breakthroughs elsewhere, riots, an oil embargo, and so forth.

This all sounds very formal, and often it is in managing organizations. However, feedback control is also characteristic of informal and personal activities. When the great Illinois Tech and professional basketball player Doug Collins was growing up in the Midwest, he would practice shooting baskets for hours in sun, rain, and snow. The goal was clear and the feedback simple. Yet, Doug learned that there were even more immediate goals and sources of feedback. Like many great shooters, he learned the feelings in the feet and fingertips that precede the swishing shot. If you can get the right feeling in the hands, the fingers pointed upward, the ball is almost certain to go in. All of this is control by feedback. It is remarkably like the potter at the wheel, where result and fingers are intimately linked with the creative vision in the brain. To be sure, the process becomes more complex as goals are defined by others, results more delayed and performance more difficult to measure, but the principle is unchanged.

Manager and Production Worker

The simple control cycle between a manager and a production worker is repeated daily in thousands of organizations. The feedback process in this instance might work as follows for Sid Blomberg, a punch press operator:

1. An industrial engineer defines management's specific goal for Sid's output on the punch press: 10 widgets per hour, 70 per day, 350 per week.
2. Each day a clerk counts the actual number that Sid completes.
3. On Monday morning Sid's total production for the past week is reported to the supervisor, who compares expected and actual performance.
4. The supervisor decides:
   a. If Sid produced 350 widgets or more, to do nothing (and if Sid turned out 400, the supervisor might compliment him).
   b. If Sid produced 285, the supervisor would probably chew him out and warn him to increase his output. Before doing this, however, the supervisor should investigate to determine if the expected standard was valid for the past week, whether the material was different than usual, or whether Sid experienced equipment problems.
   c. If conditions were nonstandard and the expected performance was unrealistic, then the supervisor would probably take steps to see that Sid is not punished for last week's output. If the nonstandard conditions will continue, the supervisor will see that the expected goal is modified.

Executive and Manager

Controlling the performance of a production worker is easy to imagine (although not always easy in practice) and relatively common in all industrialized nations. American management has also applied this process to managerial positions to a greater extent than is the case in the rest of the world, perhaps as a reflection of the individualism of our cultural heritage. In any case, budgets for individual managers are a central feature of American management. For example, Figure 14–2 is the budget statement for Joseph Figlia's Detergent Manufacturing Department at the United Basic Chemical Corporation.

Sometime in December Joe receives the printed form with the expected goals typed. Early in April he receives a second copy of the form with the actual figures written in by a cost engineer on his division manager's staff. At the bottom of the form, Whitney Anderson, the Cleaning Division manager, usually writes in some general observations, which undoubtedly will be a topic of discussion between him and Joe. Note that Whit has told Joe to provide him with answers within three days. Joe's answer might be as shown in Figure 14–3.

FIGURE 14–2

Budget for Detergent Department, United Basic Chemical Corporation

For Period _Jan 1 – March 30_   Department Head _Joseph Figlia_

Item	Expected	Actual	Comments
1. Everbrite Production	250,000 lbs.	249,802	
2. Neverscrub Production	50,000 lbs.	30,043	← action needed
3. Direct Labor Utilized (production employees)	6,000 labor-hours	5,812	good!
4. Indirect Labor Utilized (maintenance, office)	1,000 labor-hours	1,498	← why so much?
5. Rejected Product Everbrite Neverscrub	2,000 lbs. 500 lbs.	1,704 2,013	← action needed
6. Overtime	500 labor-hours	503	
7. Downtime on Production Equipment	32 hours	65	← action needed
8. Index of Productivity $\dfrac{\text{Total lbs. Produced}}{\text{Direct Labor-Hours Utilized}}$	50	48	

9. Comments by Cost Engineer

I can hardly read the production sheets kept by your office. Please try to write them more neatly.

10. Comments by Division Manager   _April 2 –_

Joe, it looks like you've got some trouble with your neverscrub cleanser. Downtime is so great, is something wrong with your equipment? Have you changed raw materials? Let me know by Wednesday. Otherwise, the figures look pretty good (but get that productivity index up). Don't forget, I want some answers by Wednesday, April 6

Whit

FIGURE 14–3

Memo
To: Whitney Anderson, Cleaning Division Manager
From: Joe Figlia, Detergent Manufacturing Department Head
Date: April 5

With reference to your questions about our performance from January 1 to March 30:

Item 2: My production of Neverscrub was down because of equipment failures early in January. We had just installed a new drive on the fluffing drum which didn't work correctly. It was February before we had it repaired, but we were so far behind that we couldn't catch up. It is working fine now.

Item 5: The rejected Neverscrub came from oil leaking from the drum drive. It is no longer a problem.

Item 7: The production equipment downtime reflects the above problem. It has been corrected.

Item 8: I believe the index of productivity was a little low strictly because of the Neverscrub problem. Everything on Everbrite is going well and the index should be over 50 next time—barring unforseen casualties.

Board of Directors and President

Although it is seldom done formally, the feedback control process might also be imposed on the corporation president by the board of directors. For example, a specific goal or budget statement for the president of United Basic Chemical Corporation is illustrated in Figure 14–4.

Depending on how well the president explains the performance, the board of directors may or may not be displeased. Perhaps the whole industry was depressed, but the market share figure suggests that United Basic is falling behind, a conclusion reinforced by its apparent inability to entice investors to purchase their entire new stock issue at the intended price. It is possible of course that the sales decline reflects an event beyond management's control: a government ban on a critical product ingredient (such as phosphates), which shifted purchasers to other products. The directors could argue that the president should have anticipated such a possibility and planned for a rapid replacement. And so the discussion could go on and on.[5]

Control before Final Results

Rather than locking the barn door after the horse is stolen, a good control system will catch the thief in the act. Immediate performance should be monitored to detect departure from expected performance when it first occurs rather than waiting until undesirable results have piled up. In this way corrective action can be initiated early. For example, both Sid, the punch press operator, and his supervisor would keep tabs on what is going on several times during the day. If Sid's production were below expectations by 10:00 A.M. or 11:00 A.M., the supervisor would stop by to see if anything were wrong. Is Sid ill? Or goofing off? Is the material nonstandard?

FIGURE 14–4

Performance of <u>United Basic Chemical Corporation</u> for period *January 1 – December 30*

Item	Expected	Actual
1. Earnings per Share of Common Stock	$2.50	$1.69
2. Net Return on Investment (net profits as percentage of net capital investment)	23%	16%

3. Net Sales
    Everbrite
    Neverscrub
	$110,000,000
	$ 40,000,000
		$109,583,600
		$ 23,453,600

4. Market Share (our sales as percentage of total industry sales)	25%	19%
5. New Capital Raised (from issuing and selling new stock)	$20,000,000	$ 11,000,000

Lack of in-process control was one of the major causes of the dismal failure of W. T. Grant Company when it went bankrupt in 1975.[6] According to court testimony: Grant's buyers often had to ask their suppliers for figures on Grant's inventories, since the firm had inadequate data; some officials requested vendors to overbill Grant and pay purchasers on the side; and store managers were not granted authority to control the stock in their own stores. Perhaps worst of all, although about 20 percent of all credit purchasers never paid their bills, the delinquencies were never detected.

In the Detergent Manufacturing Department, Joe Figlia maintains his own performance records. Each day he plots the actual figures on a chart, which gives him a continuous picture of how he is doing. For each item on his budget in Figure 14–2, Joe keeps a record like that shown in Figure 14–5. With these figures available, poor results should be no surprise to Joe. He should know when performance starts to depart from expected, so he can determine the cause and take early corrective action. He fell behind on Neverscrub production early in January—he produced none on January 4, 5, 8, and 9 and produced none later in the month. His equipment had been out of commission because of the failure of a fluffing drum drive, as he was able to tell his boss in his April 5 memorandum (Figure 14–3).

As department head, Joe probably has even earlier controls than these charts. These would most likely be quality control tests on incoming materials. For example, each incoming shipment of his basic raw material, TND, would be tested according to established procedures, and the form shown in Figure 14–6 would be completed

FIGURE 14–5 ━━━━━━━━━━━━━━━━━━━━━━━

Ongoing Production Controls in Detergent Department

Item 2: Daily Production of Neverscrub

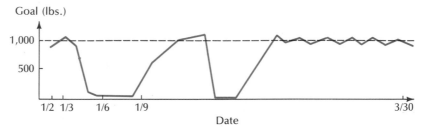

Item 2: Cumulative Production of Neverscrub

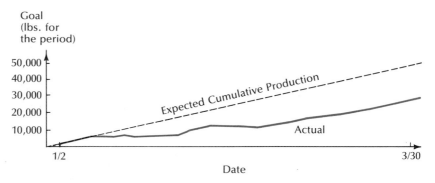

Item 3: Daily Utilization of Direct Labor

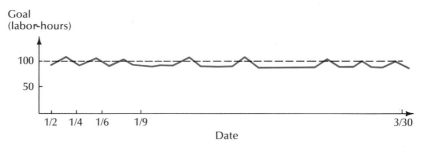

Item 3: Cumulative Utilization of Direct Labor

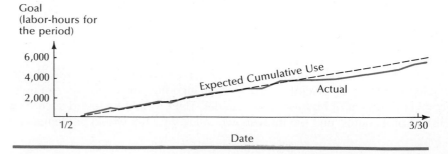

FIGURE 14–6

Detergent Manufacturing Department

Date ___2/17___   Name of Tester _Bill Simpson_

Material ___TND___

From ___Du Pont___

Test #1; Color:___✓___ Clear; _____ Clouded

Test #2; Viscosity___25.3___ (should be 23.0 to 27.0)

Test #3; Purity: ___98.5 %___ (should be above 96%)

Material Is:___✓___ Accepted;

_____ Rejected

by a technician. A somewhat similar form would be completed for each manufactured batch of Everbrite and Neverscrub, and the form and test results would be submitted to Joe before he would release the batch for packaging and distribution.

A recent review of manufacturing management practices in Japan suggests that at the heart of much of Japan's economic success has been a concern for monitoring the many little details: orderliness in the work area, proper (and usually low) inventory levels, machine loading within tolerances, acceptable levels of defective parts, and so forth. As the writer puts it, the Japanese manager constantly "pursues the last grain of rice."[7]

To follow this approach, it is necessary to break larger goals down into their smaller components, big tasks into smaller subtasks. Progress against such benchmarks can then be measured. The manager should not look to some other part of the organization to provide such control mechanism but should see that they are a normal part of making the operation contribute continually to the organization's achievement.

Control through Policies and Procedures

There are circumstances in which feedback controls are not the most appropriate. The costs of measuring progress and outcomes may be too high, or such measurement may not be feasible. As an extreme example, it is not possible at present to monitor the progress of a lunar vehicle on the far side of the moon. Activity there must be preset in the vehicle's onboard guidance computer, or it must be directed at the discretion of an astronaut on board. The latter will have been trained to make the correct decisions for accomplishing the mission. Organizations often rely on policies and procedures as management, rather than waiting for results, endeavors to control activities by limiting them in advance.[8]

From *The Wall Street Journal,* with permission of Cartoon Feature Syndicate.

Development of Policies and Procedures

Policies and Procedures
Develop to . . .
- use past experience
- avoid repeating mistakes
- use specialists
- improve coordination
- facilitate comparison and decision making

The Xerox Corporation offers an illustration of the process by which policies and procedures are developed.[9] For the past quarter century, it has been one of the most exciting businesses in America. The old, family-dominated Haloid Company, which manufactured specialized photographic products, transformed itself into the modern Xerox Corporation and jumped from $25 million from more than $1 billion per year in revenue.

In the late 1950s, the company was in a chaotic state. Offices were located all over the Rochester area, above delicatessens and in abandoned schools. Job descriptions were few, policies were broad, procedures nonexistent, and controls weak. Yet the company was successful, because of top management's ability to define direction. At that time Chairman Sol Linowitz and President Joseph Wilson saw their roles as entailing the formulation of objectives. Wilson devoted much of his time to selling the Xerox company and its objectives to his own managers, describing the revolutionary and beneficial impact of its information technology on society— and also pointing out how each manager's own interest would be served if the company advanced.

Given fantastic expansion, Wilson was aware that it would be impossible to control the entire company from the president's office. In order to take advantage of a great market opportunity and to exploit the technological breakthrough, it was essential that Xerox managers at all levels be committed to manufacturing their products and getting them out into the market as quickly as possible. Premature policies, procedures, and controls would have interfered with the spontaneous cooperation and initiative demonstrated by management. Nonetheless, policies and procedures did emerge in the Xerox Company, as they do in all organizations.

Using Past Experience.   Because Xerox was in effect a new organization designed to market a technological breakthrough, it had no policies and procedures developed from past experiences, as is the case in many companies. When an awareness develops that the company need not handle every problem as unique, policies and procedures often begin to develop. If Sam wonders how Tom has handled the problem of quality control on his gears and asks about it, Tom's answer may seem so reasonable that, rather than searching for new alternatives, Sam adopts Tom's procedures. When Sally has great success in handling rush orders, questions can uncover her methods, and an information memorandum can be drafted and distributed to let everyone know about them. The basis for policies and procedures is therefore an awareness of the stupidity of failing to use past experience. Why should management repeat the same mistakes over and over again without taking advantage of the accumulated knowledge of people in the organizations? As Justice Oliver Wendell Holmes said: "Three generations of idiots are enough!" In this way the company decides to implement a policy that trades upon experience and gives guidance to people facing similar problems for the first time.

Initially, these policies and procedures are developed from the organization's own past. After a time, however, management may believe it should take advantage of other people's experience instead of restricting itself to its own company. Experts and specialists are engaged to provide this knowledge; once they are on the payroll, it is natural for management to see that they are used. Frequently they are granted some authority to impose their experience on the rest of the organization. Such expert support can come from outside as well. At the New England Apparel Manufacturers' Association in New Bedford, Massachusetts, an industrial engineer, hired by the Association under a government grant, helped more than 20 small apparel companies to increase productivity by introducing improvements in management practices and procedures.

Improving Efficiency.   At Xerox the expansion of staff activities, job descriptions, policies, and procedures was given impetus when management became concerned about internal efficiency. When the market was free of competitors and the product was clearly superior, management's main concern was getting it made and out the door. Internal costs and efficiencies were less important, since production costs made up a small percentage of the selling or rental price. Since competition has developed for Xerox, price has become much more important, and concern about manufacturing costs has increased. Such concern inevitably brings rationalization of production operations, and rationalization means identifying the best methods, applying them throughout the organization, and seeing that people adhere to them.

Comparing Alternatives.   A Xerox research and development engineer has indicated how the elaboration of procedures has affected him. In 1959 when he had an idea that required funds, he would walk into the vice president's office with a scratch pad and pencil and sketch out the idea. A decision would be made quickly. If the idea was accepted, the researcher began working. Today, the same researcher must complete, in multiple copies, a regulation project form indicating potential equipment cost, material requirements, potential return, cash flow, and so on. This is not simply red tape; the forms are not prescribed just to complicate the lives of people in the organization. Decisions about funds allocation are now much more complex than they once were. As more and different types of projects are involved, they must be compared with one another on some consistent basis, and priority decisions must be reached with regard to organizational objectives. Standard procedures for capital fund applications facilitate comparison, prediction, and control, which are essential functions of management in any organization.

The development of policies and procedures improves efficiency by promoting coordination and predictability. When such measures are used appropriately, they can reduce costs of supervision and communication and reporting. In mature and stable markets, order, regularity, and predictability become essential in the long run—especially if the growth rate and promotional opportunities begin to decline. Nor do people necessarily dislike the development of standing plans and controls. Order will be brought out of chaos and probability out of uncertainty, and all will enjoy the relief from repeating the same mistakes over and over again. Indeed, most of us perceive the development of control instruments as progress.

Distinguishing between Policies and Procedures

The distinction between policies and procedures as aspects of control is seldom clear. Theoretically, policies are merely guidelines that higher management and staff set down to assist other managers in handling certain anticipated problems. They reflect an intention to give life to the organization's continuing objectives.

Examples of policies include such statements as:

1. *Product policy.* This company will manufacture products for the middle range of potential customers. (This policy is intended to encourage volume sales and discourage expensive, elite products).
2. *Product quality.* This company will produce appropriate quality products. (This policy is intended to discourage manufacturing products of higher quality than they need to be.)
3. *Management development policy.* This company will reward effective performance. Managers should endeavor to reward their more effective individuals with training and transfer opportunities. (Such a policy would discourage managers' efforts to hold onto good people by dumping their poorer performers on training programs and other departments).
4. *Corporate citizenship policy.* This company will obey applicable federal, state, and local statutes as well as abide by rulings of regulatory agencies. (This policy warns managers that they had better not collude with competitors in fixing prices, or at least that they shouldn't be caught.)

5. *Employee relations policy.* This company will be fair and equitable in dealing with employee absence. (About all this says is that the manager shouldn't be a villain.)

Procedures, in contrast, prescribe specific behavior for managers to follow. There is an implied threat of punishment if they fail to do so. The following are examples of procedures:

1. *Product procedure.* Widgets should be designed and manufactured to sell for between $5 and $8 in the United States; $4 and $6 in Argentina; $1 and $3 in India.
2. *Quality procedure.* Widgets shall pass the quality standards of Aero-Tech specification test number 3.
3. *Management development procedure.* Managers shall maintain a rank listing of their employees and their performance. People shall be assigned to training programs and transferred to other departments in order of their ranking, starting with the highest rated, as opportunities occur.
4. *Corporate citizenship procedure.* No manager shall formally or informally meet with any competitor's employees or agents to discuss pricing. If inadvertently in each other's company, they shall politely discuss only neutral nonbusiness topics (weather, sports, etc.) and shall endeavor to terminate the conversation as quickly as possible. Under no circumstances should they entertain competitor's employees in their own homes.
5. *Employee relations procedure.* Each manager shall notify the Personnel Department of an employee's absence by 10:00 A.M. The Personnel Department will call the employee's home to determine reason for absence. A nurse will visit the home if the absence extends to a third day. Management will pay for sick days (over two days absent) only if the nurse certifies that an actual illness exists.

The distinction between policy and procedure is often ambiguous, however. Some so-called policy manuals are actually filled with procedures, so that what higher management calls a policy is really a procedure to which lower levels had better adhere—or else. Sometimes, however, the distortion runs the opposite way. Inexperienced, insecure, and fearful junior managers may search out the "real" procedures underlying the company's general policy statements. Such managers may not believe that they have any discretion (or they may not want it), so they convert guidelines into rules.

A common situation occurs when top management declares the organization to be decentralized and publishes guideline policies for lower managers. Ambitious middle managers, however, convert the announced policies into specific procedures for which they hold junior management responsible. Because they perceive themselves as merely following narrow procedures that allow no discretion, the junior managers then complain that the top executives are either lying or ignorant in claiming that decentralization exists.

Guide and Assist Managers to Achieve Objectives

Policies

Procedures

Prescribe Specific Behavior in the Defined Situation

The Challenges of Control

We have seen that planning requires a special effort by managers to keep from slipping from a strategic into a pragmatic mode. It also suffers from several problems, to be discussed in detail in Chapter 15, including neglect, poor definition, misperception of organization and environment, the wrong people doing the planning, and inappropriate specific goals and performance indicators. Control also presents the manager with various challenges and problems. A major challenge is to allow for the coordination demanded by the complex interdependences in organizations.

Getting a particular employee or operating unit to perform its task is only part of the challenge in achieving organizational success. All organizations are faced with the problem of coordinating interdependent activities. Control systems must take such interdependence into account.[10]

Types of Interdependence
Requiring Control
- pooled
- sequential
- reciprocal

Controlling for Pooled Interdependence

Tasks in an organization may be interdependent because accomplishing them requires the use of a common resource. An example of such pooled interdependence might be seen when two salespeople must rely on a single telephone line at the local sales office. They may find it possible to handle the conflicts over using it by informal mutual adjustment, as long as the calling load remains moderate. More often procedures, rules, and schedules are needed to provide for adequate coordination under such circumstances.

Controlling for Sequential Interdependence

Tasks may also be sequentially interdependent. Task B can only be performed after Task A has been completed, as on an assembly line. Here the control of one task must be linked to progress on the other. Difficulties most often arise when there is a failure to meet expected milestones in one, thus causing unexpected disruption in the other. This requires the exchange of information. Among the coordinating devices available are schedules, routing slips, phone calls, and hand signals. Often a common supervisor is needed to assure that information flows are adequate and work flow is properly coordinated.

Controlling for Reciprocal Interdependence

Finally, tasks may be reciprocally interdependent, as in the operating room during a surgical procedure. Surgeon, anesthetist, nurse, and orderly must all interact as they carry out their tasks. Creating protocols of action for the various participants can help. This is done for launching a space craft. But most often, participants must rely on mutual adjustment, having internalized the knowledge and skills required for adequate coordinated performance.

SUMMARY

Control is achieved through two primary means: (1) policies and procedures that control behavior before it occurs and (2) feedback controls to correct behavior while it is occurring or just afterward—before too many undesired results have accumulated, it is hoped.

Policies and procedures are difficult to distinguish in practice: A policy is generally a guideline allowing discretionary application, and a procedure tells the subordinate exactly what to do in the described situation.

Actual performance is measured by performance indicators, usually by someone other than the person being controlled. The data on expected performance (unit specific goals) and actual performance are communicated to the relevant people, especially the manager and his or her superior. The superior compares expected and actual performance in order to make a decision about its status:

1. Performance is in control; no action is necessary.
2. Performance is out of control; take corrective action.
3. Performance less than expected, but effort seems satisfactory; investigate validity of the unit's specific goals and modify them as necessary.

Interdependence among tasks in organizations—whether pooled, sequential, or reciprocal—presents a special challenge to managers as they attempt to institute controls. It is important that they allow for the coordination needs that result from the interdependence.

REVIEW QUESTIONS

1. What is control through performance feedback? What are the steps?

2. What are the elements in a feedback-control system?

3. How does a manager's budget statement fit into the control process?

4. What does control before final results consist of?

5. Why should poor results be no surprise to a manager?

6. What is control through policies and procedures?

7. How are policies and procedures developed?

8. Why is it logical for an organization to utilize past experience?

9. How does complexity contribute to the development of policies and procedures?

10. What are the differences between policies and procedures?

11. How does task interdependence make control more difficult?

12. What are the three types of task interdependence?

Notes and References on Controlling Performance

1. The general study of control mechanisms is called cybernetics. For a general introduction, see W. Ross Ashby, *An Introduction to Cybernetics* (London: Methuen, 1956).

2. W. G. Ouchi and M. A. Maguire, "Organizational Control: Two Functions," *Administrative Science Quarterly,* December 1975, pp. 559–69.

In Henry Mintzberg, *The Structuring of Organizations* (Englewood Cliffs, N.J.: Prentice-Hall, 1979), it is argued that control can be achieved through behavior formalization or training and indoctrination. Behaviors are formalized through job specification and the establishment of rules and procedures. With training and indoctrination, the routines required for achieving desired outcomes are internalized by the worker to be called upon in appropriate circumstances.

3. D. M. Herold and M. A. Greller, "Feedback: The Definition of a Construct," *Academy of Management Journal,* March 1977, pp. 142–47.

The centrality of control to management is illustrated by the statement that "authority is the authorization to engage in certain attempts at control." W. R. Scott et al., "Organizational Evaluation and Authority," *Administrative Science Quarterly* 12, no. 1 (1967), pp. 93–117. The authors make an interesting distinction between four authority rights as they pertain to control:

1. Allocating right: to assign an organizational goal to a participant.
2. Criteria-setting right: to specify the performance properties to be considered, their weights and relative importance, and the standards to be used.
3. Sampling right: to select the aspects of performances or outcomes that will be observed to provide information for an evaluation.
4. Appraising right: to decide how the level of performance is to be inferred from the sample and to make an evaluation.

A complete survey of the literature and a bibliography on control is in G. B. Giglioni and A. G. Bedeian, "Conspectus of Management Control Theory: 1900–1972," *Academy of Management Journal* 17, no. 2 (1974), pp. 292–305. Some other references are R. N. Anthony, *Planning and Control Systems: A Framework for Analysis* (Boston: Harvard University Press, 1965); W. Travers Jerome III, *Executive Control: The Catalyst* (New York: John Wiley & Sons, 1961); C. P. Bonini, R. K. Jaedicke, and H. M. Wagner, eds., *Management Controls: New Directions in Basic Research* (New York: McGraw-Hill, 1964); W. H. Newman, *Constructive Control* (Englewood Cliffs, N.J.: Prentice-Hall, 1975); E. E. Lawler and J. G. Rhode, *Information and Control in Organizations* (Santa Monica, Calif.: Goodyear Publishing, 1976); and Martin R. Smith, *Manufacturing Controls* (New York: Van Nostrand Reinhold, 1981).

4. On systems, see L. Von Bertalanffy, *General Systems Theory* (New York: Braziller, 1968); J. G. Miller, "Living Systems: The Organization," *Behavioral Science* 17, no. 1 (1972), pp. 1–182; and special issue, "General System Theory," *Academy of Management Journal* 15, no. 4 (1972).

5. On the problems of evaluating corporate performance, see R. B. Buchele, "How to Evaluate a Firm," *California Management Review* 5, no. 1 (1962), pp. 5–16. See also M. L. Mace, "The President and the Board

of Directors," *Harvard Business Review,* March–April 1972, pp. 37–49.

Peter Lorange argues that one of the most important jobs of senior executives is to provide for strategic control, that is to monitor the assumption lying behind the strategic decisions of the firm. P. Lorange, "Monitoring Strategic Progress and Ad Hoc Strategic Modification," in John Grant (ed.), *Strategic Management Horizons* (Greenwich, Conn.: JAI Press, 1984).

6. S. H. Slom, "Grant Testimony Shows It Lacked Curbs on Budget, Credit and Internal Woes," *The Wall Street Journal,* February 4, 1977.

7. Robert H. Hayes, "Why Japanese Factories Work," *Harvard Business Review,* July–August 1981, pp. 57–66.

See also in the same issue, Steven Wheelwright, "Japan—Where Operations Really Are Strategic," pp. 67–74.

8. F. T. Paine and W. Naumes, *Strategy and Policy Formation: An Integrative Approach* (Philadelphia: W. B. Saunders, 1974).

9. On Xerox, see "Why Xerox's Money Machine Slows Down," *Business Week,* April 5, 1976, p. 60 ff.

10. The concept of interdependence is explored in James Thompson, *Organizations in Action* (New York: McGraw-Hill, 1967). The implications of interdependence for coordination and control are discussed in Henry Mintzberg, *The Structuring of Organizations* (Englewood Cliffs, N.J.: Prentice-Hall, 1979).

15

Problems in Planning and Controlling

With no other management function is there a greater gap between theory and practice than with planning and control. We can know what should be done, yet still experience enormous difficulty in implementing plans and controls. In this chapter we shall examine the problems encountered in formulating strategy, setting goals, and controlling results.

Pitfalls in Strategic Thinking

In the continuing definition of an organization's strategy, past success is no guarantee of future success. Changes in the names on *Fortune* magazine's annual lists of the 500 largest corporations provide dramatic evidence of this. Unless a company periodically reexamines its relationships to the environment, its strategic definitions will become obsolete and inappropriate.

In the process of examining the external world and redefining the organization, three problems arise: (1) misperception of the organization, (2) misperception of the world, and (3) conflict among executives.

Problems in Formulating Strategy
- misperceiving the organization's attributes
- misperceiving what the market wants
- conflicts among managers over different strategies

© King Features Syndicate, Inc., 1977. World rights reserved.

Misperception of the Organization

When the Columbia Broadcasting System was organized in the 1920s, it was in the radio business.[1]* Although a businessman was at the helm, most of the organization was dominated by a technical, inventive orientation which characterized the men attracted by the new technology. The essential company need was for technicians who could exploit it. As the years passed CBS added other activities, such as phonograph records, that fit with the firm's primary orientation. When television first appeared in the 1930s it seemed natural to initiate broadcasting in the new medium, because the electronics technology was similar to that used in radio broadcasting. The fact that the production of TV shows required different skills initially seemed of minor consequence. The advent of World War II, however, gave strong support to those within the CBS organization who saw it as something different— a communication company—and emphasized public service.

At the beginning of the postwar era, CBS demonstrated three orientations: It was at the same time a profit-seeking business, a technical electronics company,

---

* Notes and references will be found at the end of this chapter.

and a public service news institution. While these orientations existed together in uneasy association, a soaring economy generating substantial profits led management to look for new fields. It seemed natural to expand in areas requiring similar technical knowledge, as the larger Radio Corporation of America (RCA) had done in affiliation with the National Broadcasting Company to produce receiving equipment and electronics facilities for broadcasting. When CBS entered into the production and marketing of electronic consumer items and CBS television sets appeared on the market, however, it lost its shirt. The company had defined itself as an electronics firm and assumed that it could follow the lead of other electronics firms in vertical integration. It was mistaken. In part it had misdefined itself, and in part it did not understand what the new field required. It is relatively easy to design a television set that will be a good receiver, and the company did have the technical knowhow to do this. However, it is much more difficult to design a reliable set that is inexpensive to make and will be competitive in price. This requires a different expertise, which the company did not possess and apparently could not purchase. Consequently, although the set worked and might have been good, it was too expensive to manufacture. CBS management was even less effective in marketing and sales; they did not know how to sell a consumer item.

In this expansion and redefinition of the company's strategy, CBS management did not understand what the firm in fact was and what kinds of skills it actually possessed. Management extrapolated from a simple to a complex technology, not realizing that the knowledge and skill gap between the two was substantial. Even more costly was its failure to take stock of the kinds of manufacturing and marketing skills it possessed and what was required to break into new fields.

With individuals, such unthinking action is labeled "overconfidence," and perhaps the label also can be applied to management teams. In their eagerness to exploit a valid market opportunity, they introspectively assume the firm has the necessary skills. Because they have always succeeded, they believe they can continue to do so. Such misperception and wishful thinking mislead many expanding firms, especially those growing through acquisition of unrelated businesses—like conglomerates. Although it may yet succeed, the Boeing Vertol Company, which has been primarily a helicopter manufacturer, has experienced great difficulty in producing a "spaceage" streetcar for use in urban transit.[2] Time delays and cost overruns have been enormous because, in some critic's eyes at least, the skills of an aerospace firm are ill-suited to surface transportation with its traditionally poor maintenance and low-skilled operators.

Even a simple-appearing product, such as disposable diapers, has proved extremely difficult to produce and market in competition with Procter & Gamble. Such giants as Union Carbide, International Paper, and Scott Paper have lost millions of dollars mainly because they couldn't reliably produce a diaper that didn't leak.

To be rigorously honest in assessing one's own abilities is probably even more difficult for a management team than it is for an individual. It took several years in the 1970s of losses in excess of $100 million per year to convince Westinghouse Electric that it did not have all the required managerial skills to compete across the board with General Electric.[3] Their belated recognition, however, led to a decision to get out of appliances, television tubes, and car rentals. And these strategic eliminations increased profits from approximately $30 million to $250 million in just three years.

In the mid-1950s CBS was still generating enormous profits from radio and television broadcasting and still considering further redefinition of the company and its strategy. Gradually, management began to see the organization as "an entertainment company." It became more involved with program production, more concerned about relations with talent agencies and Hollywood producers as it belatedly realized that television broadcasting had to draw on motion-picture skills even more than on its radio experience. In addition, management invested in other entertainment media; a relatively small investment of less than $1 million in a then-new Broadway musical entitled *My Fair Lady* has since yielded many, many times its original investment. The company also brought in a new television programming vice president who examined its offerings from the entertainment point of view and quickly brought the network to a dominant rating position through such innovations as "The Beverly Hillbillies" and "Petticoat Junction." This strategy of pushing the organization into various entertainment areas was climaxed in a way by the purchase of the New York Yankees in the early 1960s. As measured by profits, the decision to move from an electronics-oriented company to an entertainment combine was spectacularly successful. The company utilized its resources more effectively; it differentiated itself from its major competitors and drew upon its strengths rather than its weaknesses.

Inadequate internal definition can be reflected in a hazy public image. And attention to clarifying the public image may help internal identification.[4] Consider United Aircraft's case of mistaken identity. While it has designed and built aircraft products for many years, the company extended its aerospace technology to a wide variety of other fields including electrical power generation, industrial processes, electronics, marine propulsion, and lasers. Yet the firm was less known than many of its subsidiaries. It continued to be identified principally with aircraft manufacture when it was not confused with United Airlines. Since the security analysts who followed the company were those who specialized in this high-risk area, the firm was unattractive to more conservative investors.

A more valid identification was developed by working from the high technology characterizing all its activities. The new name United Technologies was accompanied by a clarification and strengthening of the corporation's sense of its own future, as well as a plan for compatible acquisitions. The company has applied its high-technology capabilities to consumer products and has grown impressively in recent years.

Misperception of the Environment

Perhaps even more common, management sometimes misperceives the world to suit its own needs. That is, it correctly understands its own abilities but misperceives the environment so that the market seems to want what it has to offer.[5] Holiday Inns company lost $21 million in just three years in Europe because it built American-style, chrome-plated, interchangeable, no-surprises motels all over the place.[6] American tourists liked them well enough, but Europeans didn't. They preferred more differentiation and cultured identification.

Some years ago one of the largest worker's compensation insurance companies began to move into business liability, fire, and theft insurance.[7] This made sense. The salespeople who sold worker's compensation had access to client executives who made insurance decisions, so they could sell their expanded coverage to the same customers. The technical knowledge needed in sales and underwriting for the new coverage was quite similar to what they already had. This redefinition of organization strategy was successful. As the years passed, the company added personal insurance on homes and automobiles. The company utilized the same salespeople to sell to the same preferred-risk executives who were buying the business insurance. Again, this strategy made sense. Even though the required knowledge was somewhat different, the ease of access to these executives and their desirability as preferred risks supported the decision to expand into personal lines.

The company recently added life insurance to its line. Following its past successful strategy decisions, it is trying to sell to preferred risks, to those executives to whom it can gain access by business insurance dealings. But the skill and knowledge required for selling life insurance is different. Because of the inexperience of its sale representatives in life insurance, the company planned to sell on an order-taking basis. That is, salespeople were simply to tell the prospective purchaser of life insurance what policies and rates were available and allow the client to pick what he or she wanted. It was management's judgment that this strategy is what is desired by the managers and professional personnel to whom the company was attempting to sell. Management assumed that such purchasers desire to make their own decisions and simply want data. However, this marketing strategy is counter to the more common approach of the small life insurance companies competing with such giants as Metropolitan and Prudential. These small companies emphasize the financial consultant aspect of the insurance agent. They advertise that their agents offer advice on financial planning and family security, and their staffs will make a complete survey of the prospective purchaser's estate and give advice on personal plans.

Thus when the mutual insurance firm in our example started in life insurance sales, it chose not to emulate the other small concerns but to sell in the style of the large companies. Management argues that this is what business and professional purchasers want. This may or may not be so, but the danger is that the insurance company is defining the market's needs in terms of its own weaknesses. That is, since its agents do not have the ability or the knowledge to become financial advisers on an executive's personal estate, they simply offer a policy. The moral is that management must be very careful that it does not see market needs strictly in terms of its own abilities. It should perceive the market's needs as realistically as possible. Then it should examine its own abilities to see if ability and market correspond. This company, which was very successful with its worker's compensation, business, and personal lines, may have made a mistake in formulating its life insurance strategy because it misinterpreted the outside world to suit its own inappropriate abilities.

Sometimes environmental projections indicate that potential markets exist, but they turn out to be phantoms.[8] The needs may exist, but not the means to satisfy them. Some examples are as follows:

1. Prediction of large expansion in the production of pollution control equipment has not materialized—mainly because profit-seeking firms and debt-avoiding

governments are unwilling to purchase something that neither earns or saves money.

2. Time sharing of computers has lagged because organizations have been reluctant to change the way they process data on their own equipment, even if it costs more to do so.

3. Educational machines, such as videotape systems, are generally praised but not purchased by education-poor nations because they are also funds poor.

4. Ground fish meal has never attracted users in spite of its great nutritional advantages because of aesthetic opposition to eating the whole fish—including bones, head, and tail.

Correct perception of the external environment is becoming increasingly important and more difficult. Environmental unpredictability and turbulence are the main problems.[9] Simply put, more things are going on out there that can affect the firm: political events, technical inventions, social movements, and economic developments both at home and abroad can upset management's best laid plans. As a result of this external turbulence, management is less free and autonomous than in a simpler era. Planning must not be a one-shot affair drafted on paper, to be blindly followed without sensitivity to outside events. Rather, it must be monitored closely and the internal plans adapted as necessary.[10]

Conflict in Strategic Vision

We cannot assume that all executives in a 50-year-old corporation will agree upon strategy and mission. Even more, a young company developing new fields is certain to encounter conflict over the nature of the firm. Therefore, although examination and modification of an organization's nature and mission are necessary, they can be unpleasant. Arguments, resignations, and firings are not unlikely. At CBS the movement toward entertainment as the company's central theme led to healthy profits, but it also threatened the news department. Many respected news professionals left CBS because they disagreed with the company's direction. One news vice president resigned angrily when the president of the television network decided to show an eighth rerun of an "I Love Lucy" show rather than the first investigatory Senate hearings on the Vietnam War.

In recent years, B. F. Goodrich Company has been trying to diversify by using the profits from its number four ranking in the automobile tire business to acquire different enterprises—such as chemicals, plastics, and various industrial products.[11] A newly appointed chairperson reasoned that tire demand would grow relatively little in the 1970s as more and more cars switched to long-wearing radial tires. Yet, this perspective was not easily accepted by predominantly tire-thinking executives. With time and selling (and the replacement of the tire division president), the strategic change was effected.

The point is that strategy definition and redefinition is a political process under which one coalition of similarly minded personnel attempt to push their strategic concept while other coalitions are pushing theirs.[12] Thus conflict occurs when executives manifest strong commitments to differing concepts of the organization. They stake their careers on being able to move the company their way. And success

"I've got him softened up—now what is our
product again?"

may be only temporary. The exceptionally successful young executive who drove CBS to the top of the television ratings eventually lost his job, perhaps partially because of his very success. Higher officials were apparently upset by the declining morale in the news department, the public resignations of famous men, and critics' sarcasm about the network's "backwoodsy" programs. (Don't feel sorry for the fired vice president; he departed CBS with a million-dollar settlement on his contract, subsequently became president of MGM, and was reputed to be the model for the main character in the novel and motion picture *The Love Machine.*)

The World Changes

Time is the great enemy of all strategy and planning. The moment a plan is drafted, it starts to become outdated. A plan is always based upon an estimate of future developments drawn from past trends and present conditions.[13] Since these conditions are always changing, the plans ought to be continually modified, but this is impossible; plans can be flexible, but they cannot change continually. Research on dramatic profit declines suggests that they are caused by unfavorable changes in the environment coupled with either: *(a)* ineffective operations under existing corporate strategy or *(b)* a strategy no longer suited to its competition, markets, or economy.[14] In 1959 Apeco Corporation was one of the most successful pioneers in the photocopy industry when the corporation reportedly turned down an offer of merger with the then little-known Xerox Corporation in favor of by themselves diversifying into a miniconglomerate.[15] They invested in such noncopier fields as marinas, boat-building, and mobile homes. By 1977 they were in bankruptcy. Why? Mainly because they chose to remain with their copier technology, which required their own specially coated paper, when Xerox utilized plain paper. As the president of Apeco put it, "Our main business was supplying coated paper for our machines, but that business began eroding very rapidly and so did our financial base." Eastman Kodak's Verifax reproduction system used an even more awkward and messy wet paper process akin to conventional photography, which was even more quickly devastated by xerography. But, of course, Kodak had other products to fall back on. Only after more than 15 years did it reenter the duplicator field with its new Ektaprint technology. Clearly, size itself is no protection against obsolescence.

To reduce the possibility of obsolescence, management should identify those environmental factors relative to the firm, develop means of monitoring and forecasting change in these relevant factors, and make sure this information is assessed inside the organization. American Express Company is centered about its credit card business, which is doing well; but it must be concerned about research on electronic funds transfer (EFT), under which your bank would be connected directly to a store's cash register. When you made a purchase, no cash, checks, or credit card would be necessary; the amount would be automatically deducted from your bank balance. Perhaps AmEx should invest in the cash register business or emphasize the time-delay feature of credit cards (you don't have to pay for 30 days versus instant payment with EFT).

The ill-fated Edsel automobile provides the classic story.[16] When the idea for the Edsel originated in the early 1950s, Ford wanted to fill a gap in the middle of its product line in order to compete more favorably with General Motors in this attractive profit-margin area. When the first designs were formulated in 1954, the automobile industry was entering the era of longer, lower, heavier, fancier, and gaudier models. Extensive market surveys were conducted and the conclusion, right or wrong, was that the public would purchase a new automobile created on these lines. Consequently, the original Edsel was one of the biggest and flashiest cars in history. To go from the basic design to the first model required approximately three years, and the first cars came to the market in the fall of 1957. They apparently did fairly well initially, but then demand collapsed. The Edsel lingered near death for two more years before it expired.

There are many speculative explanations for this debacle. The simplest is that the public did not like the design, especially the radiator grille. But perhaps a more pertinent reason was the unfortunate coincidence of the model's birth with other developments. In October the Soviet Union orbited the first artifical satellite. This shocked the United States and produced a serious reexamination of American goals and strategies in the space age. For a time at least, we turned toward more austere and conservative cars, a trend strengthened by the economic recession in 1958, which was a boon to the compact automobile and American Motors. Edsel's concept and design may have been correct for its assumptions, but the world changed and the initial idea was no longer relevant. This is the danger in all planning.

Inappropriate Specific Goals

Planning should build congruity between three elements: continuing objectives, specific goals, and performance indicators. Unfortunately, this congruity is often difficult to ensure. When Joseph Figlia was a first-line supervisor in charge of a detergent mixing gang, he tried to balance long-run training, intermediate-employee morale, and short-run production. But short-run efficiency suffered so much that his superior demanded immediate results. If the specific goals are improper, immediate results could hinder long-run performance. A more extended example of the setting of inappropriate goals is given below.

An Example of Inappropriate Goals

There are cases in which goals are set and indicators are measured that do not contribute to the organization's continuing objectives. Consider the following example of a government employment office.[17] The unit's continuing objectives are to: (1) reduce unemployment, (2) reduce the welfare load for the community, (3) obtain suitable jobs for applicants (applicants may remain on welfare after turning down a job if they are overqualified for the job), and (4) serve local employers.

The office layout is as shown in Figure 15–1. Before a new supervisor joined the office staff, unemployed people would come in the entry and wait in line along the wall until they were called to the counter by the clerks. The order of attention was first come, first served. The clerk would gather enough preliminary information on the client to direct him or her to an interviewer who specialized in the jobs for which the client seemed most suited. The interviewer would learn more about the client, search the files, perhaps place some phone calls, and then refer the client to a potential employer, who might offer a job.

FIGURE 15–1

Office Layout for Government Employment Office

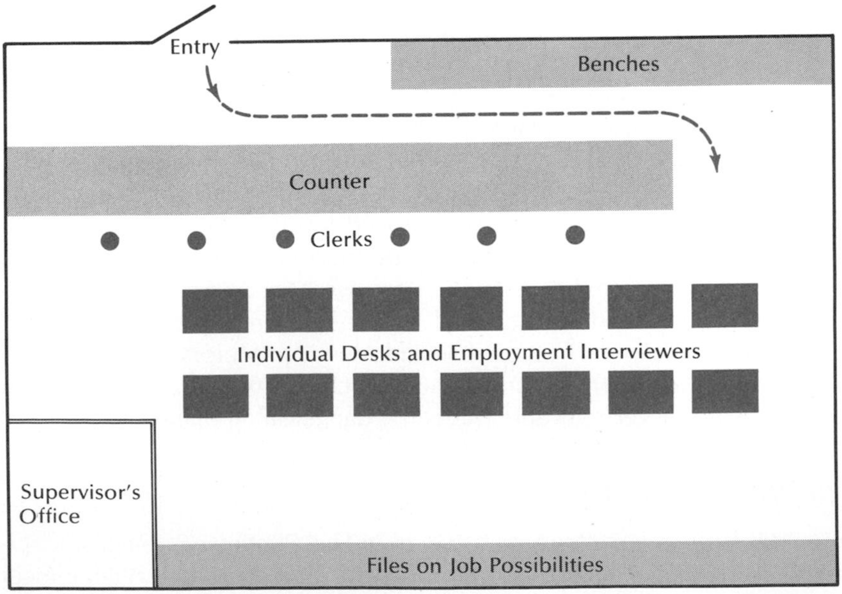

There was no control system and no performance measurement. The interviewers were all professionals, many with advanced degrees, and they worked in the manner and at a pace they deemed appropriate. They got along well with one another, and all had access to the small files of most active job possibilities they kept on their desks. If a clerk sent Bud Macmillan a client who might better be served by the jobs in Sylvia Finestein's file, Bud would just walk over to Sylvia's desk, and she would gladly allow him to look through her file.

Then a new supervisor entered the scene and introduced performance controls.

The First Performance Indicator.   Probably influenced by the slowly moving line of clients waiting to be interviewed, the supervisor decided to measure "interviews per week for each interviewer" and to post the result for each person on the office bulletin board. Also posted was an announcement that performance by this measure would be a factor in determining salary increases.

This performance indicator did work to the extent that it affected the interviewers' behavior. They conducted faster interviews, and the client line moved more quickly. But this specific goal and changed behavior did not contribute to more effective achievement of the organization's continuing objectives. Interviews were so hurried that clients were referred to inappropriate employers. Since they were not hired, they had to go through the cycle again. After a while, the line was moving faster, but it was just as long.

The supervisor clearly had set an inappropriate goal. The number of interviews was attractive as a measure because it was easy to count and reliable, but it was not valid. It distorted behavior rather than contributing to the unit's continuing objectives.

The Second Performance Indicator.   The second time the supervisor was cleaverer. Realizing that clients were not getting hired, he replaced the first measure of interviews with a ratio:

$$\text{Performance} = \frac{\substack{\text{Number of placements} \\ \text{per week per interviewer}}}{\substack{\text{Number of referrals} \\ \text{per week per interviewer}}}$$

This indicator seems more appropriate to the organization's continuing objectives of reducing unemployment and placing clients, but even this measure distorts behavior—in two ways. Some interviews became extremely long as the interviewers attempted to learn as much as they could about each client in order to refer him or her to a company that would be most likely to offer a position the client would accept. In this case, the line moved even more slowly.

Other interviewers attempted to deal with the situation in another way, by referring people to positions for which they were overqualified in hopes of increasing the probability of their being offered jobs. The interviewers soon discovered that certain visible characteristics affected how likely a client was to receive an offer; clean-shaven and fairly neat clients were desirable. Accordingly, the interviewers cultivated special relationships with clerks, plying them with gifts to influence them to send the better appearing clients to them rather than assigning clients on a random or industry basis. The interviewers also discovered that certain clients, mainly blacks, were more willing to accept jobs for which they were overqualified. So neat, conservative-looking blacks became the most desired clients, a reversal of the original condition.

Under supervisory pressure to look good in comparison with others, cooperation between interviewers was disrupted. Competition for clerks' favoritism, competition for more attractive clients, and competition for job listings became the rule. Competition may be good, but in this situation it interfered with the unit's mission. The most active files, which formerly were open to all, now became propietary information locked in a desk drawer and known only to the interviewer who had uncovered the opportunity.

Distortions of Improper Goals

The point of the foregoing story is that determining appropriate specific goals and performance indicators can be difficult. The goals and indicators may influence behavior, but not necessarily in a way that meets the organization's continuing objectives. Managers can develop elaborate devices for adapting to controls by meeting the standards on paper, but not always in ways that will promote effectiveness. Therefore, a misdirected control system is one of the gravest threats to organizational initiative. People will try to meet the numbers by which they are measured. If they cannot achieve these goals by accepted and desirable behavior, undesirable actions will result.

Studies of the impact of budgets give repeated examples of short-run compliance that adversely affects the organization in the intermediate and long run.[18] People who work under fixed output quotas tend to choose easy, rapidly completed jobs as fillers toward the end of a measurement period. For example, production supervisors sometimes ''bleed the line'' by stuffing all work in progress through the measuring point, using augmented crews, in order to meet a specific production goal. However, they lose efficiency in the succeeding period until the line is refilled with work.[19]

Deliberate evasion is also a response. ''Making out with a pencil'' is a means of giving the appearance on paper of meeting expected standards without actually doing so.[20] Some students are not unfamiliar with such techniques. In large corporations, local plant officials sometimes conspire with central office staff to evade cost control checks imposed by top executives.[21] Such managerial adaptations to controls are not culture bound. In Russia monetary rewards and prestige are granted to the Soviet plant manager who sets a new production record.[22] When pressure to achieve such records is at the expense of operating repairs and preventive maintenance, the result is lower output in the subsequent period while the delayed maintenance is performed. The manager, however, has already received a payoff for the over-quota output in the earlier period.

In many organizations there is strong pressure to meet formal performance criteria—even if in doing so, high but hidden costs are generated. It also seems that the greater the penalties incurred for failure to meet control standards, the greater the effort to demonstrate apparent success, regardless of the other costs involved.

The Dominance of Numbers

Planning may suffer from "quantiphrenia." Those objectives and goals that can be quantified tend to dominate nonquantifiable ones. For example, a few years ago a manager in charge of producing a small consumer appliance learned of a study showing that one of the component materials was toxic. Company policy called for avoiding toxic matter in consumer appliances. But replacing the stock of material in inventory would reduce his return on investment (ROI) for the quarter by increasing costs and inflating the asset base. The discarded material would not be taken off his inventory account until the next reporting period. He chose to continue producing appliances with the toxic material until the existing stock was exhausted.

Among the objectives communicated to this manager from higher executives were (1) to achieve a specified ROI (for which he earned a bonus) and (2) to avoid creating a potential product liability situation (for which he could be dismissed). The ROI objective was reinforced by a decentralized structure and profit center budgeting, which clearly indicated the manager's goals and actual performance. The product safety objective was supported by written corporate policy, but no monitoring or measurement of actual behavior. The ROI objective exerted a stronger force on managerial behavior than did the second objective. Rightly or wrongly, the manager concluded that he could reach his ROI objective only by taking a risk with the product. Rewards and punishment were more certain in the profit area than in following the policy.

If all continuing objectives could be converted into specific numerical goals, the problem would not exist; but many objectives and goals cannot be expressed numerically. In competition for a manager's time, numbers dominate. Thus for some university football teams, such measurable objectives as games won and tickets sold carry more weight than nonquantitative objectives—developing player's character or providing healthy recreation. Coaches are seldom fired for how the team played the game, but because it lost. It is the same in business. Such objectives as profits, productivity, and growth receive more attention than less quantifiable objectives, such as public responsibility, labor force development, or revitalization. Since these latter objectives are less easy to measure, evaluation is more subjective and more difficult to justify, and these objectives tend to be ignored.[23]

Quantification leads to the inflated importance of some goals. The quantifiable objectives are not necessarily more important; their importance may be artificially exaggerated just because they are measurable. Because poor results are easily detectable for these objectives, a manager attempts to avoid showing poor performance in these areas. Unfortunately, such action may harm the organization in the long run because it means the deferment of important but more subjective objectives, public responsibility for example. Unfortunately, management has not been very clever in formulating performance indicators for such objectives.[24] We can hope that as management becomes convinced of the importance of these objectives, it will become more sensitive and more effective in developing quantitative measures for them.

Common Control Problems

Among the common problems with controls are (1) resentment and rejection of controls, (2) obsolescence of policies and procedures, (3) premature rapid response, and (4) excessive cost.

Resentment and Rejection

People Sometimes Reject Control Systems because

- goals are contradictory
- results depend on factors not under their control
- results and evaluations are unpredictable
- goals are unrealistic and unattainable
- control system is incompatible with leadership climate

It is not surprising that people do not like to be controlled.[25] Even the word *control* has a negative connotation, and everyone is reluctant to face unpleasant facts. It is natural for people to resent criticism; however, this does not mean control can be eliminated. The all-too-common stressful conditions that lead to anger about controls involve evaluations that are contradictory, uncontrolled, unpredictable, or unattainable.

One of the most difficult positions in life is only being able to look good on one performance criterion by sacrificing your evaluation on another criterion. It is unsettling to be told that you must do well simultaneously on contradictory or competing criteria, as when you must take a quick bath and emerge perfectly clean.

As a manager you may be expected to demonstrate faster production and fewer rejects, stable prices and greater market share, or higher quality and less cost. Although these objectives are not always mutually exclusive, you may think that their simultaneous accomplishment is unrealistic. If you believe this strongly enough, you may reject the whole planning and control system. Ideally, management should prescribe unambiguous and mutually compatible performance goals that can be achieved simultaneously.

It is natural to be angry when you are punished for something you did not do—perhaps for leaving a confidential file unlocked overnight. You would certainly be upset if you were reprimanded for not increasing profits when the design of the product given you by the research department was totally inadequate. We all resent a control system that evaluates us for performance over which we have insufficient control because our performance depends upon others or events in the outside world. Ideally, management should hold subordinates responsible only for performance that results entirely from their behavior; they must have all the necessary authority over resources to achieve the desired goals if they manage them correctly. Task interdependence, however, often makes this impossible.[26]

A younger manager may feel extremely anxious because her inexperience makes it difficult to predict what will happen if she makes a certain decision. Desirable or undesirable results seem random and unrelated to what she does. Anxiety may turn to resentment if the criteria by which the manager thought she was being evaluated are changed in midstream, while she is acting to meet the old expectations. The young professor who is told that classroom teaching and personal counseling of students is most important for his career will become quite upset if he finds at promotion time that a status-seeking college administration has changed the criterion to articles and books published.

Subordinates should be sufficiently experienced or adequately trained to predict the relationship between their behavior and their performance. In addition, they should have sufficient in-process feedback on preliminary results so that they can judge how well they are moving toward the accomplishment of the assigned goals.

Mixed feelings, leaning toward resentment and disillusionment, characterize response to superiors whose performance goals are thought to be impossible. Objectives that are too easy are also harmful; they may prove to be self-fulfilling prophecies when performance deteriorates to the lower levels. Higher objectives motivate subordinates to better performance—but only up to the point at which the objectives are perceived as realistic.[27] It is clear that objectives should be neither too easy nor too difficult to attain, but finding the proper level can be a real challenge for management.

"You'd damn well better come up with an antidote before five o'clock, Stimson. This project has cost enough without having to pay you overtime."

Planning and controlling are ways of implementing leadership styles.[28] Subordinates will resent the superior who preaches friendship, supportiveness, and participation but does not include them in his or her formulation of plans. If the policies, procedures, and controls are so narrow and confining that no opportunity exists to vary behavior in pursuit of organizational objectives, then management's talk of democracy is a sham. If participation is desirable (and we have seen that sometimes it is and sometimes it is not), it must have been meaningfully expressed in management's planning of objectives, policies, and procedures. An executive's promise of participation will be meaningless if, for example, the procedures limit a department manager's expenditures on his or her own discretion to $25. Consistency between the superior's interpersonal behavior and the leadership style implied by the structure of plans and controls is necessary to ensure acceptance of the control systems.

Obsolescence of Policies and Procedures

If policies and procedures are followed blindly, the organization loses direction. There is an inversion of means and ends when plans and controls become ends to be followed without thought as to whether or not they contribute to the organization's objectives. Indeed, such an inversion can be seen frequently in highly formalized or bureaucratized organizations.[29]

An advertisement in a management journal showed a notebook titled "Policy Manual" suspended over an incinerator in which several similar notebooks were burning. The advertiser was a management consulting firm whose message was that management should not allow plans, policies, and procedures to exist unchanged for too long because they get out of date and hinder the organization instead of helping it. One long-time chief executive suggested that his people should periodically change their orientation to their jobs in order to forestall loss of direction and overreliance on the past.

> I would tell them that they should, a couple of times a year, pretend that they are a new man on the job. All right, one of the first things you do is just go through your desk and look at the files and clean them out; and everything that crosses your desk, you question: Why? Never take things for granted. I don't believe in tradition unless tradition is sound.[30]

The organization is in danger when spontaneity disappears. Once established and accepted, policies and procedures tend to limit flexibility and initiative. When controls are first established, management may gain in coordination and predictability what it loses in initiative. Since policies, procedures, and controls are based on the past, however, it is difficult to keep them up to date. As time passes, policies may no longer apply to new conditions; controls may come to measure irrelevant factors; and the rational plans that were developed to promote organizational effectiveness can eventually interfere with the accomplishment of objectives. If managers blindly follow established rules, spontaneity is lost.

Under long-standing restrictive control systems, some managers ignore their obligation to avoid mistakes. If they believe that punishment awaits an unsuccessful departure from procedures, they may do what only "the book" requires. When no spontaneity is demonstrated, apathy will prevail.[31]

Managers must structure organizations, allocate people to jobs, maintain communication links, and determine operational objectives. Policies and procedures based on past experience are means of attaining these goals. Such modification of the past is necessary to maintain organizational direction and momentum, but it can get out of touch with the real needs of the business. People may conform to rules without considering their contribution to goals so that the firm loses direction.

Premature Response

Upon receiving information that actual results are not meeting expected goals, a manager must take timely corrective action, but acting prematurely might make matters worse. If as a manager you observed two employees getting off the elevator 10 minutes late, you might be tempted to reproach them on the spot for being tardy. You might also distribute a memo to all employees reminding them of the rules about promptness and warning them to correct their unacceptable behavior. But do you really have a problem? If the tardiness is only a rare occurrence (the employees may have been stuck in the subway when the doors failed, for example), you would be overreacting. By criticizing them and circulating the memo, you would be acting quickly, but you would be responding to inaccurate data. You would be correcting a problem that did not exist, and your premature reaction could actually create a problem where none existed.

All managers confront this tension between responding quickly—perhaps to inaccurate information or to a random variation from desired behavior—and responding accurately. They must balance a desire for timely response with the need to wait until they are certain their information is accurate. Otherwise they may create problems where none exist.

Excessive Cost

Controlling can be so expensive that there may be times it does not pay. The federal government might be criticized for selling surplus typewriters in Boston at the same time it is purchasing the equipment in San Francisco. This appears to be a waste of taxpayers' money. However, the government cannot simply send the machines from one location to the other. Not only would the freight be expensive, but more fundamentally, it is expensive to implement a control system that would keep everyone informed about surpluses and purchases. In the long run it could cost the government less to sell the surplus typewriters in Boston and buy others in San Francisco.

It also costs money to control in business. At times management must consider whether doing away with control might be less troublesome than maintaining it. One corporation used to weigh every carton of materials purchased from suppliers, even though the contents of each box was clearly marked on the outside. Perhaps management did not trust the vendors, or maybe it was just habit. The firm saved substantial expense when it began to sample cartons randomly rather than weigh every one. This was sufficient to detect suppliers who might be cheating systematically. Although individual underweight boxes could slip through, the cost was less than the cost of the former control system.

Reasons for Neglecting Planning

Management must plan; it must separate itself from the burdens of the past and the exigencies of the present in order to be able to define conditions desired for the future. Nonetheless, many managers apparently do not plan, although most agree that planning is their most neglected duty. This is mainly because the present uses up their allocation of time. They may allow the present to dominate the future and curtail planning for several reasons: (1) Planning is unnecessary; (2) the future is just not real to them; (3) they think about the future but consider doing anything about it less than worthwhile; or (4) punishment for immediate mistakes is too close to worry about long-run failure.

It Is Unnecessary

One survey of five major U.S. corporations concluded that not one of them engaged in high-level strategic planning.[32] Of course, they planned departmental budgets and financial projections, but not integrating, future-looking strategy. Three conditions seemed to obviate the need for such planning—at least in the views of the top executives involved.

Lack of Competition.   The five organizations were not under market stress, so management "satisfied" rather than attempting to optimize performance. Either they enjoyed a near-monopoly or were in regulated industries in which rate of return was limited.

Environmental Certainty.   The firms were in fields in which uncertainty was minimal. All five companies were characterized by stable technologies in raw materials, processes, and products as well as unchanging distribution channels and markets.

Internal Simplicity.   Although large, the organizations were structured simply; authority was separated in divisions or functions that operated quite independently. Close coordination was not considered essential.

Not Thinking about the Future

The virtues of an achievement orientation can also be vices. Managers with high achievement needs desire feedback indicating they have performed effectively, but they tend to be impatient. They want results quickly, for that is the purpose of their effort and discipline. Unfortunately, overconcern with rapid progress and feedback hinders progress. Too much attention is directed to the present, to the short-run payoff, without adequate concern for the future. In the effort to act quickly, some managers fail to collect necessary information, to plan, or to think.

This predilection for action rather than thought is characteristic of American culture. Patience is an easy virtue where the prevailing cultural view of time is circular, characterized by infinite length and repetition. It is difficult, however, where time is seen as an arrow, a line going one way, as in this country. We are concerned about the future, but our future must be relatively close. Ours is not the distant future of the East, which is far beyond present influence; it is just up the road a piece.[33]

Not thinking about the future may even stem from being successful in the present and confident about the future. Franklin Roosevelt ran the presidency from his hip pocket with short-run ingenuity and tactical brilliance.[34] Apparently, the very competence of the president to manage the turbulence about him led to enormous confi-

Planning Is Sometimes Neglected because

- some managers don't think about the future
- they are impatient
- overly confident or overly pessimistic
- unable to delay gratification
- rewards and punishments based on short-run performance
- managers transfer too frequently
- planning sometimes performed by staff instead of line managers

dence that he could similarly manage the Soviet Union and post-World War II conditions. No real plan or even future philosophy was formulated to implement this confidence—and, unfortunately, F. D. R. died before he could fulfill these expectations.

Such conditions of competence in the present and perhaps overconfidence about being able to handle the future characterizes many managers, so that they never find the time to consider the future. A former chairman of RCA suggested: "You know our brain needs exercise as well as our muscle. A great many people don't go beyond today. If things are going along all right today, they are not thinking about 5, or 10, or 20 years from now."

This heedlessness for the future is characteristic of most adults in some cultures, and perhaps of everyone under certain conditions. Anthropologists have observed that for some Indian tribes, only the present has reality.[35] Similarly, in countries whose ancient glories are celebrated as if they happened yesterday, business executives have been known to invest large amounts in factories without making the slightest plan for how to use them. In this case, the future seems unreal.

Lack of Faith in the Future

A bird in the hand, cross that bridge later, and Omar Khayyam's "take the Cash and let the Credit go, nor heed the rumble of a distant Drum" appeal to all people sometimes—but especially to those who doubt what is in the bush, do not ever expect to reach the bridge, or know from experience that promises tend to be broken. Some persons have no model of parents, relatives, or friends for whom any planning has paid off.[36]

There is a story about an American agricultural expert visiting in the United Arab Republic. When the American asked the local farmer about his expected yield the Arab was insulted; he thought the American considered him crazy. To the traditional Egyptian, only Allah knows the future, and it is presumptuous even to talk about it.[37] Perhaps the Arab farmer had a certain faith, but planning requires greater faith because the expenditure of time now is an investment in the future, and sometimes it is a risky investment. It assumes that tomorrow will come and that action today will make a difference.

Thus people may not plan because they fail to think about the future or because they can conceive of nothing good there. Individually, most managers are achievement oriented, time conscious, and optimistic—at least to the extent of believing that action helps. Within organizations, however, ignoring the future is not rare. Much talk is heard about the future in business and politics, but until recently the talk was preceded by little real thought—witness the reluctance of management to think about the implications of industrial despoilment of our atmosphere, rivers, lakes, and oceans.[38]

Proximity of Reward or Punishment

The economist John Maynard Keynes once responded to the conservatives' insistence that in the long run depression would cure itself through the free market with the acid comment: "In the long run, we're all dead." For Keynes, (and for President Roosevelt) eventually, saving private enterprise and democratic society was more important than preserving a certain model of capitalism. Perhaps they were right, perhaps not; the problem is that the manager cannot wait. Without action of some sort, failure looms.

Politicians and government officials tend to concentrate on the short run because of threats in the near future: defeat of a bill, reduction of the yearly appropriation, rejection by the voters. Long-range demographic, agricultural, and environmental problems will not hurt them now (although they may not be able to say this much longer). In this short-range view, small matters loom large.

Life and death are not so close to the business manager, of course, but dominance of present over future can be as great. Short-term performance standards encourage many managers to concentrate on immediate matters. Frequently they believe that they are rewarded or punished for this year based upon short-run, objective measures of profits, costs, and growth. In the long run they will be dead—or maybe transferred.[39] A competitive business system encourages a short-time perspective, of course; only a monopoly can ignore the present. Yet, even given competition, management tends to measure performance over too limited a time span. Concentration on the present is sometimes rewarded while concern for the future is punished.

Corporate rotation and transfer policies also contribute to the dominance of short-range time orientations. Supermobile managers average a position change every 18 months; even average managers move every two or three years.[40] Transfers and shorter tenures do not reflect job mastery and threat of stagnation so much as they express impatience for signs that one is progressing up the hierarchy. Mobile managers tend to measure their success by how frequently they are promoted or transferred, not by how well they perform. They never are afforded the luxury of failure or time to learn, so their first setback is catastrophic. This lends credence to the so-called Peter Principle that every managerial slot in hierarchical organizations is filled with an incompetent because managers are promoted to the level of their incompetence, where they remain.[41] This is an exaggeration, of course, because individuals can and do grow as they move upward; but the point is clear: our national culture, organizational climate, and personal attitudes emphasize the present.

The Wrong People Do the Planning

When general managers are pressed for time, but additional activities should be performed, a common response is to create a staff group. The staff presumably should be able to concentrate on a single function, such as planning, because they have no other operational duties. This was the solution for planning as it became increasingly sophisticated with the introduction of various mathematical and statistical techniques for forecasting and decision making. Since general executives could not be experts in these techniques, planning directors and staffs began to be used with increasing frequency.[42] Their influence in corporations increased along with their prestige. Unfortunately, the planner has been less effective than hoped, for several reasons.[43]

First, staff planners are frequently frustrated. In spite of access to the company president, fancy office, and good income, staff planners possesses little real power. They can recommend but cannot execute. They want things to change, but many of the line managers they work with do not. Planners have a vision of the ideal, but the line is rooted in the practical. Thus planners are often offended by rejection or, worse, discouraged by being ignored.[44]

Second, the staff's plans are sometimes poor. Because of their isolation from the ongoing business, their proposals may ignore current realities and hence be impractical. Their forms, charts, and tables can become part of a useless ritual in which everyone engages; but this paperwork may gather dust in forgotten files and eventually be deposited in the incinerator.[45]

Increasingly, management has come to realize that planning is too important to be left only to staff planners. Line management must be involved. The planning specialist's role is to provide technical education, assistance, and encouragement to managers, not to perform their work for them. Successful staff planners are informal and unconcerned about having their name on the final documents. They act as coordinators and catalysts of the planning process, a bridge between the generalist managers and specialized computer personnel, systems engineers, and operations researchers.[46]

SUMMARY

Defining an organization's nature and essential strategy is not an easy process. Sometimes management misperceives its own abilities so that it will seem to possess what the market needs. At other times it correctly understands its own attributes but misperceives the environment, again so the market will seem to desire what it has. These examinations tend to generate substantial conflict among executives and managers.

Resistance and resentment toward control is a widespread human response, especially when goals seem unattainable or performance evaluation is unpredictable. This can also be the reaction when the control system contradicts management's professed leadership style. Time undermines all policies and procedures, and they can become inappropriate in a changed world. If management follows them blindly, they can cease to contribute to goals and become ends in themselves. Too rapid response to apparent out-of-control behavior can lead to adverse

results. By not waiting to see if the data are valid, management can create a problem where none actually existed. Finally, control can cost more than it is worth. Management should not attempt to control everything, even if this were possible. The cost might be more than might be lost if there were no control.

The purpose of controlling is to enable management to accomplish plans. Controls are subordinate to objectives. Management should not make them ends in themselves or consider them more important than what they are intended to accomplish. To do so will lead to the inversion of means and ends and result in the kind of organizational sleepwalking that seems all too common in large organizations today. Control is a means, not an end in itself. The purpose of the control system is to help the organization meet its objectives, not to find wrongdoers. In handling negative response to control, the positive approach of emphasizing the goals and objectives to be met should be taken, rather than catching and punishing the culprit. What seems to be the problem? is the question—not "Who did something wrong? or Whom can be blamed?

Several methods have been suggested to counter unrealistic plans and resented controls. One of the most promising is management by objectives (MBO), which we will examine in the next chapter.

Managers tend to neglect planning because they do not think about the future, are overconfident or too pessimistic. Most of all, they slight planning be-

cause they are too busy in the present striving for immediate rewards or avoiding punishment. Nonetheless, time and effort devoted to planning has increased, much of it performed by newly created staff planning departments. Unfortunately, staff planning is not always helpful. Such plans are sometimes unrealistic and subsequently ignored. Line managers should plan with staff assistance if plans are to have a real impact on organizational behavior.

REVIEW QUESTIONS

1. What problems arise in the continuing redefinition of an organization's strategy?
2. What is misperception of the environment, and how does it affect strategy?
3. What is misperception of the organization, and how does it affect strategy?
4. Why is strategy modification often accompanied by conflict?
5. How does the passage of time affect plans?
6. How do budget controls sometimes hinder the accomplishment of an organization's objectives?
7. Why do numbers sometimes dominate the control process?
8. Why is the control system sometimes resented and even rejected?
9. What are contradictory evaluations?
10. What is uncontrolled evaluation?
11. What is unpredictable evaluation? What causes it?
12. What is unattainable evaluation?
13. What is incompatibility between leadership style and control?
14. What is inversion of means and ends in control?
15. What is the danger in all written policies and procedures?
16. What effect stems from an overly rapid response in controlling?
17. When is it better not to control at all?
18. Why is it dangerous to see control as policing the organization?
19. Why is planning sometimes neglected?
20. Why do achievement-oriented people not think about the distant future?
21. What does it mean to lack faith in the future?
22. How do organizational rewards contribute to overemphasis on the short run?
23. Why is delegating long-range planning to staff planners not desirable?
24. What should be the relation between staff planners and line managers?

Notes and References on Problems in Planning and Controlling

1. On CBS, see D. Halberstam, "CBS: The Power and the Profits," *Atlantic Monthly,* January 1976.

2. "When Boeing Gets into the Streetcar Business," *Business Week,* September 12, 1977, p. 127.

3. On Westinghouse, see "Comeback?" *Fortune,* May 1977, p. 22.

4. W. P. Margulies, "Make the Most of Your Corporate Identity," *Harvard Business Review,* July–August 1977, pp. 66–72.

5. D. W. Ewing, "Corporate Planning at a Crossroads," *Harvard Business Review,* July–August 1967, pp. 77–86. E. Rhenman maintains that most organizational problems and failures occur when the organization's own value system is at variance with the values and demands of the environment (e.g., General Motors commitment to large automobiles when the energy crisis began in 1973–74). *Organization Theory for Long-Range Planning* (Chichester, U.K.: John Wiley & Sons, 1973). See also K. J. Hatten and D. E. Schendel, "Strategy's Role in Policy Research," *Journal of Economics and Business,* Summer 1976, pp. 195–202.

6. On Holiday Inns, see "An Idea That Didn't Travel Well," *Forbes,* February 15, 1976, p. 26 ff.

7. "Life and Casualty Insurers Meet Head on," *Business Week,* August 29, 1977, p. 86.

8. A. Wilson and B. Atkins, "Exorcising the Ghosts in Marketing," *Harvard Business Review,* September–October 1976, pp. 117–27.

9. For three articles that survey the relationship between organizations and their environments, see J. D. Thompson and W. J. McEwen, "Organizational Goals and Environment," *American Sociological Review* 23 (1958), pp. 23–31; F. E. Emery and E. L. Trist, "The Causal Texture of Organizational Environments," *Human Relations* 18 (1965), pp. 21–31; and S. Terreberry, "The Evolution of Organizational Environments," *Administrative Science Quarterly,* March 1968, pp. 590–613.

10. P. T. Terry, "Mechanisms for Environmental Scanning," *Long-Range Planning,* June 1977, pp. 2–9.

11. "Goodrich's Cash Cow Starts to Deliver," *Business Week,* November 14, 1977, p. 78 ff.

12. A. M. Pettigrew, "Strategy Formulation as a Political Process," *International Studies of Management and Organization,* Summer 1977, pp. 78–87.

13. J. O. Vance, "The Anatomy of a Corporate Strategy," *California Management Review* 13, no. 1 (1970), pp. 5–12, and B. Hedberg and S. Jonsson, "Strategy Formulation as a Discontinuous Process," *International Studies of Management and Organization,* Summer 1977, pp. 88–109.

14. D. Schendel, G. R. Patton, and J. Riggs, "Corporate Turnaround Strategies: A Study of Profit Decline and Recovery," *Journal of General Management,* Spring 1976, p. 3 ff.

15. "Why Apeco Preferred Filing for Bankruptcy," *Business Week,* November 7, 1977, p. 25.

16. John Brooks, *The Fate of the Edsel and Other Business Adventures* (New York: Harper & Row, 1963).

17. Adapted from Peter Blau, *The Dynamics of Bureaucracy* (Chicago: University of Chicago, 1955).

18. Chris Argyris, *The Impact of Budgets on People* (New York: Controllership Institute, 1952).

19. V. F. Ridgway, "Dysfunctional Consequences of Performance Measurements," *Administrative Science Quarterly* 1, no. 2 (1956), pp. 240–47; N. C. Churchill and W. W. Cooper, "Effects of Auditing Records: Individual Task Accomplishment and Organizational Effectiveness," in W. W. Cooper et al., eds., *New Perspectives in Organizational Research* (New York: John Wiley & Sons, 1964).

20. F. J. Jasinski, "Use and Misuse of Efficiency Controls," *Harvard Business Review,* July–August 1956, pp. 105–12; E. H. Caplan, *Management Accounting and Behavioral Science* (Reading, Mass.: Addison-Wesley Publishing, 1971).

21. Melville Dalton, *Men Who Manage* (New York: 1956); G. H. Hofstede, *The Game of Budget Control* (London: Tavistock, 1968); and M. E. Barrett and L. B. Fraser, "Conflicting Roles in Budgeting Operations," *Harvard Business Review,* July–August 1977, pp. 137–46.

22. On Soviet management problems, see D. Granick, *The Red Executive* (Garden City: Doubleday, Inc., 1960); J. S. Berliner, "A Problem in Soviet Business Management," *Administrative Science Quarterly* 1, no. 1 (1956), pp. 87–101; and B. Richman, *Soviet Management* (Englewood Cliffs, N.J.: Prentice-Hall, 1965).

23. W. K. Warner and A. E. Havens, "Goal Displacement and the Intangibility of Organizational Goals," *Administrative Science Quarterly* 12, no. 4 (1968), pp. 539–55.

24. One reason that numbers dominate might be that managers have allowed accountants to specify the criteria. L. N. Redman, "Planning and Control and Accounting: Divide and Conquer," *Managerial Planning,* July–August 1976, pp. 15–17.

25. An excellent survey of resistance to control is reported in W. R. Scott et al., "Organizational Evaluation and Authority," *Administrative Science Quarterly,* 12, no. 1 (1967), pp. 93–117. For a survey of the impact of accounting control on behavior, see T. R. Hofstedt, "Behavioral Accounting Research," *Accounting, Organizations and Society* 1, no. 1 (1976), pp. 43–58 and K. E. Said, "The Human Side of the Budgetary Process," *Managerial Planning,* January–February 1978, pp. 1–8.

26. R. F. Vancil, *Decentralization: Managerial Ambiguity by Design* (Homewood, Ill.: Dow Jones-Irwin, 1979).

27. For a report on the impact of superiors' expectations on subsequent performance, see S. Livingston, "Pygmalion in Management," *Harvard Business Review,* July–August 1969, pp. 81–89. In general:

Poorer subordinate performance is associated with a superior having lower personal standards for himself/herself and lower expectations of subordinates.

Better subordinate performance is associated with a superior having high personal standards and high expectations of subordinates.

The superior's personal standards seem to exert a greater influence on subordinates' performance than expectations of them. For a survey of this, see J. P. Campbell, et al., *Managerial Behavior, Performance and Effectiveness* (New York: McGraw-Hill, 1970), pp. 447–51.

28. A. S. Tannenbaum, "Control in Organizations: Individual Adjustment and Organizational Performance," *Administrative Science Quarterly* 7, no. 2 (1962), pp. 236–57. This article makes the point that influence and control run both ways. Where subordinates perceive themselves as having some control over their superior, the superior will have more control over them.

29. On the inversion of means and ends, the comments of John Knowles, former director of the Massachusetts General Hospital, are illustrative: "In the teaching hospital, it has become set that the patient exists for the teaching programs and not that the hospital exists for the patient." Quoted in J. De Hartog, "What Money Cannot Buy," *Atlantic Monthly,* July 1966, p. 113. In his Pulitzer Prize-winning study of the Kennedy presidency, Arthur Schlesinger provides several examples (almost caricatures) of the loss of direction in governmental units. A particularly disturbing chapter describes the organizational paralysis stemming from tradition and conservatism in the Department of State. *A Thousand Days* (Boston: Houghton Mifflin, 1965).

30. J. Hall quoted in *Lessons of Leadership,* by the editors of *Nation's Business* (Garden City, N.Y.: Doubleday Publishing, 1966).

31. V. Thompson describes "bureautic" and "bureaupathological" behavior in *Modern Organization* (New York: Alfred A. Knopf, 1961).

32. C. B. Saunders and F. D. Tuggle, "Why Planners Don't," *Long-Range Planning,* June 1977, pp. 19–24. Actually, the title is misleading. The article is about managers, not staff planners. Another survey indicates that most firms experience problems in implementing long-range planning, but efforts are repeated. H. W. Henry, "Formal Planning in Major U.S. Corporations," *Long-Range Planning,* Octo-

ber 1977, pp. 40–45. See also, P. Kumar, "Long-Range Planning Practices by U.S. Companies," *Managerial Planning,* January–February 1978, pp. 31–33.

33.   For an example of American views of the future, consider our history in Vietnam: For years we deluded ourselves that victory was around the bend or it was the beginning of the end. Yet the enemy's time scale for accepting warfare and delaying victory was beyond ours. Years before our military involvement in Vietnam, the anthropologist Edward Hall wrote: "While we look to the future, our view of it is limited. The future to us is the foreseeable future, not the future of the South Asian that may involve centuries." *The Silent Language* (Garden City, N.Y.: Doubleday Publishing, 1959), p. 20. Also consider the U.S. government's apparent repetition of so many of France's mistakes and even our own earlier errors in Southeast Asia. The sense of *déjà vu* is overwhelming in articles written 10, and even 20 years ago. A former Rand Corporation researcher who lived in Saigon for 15 years commented:

> Through the years, the same strategies have been used with different names, but the same old mistakes have been made. Why have these mistakes been repeated? For one thing, there is a lack of institutional memory in the American organization in Vietnam. Any lessons learned here have not been transmitted to people who followed the people who learned the lessons. This is due primarily to the short tours of duty, the rapid turnover of people. The one-year tour, especially for people in command jobs or running programs, has been disastrous. A person comes in, works hard for a year and then leaves, giving the job to someone else with no experience.

Gerald Hickey, quoted in *Newsweek,* May 3, 1971.

34.   On Franklin D. Roosevelt's presidency, see James MacG. Burns, *Roosevelt: The Soldier of Freedom* (New York: Harcourt Brace Jovanovich, 1970).

35.   For an interesting book on Indians and their time perspectives, among other things, see Peter Farb, *Man's Rise to Civilization as Shown by the Indians of North America* (New York: E. P. Dutton, 1968).

36.   For perspectives on time among some black Americans, see E. Liebow, *Talley's Corner* (Boston: Little, Brown, 1967).

37.   Hall, *The Silent Language.*

38.   That management's downgrading of social responsibility and concern for the environment also occurs out-
side of capitalism, see a description of similar practices in the Soviet Union in M. I. Goldman, *The Spoils of Progress* (Cambridge, Mass.: MIT Press, 1972).

39.   On how rewards emphasize the short run, see J. Naor, "How to Motivate Corporate Executives to Implement Long-Range Plans," *MSU Business Topics,* Summer 1977, pp. 41–49.

40.   On trends in mobility patterns, see E. E. Jennings, *The Mobile Manager* (Ann Arbor: University of Michigan Press, 1967).

41.   Laurence J. Peter and Raymond Hull, *The Peter Principle* (New York: Morrow, 1969).

42.   On the increase in staff corporate planning, see G. A. Steiner, "Rise of the Corporate Planner," *Harvard Business Review,* September–October 1970, pp. 133–39. See also C. E. Summer, "The Future Role of the Coporate Planner," *California Management Review* 3, no. 2 (1961), pp. 17–31; R. J. Litschert, "The Structure of Long-Range Planning Groups," *Academy of Management Journal,* March 1971, pp. 33–43; R. H. Mason, "Developing a Planning Organization," *Business Horizons* 12, no. 4 (1969), pp. 61–69.

43.   K. A. Ringbakk, "Why Planning Fails," *European Management,* Spring 1971, pp. 15–24. Ringbakk lists the causes of planning failure as follows: (1) corporation planning not integrated into total management system, (2) different dimensions of planning not understood, (3) management at all levels not engaged, (4) responsibility vested in planning department, (5) management expects plans to come true, (6) too much attempted at once, (7) management fails to operate by plan, (8) extrapolations and financial projections confused with planning, (9) inadequate information inputs used, and (10) too much emphasis on only one aspect.

44.   R. W. Knoepfel, "The Politics of Planning: Man in the Decision Process," *Long-Range Planning* 6, no. 1 (1973), pp. 17–21. Knoepfel noted:

> Power and politics play a very crucial role in planning. Whoever the top planning executives are, they are the target of political intrigue and "power plays" engineered by other leaders and would-be leaders. Indeed, such goings-on may affect planning even more than other leadership functions, because so many managers and employees tend to regard planning as a personal threat. Also, they may think that planning is expendable, even if it is not in fact. Unlike executives in, say, marketing and finance, the planning leader cannot count on tradition and long acceptance to establish

the need for his presence. Therefore, whether he is spending part or nearly all of his time on planning activities, he must tend his political fences assiduously or risk losing influence over others (p. 17).

See also G. G. Garbacz, "Planner-Line Conflict: Asset or Liability," *Managerial Planning* 21, no. 6 (1973), pp. 1–6, and J. Pfeffer and G. R. Salancik, "Organizational Decision Making as a Political Process: The Case of a University Budget," *Administrative Science Quarterly* 19, no. 2 (1974), pp. 135–51.

45. W. K. Hall, "Strategic Models: Are Top Managers Really Finding Them Useful?" *Journal of Business Policy* no. 2 (1973), pp. 33–42.

46. J. C. Chambers, S. K. Mullick, and D. A. Goodman, "Catalytic Agent for Effective Planning," *Harvard Business Review,* January–February 1971, pp. 110–18. This article reports on the planning in a successful corporation, Corning Glass Works. Also see G. A. Steiner, "Tomorrow's Corporate Planning and Planners," *Managerial Planning* 20, no. 5 (1972), pp. 1–7; and W. W. Simmons, "The Planning Executive of Century III—A Futuristic Profile," *Managerial Planning,* January–February 1977, pp. 19–22.

P. Lorange suggests that planners cannot concern themselves with both the substance and the process of planning. Line should take the former; staff the latter. "The Planner's Dual Role: A Survey of U.S. Companies," *Long-Range Planning* 6, no. 1 (1973), pp. 13–16. W. O. Nutt suggests that the role of the planner will be to secure concensus on an ever-widening oribit of assumptions—from which managers plan. "A Future for the Corporate Planner," *Long-Range Planning,* April 1977, pp. 90–93.

16

Management by Objectives

In the traditional, rather authoritarian approach to planning and controlling described so far, the process of defining strategy, objectives, and goals moves from the top of the organization downward; lower levels are controlled to ensure their adherence to the plans of the higher level. This top-down approach has been a powerful management technique. When it is well done, objectives are clearly defined and communicated downward to each organizational level, which then knows exactly what is expected of it. The control system provides superiors with information so they can inform their subordinates how well or badly they are doing.

As powerful as this approach is, however, we have seen that it presents problems, especially of subordinate resentment and rejection of higher management's objectives. What is now popularly known as management by objectives is a reformist approach that attempts to reverse the flow of planning so that it moves from the bottom upward in the organizational hierarchy. In this section we shall discuss the philosophy, mechanics, and problems of management by objectives (MBO).[1]*

MBO Philosophy

Under the traditional approach to planning and controlling, your parents might have announced that their specific educational goal for your senior year in high school was at least one A, only one C, and no Ds or Fs. This was in support of their continuing educational objective for you, which was admission to a good college. If you achieved the goal and objective, presumably your parents would dispense a reward: their esteem, or college tuition, or a new car. Suppose, however, that your parents took the radically different approach of management by objectives. Instead of starting with their objectives for you, the first step would have been for you to define your own educational goals and objectives. You could have proposed these to your parents and generally controlled your own behavior to reach these goals. At the end of the year (at the least, but probably more frequently), you would have reported to your parents on your evaluation of your performance in reaching your goals.

Self-Planning

This MBO approach assumes that you would have performed more effectively, having planned your own objectives and controlled your own behavior. You might have even worked harder because you would have been more committed to your plans and schooling. Perhaps these are overly optimistic assumptions, for you may not have been mature enough to define your academic goals or even to have known whether or not you wanted to go to college. Or given a chance, you might have decided that college was not your aim at all. Unfortunately, many young people are in college only because their parents expected it and structured their children's lives to that end.

Assumptions about People

At the core of MBO is a set of beliefs about people and modern organizations.[2] These beliefs hold the following to be true:

1. Most people possess higher level needs for power, autonomy, competence,

---

* Notes and references will be found at the end of this chapter.

achievement, and creativity that increasingly are motivating those who have satisfied their physiological and security needs.

2. People will want to satisfy these needs through their work if provided an opportunity to do so. Mature people are not inherently lazy; they possess an inherent drive that is released when they enjoy autonomy.

3. The educational, competence, and specialization levels of employees has increased to such an extent that they have substantial knowledge to contribute—knowledge that is often unknown to superiors.

4. Organizations are facing increasingly complex and challenging conditions beyond the capacity of old-fashioned, centralized, authoritarian management. Survival and growth will require greater effort and creativity from individuals at all levels. Past management has discouraged such creativity, so dramatic change is essential.

5. People will work harder, satisfy their higher needs, manifest greater commitment, and perform better if they determine their own objectives. Most particularly, employees with high needs for achievement will set explicit, moderately risky, and challenging objectives that may very well surpass what higher management would set for them.

6. Personal commitment and growth cannot be commanded by top management. It must be self-developed by individuals. Management's chief responsibility is to establish an organizational climate that stimulates people to strive.

7. The best indicator of a superior's performance is subordinates' growth in capacity, aspirations, and performance.

MBO Assumptions about People
- they possess higher needs
- they desire to satisfy these needs through work
- they have increasing knowledge
- they will work harder for their own goals
- they will correct their own behavior

Few techniques have caught on with organizations as much as MBO. Although often misunderstood, it has become a fad; one company called a consultant to request that he install an MBO system "next Thursday afternoon." But management by objectives is not a medicinal dose that a sick company takes to get well or a simple technique that can be applied in three hours. Rather, it is a philosophy as well as a complex technique requiring years to implement fully.[3]

The Process of MBO

The central endeavor in any MBO program is the development of understanding between every superior-subordinate pair about the subordinate's continuing objectives and specific goals.[4]

Subordinate Proposals

The first step is usually for the subordinate to draft a written statement of his or her continuing objectives and specific goals for the coming time period (usually one year). The proposal should detail how goal achievement is to be measured by the specific performance indicators described in Chapter 13. Thus the subordinate exercises the major influence in determining the criteria by which his or her performance is to be evaluated.

Joint Negotiation and Agreement

Next the subordinate submits the proposal to the superior. They meet, discuss, negotiate, and agree in writing on the subordinate's final objectives and goals for

Steps in MBO
- subordinate proposes goals for next time period
- subordinate and superior discuss, modify and reach agreement
- periodic formal and frequent informal review
- subordinate reports on performance at end of period
- repeat cycle

FIGURE 16–1

Specific Goals for Technical Sales Representative

Background

This territory covers the states of Indiana and Illinois and includes approximately 420 accounts that have been active in the past three years. The 1984 total volume will be about $4.8 million, with some 40 percent coming from four major accounts. Approximately 310 accounts will have made one or more purchases from us by the end of the year. Principal volume chemicals in this territory are DMT, RDP, and sulfuric acid, going primarily to the plastic industry.

1985 Sales Goal

The territory should be able to produce a 12-month volume of approximately $5.4 million next year; this is our sales target.

1985 Specific Goals for Marshall Greenbaum

1. To obtain a broader base of customers for DMT and RDP for the purpose of spreading our competitive risk in the plastics industry.

    This objective will have been met when initial DMT and RDP orders are booked from five accounts in the territory not sold in 1984.

2. To improve our franchise with the "big four" customers in this area, so that continuing competitive efforts do not diminish our share of the total business of these important customers.

    This objective will have been met when useful Technical Service Laboratory projects have been initiated for two of these cusotmers.

3. To improve my personal business relationships with those prospects in the area included in the group of approximately 75 companies that have purchased nothing from us in the past three years.

    This objective will have been met when I have been able to perform some gratuitous service for, or to arrange cordial social contacts with, 15 executives in at least 10 of these companies who have a voice in purchasing decisions.

4. To improve the frequency with which I am able to make in-person contact with the bulk of our customers, specifically those not included in the territory's big four.

    This objective will have been met if I have developed and am following a suitably revised basic travel plan by July 1.

5. To develop additional increments of volume with old, and also prospective new, customers in the medium-size company category.

    This objective will have been accomplished if:

    a. 1985 total volume goals are met, and

    b. such customers account for an additional 5 percent of total dollar income; i.e., 65 percent of sales.

6. To improve the ratio of the more profitable "growth" chemical sales to basic chemical sales in this territory.

    This objective will have been met when the percentage of total sales dollars accounted for by "growth" chemicals has been increased from 65 to 70 percent.

7. To hold down the direct costs of selling that are under my control with the end of contributing to optimum territorial profit.

    This objective will have been met if the year-end average of monthly expenses reported does not exceed the median range of those for territories of comparable type, volume, and geographical size.

8. To determine whether it is desirable to acquire additional resellers in the southern part of Illinois, in view of the steady growth in numbers of new, smaller end-user prospects for some of our specialty products.

    This objective will have been met if, by April 1, I am able to obtain a clear-cut policy on the appointment of resellers, together with an adequate understanding of the economics supporting this policy.

9. To gain a comprehensive knowledge of the natural gas industry, which—although not the territory's dominant industry potential in terms of pounds—represents the highest profit potential, by industry, in the territory.

    This objective will have been met when I am able to contribute one or more basic new ideas to them developed either personally or with the Technical Service Laboratory.

10. To master a thorough knowledge of all uses for RDP, the product for which there is the third largest number of individual customers in this territory.

    This objective will have been met if, by October 1, I have completed an intensive program of indoctrination at the Technical Service Laboratory of not less than three full days' duration.

the coming year. Figure 16–1 is a typical statement of the agreed-upon goals. It is for Marshall Greenbaum, a technical sales representative.

Review and Evaluation

The foregoing statement should be a working document, not engraved in stone for the ages.[5] By keeping the statement handy in their desks or enlarging it for display on their office walls, each superior-subordinate pair can refer to specific items from time to time.[6] Review should be frequent, on an opportunity basis, not saved up for a year-end inquisition.

THE BETTER HALF®   By Harris

"I'll be late. Twice a year the boss makes us all line up and kiss his feet."

The Better Half, reprinted courtesy *The Register* and Tribune Syndicate, Inc.

This is the most difficult part of MBO: Who initiates the in-process checks and discussions? And how frequently? One purpose of MBO is to create subordinate autonomy. This means that the subordinate must be left alone to achieve objectives and does not have to explain what he or she is doing as frequently as under traditional management. Too frequent checks by an anxious superior will destroy the collaborative nature of MBO. Ideally, the subordinate should initiate conversations to keep the superior informed and to obtain advice. Perhaps the key is spontaneity and casualness, where both sides utilize frequent opportunities to discuss progress on their mutually agreed-upon objectives.

Repetition

At the end of the period, the process starts anew. The orientation should be toward the future, not the past. Reasons certain objectives were not achieved should already be known to superior and subordinate; objectives not achieved should influence goal setting only to the extent of defining what remains to be done. Recriminations about the past should not be allowed to corrupt the future.

Most MBO applications include subordinates' written appraisals of their own performance, which are submitted to their superiors and jointly reviewed. This written appraisal is valuable, but the appraisal and discussion should contain no surprises. They should survey matters already discussed and acted upon by the pair.

Problems with MBO

The management-by-objectives philosophy and assumptions about people are stirring but idealistic. Unfortunately, they may not be applicable to all situations and to all people, and even when they are, application can be difficult.[7]

Distrust of the System

Like other approaches to participative management, MBO makes optimistic assumptions about human motivation: that most people possess needs for power, autonomy, competence, and achievement and that they will respond to opportunities to satisfy these needs on the job. Where traditional authoritarianism has been strong and long standing, however, middle- and lower level personnel may not be enthusiastic about MBO. They may be so distrustful of top executives that they perceive management as attempting to manipulate them into setting higher objectives and working harder.[8] They may believe that unless they set unrealistically high objectives, higher management will veto them. The whole relationship can be a very antagonistic one in which lower level employees seek to hide their true capacity from top management and endeavor to find the minimal allowable objectives. The whole thing becomes a sham.[9]

In addition, MBO strives for objective feedback, so that people know how they are performing on the basis of specific criteria, not vague, subjective judgment or suspicion. The approach assumes that people really want to know how they are doing. This may be true for those with high needs for achievement, but many others do not really want to know unless they are doing very well. Less happy truth is too upsetting, and they attempt to avoid it or do not believe it. Research suggests that the great majority of employees consider themselves above average.[10] But we all can't be better than most others, and the facts may be disappointing to the majority because they will learn that they are not as good as they think they are. Many of us would simply prefer to operate in the dark.

To avoid these adverse consequences, MBO should neither make comparisons nor rank individuals. As much as possible, individuals should consider themselves to be in competition with no one but themselves. The individuals' unit objectives should be uniquely theirs, and judgment should be based only on their performance against their objectives.[11]

Resentment of Forced Program

MBO is sometimes imposed by an authoritarian top executive who becomes aware of her or his unsatisfactory behavior and endeavors to reform the organizational

Problems with MBO
- distrust of system
- resentment of program
- resistance to paperwork
- focus too narrow and short run
- inconsistency between top and bottom plans
- evaluation not tied to MBO
- inability to measure objectives

climate in this way. In such a case a paradox exists: a nondirective system being implemented by authoritarian means. It just does not work.[12]

If subordinate personnel believe the program is being imposed on them, they may merely go through the motions of completing the forms and then ignore them. The MBO program can become an exercise in which invested time is to be minimized. Since there is no personal commitment to the program, managers do not view short-term events in the light of continuing objectives; they merely make ad hoc decisions. Top management loses credibility, and distrust increases.

Symbolic communication of top management's commitment to the program philosophy is essential.[13] It must demonstrate that adoption is voluntary; that in its own use of procedures, management will be truthful and responsive. In addition, it might make a consultant available to assist subordinate managers in implementing the program. Such a third party can be extremely valuable in instituting the initial discussions between superiors and subordinates about their expectations.

Resistance to Paperwork and Talk

Again, as in other participative practices, MBO can be very time-consuming in the short run. In comparison with the simple communications of authoritarian top-down planning and controlling, MBO is a two-way communication process of the most profound kind: an exchange of views under conditions of mutual respect. Such two-way discussion consumes much more time than one-way directives.

Shoe

Reprinted by permission: Tribune Company Syndicate, Inc.

In addition, MBO works more effectively when proposals and agreements are written. Since it is an iterative process of proposing, reviewing, and reporting, the writing time mounts up.

All of this talking and writing requires substantial time, management's most precious resource. Under short-time operating pressures, many managers resent the time demands of MBO, which seem to pay off only in the future—if ever. Some who have always considered themselves effective managers may not feel any need to invest such time and energy in an unnecessary venture.

Overly Narrow Focus

Management by objectives is individualistically oriented to appeal to upper-level ego needs. The approach intends to foster greater job commitment. Unfortunately, these laudatory intentions can have some adverse impact. The system encourages and rewards the narrow view in which each person concentrates on his or her own unit and ignores how individual objectives fit with those of the organization. Such problems are not unique to MBO of course; but under top-down planning and controlling, each higher level assumes responsibility for coordinating the activities and objectives of its subordinates. Such a hierarchical-based mechanism is the most effective integrating technique yet developed.

When planning is initiated by subordinates in MBO, they seldom anticipate how their proposals relate to those of their peers. Marketing may desire to launch a new product X, but production expects to delay it for a year until new machinery is available. Personnel may plan to expand minority hiring at the same time other departments intend to reduce total employment. These gaps and conflicts must be reconciled. An executive can do this by showing each subordinate manager how his or her proposals relate to others' and encouraging appropriate modification. The executive will probably hold joint group meetings of the subordinates to integrate their plans. Some may even require consultation among peers as part of the early stages of plan development.

Reasonable people may agree, but not always. And even such people may resent colleague and superior pressures that seem to restrict the very autonomy that the MBO system promises. Power- and achievement-oriented managers become so committed to their proposed objectives that they perceive the organization from only one perspective. They tend to believe that their own functions and proposals are most important to the organization. From time to time, the superior may have to direct plan modification. This is necessary, but can be perceived as inconsistent with MBO philosophy.

Inconsistency between Bottom-up and Top-down Plans

The traditional planning and controlling system implies a unidirectional flow of plans, with objectives and goals moving from the top downward. Theoretically, this should provide consistency and ensure that lower level goals will add up total organizational goals. This apparent predictability constitutes a great attraction of the traditional system. Unfortunately, as we have seen, top-down goals are sometimes unrealistic and impossible to accomplish.

The initial conception of MBO was just the opposite: The flow of objectives and goals was to be from the bottom upward, through successive levels to the top. The sum of the lower level goals would be the top-level goals. Unfortunately, this system does not work either, because different managerial levels get out of touch and go off in different directions.[14] Their aims can become inconsistent.

Top executives are not passive receptors of what lower managers chose to tell them. They have objectives on their minds, and it would be impossible for them not to. Top management could say nothing about its own ideas, let the bottom-up

MBO planning proceed, and hope that the resulting plans will add up to or surpass top-management hopes. If the plans fulfill the hope, fine; but if they don't, management will probably direct everyone to develop another plan—and to try harder. Such pressure undermines the philosophy of MBO, creating a manipulative game wherein every level tries to guess the minimum expectations of its superiors.

Even in the absence of explicit executive dissatisfaction with proposed objectives, most MBO systems contain an inflationary bias. It is always assumed that this year's goals must surpass last year's, even if conditions do not seem to justify the improvement. In some organizations it is worse to reduce planned goals than not to achieve them at all.

Most top-management groups announce their yearly aspirations in terms of sales, profits, expansions, and so on, generally accompanied by a short summary of salient environmental developments of which everyone might not be aware. These general objectives become guidelines for the proposals from below and constitute a warning that subordinates had better have good arguments if their proposals do not add up to management's desires. By stating its objectives, the top does exert pressure incongruent with MBO philosophy, but perhaps this clarity and honesty is preferable to the secret targets that would exist anyway.

Reconciling MBO with top-level strategic planning is a continuing problem. The top cannot abdicate its responsibility to define the organization's mission and continuing objectives and to articulate them to all personnel. This internal educational and sales effort should remain even with a bottom-up participative system. Indeed, it is even more important under MBO than under top-down authoritarianism because strategic plans should be the primary guides in integrating lower level objectives.

Lower level proposals and results should in time assist the top better to understand the organization's capabilities and its environmental realities. Information from the bottom will assist in refining and modifying basic organizational strategy.

Evaluation Not Tied to MBO

Most logically, the results as self-reported by subordinates and corroborated by performance data should serve as the basis of the dispensing of rewards. Unfortunately, in some organizations the merit review and reward system is completely separate from and inconsistent with MBO performance.[15]

There are several reasons this condition may exist. One is that management not entirely committed to MBO is reluctant to relinquish any control over the real control system, which resides in the control of rewards.

Another instance of the merit system being divorced from MBO performance occurs when managers retain secret performance goals and criteria so that subordinates are not informed of the real basis of judgment. These may be objective performance results or subjective behavior. For example, authoritarian superiors tend to rate more highly subordinates who are like themselves, even in the absence of supporting performance data.[16] We all tend to rate others more highly who are like what we imagine ourselves to be: energetic or calm, aggressive or patient, decisive or thoughtful, and so on.

Superiors also like subordinates who save time, who can accept a blanket delegation of duties and perform the task without unnecessarily bothering the superior about details. Perhaps what superiors desire most from their subordinates is reliability and loyalty. Loyalty seems to mean (1) not doing anything that might make the boss look bad; (2) not publicly embarrassing the boss; and (3) either doing what you're told or telling the superior you can't do it, resigning, and keeping your mouth shut. Reliability means if you agree to do something, do it—and on time.

Although loyalty and reliability or any other personality traits or behavior patterns may be desirable, they are highly subjective. Judgment about them depends as much on the superior as on the subordinate. In addition, they are seldom explicitly stated as criteria that are considered to be as important as objective results. The subordinate managers who achieve their apparent goals can be surprised to learn that their actual evaluation is not so high as they might expect because their superior judges them by unknown factors.

Inability to Measure Objectives

MBO does not magically provide hitherto unknown means of measuring performance. It is hoped that lower levels will become more knowledgeable about their activities and better able to determine measures. However, as was discussed in the preceding chapter, some objectives and goals may not lend themselves to measurement.

Transitory Impact

Some of the salutary effects of MBO may be the result of its novelty in a given organization. The introduction of a new, formal mechanism causes managers and subordinates to interact in new ways. This may be exciting at first. It may bring new information to the surface, leading to new insights. Over time, though, habit and inertia can lead to a return to business as usual. Such revitalizing management processes as MBO are important if they are to keep on contributing to organizational success.[17]

SUMMARY

Management by objectives (MBO) is a philosophy and technique for promoting better plans and performance. Management by objectives is a managerial philosophy and technique that attempts to draw on people's needs for achievment, competence, and autonomy by allowing them to set their own objectives, goals, and performance criteria. Planning be-

gins with subordinates proposing their periodical plans to their superiors. Negotiation, modification, and approval flow from give-and-take between the two parties.

It is assumed in this approach that most people desire to set challenging objectives, possess the capacity to do so, and will be committed to their accomplishment. Some assert that this approach is essential because increased specialization and sophistication have made it impossible for higher authority to proceed with traditional, top-down planning and controlling. In certain areas, superiors do not know as much as their subordinates do.

In spite of its apparent attractions, MBO is no simple remedy that can correct organizational ills overnight. Personnel may distrust the system if it is too great a departure from past authoritarian practice. Some employees may not like to commit themselves to anything or to really know how they are doing. Resistance and resentment will be especially strong if the chief executive imposes the system on unwilling managers. Such implementation contradicts the essence of the MBO philosophy of voluntеerism. Even some sympathetic managers will resent the time expended on paperwork and talk, which is so much greater in the beginning with this technique.

MBO does not automatically broaden a manager's horizons. It may even initially contribute to a narrower focus as each manager attempts to achieve his or her own unit's seemingly all-important objectives. For the superior, carrying out the responsibility of broadening subordinates' views can be as difficult as the job of developing consistency between what subordinates propose and what higher levels expect. Thus MBO is not a one-way flow of plans upward. It involves ongoing communication and negotiation between the various organizational levels to promote understanding and agreement.

REVIEW QUESTIONS

1. What is the difference between the setting of objectives and goals under traditional management and the use of management by objectives?

2. What assumptions about people are implicit in MBO?

3. Why is MBO a philosophy and not simply a technique?

4. What are the mechanics of MBO?

5. Why is review and evaluation such a difficult phase in MBO?

6. Why is MBO thought to be potentially superior to traditional planning and controlling?

7. What are the general problems that sometimes characterize MBO?

8. Why do subordinates sometimes distrust the system?

9. Why do some people not want honest performance feedback? How can such information actually undermine future performance?

10. How do some executives attempt to impose MBO? Why do some think that MBO should only be voluntary?

11. Why is the paperwork and talk in MBO sometimes resisted?

12. What is the inconsistency between bottom-up and top-down plans?

13. Why should performance evaluation be tied to an MBO system if it exists?

Notes and References on Management by Objectives

1. For a variety of views on MBO, see George S. Odiorne, *Management by Objectives* (New York: Pitman, 1965); J. D. Batten, *Beyond Management by Objectives* (New York: American Management Association, 1966); John W. Humble, *Management by Objectives* (London: Industrial Education & Research Foundation, 1967); R. A. Howell, "A Fresh Look at Management by Objectives," *Business Horizons,* (Fall 1967, pp. 51–58; and National Industrial Conference Board, *Studies by and with Objectives,* NICB Studies in Personnel Policy, No. 212 (New York, 1968). Also see W. J. Reddin, *Effective Management by Objectives: The 3-D Method* (New York: McGraw-Hill, 1971); F. Mali, *Managing by Objectives* (New York: John Wiley & Sons, 1972); A. C. Beck, *A Practical Approach to Organization through MBO* (Reading, Mass.: Addison-Wesley Publishing, 1972); S. J. Carroll, Jr., and H. L. Tosi, Jr., *Management by Objectives: Applications and Research* (New York: Macmillan, 1973); and P. Mali, *Improving Total Productivity: MBO Strategies for Business, Government and Not-for-Profit Organizations* (New York: Wiley-Interscience, 1977). Ronald Greenwood, in the article "Management by Objectives: As Developed by Peter Drucker, Assisted by Harold Smiddy," *Academy of Management Review* 6, no. 2 (1981), pp. 225–30, discusses one of the early efforts to systematize an approach to MBO.

2. Douglas M. McGregor, *The Human Side of Enterprise* (New York: McGraw-Hill, 1960). For other views on MBO and motivation, see A. P. Raia, "Goal Setting and Self-Control," *Journal of Management Studies* 2 (1965), pp. 34–53; G. A. Bassett and H. H. Meyer, "Performance Appraisal Based on Self-Review," *Personnel Psychology* 21 (1968), pp. 421–30; J. M. Ivancevich, J. H. Donnelly, and H. J. Lyon, "A Study of the Impact of MBO on Perceived Need Satisfaction, *Personnel Psychology,* Summer 1970, pp. 139–51; R. A. Stringer, "Achievement Motivation and Management Control," in Gene W. Dalton and Paul R. Lawrence, *Motivation and Control in Organizations* (Homewood, Ill.: Richard D. Irwin, 1971), pp. 329–36; and R. M. Steers and D. G. Spencer, "Achievement Needs and MBO Goal-Setting," *Personnel Journal,* January 1978, pp. 26–28.

3. R. A. Howell suggests a four- to five-year evolutionary plan for installing MBO "Managing by Objectives: A Three Stage System," *Business Horizons* 13, no. 1 (1970), pp. 41–45.

4. Stephen J. Carroll, Jr., Henry L. Tosi, and J. Rizzo, "Setting Goals in MBO," *California Management Review* 12, no. 4 (1970), pp. 70–78. Richard Barton, "An MCDM Approach for Resolving Goal Conflict in MBO," *Academy of Management Review* 6, no. 2 (1981), pp. 231–41.

5. J. B. Lasagna, "Make Your MBO Pragmatic," *Harvard Business Review,* November–December 1971, pp. 64–69.

6. R. H. Brady stresses the need for frequent interim meetings, especially where the performance criteria are not quantitative. "MBO Goes to Work in the Public Sector," *Harvard Business Review,* March–April 1973, pp. 65–74.

7. Stephen J. Carroll and Henry L. Tosi, "Some Factors Affecting the Success of MBO," *Journal of Management Studies* 7 (1970), pp. 209–23; D. D. McConkey, "MBO-Twenty Years Later, Where Do We Stand?" *Business Horizons,* August 1973, pp. 25–36; and R. W. Hollmann and D. A. Tansik, "A Life-Cycle Approach to Management by Objectives," *Academy of Management Review,* October 1977, pp. 677–83.

8.   D. Moreau criticizes management by objectives as "a way to extract promises from people which can later be used against them." *Look Behind You* (London: Associated Business Programs, 1973). Harry Levinson advances similar criticism in "Management by Whose Objectives?" *Harvard Business Review,* July–August 1970, pp. 125–34.

9.   Management by objectives is not a substitute for good management. Goal setting has its strongest impact when it is accompanied and followed by a supervisor who demonstrates concern about the people and their performance. W. W. Ronan, G. P. Latham, and S. B. Kline III, "Effects of Goal Setting and Supervision on Worker Behavior in an Industrial Situation," *Journal of Applied Psychology* 58, no. 3 (1973), pp. 302–7.

10.   H. H. Meyer, E. Kay, and J. R. P. French, "Split Roles in Performance Appraisal," *Harvard Business Review,* January–February 1965, pp. 123–29.

11.   Douglas M. McGregor, "An Uneasy Look at Performance Evaluation," *Harvard Business Review,* May–June 1957, pp. 89–94; P. H. Thompson and G. W. Dalton, "Performance Appraisal: Managers Beware," *Harvard Business Review,* January–February 1970, pp. 149–57; and A. L. Patz, "Performance Appraisal Useful but Still Resisted," *Harvard Business Review* (May–June 1975), pp. 74–80.

12.   B. D. Jamieson, "Behavioral Problems with Management by Objectives," *Academy of Management Journal* 16, no. 3 (1973), pp. 496–505.

13.   D. D. White, "Factors Affecting Employee Attitudes toward the Installation of a New Management System," *Academy of Management Journal* 16, no. 4 (1973), pp. 636–46.

14.   W. R. Haines, "Corporate Planning and Management by Objectives," *Long-Range Planning* (August 1977), pp. 13–20.

15.   At Corning Glass, they make an effort to link MBO and performance evaluation. See M. Beer and R. A. Rub, "Employee Growth through Performance Management," *Harvard Business Review,* July–August 1976, pp. 59–66.

16.   On how managers tend to rate subordinates like themselves more highly, see J. H. Mullen, *Personality and Productivity in Management* (New York: Temple University Publications, 1966); and J. P. Campbell et al., *Managerial Behavior, Performance and Effectiveness* (New York: McGraw-Hill, 1970).

17.   Jack Kondrasuk, "Studies in MBO Effectiveness," *Academy of Management Review* 6, no. 3 (1981), pp. 419–30.

Discussion Questions and Exercises on Planning and Controlling

Discussion Questions

1. A theologian observed that the human being is the only creature that has the ability to make promises. How is this reflected in management?

2. Modern observers of management declare that business has "multiple objectives." What does this mean?

3. In response to a criticism of his company's unpreparedness for the energy shortage and lack of availability of small economy cars, a General Motors executive exclaimed, "But you misunderstand, we are not in the transportation business, we are in the entertainment business!" How might this comment relate to corporate strategy?

4. A distinction is often made between corporate strategy and business strategy. What is the difference? Are these two concepts useful? How?

5. The absence of consistent written policies and procedures is one of the most persistent problems in small business. Why is this so?

6. Desire for equity is one of the main reasons for the development of policies and procedures, especially on personnel matters. Why? What kinds of policies and procedures are developed?

7. The effect of a manager's control system, no matter how elaborate and comprehensive, depends upon the responses it elicits from those whose performance it seeks to measure and adjust. What does this mean?

8. In a large eastern state, high school teachers are evaluated and rewarded by school administrators on the basis of their student's scores on statewide examinations, which are written by the state and graded by the teacher. What are the advantages and disadvantages of such a control system?

9. Peter Drucker has written, "Management by objectives and self-control makes the common weal the aim of every manager. It substitutes for control from the outside the stricter, more exacting and more effective control from the inside. It motivates the manager to action not because somebody tells him to do something or talks him into doing it, but because the objective needs of the task demand it. He acts, not because somebody wants him to, but because he himself decides that he has to—he acts, in other words, as a free man." What does this mean, practically?

10. Some governmental units and not-for-profit organizations particularly suffer from (and can be paralyzed by) excessive red tape and controls that were originally imposed for legitimate reasons. What causes and sustains this condition?

11. "Probably the most important thing to understand about control in organizations, and the most difficult to explain, is the paradox that managers and researchers so frequently encounter: In many circumstances the more managers attempt to obtain and exercise control over the behavior of others in the organization, the less control they have. Furthermore, often the less control they have, the more pressure they feel to exert greater control, which in turn decreases the amount of control they have." How would you explain this paradox?

12. Missing funds and unexplainable expenditures are major problems in student extracurricular organizations. Why?

13. Most corporations use both the outside-inside and the inside-outside approaches to strategy. What are the hazzards of using one approach exclusively?

14. Despite the promise of MBO, it has sometimes been a miserable failure. Even in companies that scored initial success, it has been known to wither on the vine. Can you think of any reasons for this?

15. Objectives represent both the beginning and the end of the strategic planning process. Explain.

Individual Exercises

1. Design an ideal evaluation and grading system. Clarify your values and objectives for the control system, and indicate how it meets them.

2. Draw up, in order of most dominant to most deferrable, the probable objectives of your school. What changes would you propose, if any?

3. Draw up, in order of most dominant to most deferrable, the objectives of any organization with which you are familiar. What changes would you propose, if any?

4. Describe and analyze any control system you have personally experienced, indicating (a) specific goals, (b) performance indicators, (c) measurement, and (d) corrective action taken with you. What was your response? Why?

5. Assume that you crave power and a long life and have just formed a pact with the devil in which he promises to delegate his powers to you for controlling individual behavior and to place you at the head of a large corporation. In return, you promise your soul and to make as much money from the corporation as possible for your master. For every percentage over 10 percent return on investment, he rewards you with an extra year of life, and for every point below 10 percent, you forfeit one year. What kind of a planning and control system would you devise?

6. Suppose you are a saint and you have the same powers as in question 5. You seek to make as much money as possible in order to support missionary work. What kind of a planning and control system would you devise?

Managerial Cases and Problems on Planning and Controlling

Fargo College (A)*

Fargo College has long enjoyed a reputation as one of America's finest women's liberal arts colleges. Proportionately as many of its graduates have gone on to Ph.D.s and M.D.s as those of any of the prestigious women's schools. The institution was founded early in the 19th century as a seminary for young women by a railroad baron who located it far out in the country on his main line west (unfortunately, the last train passed through in 1961). The school enjoyed little debt and flourished on the strength of its ability to attract the daughters of the "best" and most affluent families in the Midwest.

The students have generally been academically gifted. In the best years in the 1950s, Scholastic Aptitude Test (SAT) scores averaged over 1,200 combined mathematical and verbal (the national average was about 800). Each year 200 students were accepted from more than 800 applicants. The students went through a program that emphasized small classes (faculty-student ratio around one to five) and personal attention in developing the whole person and her ability to think, not on preparation for specific careers. The school gave no business courses or even applied fine arts because this was considered too vocational.

Back then, the school's financial position had been strong, and the school's endowment was relatively generous for so small an institution. All buildings were paid for, although there had been relatively little construction since the 1920s. The financial position was helped by the fact that 90 percent of the students paid full tuition, so scholarship needs were modest. One could even play on the golf course for free. Fargo was geographically isolated, all students were required to live in regulated campus dorms, and students were not allowed to have automobiles. Nonetheless, young men from all-male colleges managed to find their way to the campus through rain and snow for distances of 50 to 300 miles. It was (and is) a beautiful campus located on the southern slope of a large lake and dotted with ivy-covered buildings that intermeshed with a small town located virtually on campus.

In the 1960s the picture began to change. The proportion of scholarship students climbed dramatically as the school actively recruited minority and disadvantaged women. Applications began to decline, even from alumnae daughters who had always been a major source of students. As applications declined, enrollment also declined because of unwillingness to lower admission standards. This reduced tuition income, thereby putting great stress on endowment funds, which were not sufficient to carry the burden. To make matters worse, the yield on investments declined with adverse market conditions in the 1970s. Perhaps worst of all, the school's utility expense doubled and tripled with cold winters and inflationary energy costs.

Applications have declined to such a degree that 75 percent are now accepted. Although no policy change in admissions standards has been announced, SAT scores on the average have dropped about 150 points. The school has experienced no difficulty in holding or attracting faculty because of the depressed job market for liberal arts professors, but faculty salaries are low (the relatively large faculty, however, is an exceedingly heavy load on the school's budget).

---

* Part (B) to this case is contained in the Instructor's Manual.

In short, the school has not changed its basic strategy, but there is a growing feeling of concern.

Excerpts from an interview with Dr. Emily Mortimer, dean of faculty follows:

> Educational styles run in cycles; what is a fad today will not necessarily be so tomorrow. Right now the trend is toward co-education and vocational relevance. But I believe this is an insecure base on which to erect a whole college—especially one like Fargo, which has built such a fine reputation as a women's liberal arts college. Our approach gives a young woman a chance to find herself ,to grow and test her capacities without fear of losing her attractiveness to boys. Even more important, our liberal approach lays a foundation for a total life, not just whatever job she may have in her 20s. . . . Right now, women seem to want to work outside the home. That's fine and many of our graduates in the past have gone on to graduate school and pursued professional careers as teachers, writers, even lawyers and physicians. But my own view is that in the long run, even most college women will still place the family at the center of their lives—and I even believe that the birthrate will start back up. There is evidence that this is already occurring. I've been intrigued by some reports out of the Soviet Union that what passes as the women's liberation movement there has made as a primary goal the freedom for women to remain home, to have more children, and to rear them. In the long run, I think our traditional and current educational philosophy was, is, and will be appropriate.

Excerpts from an interview with Edward White, assistant professor of sociology and an active person in the faculty senate:

> This school is in real trouble. Our applications are declining, and the student quality is going down. What we mainly get are girls who expect this to be a finishing school or are afraid of competing with young men. They sit passively in class and expect to be told what to write. And don't accuse me of chauvinism. I had

> women in my doctoral program who were just as motivated, just as analytical, and just as outspoken as the men. We need more of that spirit here. . . . Perhaps we can get it by finding more motivated women, but I just don't think you can get them to come to an isolated campus in the country unless we become co-educational. To attract such men and women, I guess, we would have to add more career-relevant programs—tranditional ones like premed and prelaw and more applied areas like accounting and administration.

Excerpts from an interview with Sheila Whitney, a senior who is president of the Student Association:

> I love this place . . . the hills, the trees, the lake, but it does get *boring*. Sometimes I think I'm in a convent. My Mom can't understand it, you know, because boys were always coming here when she was a student. And they still do, but only if they have a date or a special relationship. Blind dates are a thing of the past, so you don't meet anyone here. . . . It really doesn't bother me so much because I intend to go to law school, but I think the classes would be more exciting at a co-educational school. Some of the administrators and professors here are just incredibly old-fashioned! I know my summer course in con-law at Old Ivy was much more interesting than class here. . . . Still, I wonder if I'd be president of the Student Association there. Here, at least, those who want to run things can. That really helped me on my law school application. . . . Would I come to Fargo again? I don't know . . . , I doubt it.

Questions on Fargo College (A)

1. What has been the school's basic stragegy?

2. Why was it successful for so long?

3. What has undermined this strategy?

4. What would you recommend to the president and board of directors?

Lanzor, Ltd.

Lanzor, Ltd., was founded in Fragertalia, a country in Western Europe in 1900 (names disguised). In its first year it employed 50 people and manufactured only automobiles. Today it employs 350,000 and, in addition to automobiles, is involved in trucks, industrial vehicles, agricultural tractors, construction machinery, steel, machine tools, and railroad rolling stock. Automobile manufacturing employs 150,000, trucks and industrial vehicles 70,000, steel

40,000, agricultural tractors 15,000, machine tools 5,000, railroad stock 5,000, and miscellaneous 65,000.

As the business has grown, its strategy has changed of course. Until the late 1960s, automobiles and trucks were virtually the exclusive thrust of Lanzor. All the other segments existed primarily to serve these products. In 1970, however, Chairman Pierre St. Foradora launched a diversification strategy designed to promote outside sales and expansion into new product lines. Because Lanzor enjoyed overwhelming success in automobiles at home (more than 80 percent of the domestic market), it was able to utilize auto profits to acquire and invest in new activities—such as steel, tractors, construction vehicles,

machine tools. Exhibit 1 summarizes how management describes its businesses. To generate greater profits, management focused its production on existing models and expanded manufacturing capacity to more than 2 million automobiles per year. Larger production runs and less frequent model changes were designed to reduce unit cost.

Opinions vary on the success of the diversification strategy. Sales have increased, and automobiles constitute a reduced proportion of the business. Nonetheless, profits have not kept pace with sales growth (and inflation), and the automobile division is running a deficit. Following are some excerpts from recent newspapers and magazine articles on Lanzor, Ltd.

EXHIBIT 1

How Lanzor Describes Its Business

1. Automobiles

The Makes

Lanzor means several different product ranges, each with a distinctive personality, marketed in 150 countries.

Lanzor: quality series production, 11 models in production.

Tanis: classic automobiles for a select clientele, 8 models.

Bianchi: top-quality compact cars, 1 model.

Zither: specializing in sports cars.

Magia: world-beater GTs and Formula I cars.

The Figures

Lanzor has no fewer than 55 production and assembly plants in the world, 36 of which are run directly (Fragertalia, Brazil, and Argentina) and 19 production and assembly plants run by associated companies or licensees.

In 1981 Lanzor built 1,450,000 cars (790,000 of which were sold in Fragertalia).

The consolidated income was U.S. $6.9 billion.

Total payroll is 159,411 (133,514 in Fragertalia).

The after-sales service network has 12,000 service points and authorized repair shops.

Models

Since 1900 Lanzor has turned out the staggering figure of 27 million automobiles (300 different models). Eight models have sold over a million units: 1100, 600, nuova 500, 850, 124, 128, 127, and 126.

2. Commercial and Industrial Vehicles

The Makes

Lanzor builds more than 250 different models (700 versions) of trucks and buses, with engines from 53 to 265 kW, both water-cooled and air-cooled. Total vehicle weights range from three tons up to the maximum permitted legal limits.

The Figures

Lanzor Truck has a total of 14 plants in Western Europe.

The Group also has 33 production and assembly plants (12 owned by subsidiaries and 21 by associated companies and licensees) in other countries plus four plants in Fragertalia that belong to other companies and are managed by Lanzor.

In 1981 Lanzor Truck built 111,500 vehicles. Of these 42,500 were exported outside the three domestic markets.

Consolidated income was U.S. $3.9 billion.

Investments in 1978 came to U.S. $395 million.

The payroll of the group was 59,289 (31,537 in Fragertalia).

EXHIBIT 1 (*continued*)

After-Sales Service

In Fragertalia: 11 centres and 361 specialized concessionaires.

3,000 service points in Europe.

200 concessionaires in more than 100 countries.

A Few More Names

The Lanzor Truck group also includes companies manufacturing fork-lift trucks, fast diesel engines, and engines for naval propulsion and industrial uses.

3. Agricultural Tractors

The Makes

An extremely wide range of tractors—both wheeled and crawler type—for all kinds of agricultural work. Powers range from 40 to 150 CV. Medium- and large-size tractors with two- or four-wheel drive; special models for orchards, vineyards and work on hilly or mountainous terrain.

Implements for working the soil, harvesters of all kinds, and in particular for forage, beet and cotton.

The Figures

Lanzor Tractor has 4 production plants in Fragertalia and 8 elsewhere in the world, plus 5 factories owned by associated companies and licensees.

Total units built in 1978: 76,000 (second largest in Europe).

Exports account for over 65% of vehicles sold.

Consolidated income was U.S. $922 million.

Payroll: 11,925 (6,405 in Fragertalia).

4. Construction Machinery

The Makes

52 models from 45 to 550 CV (DIN): dozers, wheeled and crawler loaders; motorgraders; motorscrapers; pipelayers; pipewelders; pipe carriers; wheeled and crawler hydraulic excavators.

The Figures

Lanzor-Construct has four production plants in Fragertalia, one in England, three in the United States, two in Brazil, and one in Argentina. It has granted licences to companies in Spain, Pakistan, Japan, South Korea, Australia, New Zealand, and South Africa.

Total units built in 1981: 9,500.

Consolidated income U.S. $791 million.

Payroll: 11,392 (4,575 in Fragertalia).

5. Steel

The Makes

Lanzor-Steel specializes in the conversion of special steels, iron and aluminum castings, hot and cold pressing, and the cold forming of mechanical components. It is structured according to product lines.

Steels: the product range includes flat steels (strips and sheets, steels for cold pressing and stainless steels) and long pieces in special steels (sections, semi-finished ingots, bars, rods, etc.).

Foundries: it is the biggest complex in Europe specializing in the production of parts for cars: grey pig iron castings, speroid graphite, aluminum and light alloys for special uses (aerospace quality).

Forges: they are the most complete in Europe for the forging and hot pressing of mechanical components for the motor industry.

Mechanical cold-forming: offers a vast range of cold-formed parts (extrusions, cold-heading, nuts and bolts, etc.).

Engineering and diversified: comprises Tooling which produces tools for foundries and forges; Framing, one of the principal European manufacturers of springs; Tubing, which manufactures and sells welded pipes and steel sections; and Shaping, which manufactures refractory materials for industrial applications.

The Figures

Lanzor-Steel has 35 production plans throughout the world (27 in Fragertalia).

In 1981 it converted 1,600,000 tons of steel; 180,000 tons of iron castings; 33,000 tons of aluminum castings; 65,000 tons of forged parts; 30,500 tons of nuts and bolts; 11,000 tons of cold-formed parts.

Consolidated income was U.S. $1.5 billion.

Payroll: 31,345 (29,263 in Fragertalia).

EXHIBIT 1 (*concluded*)

6. Components

The Makes

Hundreds of thousands of different products for the automobile industry, and for a variety of industrial uses (electrical home appliances in particular).

From electrical and pneumatic equipment to paints; from lubricants to cables; from flexible hoses to auto accessories; from plastics to electronic automation systems for industrial and military applications; from carburetors to locks; and from accident prevention devices to docking and loading booms for ships.

The Figures

Lanzor-Components group has 54 production plants, of which 52 are in Fragertalia, plus 22 plants owned by associated companies and licensees.

Consolidated income U.S. $1.4 billion.

Payroll 35,089 (practically all in Fragertalia).

7. Machine Tools and Production Systems

The Makes

Lanzor Tools designs and manufacturers individual machines and complete plants for the mechanical industry, particularly for automobile, commercial and industrial vehicle, and tractor production.

Machine tools; Welding systems; and Materials handling, storing and industrial washing. It also operates, through subsidiary companies, in the fields of: Dies; and Engineering.

The Figures

Twelve production plants and has awarded licences in four countries.

Consolidated income was U.S. $249 million.

Payroll: 5,432, all in Fragertalia.

8. Rolling Stock and Rail Transportation Systems

The Figures

To date Lanzor has built:

2,000 diesel railcars, 700 diesel and electric locomotives, 450 surface and underground electric railcars, 7,000 passenger carriages, 15,000 goods vans, and thousands of containers. Lanzor has 3 production plants in Fragertalia, and 2 in Argentina.

Consolidated income: U.S. $207 million.

Payroll: 6,059 (2,657 in Fragertalia).

"Lanzor Revs Up More Than Cars" (May 7, 1979)

Fragertalia's Lanzor, once monogamously married to the automobile, has finally made official its metamorphosis into a diversified conglomerate. For the past decade, Lanzor has been quietly pushing its auto-related products—steel, machine tools, components, and the like—away from captively supplying Lanzor's auto production into feeding the open market. Autos now account for only 44.5 percent of its 1978 worldwide sales of $15.5 billion (down from 70 percent or so in the late 1960s).

Lanzor's need to make the product lines autonomous profit-generators is a response to the intensifying competition in the European auto market. This was pointed up most recently by the joint marketing agreement between Honda Motor and British Motor Corporation. And Detroit's current moves toward European-size cars will mean still more market pressure for Lanzor.

So far, though, the diversification has failed to bolster Lanzor's profitability. From 1967 through 1977 the company's sales quadrupled, yet profits went up by only a third. By the late 1960s the European auto market began to sag, from a 10 percent annual growth rate to the 2-to-3 percent level of the 1970s.

In the early 1970s St. Foradora conceived his plan to push some of Lanzor's captive, auto-related products (for example, machine tools and sheet steel) out on the open market as a means of increasing profits. He also abandoned the unprofitable manufacture of aircraft and giant marine turbines.

But labor problems put a definite crimp in his slow

but steady plans to expand. In 1974, for example, the company was hit with massive wage boost requests, just as it was trying to cope with the energy crisis. Although Lanzor rang up its first operating loss ($100 million) that year, the unions refused to allow the company to reduce production. The final straw came in 1974, when the Fragertalian government slapped price controls on cars, despite slumps in auto sales. Lanzor was forced to increase its short-term debt from virtually zero in 1973 to $474.3 million and to nearly double its medium- and long-term debt to $278.2 million.

Not surprisingly, the company experienced what Managing Director Vittorio Steinhart calls a "moment of coldness toward the passenger car," and the diversification push went into high gear. The company expanded into specialty steels—last year, in fact, non-Lanzor customers purchased 40 percent of Lanzor's steel production.

Similarly, component sales to outside customers went from 30 percent of production in the early 1970s to 50 percent last year. Meanwhile, Lanzor urged its operating heads to buy about 20 percent of their own raw materials and components from outside sources, as a built-in check on the company's own pricing and quality control.

Such expansion needs capital of course, and bankers consistently point to the possible future scarcity of fresh financing as Lanzor's Achilles' heel. The company was helped mightily in 1977 when the Libyan government plunked down $415 million, half of which went to buy 10 percent of its shares, and the rest split between a convertible bond issue and a long-term loan. But such windfalls are rare. It is hard to tell how well Lanzor is doing with its reorganization thus far. The company has only been publishing worldwide group sales figures since 1976. It still does not publish worldwide group profits, and by Fragertalian law, it cannot divulge this fiscal year's profits and losses until its annual meeting in May. Although the 1978 sales figure of $15.5 billion did represent a 9 percent increase over the $13.8 billion in 1977, Lanzor does not release its profits, and bankers and other observers say the company has not been nearly as profitable as it was during its heyday of the late 1960s. The only profit figures available are for 1977 Fragertalian operations, and those are downbeat: On $4.6 billion of sales, Lanzor turned out only a $75.5 million profit.

Bankers and potential investors will have more facts to play with in 1980, when Lanzor plans to distribute its first comprehensive, worldwide financial report. Until then, chances are that the company's lackluster profits will make most investors wait.

"Lanzor, Despite Poor Auto-Business Results, Expects to Post 1979 Net Matching 1978's" (Feb. 4, 1980)

Despite a poor performance in the automobile business, Lanzor Company, Ltd. probably remained in the black in 1979.

Although precise figures won't be released until spring, company officials estimate that consolidated 1979 earnings of Lanzor equaled the current equivalent of $190 million earned in 1978 on a 20 percent sales rise to $21 billion.

The sales gain came on good results in the European tractor market; on improvements in Brazil, where Lanzor has invested heavily in automobile and steel production; and on sustained sales to Third World countries of engineering services and heavy equipment.

Auto sales, however, which usually account for 45 percent of the company's volume, remained level at $8 billion, and auto operations dropped to a breakeven point from a profit of $50 million in 1978.

The auto setback lead to repeated rumors in Fragertalian financial circles that Lanzor was headed for a net loss in 1979 and might require government aid. In particular, the Communist Party and the Communist-led trade union that represents many Lanzor workers have been pushing for state aid to bolster Lanzor's research and development.

Union leaders contend that lagging research and development is the reason for Lanzor's difficulties in competing with other European auto makers. "Lanzor doesn't have the technology," asserts Sean Frainese, a Communist Party expert on industrial affairs. Lanzor's share of the auto market, a key to its financial health, fell to 52 percent in 1979 from 54 percent the year earlier, despite a 6 percent growth in total Fragertalian car sales. A decade ago, Lanzor held 74 percent of the Fragertalian market.

But company officials insist that nonauto business and overseas activities are holding up well and compensating for the drop in auto earnings.

Engineering construction work in the Third World, particularly Africa, has continued to be strong. It has also enabled Lanzor to sell its own heavy equipment, such as engineering machinery, tools, and gas turbines.

In Western Europe a bright spot is the 2.4 percent increase in tractor sales to 64,225 units, making Lanzor the market leader with a 12.2 percent share and displacing Massey-Ferguson Ltd., the Canadian manufacturer.

Like most other large Fragertalian companies, Lanzor is experiencing high labor costs because of wage increases, low productivity, and worker disputes. The company negotiated a contract last year with the Metal Workers Union that calls for a 15 percent increase in wages over three years plus automatic adjustments to cover the cost of living, which is rising at an annual rate of 20 percent.

The political pressure to infuse Lanzor with state aid is likely to be rigorously resisted by the company, which has jealously guarded its private status. The largest and most influential private company in Fragertalia, Lanzor employs 350,000 workers—275,000 of them in Fragertalia. Although the Communist Party has for some time abandoned its efforts to nationalize industry, its leaders are convinced the state should more actively direct the activities of Lanzor and other private concerns.

"Fragertalia Debating Auto Future" (February 28, 1980)

A national debate over the future of the Fragertalian automobile industry has been set off by the publication in the Communist Party newspaper of a letter written to all Lanzor Company, Ltd. stockholders by the firm's Chair Pierre St. Foradora. The letter warned that the automobile division of Lanzor was no longer able to compete in the international markets because of high costs and low productivity resulting from strikes and other labor unrest.

"Lanzor in State of Alarm" was the front-page headline. Underneath, the article began this way: "What would happen . . . if a crisis at Lanzor endangered some of the jobs of its 200,000 workers and in addition threatened the wages of 1.8 million workers employed by factories connected with the automobile industry? These are hypothetical questions, but they have to be asked if one wants to understand what Lanzor represents on the Fragertalian scene."

The message was clear: The Fragertalian working class cannot afford to let Lanzor wither away.

By implication, the Communist Party backed Mr. St. Foradora's suggestion that the Government should subsidize part of the research that goes into new models and new engines.

Mr. St. Foradora and his younger brother, who is vice president and managing director of the company, discussed Lanzor's difficulties in a meeting with Communist Party Secretary Hans Gotenburg and other party leaders at Communist headquarters in January.

Lanzor executives are known to be concerned primarily over low standards of productivity due to labor unrest. The company says that its production last year was 200,000 cars lower than expected because of labor disputes.

A Communist Party survey of 6,000 Lanzor workers published last week showed that a majority of workers were fairly content with conditions at Lanzor.

Summing up the debate at the Lanzor party symposium, Gotenburg conceded a need for greater productivity but linked it with a demand for better planning, worker participation in company decisions, and reform of assembly-line procedures.

"Fragertalia: Lanzor Tries to Avoid the Fate of Chrysler" (March 10, 1980)

There is an old adage in Fragertalia. As Lanzor goes, so goes the country. And Lanzor is not doing so well these days. Suddenly, Fragertalians—even the Communist Party and the unions—are worried about the health of the nation's largest privately owned corporation. Lanzor executives hope that this widespread concern will give the company the leverage it needs to persuade its workers to raise productivity and hold down wage requests. If not, they say Lanzor in the 1980s could go the way of Chrysler.

Lanzor's plight is not desperate—yet. The company, which includes such operations as autos, trucks, and earth-moving equipment, had worldwide sales of $18.9 billion in 1979. Although the company had an operating loss, it managed, through deft financial management and its investments in securities, to make an overall profit estimated at $92.7 million.

Autos, which comprise 48 percent of total sales are

symptomatic of Lanzor's troubles. The group's control of the Fragertalian auto market slipped from about 75 percent in the 1960s to 51 percent in 1979. And although this home market grew by about 6 percent in 1979, Lanzor increased its sales by only 4 percent. The reason: Some 9 million hours of strikes cost the company production of some 200,000 cars that the company insists it could have sold. As waiting time for popular models rose to four months, buyers simply switched to more readily available imports. Thus, on worldwide auto sales of $9.1 billion, Lanzor actually lost $62 million. .

Lanzor calculates that its workers work 10 percent less than their counterparts in West Germany and 15 percent less than those in France. In addition, Fragertalian labor costs in December 1979 were 24 percent higher than in December 1978, compared with a 13 percent increase for Europe as a whole.

Not all of Lanzor's problems are due to labor of course. When oil prices quadrupled in 1973, management decided that the automobile could not be counted on for future growth and concentrated instead on mass transportation. "This moment of coldness toward the auto," as Lanzor calls it, made the firm late in bringing out new models. The fast-selling Spring model, which was introduced in late 1978, should have been introduced in 1976.

"Embattled Lanzor Plans Cutback" (July 13, 1980)

Pierre and Juan St. Foradora, the brothers who run Lanzor, Fragertalia's largest private enterprise, have rarely been so embattled. Their company, more than most other European car makers, has been feeling the impact of the automobile industry's worldwide crisis.

Pierre St. Foradora announced at a stockholders' meeting early this month that the company would have to cut car production by 30 percent in the second half of this year to keep its already large stock of unsold cars from growing to intolerable proportions.

Major layoffs of workers will be necessary in the fall, he said. In answer to questions, however, he declined to estimate how many people would become idle. The labor unions have reacted sharply. The cutback is certain to affect the hundreds of smaller factories and workshops that work for Lanzor.

Last year Lanzor produced almost 1.5 million cars. Its automobile division showed a net loss of about $120 million; but the company, which has become increasingly diversified in recent years, had a profit of $47.7 million.

The automobile division is the most important of Lanzor's operations, which include some 600 companies. Lanzor produces railroad rolling stock, machine tools, farm tractors, and construction machinery in addition to automobiles.

"Thank God for diversification," an executive at the group's headquarters said the other day. He added that the diversification drive of the past few years had left the conglomerate in a better position to cope with its present difficulties than it was during the automobile industry's last major crisis in 1974 and 1975.

Lanzor executives blame two things for the car division's troubles: the Fragertalian phenomenon of labor unrest and low labor productivity and the lack of coordination among European automobile manufacturers in the face of growing Japanese and American competition.

Pierre St. Foradora, at the stockholders' meeting, spoke of the "deep process of restructuration" that the world's entire automobile industry was going through as a result of the energy crisis.

"I want to remind you that in Detroit, at this moment, there are already more than 350,000 unemployed," he said. "We don't want to take Detroit as a model, but it is a reality that has to be considered." He added that the American automobile industry, in spite of its troubles, had a far greater "structural capacity" than the European auto industry and that Japanese car makers, unlike the Europeans, were able to compensate for the limitation on their domestic market by an aggressive export policy.

In an interview, another Lanzor executive predicted, "In four to five years the Europeans will be squeezed to death between the Japanese and the Americans."

The Ford Motor Company and the General Motors Corporation, he said, will be able to produce a compact "world car" by then and have plants in Europe unless the Europeans organized themselves in the meantime to reduce their costs by joint production of engines and parts and by standardization.

Comments of Various Officials.   Asked to comment on the current Lanzor situation, an American automobile company executive observed:

> Lanzor made the same mistake as some U.S. car makers. Their autos were selling well, and they didn't invest enough in product improvement and change. Of course their models were always more fuel efficient than ours because gasoline was so much more expensive in Europe. Nonetheless, their cars are technologically obsolete. And they all look like boxes! Now their problem is that it takes so much time and money to come up with new models. Even Ford, which is much bigger than Lanzor, is picking up huge losses in trying to renovate its line. I don't think Lanzor is big enough to do it. Being large in this business makes some things easier.

The owner of a U.S. Lanzor dealership also comments:

> I don't know about their home market service, but their general reputation in this country is lousy. The bodies tend to rust because Lanzor still doesn't realize how much salt is used to melt snow on our roads. And we get blamed for the unavailability of spare parts. They just won't stock parts in their warehouse. And we can't afford to because sales are so bad and they offer no financial support. But the worse problem is the lousy communication from Lanzor. They don't tell us about new models, and we hear rumors that they are eliminating station wagons, or emphasizing sports cars, or introducing diesel engines. But often as not, the rumor is unfounded. The lack of diesel engines really angers me because I know they offer them in Europe.
>
> What gripes you is the lack of response to complaints. For example, their ACA model is almost 10 years old, but its a nice car. But for all that time it's had a lousy clutch cable arrangement. It squeaks and breaks too often. Owners complain, we complain—and *nothing* is done to change the design!
>
> Personally, I like the feel of Lanzors, but I guess you have to be an auto afficianado. The public seems to prefer the Japanese cars—and I would drop my Lanzor affiliation immediately if I could get a Toyota, Datsun, or Honda dealership!

A senior executive in a very successful, smaller German automobile manufacturer gives his view:

> Lanzor tries to do too much. They have too many models—twenty to our five. Their image is too ambiguous because their cars run from glorified lawnmowers all the way to $50,000 sports cars for decadent Princes. We focus on the young and not-so-young executive and professional who wants a conservative appealing, high quality machine. Being small gives us a big competitive advantage.

A Fragertalian professor at a business school in Lanzor's home city presents his view:

> Lanzor's managers (and most all managers in this country) are not market oriented. They are almost all engineers with no management training who believe product design is *the key* element in success. And we've been good at this, but its not enough. Focus is on controlling costs, not generating profits. For example, selling prices tend to be 'cost-plus,' not based on market situations.
>
> Let me give a personal example. My car is a DMD model, one of the smaller ones. It's a good car, but the brakes squeak as they do on all Lanzors. I asked a manager about this. He said that Lanzor uses a harder brake lining than other manufacturers because it holds better and lasts longer. They tried to remove the squeak, but it's inherent in the material. They decided to leave the material unchanged because its technical advantages outweigh a minor inconvenience like squeaking.
>
> In addition, vertical communications tend to be poor. Research suggests that there is less informal participation and communication up and down than in any other industrialized culture. In a firm like Lanzor, there are probably 100 top executives, 400 senior managers called directors, 2400 middle managers called (in translation) leaders, and 10,000 supervisors. These levels are quite distinct, and not all levels identify with the firm in the same way. For example, the supervisors and middle managers have their own unions. This is just not the situation in the United States.
>
> Worst of all, we don't plan much in this country. History has been so turbulent with wars, revolutions, communist threats, and terrorism that we don't look ahead much. We think mainly of tactics, seldom of strategy.

Questions on Lanzor, Ltd.

1. What external (e.g., market, environment, etc.) factors have contributed to the deterioration in Lanzor's performance?

2. What internal (e.g., decisions, policies, etc.) factors have contributed to the decline in Lanzor's performance?

3. How would you define the problems presently confronting Lanzor?

4. What should be management's objectives in the future?

5. What recommendations would you offer top management?

Quick-Clip Printing, Inc. (A)*

Quick-Clip Printing, Inc. was a family-owned printing firm specializing in business forms, such as retail clerk order pads, billing sets, and inventory sheets. Most forms were customer designed and printed to a customer's specifications. Customers were mainly businesses, with some hospitals, government agencies, and schools. The firm had been founded 40 years earlier by Simon Grabner, who had guided the firm until his death four years ago. His philosophy had always been to control the firm's activities very closely while retaining intimate personal ties with employees. Many times he, his printing manager Herb Blacker, and his chief assistant Frank Berkowitz would work into the evenings attempting to solve customers' problems with clever designs manufactured and delivered on time. Simon's brother Abe was the primary sales manager and key salesperson. Simon kept a sharp eye on Abe (who was something of a playboy) but managed to benefit from his tremendous range of social contacts.

Simon's business strategy could be described as:

1. Giving the customers what they want, but helping them to determine what that really is.
2. Delivering the product as quickly as possible to ensure that customers were never out of forms (most customers neglected to order until they were almost out).
3. Depending on repeat business for stability and expanding through word-of-mouth reputation.
4. Considering price less important, as long as it is not unreasonable.

Simon's management philosophy could be described as:

1. We are all family or close friends, so everyone should work hard and put in as much time as necessary to do the job.
2. Because I am the senior person in the organization and family leader, I will make all important decisions

and will look out for your interests. Loyal performance and effort will be noticed and rewarded.
3. Nonfamily members will be treated as family, and I will see that they are taken care of when ill or retired.

The firm prospered and grew at a moderate pace under Simon. The income statement for his last year is given in Exhibit 1. Although there was no formal organizational chart in existence at the time, it would have looked something like Exhibit 2.

Upon Simon's death, a family conference was held. Abe Grabner thought he should take over as president, but the family thought that he was too old and a little unreliable. Accordingly, they asked Simon's son Stewart to assume his father's post. Stewart was not working for the firm at the time, although he had done so while on school vacations for many years. After graduation from the Midwestern MBA program five years earlier, Stew had gone to work as a financial analyst with a Wall Street brokerage firm. His analytical ability had facilitated his rapid advancement, especially after he had negotiated several mergers from which he and his employer benefited greatly. Stew was a hardworking and ambitious young man. He was as anxious to take over the firm as he had been to avoid working for his father earlier. He wanted

* Part (B) for this case is contained in the *Instructor's Manual.*

EXHIBIT 1

QUICK-CLIP PRINTING, INC.
Simplified Income Statement
For Last Year under President Simon Grabner

Net sales		$806,000
Expenses		
Purchases	$240,000	
Labor	252,000	
Selling	68,000	
Administration	112,000	
		672,000
Net Profit before Taxes		$134,000

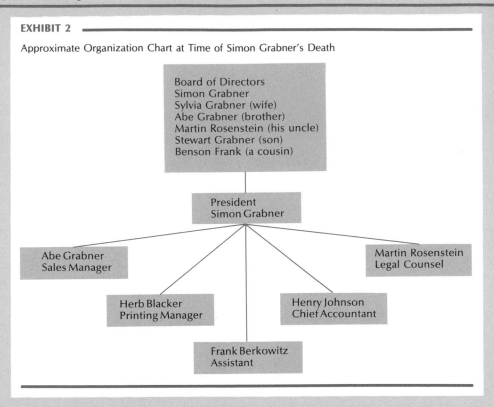

EXHIBIT 2

Approximate Organization Chart at Time of Simon Grabner's Death

Board of Directors
Simon Grabner
Sylvia Grabner (wife)
Abe Grabner (brother)
Martin Rosenstein (his uncle)
Stewart Grabner (son)
Benson Frank (a cousin)

President
Simon Grabner

Abe Grabner
Sales Manager

Herb Blacker
Printing Manager

Henry Johnson
Chief Accountant

Martin Rosenstein
Legal Counsel

Frank Berkowitz
Assistant

---

to show the family that he would be just as effective as Simon and that their trust was well placed.

After the meeting at which Stew was elected president, his great-uncle Martin Rosenstein, the firm's part-time legal counsel, stayed to talk awhile and to give the younger man some advice:

MARTIN: Stewart my boy, congratulations! I know your father would be proud to see you in the business again.

STEWART: Thanks, Uncle, I see a real opportunity here.

MARTIN: Well, I think you should remember a few things. Sure the family wants profits, but we're all doing well and there's a limit to what we all can spend. I'm already a member of two country clubs, a third would be ridiculous. I think the family is more concerned about stability than more money. They don't want anyone rocking the boat. Most of my generation are too close to those tough depression days to take many risks.

STEWART: I understand, but times have changed. A business is dead if it stands still. We must be aggressive or we'll be gobbled up by our expanding competitors. I'm not going to let them get the best of me.

MARTIN: Well, I'm an old man, but be careful.

For the next six months business continued as in the past, but then Stew began to have some troubles in marketing. Abe Grabner was spending more and more time in Miami, so Stew couldn't talk to him easily. The old customers still seemed to be reordering, but Abe wasn't getting any new customers at all. When Stew called him one night to complain, Abe quit the company right on the phone. Stew decided not to replace Abe but to undertake marketing himself. He began to call on competitors' customers and was successful in stealing some of them away by cutting his price. By the end of the year he had expanded gross sales, as indicated in the income statement for the first year in Exhibit 3.

As the second year of Stew's presidency progressed, Uncle Martin expressed concern that the firm's profit margin was dropping. Stewart responded that you had to spend money to make money and that he was going to initiate newspaper, magazine, and radio advertising to attract more customers.

Stew also sent a note to Herb Blacker ordering him to reduce manufacturing costs by 10 percent. When Herb asked how he was to do this, Stew exclaimed:

EXHIBIT 3

QUICK-CLIP PRINTING, INC.
Simplified Income Statement
For First Year under President Stewart Grabner

Net sales		$1,082,000
Expenses		
Purchases	$360,000	
Labor	346,000	
Selling	78,000	
Administration	158,000	
		942,000
Net profit before taxes		$ 140,000

EXHIBIT 4

MINELLI PRESS
Simplified Income Statement
For Last Year before Merger with Quick-Clip

Net sales		$224,000
Expenses		
Purchases	$98,000	
Labor	80,000	
Selling	4,000	
Administration	36,000	
		218,000
Net profit before taxes		$ 6,000

Must I do everything around here? Fire two warehouse workers tomorrow. Next week, I will have a plan to print standard forms that can be sold to anyone along with a rubber stamp for adding their own names. Or we could mimeo the names on the completed standard forms. This should simplify our product line and reduce costs. But really Herb, I think you should think of these things too.

Two weeks later, Frank Berkowitz learned from Herb Blacker about the policy. He was angry and ran to see Stew, but unfortunately the president was away on a sales trip and did not return for 10 days. When he came back, he called Frank into his office in great excitement and told him that he was negotiating a merger with a competitor, Minelli Press, and that he was going to put Frank in charge of the new area. Stew went on:

This is the first of several key mergers designed to promote growth. From the Minelli Press we will gain additional revenue, job shop printing know-how, production and managerial skill, and equipment. Minelli, the owner, has sort of run out of creative ideas, but you can add to that dimension. I can put Minelli in our production area as assistant printing manager, and he can help Herb Blacker in simplifying things there.

The acquired company, owned by Salvatore Minelli, was much smaller than Quick-Clip. It was more of a job shop printing concern, handling letters, stationery, wedding announcements, tickets, simple forms, and many miscellaneous items. The income statement for the company is summarized in Exhibit 4. Minelli Press consisted of Mr. Minelli, two press operators, a linotypist, and a clerk who helped Sal with customers. When asked why he had sold his firm, Sal joked that Quick-Clip was the first one to come up with $200,000. He added that he was tired and wanted to spend his remaining years just running the

presses. Besides, his linotype was very old and in need of replacement. He felt that Quick-Clip would have the money and energy to keep that place going.

At the end of the second year, Stew was disappointed at the income statement in Exhibit 5. Sales had expanded somewhat, but very little considering the substantial new business Stew had brought in. Production costs had continued to increase. At a meeting to discuss these results, the chief accountant, Henry Johnson, pointed out that the company had made some sizable equipment purchases.

STEWART: What purchases?

HENRY: A new rotary press for $18,000 and a new linotype for $40,000.

STEWART: My God, who ordered them?

HERB BLACKER: I bought the rotary press in order to improve our efficiency on these longer production runs on the new standard forms.

EXHIBIT 5

QUICK-CLIP PRINTING INC.
Simplified Income Statement
For Second Year under President Stewart Grabner

Net sales		$1,364,000
Expenses		
Purchases	$518,000	
Labor	438,000	
Selling	152,000	
Administration	198,000	
		1,306,000
Net profit before taxes		$ 58,000

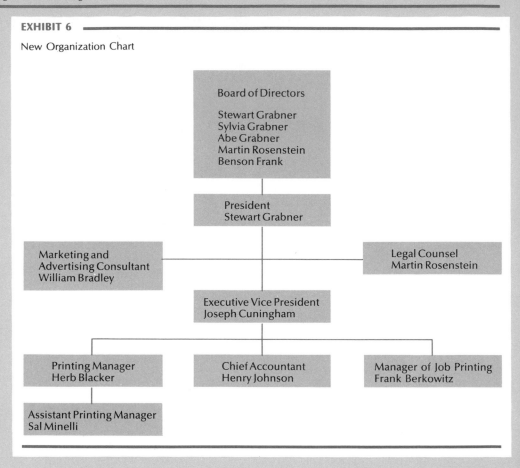

EXHIBIT 6

New Organization Chart

FRANK BERKOWITZ: And I needed a new linotype because the old one was shot, and it wouldn't handle the exciting new type faces we're using now.

Not long after, Martin Rosenberg visited his cousin Abe Grabner in Miami.

ABE GRABNER: Well, it looks like Stewart has got the business in a pretty mess. Several of my old customers have explained that they left Quick-Clip because the quality of the jobs declined and they couldn't get their jobs on time.

MARTIN: Yes, things haven't gone too well, but Stew feels he's laying a better groundwork for the future. His new standardized forms seem to be selling well and I think

they are less expensive to produce once you get geared up for them.

Last month, Stew hired an executive vice president named Joseph Cunningham, who had been marketing manager for one of the largest printing houses in the country. The appointment announcement was accompanied by the organizational chart in Exhibit 6. In private conversation, Stewart told his uncle:

STEWART: Hiring Joe should allow me to concentrate on expanding sales while he cracks down on the way the place is run. I've found I just can't trust most of the managers around here. They are too lax with the workers, unable or unwilling to control expenditures, and perhaps even a little lazy. I'm not going to let them ruin my chance to make this company into one of the most important printing firms in the country.

Questions on Quick-Clip Printing, Inc. (A)

1. What was the difference between Simon's and Stewart's basic organizational strategies?

2. What was the difference between their management philosophies?

3. What caused the firm's profit performance to decline?

4. How do you evaluate the merger with Minelli Press?

5. If he could start over again, what do you think Stewart should have done?

6. What do you recommend that Stewart do now?

Part Six

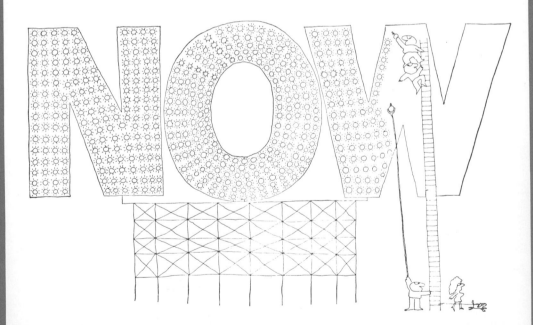

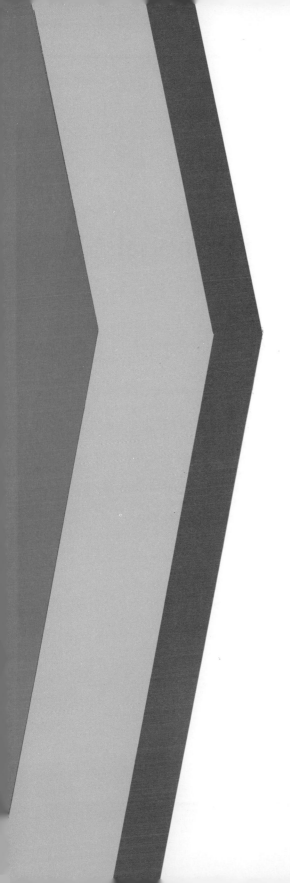

Structuring Organizational Systems

17

Basic Concepts of Organizational Structure

An apocryphal Washington story goes as follows. Democrats believe that if you hire good people, they will do a good job, no matter what kind of a confused organizational setup you put them into. Republicans, in contrast, believe that if you draw up a good organizational chart, you can hire second-rate tractor salespeople and still make things work. Of course, neither position is correct. Some great managers work well anywhere; some incompetent ones function nowhere; and the majority perform most effectively in a well-designed structure. It is difficult to attract anyone, no matter how talented or untalented, to a poorly defined position in an ambiguous structure.[1*] In this chapter we shall examine some fundamental concepts about organizational structure and some of the basic principles that have emerged from the classical writings on organization as guides for their design.

Evolving Organizational Forms

Organizations are characterized by persistent patterns in the work carried out by their members and in the means through which such work is coordinated. We can think of these patterns as constituting an organization's structure. At the most basic level, the building blocks of structure are *jobs,* as established by decisions regarding the division of labor, and *hierarchy,* as established by decisions regarding the interrelationships among jobs.[2]

Each organization has a unique configuration of these building blocks. However, with time and economic development, the general shape of organizations tends to change in certain ways.[3] Therefore, our thinking about structure can be guided usefully by a few typical forms that are sufficient to describe the overall shape of most organizations. We shall describe these characteristic forms.

Traditional Structure

Throughout most of history and even today in much of the world, the typical organization has been shaped like a small ball atop a large oval, as shown in Figure 17–1.[4] The ball represents a small owner-management group, which dominates the organization and reserves all important (and most unimportant) decisions to itself. There are few staff specialists or middle managers, as indicated by the thin line between management and the mass of employees. The workers are relatively unskilled people who do what the management tells them to do. No promotion ladder exists for these lower employees; most will remain at the same task all their lives, and that task may well be the same as their parents'.

Access to the small management group is essentially by being born into the owning family, marrying an owner's child, or perhaps being reared in the same social class and attending the same schools. Princes and dukes abound on the boards and management staffs of some European firms. Thus attaining management is mainly through heredity. Whether or not an executive possesses any managerial skills is irrelevant, and the traditional owners may not even know what such skills are.

FIGURE 17–1

Traditional Structure

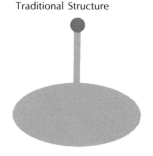

_____
* Notes and references will be found at the end of this chapter.

Ziggy

J.P. DOWD
AND
THE MESS HE
INHERITED

© 1983 Universal Press Syndicate

Because entry into management depends on birth, advancement depends mainly on death. That is, managerial performance is not systematically evaluated, and there is no promotion based on performance. A younger child is promoted when a father, uncle, or older sibling dies. Sometimes a firm may be sold or go bankrupt, but short of this, managers are seldom punished or rewarded for results.

Traditional organizations are run in the interests of the controlling group. With a family business, this means the firm's objectives are the family's objectives in the broadest sense. Profit is of course desired, but it is usually only one of several family goals, such as building and maintaining community status and political influence or providing security, educational, and recreational activities for family members.[5] The key to the ability of traditional organizations to provide these family desires is retention of family control. To this end, management may even reject expansion and profit opportunities because exploiting them would require borrowing from outsiders or hiring them to manage the more complex organization. Solvay and Company of Belgium is one of the largest chemical firms in the world; its sales figure is more than $2 billion per year. Yet, until the mid-1960s the company was run entirely by a committee of five or six Solvays.[6] Although management has now been more professionalized, the family still owns 60 percent of the stock.

Unlike Solvay a substantial proportion of family-dominated businesses seek stability and shun growth just to perpetuate the family's position. Such a no-growth policy tends to put the firm at a disadvantage in competing with more aggressive and larger, more modern organizations.

Because the objectives of the traditional organization reflect the decision-making processes of the family group, they tend to be subjective, not objective. That is, the goals are seldom quantified or explicitly defined in writing.[7] All decisions are filtered through the criteria of family or ruling interest. This is not to imply that all such businesses are heartless and cruel to their workers, although many have been. The horrors of the family mills and factories in the 19th-century Industrial Revolution outraged Karl Marx and various other revolutionists and reformers. Some traditional, family-dominated organizations serve as vehicles for improving the lot of those "less fortunate." In the spirit of noblesse oblige, paternalism, religious charity, and civic-mindedness, the family may provide housing, recreational facilities, medical care, or support to community projects. To be sure, the paternalism can be degrading because of the elite's attitude of superiority and assumption that their values should be imposed on employees (in some firms, one could be fired for not attending religious services or for being drunk in public). Still, many traditional organizations express a real sense of obligation toward employees and the community.

Rational Bureaucracy

In the industrialized nations, the small, traditional structures have evolved into the familiar pyramidal form that is most often associated with large, modern organizations, as Figure 17–2 suggests.[8] This structure developed from attempts to bring rationality and planning to organizational design.[9]

The salient difference between the traditional and the bureaucratic structures is in the middle levels. In all of the industrialized and industrializing nations, the number of managers and specialists for each 100 workers has been increasing (in the United States—from approximately 7 in 1900 to perhaps 25 in the 1980s). In just 30 years Swift and Company changed from a ratio of 500 executives for 50,000 workers to 2,150 executives for 75,000 workers.[10] Spans of control have contracted as more supervisors and specialists are added to plan, control, and maintain an increasingly complex set of relationships among more specialized, yet more interdependent, jobs. The shift toward greater specialization and interdependence comes from changes in technology and in the characteristics of the competitive marketplace.[11] Lower level positions are more defined and structured than in the traditional form. Graded levels of skill, responsibility, and reward are present, so that for even the lowest worker there is a possible ladder of succeedingly higher positions.[12] Most of the basic organizational principles discussed in this chapter were developed in rationally bureaucratic organizations.

The central aspect of this rationality is a belief that competence and performance should be the criteria for entry into the organization and promotion up the hierarchy.[13] Instead of birth and family, education and experience should determine who gets in and who goes up. In the ideal version, a young person could enter the firm at the bottom, work hard, perform well, and, with experience, be promoted up the pyramid—as in the Horatio Alger tales. It doesn't always happen like this, but it is the ideal.

In order to promote on the basis of performance, performance must be evaluated by comparing actual results and desired goals. Hence rational organizations must define their objectives more specifically than traditional organizations. These more

FIGURE 17–2

Rational Bureaucracy

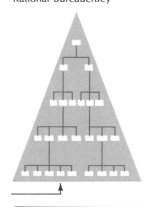

explicit objectives tend to be narrower and more impersonal than those in family firms. Since the owners of a large corporation are seldom involved in management to a significant extent, their interest is defined mainly as economic—dividends on their shares of stock or increases in the stock's value in the securities markets. Increasing the stockholders' prestige, power, or political influence cease to be goals of the rational firm. What the owners do with their dividend is of little concern to the professional managers.

The specificity and impersonality of objectives also extends to managers and executives. Their personal goals are expected to be subordinated to those of the organization. It is considered unethical to use one's position to promote one's own business interest at the expense of the firm. Indeed, even the appearance of conflicting interests is dangerous. Some years ago, a newly installed president of Chrysler Corporation was forced to resign merely because he owned an interest in a supplier. No evidence existed that he pushed orders his way, but in the rational organization one's personal position is expected to be subordinated to one's organizational role. In traditional organizations in many countries, however, a person simultaneously may be owner or executive in several firms buying and selling from each other. It is simply assumed that such a person will utilize organizational authority in his or her personal interest; no one distinguishes between organizational and personal positions. In rational bureaucracies, this is viewed as unethical.

Bureaucratic "Ideals"
- entry by credential
- promotion by merit
- clear objectives
- impersonality
- subordination of manager self-interest
- equal treatment of all outsiders

Impersonality and objectivity take another ethical form in rational organizations. Managers are expected to treat all employees, customers, and suppliers equally. A person's social status or personality should be irrelevant to treatment by the organization; managers should not play favorites; strangers and friends should have equal opportunity to obtain jobs or purchase products. Like promotions based solely on merit, this impersonality is seldom fully achieved, but merely espousing such a view is revolutionary in a world where insiders apply different rules to outsiders. The ability to be equally polite and honest with friends and strangers is historically rare, but such objectivity is achieved by modern organizations to a remarkable extent. This is especially important in a democratic nation whose citizens are assumed to be equal and in which first come, first served is the accepted norm for service.

To many people, the word *bureaucracy* has become an odious term connoting long delays, supercilious clerks, and infuriating red tape—such as college registration. These frustrations, however, reflect human problems and numbers, not necessarily organizational inadequacy. Working in large bureaucratic organizations where they are expected to treat all others equally may cause some employees to convert the impersonality of equality into the impersonality of insensitivity.[14] Eventually everyone may be treated equally badly, and no one may really care about anyone. Complaints about such treatment are certainly justified, but many complainers do not really want the equal and impersonal treatment that is the aim of bureaucracy. What they want is preferential treatment ahead of others. In spite of this, however, rational bureaucracy has made an enormous contribution to fairer and more efficient organizations.

In addition, such hierarchies promote less autocratic government than traditional structures do. Bureaucracy can strengthen the weak person and control the stronger

by limiting the authority of his or her position. Rational bureaucracies are actually less centralized than are traditional structures.[15]

Contemporary Bureaucracy

Most contemporary organizations have the general shape of a pyramid, but in today's business corporations the shape is actually a smaller pyramid atop a larger one, as indicated by Figure 17-3. The Horatio Alger myth was that a young person with no particular educational credentials could enter at the bottom and, through years of dilligent effort, work to the top on merit. This is seldom true anymore. A college degree and more are needed to gain entry to the bottom rung of the managerial ladder in the upper pyramid. The initial positions are mainly in the wings of the upper pyramid: staff professional and specialized positions in which young graduates are not managers in the sense of supervising anyone. Only as they establish and sell themselves do they move laterally or diagonally into the line management. Further movement up the hierarchy should depend on merit and performance.

A more detailed view of the large, contemporary organization suggests that the upper pyramid can be subdivided into four distinct clusters of jobs.[16] Figure 17-4 illustrates these clusters. At the top is the strategic apex. Here the key function is to assure that the organization has a clear and appropriate sense of direction or mission. Attention must also be given to ascertaining that the deployment of resources and the patterns of activity throughout the organization contribute to the achievement of key organizational goals.

Below the apex are three groups of middle-level managerial jobs: line managers, technical specialists, and support staffs. Line managers serve as the direct supervisors of the organization's operating units. Thus they provide the central link between top management and the operating core. Technical specialists undertake the investiga-

FIGURE 17–3

Contemporary Bureaucracy

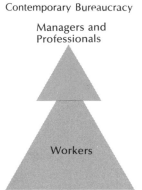

Managers and Professionals

Workers

tion and analysis that serve as the basis for defining jobs and setting standards for carrying out specific tasks and for measuring performance. The support staffs are charged with supplying the operating core and other managerial groups with smoothly running logistical support, from housekeeping functions to the operation and maintenance of highly specialized facilities and equipment, such as electronic data processing networks. Support staffs may manage such services directly, or they may establish norms for their use throughout the organization.

Classical Principles

A little book published approximately 30 years ago titled *The Golden Book of Management*[17] was not, as you might guess, a child's reader but a review of the lives and contributions of management pioneers and what they considered to be the essential principles of management and organization. At that time it was believed that the fundamental rules for structuring all organizations had been discovered. We now know that different kinds of organizations require different structures. Nonetheless, those rules are still extremely useful because they do apply to a large number of organizations—those that are relatively stable and produce standardized, unchanging products with relatively unskilled labor. The manufacture of automobiles, washing machines, television sets, and bottles only suggests the many relatively stable endeavors to which these organizational principles apply.

Nonetheless, don't be misled by the terms *principles* and *rules*. The ideas discussed in this chapter are suggestions or guidelines, not ironclad rules. Experience has shown that when they can be followed in repetitive, routinized, stable tasks, much managerial grief can be avoided. In the next chapter we shall discuss less stable organizations and tasks in which it is necessary or advisable to set aside these principles and adhere to newer and more dynamic guidelines.

Chain of Command

The chain-of-command principle is that all individuals from the bottom to the top should have a superior to whom they are accountable. From experience, military, governmental, religious, and economic organizations have discovered the value of an unbroken chain of command leading from the lowest level private, citizen, parishioner, or worker to the most elevated general, president, bishop, or executive.

The chain-of-command principle is illustrated in Figure 17–5. In this example, R might occupy a small office in Laramie, Wyoming. We can trace an unbroken chain of command to his direct superior, L, the regional manager in Salt Lake City, then to Vice President H in Chicago, and finally to Senior Vice President C and President A in New York. Everyone reports to someone else because everyone has a boss; even A reports to the board of directors. In short, everyone is accountable to someone. The certainty of being held to account should promote effort throughout the organization and discourage stealing, sleeping, goofing off, and other forms of dysfunctional behavior.

In practice, the chain of command takes on another meaning in hierarchical organizations. It is dangerous for anyone to violate the chain of command in his

FIGURE 17–5

Chain of Command in Organizational Pyramid

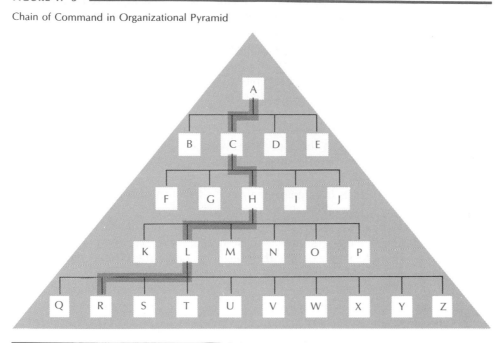

or her communications; L would probably be offended if R bypassed her and took a complaint directly to H. Similarly, a teacher might become angry if a student went directly to the school principal with a grievance, or the lieutenant would be peeved if a corporal bypassed him or her to speak with the colonel. Most superiors expect subordinates to communicate through them as a common courtesy, and subordinates violate this expectation at their peril.

The structural aspect of the chain-of-command principle is a good one. Most people like the clarity of knowing their positions on the organization chart. There are only a few situations that justify not holding people accountable to a superior (we shall discuss these in Part 7, which considers conflict resolution). Accountability is usually eminently desirable in every organization, but there is a problem when a subordinate must communicate with a higher level manager other than the immediate superior. R may have to speak with N and P or even J from time to time. For L to be offended every time R does this or to require him to communicate only through L would be inefficient. Subordinates should be able to initiate routine task communications with anyone appropriate to the task.

Unity of Command

No organizational principle is older than the rule that each person in the chain of command should have one and only one direct superior to whom he or she is accountable. Even the Bible suggests that no individual can serve two masters. R should not have to respond to instructions from both L and K. To require R to do so would place him in a potentially awkward situation. What would he do if both superiors ordered him to do two different things immediately? Who would have priority? Anyone who has experienced conflicting orders from parents (Mother: Clean up your room right now. Father: Put my tools away immediately) can appreciate the difficulties for a subordinate when unity of command is violated.

Nonetheless, this principle of command unity is widely violated, for several reasons. In a small family-owned business, middle-level personnel sometimes receive instructions from several members of the family, who are unable to establish clear-cut authority relationships at the top.[18] Two brothers who both believe that they have equal rights to tell a hired manager what to do can make life miserable in an owner-managed firm.

The problem also exists in larger organizations because of increasing knowledge specialization. When specialties develop and specialists are hired to direct them, top management may give them the right to control certain functions. For example, in Figure 17–6, which illustrates several positions in a small manufacturing company, supervisor A has a chain of command through his department head and the vice president of manufacturing to the president. He apparently enjoys unity of command. Yet the president may have granted authority to the engineering VP to determine how product X is to be manufactured, authority to the personnel VP to hire and fire people, and authority to the accounting VP to specify procedures for recording costs. The manufacturing VP has no right to order the department head and supervisor to ignore these other VPs. If the engineering VP tells the supervisor to make X using a certain machine, he must do so; if the personnel VP says he can hire only Ms. Jones and not Mr. Johannson, the supervisor must do so; and the supervisor

FIGURE 17–6

Command Unity

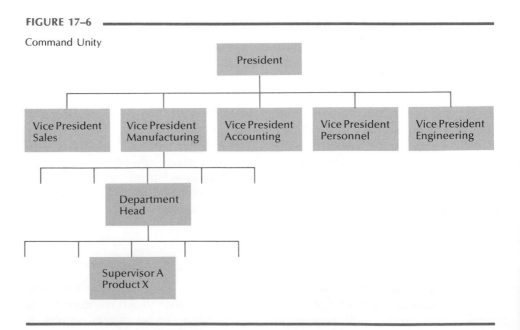

can't keep his records in pencil on looseleaf paper if the accounting VP prescribes ink on form 23b. Although these three vice presidents are not the direct supervisors of the department head and supervisors, they certainly influence them and may cause the subordinates to perceive themselves as receiving orders from multiple supervisors.

The solution to this problem is not eliminating all specialized executives. Rather, the manufacturing VP must represent his subordinates to the president and settle matters with the other vice presidents if his people receive contradictory or ineffective directives. The president should ensure that the activities of the specialized executives are complementary and not contradictory.

Span of Control

Span of control is a number that measures how many people report directly to a common superior. In Figure 17–7 A has a span of control of 2, B of 7, and C of 16.

The general principle is to assign managers the proper span of control. This once was thought to be approximately seven because it was considered to be the maximum number of people that a superior could keep track of effectively.[19] A smaller span of control would mean that the supervisor could oversee the people more closely, but this would require more managers and would be expensive. A much larger span of control would save a company a lot of money in managerial salaries, but it would run the risk that most employees would be operating without sufficient supervision, and managers might not know what was going on. The president of the United States has more than 100 people who supposedly report directly to him. History suggests that he does not know what White House personnel are doing because his span of control is too great.[20]

We can easily see that some spans of control are too small and others too large, but seven is not necessarily the optimal number. In a research laboratory that develops sophisticated products, a small span of control is desirable. In this way a manager can be freely available for extended discussion of design problems. In a mass-production, task-specialized factory, however, a manager can effectively direct more than 20 people if all are performing very similar work and their output can be easily measured (such as X number of widgets per hour).[21] One retail chain headquarters instituted a span of control of almost 100 for its regional vice presidents because it was easy for them to determine how well their store managers were performing

FIGURE 17–7

Span of Control

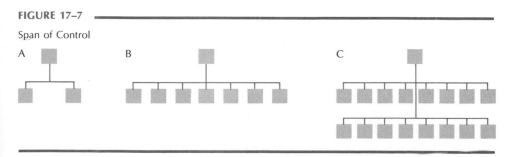

on the basis of monthly sales figures. Each vice president communicates only with the subordinates experiencing trouble; the others are left alone.

Thus managers should ask themselves whether or not the span of control is appropriate for the organization and the tasks they are supervising.[22] The guideline of seven might be less or more and still be correct. Some supervisors in mass-production plants successfully manage 40 to 50 subordinates; but engineering managers generally can handle only 5 to 10.[23] In general, the acceptable span of control *decreases* with: (1) less predictable work demands, (2) greater discretion allowed subordinates, (3) greater job responsibility—as measured by the length of time between a decision and its review or results—(4) less measurability of results, and (5) greater task interdependence among subordinates. Where subordinates work on simple, repetitive, programmed, and easily measured tasks, the span of control can be quite large.

Clarity of Delegation

Delegation probably originated with an overworked owner-manager who could not keep up with everything and hired someone to help. Without giving the new employee much authority or autonomy, the owner-manager did have her or him assume some of the owner-manager's activities. Much delegation in larger organizations shares this general theme: begrudging assignment of tasks that managers would prefer to do themselves if only they had the time. Yet all effort is not saved when managers delegate. They must still supervise, monitor, and correct subordinates, especially because initially the new employees are not as competent as is the manager.

Some supervisors think they can do the job faster without a subordinate; in the short run they are probably right. In the long run, however, delegation will enable the subordinates to develop competence and free superiors to devote time to other, longer range matters. That is, they will be freer if they have delegated responsibility clearly enough that subordinates know what to do and what is expected of them. A recurring problem is that harried superiors do not take the time to define what they expect, and inexperienced or fearful subordinates often do not ask the tough questions necessary to clarify what is expected. Both managers and subordinates should realize that there are several forms of delegation, and each group should know what form is intended between them. For example, when a superior (A) delegates to a subordinate (B), A should clarify what degree of initiative is expected of the subordinate. The superior may in effect be issuing any one of the following instructions:[24]

1. Look into this problem. Give me all the facts. I will decide what to do.
2. Let me know the alternatives available with the pros and cons of each. I will decide which to select.
3. Recommend a course of action for my approval.
4. Let me know what you intend to do. Delay action until I approve.
5. Let me know what you intend to do. Do it unless I say not to.
6. Take action. Let me know how it turns out.
7. Take action. Communicate with me only if your action is unsuccessful.
8. Take action. No further communication with me is necessary.

When delegating or accepting a delegated task, a manager should be clear about which of these patterns he or she is working with.[25] Clarity in initial instructions will save both time and embarrassment. After the pattern is defined, the superior should adhere to it consistently to the completion of the delegated task. Without such clarification and consistency, subordinates will tend toward patterns 1, 2, and 3 because they fear taking action for which they will be criticized.

President Dwight Eisenhower was said to prefer delegation styles 3 and 4. He wanted his White House assistants to supply him with a detailed proposal he could approve and implement merely with his signature. In contrast, President John Kennedy favored forms 1 and 2; he wanted to be involved in early discussions developing the facts and generating alternatives. President Harry Truman seemed to lean toward form 8—at least according to one high-level appointee, who maintained that when he once tried to report on his activities, Truman cut him short, "You're doing a good job. You'll hear from me when you're not. Now let's talk about the Civil War."[26]

Completeness of Delegation

Experience suggests that every activity necessary to achieve organizational goals must be assigned to someone. A manager may assign duties to himself or herself or to subordinates, but for every organizational activity there must be someone who is responsible. Even in operating a neighborhood lemonade stand, someone must get lemons, sugar, water, ice, cups, a table, and a sign, make and serve the lemonade, and take the customer's money. Ideally, the manager will make sure that every worker knows he or she is accountable for some activity and that every activity is assigned. In the ideal situation, if everyone performs his or her assigned task precisely and satisfactorily, the result will be the exact accomplishment of the organization's goals.

This is a valid, if optimistic, guideline if management can anticipate all activities necessary to achieve organizational goals. Such anticipation is most likely where the task is routine, standardized, and stable. In more complex, changing situations in which individuals must behave flexibly in order to contribute to goals, complete delegation is much more difficult. For example, when IBM is developing a new generation of electronic computers, the technical unknowns are so great that it is impossible to designate beforehand everything that will have to be accomplished. In such complex ventures, management should be more concerned that employees clearly understand organizational objectives than that they know precisely what duties have been delegated to them. Figure 17–8 illustrates this point.

FIGURE 17–8

Content of delegation

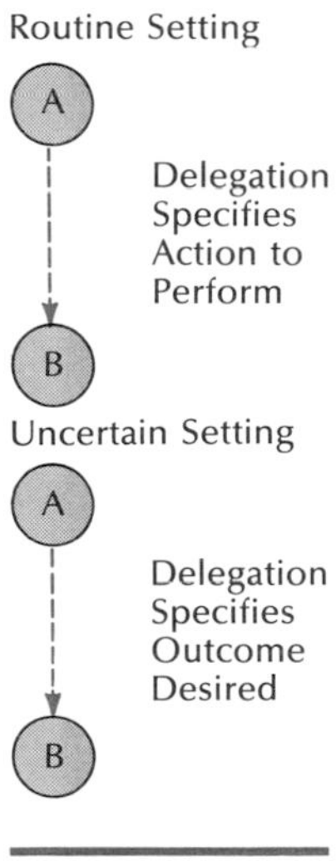

Routine Setting

A

Delegation Specifies Action to Perform

B

Uncertain Setting

A

Delegation Specifies Outcome Desired

B

Sufficiency of Delegation

One of the most hallowed of the traditional organizational principles is that authority should equal responsibility. Perhaps no other principle makes as much intuitive sense to the typical subordinate, who knows one should have authority sufficient to perform the task for which she or he is held accountable. If the boss has assigned responsibility for keeping the office clean, the worker must have authority to enter the office after working hours and to obtain the necessary cleaning supplies. Meeting this responsibility is impossible without the necessary authority. Likewise, a manager charged with increasing widget sales in Texas may be frustrated if given insufficient authority to change prices to compete, hire and discipline salespeople, pay sufficient wages and bonuses, and perhaps modify the product to customer demands.

Managers could find themselves without sufficient authority for one of four reasons: (1) It was never delegated to them; (2) it was offered, but they failed to accept it; (3) it is in the hands of specialized staff; or (4) a needed resource must be shared with another operating unit.

Lack of Delegation.   Many owners, executives, and managers complain how overworked they are but will not delegate enough to lighten their burdens. Fear deters them. The manager may be afraid that a subordinate will not be able to perform the activity as well as the manager can and therefore fears that his or her superior will be displeased with the results. Worse, an insecure manager may be afraid that a subordinate will do a better job, thus threatening the manager's security. More subtly, a manager may fear the ambiguity of not being continually on top of everything. Dependency on subordinates may create excessive anxiety for some managers who are averse to risk. This anxiety can be especially great when the superior finds it difficult to define precisely what subordinates are to do or cannot measure how well they are doing.

This fear is understandable, but a manager who cannot stand the anxiety of delegation is fleeing from the managerial role and ought to look for other work.

Failure to Accept.   Inadequate delegation is not always the superior's fault. Some subordinates resist delegation because they want to avoid anxiety, dislike their superiors, or simply do not want to be bothered.[27] Others may resist because they lack self-confidence or ability or because they are not ambitious enough to stand being criticized if things turn out badly. Finally, subordinates may not be offered sufficient incentive to accept more than the most narrow job task. If forced to do more, they may find it easier to ask the boss repeatedly for detailed instructions on each step. The superior may well conclude that attempting delegation on this task was not worth the effort.

Effects of Specialization.   Specialization, which undermines unity of command, also violates the principle of equality between authority and responsibility. Figure 17–9 illustrates the adverse effects of specialization that make the equality principle one of the most often undermined in management practice. A Texas regional manager, for example, might find that several home office specialists and managers make decisions that affect her ability to meet her sales responsibility: the engineering VP determines product design and resists modifications; the marketing VP sets prices and limits price negotiations; the personnel manager sets salary policy and specifies uniformity; the finance VP limits travel expenses. The Texas regional manager may feel so confined by her lack of authority that she considers it impossible to reach goals for which she is being held responsible.

Actual situations are seldom all this discouraging. Top managers create the higher

FIGURE 17–9

Specialization and Insufficient Delegation

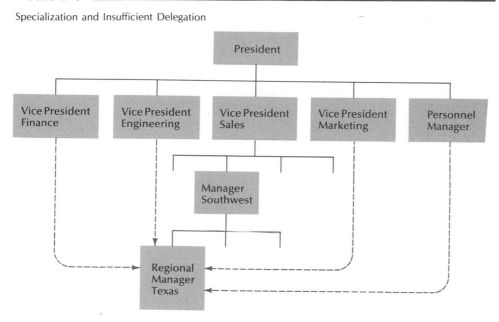

level specialist departments because they believe their people can contribute expertise to the organization. This expertise may so exceed the knowledge of lower managers that the specialists' policies contribute significantly to the total organization—even though they do frustrate some lower level personnel. Nonetheless, some larger firms attempt to preserve equality between responsibility and authority by giving lower level managers control over specialized activities that affect their units. For example, the Texas regional manager could be assigned an engineer, a marketing specialist, a personnel specialist, and an accountant—all reporting to her, as shown in Figure 17–10. Such assignment should facilitate rapid coordination and flexibility, improve the regional manager's motivation, and reduce opportunity for excuses. Unfortunately, applying this policy can be expensive because so many specialists must be employed.

Effects of Interdependence.   Often an operating unit under a given manager, A, must rely on inputs from a second unit under manager B, or it may supply parts or services to a third unit under manager C. For example, an automobile assembly plant may depend on the engine manufacturing plant and the dealer network. It may also happen that a manager's unit, X, and that of a fellow manager, Y, both depend on a third centralized unit, Z. For example, two product-line divisions may both use the services of one research and development laboratory. In such instances a manager's ability to achieve the goals for which he or she is responsible is affected by the performance of interdependent units. Some of the resources the manager needs are under the authority of other managers. The manager must develop

FIGURE 17–10

Specialization and Sufficient Delegation

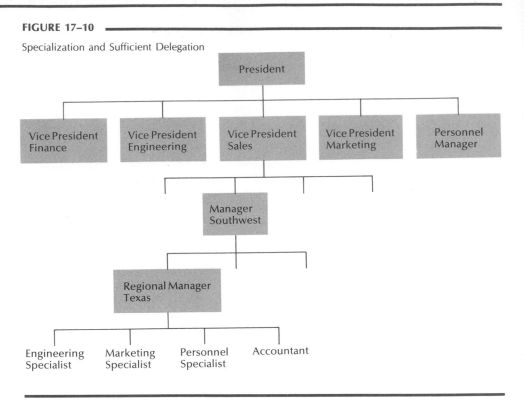

skills in communications, negotiation, and "horse trading" to overcome the imbalance between authority and responsibility.[28]

Nondelegatable Responsibility

The principle that a manager can delegate authority but not responsibility has taken on the mantle of moral law, but it is extremely difficult to follow rigorously. If A assigns certain activities and necessary authority to B, B may in turn delegate the duties and authority to C. However, if C then fails to perform the activities satisfactorily, A still holds B accountable and responsible. A would "hang" B, not C (although B may attempt to get at C). In short, B can delegate some authority and create responsibility in C, but B cannot delegate his responsibility or relieve himself of his accountability to A.

This was the essential guideline that the United States applied in the war crimes trials after World War II.[29] Prosecutors maintained that higher leaders were responsible for the atrocities committed by subordinates even if it could not be proved that they had ordered them. In the celebrated case of the Japanese General Yamashita, it was ruled that he should be executed because of actions of his troops toward American prisoners of war in the Philippines. He was held responsible for prisoner welfare and could not relieve himself of the responsibility, even though his defense

contended that it had been impossible for him to know what was going on in the field.

Such a rule seems correct and desirable, but it creates problems. A manager who really believes he or she will be punished for every subordinate mistake will delegate nothing and will forbid subordinates any autonomy for fear they will fail. Thus it may not be desirable or feasible to institute the centralization and close management control that would result from rigorous adherence to the rule forbidding delegation of responsibility.

Some years ago several managers in large electrical equipment companies were convicted of violating federal law by meeting with competitors to fix prices and territories.[30] In one company the department marketing manager was convicted because he personally participated in the meetings. The department manager and division vice president were convicted because they knew of the meetings. The product group vice president was convicted because the weight of evidence indicated that his behavior reflected knowledge of the illegal activities. The government prosecutor then went after the president, with the argument that he was ultimately responsible; but the judge ruled against this because the prosecution had no evidence that the president had known of the actions and it was considered unreasonable to expect the chief executive to know about everything in a large corporation. In short, if an organization becomes large enough, the top executives may be able to delegate responsibility and blame failure on subordinates.

Specialization

We live in an age of specialization: placekickers instead of triple threats, designated hitters instead of slugging pitchers, internists instead of general practitioners, right-fender fitters instead of automobile body crafters and quality control employees instead of general managers. Much of industrial society's great strides in productivity have come from specialization. For almost 200 years, managers have been advised to take advantage of specialization and specialize as much as possible.[31] Various kinds of specialization have resulted: task, functional, process, product, customer, and geographic.

Task Specialization. The early apostles of so-called scientific management in the 19th century criticized the managers of their day for not teaching workers exactly what to do.[32] The custom had been to allow supervisors and employees to decide how to perform each task. Advancing industrialization changed all this in various ways:

1. It brought large masses of people together to utilize a central power source (water and steam in the early days).
2. It delivered work to the workers in the plant so they could remain in one place as much as possible.
3. It specified exact hand movements on manual tasks.
4. It provided specialized single-use machines in place of the workers' general-purpose hand tools.
5. It allowed limited time for each step.

Thus discretion about task and control over work rhythms was removed from many blue-collar jobs.[33]

By specializing, the worker becomes more proficient in a narrower job and pays more attention to the task's minute elements. The proficiency and attention should improve efficiency. Industrial engineers and time and motion experts promote task specialization by studying relatively skilled jobs and simplifying them so they can be performed by employees with less skill and training. This means that management can pay lower wages and hire and train acceptable people more easily. The great contribution to manufacturing of Henry Ford and others was recognition of the economic advantage in mass production of standardized parts and products. Where volume is large enough, task specialization is economically desirable. In Chapter 4, however, we noted that task specialization can be excessive. People can become so bored by routine, narrow jobs that they quit or sabotage their equipment and machinery.[34] Short of this, however, task specialization appears economically desirable.

© Jefferson Communications, Inc., 1978. Distributed by the Chicago Tribune–New York News Syndicate, Inc.

Functional Specialization.   Functional specialization also aims to simplify complexity; few people can understand and be proficient in all aspects of medicine, law, business, or anything else. Knowledge in each of these areas has grown so dramatically that people need to concentrate on smaller parts they can master. Departments are instituted in organizations for the major knowledge specialists. A bicycle manufacturer, for example, might have various departments headed by functional vice presidents under the president (see Figure 17–11). Engineering designs the bikes; manufacturing makes them; finance obtains the necessary funds and pays the bills; industrial relations hires workers and negotiates with the union; and marketing sells the finished bikes.

Process Specialization.   Process specialization is task specialization extended to an entire department devoted to one phase of the production or service provided by the organization. In manufacturing bicycles, the Manufacturing Department might be organized as shown in Figure 17–12. The Shaping Department cuts and shapes steel tubing to form the frame and handle bars; the Stamping Department molds the sheet metal for fenders; the Painting Department paints; and the Assembly Department assembles the bicycle, which is then turned over to the Shipping Department.

FIGURE 17–11

Functional Specialization

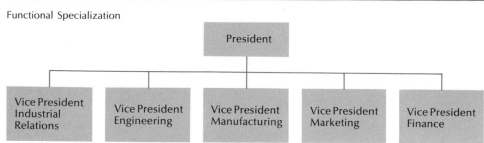

Product Specialization. If the bicycle were just one product of a larger recreational vehicle manufacturer, there would probably be no central manufacturing vice president but a series of product vice presidents. Each vice president would be responsible for design, purchasing, manufacturing, and selling of his or her product line. Ideally, each product vice president would have the greatest and most detailed knowledge of the nature of the products and customers, more than could be possessed by a single engineering or marketing VP.[35] This form is shown in Figure 17–13.

Customer Specialization. In certain cases the key component is not product or process as much as it is customer. The central organizational problem may be marketing to different kinds of purchasers. The special needs and procedures of such customers as governments, schools, wholesalers, and retailers may require the company to organize departments around them, as shown in Figure 17–14. Dealing with each requires different types of knowledge and a variety of business practices.

FIGURE 17–12

Process Specialization

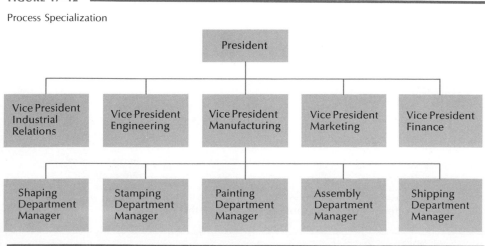

FIGURE 17–13

Product Specialization

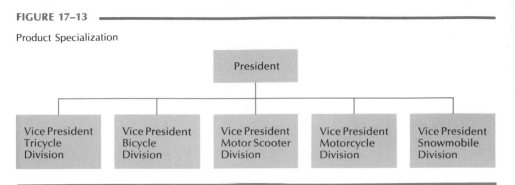

Geographic Specialization.   To deal with customers scattered over a large area in various states and nations, the firm may specialize on the basis of geography (Figure 17–15). Certain product design, pricing, and marketing decisions may be left to the discretion of the geographic region managers who are most knowledgeable about the specific conditions in their areas.

There are no reliable rules for what kind of specialization to use. Organizational design reflects management's experience and judgment about what works in each situation.[36] The vehicle manufacturer in the examples above would probably encom-

FIGURE 17–14

Customer Specialization

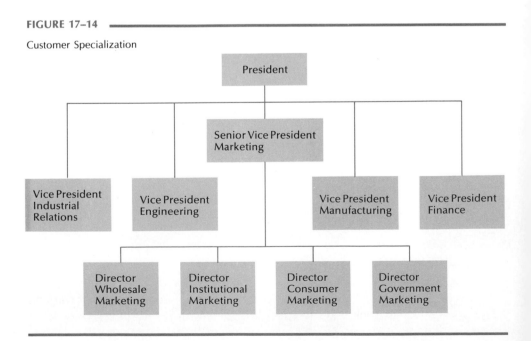

FIGURE 17-15

Geographic Specialization

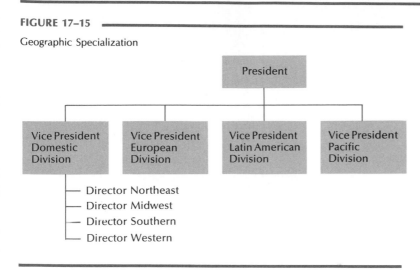

pass all forms of specialization at various levels. The partial organizational chart for such a firm would be as shown in Figure 17–16.

Managers and Specialization. On the managerial level, some people spend an entire career in a single area of knowledge specialization, such as industrial relations, but most do not. You will probably move from area to area, at least in the beginning of your career, but you will concentrate on one specialty at a time and spend several years on each. Only in this way can you find the time to master the unique aspects of a function, product, process, customer, or territory.

Specialization by managers and staff professionals is helpful for both the organization and the individual; it maximizes the expertise each individual has and can contribute to the realization of the goals of the organizations. Nonetheless, like blue-collar task specialization, knowledge specialization raises problems. A specialist may know more than anyone else in the company about one area, but this knowledge may be so concentrated that the specialist knows nothing about the rest of the organization and how her or his duties fit into it. As we shall discuss later in Part 7, specialists sometimes fight with one another because each thinks his or her area is the *most* important one in the organization.

Another potential pitfall is having a unique specialty that no other organization can use. An expert in hydrogen bomb firing devices can find only one employer, at best. If that organization does not need the expert (we hope) the specialty is worse than useless to the expert.

In short, specialization is a limited good. If the size and scope of the task warrants it, management must seek ways to specialize. However, it must always recognize the personal and organizational dangers of such an approach.

FIGURE 17–16

Various Forms of Specialization in a Single Organization

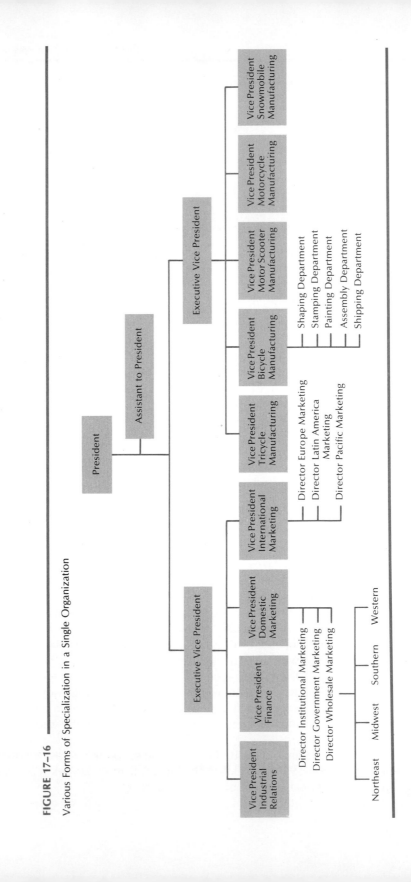

SUMMARY

Organizational structure evolves with economic development, expanding size, new technology, and increased management education. Big business in the industrializing nations moves from traditional structures to rational bureaucracies. The traditional owner-managed firm has all authority vested in a small management group reserved for the family. Objectives are seldom explicitly defined but reflect the family's interest in security, status, power, or wealth. Rational bureaucracy, however, endeavors clearly to define organizational objectives that transcend individual desires. Each of the larger number of managers and specialists is expected to subordinate personal goals to the organization and to avoid even the appearance of interest conflict. All insiders and outsiders are treated impersonally so that no customer, client, supplier, or employee is unfairly favored. Educational and managerial credentials replace birth as criteria for entry into management, and promotion up the pyramid is based on performance.

Most contemporary structures are mixtures of traditional and bureaucratic, like a small pyramid atop a larger one. A college education is virtually a prerequisite to enter the upper managerial and specialist structure, and most workers find it impossible to move from the lower to the upper areas. The pyramid may contain a strategic apex, a cluster of middle-level line managers, technical specialists, and support staffs.

Many years of management practice in relatively stable organizations have yielded some classical guidelines for organizational design. In putting together an organization's people and positions, these guidelines suggest the following:

1. A clear chain of command from the bottom to the top should be defined, promulgated, and adhered to.
2. Unity of command requires that each person be accountable to one and only one superior.
3. The span of control that defines the number of people reporting to a single manager should be appropriate for the task and people being supervised—neither too broad nor too narrow.
4. Delegation should be clear in the sense that both superior and subordinate understand what is to be done, what the subordinate is to report, and how his or her performance will be evaluated.
5. Delegation should be complete, without gaps, so that every activity necessary to achieve the organization's objectives is either performed by the superior or specifically assigned to subordinates.
6. Authority should equal responsibility so that each person possesses sufficient and appropriate authority to perform the activities for which he or she is held accountable—not too little or too much.
7. A manager may delegate activities and authority assigned by the superior, but such delegation does not relieve the manager of her or his own responsibility for how well the activity is performed.
8. Organizations and managers should take advantage of the forms of specialization appropriate for them: task, function, process, product, customer, geography, or knowledge.

These so-called principles are helpful when management designs or modifies an organization, but they are neither inclusive nor sufficient. They ignore the human dimensions: motivation, job satisfaction, knowledge differences, fears. In addition, they are difficult to follow in practice, even if management desires to do so. In fact, they are a little contradictory (for example, specialization tends to undermine chain and unity of command). In the next chapter we shall consider some of the newer guidelines for structuring organizations.

REVIEW QUESTIONS

1. What determines access to management in a traditional structure?

2. What are the objectives of a traditional organization?

3. Why is the bureaucratic form of organization termed *rational*?

4. What is the difference between a traditional structure and rational bureaucracy?

5. What determines access to management in the ideal rational bureaucracy?

6. How is the rational bureaucracy impersonal? Why might this be good? How might it be bad?

7. What is the significance of the pyramid atop a larger truncated pyramid in contemporary structure?

8. What determines entry into the upper pyramid in contemporary structure?

9. What is the principle of chain of command? What should characterize its construction? When can it be violated?

10. What is the principle of unity of command? Why is it desirable? Why is it sometimes violated?

11. What is the principle of span of control? When is a narrow span of control appropriate? When is a wide span of control appropriate?

12. Why do some managers hesitate to delegate?

13. How should a manager clarify his or her delegation?

14. What does completeness of delegation mean?

15. What does sufficiency of delegation mean?

16. Why do some subordinates fail to accept the authority delegated to them?

17. Why do some people believe they have greater responsibility than they have authority?

18. How can an organization strive to make authority equal to responsibility?

19. How is responsibility nondelegatable? Why is this principle not always followed?

20. What are the bases for specialization?

21. What is task specialization?

22. What is functional specialization?

23. What is process specialization?

24. What is product specialization?

25. What is customer specialization?

26. What is geographic specialization?

27. How might an organization utilize several forms of specialization?

Notes and References on Basic Concepts of Organizational Structure

1. Marvin Bower, *The Will to Management* (New York: McGraw-Hill, 1966).

2. Henry Mintzberg, *The Structuring of Organizations* (Englewood Cliffs, N.J.: Prentice-Hall, 1979).

3. H. Bogart, "Changing Views of Organization," *Technical Forecasting and Social Change* 5 (1973), pp. 163–77. Evolutionary theory maintains that organisms evolve on the basis of external competition; the fittest forms survive. E. Jantsch argues that organisms also evolve internally, but on the basis of cooperation, not competition; the most cooperative survive. "Organizing the Human World: An Evolutionary Outlook," *Futures* 6, no. 1 (1974), pp. 4–15. See also J. Hutchinson, "Evolving Organizational Forms," *Columbia Journal of World Business* Summer 1976, pp. 48–58.

4. C. J. McMillan et al., "The Structure of Work Organizations Across Societies," *Academy of Management Journal* 16, no. 4 (1973), pp. 555–68.

5. C. J. Haberstroh, "Organization Structure: Social and Technical Elements," *Industrial Management Review* 3 (1961), pp. 64–77.

6. "A Cottage on the Cap," *Fortune,* September 1977, p. 24.

7. McMillan et al., "Structure of Work Organizations." The authors show that U.S. firms are more formalized and utilize more paperwork. Traditional societies seem to have less formalized structures and greater centralization.

8. A multivariate statistical project indicates that size, dependence on other organizations, and technological complexity demonstrate the strongest relationship to structure; increase in these factors leads to bureaucratization and formality. D. S. Pugh et al., "The Context of Organization Structures," *Administrative Science Quarterly* 14, no. 1 (1969), pp. 91–114. Other studies on the impact of size include T. R. Anderson and W. Seymour, "Organizational Size and Functional Complexity," *American Sociological Review* 26, (1961), pp. 23–28; B. P. Indik, "The Relationship between Organizational Size and Supervision Ratio," *Administrative Science Quarterly* 9, no. 3 (1964), pp. 301–12; L. R. Pondy, "Effects of Size, Complexity, and Ownership on Administrative Intensity," *Administrative Science Quarterly* 14, no. 1 (1969), pp. 47–60; S. R. Katsky, "Relationship of Organizational Size to Complexity and Coordination," *Administrative Science Quarterly* 15, no. 4 (1970), pp. 428–38; and J. Child, "Predicting and Understanding Organization Structure," *Administrative Science Quarterly* 18 (1973), pp. 168–85.

9. The classic analysis of bureaucracy was by Max Weber. See *The Theory of Social and Economic Organization,* translated by A. M. Henderson and Talcott Parsons (New York: Free Press, 1947) and *From Max Weber,* ed. Hans H. Gerth and C. Wright Mills (Oxford: Oxford University Press, 1946). See also R. L. Merton, et al., ed., *Reader in Bureaucracy* (New York: Free Press, 1952). For a complete discussion of organizational rationality, see S. H. Udy, Jr., "Administrative Rationality, Social Setting, and Organizational Development," *American Journal of Sociology* 68 (1962), pp. 229–308. An extensive discussion of organizations and rationality is in William G. Scott and Terrence R. Mitchell, *Organization Theory: A Structural and Behavioral Analysis,* rev. ed. (Homewood, Ill.: Richard D. Irwin, 1972).

10. For discussion of the process of bureaucratization, see N. P. Mouzelis, *Organization and Bureaucracy* (Chicago: Aldine, 1967); Reinhard Bendix, *Work and Authority in Industry* (New York: John Wiley & Sons, 1956); John Child, "Parkinson's Progress: Accounting for the Number of Specialists in Organizations," *Administrative Science Quarterly* 18, no. 3 (1973), pp. 329–48. N. Toren, "Bureaucracy and Professionalism: A Reconsideration of Weber's Thesis," *Academy of Management Review,* July 1976, pp. 36–46; and L. G. Hrebiniak, "Size and Staff Professionalization," *Academy of Management Journal,* December 1976, pp. 662–69.

11. Michael Porter, *Competitive Strategies* (New York: Free Press, 1980).

12. There is much debate over whether bureaucracy is a single-dimensional concept or contains independent dimensions. For arguments that it is a single dimension, see John Child, "Organization Structure and Strategies of Control," *Administrative Science Quarterly* 17, no. 2 (1972), pp. 163–77. For arguments that decentralization, specialization, and formalization are independent, see B. C. Reimann, "On the Dimensions of Bureaucratic Structure," *Administrative Science Quarterly* 18, no. 4 (1973), pp. 462–76.

13. On the personnel differences between traditional and modern organizations, see R. N. Farmer, "The Revolutionary American Businessman," *California Management Review,* Summer 1967, p. 81 ff.; and O. Grusky, "Corporate Size, Bureaucratization, and Managerial Succession," *American Journal of Sociology* 67 (1961), pp. 261–69. For an example of family management passing to an outsider, see "Irving Shapiro Takes Charge of DuPont," *Fortune,* January 1974, p. 79 ff.

14. See V. A. Thompson, *Modern Organization* (New York: Alfred A. Knopf, 1961); R. K. Merton, "Bureaucratic Structure and Personality," in *Social Theory and Social Structure,* rev. ed. (New York: Free Press, 1957), and Michael Crozier, *The Bureaucratic Phenomenon* (Chicago: University of Chicago Press, 1964).

15. Child, "Organization Structure and Strategies of Control"; R. Mansfield, "Bureaucracy and Centralization: An Examination of Organizational Structure," *Administrative Science Quarterly* 18, no. 4 (1973), pp. 477–88.

16. Mintzberg, *The Structuring of Organizations.*

17. Lyndall F. Urwick, ed., *The Golden Book of Management: A Historical Record of the Life and Work of Seventy Pioneers* (London: N. Neame, 1946). The best early summaries of the classical principles are in Henri Fayol, *Industrial and General Administration* (Paris: Dunod, 1925); J. O. Mooney and A. C. Reiley, *Onward Industry* (New York: Harper & Row, 1931); Luther Gulich and Lyndall F. Urwick, eds., *Papers on the Science of Administration* (New York: Columbia University Press, 1937); and Lyndall F. Urwick, *The Theory of Organization* (New York: American Management Association, 1952). All of these principles are reexamined and tested in Alan C. Filley and Robert J. House, *Managerial Process and Organizational Behavior* (Glenview, Ill.: Scott, Foresman, 1969). Also see T. E. Stevenson, "The Longevity of Classical Theory," *Management International Review* 8 (1968), pp. 77–94.

18. Harry Levinson, "Conflicts That Plague Family Business," *Harvard Business Review,* March–April 1971, pp. 90–98.

19. Lyndall F. Urwick, "The Manager's Span of Control," *Harvard Business Review,* May–June 1956, pp. 39–47; G. A. Miller, "The Magical Number Seven, Plus or Minus Two: Some Limits on Our Capacity for Processing Information," *Psychological Review,* March 1956, pp. 39–47.

20. According to Arthur Schlesinger, President F. D. Roosevelt never had more than 11 White House assistants; Truman, 13; Eisenhower, 37; Kennedy, 23; Johnson, 20. President Nixon reportedly had 48. The Executive Office staff similarly grew from 1,175 in 1954 to 5,395 in 1971. *The Imperial Presidency* (Boston: Houghton Mifflin, 1973), pp. 221.

21. Research in industrial manufacturing indicates that group size is positively related to both productivity and leader-member relations for highly structured tasks. Thus a supervisor of a structured task is likely to have a better performing group and more cooperation if he or she is *unable* to pay close attention to each individual member. R. C. Cummins and D. C. King, "The Interaction of Group Size and Task Structure in an Industrial Organization," *Personnel Psychology* 26, no. 1 (1973), pp. 87–94.

22. W. W. Suojanen, "The Span of Control—Fact or Fable," *Advanced Management,* November 1955, pp. 5–13; G. D. Bell, "Determinants of Span of Control," *American Journal of Sociology* 73 (1967), pp. 90–101; Harold Stieglitz, "Optimizing Span of Control," *Management Record,* September 1962, pp. 25–29. A complete survey of span of control is in W. F. Whyte, *Organizational Behavior: Theory and Applications* (Homewood, Ill.: Richard D. Irwin, 1968).

23. Joan Woodward, *Industrial Organization: Theory and Practice* (Oxford: Oxford University Press, 1965). It has been suggested that the more experts in the organization, the more superior-subordinate communications there are, the smaller the span of control, and the greater the number of supervisors that are necessary. See M. W. Meyer, "Expertness and the Span of Control," *American Sociological Review* 33 (1968), pp. 434–40, and J. Brewer, "Flow of Communications, Expert Qualifications and Organizational Authority Structures," *American Sociological Review* 36 (1971), pp. 475–84. Meyer also suggests that it might go the opposite way: the more supervisory positions, the more experts needed; the more experts, the fewer the supervisory positions. "A Note on Expertness and the Supervisory Component in Organizations," *Human Organization* 32, no. 4 (1973), pp. 379–84.

24. Harvey Sherman, *It All Depends: A Pragmatic Approach to Organization* (Tuscaloosa: University of Alabama Press, 1966). Misunderstanding of a manager's authority appears to be widespread. In one research effort, approximately 50 percent of the time a first-line supervisor and the person's superior disagreed on the former's authority. There was either substantial overestimation or underestimation of the subordinate's authority, and the subordinate seldom demanded clarification. B. B. Boyd and J. M. Jensen, "Perceptions of the First-Line Supervisor's Authority," *Academy of Management Journal* 15, no. 3 (1972), pp. 331–42.

25. N. R. F. Maier, "The Subordinate's Role in the Delegation Process," *Personnel Psychology* 21, (1968), pp. 179–91.

26. The subordinate was J. J. McCloy, then Allied High Commissioner of West Germany.

27. Chester Barnard indicated that a person will accept delegated authority only when four conditions simultaneously apply. The person: (1) can and does understand, (2) believes, at the time of the decision that it is not inconsistent with the purpose of the organization, (3) believes it to be compatible with his/her personal interest as a whole, and (4) is mentally and physically able to comply with it. *The Functions of the Executive* (Cambridge, Mass.: Harvard University Press, 1938).

28. Richard F. Vancil, *Decentralization: Managerial Ambiguity by Design* (Homewood, Ill.: Dow Jones-Irwin, 1979).

29. See T. Taylor, *Nuremberg and Vietnam: An American Tragedy* (Chicago: Quadrangle Books, 1970), and A. F. Reel, *The Case of General Yamashita* (Chicago: University of Chicago Press, 1949).

30. C. C. Walton and F. W. Cleveland, Jr., *Corporations on Trial: The Electrical Cases* (Belmont, Calif.: Wadsworth, 1967).

31. One of the earliest and most famous descriptions of the advantages of task specialization is in Adam Smith, *The Wealth of Nations,* originally published in 1776. He describes how one person could make 20 ordinary pins per day, but 10 specialized workers made 48,000 per day.

32. Frederick W. Taylor, *The Principles of Scientific Management* (New York: Harper & Row, 1911); Frank B. Gilbreath, *Motion Study* (New York: Van Nostrand Reinhold, 1911). On Harrison Emerson and others, see Ernest Dale, *Management: Theory and Practice* (New York: McGraw-Hill, 1965). For a discussion of how management initially opposed scientific management, see Reinhard Bendix, *Work and Authority in Industry* (New York: John Wiley & Sons 1956).

33. A tragic comment on the permanent displacement of skilled labor by scientific management is provided by the Joint Committee on Atomic Energy hearings on the loss of the nuclear submarine *Thresher*. The lament is frequently heard that it is impossible to replace the old type of crafter who could labor to exact specifications, who took initiative to point out errors, and who could be trusted with complex work. As they die off, it is becoming impossible accurately to complete any complex piece of construction. In the case of the *Thresher,* this proved fatal to more than 100 men. The hearing revealed that in some industries the business is mainly carried on by 70-year-old crafters whom the owners fear to retire because they cannot be replaced. J. A. Merkle, "The Forgotten Revolution," (doctoral dissertation, Department of Political Science, University of California, Berkeley, 1973), p. 150.

34. For a thorough review of the impact of technology, see Charles R. Walker, *Modern Technology and Civilization* (New York: McGraw-Hill, 1962).

35. Functional organization seems to lead to better results in a situation in which stable performance of a routine task is desired, and product organization leads to better results where the task is less predictable and requires innovative problem solving. Functional organization makes coordination among the various units difficult; product organization eases such problems but reduces the identification of functional specialists with functional goals. A. Walker and J. W. Lorsch, "Organizational Choice: Product versus Function," in Jay W. Lorsch and Paul R. Lawrence, *Studies in Organization Design* (Homewood, Ill.: Richard D. Irwin, 1970).

36. E. A. Dale, *Planning and Developing the Company Organization Structure,* Research Report No. 20, (New York: American Management Association, 1959) and R. H. Hayes and R. W. Schemenner, "How Should You Organize Manufacturing?" *Harvard Business Review,* January–February 1978, pp. 105–18.

18

Advanced Guidelines for Organizational Design

The design of most organizations may not be entirely rational or perfect, but in a general way all are structured to suit their tasks, technology, and environments. For instance, the Catholic church or an automobile assembly plant tends to foster centralized decision making and stable hierarchical relationships. This can be contrasted with the decentralization and dynamism of a research laboratory or university. These differences exist because organizational principles are not absolutes; they are contingent on the task being performed, the technology being used, and the environment confronted.[1]* Under certain conditions, more effective organizations adhere to the traditional rules set forth in Chapter 17. With different conditions and organizations, these rules are less important than more recently developed guidelines. In this chapter we shall explore three additional approaches to defining structure upon which these guidelines rest. This will set the stage for the discussion of design contingencies in Chapter 19.

Extensions of the Concept of Organizational Structure

Today's manager can supplement the classical view of organizational structure, developed in the writings of the scientific management and administrative science traditions, by drawing from the social sciences and the decision sciences. We will look briefly at three such extensions of the concept of organizational structure: organizations as decision-making and information processing systems, organizations as social systems, and organizations as open systems.

Organizations as Decision-Making and Information Processing Systems

The persistent patterns of activities and relationships that constitute an organization's structure can be analyzed in terms of their contributions to key decision-making processes. As we argued in Part Five, organizational performance is the outcome of a multiplicity of interrelated decisions and the actions resulting therefrom. When these decisions form a harmonious, integrated whole consistent with the organization's strategic focus, we expect outstanding performance. When they are disjointed and unfocused, the firm will have difficulty holding its own in a competitive setting.

Effective decision making depends on two interrelated factors—access to pertinent information and the ability to exercise judgment and choice. By looking at how jobs are defined and how hierarchical relationships are established we can learn much about where information enters the system, how it flows within the system, and where, how, and by whom critical judgments and choices are made.

In organizations facing stable, predictable environments it is possible for tasks to be specified with precision and for needed coordination to be routinized. Few demands arise for resolving nonroutine dilemmas or cross-functional conflicts. Those that do come up can be handled easily within a traditional hierarchy. Operating decisions tend to be assigned to specialized operating units linked together by a

---

* Notes and references will be found at the end of this chapter.

Reprinted by permission: Tribune Company Syndicate, Inc.

chain of command. Information flows tend to be vertical, with task specification flowing downward and requests for coordination and conflict resolution flowing upward. This picture is very much in keeping with the traditional view of organizations set forth in Chapter 17.

When organizations face changing, unpredictable, and complex environments, however, it becomes difficult to predetermine the specific tasks to be carried out or how coordination among tasks is to be achieved. The demand for information processing increases as the environment must be monitored more frequently and as coordination becomes more problematical. Reliance on specialization and formal hierarchies tends to give way to an increased use of lateral communication for coordination among tasks. Vertical communications also increase, but their content changes. The critical dialogue is now around setting objectives and monitoring outcomes, rather than the specification of activities to be performed.[2]

Organizations as Social Systems

Organizations are clusters of people that work together.[3] This is a central theme of the first three parts of this book. From the thinking and writing of social-psychologists, we know much about the nature of social groups in the workplace.[4]

The Stable Work Group.   When a group of individuals is drawn together over a lengthy period of time in tasks that cause them to share the same physical space, to exchange material resources or information on a regular basis, and to become dependent on each other for task accomplishment, a stable work group is likely to be formed. In addition to task, information, and resource commonalities, the group's members will form shared beliefs, values, feelings, and norms about the important events surrounding them. A social hierarchy is likely to emerge as well with individuals occupying positions with varying degrees of status and influence.[5]

The resulting social system of the stable work group is often referred to as the informal organization. It conditions the ways in which its members respond to the formal organizational arrangements set up by higher levels of management and to instructions and information circulated through formal channels of communication. Inexperienced managers are often puzzled when behaviors within organizational units do not conform to the dictates of the formal system. Knowledge of the characteristics of the stable work group can frequently explain the anomalies.

External Reference Groups.   Members of organizations are simultaneously members of other social groupings, such as families, ethnic neighborhoods, religious communities, professions, trades, unions, fraternal organizations, and political parties. Their beliefs, values, and goal orientation are influenced in important ways by such external reference groups. For example, a physician is a member of the hospital staff but also sees herself as a member of the medical profession. Her judgment in providing treatment for a patient is often influenced more by the standards and practices accepted by the profession and propagated through training in medical schools than by administrative, financial, or other organizational aspects of the particular hospital within which she is practicing. Similar arguments can be made about other professions, such as accounting, law, and engineering. Thus the organization designer must recognize that activities and relationships in the organization may well reflect the structural influence of external groups as well as internal structural arrangements.

Corporate Culture.   There is growing evidence that members of a specific organization share a core of common interpretations of the social world around them. This view encompasses the values and meanings attached to certain symbols and behaviors, both within and outside the organization. We can think of this shared view of reality as a corporate culture with its own unique structure. In some organizations the shared view is pervasive, touching on many aspects of life and work, and serves as a strong common bond. In others it is more diffuse and may encompass only a small number of events. In any case, such common shared values will have a marked influence on how other dimensions of structure shape choices and actions of the organization's members.

Organizations as Open Systems

Contemporary models of organizations—whether based on information and decision theory, social psychology, or microeconomics—are best understood as open-system models. By this we mean systems whose internal patterns of behavior are influenced in significant ways by linkages to elements of the surrounding external environment. Earlier thinkers tended to view organizations as closed systems, whose internal patterns of behavior were self-contained. Exchanges with the external world were not seen as having an important influence.[6]

The open-systems perspective invites us to think of organizational structure as including the key linkages with the environment. Thus an enriched view of structure might include the following elements and the relationships among them:

Internal elements—the organization's members, its physical resources, formal administrative arrangements, internal communications and information processing networks, and the internal social system.

External elements—suppliers, competitors, and customers; pertinent dimensions of the national and world economies; the social system of the community; and the governmental and other external controls and regulations.

Figure 18–1 is a representation of these relationships.

FIGURE 18–1

The Elements of Organizational Structure

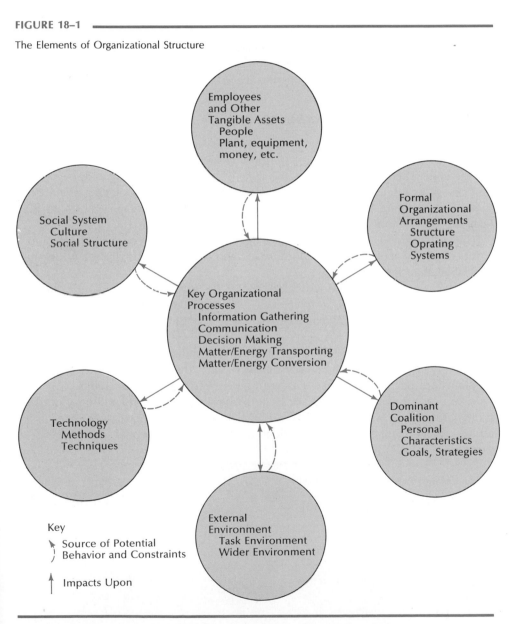

Source: John Kotter, *Organizational Dynamics* (Reading, Mass.: Addison-Wesley, 1978).

Design Guidelines

From these three diverse views of organization structure come some additional guidelines for the manager and the student concerned with the issue of organizational design. As with the classic principles set forth earlier, these should not be seen as ironclad rules. They are merely insights that seem to mesh with experience in innovative organizations that produce sophisticated knowledge or complex products.[7] These guidelines are not replacements of the earlier principles, rather they are extensions of them.

We shall examine several guidelines including: unity of authority and knowledge, tailoring line and staff authority, balancing centralization and decentralization, and maintaining organizational and status flexibility.

Unity of Authority and Knowledge

In the rational or hierarchical structure it has been assumed that good people enter at the bottom, and the best performers are promoted as they demonstrate competence. The key assumption in this view is that successively higher level managers possess greater competence and knowledge consistent with their greater authority to make decisions. Optimistically, it has been thought that equality between position level, formal authority, and personal knowledge would thus exist.

This assumption is no longer valid, if indeed it ever was. In complex organizations a superior may have several subordinates who are more knowledgeable in their specialties than he or she could be.[8]

In the example illustrated in Figure 18–2, the manager of emission control is charged with responsibility to develop a feasible pollution control device for the company's automobiles. He has four managers reporting to him. The department manager may be an expert in one area and be knowledgeable in another, but of the other two areas he knows relatively little. Although he retains the formal authority to make decisions, he does not personally possess the requisite knowledge. Such situations are occurring with increasing frequency in many organizations.

Wherever effective decisions are to be made, knowledge and authority must be brought together. One way to do this is by collective decision making. In the example above, all five managers in the emission control department could discuss the issue

FIGURE 18–2

A Manager with Specialized Subordinates

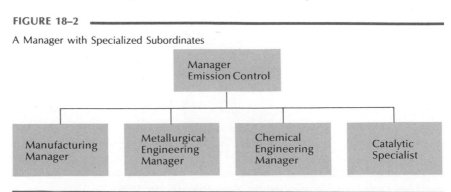

fully and attempt to reach a consensus. The department manager would act less as a hierarchical superior than as a group leader.

In the long run, the unification of authority and knowledge means better design of organizational communications. Information flow should be as much an object of conscious design as are the authority system and job descriptions.[9] It cannot be assumed that communications flow in accord with the formal organizational chart. Information is power, and the person who controls the critical communication links exercises influence far beyond that of others who might have higher formal status or authority. In traffic court, for example, the clerk possesses substantial power (and opportunity for graft) because he or she is the first person to receive both copies of the summons. If they are dropped in the wastebasket, the case is closed.

In designing an organization, attention must be paid to a series of questions: What information is needed to make what decisions? Who has it or can get it? Who is to communicate with whom? Who initiates? Who responds? As we shall see in Part 7, most prophecies about future structure foresee a central, powerful role for data processing and management information specialists.

Tailoring Line and Staff Authority

Most organizations contain two kinds of organizational units: line and staff. These terms come from the military; the line officers give direct battle orders, and staff officers are specialists and planners who advise.[10] The traditional rule is that staff should have no authority to make decisions, only to advise.[11] If advisors give orders on their own, it is believed, unity of command is destroyed and confusion results. However, a decision-making system view of structure suggests that we might need to tailor the roles of line and staff managers depending on the nature of the decision situation being faced. We can thus distinguish between kinds of staffs and the ways they operate.

Personal Staff.   The simplest kind of staff is formed when an overworked manager engages a secretary or assistant to help her with her work. On the organization chart, such assistants would appear as a box to the side of the chain of command (see Figure 18–3). Personal staff assistants have no status or authority independent of the executive. They are available to do whatever A wants them to: draw up complex documents or answer the phone. Before anything the assistant recommends can be implemented, it must be approved by A. To ease the burden, some line executives delegate authority to their assistants to sign their names so that lower personnel think a directive orginates with the executive when in fact it comes from the assistant. This practice can be dangerous, however, because the executive may inadvertently abdicate responsibilities to the personal staff.

Although a staff assistant B may possess no formal authority, he can still exercise substantial influence. If the department heads perceive that A trusts her assistant B and listens to him more than she does to the department heads, they may begin to court B in the hope that he will put in a good word for them with A. They may even go to B for instructions so that A is not bothered. Senator Charles Percy of Illinois began work at Bell & Howell as a young assistant to the president; he

FIGURE 18–3

Personal Staff

Vice President A

Assistant to Vice President

Department Managers

"Why complain now? You should have asked what 'Special assistant to the President' meant before you took the job."

quickly impressed the boss and others and learned the business so rapidly that he was elected president of the company at age 29. In most cases, however, young staff assistants are transferred to lower line executive positions after a year or two.

Advisory Staff.   Specialists are hired to work in staff units to take advantage of the contributions to organizational goals that specialization can make. (See Figure 18–4.) Initially, it is expected that these staff specialists will be consulted when line managers need advice, as in the interaction shown in Figure 18–4. In this flow of communications, the staff posses no authority and only gives advice. A production manager having trouble with equipment might call an engineering specialist; a manufacturing supervisor having continual discipline problems with a particular worker would call a personnel specialist, and so on.

Unfortunately, in spite of the fine degree they hang above their desks, newly hired staff specialists may find that they are not called upon for advice. Then they might be instructed by colleagues and staff superiors to "sell" themselves to line managers, as in the interaction illustrated in Figure 18–5. Such selling requires frequent, vigorous overtures to line management, a reverse of the behavior usually required of an advisor—salespeople initiate, advisors respond. Moreover, in order to have something to sell, a specialist must have greater familiarity with the line's

FIGURE 18–4

Advisory Staff

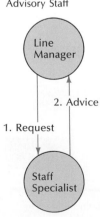

problems and possibilities than he or she would derive from passively waiting to be called. In order to engage in such selling, staff must have a little authority— that of right of entry to line departments. Such a right cannot be assumed because some line managers forbid staff from entering if they can. A higher line executive may have to order line management to allow staff entry. To preserve the separation of line authority and staff advice, however, line management would have to remain free to reject staff's proposals.

Top management may soon discover that hiring specialists, providing them with luxurious offices, and giving them right of entry into line departments does not guarantee that they will be consulted or heeded.[12] To make sure that staff expertise is being utilized, management may then delegate additional authority to staff. (See Figure 18–6.) The staff can be strengthened by movement along a continuum of staff influence beyond availability and entry rights to compulsory consultation, concurrent authority, and functional authority.

Compulsory Consultation.   To ensure that line consults staff on specific matters, top management may refuse to discuss lower line proposals unless staff has first been consulted. In the example illustrated in Figure 18–7, vice president B may refuse to discuss department head C's request to replace manufacturing equipment until C has consulted with staff specialist E in the Engineering Division. President A insists on this to ensure that the engineering specialists have an opportunity to influence manufacturing methods.

Concurrent Authority.   Wanting to give staff a little more influence, top management may require staff approval or concurrence on all line decisions. In effect, this gives a staff specialist veto power over a line manager if the specialist disagrees with the manager's proposal. Figure 18–8 illustrates how president A may require that manufacturing obtain the concurrence of the Industrial Engineering Department before scheduling overtime. Thus department head D will have to request that specialist F sign the overtime schedule, and this will serve as a check against poor planning and excessive overtime expense.

Such checks through concurrent authority are common in government, where it is desirable to keep many interdependent persons informed of what others are doing. It can prevent mistakes by ensuring that every relevant specialist has an opportunity to block potential disasters. Unfortunately, in blocking mistakes a system of multiple concurrences can lead to overconservatism and rejection of promising innovation. Multiplying the number of people who can say no probably has the effect of reducing both errors and creative breakthroughs.

Functional Authority.   Management can go so far in its support of staff that the distinction between line and staff is dissolved.[13] Each functional unit is assigned authority to initiate, veto, and control policies and procedures in its area of expertise. Thus in Figure 18–9 the personnel vice president may be responsible for all employment and training; the engineering VP for all product design; the director of industrial engineering for setting all production methods and incentive standards; and the finan-

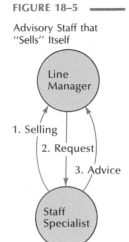

FIGURE 18–5

Advisory Staff that "Sells" Itself

Line Manager

1. Selling
2. Request
3. Advice

Staff Specialist

FIGURE 18–6

Staff "Authority"

Increasing Staff Influence

• Functional Authority

• Concurrent Authority

• Compulsory Consultation

• Right of Entry

• Availability

FIGURE 18–7

Compulsory Consultation Staff

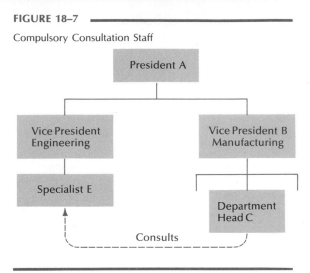

cial VP for all cost control and accounting procedures. Each is supreme in an area as long as top management supports and validates the VP's decisions.

Functional authority ideally ensures that persons with expertise have authority in their areas, independent of anachronistic boundaries between staff and line. Nonetheless, there are some problems.[14] As we saw in the preceeding chapter, widespread functional authority undermines the principle of unity of command—especially for line managers at lower and middle levels. So many functional authorities can influence line activities that a manager receives contradictory directives from different special-

FIGURE 18–8

Concurrent Authority Staff

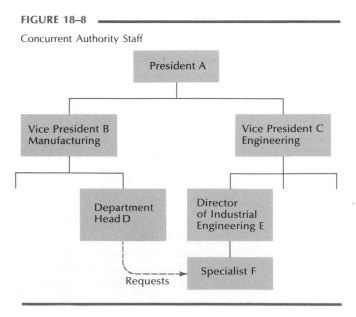

FIGURE 18–9

Functional Authority Staff

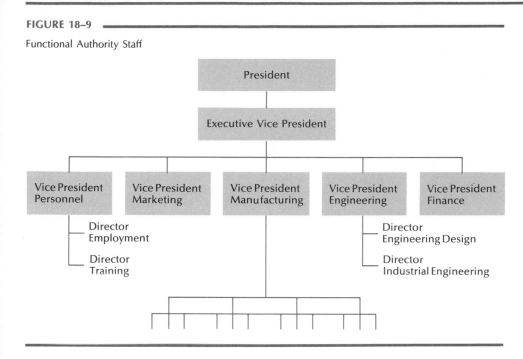

ists. And each function tends to see its responsibility as most important, when in fact they are all equally important and dependent on one another. Coordination of these different functions is the responsibility of top management, but it is a difficult task.

No single location along the continuum of staff influence is ideal. It is a practical issue, not a theoretical dispute. Management must balance the desire for high-level expertise and standardized plans against the advantages of lower level control, especially when pertinent knowledge and information is located at lower levels.

Balancing Centralization and Decentralization

Centralization is not like a disease you either have or do not have. The range from centralization to decentralization is a continuum, not an either/or dichotomy. We cannot say that one firm is centralized and another is decentralized. We can only state that company A is relatively centralized in some functions and relatively decentralized in others.

Theoretically, a perfectly centralized organization would have one authoritative person at the top who would be all-knowing and perfectly wise. Therefore that person could make all the important decisions. The resulting organizational performance would be exactly the same as with a completely decentralized organization in which each lowest level manager is perfectly knowledgeable and wise about his or her area of responsibility. Thus there is no theoretical advantage to either centralization or decentralization; it depends on those deceptively simple terms

FIGURE 18–10

Centralized Functional Staff

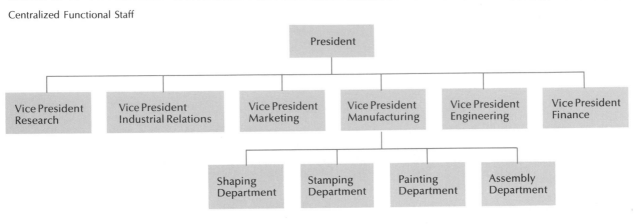

knowledgeable and wise.[15] In fact, perfect centralization and perfect decentralization are both impossible, and every organization must adjust to an intermediate system.

The relative centralization of a company is suggested by the location of its functional staff. If they are attached high in the structure and report directly to the top, above product or operating line managers, the firm is probably quite centralized (Figure 18–10).

In contrast, if staff and functional specialists are located lower down in the chain

FIGURE 18–11

Decentralized Functional Staff

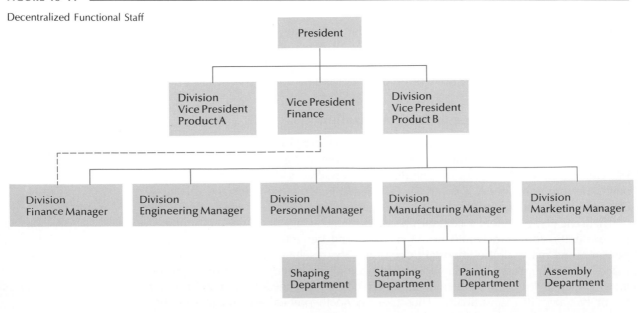

of command, below product managers, the organization is probably relatively decentralized (Figure 18–11).[16] The product or operating line manager controls the physical and human resources necessary to design, manufacture, and sell the product. The manager's responsibility is especially clear if he or she is held accountable for profits generated by the division. Of course, a product manager is not entirely autonomous, and the firm is not completely decentralized. The vice president of product B may not spend whatever she wants; she must clear large expenditures with the president. To see that she does, the division finance manager has a dual reporting relationship to the division VP and to the corporate finance VP, who can thus keep tabs on what is going on in the various "decentralized profit centers" that are the product divisions.

The balance between centralization and decentralization is seldom permanent. As conditions change the firm moves in one direction, then in another.[17] In general, when business declines, competition increases, and profits lessen, organizations tend to centralize. When a market is expanding and a business is seeking energetic exploitation, decentralization tends to increase. Excessive decentralization, however, can lead to conflicts among executives within a company. In competing with outsiders, profit centers may compete with each other to the detriment of the total organization. Thus the Mustang people at Ford Motor Company were not happy when the Lincoln-Mercury Division took business away with the Cougar (as well as luring away several outstanding executives).[18]

The tension between centralization and decentralization is reflected in the arguments that have been advanced for both. A summary of these arguments is as follows:[19]

Arguments for Centralization

1. Brilliant, energetic, and knowledgeable people are rare. Therefore, it is appropriate to concentrate authority in them.

2. Whether small or large, organizations require coordination and integration of their various activities. This is best accomplished by a centralized authority who can see overall needs.

3. In a fairly sizable and diversified organization, different functional and operating managers will come to think differently and to focus on their own units, perhaps exaggerating their importance to the whole. From time to time, overall organizational interest will require unpopular decisions that most personnel will disagree with. Only a centralized management can make such decisions.

4. Confidentiality of strategic plans and tactical decisions can be better maintained if restricted to a small group at the top.

Arguments for Decentralization

1. As an organization becomes larger and more complex, top management only deludes itself if it thinks that it can maintain central control. This is a physical impossibility. Since deteriorating central control is inevitable, delegation should be conducted logically through decentralization.

2. Decentralization lodges authority in the managers most knowledgeable about the specific details of their products, customers, and market conditions. Hence their policies and procedures will be more appropriate than those set by centralized authorities.

3. Decentralization will create organizational units small enough for managers to fully understand and identify with. If a manager is given sufficient authority, the organization can benefit from the same kind of commitment and motivation as that of the owner-manager.

4. Pushing decision-making authority down the organization will provide more people with an opportunity to participate. General motivation and job satisfaction will be greater and management development more effective.

These are all plausible arguments, but no one of them is always true or always false. The degree of centralization depends on the particular organization, its situation, and its managerial capacities. Each must work out a location along the centralization/decentralization continuum that best suits its needs. Seeking answers to the following questions may help determine the extent to which centralization or decentralization will be effective:

1. Who knows the facts on which the decisions will be based?
2. Who can get the information most readily?
3. Who has the ability and knowledge to make sound decisions?
4. Must speedy decisions be made to meet local conditions?
5. Must local decisions be carefully coordinated with other activities, or are local units fairly independent?
6. How busy are top-level executives? Who has the time to plan versus making operating decisions?
7. Will initiative and morale be improved by decentralization? Will this help the organization?[20]

The central criteria in the centralization/decentralization decision are ease and cost of communications, access to necessary information, and necessity of rapid response. If an organization can obtain information easily and transmit it quickly, it can centralize more and take advantage of specialized or more experienced personnel at headquarters. If not, it will be more likely to decentralize. However, decentralization can be achieved only when higher executives realize that authority genuinely delegated to lower echelons cannot also be retained by them. Second-guessing and overly detailed review of subordinates will create confusion that hinders the growth of self-reliant individuals. In return for this delegation, of course, subordinate managers must truly accept and exercise decentralized authority.

In practice the centralization/decentralization dichotomy becomes an unresolvable conondrum. There is a need to delegate authority and responsibility to match the dispersal of knowledge, information, and resources throughout the organization; but there is also a need to maintain cohesion and strategic focus in the overall pattern of decisions and actions. Hence senior managers tend to use multiple design devices, including formal structural arrangements, performance measurement systems, promotion, reward and sanction systems, ad hoc devices (such as temporary committees and field visits), and the creation of specific symbols, images, and shared expectations to bring about simultaneously the dispersal of decision-making authority and a set of forces that bound and constrain the areas of discretion for the exercise of that authority.[21]

Organizational and Status Flexibility

Although it is generally recognized that organizations should maintain sufficient structural and status flexibility, history and human nature tend in a different direction. Pyramid-shaped organizations demonstrate similarly shaped status systems: the higher a person is, the more rewards and status symbols that person receives. To some extent this makes sense as a means of differentiating between positions and providing incentives. Nonetheless, it can be overdone to the extent that pyramidal organizations come to emulate the Egyptian pyramids as tombs for the dead.

Flexible Rewards.   Closely associated with the traditional hierarchical assumption of unity between authority and knowledge has been a further assumption that position level equals contribution, and contribution equals rewards. That is, the higher individuals are in the organization, the more authority they have, the greater knowledge they possess, the more they contribute, and the more they should be rewarded. There are few organizations today in which there is no direct correlation between position level and rewards.

Authority and Salary Increase with Level in Most Organizations

This assumption is not always valid, however. Today contribution to an organization may reflect a person's specific knowledge, not title or level. A junior faculty member joining the faculty of a state university may not understand why a 61-year-old professor receives $2,000 for teaching an evening course and a 31-year old assistant professor receives only $1,400 for teaching another section of the same course—especially since the younger scholar has just published two innovative research papers and the older one has produced nothing for years. Deans and presidents may maintain that greater experience leads to better performance or that seniority should be rewarded to encourage loyalty. These are plausible arguments, but such policies can lead to a contradiction between current contribution and reward. The future of some automobile company may rest less on any vice president than on an obscure engineer or scientist working to tame the polution evils of the internal combustion engine.

Unfortunately, few organizations have sufficient wage, salary, and bonus flexibility to reward contributions independent of organizational level. In some, a person must be promoted to receive more money and status. Nonetheless, some companies have instituted two other practices to give flexible rewards to nonmanagerial people: (1) dual ladders and (2) flexible bonuses. In some science-based companies, management has created two promotion ladders—one managerial, the other professional.[22] For example:

Managerial Ladder	Professional Ladder	
Research manager	Research fellow	Money and status increase equally as one moves up either ladder.
Department manager	Senior researcher	
Group supervisor	Research associate	Research fellows and senior researchers might report to a team leader making
Team leader	Research assistant	less salary than they are.

This system was introduced to keep effective researchers in research rather than having them become ineffective managers just to make more money. Unfortunately, it does not always work because some professional ladders stop too soon, or higher professional titles are given only to managers, or the professionals feel frustrated because the titles are in lieu of any real power to affect decisions.

Many firms tie bonuses strictly to managerial positions or past income. For example, a vice president might be paid $5,000 for meeting her budget and a department head awarded $2,000 for meeting his. Or a person earning a salary of $30,000 would be awarded a bonus of 10 percent, and so would a subordinate earning $15,000. Such systems do not really recognize contribution. A more flexible reward system would evaluate each person's unique contribution and reward him or her on the basis of contribution to the firm for that year. A $20,000-per-year department head who successfully introduced a new product might earn a bonus of $10,000 for the year, and a vice president with no special accomplishment might be awarded only $2,000. This kind of flexibility can only be promoted by a chief executive or a high-level bonus committee that can analyze individual performance and reach individual decisions.

Flexible Structures.   Hierarchical structures borrow too much from ancient kings. Lavishly decorated offices and executive perquisites may in fact interfere with task performance. There are production supervisors who will not consult their department heads because they feel uncomfortable in their posh offices. Some critics suggest that reserved parking spaces and exclusive lunchrooms for executives are obsolete; executives should be at work earlier than others, anyway, and they should eat with the rank and file to find out what's really going on.[23] Some companies have even emulated the Chinese practice of requiring high-level executives periodically to spend a day at low-level operating jobs to keep them both knowledgeable and humble.

Of greater concern, some organizational units outlive their usefulness yet remain in existence only to consume resources and block initiatives.[24] Especially when staffed with less mobile members receiving fewer promotions, they will fight for survival and become very articulate in justifying their existence long after their original mission has evaporated. Whatever departments are born seem to become immortal—or at least to live on until the whole organization fails.

There is more rigidity in traditional hierarchical organizations because promotions tend to be one way. Except in relatively rare instances of massive personal failure, managers are not demoted. When appointed to particular positions, managers tend to see the position as their own. If the managers subsequently find themselves working for a former subordinate, they are likely to perceive themselves as experiencing relative demotion. This inflexibility hinders the bringing together of authority and knowledge.[25]

Temporary Structures.   The temporary structure is one way of promoting and maintaining organizational flexibility. Through independent, limited-life project, product, problem, or venture teams, specialists necessary to accomplish a mission are brought together for as long as necessary, but no longer.[26] For example, Figure 18–12 illustrates another way of handling the pollution-control activities illustrated earlier in Figure 18–2. There is a project team that consists of the same people, but the assignment is temporary. This structure is based more on a presumption of

FIGURE 18–12

Project Team

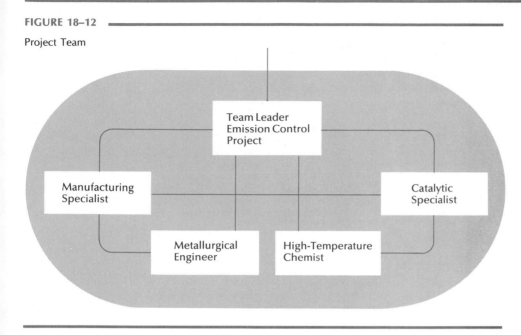

basic equality among the team members than is the formal organizational hierarchy. Given the temporary nature of the arrangement, group leaders should perceive their positions as related to the task and not to higher status. Their offices are likely to have few or no status distinctions from those of team members.

When a project is completed or specific problems have been solved, the temporary team is dissolved and members reassigned. On the next team, relationships may be different. Perhaps it will be a project in which metallurgical knowledge is central, so that the metallurgical engineer will be appointed group leader and the former pollution project leader may be just a team member. Neither person should perceive this as a promotion or demotion but as evidence of organizational flexibility, which makes it possible to bring knowledge and authority together.

The matrix structure illustrated in Figure 18–13 is a way of promoting status flexibility and temporary organizations.[27] The most common matrix structures appear in technical organizations in which many specialists, such as scientists and engineers are employed to work on sophisticated projects or programs. The specialists are assigned to functional departments until they are needed on projects. The staff is attached to the project on a full-time or part-time basis. Three situations can be distinguished here:

Situation 1. The project manager instructs the various department heads to produce a certain result. Each department head acts as a subcontractor, responsible for delivery of the result on time and at the right cost and quality. This situation gives a clear relationship between the project manager and the department heads. The staff performing the work does not have to cope with the project manager because their responsibilities remain with their usual managers.

FIGURE 18–13 ━━━━━━━━━━━

Matrix Structure

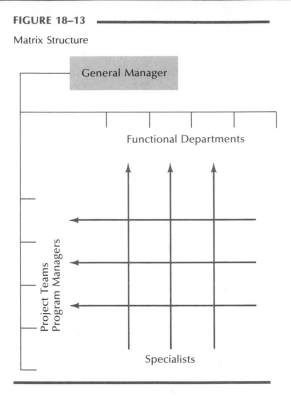

Situation 2.   The project manager leads the staff that contributes to the project and determines the sort of activities required and their timing. The department head is responsible for choosing the right personnel and for instructing them regarding the performance of the work. She or he is also responsible for the quality, quantity, and costs of the contribution they make. In this situation the relationship between the project manager and the department head is clear.

Situation 3.   The project manager is furnished with personnel and equipment from various departments. The product manager is responsible not only for the results in the various departments, but also for giving orders and for the amount, quality, and costs of the contributions.

Figure 18–14 illustrates the organization of a nuclear engineering firm, which in part demonstrates the matrix system. Across the top are the permanent functional departments into which specialists are hired, and down the left side are three projects currently being pursued. The development of a nuclear-powered rocket is the largest project, so it is composed of a person from each of the functional departments and the production manager. The other two projects are somewhat smaller: (1) the development of more effective shielding for a nuclear reactor and (2) preliminary investigation on the use of nuclear explosives for large excavations, canals, for example. These teams draw on only the most appropriate functional specialists. For the duration of the project, the individual team members are under the direction of the project manager. However, their permanent corporate homes remain in the

FIGURE 18–14

Matrix Structure for Nuclear Engineering Company

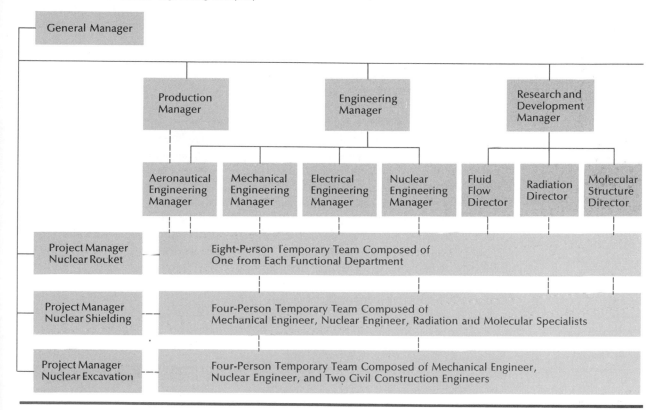

functional departments, which continue to handle such routine administrative tasks as keeping personnel files, maintaining office space, and supervising employee fringe benefit programs.

As vehicles for uniting knowledge and authority, status flexibility and temporary teams can promote more open communication about the task between all relevant parties. Such all-channel networks make it possible for each person to feel free to ignore the chain of command on task matters and communicate directly with the appropriate people. Matrix organizations aim to promote coordination among various functional specialists.[28]

This concept of temporary structure can be extended to quite traditional organizations by setting the time limits on the existence of all departments. No department is permanent; for it to continue past a certain time period would require a conscious, higher level decision. For example, some academic institutions are promoting flexibility by limiting the time in office for deans and presidents to 7 to 10 years and making all departments temporary ones required to expire in 3 to 5 years unless continuation is justified. Such rules force the organization to examine whether or not current officials should be maintained in office and whether established specialized departments have any relevance to today's organizational goals.

Problems of Flexible and Temporary Structures. The implementation of status flexibility and temporary structures is not without problems.[29] We are accustomed to the clarity and definiteness of hierarchical organizations. Most of us enjoy status distinctions and are jealous of our prerogatives, so that matrix forms of organization and temporary teams seem vague and threatening.

Aerospace and electronics firms, which pioneered in these structural approaches, have met with resistance for several reasons. First, some people feel lost without a permanent department with which they can identify. The organization or corporation is too large to provide any sense of affiliation, and the immediate group is too transient. Second, security for some people is threatened when it appears that the organization's only commitment to them is a temporary project. They fear that the completion of the project will mean the end of their jobs, and experience with government contracts suggests that this may indeed be the case. Understandably, such a possibility can encourage project slowdowns. Even in a successful and secure organization, there can be insecurity when engineers are not reassigned quickly enough. When delays of one or two months occur between project assignments and engineers have little to do during this time, they begin to worry about their importance to the company.[30]

SUMMARY

Experienced managers know there is more to an organization's structure than what can be captured in the organization chart. There is structure in the flow and use of information, in the processes of decision making, and in the organization as a social system. The open-system view of organizations suggests that linkages to relevant dimensions of the surrounding world are also important aspects of an organization's structure.

The increasing complexity and sophistication of modern products, services, markets, and technologies have caused organizations to become more heterogeneous and differentiated among various specialties. Where these tasks can be simplified and routinized in a stable environment, the traditional classical organizational principles may suffice. Where activities are unique, unpredictable, and cre-

ative, more flexible organizational processes are needed to unite authority and knowledge so that decisions can be made by the most knowledgeable individuals and groups. We have discussed some emerging guidelines for doing this.

Staff should possess the authority necessary to allow them to contribute effectively to the organization. This may require (1) compulsory consultation so that line must seek staff advice, (2) concurrent authority so that line must request staff's joint approval, or (3) functional authority, in which the distinction between line and staff evaporates as specialists achieve full authority in their area of expertise.

Centralization and decentralization should be balanced in a relationship appropriate to each organization. Under the following condition, leaning in the centralized direction is desirable: (1) close coordination of activities around an overall perspective is required; (2) unpopular decisions must be made frequently; and (3) confidentiality of top-level strategy and tactics is desirable. Leaning in the decentralized direction is appropriate when: (1) the organization has become very large and diversified; (2) local geographic and product managers are more knowledgeable about their products and markets; (3) commitment and initiative from lower level managers is required; and (4) more widespread on-the-job management development is desired. Balancing centralization and decentralization is one of the most difficult challenges facing top management.

Organizations require increasingly greater structural and status flexibility in order to balance centralization and decentralization and unite knowledge and authority in changing, turbulent environments. Temporary project, product, or problem teams and matrix organizations are vehicles for bringing specialized people together in flexible groups for as long as a particular need exists, but no longer. Such an approach reduces the inflexibility and inefficiency of traditional organizational structures in which permanent departments tend to remain after they have outlived their usefulness. In addition, reducing status destinctions should facilitate more open communication.

Organizational flexibility should include flexible rewards that reflect actual recent contributions to the organization, not level in the hierarchy, office size, title, or base salary.

REVIEW QUESTIONS

1. What does it mean to bring authority and responsibility together?

2. What assumption did traditional hierarchical organizations make about authority and knowledge? What has undermined this assumption?

3. What is the traditional role of staff?

4. What is a personal staff?

5. What is an advisory staff? How does such a staff operate?

6. What is the continuum of staff influence?

7. What is compulsory consultation in line-staff relations? When is it desirable?

8. What is concurrent authority in line-staff relations? When is it desirable?

9. What is functional authority in line-staff relations? When is it desirable?

10. What is the difference between centralized and decentralized organizational structures?

11. What suggests that an organization is relatively centralized?

12. What suggests that an organization is relatively decentralized?

13. Why do organizations change from centralized to decentralized? And vice versa?

14. What are the arguments for centralization?

15. What are the arguments for decentralization?

16. How is a structural decision regarding centralization/decentralization made? What questions should be asked?

17. What is the difference between flexible and inflexible organizational rewards?

18. Why should lower level people sometimes receive greater rewards than higher level people?

19. What are the dual ladders in some organizations?

20. Why are flexible and temporary structures sometimes desirable?

21. What is a matrix organization?

22. How do project teams interact with functional departments in a matrix structure?

23. What problems exist with temporary structures?

Notes and References on Advanced Guidelines for Organizational Design

1. F. E. Kast and J. E. Rosensweig, *Contingency View of Organization and Management* (Chicago: Science Research Associates, 1973).

2. For a fuller discussion of the information processing view of organization design, see Jay Galbraith, *Designing Complex Organizations* (Reading, Mass.: Addison-Wesley Publishing, 1963).

3. C. Barnard, *The Functions of the Executive,* 30th anniversary ed. (Cambridge: Harvard University Press, 1976).

4. Early contributions to the stream of thinking about organizations as social systems include Talcott Parsons, *The Structure of Social Action,* (New York: McGraw-Hill, 1937); and Kurt Lewin, *A Dynamic Theory of Personality* New York: McGraw-Hill, 1935). More recent works are Harry Levinson, *Emotional Health in the World of Work* (New York: Harper & Row, 1964); D. Katz and R. Kahn, *The Social Psychology of Organizations* (New York: John Wiley & Sons, 1966); and R. Tagiuri and G. H. Litwin, *Organizational Climate: Explorations of a Concept* (Boston: Graduate School of Business Administration: Harvard University, 1968.)

5. Roosevelt Thomas, "Managing the Psychological Contract," in Paul Lawrence, Louis Barnes, and Jay Lorsch, *Organizational Behavior and Administration: Cases and Readings,* 3d ed. (Homewood, Ill.: Richard D. Irwin, 1976).

6. Formal treatment of the ideas of closed and open systems can be found in texts on cybernetics and systems theory. See, for example, W. Ross Ashby, *An Introduction to Cybernetics* (London: Methuen, 1956).

7. Peter Drucker, "New Templates for Today's Organizations," *Harvard Business Review,* January–February 1974, pp. 45–52.

8. Victor A. Thompson, *Modern Organization* (New York: Alfred A. Knopf, 1961). One empirical study traced communications and concluded that "the influence of subordinates over superiors on nonprogrammed choices is greater than the influence of superiors over subordinates." This was because of their greater specialized knowledge. B. Walter, "Internal Control Relations in Administrative Hierarchies," *Administrative Science Quarterly* 11, no. 11 (1966), pp. 179–205. See also W. H. Read, "The Decline of the Hierarchy in Organizations," *Business Horizons,* 8, no. 3 (1965), pp. 71–75.

9. Eliot D. Chapple and Leonard R. Sayles, *The Measure of Management* (New York: Macmillan, 1960). Herbert A. Simon maintains that organizational problems are best attacked by examining the information system in abstraction, apart from department structure. "Applying Information Technology to Organizational Design," *Public Administration Review* 33 (1973), pp. 168–278. See also J. R. Galbraith, "Organization Design: An Information Processing View," *Interfaces,* May 1974, pp. 28–36, and R. V. Farace et al., *Communicating and Organizing* (Reading, Mass.: Addison-Wesley Publishing, 1977).

10. J. D. Hittle, *The Military Staff: Its History and Development* (Harrisburg, Pa.: Stackpole Books, 1961).

11. E. Dale and L. R. Urwick, *Staff in Organization* (New York: McGraw-Hill, 1960).

12. R. C. Sampson, *The Staff Role in Management* (New York: Harper & Row, 1955); L. A. Allen, "The Line-

Staff Relationship," *Management Record* 16, no. 9 (1955), pp. 346–49.

13. G. C. Fisch, "Line-Staff Is Obsolete," *Harvard Business Review,* September–October 1961, pp. 67–79.

14. Wendell French and Dale Henning, "The Authority-Influence Role of the Functional Specialist in Management," *Journal of the Academy of Management* 9, no. 3 (1966), pp. 187–203.

15. James G. March and Herbert A. Simon, *Organizations* (New York: John Wiley & Sons, 1958).

16. R. A. Pitts, "Diversification Strategies and Organizational Policies of Large Diversified Firms," *Journal of Economics and Business,* Summer 1976, pp. 181–88.

17. A. R. Negandhi and B. C. Reimann, "Correlates of Decentralization: Closed and Open System Perspectives," *Academy of Management Journal* 16, no. 4 (1973), pp. 570–82.

18. T. Metz, "The Enemy Within," *The Wall Street Journal,* January 16, 1969.

19. Increasing size and decentralization tend to be associated together, along with greater formalization of organizational positions and policies. In general, decentralization is a means for maintaining management control. See R. Mansfield, "Bureaucracy and Centralization: An Examination of Organizational Structure," *Administrative Science Quarterly* 18, no. 4 (1973), pp. 477–88, and Thomas J. Whisler et al., "Centralization of Organizational Control: An Empirical Study of Its Meaning and Measurement," *Journal of Business,* January 1967, pp. 10–26.

20. J. C. Worthy, "Organizational Structure and Employee Morale," *American Sociological Review,* April 1950, pp. 169–79; and R. J. Cordiner, *New Frontiers for Professional Managers* (New York: McGraw-Hill, 1956). Decentralization in government seems to increase citizen sense of power, but it has no effect on sense of trust and may even reduce it. R. K. Yin and W. A. Lucas, "Decentralization and Alienation," *Policy Sciences* 4 (1973), pp. 327–36.

21. R. F. Vancil, *Decentralization: Managerial Ambiguity by Design* (Homewood, Ill.: Dow Jones-Irwin, 1979).

22. F. J. Holzapfel, "Multiple Ladders in An Engineering Department," *Chemical Engineering,* February 27, 1967, pp. 124–27. Edgar Schein maintains that the dual-ladder concept of rewarding technical people is more myth than reality; that even Ph.D.s in technical jobs have lower salaries and are less satisfied than general managers with a bachelor's degree. Address to the American Psychological Association, September 5, 1971.

23. R. Townsend, *Up the Organization* (New York: Alfred A. Knopf, 1970).

24. C. N. Parkinson, *Parkinson's Law on the Pursuit of Progress* (London: Murray, 1958).

25. Half in jest, half in deadly seriousness, the "Peter Principle" contends that in a hierarchy, every employee tends to rise to his/her level of incompetence. Employees are promoted for good performance until they reach a level where they cannot perform well, and there they supposedly remain. This pessimistic view ignores the possibility of personal growth. See Laurence J. Peter and Raymond Hull, *The Peter Principle: Why Things Always Go Wrong* (New York: Morrow, 1969). A humorous rebuttal maintains that the principle may indeed be true, but organizations can still perform satisfactorily because there are competent people who do not want promotions or who are blocked because they did not go to college, are black, or females. Lane Tracy, "Postscript to the Peter Principle," *Harvard Business Review,* July–August 1972, pp. 65–71.

26. J. D. Hlavacek and V. A. Thompson, "Bureaucracy and New Product Innovation," *Academy of Management Journal* 16, no. 3 (1973), pp. 361–72. The authors argue that the venture team should be protected from the rest of the company administratively, financially, spatially, and sometimes, legally. See also Jay W. Lorsch and Paul R. Lawrence, "Organizing for Product Innovation," *Harvard Business Review,* January–February 1965, pp. 109–18; J. M. Stewart, "Making Project Management Work," *Business Horizons* 8, no. 3 (1965), pp. 54–70; C. J. Middleton, "How to Set up a Project Organization," *Harvard Business Review,* March–April 1967, pp. 73–81; M. Hanan, "Corporate Growth through Venture Management," *Harvard Business Review,* January–February 1969, pp. 43–61; and R. M. Clewett and S. F. Stasch, "Shifting Role of the Project Manager," *Harvard Business Review,* January–February 1977, pp. 65–73.

27. J. R. Galbraith, "Matrix Organization Designs," *Business Horizons* 14, no. 1 (1971), pp. 29–40; A. L. Delbecq et al., *Matrix Organization: A Conceptual Guide to Organization Variation* (Madison: Graduate School of Business, University of Wisconsin, 1969); and S. M. Davis and P. R. Lawrence, *Matrix* (Reading, Mass.: Addison-Wesley Publishing, 1977).

28. On the matrix in hospitals, see M. P. Charna, "Breaking the Tradition Barrier: Managing Integration in

Health Care Facilities," *Health Care Management Review,* Winter 1976, pp. 55–67.

29. C. Reeser, "Some Potential Human Problems in the Project Form of Organization," *Academy of Management Journal,* (December 1969), pp. 459–67; D. L. Wilemon and J. P. Cicero, "The Project Manager: Anomalies and Abiguities," *Academy of Management Journal,* September 1970, pp. 269–82; D. L. Wilemon and G. R. Gemmill, "The Venture Manager as a Corporate Innovator," *California Management Review* 16, no. 1 (1973), pp. 49–56; S. Dietz, "Get More out of Your Brand of Management," *Harvard Business Review,* July–August 1973, pp. 127–36.

30. On engineers in temporary structures, see R. R. Ritti, *The Engineer in the Industrial Corporation* (New York: Columbia University Press, 1971).

19

The Contingency Approach to Organization Design

Some years ago a very successful executive was attracted away from a large, nationally known industrial corporation to head up a major division of a growing high-technology company. He was distressed to find that his new organization had a poorly defined management hierarchy and few clear reporting procedures and that everyone seemed to spend inordinate amounts of time in aimless meetings in the many conference rooms near the laboratories. Within six months he had moved on to a high position with a competitor of his original employer. There the administrative arrangements were again orderly and to his liking. Although this manager didn't feel at home in the second company, it (like the other two) was considered to be successful, a leader in its industry. In this chapter we will examine some ways of thinking about structure, collectively known as the contingency approach.[1]* The examination should help us understand why such differences arise, as a matter of course, in the organizational patterns of a variety of successful institutions.

Organizations, Environments, and Task Complexity

The basic premise underlying the contingency approach is that each organization interacts with a specific task environment and with a broader general environment. (See Figure 19–1.) The task environment may consist of suppliers, customers, unions, regulatory agencies, professional associations and competitors, or possibly of some other mix of actors and institutions with which the organization has frequent and significant interactions.

For example, a tire company must deal with the chemical and rubber industries, automobile and truck manufacturers, specialized research laboratories at some major universities, the Federal Trade Commission, various transportation and product-safety lobbying groups, tire wholesalers and retailers, and vehicle purchasers—both individual and institutional. In contrast, an integrated circuit board manufacturer must focus on relationships with silicon suppliers, the major electronics and computer companies, various small (and possibly transient) computer assembly companies, a different set of specialized research facilities around the world, a host of potential users of electronic and digital components (such as appliance and automobile makers), and agencies of certain governments (such as in Japan and East Germany) that are sponsoring the growth of this field within their own economies.

As task environments differ, so do the activities that must be performed in order to deal successfully with each environment. Organizing to carry out these activities effectively, then, may require the use of different patterns in different settings.

Research on communication and leaderships in networks is relevant here. Some studies have explored behavior in five-person groups when the experimenter modifies the task being performed.[2] It has been shown that an all-channel communication network tends to transform itself into a wheel network with centralized decision making when presented with a simple, repetitive task (such as determining the color of a marble or letter common to all group members.) When the task is changed to a more complex and integrative process such as building words from the letters, the centralized structure breaks down, unused communication links are activated,

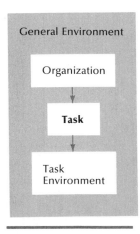

FIGURE 19–1

Organization, Task, and Environment

General Environment

Organization

Task

Task Environment

---

* Notes and references will be found at the end of this chapter.

and the task is solved through a more decentralized participatory process. (See Figure 19–2.) These changes seem to occur irrespective of the personalities of group members. Through intuition, trial and error, or analysis, most groups conclude that: (1) repetitive, routinized, simple tasks are best handled through formal, centralized organizational structures and (2) integrative, complex, and creative tasks are better handled through informal, decentralized structures.

Managers and organization design specialists are interested in finding generalized principles that can help them anticipate what organizational forms are likely to work well under specific circumstances. Although the appropriate design solutions for any given organization are unlikely to fit a predetermined prescription, there are a number of generalizations that have gained widespread support. These suggest that organization design choices should take into account such contingencies as (1) the nature of the technologies employed; (2) the degree of stability in the environment, measured in terms of the rate of change, the amount of uncertainty, and the time lags for obtaining feedback; and (3) the competitive and institutional structure of the environment itself.

Technology and Structure

The technology required in the operations of various types of organizations will have an effect on structure. A study of leadership styles contrasted container manufacturing plants, wherein the technology was sophisticated and highly mechanized so that management's task was simply to keep it working, with research laboratories, wherein the technology was not specified but rather dependent on individual and team creative efforts.[3] Results of the study showed the following differences between the more effective and less effective in each of the two pairs of organizations studied:

The more effective container manufacturer was characterized by formal, centralized structure, policy, and decision making.

The less effective container manufacturer was characterized by less formal structure and more participation.

The more effective research laboratory demonstrated more ambiguity in policy and structure, as well as more participation.

The less effective research laboratory demonstrated formalized and centralized structure, policy, and decision making.

Research in many other firms further supports these observations.[4] In production companies, there are three basic technologies:

1. Mass production or large-batch production of a large number of very similar items with substantial interchangeable parts. Assembly lines turning out Chevrolets, RCA television receivers, and Westinghouse lamps fall into this category.
2. Job shop or small-batch manufacturing includes the design and production of a unique product, singly or in small numbers. Rather than assembly lines, a more craftlike technology is involved in which the workers build from the ground up. Examples include the design and construction of IBM computers, Boeing 747s, or GE nuclear reactors. This technology is usually diffuse because it is

FIGURE 19–2

Task and All-Channel Networks

All-Channel (initial state)

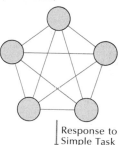

↓ Response to Simple Task

Wheel

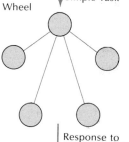

↓ Response to Complex Task

All-Channel

flexible and can produce a variety of products. For example, Boeing Vertol, which constructs helicopters on a small-batch basis, utilizes the same facilities and people to make streetcars.

3.   Continuous processing turns out a nondifferentiated product flow from automated equipment that operates around the clock and calendar (except for infrequent repairs). Such products include Detroit Edison electricity, Mobil gasoline, and Du Pont nylon. This technology is specific and inflexible. A petroleum refinery may vary the proportion of fuel oil to gasoline that it produces, but it can't be converted to manufacturing helicopters or generating electricity.

Effective mass production and large-batch plants tend to adhere to traditional static organization principles. The relatively stable, routine, long-linked sequences of tasks in these organizations are well served by a clear-cut hierarchical structure and centralized decision making.[5] In fact, most of the static principles were developed from the experience of executives with mass-production technology.[6] In contrast, custom, small-batch and continuous-processing organizations frequently depart in different ways from some of the static rules in order to follow the more dynamic guidelines. Thus continuous-processing firms, with their intensive technologies, tend to have narrow spans of control with substantial authority vested in high-level staff personnel who design, plan, and control the operation of what is usually quite expensive equipment. These specific, inflexible technology organizations are generally even more rigidly structured and mechanistic than mass-production firms. Custom or small-batch operations tend to have sizable teams of relatively equal-status specialists who interact freely to solve unpredictable problems.[7]

In summary, more predictable and routine tasks and technologies are suited to structures adhering to the traditional hierarchical principles. Such "performance" or "mechanistic"[8] structures dominate mass-production, large-batch, and routine service organizations where the product or service and technology are relatively stable, as with assembly lines, building construction, transportation, and banking. (See Figure 19–3.) More ambiguous, unpredictable, and creative tasks are more

FIGURE 19–3 _____

Technology and Structure

Technology		*Structure*
Mass production, large-batch, long-linked	←→	Static, mechanical principles
Job-shop, small-batch, diffuse	←→	Dynamic, organic guidelines flexible
Continuous processing, specific	←→	Combined static and organic, but specialized and centralized

likely to be handled in all-channel, flexible groups openly communicating to bring knowledge and authority together. Such "problem-solving" or "organic" structures are common in research labs, hospitals, schools, new-product development, long-range planning, and top-management groups, such as executive committees and "the president's office."[9]

An example of the problem-solving structure is the five-person executive committee of one large company. This committee is composed of the chairperson of the board of directors, vice chair of the board, president, general manager, and chairperson of the executive committee. All are full-time employees, and the status relationship is ambiguous. Their offices on the top floor of company headquarters are arranged in a pentagon around a central meeting room. Secretaries are located around the outer perimeter. The executives maintain that their interior doors are always open to facilitate communications on joint problems.

Environment and Structure

In additon to its own technology and purposes, an organization's structure must be suited to the world in which it exists—scientific and technological changes, market and economic conditions, political trends, and social climate.[10] A firm that produces a stable product in a mature market with little innovation and relatively few competitors confronts a different problem than does a business that provides a rapidly changing service in a growing market and has many competitors.[11] The first environment is stable, the second may be changing or turbulent.[12]

Stable Environment

A stable environment is characterized by the following:

1. Products and services that have not changed much in recent years.
2. A stable set of competitors and customers with few entries or departures.
3. Consistent government policies toward regulation and taxation.
4. Lack of technological innovation in competitive fields.
5. Consistent labor-management relations.
6. Stable social and political conditions.

Since firms operating in such an environment are likely to routinize their operations, a formalized, centralized structure is appropriate. Top management can keep track of what is going on and make necessary policy decisions. Such a system is likely to be effective as long as the environment remains stable. If it begins to change, management may not detect what is happening for some time, and at this point the organization may be too inflexible to adapt quickly enough.

Few organizations admit to being stable in stable environments. It is not glamorous, and it implies that management is easy. Nonetheless, some organizations have faced stable environments for substantial time periods. The Roman Catholic Church during the 1930s to 1950s operated in an environment that was quite stable in relation to the Church. Although pressure was building up, the doctrine, liturgy, and regulations did not begin to change until the late 1950s and 1960s. Some businesses

Characteristics of a Stable Environment
- unchanging products and services
- few new competitors
- consistent government actions
- little technological innovation
- mature labor relations
- stable political and economic conditions
- observance of static principles of organizations
- formalized and centralized structure

have also operated in quite stable worlds: leather tanning, coal mining, such agricultural staples as flour and gelatin, and such household familiars as brooms and candles. Many people make good livings in these fields, even though technological change has been minimal and growth absent or small.

Changing Environment

A changing environment is characterized by the following:

1. Products or services that have been changing moderately.
2. A stable set of larger competitors, with others entering and leaving from time to time.
3. Government regulations that have been moving in a predictable direction (generally toward closer control).
4. Moderate and incremental technological innovation, each step forward building modestly on the preceding one.
5. Evolutionary (not revolutionary) labor-management, political, and social trends.

Characteristics of a
Changing Environment

- moderately changing products or services
- stable large competitors with others entering
- predictable change in government actions
- incremental technological innovation
- evolutionary external trends
- mixture of static principles and dynamic guidelines
- functional staff and moderate decentralization
- observance of environment

Firms confronting such an environment will probably be fairly formalized and centralized in decision making but will have a specialized staff or decentralized line managers responsible for monitoring the environment to learn what is happening. Marketing managers will submit periodic reports on customer desires; engineers will read technical publications to learn of advances; a government liaison specialist will maintain contacts with federal and state legislatures. Response to local, national, and international changes in any of these dimensions may be centralized. However, if the firm is large and diversified, such response may be delegated to decentralized managers. Nonetheless, since predictability characterizes the changes in such an environment, top management and centralized specialists can retain control over important policy decisions.

An automobile assembly plant in 1962 was an example of a company confronting a changing environment. Technological changes were incremental—improvements in automatic transmission, steering, and braking and automated manufacturing techniques—but nothing that was a dramatic breakthrough (advertising claims notwithstanding). No radically new power plants or basic designs emerged in the 1950s and 1960s (with the possible exception of the rotary engine). Only relatively minor government regulations on safety and pollution were imposed, and competition changed little, at least until the entry of foreign manufacturers into the market.

Most businesses have existed in changing environments. By monitoring social, economic, and technological trends, top management is able to hire appropriate experts, introduce technical improvements, and maintain capabilities. Change is constant and fairly predictable for such consumer durables as washing machines, residential construction, insurance, and chemical manufacturing.

Turbulent Environment

Most managers believe a turbulent environment is what they face today. It is characterized by:

1. Continually changing products or services.
2. An ever-changing array of competitors, including market entries by large businesses.
3. Unpredictable governmental actions reflecting political interactions between the public and various advocacy groups for consumer protection, pollution control, and civil rights.
4. Major technological innovation, including introduction of radically different technology, which is obsoleting the old.
5. Rapid changes in the values and behavior of large numbers of citizens.

Successfully dealing with such a world puts a premium on sensitivity, commitment, and creativity. It demands a fairly decentralized structure in which many people feel a responsibility to keep informed about external developments, a flexible communication system that bypasses the formal hierarchy when necessary to bring various specialists together quickly, and a structure that can change to give emphasis to new products and services when opportunities are detected.[13] Perhaps most of all, it requires boundary-spanning people who can accept ambiguity as they change tasks and positions on various teams where they must cooperate with people of differing backgrounds and perspectives.[14]

Automobile companies have entered an era of turbulence. Gasoline shortages, safety requirements, and pollution controls are making it more difficult to predict what the firms will need to compete or to meet social demands. Will they have to replace the internal combustion engine? Will merely reducing its pollution effects suffice? Will economic and energy conditions eliminate the big car as a status symbol? Will changing attitudes toward work require revolutionary changes in the design of work and management systems? These are all questions management must ask when confronting turbulence. Similar problems face the energy companies, given limited and unstable supplies of oil. They must explore the alternatives: coal, nuclear fission, nuclear fusion, thermal energy, water, and perhaps wind. But these alternatives raise other technical, economic, and pollution problems. Even on university and college campuses, the world became turbulent in the 1960s and 1970s. Student complaints, legislative anger, declining applications, soaring costs, demands for immediate equal opportunity, and political upheaval destroyed the myth of academic tranquility.

Response to such turbulence will require much flexibility and interest on the

Characteristics of a
Turbulent Environment
- continually changing products or services
- changing competitors
- unpredictable government actions
- major technological innovation
- rapid social change
- fairly decentralized structure
- flexible structure
- search for dynamic guidelines
- sense of greater system

Hagar the Horrible by Dik Browne

part of individuals, groups, and organizations. No central authority can possibly provide all the answers, although an attempt should be made to articulate the organization's essential nature and aspirations and set personal examples of commitment and concern. Participation, open communication, and innovative organizational forms will be essential.[15]

If an organization is to be structured appropriately for its environment, management must keep informed about external developments.[16] Even more, management must expand its view of the organization to see it not as a narrow, closed system of owners, managers, and employees—but as part of an open system also encompassing suppliers, customers, competitors, government, and a multiplicity of action groups (such as those on civil rights, consumer protection, and environmental cleanup).[17] Structure should facilitate the collection of information from these external groups so that management can make better decisions. All organizations should realize that insulation breeds disaster; they must be open to influence from the surrounding world.

Integrating Frameworks

Three conceptual schemes have shown themselves to be particularly valuable in thinking through the implications of the contingency approach. They grow out of the views of organizational structure presented in Chapter 18: organizations as information processing systems, organizations as social systems, and organizations as open systems.

Differentiation and Integration

In a large organization, the subenvironments of all parts are not identical.[18] Some of General Electric's departments operate in fairly stable subenvironments and markets, others in more changing and turbulent ones. To be effective, such a firm must facilitate the differentiation of structure and attitudes toward tasks and goals. Those operating in the most stable subenvironments will have the most formalized and static structures as well as task-oriented leadership. Units confronting moderately unstable subenvironments may demonstrate more social and human relations concerns.

Effective organizations balance differentiation among units and specialists with integration of managers, coordinators, committees, and teams. Integration refers to the quality of collaboration among departments to achieve unity of effort.[19] Integrators are concerned with and rewarded for the performance of the total, not individual parts. Their effectiveness rests less on their formal power than on their energy and knowledge. One of the most complex differentiated organizations in the world is NASA, the National Aeronautics and Space Administration. An extensive study found that NASA's great success in space was due to the integration of the activities of its far-flung offices, centers, contractors, and subcontractors.[20] Computer systems and quantitative techniques helped of course, but the single most important integrative element was the energy and commitment of various persons who traveled between

FIGURE 19–4

Common Relationships among Environment, Structure, and Task

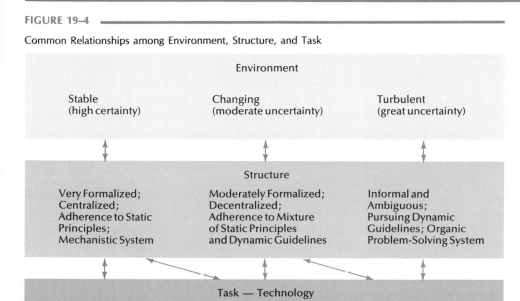

the various differentiated units to discuss problems and promote concern for the total mission.

Structure should be derived not from abstract principles but from the organization's tasks, technology, and environment.[21] Standarization and stability are desirable in predictable organizations operating in stable environments, but such is not the case with unpredictable, innovative organizations in turbulent environments that require more differentiation and flexibility. Although the relationships are neither inevitable nor certain, the usual association of structure, task, and environment is as illustrated in Figure 19–4.

Stakeholder Analysis

Because organizations have important interactions with their environments, the structure of those environments can have a significant bearing on what constitutes an effective organizational structure. Outside the firm are a set of actors and institutions with identifiable interests in its performance.[22]

The traditional microeconomic model of the firm identifies suppliers, customers, owners, lenders, and the govenment. To this list, recent research has added competitors—more specifically, the structure of the competitive arena.[23] Firms that compete in an oligopolistic setting, with only a few other significant competitors, must organize to deal with information about product innovation, for example, differently than would firms faced with a large number of small, scattered competitors. When the costs of entering the business are high, the firm may rely on these entry barriers to keep potential rivals at bay. Under such conditions it may be possible to concentrate more on internal issues when considering organization design decisions. When no such barriers exist, however, it may be essential to use design decisions to help create an advantageous competitive position. For example, a company may decide to automate its new manufacturing plant or its management information systems. Such measures will affect in significant ways how the organization's structure should evolve.

Stakeholder analysis must move beyond the economic actors in the firm's environment and encompass social and political forces as well. In today's world, consumer action groups; environmental protection associations; governmental agencies concerned with human rights, worker health and safety, and socioeconomic decay in large urban areas; labor unions; and organizations that press for the rights of such specific social groups as women, handicapped persons, the elderly, and ethnic minorities—all may add to the pressures on the structure of an organization. Many companies find it necessary to establish specialized units to serve as conduits for information exchanges with specific outside groups. Others have revised internal planning and reporting relationships to assure that critical information about significant stakeholders is circulated and appropriately used in the decision-making and coordination processes within the firm.

Organizational Evolution

No structural arrangement should be permanent. This is so because often major changes occur in the environment. Even if the environment remains fairly stable, an organization should change as it grows and matures.[24] What works during the birth of an owner-dominated firm must pass on to more bureaucratic and professionally managed phases.

An organization's life can be conceived as an evolutionary process punctuated by certain crises.[25] At each juncture the old structure and style become so out of

FIGURE 19–5

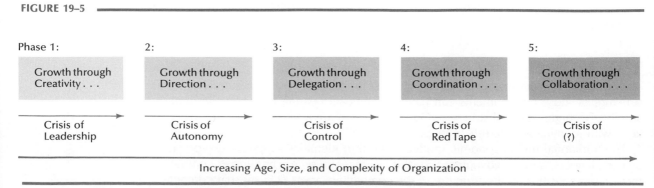

Source: L. E. Greiner, "Evolution and Revolution as Organizations Grow," *Harvard Business Review,* July–August 1972, p. 38.

step with what the organization then needs that revolutionary change is required. The various phases in organizational evolution are shown in Figure 19–5. They can be described as follows:

Phase 1: Growth through Creativity.   Creativity during organizational birth rests upon the founder's technical or entrepreneurial activities; structure is rudimentary and communications frequent and informal. Everyone is aware of how well the new firm is doing, and most feel involved. But success leads to a crisis of leadership. The founder needs to hire more people as he or she becomes burdened with managing rather than doing. However, the founder may find it difficult to delegate as to be able to concentrate on structuring and managing rather than doing the work.

Phase 2: Growth through Direction.   Organizations that survive the first phase usually grow with the implementation of formalized and usually centralized structure and decision making. They evolve smoothly until lower managers rebel against their lack of autonomy and authority.

Phase 3: Growth through Delegation.   With increased size, continued central direction becomes impossible, and greater authority is delegated. Decentralized, georgraphically dispersed profit centers become common. This heightens managerial motivation and fosters continued growth. But, once again, growth creates further problems—those of control. Autonomous field managers will tend to push their units' interest, even at the expense of the whole organization.

Phase 4: Growth through Coordination.   If the firm has the information capability, it might respond with recentralization, but more likely a more modest form of central coordination will be developed. Through planning, product groups, committee meetings, and staff expansion, the various managers must confront each other and top management in order to make their activities compatible.

This solution is complex; as a result, the monster of bureaucracy and red tape may rear its ugly head. Staff and line tend to fight, and managers complain that they waste so much time "coordinating" that they have no time to do anything else.

Phase 5: Growth through Collaboration.   Solutions to the red-tape crisis are by no means certain. They lie in the development of collaborative mechanisms along the lines of the dynamic guidelines discussed: bring knowledge and authority together, eliminate the distinction between line and staff, develop more flexible organizations.

Possible Future Organizations

For a long time, the pyramid has been regarded as the ideal command structure. Most contemporary organizations build upon this general model because there is no better way to define accountability and to pass orders from the person at the top to subordinates. A general's battle orders can be passed to 10 senior officers. They in turn can each inform 10 noncommissioned officers, each of whom tells 10 soldiers. Thus orders are speeded from one person to 10,000 in four simple steps.

In spite of this advantage, however, most predictions about future organizations suggest that the primacy of the pyramid will lessen.[26] Greater educational levels, specialization, and technological complexity supposedly will lead to forms that tone down the autocratic nature of the pyramid, which is accentuated by its sharply defined apex. A warning: some of the future can be perceived in the present. The signs are about us, but so are the signs of things that will never be. It is difficult to tell the difference.

FIGURE 19–6

Possible Future Organization

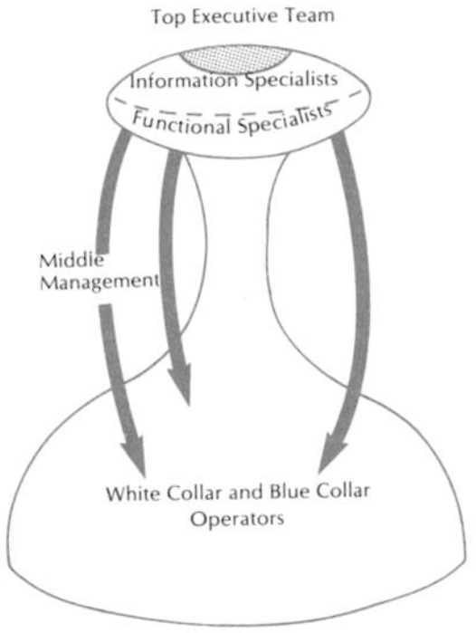

Extreme Centralization in Collective Leadership.   Drawing on the capacities of graduate degree specialists in computers and information systems, organizations may become ultracentralized as suggested by Figure 19–6.[27] The key decision makers might be grouped around an executive team at the very top that would exercise collegial leadership.[28] The person with the necessary credentials would enter the organization directly into one of the specialized sections of the decision-making power center at the top. The centralized planning and control center would send instructions directly to the white- and blue-collar employees grouped in the lower portion of the bell-shape structure. The lower jobs would be highly programmed and probably boring. Working hours might be shortened for these personnel so that life would be divided into on-job and off-job segments.

This future model suggests that middle management would shrink. With decision knowledge and authority concentrated at the top, middle management would be bypassed on most communications. Only a vestigal middle management would be required for personnel and nontechnical duties. Hence the central portion of the structure would be narrowed.

Support for this prediction is mixed. People with graduate degrees are increasingly appearing at the top of business corporations. In the early 1970s, perhaps 50 percent of top executives possessed master's degrees and 25 percent had doctorates.[29] In addition, organizations have been centralizing to take advantage of specialists and new information technology. Yet, at the very top major strategic decisions are still made by generalists without great reliance on mathematics or computers,[30] and middle managers are not disappearing. The introduction of computers and management information systems reduces the technical requirements for middle management, but this apparently leaves more time to devote to human relations and planning. Many middle managers report that they consider their jobs relatively more important and satisfying than in the past.[31]

Smart Chart
by Stansbury

"Thank goodness we're all retiring before the MBAs get us."
Reprinted with the permission of Herbert E. Stansbury.

The Expansion of Specialists.   "The engineer is the proletariat of the future," according to a governmental report on employment trends. It is by no means clear that only engineers will predominate, but knowledge workers will come to dominate organizations numerically as technologies change and older production jobs are automated. This may lead to a structure that looks like a football on end, as in

Figure 19–7. At the top would be the few generalists and graduate degree functional specialists. Below them would be a large number of lesser college-trained knowledge workers. At the bottom would be the operators. Thus the organization would be divided into three segments, with little movement between them.

The very top of this organization would operate much like the top of the bell structure (see Figure 19–6): collective team decision making, drawing on the staff work of the specialists below. These specialists would not be part of the vaguely pyramidal shape above them. Managers would directly contact whomever they wanted, without regard to status or chain of command.

This prediction is not optimistic about the quality of work in the swollen middle. These knowledge jobs would be quite highly programmed and formalized so that challenge would be relatively limited. Many graduate engineers already complain that they are underutilized, and this prediction suggests that this attitude will increase. It is likely that college graduate knowledge workers would come to express antimanagement views and join unions, much as unskilled and semiskilled blue-collar workers have done in the past. The strongest support for this type of organization is the expansion of white-collar specialist and professional positions over the past 20 years, while blue-collar operating positions have been declining as a proportion of jobs.[32]

Organizational Democracy.   "Democracy Is Inevitable" was the title of a popular article some years ago.[33] Its theme was that the increased educational and ability level of employees would ultimately lead to a decline in the traditional hierarchical structure, with its differentiated power and status levels. The structural form that such a development might take is uncertain, but one representation utilizes concentric circles, as in Figure 19–8.

The form implies a high degree of communication among managers, regardless of status. To some, it implies that ultimate authority would reside in the mass of organizational members. They would grant authority to certain individuals by electing them to managerial office for limited terms. Such elected managers would enjoy some status and pay differentials as in traditional hierarchies, but to a less marked degree. More important, they would recognize what is increasingly a reality in many organizations: that superiors are just as dependent on subordinates as the latter are on them. Therefore, mechanisms would be instituted to see that organizational members have a voice in policy decisions, and elected managers would know that they could be removed from office by these subordinates.[34]

Organizations already exist with such characteristics. This is essentially a political structure and has the strengths and weakness associated with politics. Some departments in academic institutions elect faculty department heads. More significant, however, is the business development of this form in some European countries, particularly Yugoslavia.[35] In that nation's blend of socialism and capitalism, the firm is owned by the employees, who are motivated to increase profits. They elect managers who they believe will contribute to their objective.

The form of industrial democracy exists, but some skeptics question whether it really works. Most workers apparently do not aspire to be managers, and incumbent executives are almost always reelected. Like an American labor union leader or an entrenched congressional representative, executives come to consider the position

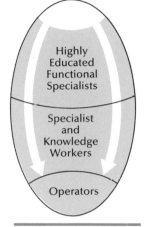

FIGURE 19–7

Possible Future Organization

Top Executive Team

Highly Educated Functional Specialists

Specialist and Knowledge Workers

Operators

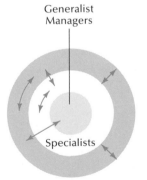

FIGURE 19–8

Possible Future Organization

Generalist Managers

Specialists

as their own and operate quite independently of the constituency. Management in this structure may become almost as hierarchical and unilateral as in the old pyramids.

Free-Form Organizations. Descriptions of free-form structures visualize something like an amoeba constantly changing shape as it needs to.[36] A better description is a multiform organization with a permanent management team and various specialists in the center surrounded by an array of permanent hierarchies, temporary teams, and matrix structures, as in Figure 19–9.[37] Each of these units would be designed to suit the production technology, service process, and external environment in accordance with the contingency views discussed.

FIGURE 19–9

Multiform Organization

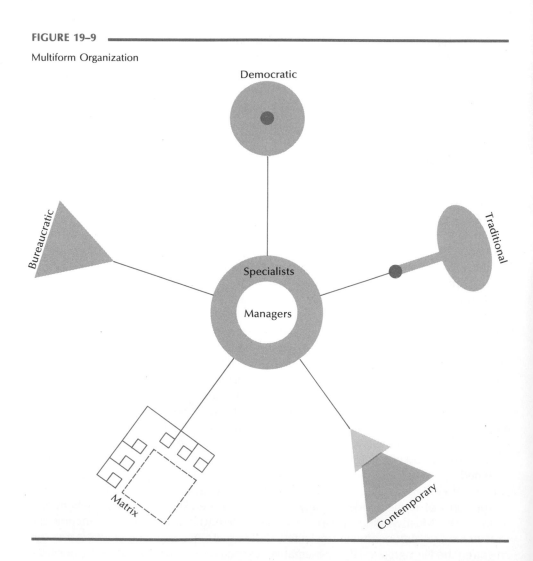

SUMMARY

Organizations facing different environments have differing structural needs. These relate to task complexity, technology, and environment. Environments vary in terms of the rate of change, the degree of uncertainty, and time lag for feedback. Thus they place different demands for information processing, differentiation in task orientation, and coordination on each organization.

Within a given organization consistency is not necessarily a virtue. All parts of a large organization need not be similarly structured. Manufacturing electric lamps, for example, is much different from designing community transportation systems, although both are activities at General Electric. Organizations need both standardization and differentiation to varying degrees. Differentiation refers to the variety of fairly independent functions, specialties, and departments that must develop their own mechanisms for performing their tasks and dealing with the world. Since manufacturing an automobile is different from designing an aircraft engine, these two units in General Motors should not be similarly structured; nor should they be held rigorously to the same personnel policies in a misguided search for standardization. The need for different time perspectives, creativity, reliability, and flexibility in the two activities is too great for them to be managed similarly. Differentiation must be counterbalanced by integrative mechanisms sufficient to deal with the interrelatedness of the tasks assigned to the various units.

Organization design features of today's organizations must be flexible and adaptable in order to fit the evolving stages of the organization's life. They must also be sufficiently elaborate to provide for adequate interactions with a complex web of external stakeholders.

Among the various predictions of future organizational forms are the following:

1. Extreme centralization in a relatively small, highly educated managerial and professional specialist group that will bypass (and perhaps greatly reduce) middle management.
2. Expansion of specialists who will replace white- and blue-collar operating employees as the largest category of personnel. These college-educated specialists will be knowledge workers performing relatively programmed and non-satisfying tasks. Such organizations will probably also demonstrate substantial centralization of decision making.
3. Organizational democracy in which managers are answerable to their subordinates, who will have formal mechanisms for influencing organizational policy.

No single one of these forms is likely to dominate because organizations will vary with task, technology, situation, and people. Some organizations will continue in the form of the older traditional, bureaucratic, and contemporary structures. While recognizing the limitations of the pyramid, most companies will seek to modify it rather than abandoning it entirely.[38] In the final analysis, management must conclude that there must always be accountability and ultimate authority in an organization. But what is most important is that we combine stability and flexibility, rationality and feeling; that we learn how to design systems that treat employees, customers, and clients competently, equitably, *and* personally.

REVIEW QUESTIONS

1. In network experiments, what tasks were best performed with a wheel structure?

2. In network experiments, what tasks were best performed by an all-channel structure?

3. The more effective container manufacturing firm was characterized by what kind of management and structure?

4. The more effective research laboratory was characterized by what kind of management and structure?

5. What is mass-production or large-batch technology? What organizational princples or guidelines do such organizations tend to follow?

6. What is job-shop or small-batch technology? What organization principles or guidelines do such organizations tend to follow?

7. What is continuous-processing technology? What organizational principles or guidelines do such organizations tend to follow?

8. What are mechanistic structures? Where are they found?

9. What are organic structures? Where are they found?

10. What is a stable environment? What structure tends to characterize organizations in such an environment?

11. What is a turbulent environment? What structure tends to characterize organizations in such an environment?

12. What is differentiation in an organization? Why is it necessary?

13. What is integration in an organization? Why is it necessary?

14. What stakeholders are highlighted in traditional microeconomic theory?

15. In what ways can the structure of the competitive arena affect the structure of an organization?

16. Why are stakeholder interests originating in political and social groups of importance in thinking about the structure of a business firm?

17. How are organizations likely to evolve? What are the phases they may pass through?

18. Why do some predictions suggest that future organizations will be less pointed at the top?

19. Why might such future organizations appear *more* centralized to middle and lower managers and workers?

20. Why might graduate education be of growing importance at top levels in the future?

21. Why are some predictions pessimistic about the intrinsic work satisfaction of many college graduates in future organizations?

22. What form might organizational democracy take in future organizations?

23. What is free-form organization? Is it really free?

Notes and References on the Contigency Approach to Organization Design

1. The term *contingency theory* has become widely used to describe the literature appearing from the late 1950s through the 1970s, dealing with the environmental circumstances that seem to be related to various patterns of organizational structure. See Joan Woodward, *Management and Technology* (London: H. M. Stationary Office, 1958); T. Burns and G. M. Stalker, *The Management of Innovation* (London: Tavistock, 1961); Paul Lawrence and Jay Lorsch, *Organization and Environment* (Homewood, Ill.: Richard D. Irwin, 1969); and Howard Aldrich, *Organizations and Environments* (Englewood Cliffs, N.J.: Prentice-Hall, 1979).

2. Alex Bavelas, "Communication Patterns in Task-Oriented Groups," *Journal of the Acoustical Society of America* 22 (1950), pp. 725–30; Harold Guetzkow and Herbert A. Simon, "The Impact of Certain Communication Nets upon Organization and Performance in Task-Oriented Groups," *Management Science* 1, nos. 3 & 4 (1955); and C. Faucheux and K. D. Mackenzie, "Task Dependency of Organizational Centrality; Its Behavioral Consequences," *Journal of Experimental Sociology and Psychology* 2, no. 4 (1966), pp. 361–75.

3. J. J. Morse and J. W. Lorsch, "Beyond Theory Y," *Harvard Business Review,* May–June 1970, pp. 61–68.

4. Joan Woodward, *Management and Technology* (London: Her Majesty's Stationery Office, 1958), and *Industrial Organization: Theory and Practice* (Oxford: Oxford University Press, 1965). Also see A. H. Van de Ven and A. L. Delbecq, "A Task Contingent Model of Work-Unit Structure," *Administrative Science Quarterly* 19, no. 2 (1974), pp. 183–97; E. Harvey, "Technology and the Structure of Organizations," *American Sociological Review,* April 1968, pp. 247–59; and M. Jelinek, "Technology, Organizations and Contingency," *Academy of Management Review,* January 1977, pp. 17–26.

5. J. D. Thompson, *Organizations in Action* (New York: McGraw-Hill, 1967); J. Hage and M. Aiken, "Rela-tionship of Centralization to Other Structural Properties," *Administrative Science Quarterly,* June 1967, pp. 72–92; M. Aiken and J. Hage, "Organizational Interdependence and Intraorganizational Structure," *American Sociological Review* 33 (1968), pp. 912–30.

6. E. J. Miller and A. K. Rice, *Systems of Organization* (London: Tavistock, 1967).

7. Production management predominates in mass-production firms because this is the key organizational activity, but engineering managers predominate in custom and small-batch firms because product design is not routinized, hence less predictable. In continuous-processing technology, marketing tends to be critical because output is difficult to shut off or inventory; customers must be found. Joan Woodward, ed., *Industrial Organization: Behavior and Control* (London: Oxford University Press, 1970). See also R. T. Keller, J. W. Slocum, Jr., and G. I. Susman, "Uncertainty and Type of Management System in Continuous Processing Organizations," *Academy of Management Journal* 17, no. 1 (1974), pp. 56–68.

8. The terms *mechanistic* and *organic* are from T. Burns and G. M. Stalker, *The Management of Innovation* (London: Tavistock, 1961).

9. One study observes that line organizations tend to be structured like erect pyramids: ▲. But staff structures are inverted: ▼. H. Kaufman and D. Seidman, "Morphology of Organizations," *Administrative Science Quarterly,* December 1970, pp. 439–51.

For an overview of technology and structure, see R. G. Hunt, "Technology and Organization," *Academy of Management Journal* 13, no. 3 (1970), pp. 235–52. Also see J. D. Thompson and F. L. Bates, "Technology, Organization, and Administration," *Administrative Science Quarterly* 2 (1957), pp. 325–42; D. J. Hick, D. S. Pugh, and D. C. Pheysey, "Operations Technology and Organization Structure: An Empirical Reappraisal," *Administrative Science Quarterly* 14 (1969), pp. 378–97;

E. Harvey, "Technology and the Structure of Organizations," *American Sociological Review* 33 (1968), pp. 247–59; L. B. Mohr, "Organizational Technology and Organizational Structure," *Administrative Science Quarterly* 15 (1970), pp. 444–59; H. Aldrich, "Technology and Organization Structure: An Examination of the Findings of the Aston Group," *Administrative Science Quarterly* 17 (1972), pp. 26–43; and Charles Perrow, *Organizational Analysis: A Sociological View* (Belmont, Calif.: Wadsworth, 1970).

Debate continues about how important technology is as a determinant of organizational structure. The "technological imperative" maintains that it is the major factor in overall structure, but most research suggests that its influence is mainly on the lower hierarchical levels. At high levels, environment factors and general strategy affect structure more. Thus, because individual departments within a large organization may utilize different technologies, their departmental structures should differ. A. J. Grimes and S. M. Klein, "The Technological Imperative: The Relative Impact of Task Unit, Modal Technology and Hierarchy on Structure," *Academy of Management Journal* 16, no. 4 (1973), pp. 583–97.

10. R. C. Hood, "Business Organization as a Cross Product of Its Purposes and of Its Environment," in Mason Haire, ed., *Organizational Theory in Industrial Practice* (New York: John Wiley & Sons, 1962), p. 73; Jay Galbraith, "Environmental and Technological Determinants of Organizational Design," in Jay W. Lorsch and Paul R. Lawrence, *Studies in Organization Design* (Homewood, Ill.: Richard D. Irwin, 1970); and D. V. Nightingale and J. Toulouse, "Toward a Multilevel Congruence Theory of Organization," *Administrative Science Quarterly*, June 1977, pp. 264 ff.

11. B. R. Scott maintains that firms are becoming more sensitive to their markets. "The Industrial State: Old Myths and New Realities," *Harvard Business Review*, March–April 1973, pp. 133–48.

12. F. E. Emery and E. L. Trist, "The Causal Texture of Organization Environments," *Human Relations* 18 (1965), pp. 21–32. They describe environment categories as: (1) placid, randomized (the economist's perfect competition); (2) placid, clustered (the economist's imperfect competition); (3) disturbed, reactive (oligopolistic market); and (4) turbulent, relative uncertainty. On judging an environment, see H. Tosi, R. Aldag, and R. Storey, "On the measurement of the Environment," *Administrative Science Quarterly* 18, no. 1 (1973), pp. 27–36; R. B. Duncan, "Characteristics of Organizational Environments and Perceived Environmental Uncertainty," *Administrative Science Quarterly* 17, no. 3 (1972), pp. 313–27; and R. N. Osborn and J. G. Hunt, "Environment and Organizational Effectiveness," *Administrative Science Quarterly* 19, no. 2 (1974), pp. 231–46.

13. One study indicates that the most important cause of decentralization is management's sensitivity to and concern about the environment, more than the technology involved or even the size of the firm. A. R. Negandhi and B. C. Reimann, "Correlates of Decentralization: Closed and Open Systems Perspective," *Academy of Management Journal* 16, no. 4 (1973), pp. 570–82.

14. Environment forces can virtually take over an organization. See J. Maniha and C. Perrow, "The Reluctant Organization and the Aggressive Environment," *Administrative Science Quarterly* 10, no. 2 (1965), pp. 238–57, and R. Leifer and G. P. Huber, "Relations among Perceived Environmental Uncertainty, Organizational Structure and Boundary-Spanning Behavior," *Administrative Science Quarterly*, June 1977, pp. 235–47.

15. M. Anshen, "The Management of Ideas," *Harvard Business Review*, July–August, 1969, pp. 99–106. Perhaps the most turbulent business environment is the popular music business, with its overnight hit tunes. Musical artists and recording entrepreneurs attempt to retain great flexibility; all relationships are temporary to avoid being stuck with a producer who "loses his or her ear" R. A. Peterson and D. G. Berger, "Entrepreneurship in Organizations: Evidence from the Popular Music Industry," *Administrative Science Quarterly* 16, no. 1 (1971), pp. 97–106.

16. S. Terrebury maintains that (1) contemporary changes in organizational environments are such as to increase the ratio of externally induced change to internally induced change and (2) *other* formal organizations are, increasingly, the important components in the environment of any organization. "The Evolution of Organizational Environments," *Administrative Science Quarterly* 12, no. 4 (1968), pp. 590–613.

17. C. J. Haberstroh, "Organization Design and Systems Analysis," in James G. March, ed., *Handbook of Organizations* (Skokie, Ill.: Rand McNally, 1965), pp. 1171–213.

18. Peter M. Blau, "A Formal Theory of Differentiation in Organizations," *American Sociological Review* 35, no. 2 (1970), pp. 201–18; Richard N. Hall, "Intraorganizational Structural Variation: Application of the Bureaucratic Model," *Administrative Science Quarterly*, December 1962, pp. 295–308.

19. Common errors in organization design include:

1. Combining two different major tasks in the same unit.
2. Placing similar tasks in separate units, with consequent conflict and redundancy of effort.
3. Using the management hierarchy as the major integrating device in highly differentiated organizations.
4. Using integrating devices between mildly differentiated units, which merely adds "noise" to the system.
5. Structuring and orienting an integrating unit so much like one of the sections being linked that it loses contact with the other.

See P. R. Lawrence and Jay W. Lorsch, *Organization and Environment: Managing Differentiation and Integration* (Boston: Graduate School of Business Administration, Harvard University, 1967); P. R. Lawrence and J. W. Lorsch, "Differentiation and Integration in Complex Organizations," *Administrative Science Quarterly* 12, no. 1 (1967), pp. 1–49; J. W. Lorsch and P. R. Lawrence, *Studies in Organization Design;* J. W. Lorsch and S. A. Allen III *Managing Diversity and Interdependence* (Boston: Graduate School of Business Administration Harvard University, 1973); and P. N. Khandwalla, "Viable and Effective Organizational Designs of Firms," *Academy of Management Journal* 16, no. 3 (1973), pp. 481–95.

20. L. R. Sayles and M. Chandler, *Managing Large Systems* (New York: Harper & Row, 1972).

21. J. D. Ford and J. W. Slocum, Jr., "Size, Technology, Environment and the Structure of Organizations," *Academy of Management Review,* October 1977, pp. 561–75.

22. For a comprehensive examination of the issues involved in the management of the stakeholder context, see R. Edward Freeman, *Strategic Management: A Stakeholder Approach* (Boston: Pitman Publishing, 1983).

23. Michael Porter, *Competitive Strategies* (New York: Free Press, 1980).

24. E. T. Penrose, *The Theory of the Growth of the Firm* (Oxford: Blackwell, 1960).

25. L. E. Greiner, "Evolution and Revolution as Organizations Grow," *Harvard Business Review,* July–August 1972, pp. 33–42.

26. David Oates, "Is the Pyramid Crumbling?" *International Management* 26, no. 7 (1971), pp. 10–13; A. C. Filley and R. J. House, "Management and the Future," *Business Horizons* 13, no. 2 (1970), p. 7; F. E. Emery, "Bureaucracy and Beyond," *Organizational Dynamics* 3, no. 3 (1974), pp. 3–13; P. G. Herbst, *Alternatives to Hierarchies* (Leiden, Neth.: M. Nijhoff, 1976).

27. H. J. Leavitt and T. L. Whisler, "Management in the 1980s," *Harvard Business Review,* November–December 1968, pp. 41–48; H. A. Simon, "The Corporation: Will It Be Managed by Machines?" in H. J. Leavitt and L. Pondy, eds., *Readings in Managerial Psychology* (Chicago: University of Chicago Press, 1964); T. L. Whisler, *Information Technology and Organizational Change* (Belmont, Calif.: Wadsworth, 1970); R. Stewart, *How Computers Affect Management* (Cambridge, Mass.: MIT Press, 1972).

28. S. C. Vance, "Toward a Collegial Office of the President," *California Management Review* 15, no. 1 (1972), p. 106. Three executives is most common, but the range is from two to seven (with one 12-person office of the president). See also Peter Drucker, "New-Old Top Management Aid: The Executive Secretariat," *Harvard Business Review,* September–October 1973, p. 6 ff.

29. E. E. Jennings, *The Mobile Manager* (Bureau of Industrial Relations, Graduate School of Business Administration, University of Michigan, 1967). J. E. Steele and L. B. Ward observe that the most striking change in educational backgrounds of top executives between 1964 and 1972 is the appearance of much greater numbers of M.B.A.s. "MBA's: Mobile, Well Situated, Well Paid," *Harvard Business Review,* January–February 1974, pp. 99–109.

30. John Dearden, "Computers: No Impact on Divisional Control," *Harvard Business Review,* January–February 1967, pp. 94–105.

31. K. E. Knight and J. A. Miller, "Impact of Computers on Management," unpublished manuscript, Stanford University, 1966; L. G. Wagner, "Computers, Decentralization and Corporate Control," *California Management Review,* Winter 1966, pp. 25–32.

32. See A. M. McDonough, *Information Economics and Management Systems* (New York: McGraw-Hill, 1963) on the expansion of knowledge jobs.

33. P. E. Slater and W. G. Bennis, "Democracy is Inevitable," *Harvard Business Review,* March–April 1964, pp. 51–59. See also W. G. Bennis, "Organizational Developments and the Fate of Bureaucracy," *Trans-Action* 2, no. 5 (1965), pp. 31–36. L. E. Preston and J. E. Post call this, "The Third Managerial Revolution," *Academy of Management Review,* September 1974, pp. 476–86.

34. It was reported at the convention of the American Association for the Advancement of Science, December

28, 1971, that at the Gaines pet food plant in Topeka, Kansas, policy decisions and all aspects of work are controlled by teams of workers. According to a company executive, the results of the experiment have been high performance, controllable costs, and an increase in productivity of 10 to 40 percent. No independent verification has been published.

The Scott Paper Company of Philadelphia has announced a plan for a new 75-person plant to be operated according to "a new industrial democracy" under which an operating committee composed of six administrative officials and various delegates will make major decisions. Work teams will also supervise their own operations. *Philadelphia Inquirer,* July 1, 1973.

35.   On practice in Yugoslavia, see I. Adizes, *Industrial Democracy: Yugoslav Style* (New York: Free Press, 1971); H. W. Wachtel, *Workers' Management and Workers' Wages in Yugoslavia,* (Ithaca, N.Y.: Cornell University Press, 1973); F. H. Stephen, "Yugoslav Self-Management 1945–74," *Industrial Relations Journal* 7, no. 3 (1976), p. 56 ff.

For a counterview that the working class in Yugoslavia has much less influence than in Western countries, see M. Djilas, "The Slow Strangulation of the Socialist Working Class," *Business and Society Review/Innovation,* no. 6 (1973), pp. 4–7.

For more on various forms of industrial democracy, see A. Sturmthal, *Workers Councils* (Cambridge, Mass.: Harvard University Press, 1964); D. Jenkins, *Job Power: Blue- and White-Collar Democracy* (Garden City, N.Y.: Doubleday Publishing, 1973); J. Mire, "European Workers' Participation in Management," *Monthly Labor Review* 96, no. 2 (1973), pp. 9–15; L. A. Brua, "Worker Groups Gain Power in Common Market Companies," *Harvard Business Review,* November–December 1973, p. 8 ff; G. D. Garson and J. Case, *Worker's Control: A Reader on Labor and Social Change* (New York: Random House, 1973); E. Rose, "Work Control in Industrial Society," *Industrial Relations Journal* 7, no. 3 (1976), pp. 20–30.

For a skeptical view of the whole movement, see H. R. Northrup, "Worker Participation: Industrial Democracy or Union Power Enhancement," *Vital Speeches of the Day,* January 1, 1978, pp. 184–186; and also R. Edwards, *Contested Terrain: The Transformation of the Workplace in the Twentieth Century* (New York: Basic Books, 1979).

36.   J. J. Pascucci, "The Emergence of Free-Form Management," *Personnel Administration,* September–October 1968, pp. 33–41. In a *Fortune* list of 46 conglomerates, 12 are considered to use free-form structures. See T. O'Hanlon, "The Odd News about Conglomerates," *Fortune,* June 15, 1967, pp. 175–77.

37.   J. W. Forrester, "A New Corporate Design," *Industrial Management Review* 7, no. 1 (1965), pp. 5–17.

38.   R. D. Miewald, "The Greatly Exaggerated Death of Bureaucracy," *California Management Review* 13, no. 1 (1970), pp. 65–69. P. A. Clark argues that behavioral scientists and such theories as job enrichment, Theory Y, and participative management have had little impact on actual organizational structures. Managers still like Theory X and hierarchies. *Organizational Design: Theory and Practice* (London: Tavistock, 1972). R. Reich argues that the most important challenge to American managers is to develop an adequate institutional framework for incorporating human potential into organizational systems. *The Next American Frontier* (New York: Penguin Books, 1983).

20

Managing the Structuring Process

In the mid-1970s, a large manufacturing concern saw a precipitous drop in the demand for its major product. As orders fell and production schedules were reduced, the inventory of unassembled components began to rise. The company's president asked his principal line managers to bring the inventory situation under control. During the next month, the inventory crisis worsened. Again the president issued instructions calling for a reduction in inventories. In the following weeks they continued to rise. Somehow the actions he was taking had had little effect on decisions about the ordering and receipt of components from the company's suppliers.

It became clear, upon investigation, that existing organizational arrangements isolated the purchasing department from information about the inventory accumulation that was available in the manufacturing plants. At the same time, the company's purchasing agents were in daily contact with component suppliers. This arrangement had worked well for many years, as growth in demand had outstripped the production capacity of the plants and good relations with suppliers had been critical for keeping production from lagging.

How was the president to alter the situation? What decisions could he take that would change the way in which purchasing agents went about their jobs? Senior managers are often confronted with puzzles of this type. When problems arise, it is not always clear where within the complex web of organizational arrangements the causes lie. Nor is it obvious which administrative mechanisms can be used effectively to bring about change. In this chapter we will consider some of the forces that shape and change the structured patterns of activity in organizations and explore some of the challenges faced by managers as they attempt to deal with them.[1]*

Shaping Organizational Structure

So far in Part Six, we have discussed what structure is and under what conditions different kinds of structure seem to work best. We have yet to address the issue of how structure comes to be. To do so we need a model of the structuring process in organizations, such as the one in Figure 20–1. This model makes a distinction between (1) administrative arrangements established in designing tasks, assigning responsibilities, specifying communications channels, and providing for coordination and (2) structured patterns of behavior within the organization. Managers can change the former directly, but the latter can only be influenced indirectly.

A simplistic view of the structuring process is that top management specifies what the structure is to be, and the members of the organization then pattern their activities to conform to it.[2] In a small, owner-managed firm, such a description may be close to the reality of the situation. But in examining an organization of even moderate size and having some degree of specialization, it soon becomes clear that many individuals are making choices every day that shape the actual structural patterns. Managers, then, must find ways to influence those decisions if they wish to maintain or change some dimension of the organization's design.[3]

---

* Notes and references will be found at the end of this chapter.

FIGURE 20–1

A Model of the Structuring Process

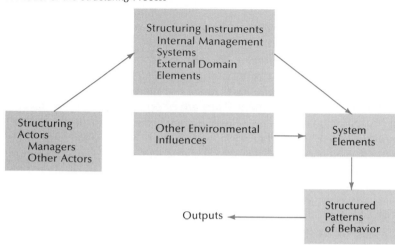

Structuring Actors

The stakeholder perspective discussed in Chapter 19 suggests that managers are not alone in their attempts to influence the structural patterns within an organization. There are many actors that participate in the structuring process.[4] In the recent drama through which the American Telephone and Telegraph Company has been reorganized, AT&T managers shared the stage with the Justice Department, the Federal Trade Commission, a federal judge, the U.S. Congress, several competitors in the areas of telecommunications equipment and long-distance service, regulatory commissions at the state level, labor unions, and the managers of the Bell System operating companies (which on January 1, 1984, became free-standing corporations).

The set of structuring actors can include many individuals, both within and outside the organization. Figure 20–2 provides an illustration of the structuring actors for one organization. There is no list of structuring actors that can be applied to organizations in general. Identifying them is a key analytic task. Some should be considered individually because of the striking personal influence they are seen to have. More often, however, they should be treated as several relatively homogeneous groups of individuals. It is assumed that structuring actors are not constrained to share a common perception of the state of the organization, nor need they act in harmony. It is possible, then, that different actors may seek to influence the structure in conflicting ways.

Top management has a primary stake in the proper functioning of the overall system, and other structuring actors are interested in partial segments of the system. Top management must be able to identify the network of structuring actors and to understand how and why they seek to influence the organization. Top management thus puts itself in a position to develop strategies for harmonizing the multiple influ-

FIGURE 20–2

Typical Structuring Actors

- top management
- technical specialists
- middle management
- union officials
- suppliers
- regulators
- legislators
- community leaders

ences of structuring actors in order to create an organization that can adapt and readapt to the critical aspects of its environment.

Structuring Instruments

The various actors bring their influence to bear on the structured patterns of behavior in an organization through a variety of devices. Perhaps the more obvious of these are the administrative arrangements that are the subject matter of innumerable works on organization and management. They are of primary concern in classical management theory. Structure is often defined as being these very arrangements. It is helpful to distinguish them from other aspects of structure as internal management systems. The particular details of management systems vary from one organization to another, but they generally serve four functions: planning, resource allocation, the organizing of operations, and monitoring and controlling performance.

THE BETTER HALF.   By Harris

"Have I told you about my boss's new incentive program?"

The Better Half, reprinted courtesy *The Register* and Tribune Syndicate, Inc.

It is easy to be trapped by the assumption that the managers in an organization have absolute control over their own management systems. For many management systems this is so. These are discretionary management systems. Often, however, external legislative, regulatory, and professional bodies set down guidelines for management systems or actually specify what they shall be and how they shall operate. Consider, for example, the influence of the accounting profession on the design of financial control systems. These are externally influenced management systems. Recognizing this distinction can be important in devising plans for managing the structuring process or for seeking to understand why structuring actors choose particular approaches.

Another set of structuring instruments lying outside the organization can be thought of as external domain elements. Usually ignored in discussions of structure and lumped into a general category of environmental constraints, domain elements can, nonetheless, be used explicitly by structuring actors to influence patterns of behavior within the organization.

The most fundamental domain element is the social contract under which the organization exists. An example from the world of communications can illustrate the point. The U.S. Postal Service is run by the federal government, for in the United States there is a general and long-standing social and political commitment to a governmental role in providing universal basic postal services. On the other hand, the provision of telecommunications services has been reserved for the private sector.

Other domain elements often include an organization's formal charter, external reporting requirements, factor markets, and complementary and competing industries. What distinguishes these as domain elements is that structuring actors can use them to influence patterns of behavior within the organization. If they are not used for such a purpose, they are merely additional elements in the environment. Managers should be sensitive to them, nonetheless, because they may be potential domain elements to which structuring actors can turn if they believe it will give them leverage that they need.

There are other environmental constraints not accessible for use in influencing the structure of an organization. These include available technology, the general sociopolitical environment, and most psychological dimensions of organization members. Such elements are important for understanding the structuring process, even though they cannot be used as structuring instruments. They serve as forces that condition how the basic system elements will respond to the use of structuring elements. The structured behavior patterns emerge from the interplay of structuring instruments and environmental constraints.

Managing the Process

The challenge facing managers concerned with organization design is to influence and channel the activities of organization members so that they take on patterns that lead to successful performance. There are several avenues open to them.

Direct Intervention

Several years ago Robert Cushman of the Norton Company, a manufacturer of abrasives and a variety of other industrial and consumer products, became convinced that his company was initiating too many new ventures without appropriate concern for profitability. He created a committee to review each product line. By chairing the committee himself and involving a wide range of middle-level line and staff managers in the review process, he was able to focus the company's attention and resources on its strongest competitive offerings.

This vignette illustrates two aspects of direct intervention in shaping organization design. A manager can create a new or altered component of the formal organization, such as the committee to review product lines. This may alter information flows, bring different people together, and change authority relationships. It may, or may

FIGURE 20–3

Approaches to Managing the Structuring Process

- Direct intervention
- Signaling
- Supportive intervention
- Orchestration

not, affect the underlying decision patterns. A manager can also use personal leadership, as did Cushman, to direct the attention of other managers at critical issues.

Direct intervention can also be targeted at administrative practices, such as the format and content of financial reports, performance evaluation practices, and the specification of job content. When management chooses to intervene directly to alter the organization's structure, it must be prepared for many of the challenges discussed in Part Seven on managing change and conflict.[5]

Signaling

During an indoctrination training session for new junior managers, it is not uncommon for a high-level company official to tell a few anecdotes about the founder of the firm or one of its early heroes in the laboratory or on the shop floor. Such stories can contain strong symbolic messages that help establish and maintain a common understanding among organization members as to important corporate values and sanctioned behavior patterns. For example, some stories encourage risk taking, others emphasize loyalty.

Such management actions serve as signals to organization members. These help them interpret in a consistent fashion the component parts of the organization's formal structural arrangements. Signals can make it clear whether the annual planning calendar is a serious part of the strategic decision-making process or whether it is merely window dressing. They may reinforce a rigid chain-of-command or may encourage lateral communications.

Managers can send signals about the meaning of the organization's structure in many ways.[6] Among them might be the content and weightings in performance appraisals, the agendas for interdivisional meetings, the degree of realism or arbitrariness in the assignment of corporate overhead to profit centers, or statements to the press.

Supportive Intervention

During the 1970s the U.S. Postal Service faced a pressing need to achieve cost savings through extensive mechanization of the mail-processing function.[7] The organizational changes that were a direct result of the introduction of the new technology were dictated by (1) the size, speed, and operating characteristics of the new machines, (2) mail flow patterns, and (3) the available transportation network. Because these were all technical issues, top management left the design and implementation of the change in the hands of the organization's technical specialists.

During this same period, nonetheless, top management invested significant amounts of time, energy, and organizational resources in bringing about dramatic changes in postal service relations with the labor unions and in the organization's labor practices. Perhaps because of this concerted effort, the attitudes of the work force toward the massive mechanization of mail processing was mostly positive. Occasional grievances that did arise were not actively pursued by the unions.

Often, for one change in an organization's design to be effective it is necessary for other changes to be undertaken simultaneously. Such supportive intervention can be seen in the story of the U.S. Postal Service, wherein changes induced by a new technology were supported by changes in labor practices. Managers must become keen students of the intricate interrelationships among organizational components if they wish to master the art of supportive intervention.

Orchestration

Earlier we alluded to the major changes that have recently taken place at AT&T. During the late 1970s and early 1980s, much ·of upper management's time and attention has been devoted to an elaborate process of balancing the interests of a wide range of stakeholders, each occupying a position in a different sphere of the company's complex environment.

AT&T management, whether dealing with issues of technology, competitive posture, or marketing, was obliged to confront external and internal structural constraints. For instance, much time and effort and many resources were directed at influencing the political processes (especially at the federal level) through which the rules of the game for the communications industry are established and changed. The Justice Department's antitrust litigation that led to the proposals to reorganize the AT&T family through divestiture of the operating companies provides a striking example of how external actors bring pressure to bear on an organizational system's structure. It also illustrates well how top management often opts for an active role in orchestrating the outcome. AT&T senior managers spared no effort to assure that the company attained the freedom to enter unregulated markets in exchange for the surrender of control over half of the company's assets.

Because the structuring process often involves many actors with disparate points of view and objectives, a key job for management is to seek a set of simultaneous actions across multiple fronts that brings the many pressures into a harmonious balance. The skills required include strategic insight, analytical aptitude, competence in technical aspects of organization design, and a high degree of political acumen.

SUMMARY

Managers can improve their understanding of the dynamics of structure by giving attention to the relationships between patterns of behavior and the instruments through which they can be shaped. This in turn can make them more effective in coping with the pressures for adaptation generated by changes in the organization's environment or in the definition of its mission.

Multiple actors seek to influence the structured patterns of action that make up an organization. They do so through a variety of instruments, including internal management systems and external domain elements.

Managers may attempt to manage the structuring process through direct intervention, signaling, supportive intervention, and the orchestration of the many influence attempts that impinge upon the system's structure.

REVIEW QUESTIONS

1. Why must managers be concerned with the forces that shape their organization's structure?

2. What is meant by structuring actors?

3. How are structuring actors different from stakeholders in general?

4. Provide some examples of structuring instruments?

5. Why should managers distinguish between internal management systems and external domain elements?

6. In what ways can outsiders influence internal management systems?

7. What is direct intervention?

8. What is supportive intervention?

9. How do signals influence structure?

10. What is meant by orchestration in the context of the management of the structuring process?

Notes and References on Managing the Structuring Process

1. A good recent review of the literature about the complex phenomena called structures, the forces that shape them, and how managers work with those forces is available in Henry Mintzberg, *The Structuring of Organizations* (Englewood Cliffs, N.J.: Prentice-Hall, 1979).

2. An extreme example of such dominance by an organization's leader can be found in the cases of some charismatic religious leaders, as in the case of the mass suicide at Jonestown, Guayana, under the strong influence of cult leader Jim Jones.

3. Joseph Bower reports that managers at higher levels in complex organizations often do not participate directly in making key decisions but rather influence those decisions by shaping the decision context. *Managing the Resource Allocation Process* (Homewood, Ill.: Richard D. Irwin, Inc., 1972).

4. For a discussion of the role of coalitions in the management process, see R. M. Cyert and J. G. March, *A Behavioral Theory of the Firm* (Englewood Cliffs, N.J.: Prentice-Hall, 1963).

5. A good guide to the issue involved in managing change in organizations is Richard Beckhard and Reuben Harris, *Organizational Transitions: Managing Complex Change* (Reading, Mass.: Addison-Wesley Publishing, 1977).

6. For a discussion of the intricate web of influence that managers use to condition decision-making in diversified corporations, see Richard Vancil, *Decentralization: Managerial Ambiguity by Design* (Homewood, Ill.: Dow Jones-Irwin, 1979).

7. For a fuller discussion of the management of organizational changes in the postal service following its establishment in 1970, see John T. Tierney, *The Reorganization of Postal Management: Problems in applying the Law to the Letter* (doctoral thesis, Department of Government, Harvard University, 1979); and Paul Browne, *The Roles of Top Management in Shaping Organization Design: Evidence from the United States Postal Service* (doctoral dissertation, Graduate School of Business Administration, Harvard University, 1981).

21

Pragmatic Organizational Designs

"One picture is worth a thousand words" goes the old Chinese aphorism. Therefore we should look at some illustrations of organizational structure and design in a variety of actual organizations.[1]* We will use organization charts accompanied by a verbal description. Charts by themselves are rarely sufficient to explain how an organization really works. Inexperienced managers occasionally get in trouble by assuming that the chart is the reality.

Each organization is described in the context of the main structural purpose it is designed to achieve: maintaining stability in a small print shop, ensuring reliable response on a warship, guiding growth in a stable utility, maintaining control in a large automobile manufacturer, balancing initiative and control in a decentralized electrical firm, reconciling centralized policy and dispersed implementation in an insurance company, meshing divergent interests in a hosptial, and integrating organizations in a conglomerate.

A warning to keep in mind: Management frequently modifies organization charts to reflect personnel transfers and regroupings of responsibilities. We will describe each organization in the present tense, but this doesn't mean, for example, that the organization at General Electric today is structured exactly as described here. Some large corporations have one department devoted entirely to keeping organization charts up to date! Therefore, the charts in this chapter are not exact or official representations of what currently exists. They do, however, accurately reflect the more persistent organizational strategies of the firms involved: the use of staff and line, relative centralization and decentralization, basis for specialization, use of matrix arrangements, and so on. In addition, the charts are not complete in showing every organizational unit. To do so would be impossible without large sheets of paper. What you will examine will be the basic structure with selected detail to illustrate lower organizational levels.

Organizations Described
- small print shop
- warship
- utility
- automobile manufacturer
- electrical manufacturer
- insurance company
- hospital
- conglomerate

Maintaining Stability in a Small Business

The Modern Press is a small owner-managed print shop. Customers come in the door or call on the phone and place their orders with the owner or the secretary/bookkeeper (the owner's sister). The copy goes to the shop supervisor (the owner's brother), who gives it to the linotypist, who casts the type. This goes to a compositor, who adds hand type and sets it in a frame. The printer then runs it on a press after obtaining paper from the supervisor, who also is the paper cutter and purchasing agent. An office assistant collates, staples, binds, and packages the printed material. The owner calculates the prices, and bills are typed by the secretary.

As Figure 21–1 illustrates, the organization is very simple. Everyone specializes by task; chain and unity of command are maintained. Spans of control are small, delegation is clear. The static principles are followed, and decision making is highly centralized in the owner-manager. The basic organizational strategy is to promote predictability and quality so that the owner can promise a good job by a specific time. High quality and rapid service are the key to ensuring stability through repeat business and word of recommendation to attract new customers.

---

* Notes and references will be found at the end of this chapter.

FIGURE 21-1

Organization Chart of The Modern Press

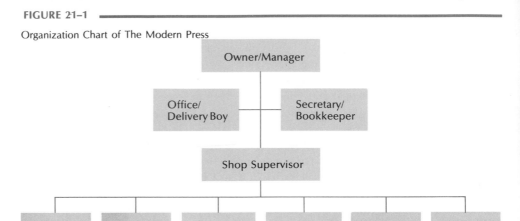

The system works extremely well as long as customer desires are within the limited range of the firm's capabilities. A customer who wants color pictures or engraving is out of luck. One who wants a less expensive process—mimeograph or offset—must go elsewhere. By refusing to provide these services, the owner-manager loses some business but maintains simplicity, predictability, quality, and stability in the short run.

"What's the good of owning the company if you can't give yourself a raise whenever I want one?"

From *The Wall Street Journal*, with permission of Cartoon Features Syndicate.

Ensuring Reliable Response on a Warship

The U.S.S. *Hero* is a U.S. navy destroyer designed to provide antisubmarine and aircraft protection to larger surface ships as well as to perform miscellaneous gunfire, missile, communications, and transportations missions. Its total crew is approximately 16 officers and 300 enlisted assigned as in Figure 21–2.

The Positions

The commanding officer is in overall charge, and his formal authority over the crew is substantial—even if reduced from the omnipotence of sailing ship days. He operates through an executive officer whose responsibility is ensuring routine and discipline through scheduling of the ship's controllable daily activities.

The Operations Department is vested with informing the commanding officer of where, when, and what the ship is to be and do as well as maintaining and operating the electronic equipment necessary to do this. The Gunnery Department is responsible for guns, missiles, and torpedoes and associated computing and directing equipment. The Engineering Department maintains and operates firerooms, engine rooms, and auxiliary machinery to provide power to the vessel. The Supply Department handles ordering supplies, payroll disbursement, food preparation, and service.

Each of the department heads has division officers who supervise technical and administrative activities. These division officers are unusually young lieutenants (junior grade) and ensigns. In general, each division is responsible for certain physical compartments and the equipment therein. For example, the radio operators in the Communications Division must maintain their equipment, but they are also responsible for cleaning and painting their living space. Direct supervision is handled through the petty officer ranks: chief petty officer, first-class petty officer, third-class petty officer. The petty officers are distinguished by technical skills. Thus the Operations Department contains; radiomen, radarmen, signalmen, and electronics technicians. The Gunnery Department: gunner's mates, bosun's mates, fire controlmen, and sonarmen. The Engineering Department: boilermen, machinist mates, and auxiliarymen. The lowest ranking enlisted men are called seamen or firemen depending on the departments they are in.

The Strategy

The essential organizational strategy is to ensure rapid decisions and predictable member response to emergency conditions and central orders. Chain of command is clear and spans of control small. Duties of specific positions are quite clearly defined and standardized so personnel can be easily replaced in case of transfer or injury. The basic organizational criteria are military rank, functional specialty, and ship's space.

The structure follows all of the static principles, but certain conditions make reality a little different than the formal structure suggests. The division officers tend to be inexperienced young people just out of college. Most will spend only three or four years in the service. Therefore, they possess rank and formal authority over career,

FIGURE 21–2

Partial Organization Chart of U.S.S. *Hero*

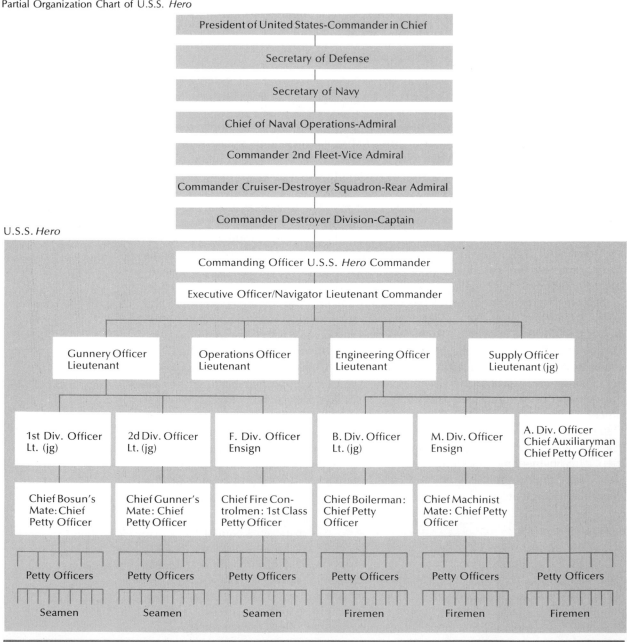

older petty officers who have greater technical knowledge developed through 10 to 20 years. The junior officers are very dependent on these senior enlisted men for effective divisional performance. This situation counters the commissioned officers' formal authority, so actually more joint discussion and decision making occurs than the hierarchical structure implies.

In addition, the structure relies greatly on the chain of command for handling grievances and personnel problems. Unfortunately, this doesn't work very well because intervening levels are loath to communicate matters that reflect adversely on them.[2] Problems of black enlisted men have especially not lent themselves to effective management through the command structure. Accordingly, commands are instituting human relations councils composed of representatives of the officers, petty officers, and nonrated personnel. Complaints can be brought to the council meetings in a way that legitimizes bypassing the chain of command and ensures that the commanding officer will investigate the matter, if not act upon it. Thus the military structure designed to promote standardized, routine, and rapid behavior must adjust to less predictable and more subtle people problems.

Guiding Growth in a Stable Utility

No organization is entirely stable or unstable, all routine or all innovative. In all institutions some aspects and activities are fairly fixed and others are changing. Nonetheless, in broad terms we can locate organizations along a stability-instability continuum and examine their organizational strategies for dealing with the environment and achieving their objectives. Philadelphia Electric is a relatively stable concern whose main objective has been responding to demands for energy with appropriate growth.

The Strategy

Electricity is a product that doesn't change, and generating technology has developed quite slowly. Therefore, structure tends to be quite simple, even though the company is large and its equipment complex. As Figure 21–3 illustrates, the general organizational structure of Philadelphia Electric makes use of central organizational strategy of functional specialization through the Departments of Electric Operations (generating and distributing electricity), Gas Operations (distributing natural gas), Engineering and Research (designing and constructing generating and distributing facilities). Principles of chain and unit of command are closely followed in most areas, but Personnel has been assigned functional authority over such matters as pay policies and fringe benefits in order to promote standardization in this organization in which security and fringe benefits are the main attractions to employees.

Marketing is quite unimportant. In recent years demand has outstripped supply, so the company discourages new customers. In addition, Philadelphia Electric enjoys a monopoly in its geographic area of southeastern Pennsylvania. Investment in facilities is so great that it would be too expensive for society to permit competition; the duplication of physical facilities would be prohibitively expensive and would utilize too much land. Marketing's activities have increasingly shifted to public rela-

FIGURE 21–3

Partial Organization Chart of Philadelphia Electric Company

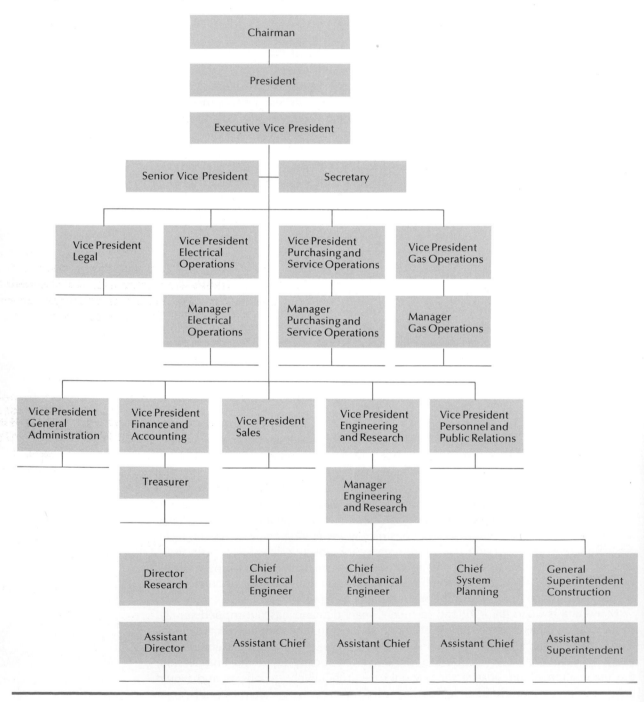

tions. This includes explaining to the community why a rate increase is necessary to pay for less polluting fuels, representing the firm at legislature hearings, and debating with various environmental protection groups.

The president and the chairperson traditionally are an engineer and a finance specialist. The engineer comes from a background in operations and engineering; the other top executive is experienced in raising capital funds from loans, bonds, and stock issues. Raising money is the essential precondition for engineering to proceed with design and construction of extremely expensive generating and distributing facilities.

One-on-One Structure

In short, the organization of this public utility is quite simple. The only distinctive feature is the frequency of one-on-one relationships. Most vice presidents and division managers have a manager directly under them with essentially the same title as their own. This is similar to the military, in which a commanding officer will have a span of control of one: an executive officer or adjutant who reports directly to him or her. The one-on-one concept reflects a desire to have one person in authority at all times who can deal with emergencies that can arise at any time in an organization that must operate continuously around the clock.

Maintaining Control in a Large Corporation

Few firms are larger than General Motors, which has thousands of employees in many countries. Yet, a recent chair of the board claims that "G.M. is basically a simple company."[3] Well, it's not that simple, but it has developed an easily understood system for handling its major problem—controlling the activities of this multi-faceted giant. Figure 21–5 presents the essential structural elements of General Motors. The company has been called "decentralized" because the general manager in charge of Pontiac Division has authority over a staff to manufacture, advertise, and sell the vehicles. Nonetheless, GM is really quite centralized in critical areas of finance, styling, and personnel.

The Dual-Overlap Structure

The finance arrangement was the great contribution of GM's longtime chief executive Alfred Sloan. Note that the chair of the board has a small span of control; only one of the executive vice presidents reports to the chair and the other three report to the president. This is the key to the dual-overlap structure of General Motors. Under the executive vice president of finance is a fully developed hierarchy of finance people, but most of these people are physically located among the worldwide operating units reporting to the president. Thus a Chevrolet plant in Ohio will have a plant manager reporting up the chain of command, but it will also have a plant finance manager whose primary orientation is up the separate finance hierarchy. Of course, the local finance person must cooperate with the plant manager, but their futures lie up two different ladders. What this provides the top is two

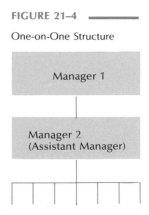

FIGURE 21–4

One-on-One Structure

FIGURE 21–5

Partial Organization of General Motors Corporation

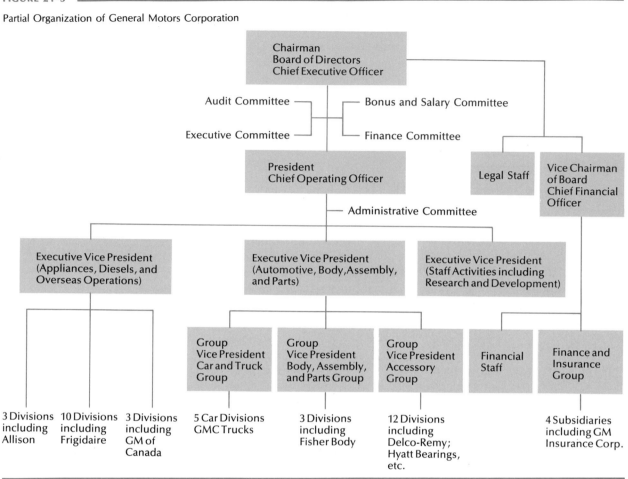

communication links to what is going on throughout the organization. The chair is not entirely dependent upon what operating managers choose to tell because independent information is received from the finance organization.[4]

Purpose of Dual-Overlap Structure

- supplemental communication channels
- more accurate information to top
- separate loyalties

The centrality of finance at GM, of course, reflects the critical importance of money. A general manager of Oldsmobile can decide to offer a horizontal, eight-cylinder engine, but can't unilaterally expend unapproved funds. The general manager must apply up the chain of command to the Finance Committee for permission. This form of control reflects the company's history. General Motors was put together from already existing concerns, such as Chevrolet, Olds, Fisher, and Delco. In the beginning, the companies had their own bank accounts, and corporate headquarters had no money because it sold nothing. Alfred Sloan used to ask Buick Division for funds to run the corporation headquarters, but he soon put a stop to this by announcing that henceforth all the money paid by customers would go into one

FIGURE 21-6

Dual-Overlap Structure

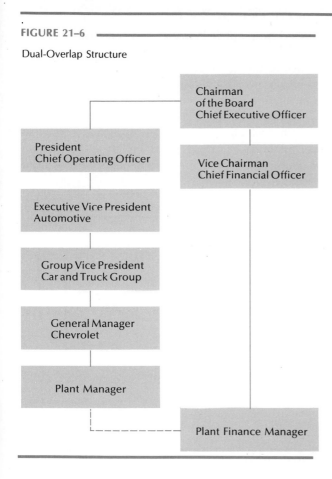

bank account—the corporation's. A division requiring funds was to ask him, not go to anyone else for loans.

The Bonus and Salary Committee has also been a source of high-level control because it evaluates and rewards the performance of several thousand General Motor's executives and managers. By concentrating the process at the very top, control is maintained over a critical corporate resource. Middle-level managers are encouraged by the assurance that they won't be lost in the shuffle. Finally, by vesting the tough bonus decisions in a committee, the company distributes some of the burden of difficult decision making that would otherwise fall on a few individuals. As a result, General Motors is remarkably successful in knitting managers to the organization and generating their commitment.

Problems of Dual-Overlap Structure
- local tension or collaboration
- line distrust of staff
- ambiguous chain of command

Centralized Activities

So authority over investment and management resources is vested high in GM's structure to provide high-level control of a vast system. Two other activities are also controlled similarly: industrial relations and styling. Negotiation of labor contracts is handled on high because the United Automobile Workers and some other unions are enormous, national organizations themselves. General Motors must ensure standard policy and consistent adherence to the contracts at all locations.

Styling is also quite centralized because of GM's traditional strategy of a product line that looks similar enough to facilitate a young person's continuing to purchase General Motor automobiles as his or her economic and social position changes. The external styling graduated from Chevrolet to Cadillac must be centrally designed and coordinated. What goes under the hood can more safely be left to the division general managers. In addition, of course, there are economic benefits derived from sharing some parts between the various models.

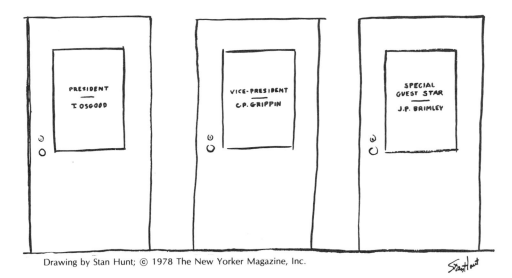

Drawing by Stan Hunt; © 1978 The New Yorker Magazine, Inc.

Thus General Motors is a mixture of centralization and decentralization knit together by close financial control. The dual system offends the unity of command principle, but it is deemed necessary to allow top management to control overall organizational activities across great hierarchical and geographical distances. All this effort is expended to see that the multiple parts fit together. They are coordinated by meticulous attention to detail demonstrated by committees and individuals at the very top (one topic at a meeting of the executive committee was duration of pregnancy leaves for hourly workers). A Chevrolet general sales manager once sent out 2 million letters to Chevy owners inviting them to contact him directly if they had troubles. He listed his home phone number! You can imagine the calls from people unable to get to work or to drive their children to school. The executive quickly changed the advertisement, but not before he saw that local General Motors agencies responded to every complaint.

Balancing Initiative and Control in a Decentralized Firm

General Electric is not as large as General Motors, but it is a more complex company because it manufactures a wider range of products in a large number of organizational units. GE was one of the pioneers of decentralization, and it made a great effort to adhere to the traditional principle of "authority should equal responsibility" by pushing control over staff down to the operating level.[5]

The Strategy

Figure 21–7 represents the overall structure of General Electric in the mid-1970s with its more than 250,000 employees. The line organization is built around product groups with four- or five-product, customer, or geographic divisions under each. Across the bottom under the divisions are more than 150 departments. These departments are the key units at GE. Management's intention was to create small- to medium-size businesses that department managers could wrap their arms around and run like their own. Their performance is measured against their budgets and profits. Thus the main intention in decentralization is not to democratize the organization but to create greater control at the operating level.

To assist the department managers, each is given a staff of five functional managers. By vesting authority in the department manager, the system hopes to foster initiative and effectiveness because those most knowledgeable about a particular product and industry are in command.

Note that the group vice presidents and division vice presidents possess little functional staff. They have assistants of course, but their staffs are small. They don't have enough people to closely control the departments on a daily basis. They are available to give advice to department managers, to ask questions, and to evaluate performance periodically. Most important, they play a central role in investment decisions.

The Multiple-Overlap Structure

At the top of the organization also reporting to the president are the vice presidents of the various overall corporate functional components. This creates a multiple-overlap structure by which several headquarters staff members frequently visit the line departments. Some staff possess functional authority to impose their views on the operating departments (such as accounting and others under the corporate administrative staff), but most senior vice presidents are in more ambiguous positions. They employ specialists who are available to advise line managers who consult them. Specialists enjoy right of entry, and they spend substantial time traveling among the various operating departments observing and talking to line management. Some staff groups also possess authority of joint consultation because a division vice president may refuse to discuss a department manager's proposal unless a central staff specialist is present or has been consulted.

In most cases, staff's formal authority stops here. Line managers retain the right to refuse staff's advice and go their own way. But they do so at their own peril, for if they exceed their budget or miss their profits, higher management will demand an explanation of why they ignored the advice. The staff soon develops substantial power even in the absence of formal authority. Since the top executives and functional staffs are physically located at corporate headquarters (formerly in New York City,

Purpose of Multiple-Overlap Structure
- supplemental communication links
- more accurate information to top
- opportunity for staff to integrate organization parts

FIGURE 21-7

Partial Organization of General Electric Company

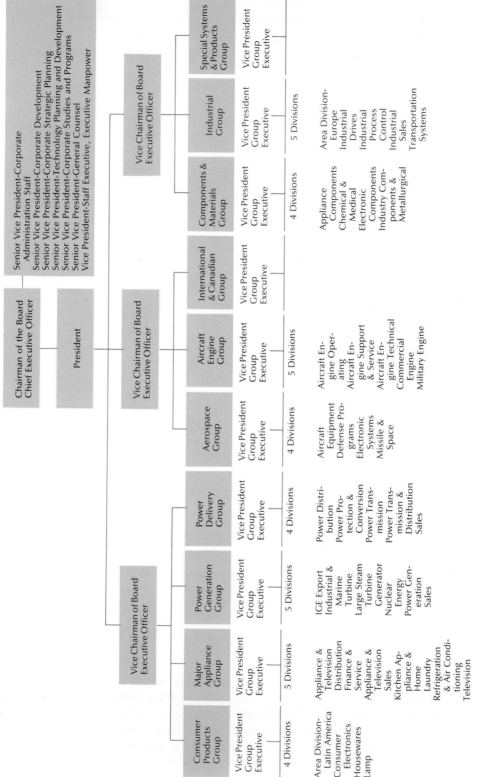

FIGURE 21–8

Decentralized Department

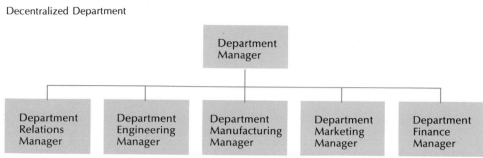

now in Connecticut) and divisions and departments are spread over the world, operating line managers know that staff specialists will meet group vice presidents from time to time. At these informal meetings the staff will communicate their observations of field events. The several functional staffs thus serve a communication function similar to the finance organization at General Motors. Multiple communication links extend from the bottom to the top to help the latter keep track of what is going on. Some central staff even refer to themselves as the police officers of the company— a phrase not likely to endear them to the line departments and divisions.

What the elaborate system is designed to do is strike an optimum balance between department manager autonomy and presidential office control. It is an uneasy balance, for the pendulum swings back and forth according to economic conditions and company performance. In good times autonomy is greater as the department managers take advantage of opportunities. In bad times the top's need to reduce expenses and eliminate fat tends to prevail. In the past decade, however, central control has been growing in order to maintain order and central direction. The three executive vice presidents were added above the group vice presidents. This added more line management and reduced top-level span of control. In addition, a label of "services" which followed the title of the vice president of each corporate function, was eliminated to recognize that these staffs are more than just services; they make up a vital part of management's control system. Finally, corporate strategic planning, development, and studies are receiving increased attention.

FIGURE 21–9

Multiple-Overlap Structure

Problems of Multiple-Overlap Structure
- line distrust of staff
- ambiguous chain of command
- role stress for staff
- line complaints of responsibility without power
- excessive power shift to staff

Reconciling Centralized Policy and Dispersed Implementation

Liberty Mutual Insurance Company is a nationwide organization of 13,000 employees providing all kinds of insurance to business and personal policyholders. Figure 21–10 illustrates the major units. In the home office in Boston, the vice president of finance is responsible for investment of reserve funds from which insurance companies derive most of their profits. From a narrow business perspective, the rest of the organization exists to obtain money to loan and invest.

FIGURE 21–10

Partial Organization Chart of Liberty Mutual Insurance

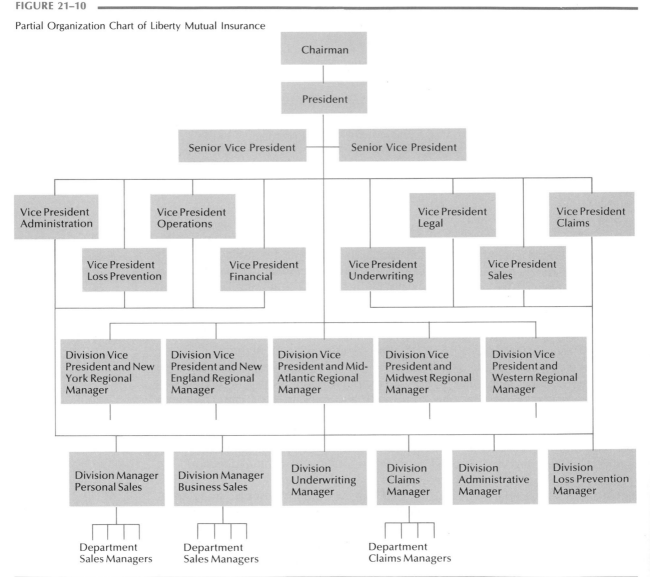

The home office functional departments are powerful because Liberty Mutual is a national company selling insurance to national clients who expect standard service. A policyholder, such as Sears, must be confident that it will be treated equitably whether an accident occurs in Massachusetts, Georgia, or Oregon.

The Positions

The vice president of underwriting heads the unit that designs policies, determines risks, sets premium rates, and defines which policyholders are desirable. Operations is responsible for the actual physical completion of policies, data collection, and office policy and procedure. Claims handles the investigation of accidents and payment to policyholders and other claimants. Loss prevention inspects policyholder property and helps policyholders prevent accidents and reduce claims. Sales is responsible for the entire field force of sales managers and salespeople.

The distinction between line and staff is hazy in this company. Each of the major functions tends to consider itself of greatest importance. A sign in one sales office states, "Sales is not the most important department, it is the *only* department." None of the functional departments is just advisory. Each possesses authority in its area of specialization. Each home office functional department sets policy and procedures in its function. These are applied in the various geographic areas by the regional functional manager.

The Multiple-Links Structure

This strong home office functional authority means that the functional managers located in the regional offices report to at least two superiors: the regional vice president and their home office functional vice president. It is not clear who is really the stronger superior. In the short run the regional vice president evaluates the local functional manager's performance and makes salary recommendations, but in the long run the manager's promotions depend more upon his or her relations with the functional specialists in Boston.

This structure can be described as a multiple-links structure because multiple home office and regional functional personnel are linked through the regional office and the person of the regional vice president. (See Figure 21–11.) This vice president is to be an integrator who coordinates regional activities to sell insurance and provide service in his or her geographic area. The VP usually comes from a sales background and may even double as a regional sales manager. Nonetheless, some regional vice presidents have come from underwriting and claims. Regional vice presidents are important persons, but they do not have final authority over the functional managers who report to them. They cannot order the regional claims manager to violate home office claims policy, but they can encourage the manager to depart from it when they think it is nececssary—and agree to fight the home office in behalf of the regional claims manager if necessary.

The unity of command principle appears to be bent if not broken, but it is done in order to balance the conflicting needs for standardized central policy and procedures while providing local effort and initiative. The system succeeds only if the regional vice presidents enjoy the confidence of the home office executives by virtue of their regional performance while also commanding the respect of their regional functional managers through their ability and upward influence.

Meshing Divergent Interests in a Hospital

Evans Memorial Hospital (name is disguised) is a private, nonprofit general hospital located in a suburb of St. Louis. It has 430 full-time employees and a nursing school

Purpose of Multiple-Links Structure
* balance central policy and decentralized implementation
* coordination of functions close to market
* provide integrating leadership in functionalized organization

FIGURE 21–11

Multiple-Links Structure

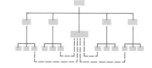

Problems of Multiple-Links Structure
* ambiguous chain of command
* role stress for the integrator
* power struggle between home and region

FIGURE 21–12

Partial Organization of Evans Memorial Hospital

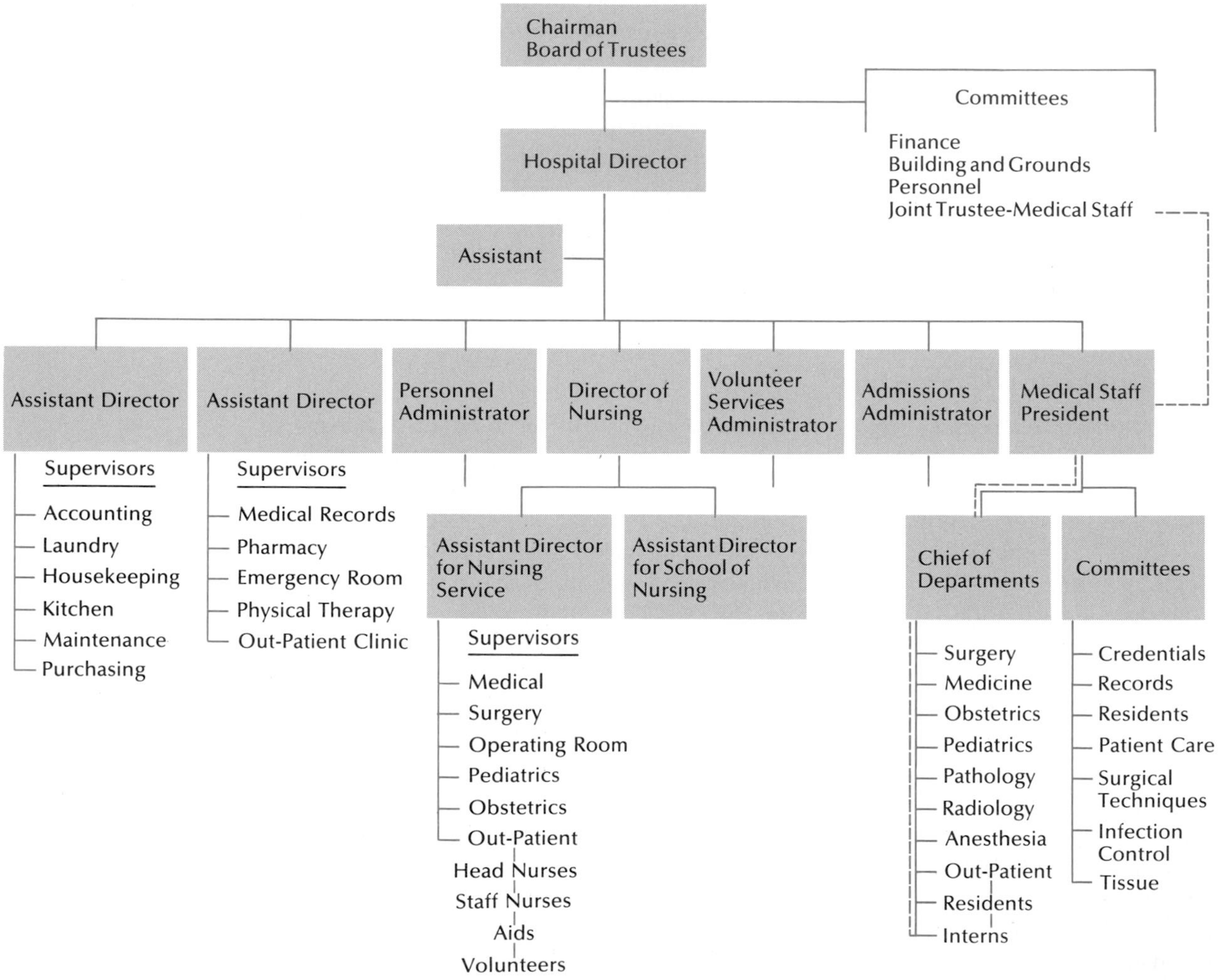

of 120 students. Atop the structure illustrated in Figure 21–12 is the board of trustees composed of 50 local citizens of some standing in the community. Most boards of hospitals are large in order to involve as many influential people as possible.[6] The board is responsible for the general administration of the hospital, and it appoints important administrators and all members of the medical staff. Because the board is large and composed of volunteers whose time is limited, it is subdivided into smaller standing committees to deal with policy matters in their areas of responsibility: (1) budget and finance, (2) buildings and grounds, and (3) personnel.

The Positions

The chief full-time administrator is the hospital director (who is more often a professional administrator, not a medical doctor). The director has two assistants, who supervise the various service activities, but medical and nursing staff directors report directly to the hospital director.[7]

The medical staff is composed of eight departments, each headed by a chief. The staff itself falls into three categories: (1) full-time employees, such as interns and residents; (2) part-timers, such as the chiefs themselves. (They are frequently present in the hospital and receive a salary but also engage in private practice); and (3) the affiliated physicians, who utilize the hospital for their private patients.

As in many hospitals, Evans experiences some conflict among the medical staff. The affiliated private physicians tend to perceive the hospital and its staff as existing to service their individual patients and the nurses and interns as available to follow only their orders. But the full-time hospital personnel tend to be more concerned about the operation of their total unit or even the whole hospital. The interns want to be taught medicine, not just how to take orders; the department chiefs desire

Source: Aetna Life and Casualty, *Business Week,* December 12, 1977.

effective units that treat interesting cases and provide some opportunity for research. As indicated in Figure 21–12, the medical staff has established several committees to police itself and coordinate its activities.

The director of nursing is responsible for nursing services and the three-year school of nursing. Assistant directors assist her, and supervisors are in charge of each of the major medical care units and the nurses and aids on the floors. The floor nurses, of course, perform their duties around the clock every day of the year. They receive instructions sometimes under conditions of great task and organizational strain. For example, requests, orders, and demands emanate from many individuals: head nurses, hospital administrators, hospital medical staff, affiliated staff, patients, and their families. The concept of unity of command has little relevance under such circumstances.

The Political Structure

What is most striking about the organization is the enormous complexity and variety of specialists. Specialized tasks and knowledge is the basic organizational criteria, but this creates great interdependence among different status functions. Laundry with its washers and dryers is essential, just as is radiology with its X-ray equipment. People of varying educations from grammar school to postmedical school training must interact to meet the patients' needs. When an attending affiliated physician prescribes certain drugs and diet for a patient, the order must be relayed by the nurse to the pharmacy, which prepares the desired dosages to be delivered by other nurses; and the special diet must be prepared by the kitchen to be delivered by various aides. Errors could be fatal. All of this is not easy or harmonious, so the administrator requires a complex mixture of business skills, technical knowledge, and human relations finesse. More than anything else, the effective hospital director is a politician—in the best sense, a person who works for human cooperation among people over whom he or she has limited authority.[8] Don't be misled because the organization chart looks like a hierarchy. The director is actually not a boss over the medical staff (nor sometimes even over the nursing staff). Notice that through the joint trustee-medical staff committee, the physicians have a direct line to the trustees. Some department chiefs and affiliated physicians may even have more influence with the trustees than the director enjoys. The top organizational power is more a triumvirate among the chair of the board (or the chairs of its relevant committees), the hospital director, and the medical staff president (see Figure 21–13). Each endeavors to develop coalitions among trustees and hospital personnel in support of his or her desired policies.

The system is effective to the extent that: (1) all necessary specialists and services are staffed by competent people; (2) communication is so effective that each generally understands what he or she must do; (3) essential agreement exists about the hospital's mission; and (4) the individuals respect each other, so they are cooperative and flexible.

Integrating Organizations in a Conglomerate

A conglomerate is difficult to define, but it includes firms with many and diverse subsidiaries engaged in a variety of related and unrelated businesses.[9] The element

FIGURE 21–13

Power Triumvirate in Hospital

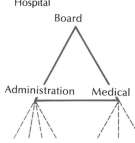

holding the units together is that they are owned by common owners and directed by a common management team seeking profits. The critical function in such an organization is integration—coordinating the various activities so that subsidiaries don't damage each other. This is an extremely difficult task because of the diversity of industries and markets dealt with. Some conglomerates handle the problem merely by looking at yearly profit statements, rewarding those managers who do well, punishing those who do poorly. As Ling-Tempco-Vought (LTV) Corporation discovered, the problem with this approach is that it is backward looking and slow.[10] When a subsidiary president is replaced for unsatisfactory performance, it is a whole year until the top knows how well the replacement is doing—and by then it may be too late to save the subsidiary.

The Strategy

Johnson & Johnson has developed a different approach for managing its subsidiaries and employees. Integration succeeds so well that corporate management denies that it is a conglomerate even though its diversity of subsidiaries and products indicate that it really is. Figure 21–14 summarizes the overall structure of subsidiary companies based on product and geography. Johnson & Johnson Domestic Operating Company is the concern most of us identify as J&J: it produces the Band-Aids and baby products. Ethicon manufactures surgical instruments and sutures; McNeil is a pharmaceutical firm; Stim-u-Dents makes gum massagers. All of these are quite medical, but other subsidiaries make sausage casings, cigarette filters, and cellophane tape.

Over each subsidiary is a chairperson of the board, a person who is also the chair of 5 to 20 other companies. Some of these companies perform all business activities—such as research, engineering, manufacturing, and marketing. Others like J&J Thailand merely market other subsidiary products in that country.

Each subsidiary is organized as if it were an independent company, even though almost all are entirely owned by Johnson & Johnson and no stock exists in their names (see Figure 21–15). Most have a chain of command that includes a chair, president, and various functional vice presidents of manufacturing, research, engineering, personnel, and so on. The full-time salaried executives constitute the subsidiary's board of directors. Although this arrangement is essentially fictitious because the companies are not independent, it is motivating for subsidiary officers who feel that they control their company. In the small subsidiaries, the system allows a relatively young vice president to serve on a board, which can be very educational in promoting cross-functional views—another device for lower level integration.

All of the various chairpeople have offices at the company headquarters in New Brunswick, New Jersey, but they spend substantial time visiting their respective companies. None of them has much staff, and in fact the entire headquarters' complement is quite small. In New Brunswick, there is a large and beautiful Georgian colonial building with powder blue carpeting and Williamsburg chandelier. The receptionist politely informs the visitor that this is not the corporate headquarters but the office of the Johnson & Johnson Domestic Operating Company. Across the street is a nondescript converted factory that is the corporate headquarters. This contrast is striking and symbolic. The central staff is small; no specialists continually travel among the subsidiaries as at General Electric; no financial organization knits the

FIGURE 21–14

Partial Organization of Johnson & Johnson

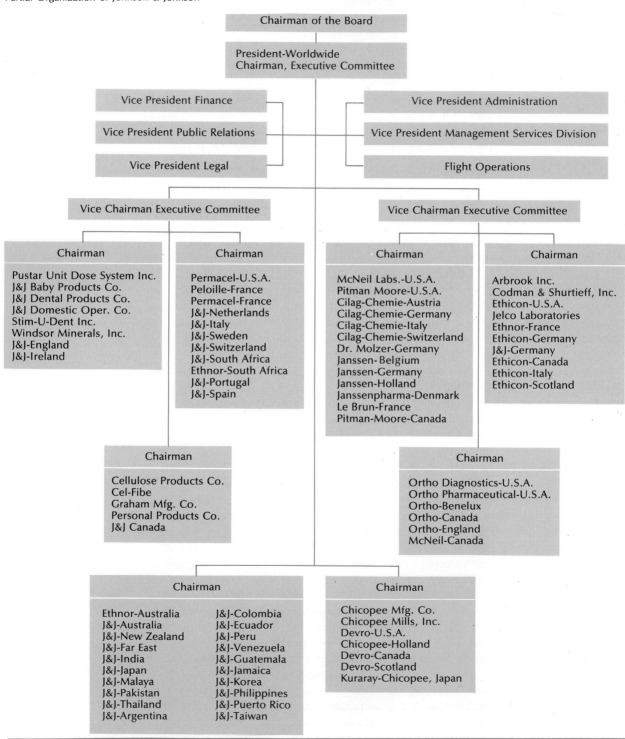

Chairman of the Board

President-Worldwide
Chairman, Executive Committee

Vice President Finance

Vice President Public Relations

Vice President Legal

Vice President Administration

Vice President Management Services Division

Flight Operations

Vice Chairman Executive Committee

Vice Chairman Executive Committee

Chairman

Pustar Unit Dose System Inc.
J&J Baby Products Co.
J&J Dental Products Co.
J&J Domestic Oper. Co.
Stim-U-Dent Inc.
Windsor Minerals, Inc.
J&J-England
J&J-Ireland

Chairman

Permacel-U.S.A.
Peloille-France
Permacel-France
J&J-Netherlands
J&J-Italy
J&J-Sweden
J&J-Switzerland
J&J-South Africa
Ethnor-South Africa
J&J-Portugal
J&J-Spain

Chairman

McNeil Labs.-U.S.A.
Pitman Moore-U.S.A.
Cilag-Chemie-Austria
Cilag-Chemie-Germany
Cilag-Chemie-Italy
Cilag-Chemie-Switzerland
Dr. Molzer-Germany
Janssen-Belgium
Janssen-Germany
Janssen-Holland
Janssenpharma-Denmark
Le Brun-France
Pitman-Moore-Canada

Chairman

Arbrook Inc.
Codman & Shurtieff, Inc.
Ethicon-U.S.A.
Jelco Laboratories
Ethnor-France
Ethicon-Germany
J&J-Germany
Ethicon-Canada
Ethicon-Italy
Ethicon-Scotland

Chairman

Cellulose Products Co.
Cel-Fibe
Graham Mfg. Co.
Personal Products Co.
J&J Canada

Chairman

Ortho Diagnostics-U.S.A.
Ortho Pharmaceutical-U.S.A.
Ortho-Benelux
Ortho-Canada
Ortho-England
McNeil-Canada

Chairman

Ethnor-Australia
J&J-Australia
J&J-New Zealand
J&J-Far East
J&J-India
J&J-Japan
J&J-Malaya
J&J-Pakistan
J&J-Thailand
J&J-Argentina

J&J-Colombia
J&J-Ecuador
J&J-Peru
J&J-Venezuela
J&J-Guatemala
J&J-Jamaica
J&J-Korea
J&J-Philippines
J&J-Puerto Rico
J&J-Taiwan

Chairman

Chicopee Mfg. Co.
Chicopee Mills, Inc.
Devro-U.S.A.
Chicopee-Holland
Devro-Canada
Devro-Scotland
Kuraray-Chicopee, Japan

whole together as at General Motors. The integrating force has been mainly the president and the various chairpeople.

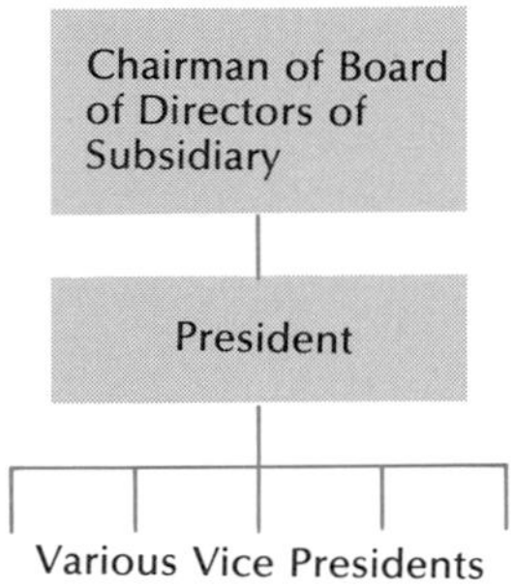

The Multiple-Roles Structure

The chairpeople are integrators because they perform multiple roles (see Figure 21–16). They are line officers atop their respective subsidiaries, but they are also personal staff to the president and the corporate chairperson, who don't have many others. The corporate officers utilize them as advisers and project leaders as well as communication links to the subsidiaries. Thus each chairperson is expected to control and represent subordinates while also being involved in corporate problem solving. For example, yearly all the presidents and chairpeople meet with the corporate executives to formulate budget and investment schedules for the next year. Each chairperson is expected to push for his or her companies but also participate in the overall corporate planning. Thus the president of Ortho may argue that since Ortho's net return on investment is greater than that at the more mature Personal Products subsidiary, Ortho should receive its own profits plus some of Personal Products to invest. Or the president of Devro may argue that although the return on investment is not very good yet, future projections suggest that substantial investment now will pay off in the future. Thus the president wants someone else's profits when Devro has generated very little itself. The corporate executives and chairpeople must reconcile these conflicting requests.

The system is intended to foster an overall corporate perspective while retaining independence among the subsidiaries. Nonetheless, the organization is not entirely successful because parochial views predominate from time to time. This is difficult

FIGURE 21–15

Subsidiary Structure

Chairman of Board of Directors of Subsidiary

President

Various Vice Presidents

FIGURE 21–16

Multiple-Roles Structure

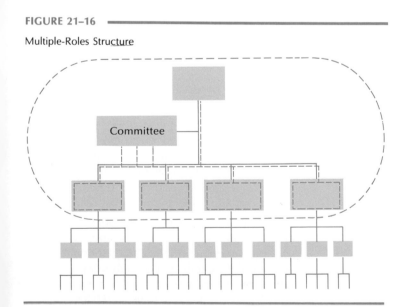

Committee

Puprose of Multiple-Role Structure
- provide executive officers for parts
- represent part in decisions on whole
- provide integrating perspective on whole

to prevent because of the extremely small central staff. Finance is fairly well controlled at the top through the vice president of finance, who has functional authority, but personnel and research present problems. Since there is no strong central industrial relations staff, each subsidiary hires and promotes independently. This causes the corporation to lose some good people because a young manager whose promotion is blocked at Chicopee Manufacturing Company in Rhode Island may leave J&J, when in fact openings exist to suit that person at Ortho Pharmaceutical in New Jersey. Without central staff, there was no way for the individual or the corporation to know. In recent years, the corporation has been developing a central data file on jobs and people in the employ of all the subsidiaries. It has also been instituting a system under which each subsidiary must report any position openings before they are filled. They are to be listed in all of the other subsidiaries so that employees can apply for positions at other units.

Problems of Multiple-Role Structure
- inadequate central control of overlapping parts
- inefficient time use of multiple role persons
- role stress

Research has suffered from a similar lack of information. Research is conducted within each subsidiary, leading to substantial overlap and wasted effort. One company may be developing a product that will put another subsidiary out of business!

In recent years, as at General Electric, there has been pressure toward increased centralization through enlarging corporate staff. Particularly in administration, labor force development, and research, it appears to be desirable to increase central control to prevent losing good people and duplicating efforts. Yet, the overall structure has been and must remain decentralized to allow the companies to pursue their opportunities in diverse areas.

SUMMARY

Designing organizations is not a science. Rather, it is a pragmatic process that draws on static principles and dynamic guidelines. We have examined how several organizations deal with their structural problems.

A small printing shop strives for stability, predictability, and quality through centralized decision making and adherence to the static principles.

A warship emphasizes the static principles, especially chain of command, and impersonal functional response to emergency conditions.

A large utility company promotes stability and growth by following the same static principles.

A giant automobile manufacturer maintains top-level control by violating some static guidelines and instituting dual communication chains through the operating and finance hierarchies.

An extremely diversified electrical concern attempts to balance local initiative and top-level control by decentralizing authority while developing an elaborate corporate functional staff which monitors operations at lower levels.

A geographically dispersed insurance company balances strong central policy and decentralized implementation through a regional executive who must coordinate subordinates over whom he or she enjoys limited authority and who have loyalties up their specialized functional ladders.

A hospital creates a political organization with a triumvirate of power in administration, trustees, and medical staff. These represent divergent parties and interest that must be integrated if the institution is to be effective.

A multisubsidiary conglomerate seeks integration of activities without developing a large central staff. The chairs of subsidiaries play several roles—as line managers of the companies, as corporate executives, and as personal staff to the corporate chair and president.

These examples do not include all existing organizational problems or strategies. Nonetheless, they should provide you some insights into the common ones.

REVIEW QUESTIONS

1. What structure characterized the small owner-managed print shop? What was the organization designed to achieve?

2. What characterizes the structure of the U.S. Navy warship? What is the design intended to achieve?

3. What is the relation of junior division officers to senior petty officers?

4. What is the basis of organization in the electric utility?

5. Why does the utility have a one-on-one structure?

6. How does the large automotive firm maintain some central control?

7. In what areas is General Motors quite centralized? Why?

8. How is General Motors a mix of centralization and decentralization?

9. How can decentralization lead to greater control in the complex electrical company?

10. How does General Electric strive to equate authority and responsibility?

11. What is the role of the corporate staff at General Electric? What formal authority does the staff possess? What informal influence?

12. How has General Electric seemed recentralized a little in recent years? Why has it done so?

13. What specialization characterizes the home office in the large insurance firm? Why?

14. What is the difference between line and staff at Liberty Mutual?

15. How and why is home office functional authority so strong at Liberty Mutual?

16. Who is to provide the "integrator" function in Liberty Mutual? How is it difficult?

17. What is the triumvirate of control at the top of the hospital?

18. What is the relationship of the medical staff at Evans Hospital to the director? Why does this violation of chain of command exist?

19. What is required to integrate and coordinate the specialist's activities at Evans?

20. What characterizes the corporate-level organization of the conglomerate?

21. How can Johnson & Johnson be termed *decentralized* when most subsidiaries are considered *centralized*?

22. How and why does J&J maintain the impression of independent subsidiaries?

23. Who performs the integrating role at J&J? How?

24. What are the problems of Johnson & Johnson's structure?

Notes and References on Pragmatic Organization Designs

1. For two fine surveys of actual business organizations, see E. Dale, *The Great Organizers* (New York: McGraw-Hill, 1970); and A. D. Chandler, *Strategy and Structure* (Cambridge, Mass.: MIT, 1962). Also P. E. Holden, C. A. Pederson, and G. E. Germane. *Top Management* (New York: McGraw-Hill, 1968); H. Schollhammer, "Organization Structures of Multinational Corporations," *Academy of Management Journal,* September 1971, pp. 345–66; and P. N. Khandwalla, "Viable and Effective Organizational Designs of Firms," *Academy of Management Journal,* September 1973, pp. 481–95.

For a survey of various organizations, see Peter M. Blau and W. Richard Scott, *Formal Organizations: A Comparative Approach* (San Francisco: Chandler, 1962); J. D. Thompson, *Comparative Studies in Organization* (Pittsburgh: University of Pittsburgh Press, 1959); A. Etzioni, *A Comparative Analysis of Complex Organizations* (New York: Free Press, 1961); S. H. Udy, "The Comparative Analysis of Organizations," J. G. March, ed., *Handbook of Organizations* (Chicago: Rand McNally, 1965), pp. 678–710; C. A. Perrow, "A Framework for the Comparative Analysis of Organizations," *American Sociological Review* 32 (1967), pp. 195–208; G. S. Pugh, D. J. Hickson, and C. R. Hinings, "An Empirical Taxonomy of Work Organization Structures," *Administrative Science Quarterly,* 1969, pp. 115–26; and P. M. Blau and R. A. Schoenherr, *The Structure of Organizations* (New York: Basic Press, 1971).

Probably the most extensive examination of structure is R. H. Kilmann, L. R. Pondy, and D. P. Slevin, *The Management of Organizational Design* (New York: Elsevier-North Holland Publishing, 1976).

Some managers have provided us with insightful descriptions of the companies with which they have been associated. Two of the best known books of this kind are Alfred P. Sloan, *My Years with General Motors* (Garden City, N.Y.: Anchor Books, 1972); and Ralph Cordiner, *New Frontiers for Professional Managers* (New York: McGraw-Hill, 1956). Cordiner based his book on experiences at General Electric.

2. On the restrictive behavior that develops in peacetime, see A. K. Davis, "Bureaucratic Patterns in the Navy Officer Corps," *Social Forces* 27 (1948), pp. 143–53. Davis hypothesizes that "the effectiveness of military leaders tends to vary inversely with their exposure to a conventionally routinized military career." This study is reproduced in R. A. Merton, et al., eds., *Reader in Bureaucracy* (New York: Free Press, 1952).

3. Frederic G. Donner, quoted in *Newsweek,* February 25, 1963, p. 67. Also Jerry M. Flint, "G. M. Shifts Management Gears Again," *New York Times,* March 3, 1970. For two books on General Motors, see Alfred P. Sloan, *My Years with General Motors;* and Peter Drucker, *The Concept of the Corporation* (New York: Day, 1946). Also E. Dale, "Contributions to Administration by Alfred P. Sloan, Jr., and G. M.," *Administrative Science Quarterly,* June, 1956, p. 41.

The original strategy at General Motors was to offer a graduated line of automobiles that a customer could comfortably move up as one's economic situation improved. Sharp demarcations in prices existed. With time, styling similarity, manufacturing commonality, and inflation, the product boundaries have become hazy. Consider a series of advertisements by the Chevrolet Division in 1977. The illustration shows four similarly appearing compact models: Chevrolet Nova, Pontiac Ventura, Oldsmobile Omega, and Buick Skylark. The copy read, "If you can't figure which emblem goes with which car, you'll see why it pays to save hundreds on the one which wears the Chevrolet emblem."

4. For further documentation, see G. C. Athanassiades,

"The Distortion of Upward Communication in Hierarchical Organizations," *Academy of Management Journal,* June 1973, pp. 207–26. In a historical study of the American presidency, Arthur Schlesinger writes: "The President will always need a small and alert personal staff to serve as his eyes and ears and one lobe of his brain, but he must avoid a vast and possessive staff ambitious to make all the decisions of government. Above all, he must not make himself the prisoner of a single information system." *The Imperial Presidency* (Boston: Houghton Mifflin, 1973), p. 408.

General Motors is constructed quite similarly to the managerial structure of the Soviet Union. Two chains of command exist side by side under the government premier and first secretary of the Communist Party. The manager of a ball bearing plant in Minsk reports up a chain of command headed by the premier. Yet, in the plant there is a political commissar or party leader. The party representative acts as sort of a personnel officer for the plant, but really is a means for the top to keep tabs on what is going on at lower levels through parallel communications.

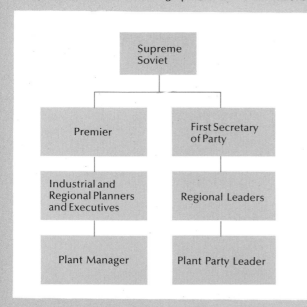

J. A. Merkel writes:

For the Soviet revolutionary army, Trotsky established a new mix of charismatic leadership, propaganda, and strong discipline. Taking over the Commissariat of War in early 1918, he came out in direct opposition to previous Bolshevik military propaganda in his speech, "Work Discipline, and Order Will Save the Soviet So-

cialist Republic," in which he called for a return of the bourgeois specialists, the technicians, engineers, doctors, teachers, and former officers because in them is invested our true people's national capital, which we are obliged to exploit, to use, if we want to resolve the basic problems which stand before us. Both in the army and in the armaments industry, the luxury of eliminating the technicians as ideologically unfit had to be foregone. Trotsky brought the "bourgeois" officers back into service, and to ensure their loyalty, established a parallel system of ideologically reliable political commissars, whose countersignature was required on every order. Of necessity, he found that he had to hold the balance of power between these two hierarchies himself.

"The Forgotten Revolution" (unpublished doctoral dissertation, Department of Political Science, University of California, Berkeley, 1973), p. 174.

On the advantages of multiple hierarchies, see P. B. Evans, "Multiple Hierarchies and Organizational Control," *Administrative Science Quarterly,* June 1975, pp. 250–59.

5. On General Electric, see Ralph J. Cordiner, *New Frontiers for Professional Managers* (New York: McGraw-Hill, 1956); "G.E.'s Jones Restructures His Top Team," *Business Week,* June 30, 1973, p. 38.

6. G. G. Howard, "Anatomy of a Hospital Trustee," *Harvard Business Review,* May–June 1973, pp. 65–71; J. Pfeffer, "Size, Composition, and Function of Hospital Boards of Directors: A Study of Organization-Environment Linkage," *Administrative Science Quarterly,* September 1973, pp. 349–64. One study demonstrates that firms with representatives of important sectors of their environments on their boards of directors tend to exhibit better performance. J. Pfeffer, "Size and Composition of Corporate Boards of Directors: The Organization and Its Environment," *Administrative Science Quarterly,* June 1972, p. 218.

7. On management in hospitals, see S. Levey and N. Paul Loomba, *Health Care Administration: A Managerial Perspective* (Philadelphia: Lippincott, 1972); C. Perrow, "Hospitals: Technology, Structure and Goals," chap. 22 in J. March, ed., *Handbook of Organizations* (Skokie, Ill.: Rand McNally, 1965); E. Friedson, ed., *The Hospital in Modern Society* (New York: Free Press, 1963); R. L. Coser, "Authority and Decision Making in a Hospital: A Comparative Analysis," *American Sociological Review,* February, 1958.

8. H. Levinson, ''The Changing Role of the Hospital Administrator,'' *Health Care Management Review,* Winter 1976, pp. 79–89.

9. N. A. Berg, ''What's Different about Conglomerate Management?'' *Harvard Business Review,* November–December 1969, pp. 112–20. He argues that it is small, generalist staffs in corporate headquarters. See also A. M. Louis, ''Ten Conglomerates and How They Grew,'' *Fortune,* May 15, 1969, p. 152.

10. ''L.T.V.: Weak Growth in Mature Industries,'' *Business Week,* April 5, 1976, pp. 50–51.

Discussion Questions and Exercises on Structuring Organizational Systems

Discussion Questions

1. What are the advantages of hierarchical structures?

2. What are the elements of delegation and the principles governing its use?

3. Organization has been described as a patchwork quilt of compromise. Which principles may conflict—and why?

4. A persistent problem in organization is whether a staff in a local plant should be responsible to the plant manager or the staff group at corporate headquarters. What are the advantages and disadvantages of each arrangement for: (a) a plant personnel manager, (b) a plant comptroller, and (c) a plant industrial engineer?

5. Under what conditions should a structure be designed in which staff specialists can give orders to lower line managers?

6. Does decentralization increase or decrease the control of the chief executive?

7. A former chair of Standard Oil of Ohio has stated, "I think that decentralization is not only a form of organization, but decentralization when you get its full implications is a way of life. That is the thing I want to stress. Decentralization is ideal." Do you agree or disagree with this statement? Why?

8. Why does the government of even the most democratic nations tend to become centralized and autocratic in time of war?

9. For many years, management practitioners and theorists attempted to define general principles of organization. These principles are increasingly being violated in modern organizations. Why?

10. Some organizational theorists suggest that the vast decentralization movement that characterized American corporations in the 1950s and 1960s was just a temporary departure from past central control. Why did businesses tend to decentralize in the past, and why might they recentralize in the future?

11. What are the major organizational problems of complex, multiproduct organizations? What mechanisms are used to handle them?

12. What are the major organizational problems of conglomerates? What mechanisms are used to handle them?

13. Many union leaders strongly opposed the clauses in the Landrum-Griffin Act that promoted democracy and member participation in union policymaking. What might be the personal and organizational reasons for such opposition?

14. Critics of modern business (and especially critics of banks, insurance companies, and brokerage firms) have complained about management's "irrationality" in hiring and promoting executives on the basis of coming from the "correct" social background, attendance at "prestige" colleges, and wearing "conservative" clothes. What are the advantages and disadvantages of such criteria?

15. What is meant by open systems theory? How does it extend our understanding of an organization's structure and the challenges facing managers?

16. Describe three ways of supplementing the staff chair-of-command and unity-of-command principles in organizations in order to assist top management in control. What are the advantages and disadvantages of each method?

Individual Exercises

1. Imagine yourself in the role of tyrant ape in a baboon pack. What is the maximum number of apes you could manage in your pack. Why?

2. Imagine yourself in the role of sales manager in a corporation. What is the maximum number of salespeople you could manage in your sales force? Why?

3. Suppose you have been appointed registrar of your school. Specifying your objectives, design a system to facilitate student registration.

4. Suppose you have been appointed head librarian of your school library. Specifying your objectives; design an appropriate organizational system.

5. Draw an organization chart of your school and indicate (a) the specialization criteria, (b) how power flows, (c) structural weakness, and (d) how you think it should be modified.

6. Draw an organization chart of any organization with which you are familiar indicating (a) the specialization criteria, (b) how power flows, (c) structural weakness, and (d) how you think it should be modified.

7. Describe the "rational" attributes of a formal organization with which you are familiar (e.g., a bank, automobile dealership, hospital).

8. Several recent books on Japanese management stress conscensus decision making and long-term employment stability. Explain the influence such traits would have on the structuring of a large industrial corporation. Assess the appropriateness of such organization attributes for a business firm in the United States.

Managerial Cases and Problems on Structuring Organizational Systems

Sherman and Jackson Stores, Inc.

Sherman and Jackson's department stores form a chain of more than 100 retail establishments across the country. The chain began as a 5- and 10-cent store 70 years ago. Over the years it has expanded its outlets, built new ones, and changed its style. Product line has grown to include expensive items—such as color television sets and furniture—that were never found in the old 5 and 10s. Most of the firm's older stores were located in downtown areas where they catered to lower and lower middle-income residents. Recent expansion has been into suburban areas, where a shopping center often grows around a large S&J.

Sidney Sherman is grandson of a founder and is now company president. He states that the company's success has been due to the following factors: (1) loyal personnel; (2) many stores in convenient locations; (3) large batch purchasing, with its associated bargaining power over supplier prices; (4) standardized, modestly priced merchandise that appeals to the mass market.

The stores are organized on a regional basis; general managers of stores report to an assistant regional manager. Exhibit 1 illustrates the company structure. Marketing and advertising and merchandise purchase and distribution are highly centralized. Promotional campaigns and advertising circulars are planned months in advance at the regional and national level. Distribution is effected through regionally located central warehouses, each of which supplies all the stores in its region.

Store layouts are standardized, with few exceptions. Every store carries the same products and brands in roughly equal quantities. When a new store opens, merchandise arrives from the warehouse automatically and continually. What items are sent and how many of each is predetermined; the store manager has little to say about this ordering. After the store has been in operation for a time, individual department supervisors and local buyers may order merchandise from the standard catalog, but goods still arrive unsolicited from the central warehouse.

The managerial structure of each store is as follows. A store is run by a general manager, who usually has been with the company for at least five years. There is also a merchandise manager, who is responsible for the kind and amount of merchandise on hand as well as for the management of local advertising and promotions. An operations manager handles the day-to-day operations of the store. The manager is responsbile for salesclerks, maintenance, and security.

Exhibit 2 illustrates the organization of Store No. 98, located in the suburbs of a medium-sized western city. The city, which is the focus of an agricultural and industrial county, has about 250,000 people and is generally considered to be deteriorating somewhat from its former prominence. Efforts by city officials and business leaders have not stemmed the flow of people and money to the suburbs. The suburbs, in an area extending for a radius of perhaps seven miles have been developing on their own and have had much industrial, commercial, and residential growth. The entire area has a population of about 720,000.

Store No. 98 is one of three similar stores constructed by the chain in the past three years in the area. The other two, which were also recently opened, are located in the northwest and eastern suburbs. The market in the area has been growing steadily as new people move in to work in local industries. Other chains and many independents have recently opened department stores similar to Store No. 98 in the area. Total sales have been good, but a number of stores are in financial trouble.

EXHIBIT 1

Partial Organization Chart

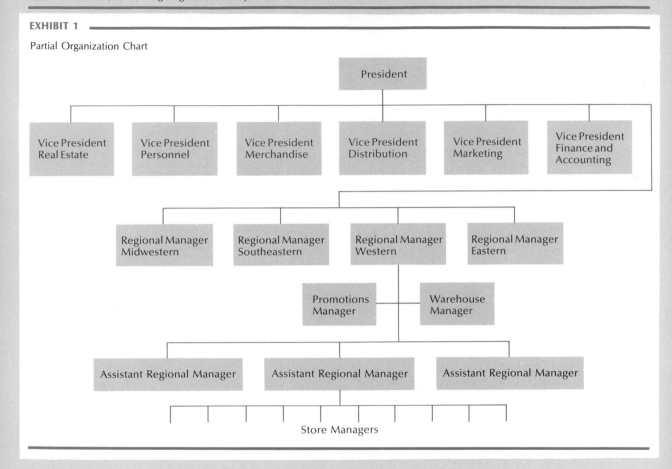

During a certain week late last June, the following events took place: Appleton, the store manager, asked Benedetto, the merchandise manager, how the plans for the big July 4th promotional sale were coming along.

BENEDETTO: We have the thousand cartons of Coke we brought in for the giveaway. The only problem is that we have no place to put them. The stockroom is jammed as it is. The salespeople have a hard time knowing what merchandise is there, let alone getting to it. Since Davis [former stock supervisor] quit three weeks ago, it's been chaos. Chase [operations manager] has tried to pick up the slack, but he's got other things to worry about. I wish you would pressure the central office to send a replacement for Davis.

APPLETON: Well, I'm sure they appreciate our problem and are working on it. Can anyone else help out?

BENEDETTO: I know I can't. With the promotional sale coming up, and the way merchandise has been piling up on me, I can hardly keep up. The warehouse keeps sending merchandise even when we're full up with the same items. I can't unload things fast enough, and sales haven't been that hot recently. You know those radios and TV's we let go below cost last week? We have to do that just to get people in the store.

APPLETON: It takes time to build a reliable group of customers. When I opened a store in Pittsburgh, it was a year before we got in the black, and longer before we began to get even a half-decent return.

BENEDETTO: I'm sure that's true. But how long can we afford to take the loss while the merchandise piles up in the back? I've had to start loading up the aisles with stacks of extra stuff that's been coming in. You should tell them to hold off sending new merchandise for awhile.

APPLETON: Well, we'll be in a better position to argue with these people when we start showing a profit.

EXHIBIT 2

Organization of Store No. 98

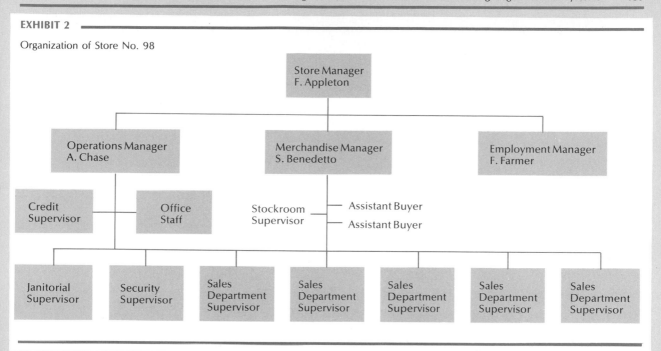

BENEDETTO: I think maybe we need some different merchandise also. The people around this area want more variety and better quality than the goods we stock. For example, Fran Epstein [Appliance Department supervisor] tells me that our best stereo sets just don't compare with many stocked by Winston's Electronics across the mall. We should be more competitive. Frankly, I think there are too many discount department stores like us in the area. We need to be different to compete.

APPLETON: We can't do anything about that. S&J has grown doing things a certain way, and I'm sure the central office knows what they're about. Some stores will survive, others won't. We can take losses longer than other people. The guys upstairs will see that the managers here will have a bright future in S&J somewhere. In fact, I'm working on my promotion to assistant regional manager in Georgia. That would create a new opportunity here.

BENEDETTO: I also have a problem of sales and promotions. The region sends down promotionals and places advertising in newspapers without my knowing about it. Customers come in with ads and the sales personnel don't know what they're talking about. They're caught in the middle and are unhappy. They complain to Chase, but he doesn't help much.

APPLETON: Some grumbling is inevitable when a store is starting up.

When requested to comment on Benedetoo's observations, Chase Expressed some different views:

CHASE: Benedetto lives in a dream world. He thinks everyone wants Mercedes quality, but this company has grown by selling Chevrolets. Our stuff is good and it works, even if it's not fancy. In fact, maybe we should concentrate more on the less-expensive lines at this store. The people out here aren't that well off. Most of them saved their pennies to get a split-level away from the ills of the city, but they are now house poor. And some had to purchase a second car they wouldn't have needed in the city. I think they may just have less money to spend than they did when they lived with one car in a crowded apartment in the city.

My biggest problems are the poor stockroom service and lazy salesclerks. Most of the clerks are part-timers: homemakers and school kids earning a little extra money. But they are neither motivated nor loyal. No sooner will they get established in a job, learn the merchandise, and begin to recognize customers than they quit. And Benedetto doesn't help. He's always giving orders to push this item, set up that special display.

He should keep his nose out of my business. And without a stock supervisor, clerks sometimes can't or won't obtain the merchandise they should be selling. They could just walk back to the stockroom themselves, but most are too lazy to do it. Rather than leave their counters, they tell the customer that we're out of a product and we lose a sale. I could really straighten things out if I ran the stockroom and if I could get rid of the Mickey Mouse supervisor of janitorial and security services.

Questions on Sherman and Jackson Stores, Inc.

1. What has been the organizational stragegy of S&J Inc?
2. What problems may exist with this structure?

3. What are the problems at Store No. 98?
4. What are the causes of the problems at Store No. 98?
5. What modification in S&J structure would you recommend?
6. What other recommendations do you have for Store No. 98?

Senator Judson Blair's Office (A)*

Judson Blair is a newly elected U.S. senator from a southern state. He is in the process of putting together an office staff and defining its organization. Based on his experience in state government (he had been governor of his home state), familiarity with Washington, D.C., and a conversation with his predecessor, Senator Blair understands that the duties of his office will include:

1. Voting on bills on the Senate floor (which only the senator personally can do). Votes average about five to six a day when the Senate is in session (approximately 10 months a year). Votes are spread out but generally occur in the afternoon and early evening. The senator must go to the Senate floor for each vote, a trip of about seven minutes each way.
2. Monitoring all legislative debate in the Senate and reading all proposed bills.
3. Drafting proposed legislation (mainly amendments; most bills as a whole come from committees).
4. Attending and voting at committee meetings. Anyone can listen to most committee deliberations and hearings, but only the senator member can ask questions, participate in the debate, and vote. Senator Blair expects to be assigned to four committees that generally meet in the morning (but committee chairpersons do

not coordinate scheduling meetings, so conflicts are frequent).
5. Responding to constituent mail. This tends to fall into three categories: *(a)* mail commenting on how senator votes or expressing criticism or support for his positions; *(b)* requests for assistance on a wide variety of personal matters ranging from social security benefits, to stationing of a child in the military service, to job requests; and *(c)* local governments seeking assistance in dealing with some department of the executive branch of the federal government. Based on the experience of the other senators from similar states, category *(a)* should run about 2,000 letters per week; category *(b)*, 500 letters per week; and *(c)*, 10 per week.
6. Responding to personal, political, and all other mail (approximately 100 letters per week).
7. Receiving telephone calls and visitors to the office. These include constitutents visiting Washington, D.C., and wanting to say hello to their senator and lobbyists wanting to argue for or against proposed legislation. Senator Blair expects about 100 visitors per week.
8. Attending various functions in Washington and the home state as political and social demands arise. Most senators believe this is necessary in order to return favors and keep in touch with home state conditions. Blair expects to return to his home state approximately three times a month when Congress is in session and to spend four weeks a year there when not in session.

* Part (B) of this case is contained in the Instructor's Manual.

EXHIBIT 1

Organizational Chart for Comparable Senator's Office

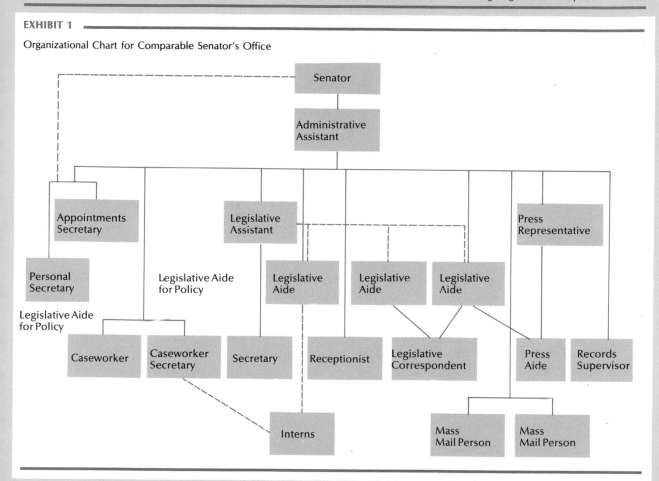

The Senate offers little guidance on dealing with these duties, although there are certain traditional positions across all 100 offices. The title and position of administrative assistant is universal as that of the principal aide to the senator and general staff administrator. A position of executive, personal, or appointments secretary is also extremely common as is that of press representative, assistant, or secretary. A distinction between professional and nonprofessional staff is common to all officers. Professional staff usually consist of young (under age 35) college graduates, many with masters or law degrees, who are variously called legislative assistants, legislative aides, or staff assistants. The nonprofessionals are frequently categorized as support staff and include such position titles as secretary, support aide, staff aide, typist, and file clerk. Most of them are young college graduates; a few part-timers are current undergraduate, graduate, or law students.

Most offices also have a position called caseworker,

which is usually seen as a nonprofessional except in a few offices where casework (response to requests for assistance) is assigned to professional staff. About one half of the senators have their caseworkers located in offices in the home state because they believe these people should be close to constituents. This also saves room in the Washington offices, which are very crowded. The other senators have the caseworkers located in their Washington office because they are easier to supervise and most of their work involves telephone contacts with executive branch officials located in Washington. Exhibit 1 gives the organization chart for one senator's office that is fairly typical. Exhibit 2 summarizes the self-described duties of these personnel.

Senator Blair is both idealistic and pragmatic. He wants to respond to constituents and to reflect their views in his voting if they are consistent with his personal views (or not *too* inconsistent), but he also desires to be re-

EXHIBIT 2

Summary of Self-Described Job Duties by Personnel in a Comparable Senator's Office

A. Activities and responsibilities of personal secretary and appointments secretary.
  1. Personal secretary:
    a. Takes personal dictation.
    b. Handles office accounts, personal checking account, political account, and charitable account.
    c. Prepares tax information for accountants.
    d. Performs personal errands for senator.
  2. Appointments secretary:
    a. Answers telephone; take messages.
    b. Schedules appointments; coordinates office appointments, speeches, and staff.
    c. Makes travel arrangements.
    d. Takes and transcribes dictation; types.
    e. Files.
B. Legislative assistant and legislative aides.
  1. Legislative assistant:
    a. Has general responsibility for all legislative action.
    b. Has specific responsibility for matters arising from several committees.
    c. Writes speeches and floor statements in specific areas.
    d. Reviews all floor statements prepared by other legislative staff.
    e. Handles constituent mail in specific area.
    f. Reviews policy establishing constituent responses prepared by other legislative staff.
    g. Oversees Senate floor activities to make sure the senator is prepared for floor action by appropriate staff member.
    h. Oversees keeping of records of senator's legislative activity.
  2. Legislative aide 1:
    a. Takes care of all legislation in energy, civil service, and post office.
    b. Supervises mass mailings with interns.
    c. Coordinates intern program.
    d. Performs administrative duties.
  3. Legislative aide 2:
    a. Follows and initiates legislation in committees on human resources and finance.
    b. Writes speeches in specific area.
    c. Answers constituent mail in specific area.
    d. Oversees agency in specific area.
  4. Legislative aide 3:
    a. Covers committees in commerce, judiciary, armed services, banking, housing, urban affairs, and related matters.
    b. Drafts speeches, position papers, and statements in specific areas.
    c. Drafts legislation in specific areas.
    d. Advises senator on bills reaching Senate floor from committees.
    e. Works out approaches to some of the more complex cases arising in home state.
    f. Drafts responses to legislative mail in specific areas.
    g. Assists constituents with federal agency problems.
C. Caseworkers.
  1. Caseworker 1:
    a. Receives, researches, writes, and types answers to constituent inquiries in specific areas.
    b. Liaisons with federal agencies and state and local officials.
    c. Counsels constituents on problems.
    d. Performs administrative duties.
  2. Caseworker/secretary 2:
    a. Receives, answers, and types responses to inquiries from constituents.
    b. Does casework for constituents.
    c. Assists legislative aide in supervising interns.
    d. Helps elsewhere in office when needed.
    e. Takes dictation from administrative aide or legislative aide when needed.
    f. Takes over reception desk when receptionist is away.
D. Support staff.
  1. Receptionist:
    a. Opens, reads, sorts, and delivers mail.
    b. Answers telephone; takes messages; transfers calls.
    c. Places phone calls for senator.
    d. Handles walk-in constituent requests for information.
    e. Answers some constituent mail.
    f. Meets and greets all incoming people.
    g. Orders office supplies for Washington and home state offices.
  2. Secretary to legislative assistant:
    a. Researches, drafts, and types constituent correspondence.
    b. Catalogs Congressional Record activities.
    c. Handles Interior Committee for office.
    d. Works on special legislative projects.
    e. Catalogs senator's voting record and voting record scores.
    f. Files legislative records.
  3. Press aide (press representative position was vacant):
    a. Writes and processes press releases.
    b. Clips and files news items referring to senator.
    c. Handles legislation and correspondence with regard to Agriculture and Forestry Committees.
    d. Assists legislative aides in their specific areas including doing casework.
    e. Does typing for legislative aides.
    f. Makes up speech scheduling.
    g. Handles press inquiries.
    h. Writes some statements for media.
    i. Lays out and types newsletter.
    j. Produces tri-weekly TV show for two senators.
  4. Legislative correspondent:
    a. Has secretarial responsibility for two legislative aides.
    b. Drafts, types constituent mail in specific areas of people for whom correspondent works.
    c. Acts as backup receptionist.
    d. Answers phone; welcomes visitors; makes appointments.
  5. Records supervisor:
    a. Classifies all mail done in office.
    b. Sets up files for home staters and controls.
    c. Handles all calls and questions with respect to files.
    d. Sets up home state files and control.
    e. Sets up subject files and control

EXHIBIT 3

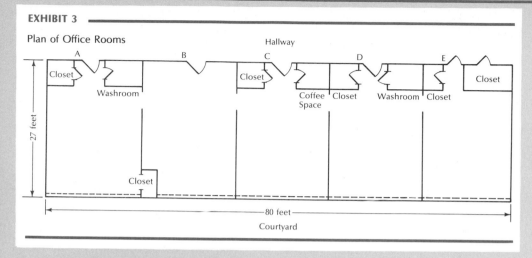

Plan of Office Rooms

elected. The importance of his constituents to him is reflected in his belief that *all* letters should receive replies, even if they are just handwritten diatribes against him. And he would like replies to get back to the writer in a week. He deems it essential that all letters have precisely the correct degree of formality in salutations and closing. That is, if the letter is from someone who knows him personally, he wants the response letter to be headed "Dear (first name)" and signed either "Jud Blair" or "Jud" depending on how close they are. More formal letters should be more conventionally addressed—"Dear Mr./ Ms. (last name)" and signed "Judson Blair." This consistent differentiation is very important to maintain political relationships and the image of friendship or approachability.

As a junior senator he realizes that his direct influence as committee member and legislator will be limited unless his legislative initiatives are extremely well researched and drafted.

Blair has been assigned office space in the Dirksen Senate Office Building. His space consists of five rooms as indicated in Exhibit 3. He is also allowed a room across the street in an old apartment house the Senate has taken over. Most senators put their part-time mail openers and handlers there. For additional Washington space he would have to pay out of his personal funds (as far as he knows,

only two senators do this—space in the home state in various federal buildings is free and virtually unlimited). His budget will allow him to hire from 15 to 25 people, depending on the relative salaries and proportions of professionals and support staff. Blair has already promised positions to four of his long-term state government staff. They have been approximately equals in terms of past duties, status, and friendship. They include: Sylvia Conrath, personal secretary; Frank Wilson, former state budget director; Samuel Jamison, former state legislative liaison; and Anthony Kingsley, former state transportation department head and primary political manager. Blair has not yet told them what positions or duties they will have in his Senate Office.

Questions on Senator Blair's Office

1. What are some possible strategies for Senator Blair in developing an organization chart for his office?

2. What are the criteria for selection?

3. Propose an organization chart defining the duties of each position.

4. Propose an office layout locating the various people in the space. What guided your assignments?

Closing Small Post Offices

The year 1970 witnessed a substantial increase in the control of postal managers over the management of the nation's postal enterprise. During that year, a major reorganization of the United States postal system took place.

Following extensive technical studies, political debate, and horsetrading among interested parties, Congress approved a law that created the U.S. Postal Service.

A key principle underlying the adoption of the change

was that congressional participation in staffing and operating decisions of the postal system should come to an end. The political appointment of postmasters was terminated. Labor relations were removed from the arena of the federal civil service, to be placed under the umbrella of the National Labor Relations Act. The postal unions became affiliated with the AFL-CIO. Postal management was given authority to borrow independently for capital investments. However, the autonomous Postal Rate Commission was established to review postal management's plans for changes in pricing and the nature of services offered.

The primary thrust of the Postal Service strategy was to maintain and enhance service levels for traditional postal services while achieving significant productivity gains by moving the system toward administrative efficiency and economic self-sufficiency.

Under the new labor relations setup, there were dramatic increases in labor costs per time unit of effort, as management and the unions sought a new equilibrium based on comparability with the private sector. At the same time, there were political pressures for keeping postal rates low, and the Postal Rate Commission adopted traditional technical criteria with regard to cost accounting, pricing, and the definition of acceptable service offerings. This placed severe constraints on the growth of revenues.

As a consequence, postal management opted for a two-pronged effort in pursuit of its strategy. Substantial resources were committed to investment in equipment and facilities for the mechanization of mail processing. A number of initiatives were taken to bring about administrative rationalization and cost savings throughout the organization. One of the measures was to reduce the number of post offices serving small communities, replacing them with other forms of rural delivery.

The history of the postal system was for many years a story of a continuing expansion of the network of postal facilities. In the years prior to the reorganization of 1970, the growth of this network was influenced primarily by the interplay of demographic and political forces. Westward migration and government policies that supported homesteading, railroad development, and continued European immigration played important roles. As agriculture and commerce flourished, the demand for communication links grew apace. Congress responded by authorizing a rapid expansion of the network of post roads and small local post offices. By 1901 there were nearly 77,000 post offices in the United States, most of them in small towns or at rural crossroads.

With the end of the era of the frontier, increased industrialization, and the advent of motorized vehicles and mechanized agriculture, patterns changed. Many of the small towns blossomed into cities. Of the farm families that remained, many were served by rural mail carriers as rural free delivery service expanded. During the ensuing decades, the number of post offices decreased dramatically. By 1971 the number had dropped to 32,000. Most of those closed were small post offices.

Before the reorganization, the process of closing a small post office had involved Congress as well as postal managers. Officers of the U.S. Post Office Department and members of the committees of Congress that oversaw postal affairs developed an informal process for determining where and when small offices would be replaced by other modes of service to rural patrons. In a nutshell it was as follows.

When a postmaster retired and the nature of the customer group being served allowed for adequate replacement service by rural or contract carriers operating from another nearby office, the Post Office Department might recommend to Congress that funding for a particular post office be dropped from the budget. Specific and detailed criteria for initiating such a recommendation were developed and issued as written procedural instructions for use by field managers.

Congress would then consider such proposals during the annual budgeting cycle. If the decision to close a particular office posed a problem of a political or community nature for a congressional representative from the district or state involved, it could easily be deferred by simply continuing to provide budget authorization for the office's operation. Local citizens and groups would bring their opinions about the closing to their representative, who would then assess the political weight and importance of these opinions against considerations of economy and efficiency. In addition, a representative who was a member of the majority party would need to consider the advantages and disadvantages of having to appoint the new postmaster.

Prior to the reorganization, then, decisions to close small post offices were triggered by information from the field about staffing and service conditions, but final determination to act was taken in Washington by Congress and senior officials in postal headquarters weighing both technical and political considerations.

Following the reorganization, Congressional involvement through the budgeting process ceased. Furthermore, the Postmaster General and key aides believed it was important to decentralize the management of operations and concomitantly to improve the quality of managerial decision making at the local level. Among the decisions that were delegated during the ensuing months to regional, district, and sectional center managers were those pertaining to the closing of small post offices.

This made little immediate difference in the rate of closings, but it did have consequences in terms of *how* the decisions were reached. There was a shift in the criteria applied in choosing when and where to close offices. In keeping with the strong emphasis placed by postal management and the Postal Reorganization Act on efficiency and cost control as performance criteria, signals from above tended to focus the attention of local managers on opportunities for cost savings. Thus closing decisions came to be framed mostly in terms of the potential for cost reduction. Local managers gave little attention to community concerns. Both Congress and postal management remained committed, nonetheless, to maintaining service levels.

Decisions on post office closings were also affected by the organization's no-layoff policies and a commitment to reducing the size of the work force by attrition. These emerged from the negotiations with labor unions and middle-management associations.

The situation soon led to difficulties. Although Congress no longer had a formal role in the decision-making process, local citizens and groups unhappy with Postal Service decisions continued to bring their concerns to their congressional representatives. In some isolated instances local managers turned to simultaneous multiple closing of small offices as a means of achieving substantial savings. Since many such offices might be located within the boundries of a single congressional district, the result was a large volume of negative mail and telephone messages to that district's representative. Such episodes led some members of Congress to conclude that the USPS was handling the matter of small office closing in an irresponsible manner.

In 1975 the General Accounting Office issued a report suggesting that closings of small post offices should be accelerated as a cost-saving move. Seeing this as a harbinger of congressional opinion, postal management took steps to relax some of the restrictions in the guidelines to local managers for initiating closings. Among the changes was the removal of the need to wait for a postmaster vacancy to consider such a move. This brought the national postmasters' association into the fray. Calling on old friends in Congress, leaders of the association criticized postal management as being too cavalier in handling the matter.

Shortly thereafter, Congress amended the Postal Reorganization Act. It required explicitly that postal management consider the effect of any proposed closing on the local community and provided local patrons with the right to appeal any closing decision to the Postal Rate Commission.

Questions on Closing Small Post Offices

1. What led to the change in the overall structure of the U.S. postal system? What were the salient features of the change?

2. Why was there a change in the way decisions to close small post offices were made?

3. Explain the lack of communication between patrons in small communities and postal management.

4. If you were the Post Master General, how would you respond to the expansion of the oversight role of the Postal Rate Commission?

5. How much change has there really been in the discretion of postal managers over the structuring of the organization?

Part Seven

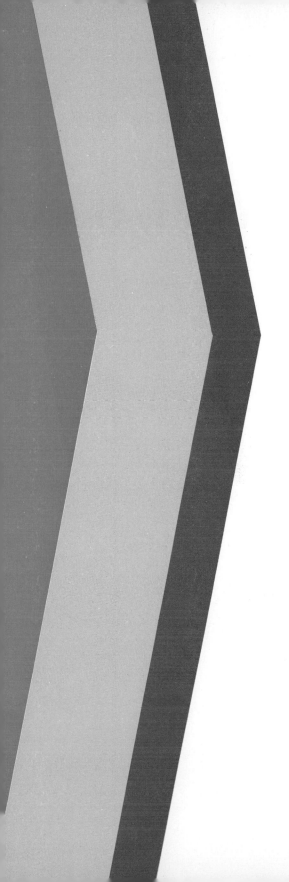

Managing Change and Conflict

22

Resistance to Change

A tale of unknown veracity is told about the British Army's use of a venerable, formerly horse-drawn artillery piece in the early days of World War II.[1]* Guns were in short supply, and this piece dating back to the Boer War was being used for coastal defense. Because it was so slow firing, a time study expert had been brought in to determine how the firing rate could be improved.

The engineer observed a five-man crew in action and took some slow-motion pictures. Studying the actions of the crew, he noticed something odd: A moment before firing, two members ceased all movement and came to attention for a three-second interval extending through the firing of the weapon. He consulted an elderly colonel of artillery. The colonel was also puzzled but finally exclaimed, "I have it! They are holding the horses." The horses had of course long since gone the way of the Boer War.

This tale suggests the difficulty with which people accommodate to changing conditions. We try to protect ourselves against the shock of change by continuing the familiar habits of the past—even when they are incongruous to the present.

With his two faces on one head, Janus, the Roman god of beginnings and endings, looked backward and forward. Managers similarly stand between two dimensions — internal and external environments, past and future, stability and change. One of their most difficult responsibilities is to mediate between the demands of the organization and the environment.[2] This task frequently requires managers to initiate change. When they initiate change, however, they must usually overcome some resistance from subordinates, peers, and superiors. Not everyone resists all change of course, but resistance commonly occurs when people reject the change agent, are satisfied with the present, are unwilling to admit past error, and are anxious to protect established authority. We shall consider each of these in detail.

Rejecting the Change Agent

Initiating change can require courage because a manager or change agent can be rejected along with the proposed change. Consider the introduction of continuous-aim gunfire into the U.S. Navy early in the 20th century.[3]

When two ships in the 19th century went into battle at sea, each would attempt to maneuver upwind of the other, shoot the other's marines out of the rigging, come alongside, throw a boarding ladder across, and claim the other vessel as prize. Such a sequence resulted in a capture and demonstrated the victor's superior sailing ability. But actually the main reason for getting so close was that it was extremely difficult to hit the target. The problem was that even after ships were made of steel and began to look "modern," the guns were basically fixed in elevation with respect to the deck. As the ship rolled, the gun rolled. Thus the gun had to be fired in anticipation of the roll, and the process was inaccurate.

In 1898 a British Navy officer named Sir Percy Scott introduced a change in the gearing mechanism on his guns that allowed a pointer to continuously elevate and depress the barrel, thus keeping it on target as the ship rolled. Improved accuracy was astounding—almost 3,000 percent.

Sources of Resistance to Change
- inertia of groups and organizations
- ignorance of trends
- investment in what will become obsolete
- preference for present system
- fear of loss (of security, status, power)
- rejection of change source
- fear of unknown

---

* Notes and references will be found at the end of this chapter.

The U.S. Navy knew nothing of this innovation until 1900, when a young lieutenant named William Sims observed some British test firings. He was impressed and promptly reported his observations via the chain of command. At first he received no reply; his letters were merely filed. Sims, however, was persistent (and a little abrasive) and kept up the pressure by writing to the Bureau of Ordinance in Washington. The Navy eventually ran a test at the Washington Naval Shipyard, which (they contended) disproved Sims's report. The experimenters said they couldn't find anyone strong enough to continuously elevate and depress the gun.

Sims was extremely persistent and eventually contacted President Theodore Roosevelt, who listened and appointed Sims as an inspector of naval ordinance. The change was soon introduced, and Sims ended up as an admiral in the World War I era. But why was this clear-cut improvement initially rejected?

The Washington Navy Department gunnery officials did not see Sims as a legitimate source of change. After all, he was just a young line officer with no special expertise in ordinance. Besides, he was literally half a world away. The "not invented here" syndrome undoubtedly also played a role. Sims's initiative might have been threatening to the Washington experts. He was asking them to change the very guns they had designed. If the innovation was so good, their superiors might well have inquired why the headquarters specialists hadn't thought of it.

Too often, conspiratorial attitudes shape the organizations's perception of people who initiate change.[4] Less secure organizational members will be especially likely to resist such initiatives by increasing their commitment to previous choices.[5]

In effect, any creative idea implicitly criticizes that which already exists—and this is one of the reasons creative ideas are so frequently rejected, even (and especially) by those who were the leaders in some previous innovation.[6] In fighting for their own changes, they have committed their personalities, reputations, and careers to the correctness of their earlier decisions. They often find it difficult to believe that conditions have changed so much so rapidly that further change is necessary so soon.

Satisfaction with What Exists

A profound cause of resistance to change is that people may feel no need to change. They perceive no threat requiring them to change what has worked in the past.

The U.S. Navy in 1900 was still basking in the glow of the glorious victory at Manilla Bay in the Spanish-American War. Admiral Dewey had led his flagship, the U.S.S. *Olympia,* and his fleet in defeating the supposed power of the Spanish monarchy (in fact, the Spanish ships were rusting to pieces). Americans were exulting in their newly acquired world power. The old gunnery system had triumphed. Nonetheless, when Sims finally achieved power in Washington, he checked all the reports on Manilla Bay and determined that of 9,500 shots fired, only 121 had hit their targets! However, this had been enough to win the battle, and it might have been good shooting for the old technology.

This bias toward the past may also have distorted the experiment conducted by ordinance officials. Rather than on the deck of a rolling vessel at sea, the test had been conducted on concrete in a shipyard. Officials attempted to simulate the roll of the ship by having the pointer continuously elevate and depress the gun. It was extremely hard doing, requiring tremendous strength to move the gun. Sims, however, had written that the maneuver was so easy at sea. The experimenters thought he must be wrong.

But Sims was not wrong. At sea Isaac Newton's first law of gravity works for the pointer; on land it works against the pointer. That is, a body at rest tends to stay at rest. On land the Navy's experimenters attempted to continuously move the gun, but at sea the pointer merely holds the gun fixed in space while the ship rolls around it. The difference in force required is enormous.

Were the Washington experimenters intentionally sabotaging the test? Probably not. More likely they were just not enthusiastic about it because it wasn't their idea.

The great danger of success is that we assume that it will continue.[7] Consequently, the value perspectives that brought us that success become inflexible. It is extremely difficult to let go of an idea that has worked in the past and appears still to be working.[8] As a result, we sometimes blind ourselves to obvious trends and deny our own ignorance.

Ignorance of Trends

"All history is bunk," Henry Ford is reputed to have announced, suggesting that the manager should be concerned with the future—future returns, future events, and future market conditions. Ironically, the Ford Motor Company illustrates the relevance of the past to present decisions.[9] Henry Ford's inadequate understanding of history contributed directly to the late 1920s decline in the company's fortunes. In his memoirs, Alfred P. Sloan, long-time chief executive of General Motors, points out that Ford did not recognize the historical development of the public's taste and its desire for a wider choice and greater luxury.[10] Because Sloan understood this, General Motors designed more attractive cars. When Ford did not, sales of the model T declined as precipitously as had sales of horse-drawn buggies a generation before. In 1927 almost no Fords were sold, and the company had nothing else to offer until a year later when the model A was introduced—a model that some thought to be old-fashioned even at its introduction.

Consider the owner-manager of a small printing establishment who had achieved success by concentrating on letterpress printing for a wide variety of local and regional customers. When lower cost but lower quality offset printing came along, the owner felt little need to add the new technology and offered a variety of excuses: "I don't have room. I don't have time. It produces lousy copy. None of my customers would accept it." This resistance to new technology went along with a backward view toward certain local institutional customers—the largest of which was the local government, followed by the hospital, schools, and churches. They were good customers, even if slow payers, but the owner-manager's perception of them was distorted by his contempt for nonprofit institutions, believing them to be badly managed, inefficient, and not greatly concerned about costs (especially politicians, who he felt only collected taxes and spent money). But he was wrong. As the cost pressures on these institutions increased, quality became a lesser concern (and offset quality

"You're living in the past, I'm not too sure you don't have the right idea."

From *The Wall Street Journal,* with permission of Cartoon Features Syndicate.

improved with time, anyway). He lost an opportunity to grow because of his misperception of historical trends.[11]

Unwillingness to Admit Ignorance

The not-invented-here syndrome rests on the difficulty of admitting that you didn't know there was a better way. Such admission can be extremely trying if it means facing your own guilt in causing harm.

A classic illustration of such resistance comes from the history of medical science. Ignez Semmelweis[12] was a physician in charge of the maternity clinic at Vienna University Hospital in 1847. At the time, the death rate in childbirth was very high—more than 12 percent at his hospital. He sharply reduced this rate (to approximately 1 percent by 1848) by having physicians disinfect their hands in carbolic acid before examining patients. Before this time, attending doctors had just lightly washed or wiped their hands on their aprons and moved directly from pathology examinations (even autopsies) to women in labor.

The physicians didn't like the change because the acid irritated their skin, and Semmelweis was dismissed from his post in 1849. By the following year, however, he had begun to repeat his success at the maternity ward in Budapest, achieving mortality rates under 1 percent. He published his findings in 1861, but once again he was rejected by the leading medical authorities. In 1865 he died in an insane asylum, his discovery mainly forgotten.

Joseph Lister is not forgotten, however. Two years later, in 1867, this English physician published a paper describing how he used carbolic acid to clean the

[handwritten margin note:] DOCTORS NOT WILLING TO ADMIT THAT THEY WERE WRONG

site of compound bone fractures (where the skin had been punctured). His innovation rapidly became widely celebrated in the medical world.

Almost 20 years later, in the 1880s, a Hungarian doctor wrote Lister, telling him how Semmelweis had anticipated the use of a disinfectant. To his credit, Lister acknowledged Semmelweis's prior innovation and used his own great authority to get it accepted as standard procedure in maternity hospitals—fully *40 years* after the Hungarian had demonstrated that it could reduce maternal mortality by more than 90 percent.

Why was Lister's procedure so easily accepted by physicians while they fought Semmelweis's for so long? Perhaps it was because the former's was consistent with the doctors' own self-image; that is, they treated the wound to heal the patient. They were agents of healing. In Semmelweis's case, however, adopting his procedure would have required tacit admission that the doctors themselves had been the agents of infection and death. This required a change in self-image that was unacceptable. (Besides, in the early 19th century physicians derived status from having blood and pus on their aprons; this showed they were busy and in demand.)

A more cynical view maintains that the general public shared in the blame for the unnecessary deaths of so many young women. In a world in which divorce was impossible or cause for scandal, the mortality rate in childbirth enabled men to live longer than women and to enjoy a sequence of wives, each succeeding one younger than her predecessor, of course. According to this jaundiced view, it was a man's world, and men felt no need to change the mortality rate in childbirth.

Dominance of the Past

People can be so busy with their current problems that they do not take time to explore ways of preventing future problems. Neither Semmelweis's nor Lister's change reflected such great scientific creativity as Louis Pasteur's painstaking development of germ theory. They were merely procedural innovations that many physicians might have introduced. But these physicians didn't seem to take the time to explore alternatives. The old way persisted.

To business managers, these military and medical stories may epitomize the limitations of noneconomic minds. But all minds are quite similar in this regard. Consider a situation at Eastman Kodak, certainly one of the world's best managed firms.[13]

Since silver is the most expensive raw material in photographic film (to make the light-sensitive emulsions), it pays Kodak to reprocess old and scrap film to recover the silver. Outdated film, production waste, and worn motion-picture reels are sorted, chopped, and chemically treated to recover the silver and reuse the flexible base. One group concentrated on old motion picture film sent from studios and distributors.

The department reported monthly to corporate headquarters on the count and physical condition of the film. When asked why the report was made, the department manager replied that it was required by higher management. When asked if he used the data in the report in managing the department, he answered no.

Inquiry at the corporate office uncovered the files of several years reports. But the clerk indicated that no one ever looked at them. Some digging revealed that

[handwritten margin notes: KODAK CORPORATION Still doing a Process that is Now serving no purpose now that NEW TECHNOLOGY WAS developed They Just kept on doing their thing BUSINESS AS USUAL]

the report originated in the 1920s, when motion picture film was on a nitrate base. Such material was extremely dangerous; it deteriorated with age, temperature, and humidity, becoming spontaneously combustible and nearly explosive in the presence of a spark or flame. Thus the older, more dangerous reels were to be sorted first and close attention paid to film condition.

In the 1960s management was still making the report, but nitrate-base film had been replaced almost 30 years earlier. In the mid-1930s Kodak had replaced the nitrate base with an acetate base, which was much more stable and much safer (the firm won a belated Academy Award for this in 1979). Yet the report on nitrate film was still being made years after the last reel had passed through the department. Thus even well-managed businesses become slaves of the past.

Protecting the Past

A past that has been successful is often protected. To allow change would undermine the very authority structure that benefited from past changes. Another military story illustrates this problem. The *Wampanoag* was one of the most successful U.S. naval vessels.[14] Commissioned in 1868, it was 355 feet long, displaced 4,200 tons, and was heavily armed. Primary propulsion was by steam and by a screw propeller 19 feet in diameter. On its sea trials it averaged almost 17 knots, making it the fastest ship in the world. Its commanding officer reported that it rode well and was "faultless." Many years later a marine historian stated that it was a magnificent success in every way, perhaps the most successful steam war vessel the world had ever seen.

Nonetheless, two years after the trials, a naval board recommended getting rid of the *Wampanoag,* and it subsequently became a floating office permanently tied to a pier. The board maintained that it wouldn't ride well because it did not fit the traditional design rules (it was judged too narrow in beam for its length). The fact that the vessel had actually proved seaworthy in trials was ignored.

Protection of Established Authority

Changes in the system of authority and status especially provoke resistance. The fundamental reason for the board's rejection was a fear of how steam vessels would change the U.S. Navy's culture. The board observed in 1870:

> Lounging through the watches of a steamer, or acting as firemen and coal bearers, will not produce in a seaman that combination of boldness, strength and skill which characterized the American sailor of an elder day; and the habitual exercise by an officer of a command, the execution of which is not under his own eye, is a poor substitute for the school of observation, promptness, and command found only on the deck of a sailing vessel.

In their fears about the social impact of this new technology, the resisting naval officers were perceptive and correct. The steam vessel did contribute to the reduction in the deck officer's status and authority, but its dominance over sailing ships was inevitable.

Even such a pioneer of change as Sigmund Freud seemed to have caved in to pressure from the establishment.[15] His earliest papers explained the psychological illness of his female patients as effects of sexual abuse from their fathers. That is what they told him, and that is what he initially believed. The notion of such abuse was impossible for 19th century society to accept, however. Because it seemed so preposterous, consciously or unconsciously, he turned the explanation on its head.[16] Thus he developed the Electra complex, which maintained that the women had wanted to be abused in childhood; that they had not actually been so abused; but that they felt guilty in adulthood for these repressed desires and were punishing themselves. Recent revelations about the unhappy frequency of child sexual abuse suggests that Freud's original interpretation was closer to the truth.

In summary, individuals and groups may be motivated to resist innovation and change for a variety of reasons:[17]

To protect social status or prerogative.

To protect an existing way of life.

To prevent a devaluation of capital invested in existing facilities.

To prevent a reduction of livelihood because the innovation or change would devalue present knowledge or skill.

To prevent the elimination of a job or profession.

To avoid the cost of replacing or modifying present systems.

Blocking Undesired Change

Managers cannot always initiate change or accept all change proposals. At times they must block change because stability is also very important to organizations.[18]

Three hundred years ago a religious philosopher observed: "When it is not necessary to change, it is necessary not to change." Most of the time, managers are trying to maintain predictability in work flow and human relations not necessarily because they fear change, but because individuals and systems can absorb only limited innovations.[19]

Managers must also take the wider and longer view. They must consider how a local change that is desirable in the short run will affect the rest of the organization in the long run.

The story of the *Wampanoag* can be seen as just another example of obstinacy and conservatism. Nonetheless, there is another side to that tale. The *Wampanoag* was ahead of its time: No other ship equaled it for 20 years. It had no natural opponent. In fact, its very existence could be interpreted as a threat by others, especially the Royal Navy of Great Britain. To them, the American vessel was an offensive weapon designed to attack, rather than defend against the British. This possible interpretation worried America's policymakers, since the United States in 1870 was still essentially following the isolationist policy of George Washington. It was trying to stay out of the affairs of European nations and, most important, trying not to threaten them. The United States had no intention of attacking and preferred not even to have the capacity to do so. Consequently, the *Wampanoag* seemed

to have no purpose, and its existence was dangerous. Getting rid of it reflected a legitimate and necessary management function: to maintain stability and block unnecessary change.

As you read Chapter 23, keep in mind managers' dual responsibilities to maintain stability but promote necessary change; to preserve the good aspects of the organization's social system but foster needed innovation; to define organizational procedures but encourage flexible new practices when desirable.

SUMMARY

Resistance to innovation and change is not universal and inevitable, but it is very common because people have many reasons for such resistance. We may reject the change agent because he or she lacks credibility or is telling us something we don't want to hear. We may not want to hear the message because our present behavior and system have led to great success in the past and still seem to be working. We may not be aware of any threats. Satisfaction with the present is one of the most profound causes of change resistance.

Not perceiving threats may reflect ignorance of external trends or unwillingness to admit that igno-

rance, because such admission might undermine our status and reduce our power. So we reject changes that would modify the existing authority structure. As a result of all this rejection, we can find ourselves to be enslaved by the past, behaving in ways that no longer are relevant to the current situation.

Not all changes are desirable, however. A manager has a critical responsibility to reject unnecessary changes, changes that might undermine the essential stability and viability of the organization. Balancing stability and change is one of the most sensitive executive tasks.

REVIEW QUESTIONS

1. How does the source of a change proposal affect its reception?

2. Why are experts sometimes resistant to the suggestions of generalists?

3. Why is past success such a threat to a person or organization?

4. How does ignorance of what is occuring elsewhere contribute to a resistance to change?

5. Why is change sometimes so threatening to an individual's or group's self-esteem?

6. How can the past dominate over the present?

7. Why is an established authority structure so often resistant to change?

8. Why should managers sometimes block attractive changes?

Notes and References on Resistance to Change

1. E. E. Morison, *Men, Machines and Modern Times* (Cambridge: MIT Press, 1966). See also E. E. Morison, *From Know-How to Nowhere: The Development of American Technology* (New York: Basic Books, 1974).

2. R. Leifer, and A. Delbecq, "Organizational Environmental Interchange: A Model of Boundary Spanning Activity," *Academy of Management Review* 3, no. 1 (1978), pp. 40–50.

3. E. E. Morison, "A Case Study of Innovation," *Engineering and Science Monthly*, April, 1950, pp. 5–11.

4. J. F. Steiner and S. W. Edmunds, "Ascientific Beliefs about Large Organizations and Adaptation to Change," *Academy of Management Review* 4, no. 1 (1979), pp. 107–12.

5. F. V. Fox and B. M. Staw, cited in "Trapped Managers Stand Their Ground," *The Wharton Magazine* 4, no. 3 (1980), p. 8.

6. Maxwell Hunter II wrote:

> All of this strongly suggests that top management should turn its back on the future ideas of the revolutionaries who have just succeeded. . . . If an organization is really going to be in the forefront with respect to technological progress, it must figuratively shoot the leaders of each successive revolution the morning after their great triumph. It is a safe bet that most of today's managements wait too long to pull the trigger.

"Are Technological Upheavals Inevitable?" *Harvard Business Review*, September–October 1969, p. 83. But will anyone lead a revolution if they know this lies in store for them?

7. T. V. Bonoma, "Market Success Can Breed Marketing Inertia," *Harvard Business Review*, September–October 1981, pp. 115–20.

8. Over the years, the Detroit-based American automobile firms have been very resistant to learning from outsiders, but that attitude is changing. As Robert Coles puts it, "The recognition is sinking in fairly rapidly that business-as-usual won't get us through this crisis." Quoted in C. G. Burck, "Can Detroit Catch Up? *Fortune*, February 8, 1982, p. 35.

9. See A. Nevins, *Ford*, 3 vols. (New York: Scribner's, 1954–1963), esp. vol. 3, *Decline and Rebirth*.

10. Alfred P. Sloan, Jr., *My Years with General Motors* (Garden City, N.Y.: Doubleday Publishing, 1964). A psychoanalytical book suggests that Henry Ford stuck with the Model T to show his estranged father that he (the son) was correct. A. Jardim, *The First Henry Ford: A Study in Personality and Business Leadership* (Cambridge Mass.: MIT Press, 1970). For a description of Henry Ford II's refusal to down-size Ford's automobiles after the oil shortage in the early 1970s, see V. Lasky, *Never Complain, Never Explain: The Story of Henry Ford II* (New York: Richard Marek, 1981).

11. One way to recognize the difficulty of change is to understand that no organization is absolutely stable. All are in the midst of some trend. It is arresting the trend and turning it around that makes adaptation so difficult. D. Miller and P. H. Friesen, "Momentum and Revolution in Organizational Adaptation," *Academy of Management Journal* 23, no. 4 (1980), pp. 591–614.

12. F. Kaufmann, "Hard and Soft Health Technology of the Future," *Technological Forecasting and Social Change* 5 (1973), pp. 67–74. The majority of drivers still do not buckle their seat belts in spite of the clear evidence that they reduce injuries in accidents. B. Simmons, "The Law Can't Save Us from Ourselves," *Philadelphia Inquirer*, August 23, 1981, p. 45.

13. R. A. Webber, *Time Is Money* (New York: Free Press, 1980).

14. Morison, *Men, Machines and Modern Times*.

15. R. Blumenthal, "Did Freud's Isolation, Peer Rejection Prompt Key Theory Reversal?" *New York Times*, August 25, 1981, p. C1.

16.   Persons with low tolerance for ambiguity tend to judge new items and novel phenomena as being *more* different and *newer* than persons higher in tolerance for ambiguity who are aware of similarities to the past. B. F. Blake et al., "The Effect of Intolerance of Ambiguity upon Product Perceptions," *Journal of Applied Psychology* 58, no. 2 (1973), pp. 239–43.

17.   James R. Bright, *Research, Development and Technological Innovation* (Homewood, Ill.: Richard D. Irwin, 1964); E. A. Gee and C. Tyler, *Managing Innovation* (New York: John Wiley & Sons, 1976).

18.   R. E. Callahan, "A Management Dilemma Revisited: Must Business Choose between Stability and Adaptability?" *Sloan Management Review,* Fall 1979, pp. 25–33.

19.   R. Albanese, "Overcoming Resistance to Stability," *Business Horizons* 13, no. 2 (1970), pp. 35–42.

23

Creativity and Innovation

During a period of severe electricity shortage, a university tried to help out in two ways: cards reading "save a watt—turn off a switch" were placed everywhere, and janitors removed half the light bulbs from all fixtures.[1]* These are the two principal approaches to change: change the people or change the situation. Use of the cards is based on the assumption that people can be taught to change their habits and will remember to switch off unused lights. Removing the bulbs assumes that people will not change, and the situation must be modified so that even if they leave the switches on electricity will be saved.

Most intervention strategies reflect these two dimensions, whether the device is asking drivers to save gasoline or rationing its purchase, showing antismoking television commercials or restricting sales, frightening children with the dangers of dope or stopping its distribution. The structural approach concentrates on impersonal organizational structure, policies, and procedures; the people approach works directly on organizational members through training and organizational development.[2] The dichotomy is a little artificial because, as we shall see, the best change efforts include both approaches, but distinguishing between them is helpful in gaining understanding (see Figure 23–1). A change agent is ultimately interested in modifying human behavior and organizational performance. In the people approach the change agent/manager's effort start with the attempt to change human attitudes, which he or she hopes will lead to modified behavior, which in turn will result in improved performance. The structural approach bypasses attitudes to work directly on behavior. By modifying the structure, technology, communications, rewards, or physical surroundings, the change agent/manager hopes to create a changed environment in which people will automatically change their behavior in the desired direction. In the structural approach human attitudes are irrelevant. Actually, we shall see that changing the system will as a by-product also inevitably change attitudes, which may help or hinder the intended change process.

In this chapter we shall examine change through technological innovation. In the next chapter, we shall describe behavioral and attitudinal change.

FIGURE 23–1

Two Approaches to Change

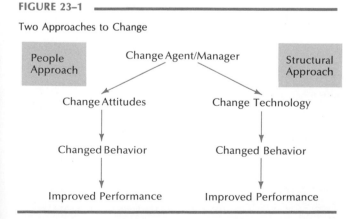

_____
* Notes and references will be found at the end of this chapter.

From Creativity to Innovation

Most literature on creativity emphasizes the dramatic role of the creator. In our individualistic tradition, our heroes are identified with great achievements: Michelangelo, Edison, Galileo, Einstein, Salk, and so on. Nonetheless, it is improtant to recognize that individuals alone are seldom responsible for creativity and even less for innovation. They build upon the work of predecessors and frequently require organizational assistance. Therefore, our concern should include the interplay between individuals, groups, and organizations in the process of creation, innovation, and change.

The terms *creativity, innovation,* and *change* are used in a multitude of ways by theorists and practitioners. To establish consistent definitions, we shall define creativity as the generation of an idea; innovation as modification of product, service, production process, or technology; and change as alteration of organizational policy, structure, or human attitudes and behavior in order to improve performance (see Figure 23–2). Thus creativity may become manifest in a new machine, a new department, or a new training program. And we shall see that most technological innovations affect organizational structure and human behavior, resulting in turn in planned and unplanned organizational and social change.[3]

Because creativity is merely the generation of new ideas, much of it exists. Real innovation is rarer, for it includes the application of the creative idea to the solution of a problem. Creativity applied in innovation includes the application of any idea, borrowed or original, to a situation in which it has not been employed before. Innovation, then, is creativity followed up by management action to the point at which it has an economic impact.[4] Indeed, the creator and the innovator may be different persons, for the creator may lack the desire or means to innovate.[5] Thus the three phases of innovation are:[6] (1) creative idea generation, (2) problem solving, and (3) implementation through innovation in product or service, production or

FIGURE 23–2

Creativity, Innovation, and Change

FIGURE 23–3

From Creativity to Innovation

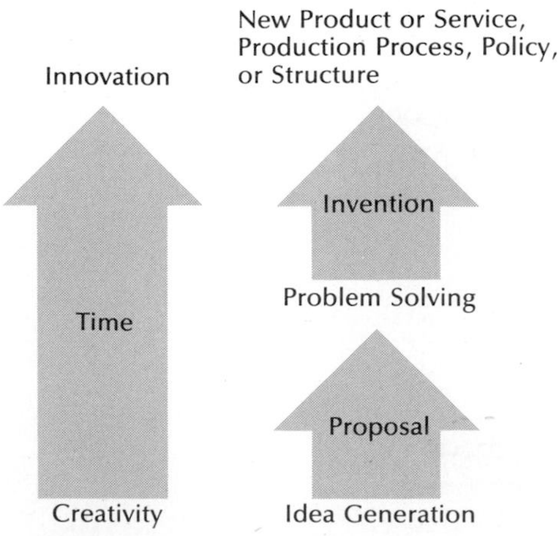

process (see Figure 23-3). Most technical innovation grows out of recognition of a customer or user need, although some comes from knowledge of a technology that is followed by a search for its application.

Aspects of Creativity

We know much and at the same time little about creativity; that is, there are many descriptions but no accepted theory. The problem is that the creative process is usually obscure, unperceived, and unverbalized even by the creator, and therefore it is uncommunicated to others.[7] We shall describe some of the common observations about creation and relate them to the kind of organizational climate that is needed for creativity to flourish.

Creation and *innovation* are not absolute terms but encompass a hierarchy of achievements, most of which do not result in a Mona Lisa, the transistor, or any dramatic discovery that soars beyond the past and present in one gigantic leap. Most creative steps are only marginally different, representing a quality of planning that adds some new or useful element, and most innovation is the sum of many routine improvements. Only a small number of men and women will ever achieve the highest levels of creativity, but most of us can be creative from time to time, perhaps by applying only a little more originality than in our regular activities. Homemakers, chemists, and painters all go about their tasks in quite similar ways; these tasks become creative only when the doer cares about doing them better.[8]

Thus creativity is manifested at many levels and takes a variety of forms, most of which depend upon borrowing, recognizing analogies, and organizing familiar things differently. From coats to boats, most innovations are adaptations of natural phenomena: fur-clad bears and floating logs. Of course, creativity is more than merely borrowing because humans enjoy the gift of imagination, the ability to conceive of a situation never experienced, to start with the word *"If. . . ."* ——→ "WHAT IF"

H. P.

COMMERCIAL
SUN DURING
BEARS GAME

Creativity is rarely a single flash of intuition; it is a process that usually requires extensive analysis of a great many observations to separate the significant from the irrelevant. Most creativity is by direct frontal assault and hard work: marshaling facts and information of all kinds, analyzing and playing with various combinations, and being alert for novel relationships. Thus Einstein, out of data available to almost any scientist of his day, formulated startlingly new concepts, but even these were latent in earlier theories.

idea comes to you in the
middle of the
night.

The bright idea that comes unbidden and naggingly, often in the middle of the night, is familiar to almost everyone. Nonetheless, the vast majority of "spontaneous" visions arrive only after the individual has been involved in conscious and often frustrating problem solving, full of spurts and lags.[9] The creative process can be traced through several steps, which are desire, saturation, manipulation, incubation, illumination, and accommodation.

Creative Steps
- desire
- saturation
- manipulation
- incubation
- illumination
- accommodation

CREATIVE PROCESS

Desire. Like all change, creation starts with dissatisfaction, the recognition of the need to fill a gap or bring a new realization. No organization is likely to change unless it is dissatisfied with the present or conceives of a better future, and no creation is undertaken unless some achievement-oriented individual or group believes it can create something better than that which exists. This is the dynamic of the achievement need. The impetus may be a recurring problem that must be responded to, a possibility presented by a development elsewhere and accidentally learned about, or a fitful night of dreams. In any case, this stimulus energizes motivation.

Saturation.   Creators review the parts of their memory and knowledge which bear directly or indirectly on the problem. They search for further information from associates and publications in an effort to make the unfamiliar familiar.

Manipulation.   With all their intellectual material before them on slips of paper, in physical shapes, or as concepts in their brains, the creators look for patterns. They poke the information, shuffle it around, turn it upside down, look at it sideways, and imagine themselves inside it. They may seek metaphors or anything to fit the various pieces together. Often they seem to do so (to premature excitement), only to collapse with further thought.

Incubation.   Somewhere frustration can be expected to clamp its grip on creative people and make them discard their seemingly insoluble problems. It seems like defeat, and many times it is. They turn to something else. But a persistent brain may not stop, and the subconscious (for want of a better term) goes on playing with the idea, perhaps freer from social and cultural restraints than the conscious mind would allow.

Illumination.   For the fortunate, the frustration and anxiety give way to a flash of insight that leads the way to a solution—like an inventive mathematician's basic theory coming to him as he steps onto a Paris bus or a writer's seeing the three acts of a play written on the ceiling over her bed.[10]

Accommodation.   The bright idea must be tested and verified to determine whether or not it really provides the answer. This can be difficult and frustrating for those midnight flashes have a way of appearing dull in the cold morning light. If the idea appears sound, it must be trained and disciplined. This stage illustrates that creativity is the union of two opposites: the uninhibited energy of the child, and a sense of order based on adult intelligence.[11] When order is missing, we get the phony creativity of the 1960s hippy movement; when childish insight is absent, we get the government's sterile response during the same period.

Innovation Categories

Technological innovation includes three broad categories:[12] routine, distress, and opportunity (see Figure 23–4). Routine innovation is programmed by management so that well-defined positions and procedures exist for developing, evaluating, and implementing an idea. Such routine innovations are usually minor product changes designed to keep them stylish. Basic structural and performance characteristics change

Drawing by Levin; © 1978 The New Yorker Magazine, Inc.

little, but shapes, colors, and options are varied from year to year. These changes seldom affect formal organizational policies and structures or the informal social system.[13] Automobiles, home appliances, and most consumer goods companies program routine innovation.

Distress innovation is undertaken by the firm in trouble. Under economic pressure, such innovation usually looks for ways to reduce product, service, or process costs.

FIGURE 23-4 ━━━━━━━━━━

Categories of Technological Innovation

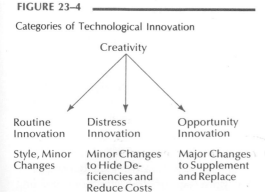

Creativity

Routine Innovation	Distress Innovation	Opportunity Innovation
Style, Minor Changes	Minor Changes to Hide Deficiencies and Reduce Costs	Major Changes to Supplement and Replace

In general, the firm will not have sufficient financial or personnel resources to redesign substantially.

Opportunity innovation is the goal of successful firms with sufficient (and excess) resources. Research is conducted to supplement or replace existing products, services, and processes.

The Innovation Process

Creative ideas must be converted into innovations in order to have an impact on the organization. Getting an idea actually implemented is a political process in which management support must be secured in order to persuade or pressure others.

The Politics of Innovation

Most organizations do not automatically recognize their creative geniuses and accept their proposals. This situation creates another paradox for management: Creative people dislike but still desire management supervision. They tend to be reserved and self-reliant introverts who desire personal autonomy and are resentful of overly close or authoritarian supervision of their technical effots.[14] They do not want to have to continually justify their time expenditures and defend their ideas. Management errs if it runs a creativity-based organization like a factory. In addition, creators and intellectuals are often disdainful of administrators. In educational and research institutions, the creators tend to see managers as hacks who exist only to serve them. The social reformers on the New Frontier with John Kennedy looked down upon Lyndon Johnson because he was a mere politician and arm twister. This is pure snobbery and elitist nonsense. As a rule, teachers, scientists, researchers, and reformers underestimate the pressure on operating executives and do not understand organizational complexity.

In business, technical people often advance good ideas with great force but only naive understanding of market forces.[15] Many innovations are not demanded by customers (when Bell first offered his telephone for sale, it was turned down because "there was no need for it," and the Xerox copying process was available for four years before anyone wanted it). Selling is essential. Some creators seem to believe that firms are omnipotent and can impose their wills on the marketplace, but the people "out there" must be educated, and a want must be created. This is where management comes in on the creative process.

Creators need doers and champions—managers—who can convert ideas into organizational reality.[16] Often the creator just proposes and then loses interest when prolonged effort is needed to implement his or her suggestions. Perceptive creative people soon learn that they do not want totally withdrawn or abdicative superiors. They want a collaborative manager who will give them advice on the political implications of their ideas as well as support in whatever battles are necessary to obtain the required financial resources.[17] The probability of a creative idea being implemented depends heavily on the relationship between the staff initiators and line management.[18]

[handwritten margin note: AT CERTIAN TIME CERTIAN NEW INNOVATIONS MAY NOT BE NEEDED BY THE MARKET.]

Implementation

Corporate responsiveness to innovation opportunity (such as initiating a new business) depends on the perceived need for the proposal—and this is related to prior familiarity with the technology, product, or markets. Most innovation is conservative adaptation to external changes in its own field.[19] People are more optimistic about changes in a familiar industry. Studies of industries have shown that although most innovations come from within, most *radical* developments come from outsiders who are less familiar with the industry but more competent in a new technology. The developers of the jet aircraft engine were not existing piston engine manufacturers but airframe companies and firms producing electricity-generating turbines. The innovators in wireless telephone were not the telephone and telegraph utilities but radio and electronics companies. Similarly, land-grant state universities, one of the great American educational innovations, did not spring from the 19th-century established private educational institutions.[20]

Most technological innovation is slow in being utilized; the delay in the use of available public technology runs from 10 to 20 years—although this lag is probably decreasing.[21] And business firms tend to innovate mainly in short-term profit areas. A company president might reject an innovation of long-term promise because it could not produce an income within the firm's two- or three-year planning horizon. As we noted in Part 5, "Planning and Controlling," not thinking about the longer run is easy; it is more necessary to prepare for tomorrow's problems than to dream about a remote future. Unfortuantely *any* long-range thinking can be discarded on these grounds, with the result that more must be spent to innovate later on a crash basis.

Risk in Innovation

Inspiration is open to all, but realizing one's objective depends upon self-discipline, almost obsessive perseverance, and enormous faith in what one is doing.[22] This commitment is not entirely rational. No application of management theory, quantitative analysis, and decision planning can change the fact that most innovation and change is charged with both personal and organizational risk. From the mythological Prometheus, who was punished for bringing creativity to earth, through Galileo, who saw Man as not being the center of the universe, to today, many innovators are initially rejected and vilified (but of course, being rejected is no proof of innovation). Unfortunately, education can promote either increased knowledge on which to build or a pseudo sophistication, which can block anything new. Innovation that is subjected to overanalysis and treated as if it were entirely logical will largely be destroyed. Our own experience in discussing cases with undergraduate and graduate management students suggests that the latter may be less willing to initiate entrepreneurial ventures than the former. Knowledge may lead to fewer mistakes, but unfortunately it also leads to more conservatism and fewer big successes. A certian amount of faith will always remain at the core of innovation.

Fear and anxiety are endemic to creative people because they always know they might fail; reputations and egos may be damaged. This anxiety is internally generated and does not need management reinforcement. Consequently, some suggest that management should create job security in positions where creativity is essential because it would encourage initiative and independence. Whatever the demerits of guaranteed tenure for professors, it does facilitate their criticism of contemporary institutions. The saint or hero without security might still question the irrational, time-honored patterns of past and present authorities, but those who are less courageous need a solid place on which to stand before they rock the boat.

The Climate for Creativity and Innovation

An organizational climate that will encourage creativity is characterized by open communications, cooperation and support, partial isolation, excess resources, delayed criticism, organizational honesty, mutual respect, and courage and commitment. We shall examine each. The specific characteristics of the creative individuals and organizations that make up such a climate are listed in Figure 23–5.[23]

Open Communications

Climate for Creativity and Innovation
- open communications
- cooperation and support
- partial isolation
- excess resources
- delayed criticism
- openness
- honesty
- mutual respect
- courage
- commitment

We have seen that creative success is usually related to and built upon the previous work of others. Innovative modern artists, such as the abstract expressionists, did not begin by throwing paint at the canvas; the creative ones began with classical draftership and realism and moved on to recreate most of the evolution of painting before developing novel forms. In science, also, each experiment builds upon the work of earlier, more limited ones. Such building is dependent on a free information flow and access to the findings of others.[24] This is one reason secrecy and censorship are an anathema to most scientists and writers.

Inability to gain access to necessary information is a powerful block to creativity and change. For example, interdepartmental and intergroup conflicts often curtail communication exchanges. By blocking information, even a minor official can hamper the innovative process at its most crucial stage—the discovery of a problem. In general, the greater the communication between a business firm and its environment at each stage of the innovation process, the more effective it will be in generating, developing, and implementing innovation.[25]

Managers and organizations need to face reality, to obtain frank feedback on their performance, and to be sensitive to the state of the outside world. These are essential conditions for adapting to conditions by internal change. Organizational structure and personal attitudes should facilitate a positive attitude toward this sensitivity. It is not just accepting incoming information, but includes both surveillance (general exposure to external information where the viewer has no specific purpose in mind other than exploration) and search (a relatively limited investigation seeking out specific information). This information from the outside world must be imported into the organization and communicated to relevant authority figures.[26] It is not sufficient for isolated and impotent staff specialists to have such information; it must become part of the planning premises for line management.

Cooperation and Support

Because of this dependence on information flow, creativity may prosper most in a friendly atmosphere of cooperation. To expect complete coopration from any

FIGURE 23–5

Characteristics of Creative Individuals and Organizations

The Creative Individual	*The Creative Organization*

Conceptual fluency . . . is able to produce a large number of ideas quickly.	Has idea specialists with opportunity for private thought.
	Open channels of communication; little secrecy.
	Ad hoc devices:
	  Suggestion systems.
	  Brainstorming.
	  Idea units absolved of other responsibilities.
	Encourages contact with outside sources.

Originality . . . generates unusual ideas.	Heterogeneous personnel policy:
	  Includes marginal, unusual types.
	  Assigns nonspecialists to problems.
	  Allows eccentricity.

Separates source from content in evaluating information . . . is motivated by interest in problem . . . follows wherever it leads.	Has an objective, fact-based approach.
	Ideas evaluated on their merits, not status of originator.
	Ad hoc approaches:
	  Anonymous communications.
	  Blind votes.
	Selects and promotes on merit only.

Suspends judgment . . . avoids early commitment . . . spends more time in analysis, exploration.	Sufficient financial, material, human and time resources. Invests in basic research; flexible, long-range planning. Experiments with new ideas rather than prejudging on "rational" grounds; everything gets a chance.
Less authoritarian . . . has relativistic view on life.	More decentralized; diversified. Administrative slack; time and resources to absorb errors. Risk-taking ethos; tolerates and rewards taking chances.
Accepts own impulses . . . playful, undisciplined exploration.	Not run as "tight ship." Employees have fun. Allows freedom to choose and pursue problems. Allows freedom to discuss ideas.
Independence of judgment, less conformity . . . deviant, sees self as different.	Organizationally autonomous. Original and different objectives, not trying to be another "X."
Rich, "bizarre" fantasy life and superior reality orientation, control.	Security of routine . . . allows innovation; stable, secure environment that allows "creators" to roam. Has separate units or occasions for generating versus evaluating ideas; . . . separates creative from productive functions.

Source: G. A. Steiner, ed., *Creative Organization* (Chicago: University of Chicago Press, 1965).

group is naive, of course, because creative people, even research scientists, are ambitious and sometimes jealous of others' success.[27] Nonetheless, the value system of science tends to cooperation rather than competition. Business management places a higher value on competition as a way of bringing out the best in people, but researchers believe that intergroup competition hinders creativity by reducing information flow and forcing premature "hardening" of proposals. Rather than exploring half-baked ideas in the critical early stage of creation, they do not communicate until the proposal is solid, packaged, and ready for selling. Unfortunately, such solidified proposals often suffer from being frozen short of their potential.[28]

One of the greatest boons to the innovator is an intellectual collaborator who will provide sympathetic reassurance, a person who may not supply original ideas but understands and supports the activity with constructive criticism. The presence of supportive others can be especially helpful when their knowledge is complementary. Bringing together people with a variety of skills and experiences can create the rich mix in which creative borrowing occurs. A brainstorming group that included an architect, an engineer, and an ichthyologist designed the roof for a building in the semitropics to resemble a flounder—able to change color through inflating bubbles that absorb or reflect heat.[29] Diversity stimulates the generation of new ideas. More creative people, for example, seem to have more varied and random reading habits, are more open to the experiences of others, and are involved with others, as in consulting off the job. They act as the gatekeepers for incoming information and as resources for others.[30]

Partial Isolation

Partially isolating the innovator from operating pressures may be helpful for innovation. To create an independent environment that is not time pressured, many industrial research and development laboratories have been constructed on suburban campus-like grounds away from manufacturing activities. The independence of the scientists is dramatized by the relaxation of bureaucratic rules about working hours and dress, in hopes of promoting personal commitments and freer interchange of ideas. In short, the creative scientists are insulated from the firm.

The paradox is that creative persons should be both part of and not part of the organization. They must feel a sense of mission, a desire to contribute, and concentrate much of their time on a single important project, but they must not be dominated by the organization's commitment to the status quo.[31] The creative staff people need to understand the line operating process, but the more they become involved in handling operational problems, the greater their proclivity to accept the organization's bias toward stability.

Excess Resources

Some managerial "sloppiness" is apparently conducive to innovation. "Slack" or excessive resources provide time and opportunity to engage in creative activity that is impossible in a more tightly constrained operation that has no excess resources.[32] Excessive concern for efficiency seems to hinder organizational creativity and adaptability.[33] Such firms search vigorously only for distress innovations, solutions to immediate problems of cutting costs or changing output.[34]

Scarce executive time is a major block to the ability to take advantage of opportunity. Part of the problem (for smaller firms, especially) is that managers are so busy with today's activities that they cannot create for tomorrow. If there is not sufficient time, no one can engage in the random search for solutions to problems that may not even be apparent.[35]

To the innovator, necessity may be the mother of invention, but if others do not feel the necessity, the creator must point it out.[36] Nonetheless, the manager who allows slack without limit abdicates responsibility. Not only is this wasteful, but too many people and resources eventually will undermine creativity itself.

Kudzu

Reprinted by permission: Tribune Company Syndicate, Inc.

Delayed Criticism

Creative ideas must eventually prove their validity in the real world, where vested interests will oppose them. In business profits must be generated, but it helps if these hard tests don't come too soon. If tested too early, almost all innovation will be found wanting and discarded because premature criticism can destroy all but the most superior ideas. The effective manager of creative people should provide some protection by buffering them from untimely pressure to produce results.[37] It took almost five years for the Manhattan project to develop a successful atomic bomb. Nazi Germany was farther along when it began its parallel project, but Hitler became impatient with slow progress and stopped it. The values of an organization's leaders and policy-making elite are more related to subsequent innovation than its structure is.[38]

Honesty

Some organizations that fail to change adequately know beforehand that they are in trouble. Though they know this, they really do not see it; they refuse to examine themselves honesty.[39] The tragedy is that there seems to be a kind of iron law of decadence by which organizations lose their revitalizing spirit once they become successful.[40] Anyone who threatens their self-delusion can be dangerous. Few incidents are more demoralizing than government officials who are persecuted for communicating the truth about cost overrides, official deception, or executive malfeasance. No wonder some high-ranking people conclude that they have a right and even an obligation to block information that might upset their superiors.

Refusal to communicate reality because of feared consequences can be utterly destructive to an organization.[41] When Nazi Germany attacked the Soviet Union in 1939, Stalin at first refused to believe it because the nonaggression pact, which he considered a monument to his wisdom, was thus destroyed. Even when the reality of the war became evident, the Russian military still feared sending truthful messages because they were sure they would be punished, either for lying or for failing. Consequently, for precious days Moscow thought things were going well, when in fact disaster had taken hold. At a later stage in the war, the German government suffered from a similar communication distortion.[42]

Organizations should have provisions for self-criticism, a climate in which uncomfortable questions can be asked and the dissenters can be protected. No top management should be trusted to be adequately critical of itself; self-deception is too easy. The organization must be hospitable to its internal critics as well as to outsiders who ask unpopular questions. From the ranks of the critics come not only troublemakers but also saviors.

In addition to such a spirit of acceptance of criticism, formal guarantees must be given, and conflict procedures must be instituted as discussed. No organization should trust its top officials to be always fair and tolerant in the fact of criticism; they should be constrained by rules. Perhaps all innovation proposals not approved by the normal hierarchy should have the right of appeal to a high-level innovation committee or even a "vice president of revolution."[43]

Mutual Respect

Managers and change agents should not assume that everyone always resists change. Such an expectation tends to be self-fulfilling; it misleads a change-initiating elite into believing that the masses must be pushed, cajoled, or manipulated into changes they would not understand. This is nonsense; more organizational change ideas have their origins in the middle levels than at the top. And people are willing to change when they perceive change to be in their interest.[44]

Americans in particular have been seen by other nations to be remarkably adaptable to change, even anxious for it. In 1835 a foreign visitor asked a sailor in Boston why American ships were built to last only a short time. According to the tourist:

> The sailor answered without hesitation that the art of navigation is making such rapid progress that the finest ship would become obsolete if it lasted beyond a few years. In these words which fell accidentally from an uneducated man, I began to recognize the general and systematic idea upon which your great people direct all their concerns.[45]

Those concerns constitute America's preoccupation with change.

Perhaps we have lost some of this drive, but by no means should we assume that the status quo is widely worshipped. Ideally the various organizational levels should respect the others' initiation of or resistance to change.[46] Resistance should be interpreted not as blind but as a rational message that something is wrong with the change plan proposed.

Courage and Commitment

To effect change, managers and other organizational members must have the flexibility to initiate and accept technological, social, and behavioral innovation. This willingness rests upon the individual's commitment to the goals of the organization and the integration between one's personal aims and these goals. People have to believe that what they and the organization do makes a difference.[47] Change is always risky and often threatening and uncomfortable. Because apathetic people seldom change, a desirable precondition is that people care. Only with such commitment and caring can an organization sustain the fluidity of structure and continuous self-renewal required to overcome the vested interests that bedevil institutions. Every change affects someone's privileges, status, or authority, but stagnancy threatens the whole organization.

SUMMARY

Creativity is the generation or transference of ideas to a new setting; innovation is the application of creativity to technology, products, services, and processes. Such innovation may be routine, distress, or opportunity innovation.

Creativity is a complex and ambiguous business, but it is rarely a single intuitive insight. The steps include: desire, saturation, manipulation, incubation, illumination, and accommodation. The climate for facilitating creativity requires open communications, cooperation and support, partial insulation of creators, excessive resources or some organizational "slack," and delayed criticism so that it is not premature.

Creators and creativity are not sufficient to convert ideas into reality; innovators and managers are needed for this. This conversion is not automatic, for resources must be assembled and potential users educated. Most innovations are incremental rather than radical because firms generally innovate only in familiar areas. Major revolutions tend to originate with outsiders who are not tied to the old technology.

Innovation is not entirely logical. The uncertainties and risks are often so great that substantial faith and courage are essential. Nor is innovation always desir-

able. To maintain necessary stability, management must sometimes block change.

The ideal organizational conditions for innovation and change appear to include: (1) energetic search for and openness to information about the external world, (2) respect and encouragement for honest communication, including formal safeguards for critics, (3) mutual respect between managers, change agents, and other organizational members, and (4) courage and commitment to the organization and its objectives. People must care enough to confront the risks involved in change.

Creativity is not a "you have it or you don't" proposition. It is a continuum and a fundamental attribute of all humanity. No organization can tap all the creativity that resides deep within the individual, and we do not want or cannot expect to make things so easy and secure that all the views of even the most timid individual will be accepted. Only the incredibly naive expect complete and immediate responsiveness of the organization to the individual. However, whether or not most people have innovative qualities is almost irrelevant. The important point is that the organization must not operate in a manner that poses insurmountable obstacles to all but the most creatively gifted or most aggressive individuals.

REVIEW QUESTIONS

1. What is the difference between creativity and innovation?

2. What are the three phases in innovation?

3. What are the categories of innovation? How do they differ?

4. What are the possible steps in the creative process?

5. In what way is innovation a political process?

6. How and why are creative people sometimes naive about innovation?

7. What factors influence whether or not a creative idea will actually become an implemented innovation?

8. How might security help the creative individual?

9. What are the attributes of a creative climate?

10. Why are open communications helpful to creativity?

11. What are the dangers to creativity of excessive competition?

12. Why is partial isolation helpful to creativity? Why not total isolation? Or immersion in the organization?

13. How do excess resources contribute to organizational creativity?

14. How does premature criticism affect creativity and innovation?

15. How can an organization provide for self-criticism?

Notes and References on Creativity and Innovation

1. Amitai Etzioni, "Human Beings Are Not Very Easy to Change after All," *Saturday Review,* June 3, 1972, p. 45. Also see James S. Coleman, "Conflicting Theories of Social Change," *American Behavioral Scientist* 14 (1971), pp. 633–50.

2. Harold J. Leavitt, "Applied Organizational Change in Industry: Structural Technological and Humanistic Approaches," In *Handbook of Organizations* (Skokie, Ill.: Rand McNally, 1965), ed. James G. March; Newton Margulies and J. Wallace, *Organizational Change: Techniques and Applications* (Glenview, Ill.: Scott, Foresman, 1973).

3. J. R. Bright, *Research, Development and Technological Innovation* (Homewood, Ill.: Richard D. Irwin, 1964); G. Zaltman, R. Duncan, and J. Holbek, *Innovation and Organization* (New York: John Wiley & Sons, 1973); G. D. Brewer, "On Innovation, Social Change, and Reality," *Technological Forecasting and Social Change* 5, no. 1 (1973), pp. 19–24.

4. D. G. Marquis, "The Anatomy of Successful Innovations," *Innovation* 1, no. 7 (1969); and F. A. Webster, "Entrepreneurs and Ventures: An Attempt at Classification and Clarification," *Academy of Management Review,* January 1977, pp. 54–61.

5. W. H. Gruber and D. G. Marquis, *Factors in the Transfer of Technology* (Cambridge, Mass.: MIT Press, 1969).

6. J. M. Utterback, "The Process of Technological Innovation within the Firm," *Academy of Management Journal* 14, no. 1 (1971), pp. 75–88; and J. L. Pierce and A. L. Delbecq, "Organization Structure, Individual Attitudes and Innovation," *Academy of Management Review,* January 1977, pp. 27–36.

7. On the nature of creativity, see W. I. B. Beveridge, *The Art of Scientific Investigation* (New York: Norton, 1957); H. H. Anderson (ed., *Creativity and Its Cultivation* (New York: Harper & Row, 1959); A. Roe, *The Making of a Scientist* (New York: Dodd, Mead, 1961); J. W. Hae-fele, *Creativity and Innovation* (New York: Reinhold, 1962); H. E. Gruber, G. Terrell, and M. Wertheimer eds., *Contemporary Approaches to Creative Thinking* (New York: Atherton Press, 1963); D. Fabun, *You and Creativity* (Beverly Hills, Calif.: Glencoe Press, 1968); and G. M. Prince, *The Practice of Creativity* (New York: Harper & Row, 1970).

8. Abraham Maslow, "Creativity in Self-Actualizing People," in H. H. Anderson, ed., *Creativity and Its Cultivation* (New York: Harper & Row, 1959).

9. D. N. Perkins, *The Mind's Best Work* (Cambridge, Mass.: Harvard University Press, 1982).

10. S. M. Maini and B. Norbeck, "Critical Moments, the Creative Process and Research Motivation," *International Social Science Journal* 25, nos. 1–2 (1973), pp. 190–204.

11. D. Goleman, "The Fertile Tension between Discipline and Impulse," *Psychology Today,* October 1976, p. 53 ff.

12. K. E. Knight, "A Descriptive Model of the Intrafirm Innovation Process, *Journal of Business of the University of Chicago* 40, no. 4 (1967), pp. 478–96.

13. On the short-run views and minor innovation of most new products, see M. A. Johnson, "New Product Planning in an Age of Future Consciousness," *California Management Review* 16, no. 9 (1973), pp. 25–33. "While industry's R&D expenditures approached $34 billion last year, managers acknowledge that most of the research they sponsor nowadays is aimed at minor improvements in existing products rather than the high-risk investigations that produce scientific breakthroughs." T. Alexander, "The Right Remedy for R& D Lag," *Fortune,* January 25, 1982, p. 61.

14. R. B. Cattell and J. E. Drevdahl, "A Comparison of the Personality Profile of Eminent Researchers with that of Eminent Teachers and Administrators and of the General Population," *British Journal of Psychology* 46 (1955), pp.

248–61. See also S. Marcson, *The Scientist in American Industry* (New York: Harper & Row, 1960); D. C. Pelz and F. M. Andrews, *Scientists in Organizations* (New York: John Wiley & Sons, 1966); and W. Kornhauser, *Scientists in Industry* (Berkeley: University of California Press, 1963).

15. T. Levitt, "Creativity Is Not Enough," *Harvard Business Review*, May–June 1963, pp. 72–83. See also, A. A. Marcus, "Policy Uncertainty and Technological Innovation," *Academy of Management Review* 6, no. 3 (1981), pp. 443–48.

16. D. R. Schoen, "Managing Technological Innovations, *Harvard Business Review*, May–June 1969, p. 156 ff; and Maxwell R. Morton, "Technology and Strategy: Creating a Successful Partnership," *Business Horizons*, January–February 1983, pp. 44–48.

17. A. K. Chakrabarti, "The Role of Champion in Product Innovation," *California Management Review*, Winter 1974, pp. 58–62; and G. Kelley, "Seducing the Elites: The Politics of Decision Making and Innovation in Organizational Networks," *Academy of Management Review*, July 1976, pp. 66–74.

18. William Evan, "Organizational Lag," *Human Organization*, Spring 1966, pp. 51–53.

Many, perhaps most, change proposals come from middle managers who then must solicit higher level support. M. Aiken. S. B. Bacharach, and J. L. French, "Organizational Structure, Work Process, and Proposal Making in Administrative Bureaucracies," *Academy of Management Journal* 23, no. 4 (1980), pp. 631–52. See also R. M. Kanter, "The Middle Manager As Innovator," *Harvard Business Review*, July–August 1982, pp. 95–105.

19. S. L. Westfall, "Stimulating Corporate Entrepreneurship in U.S. Industry," *Academy of Management Journal*, June 1969, pp. 235–46. For a view of the difficulties of governmental implementation, see J. L. Pressman and A. Wildavsky, *Implementation* (Berkeley: University of California Press, 1973).

20. Knight, "Descriptive Model of Intrafirm Innovation Process."

21. For examples of how far hardware is ahead of its utilization, see F. Kaufmann, "Hard and Soft Health Technology of the Future," *Technological Forecasting and Social Change*, 5 (1973), pp. 67–74.

22. J. Jewkes, D. Sawers, and R. Stillerman, *The Sources of Invention* (London: Macmillan, 1958).

23. C. W. Taylor, *Climate for Creativity* (Elmsford, N.Y.: Pergamon Press, 1972): M. J. Stein, *Stimulating Creativity* (New York: Academic Press, 1974); and L. L. Cummings, B. L. Hinton, and B. C. Gobdel, "Creative Behavior as a Function of Task Environment," *Academy of Management Journal*, September 1975, pp. 489–99.

R. B. Miller has suggested the following characteristics of innovative organizations:

1. Program ideas of relevance for innovation by organizations originate largely from the technological task environment.
2. Innovative organizations are aware of their interdependence with the technological task environment and exploit a diversity of external organizations, while sluggish organizations are less aware of their interdependence and rely heavily on their internal creativity and on a limited number of external organizations.
3. Initiation and search in innovative organizations take place in boundary units which have a diversity of contacts with both internal units and external organizations, while initiation and search in sluggish organizations occur in units which have fewer contacts with other internal units and external organizations.
4. Initiation and search in highly innovative organizations originate from units in which members exhibit a diversity in educational background and extra organizational experience, while initiation and search in sluggish organizations originate from units in which members exhibit inbreeding and less diversity in educational background.
5. Highly innovative organizations exhibit a lower degree of structure than sluggish organizations do.
6. Innovative organizations achieve higher levels of performance than sluggish organizations do.

Innovation, Organization and Environment: A Study of Sixteen American and West European Steel Firms (Sherbrooke, Canada: Institute of Research, University of Sherbrooke, 1971).

24. R. G. Corwin, "Strategies for Organizational Innovation: An Empirical Comparison," *American Sociological Review*, August 1972, pp. 441–54, and J. R. Schermerhorn, Jr., "Information Sharing as an Interpersonal Activity," *Academy of Management Journal*, March 1977, pp. 148–53.

The Soviet Union experiences great difficulty in industrial innovation—perhaps because of communication blocks. J. S. Berliner, *The Innovation Decision in Soviet Industry* (Cambridge, Mass.: MIT Press, 1976).

25. J. M. Utterback, "Process of Technological Innovation," See also T. S. Robertson and Y. Wind, "Organizational Cosmopolitanism and Innovativeness," *Academy of Mangement Journal* 26, no. 2 (1983), pp. 332–38.

26. M. L. Tushman and T. J. Scanlan, "Characteristics and External Orientations of Boundary-Spanning Individuals," *Academy of Management Journal* 24, no. 1 (1981), pp. 83–98.

27. Of course, conflict often occurs among co-workers in innovation, and double-crossing is not unknown in science. For the battles in the discovery of the DNA molecule structure, see H. F. Judson, *The Eighth Day of Creation* (New York: Simon & Schuster, 1979).

28. Ross A. Webber, "Case Studies of Three Companies: Barriers to Innovation in the Large Organization," in Leonard R. Sayles, *Individualism and Big Business* (New York: McGraw-Hill, 1963).

29. W. J. J. Gordon, *Synectics: The Development of Creative Capacity* (New York: Harper & Row, 1961). "Brainstorming" was developed in A. F. Osborn, *Applied Imagination* (New York: Charles Scribner's Sons, 1960).

30. G. Gordon and E. V. Morse, "Creative Potential and Organizational Structure," *Proceedings of the Academy of Management* (1968); J. Hage and M. Aiken, *Social Change in Complex Organizations* (New York: Random House, 1970).

31. Howard Gruber, *Darwin on Man: A Psychological Study of Scientific Creativity* (Chicago: University of Chicago Press, 1981).

32. R. M. Cyert and J. G. March, *A Behavioral Theory of the Firm* (Englewood Cliffs, N.J.: Prentice-Hall, 1963); M. M. Rosner, "Economic Determinants of Organizational Innovation," *Administrative Science Quarterly* 12, no. 4 (1968), pp. 614–25.

Up to a point, increasing organizational size seems to provide for excess resources and hence more innovation. J. E. Ettlie, "Organizational Policy and Innovation among Suppliers to the Food-Processing Sector," *Academy of Management Journal* 26, no. 1 (1983), pp. 27–44.

33. Herbert Kaufman argues that larger and older organizations may be more flexible and changeable than smaller and younger ones because they can: (1) more easily avoid death, (2) provide opportunities for resource concentration and intermingling of people with different perspectives, and (3) create isolated havens where innovators are freed from hampering rules and regulations. *The Limits of Organizational Change* (University, Ala.: University of Alabama Press, 1972).

34. E. Mansfield, "The Speed of Response of Firms to New Techniques," *Quarterly Journal of Economics,* May 1963, pp. 290–311; and E. Mansfield, *Industrial Research and Technological Innovation: An Econometric Analysis* (New York: W. W. Norton, 1968). See also, J. R. Kimberly and M. J. Evanisko, "Organizational Innovation: The Influence of Individual, Organizational, and Contextual Factors on Hospital Adoption of Technological and Administrative Innovations," *Academy of Management Journal* 24, no. 4 (1981), pp. 689–713.

35. James G. March and Herbert A. Simon, *Organizations* (New York: John Wiley & Sons, 1958).

36. See K. Holt, "Need Assessment in Product Innovation," *International Studies of Management and Organization,* Winter 1976–77, pp. 26–43.

37. E. B. Peters, "Job Security, Technical Innovation and Productivity," *Personnel Journal,* January 1978, pp. 32–35.

38. J. Hage and R. Dewar, "Elite Values versus Organizational Structure in Predicting Innovation," *Administrative Science Quarterly* 18, no. 3 (1973), pp. 279–90.

39. John W. Gardner, *Self-Renewal: The Individual and the Innovative Society* (New York: Harper & Row, 1964); R. Radosevich, "Designing Innovative Systems," *Long-Range Planning,* April 1977, pp. 79–84.

A person who is intolerant of ambiguity is upset by and avoids ambiguous or unfamiliar stimuli. S. Budner, "Intolerance of Ambiguity as a Personality Variable," *Journal of Personality* 30 (1962), pp. 29–50. In a specific test of change attitudes and personal attributes, one study found the following:

Conservatism is related to older age, lack of confidence, contentment, emotional introverts, and stable extraverts.

No relation to status or education.

Radicalism is related to younger age, self-confidence, frustration, stable introverts, and emotional extraverts.

But self-interest can radicalize conservatives and make innovators cautious. M. J. Kirton and G. Mulligan, "Correlates of Managers' Attitudes toward Change," *Journal of Applied Psychology* 58, no. 1 (1973), pp. 101–7.

40. On the iron law of decadence, and for a suggestion on periodic revolution and chaos, see T. J. Lowi, *The Politics of Disorder* (New York: Basic Books, 1971). See also P. H. Thompson and G. A. Dalton, "Are R&D Organizations Obsolete?" *Harvard Business Review,* November–December 1976, pp. 105–16.

41.   S. L. Fink, J. Beak, and K. Taddeo, "Organizational Crisis and Change," *Journal of Applied Behavioral Science* 7 (1971), pp. 15–37.

42.   On events in the Soviet Union at the outbreak of war, see Harrison E. Salisbury, *The 900 Days* (New York: Harper & Row, 1969). On Nazi Germany, see William L. Shirer, *The Rise and Fall of the Third Reich* (New York: Simon & Schuster, 1960).

43.   The vice president of revolution is suggested by T. Levitt, "Creativity Is Not Enough," *Harvard Business Review,* May–June 1973, pp. 72–83.

44.   B. Walter, "Internal Control Relations in Administrative Hierarchies," *Administrative Science Quarterly,* September 1966, pp. 179–205.

45.   The tourist was Alexis de Tocqueville, and the story is retold in W. G. Bennis and P. E. Slater, *The Temporary Society* (New York: Harper & Row, 1968), p. 53.

46.   Mutual respect appears to be more common in organizations in which line managers have specialist backgrounds. W. J. Bigoness and W. D. Perreault, Jr., "A Conceptual Paradigm and Approach for the Study of Innovators," *Academy of Management Journal* 24, no. 1 (1981), pp. 68–82.

47.   The commitment of a few individuals is a major point in H. O. Ronkin and P. R. Lawrence, *Administering Changes: A Case Study of Human Relations in a Factory* (Boston: Graduate School of Business Administration, Harvard University, 1952). See also A. Abbey and J. W. Dickson, "R&D Climate and Innovation in Semiconductors," *Academy of Management Journal* 26, no. 2 (1983), pp. 362–68.

24

Initiating Change

Technological change always results in changed attitudes as well as changed behavior. Therefore, another approach to change is to deal with attitudes first in a sequential process of unfreezing, conversion, and refreezing—the stages summarized in Figure 24–1.[1]*

FIGURE 24–1

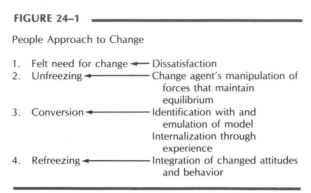

People Approach to Change

1. Felt need for change ◄— Dissatisfaction
2. Unfreezing ◄——————— Change agent's manipulation of
                              forces that maintain
                              equilibrium
3. Conversion ◄——————— Identification with and
                              emulation of model
                              Internalization through
                              experience
4. Refreezing ◄——————— Integration of changed attitudes
                              and behavior

The Phases of Change

The most profound and seductive cause of resistance to organizational change and technological innovation is past success. Such success leads us to be satisfied with what exists. Therefore attitudinal and behavioral change begins with the premise that dissatisfaction must precede change.[2] Such dissatisfaction will produce a desire to change that will allow the sequential phases to unfold.

Creating Dissatisfaction

To achieve the desired condition of dissatisfaction, the change agent could do nothing—just wait until people become dissatisfied with their behavior. Possessing confidential information about impending external events that will adversely affect the organization, one may still decide not to warn the members. One might withhold the information because of fear that it would be too much of a shock or that they would not believe it or might question the motive for presenting the information. President Franklin D. Roosevelt was accused of not warning the American people about a possible Japanese attack, but he may have thought we wouldn't have believed him anyway, that we were so committed to isolationism that only an actual attack would generate dissatisfaction with the present policy.

Thus the classic change scenario begins with a catalytic (and often cataclysmic) external event that produces crisis.[3] In this path (summarized in Figure 24–2) the environment forces an adjustment of strategic thinking that leads to redefinition of task and structural changes.

A change agent does not have to be so passive, however, but can endeavor to generate fear or dissatisfaction with the present (see Figure 24–3). A change agent fortunate enough to possess formal authority or informal prestige may simply tell

---

* Notes and references will be found at the end of this chapter.

FIGURE 24–2

The Classic "Change" Scenario

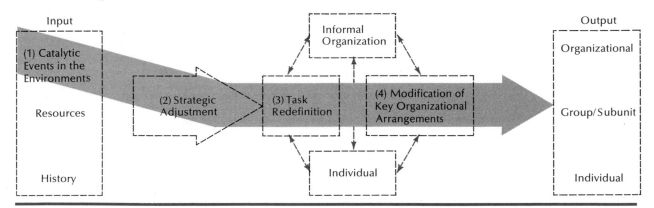

From: David A. Nadler, "Managing Transitions to Uncertain Future States," *Organizational Dynamics,* Summer 1982, p. 40.

organization members that their behavior and performance are unsatisfactory. The agent may suggest there are threats that will render the past irrelevant, and all will suffer unless they give up their comfortable habits. Winston Churchill tried to warn Great Britain and the world about the growing menace of Nazi Germany during the years he was out of office in the 1930s, but few listened because they did not want to give up the appeasement behavior they mistakenly thought would guarantee "peace in our times."

FIGURE 24–3

Change Agent's Methods of Creating Dissatisfaction and Felt Need for Change

1. Do nothing:
   Wait until people become aware of need for change.
2. Generate fear:
   Tell them of coming events that will harm them unless they change.
3. Create hope:
   Tell them of how much better things could be if they change.

Catfish

Reprinted by permission: Tribune Company Syndicate, Inc.

As another method of initiating stress, the creative change agent could create hope by articulating the possibilities of a better tomorrow if behavior were changed. Even if people are satisfied with existing behavior, performance, and rewards, the change agent might be able to create a hope of something even more rewarding. The agent would be generating a sense of opportunity cost, of relative dissatisfaction because it is possible to have more or better conditions. This is what Martin Luther King, Jr., attempted to do with his dream for black *and* white America: to make them dissatisfied with the present in comparison with the glorious society he envisioned.

These examples of Roosevelt, Churchill, and King are all testimony to the difficulty of creating the precondition for change when free people are not dissatisfied. It is much easier where organizational members are not free to leave or have voluntarily committed themselves to staying, as in the case of the military recruit.

Unfreezing

The essential elements of unfreezing are removal of support for old attitudes, saturation of the environment with new values to be acquired, minimization of threats against change, and maximization of reinforcement for change in the desired direction.

Consider the young recruit undergoing basic military training. Fundamentally, the recruit has no choice; he or she cannot leave. The military change agents exert pressure to generate stress and unfreeze the recruits.[4] They are separated physically from their families, friends, and the whole civilian world. Even their civilian clothes may be removed, and they are forbidden to leave the base. The instructors drill into the recruits the idea that their old self-centered, civilian habits are bad; individually they are weak; and only through adopting military bearing and behavior can they amount to anything and be rewarded by the system.

Unfreezing is a slightly misleading term because most people are not totally frozen in the behavior that the change agent is attempting to modify. Rather, people are changing a little most of the time.[5] Thus we have *just* achieved our current situation and can be very defensive toward proposals that reverse the trend of change or move in another direction. This seems a repudiation of our past difficult change. Momentum in life, as well as sports, is difficult to reverse.

Conversion

Needless to say, many recruits become unhappy and would prefer to leave. When this isn't possible, they become receptive to the military's pressure to change. This change or conversion is helped along by the change agent's presentation of a model to identify with and to emulate, usually a soldier whose appearance and behavior are the epitome of what the recruits are to become.[6] Your second-grade teacher, angry with undesired "childish" behavior, might have pointed to polite little Homer and asked why everyone couldn't be like him, sitting quietly at his desk with pencils neatly in place and hands folded. It was implied that you would be happier if you were like Homer—and the teacher would see that you'd be miserable if you weren't.

To the harried military recruit, an impressive example can evoke positive sentiments.[7] Consider an early training experience with the U.S. Marines. The platoon leader was a gray-haired veteran sergeant-major who had been twice selected as enlisted man of the year. He was immaculate in appearance, wise in judgment, and gracious in demeanor. He never uttered an oath, and his toughness was cushioned by compassion. To a group of college teenagers, he was an admirable model who obviously knew how to behave and was rewarded by the system. Everyone tried to be like him. A similar situation confronts the young woman who enters a convent. Symbolically and actually, her ties with family are severed; the order of nuns informs her that her former behavior is no longer acceptable. One of the older sisters is usually presented as an example of humility, unselfishness, and helpfulness.

Change is facilitated and strengthened if emulation is supplemented by internalization (see Figure 24–4). A learning experience is designed so that through trial and error a person learns the attitudes and behavior that are needed. For example, if the sergeant wants to teach the recruits to keep their heads down while advancing, he can set up machine guns that fire live ammunition at a height of 36 inches above the path. After showing the recruits how to do it, he has them transverse the path, and they quickly learn why they must keep their heads down.

More complex, the military training group can design a mock battle problem in which soldiers who persist in independence or self-seeking behavior are captured or slain symbolically (by having a bag of flour broken over their heads). If the exercise is properly executed, the trainee will internalize the lesson through improvisation: to survive, one must be part of a team whose members look out for one another.[8]

To persist for very long, any new behavior must be personally satisfying—not at an intellectual level, but on a gut basis. A therapist who helps people to change their exercise habits observes, "If people say they're doing it for their health, I know they won't stick with it more than a week. The only thing that will make a person succeed is pure narcissism. If you can get someone to admit that, he or she is hooked for life. People will do anything to get in shape if they feel it's going to make them look good and be sexy."[9]

FIGURE 24–4

Changing by Conversion

Emulation
- Change agent presents model of attitudes and behavior

Precondition — Dissatisfaction

Internalization
- Change agent structures a training experience that encourages learning of desired attitudes and behavior

Refreezing

Once the conversion process has occurred or the training is concluded, the change agent faces another difficult step in the change process—that of refreezing the new attitudes and behavior (see Figure 24–5). The organization member must be supported and rewarded for continuing his or her new behavior. After leaving the intensive and isolated recruit training, the military recruit moves to an assignment where he or she is less separated from civilian life. The soldier can go off the base in street clothes and may even live elsewhere. Civilian friends and family may not appreciate new military attitudes and behavior; indeed, they may even ridicule the soldier's hairstyle and polished shoes. This presents the service with the problem of continuing

FIGURE 24–5

Refreezing of Newly Learned Attitudes and Behavior

1. Continued rewards from the change agent or organization.
2. Continued support from fellow organization members.
3. Support, tolerable criticism, or continued insulation from former social set.

to support the values inculcated at recruit camp. If it does not, and especially if even military colleagues criticize the military way, attitudes and behavior that have been painfully learned will fade.

It is the same with the young nun who, after her postulate, at least partially reenters the world. She can see her family again, and more important, she begins to work, to teach, to nurse, and to counsel. Interaction with the world can lead away from the old ways or toward something entirely different from home or order.

Change through Training Programs

The most common managerial applications of this change model are through various kinds of training programs.[10] We shall examine organization programs, university executive education, sensitivity training, and organizational development.

University Management Development Programs

An expensive but modest approach to change is to send a manager to a resident executive program on a university campus for periods of two weeks to nine months. If the manager has explicitly requested to be sent to such a program because he or she feels inadequate in some aspect of management, such as accounting or human relations, the change precondition might be favorable. More frequently, however, being selected is a mark of status and a promise of future promotion.

Unfreezing does tend to be quite effective because those attending are isolated from job and family. If an effective faculty can create a sense of possible improvement, the possibility for changed knowledge is good. Simply sitting in lectures or discussion groups is unlikely to change the attitudes and behavior of basically satisfied managers, however. Whether the new knowledge will be applied in the sponsoring firm depends on whether or not it meets a felt need for the organization so that others will support it. If the organization feels no need for new planning techniques, they are unlikely to be used because only the one person who has attended the program understands and believes in them. The burden of change thus rests on the ability of the returning manager to persuade others of how the proposed change could improve performance.[11]

Organization Programs

More managers are trained through programs composed of participants from the same organization. Some are conducted full time in an isolated location for several days or weeks, but most take place perhaps one day a week for several months. Management may explicitly define its change desires and thus create some precondition for change, but in general the acceptance of change depends on the individual's degree of satisfaction, as in the university programs.

The actual learning process is probably inferior to the university program because unfreezing is difficult.[12] The participants usually do not feel separated from their jobs; their thoughts and concerns remain with them, and frequently phone calls interrupt class meetings. In addition, since the learning group is composed of members from a single company, the trainees are less likely to learn from each other than they would at more heterogeneous university programs.

If an idea learned during a company program is considered attractive and useful, however, the probability of actually introducing it is better because the company social system should be more supportive of the change.[13]

Good Reason in support of Organization Programs

Sensitivity Training

Traditional lectures and discussion programs do not seem to have a profound impact on attitudes and behavior. In particular, they have little effect on how managers treat subordinates and one another. The authoritarian boss is not likely to change style because a university or company psychologist tells him or her about the supposed advantages of participative management. The manager may not even be aware of being perceived as tough and insensitive.

Laboratory training, sensitivity training, and T-groups grew out of efforts to develop a training process that would exert a more profound impact on participants.[14] The content of sensitivity training is not planning, structuring, or even change. The content is what goes on in the room while the training takes place: interpersonal dynamics, not organizational principles. The group is unstructured in the sense that there is no appointed leader and no assigned topics. Under the guidance of a skilled trainer and planned activities, the group members explore their relationships with one another. The aim is to develop a participant's self-insight and self-awareness, to increase sensitivity to one's effect on others and theirs on the participant, and to bring to the surface factors that lie below the level of acute consciousness. However, it is not an exercise in individual or group psychoanalysis. Childhood traumas and adult fixations are not explored, except as members raise them to explain their behavior.

The hope is that new knowledge and understanding will assist participants to modify their behavior, become more interpersonally effective, and stop attributing their own faults to others.[15] The mechanism for change is openness and candid feedback. By communicating authentically how they perceive and respond to each other, participants should grow in understanding. Thus Bob may have a habit of interrupting people whose opinion he does not respect, but he may not be aware of it. Sean and Martin may point this out, perhaps even with oaths about Bob's cruelty. Or Annette may only talk when she agrees with someone. Judy may comment about this to Annette: "Are you just a puppet? Don't you ever have anything of *your own* to say? Don't you ever disagree with anyone? I think you're a phony." Annette may be offended, but it is hoped that she will accept the communication and deal with it.

To promote openness, the group trainer tries to create a climate of trust and helpfulness. The trainer does not dominate but provides an emulation model of personal congruency and social concern. The trainer should also keep the group's communications on the here and now and guide them toward the joys of open, authentic, and effective interpersonal relations.

Most early sensitivity training was with "stranger" groups—the participants were from different organizations and did not know each other beforehand. The general norm was that status elsewhere was irrelevant to the group. The sessions (which ranged from a few days to several weeks) were frequently held in isolated settings away from job and families. With busy managers, separation, relaxation of pressure, and ambiguous status can generate substantial stress and thus promote unfreezing. The lack of an authority structure or task agenda and the availability of wide-open time can be threatening but conducive to learning a different set of attitudes and behavior.

The majority of T-group attendees report very favorably on the experience and also report that their attitudes and behavior back on the job have been changed in the direction of greater sensitivity to others, more egalitarian attitudes, and improved communication and leadership skills, including more consideration for others. In spite of these favorable views by participants, others are not so sure there is much lasting impact. Only a minority of attendees are perceived *by others* as actually demonstrating changed attitudes or behavior, and little firm evidence exists that the programs have any lasting beneficial effect on organizational performance.[16]

Although stranger-group sensitivity training is fairly effective at unfreezing and conversion through emulation and integration, application of the lessons back on the job is weak. A lone individual returns from two weeks on a mountain in New England with greater sensitivity to self and others. But a person who attempts to act upon these new insights may be in trouble because peers, superiors, and subordinates have not attended the program. They are still behaving in the old patterns, oblivious to T-group values. Their behavior and expectations about the returned participant's behavior are likely to push the individual back to habitual pretraining behavior patterns. The person who tries to behave openly and authentically may hurt oneself. Others may perceive the behavior as weakness and take advantage.

Indeed, a sensitivity or laboratory experience can "develop" the individual but not help the organization.[17] Some people fear that a narrow, obsessive automobile

Reprinted by permission of the Chicago Tribune—New York News Syndicate, Inc.

sales manager who eats, sleeps, and dreams of selling cars might conclude that this pursuit is meaningless after having been broadened by sensitivity training. The company could lose an effective sales manager—and the manager might lose a job.[18] A small number of participants are even psychologically harmed by sensitivity training, to the extent that they are less interpersonally competent. The probability of such casualties is small with a competent T-group trainer, but it increases with one who uses the group as a vehicle for his or her own ego trip in exercising power.[19]

Organizational Development

To overcome some of the defects in stranger-group sensitivity training, change practitioners began transferring the process inside organizations, utilizing teams of managers who work together on a daily basis. Initially these were traditional T-groups, but composed of superiors, subordinates, and peers. The sensitivity training is still part of organizational development, but the approach has expanded to include working on current managerial problems as well as changing beliefs, attitudes, values, and structure so that the organization can adapt to new technologies, markets, and challenges.[20]

Organizational development (OD) is an effort that is planned and organizationwide and is managed from the top to increase organizational effectiveness and health through planned interventions in the organization's processes, using behavioral science knowledge.[21] The objective is to create a management team that is proactive with respect to the environment. Rather than defending what exists, or merely defensively responding to external events, change-oriented firms prospect for new opportunities.[22]

Organizational development programs frequently commence with intensive lectures and T-group sessions. Then periodic meetings are held to follow up on the sensitivity training, and there will be a gradual shift to discussions of concrete problems and possible solutions. Organizational development is not just a one-shot program, for it implies a long-term effort to exercise and strengthen team problem-solving ability at all levels. Inflated short-run expectations and executive impatience can sabotage the effort. Figure 24–6 summarizes a typical flow of events in OD.

The assumptions on which the change strategy of organizational development rests include the following:[23]

1. Neither evolutionary change via ad hoc improvements nor revolutionary overturn of past and present is as desired as systematic development that incorporates the best of the past while striving for the ideal.
2. The basic building blocks of an organization are groups (teams).
3. An always relevant change goal is the reduction of inappropriate competition between parts of the organization and the development of more collaboration.
4. Decision making in a healthy organization is located where the information sources are, rather than in a particular role or level of hierarchy.
5. Organizations, subunits of organizations, and individuals continuously manage their affairs to achieve goals.

FIGURE 24–6

Example of Organizational Development Process

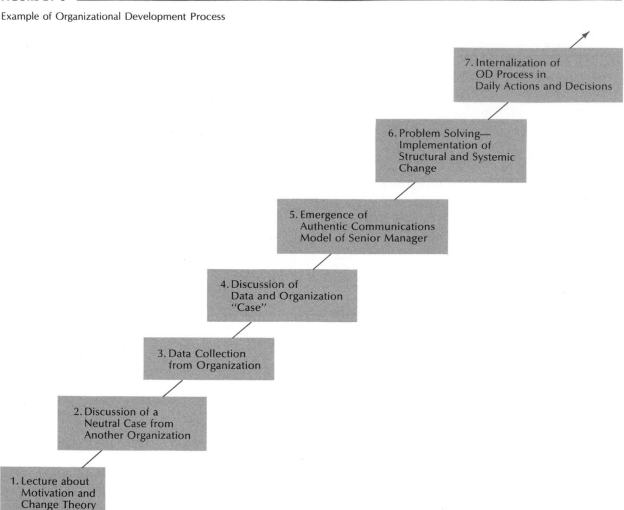

6. One goal of a healthy organization is to develop generally open communication, mutual trust, and confidence between and across levels.
7. People support what they help create. People affected by a change must be allowed active participation and a sense of ownership in the planning and conduct of the change.

The potential advantage of such an approach is in the refreezing stage. If the group actually experiences success in developing new interpersonal attitudes and behavior, it should be much easier to continue them on the job, since the same people will be involved. Actually making progress on some long-standing problem is the most potent internalization mechanism.[24] For example, if the heads of mechanical engineering and electrical engineering learn that their joint projects are improved by more open dealing with their conflict, this behavior is more likely to be accepted and supported later than if just one or even both had attended a stranger T-group.

The difficulties of the team-OD approach are at the other end of the change process—unfreezing. The habits of work may dominate the training. If the superior has been dominant, the group is likely to engage in little authentic communication; everyone will address remarks to the boss in hopes of making a favorable impression. Successful unfreezing and change are dependent on the model presented by the senior participant.[25] If this person avoids domination, accepts open communication without retaliation, and is strong enough to accept status ambiguity, the OD process has a chance.

The Consultant's Role

One of the trainer-consultant's responsibilities is to assess the top manager's feelings and help him or her understand what is happening.[26] It sometimes happens that the boss attends a stranger T-group session, is impressed, and wants to apply it in the organization. The boss understands the program intellectually but may not be emotionally aware of how open relations with subordinates differ from those with strangers. If the manager enters the program with good intentions but subtly communicates to subordinates that they run a risk of being too frank, the program may collapse quickly.

If sufficient unfreezing occurs, the change process rests on emulation of the boss (and the consultant), with internalization through the experience of solving real organizational problems. Each participant should gain a feeling of personal growth through the OD sessions. The consultant helps schedule the problems to be attacked, provides substantive knowledge from theory and others' experience, and encourages frank communication.

Managers tend to underestimate their ability to confront each other on these matters. They avoid discussing their own attitudes or emotions because they consider them as either irrelevant to or disruptive of smooth organizational operations. Therefore feelings are swept aside, to focus on the task at hand. This pattern is detrimental to management and organizational development, since a change in style requires recognition of the feelings evoked in others. It is the OD consultant's task to control the confrontation and teach the participants that authentic discourse is possible and rewarding.[27]

Values Implicit in Organizational Development

Like the trainers in laboratory consultants in organizational development have personal values they believe must come to characterize modern organizations. To the classic management problem of optimally mobilizing human resources and energy to achieve the organization's mission, OD adds the maintenance of a viable, growing organization of people whose personal needs for self-worth, growth, and satisfaction are met at work.[28] These consultants assume that the old bureaucratic organization is increasingly ineffective because task and environment are changing. Problems cannot be routinized but are novel and individual; human beings demand to be treated as individuals rather than impersonal categories. Two OD practitioners candidly list their personal values (and the supposed trend of the future) as follows:[29]

Away from a view of humans as essentially bad and toward a view of them as basically good.

Away from avoidance or negative evaluation of individuals and toward confirming them as human beings.

Away from a view of individuals as fixed and toward seeing them as being in the process of continually changing.

Away from resisting or fearing individual differences and toward accepting and utilizing them.

Away from utilizing individuals primarily with reference to their job descriptions and toward viewing them as whole persons.

Away from repressing feelings and toward making effective use of them.

Away from masking and game playing and toward authentic behavior.

Away from use of status for maintaining power and personal prestige and toward use of status for organizationally relevant purposes.

Away from distrusting people and toward trusting them.

Away from avoiding facing others with relevant data and toward appropriate confrontation.

Away from avoidance of risk taking and toward willingness to risk.

Away from a view of process work as unproductive effort and toward seeing it as essential to effective task accomplishment.

Away from a primary emphasis on competition and toward a much greater emphasis on collaboration.

These are feelings of faith rather than proven fact, and they are not shared by all OD consultants. So like T-groups, OD programs can develop feelings of trust and openness that could be inappropriate if the general organization still values the traditional bureaucratic virtues of conformity and obedience.[30]

Systemic Change

Successful change usually changes multiple factors simultaneously.[31] Structural changes affect attitudes and feelings, and these sentiments affect the response to technological innovation. Organizational development programs working with management teams endeavor to foster more flexible attitudes and authentic communications, but structural answers to real organizational problems are what keep the program going.[32] And structural reorganizations are much more likely to actually be translated into changed behavior and improved performance if they include a wide range of people in the deliberation that prepares attitudes.

Primacy Life Insurance Company (name disguised) offers a large-scale example of systemic change.[33] The company was one of the oldest and largest in the world, but its growth had slowed, and a younger competitor had passed it in new sales.

Management believed that field sales personnel had not been aggressive enough in obtaining the right volume and mix of insurance policies. It concluded that closer and more personal managerial direction of agents was needed and contracted a prominent management consulting firm to assist in analysis and implementation.

The consultants quickly observed that agents had not been aggressive and that stronger direction was required if the firm was to end its relative decline. This of course pleased company management because its own analysis was corroborated, and it readily made the first payment on a large consulting fee. This fee was earned by the consulting firm because, in addition to exhorting agents and managers to try harder, it designed and implemented a comprehensive change program that touched everyone and everything in the insurance company: structure, job descriptions, communications, rewards, office layout, and furniture.

Before the Change

Figure 24–7 illustrates the relevant portions of the former organization chart. Under the senior vice president were six territorial supervisors covering the entire United States. Reporting directly to them were approximately 800 branch managers. It was basically a centralized system of procedural controls that had remained unchanged for many years while spans of control had increased.

At the territorial level there was little possibility of close supervision or communication between the territorial supervisor and individual branch managers, since a typical branch manager engaged in substantial conversation with his or her immediate superior only once every 18 months. Even at the level of branch manager, close supervision was difficult. The assistant managers were not really managers but super salespeople, as most of their income was derived from commissions on their own sales. In effect, branch managers in a typical office had spans of control of about 35 people.

Regular agents constituted the bulk of the sales force. Some were old-timers who had started when most policies were sold to people of modest income who were not in a position to save for large annual premiums, so agents personally collected the cash and checks monthly or even weekly. Some of this type of collections remained, but most of the post–World War II market growth for life insurance had taken place in the suburbs, where most people preferred to pay premiums by mail on receipt of a notice. Unfortunately, the company had been slow and incomplete in its response to these changed market conditions.

Most of the regular agents were 20- to 35-year-old high school graduates with a little college training. Turnover was extremely high among these young agents— up to 70 percent left within two years of being hired. The typical pattern was that a regular agent would rather easily sell term and whole-life policies to relatives and friends during the first year; the crunch would come when the agent tried to shift to "cold calls" and sales to strangers. Most could not make the transition even though they were assigned territories near their homes and sales were restricted to geographical boundaries. About one third were members of the Insurance Workers International Union (AFL–CIO), which was engaged in active organizing.

Special agents were a fairly recent innovation designed to upgrade the status and attractiveness of life insurance sales at Primacy. They were college graduates

FIGURE 24–7

Primacy Life Insurance Company: Partial Organization Chart before Change

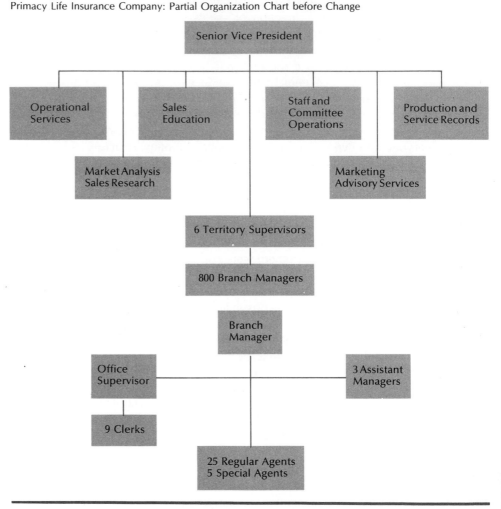

who were given additional training in sales of more sophisticated endowment and annuity policies and were qualified to give financial planning advice. Their potential buyers were the educated, affluent managers and professionals who had been the primary sales targets of the company's smaller, more aggressive, and faster growing competitors.

The office layout was as indicated in Figure 24–8. Arrangements had been fairly consistent all across the country. Only the branch manager had enjoyed a private office, while all agents and assistant managers possessed similar desks and telephones in a large common room. No status distinctions were evident. Agents would come into the office on Friday morning for an all-personnel meeting, but the rest of the time they controlled their own movements—in the office, making calls, or at home.

FIGURE 24–8

Primacy Life Insurance Company: Prechange Branch Office Arrangement

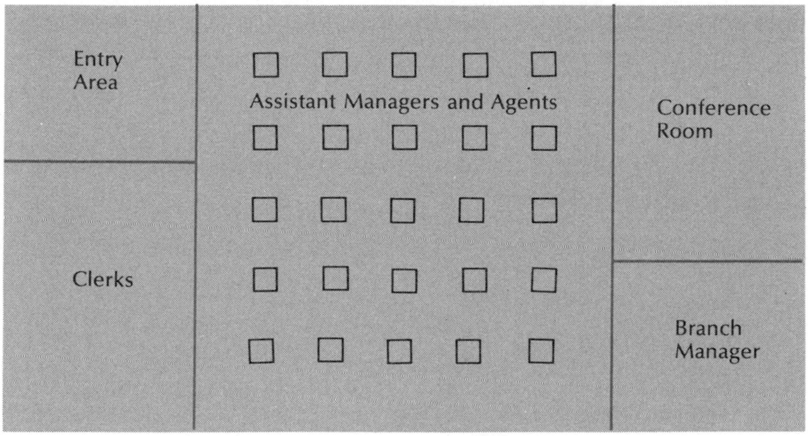

The Change

Figure 24–9 shows the new structure that was implemented to promote closer direction of the sales effort. In effect, two more supervisory levels were added. A managerial position, regional manager, was created between the territorial vice presidents and branch managers to facilitate communications between branch managers and higher management. In addition, the assistant manager's duties were redefined to include supervision, and they were interposed between branch managers and agents. All communications to and from the agents were funneled through the assistant managers in order to make them part of the work flow. At all levels, spans of control were reduced to allow supervisors to spend more time with subordinates in planning, advising, controlling, and motivating, in the spirit of a management by objectives program.

The reward system was modified so that a manager's income was a combination of salary and bonus based on their direct subordinates' sales, not their own. This motivates managers to train and supervise the salespeople under them. They should come to expect more of their sales personnel, and nothing exerts a stronger influence on a young salesperson's performance than his or her first supervisor's high expectations.[34]

In addition to this structural change, extensive physical alterations were instituted in the branch offices. Partitions were erected in the offices to provide each of the former assistant managers with a private office (see Figure 24–10). This reinforced their status as managers by giving them a place to advise, train, or criticize their subordinates. In addition, the special agents' desks were moved into the former conference room. These changes left insufficient room for the regular agents' desks, which were eliminated; file cabinets were pushed against a wall, and a single long table was provided for their paperwork. The changes were tested in one state and

FIGURE 24–9

Primacy Life Insurance Company: Partial Organization Chart after Change

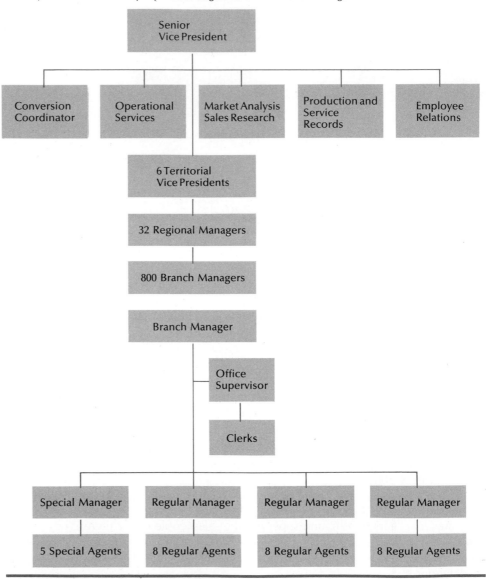

then applied throughout the nation in a logistics maneuver rivaling a military campaign.

The modified office made it impossible to hold general all-personnel meetings. Space was so limited that it was not even possible for all the regular agents to be in the office simultaneously, and they were arbitrarily divided into four sections and assigned days and hours when they could work there. One tale that made the rounds was that this change was instituted because one of the consultants had

FIGURE 24–10

Primacy Life Insurance Company: Postchange Branch Office Arrangement

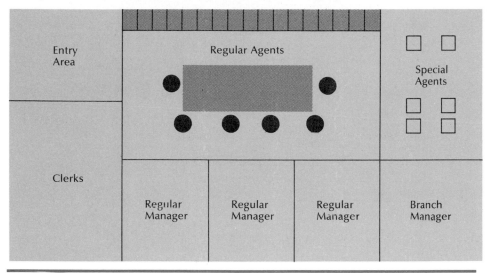

come into an office at 10:00 A.M. on a Wednesday to find regular agents playing cards. (The agents argued that you just can't sell insurance at this time; people aren't available, and the poker players might well be out working at 9:00 that evening.) The sectioning and scheduling broke up many long-standing social groups and made the agents feel unwanted in the office.

The dramatic changes in structure, communications, rewards, physical facilities, and social conditions elicited a strong reaction from the agents. One complained that after 25 years his position had been reduced to one file drawer. Another said that the annual family Christmas party had been canceled in his office because no one wanted to bring children into the office and not have a desk to show them where Daddy worked—a desk being a potent symbol of status and individuality.

The greater differentiation between regular and special agents was also resented. The union newspaper ran pictures contrasting the regular agents in one office crowded around their single work table, piled high with papers, while the nonunion special agents enjoyed separate and relatively spacious quarters.

The Result

An important phase in any change process is follow-up, which consists of the measurement of behavioral and performance change to see if the desired change has occurred. At Primacy Life, the answer was both no and yes—no in the beginning and yes eventually (see Figure 24–11). A change agent endeavors to change behavior in a desired direction so that performance will improve: Agents will be better trained and more aggressive; managers will supervise more closely; and sales of new policies will increase more rapidly. At Primacy after the change, however, behavior changed

FIGURE 24–11 ━━━━━━━━━━━━━━━━━━━━━━━━

Primacy Life Insurance Company: The Path of Change

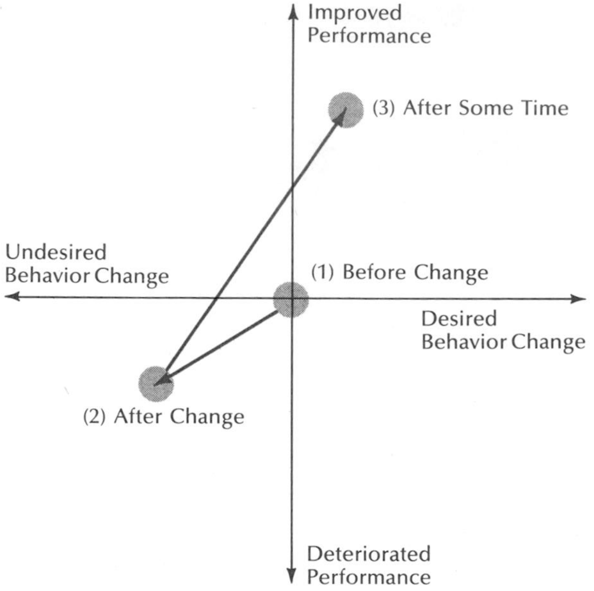

in an undesired direction and performance deteriorated for about a year. Behavior deteriorated because the system change unintentionally affected attitudes. Some of the older agents went to the movies or just went home; they literally retired early without informing the company. Rather than selling new policies, they merely serviced old policyholders and collected commissions from their renewals. To be sure, their incomes dropped because renewal commissions are much less than those on new premiums, but the older ones could get by. The younger sales personnel complained, and many left just as before.

In spite of all this bitterness, with time behavior and performance began to move in the desired direction. The older regular agents began to formally retire, and newly hired agents who had not experienced the change did not feel deprived. Their indoctrination and training were improved, along with subsequent closer supervision. The high turnover of regular agents actually helped the company to renew the sales force. The various managers became more proficient and motivated as they discovered they could have an impact on subordinate performance and on their own incomes.

In total, this large change process must be considered successful because behavior and performance eventually improved. Consider the variety of things that were modified: organizational structure, authority, status, communications, rewards, titles, job responsibilities, offices, and desks. The performance improvement might have been accomplished with greater human sensitivity to attitudes and less disruption of social systems, but no change is achieved without some stress. "Creative destruction" from time to time of what exists is part of management's job.

Subordinate Participation in Change

A manager initiating change could use three general styles allocated along a continuum from unilateral action based on power to shared authority to delegating the decision to subordinates:

Unilateral imposition by authority	Shared authority in problem solving	Decision delegated to subordinates

Most successful change implementation falls in the middle range.[35] The sequence of events can be summarized as follows:

1. Stress arises or is created so that many people, but especially the senior manager, are under pressure and dissatisfied with present behavior and performance.
2. A respected and influential new person acts as change agent. He or she may be a senior manager, a company staff specialist, or an external consultant who deals directly with the senior manager.[36] An outsider has a freedom of pressure from the organization's part. No staff specialist or consultant, however, can replace the manager. They can assist, but management must make the commitment.
3. Under the guidance of the change agent/manager, a frank examination of past and present, policy and practice is conducted to define inadequacies in relation to the future.
4. Top management of the relevant unit becomes intimately involved in the change process, including support for the examination of the past and present.
5. The change agent involves multiple organizational levels in fact finding and analysis of present problems before change proposals are formulated.
6. The change agent provides new ideas that depart from the organization's practices.
7. Problem solutions and changes are tested on a small scale and checked with personnel at various levels to determine unrealistic aspects or planning gaps.
8. The success of small changes creates a climate for subsequent change so that an expanding number of people perceive their personal interests as being served by organizational change.

This pattern underscores the concept that change is not a plan that should be created unilaterally by top management for subordinates to implement by modifying their behavior. Rather, development and implementation should include a heavy flow of communications up and down. An effective manager allows the people involved to play a major role in determining the details of change and implementation methods but retains the authority to initiate change, whether agreed to or not. This approach requires a respected, knowledgeable, and articulate change agent-manager with a high probability of persuading the people involved that objective conditions demand change. Through agreement or faith, they come to believe that present

Pattern for Successful Change
- stress
- respected change agent
- examination of past
- top management involvement and support
- multiple levels involved
- new ideas introduced
- solutions tested on small scale
- test success creates climate for change

ways will no longer suffice. It is important that the agent develop general agreement on the organization's objectives, basic problems, and why current behavior will not work. Once this basic consensus is gained, either the solution is self-evident or the agent can safely delegate, confident that most people will be striving toward the desired end.

A change agent-manager who takes the high road of rational persuasion and unifying interests may simultaneously be communicating a message of fear. While arguing that objective conditions make change inevitable, the threat may be implied that if subordinates do not agree and participate, the change will unilaterally be imposed anyway. Therefore, they might get a better deal if they join in the process and share some of the responsibility.

Participation by subordinates in the formulation of change may improve its implementation, but it is no panacea, and it certainly does not guarantee that resistance will magically disappear.[37] Participation through discussion has its greatest positive impact on creating the precondition for change—the desire for it. Listening to a scholar or supervisor lecture on the need for change generally is less effective than open discussion of future trends and why present behavior is ineffective. If the group discussion leads to a consensus that change is desirable, the change plan is more likely to be followed.[38] Japanese organizations are reported to be slow in initiating change because extensive lateral talks are regularly held, not about any particular plan but on whether the status quo is still viable. Once these groups achieve consensus on the need for change, however, change implementation is rapid.[39] In contrast, many American organizations begin developing a change plan (and even implement it) before there is widespread agreement on the desirability of change. In such a case opposition can severely hinder the process.

Dangers of Participation

A manager can be faced with a dilemma when, on the basis of confidential information or greater perceptiveness of environmental trends, he or she concludes that present organizational behavior will become ineffective but is not sure of being able to convince subordinates of this view. If subordinates are satisfied with the present, and if until now the manager has expressed satisfaction with their performance, they may be reluctant to change on the basis of the boss's perceived need, not their own. Inviting subordinate participation in a general discussion of the desirability of change runs the risk that they may conclude change is not needed. The manager is then faced with either unilaterally imposing change anyway or abdicating to their decision. Neither of these alternatives is very attractive. Imposing change after subordinates have discussed and rejected the matter may cause the manager's solicitation of their opinions to be interpreted as a show; "participation" was really an attempt to manipulate them into thinking they were participating, when in fact the boss had already decided. Thus the door to future authentic participation may be closed.

Congressional disenchantment with President Richard Nixon rested partly on its interpretation of his elicitation of its participation as a charade. The legislators believed he fled to Maryland, Florida, or California for publicized deliberation and returned with a decision in which he invited them to join—over coffee in the oval office. Their opinion was that the talk had no meaning because the decision had already been made, and any conversation with Congress should take place *before* the president worked it out on his yellow legal pads. Similarly, the widespread skepticism by workers and unions about participation reflects management's improper and sometimes dishonest use of this approach in the past. This skepticism restricts a manager to unilateral implementation, the success of which depends on having the power to punish or reward.[40]

Thus the central danger of all efforts to solicit opinions or hold formal votes is that subordinates may recommend something different from what the superior wants. Before initiating such democratic or participative methods, managers must ask whether they are willing to live with a subordinate decision against change. If not, some other approach is desirable.

Of course, an effective change agent-manager must also be a politician.[41] Informal communications and contacts should facilitate a fairly good understanding of attitudes and interests before the manager actually goes to subordinates with a proposal. A change agent who concluded that a majority already recognized the problem and was receptive to change, might expect a participative approach to be well received and would probably be widely admired for using it. However, the manager should avoid taking a change issue to people who (as concluded from intelligence gathering) are deeply divided. In such a case a participative approach might exacerbate resentment and lead to organizational paralysis.

SUMMARY

The process of changing attitudes and behavior includes four major aspects: (1) dissatisfaction with what exists, (2) unfreezing so that old behavior is no longer supported, (3) conversion or behavior modification by identification with and emulation of a model or by internalization of new attitudes and behavior through improvisation and experience, and (4) refreezing of the modified attitudes and behavior by continued social support in real life.

Training and development programs implement this change process by endeavoring to improve the appropriate technical, human, and conceptual skills. University management development programs are fairly good at unfreezing and transferring new knowledge but not very effective in modifying behavior or supporting the participant back on the job. Company programs experience great difficulty in unfreezing because they are so close to the job. Actual modification of behavior is probably rare, although when it occurs it may be supported back on the job.

Sensitivity training can exert a profound unfreezing and conversion influence on an individual who attends away from the job. The person may well emulate and internalize new values of openness and authenticity as well as greater awareness of interpersonal relations. However, the individuals will probably experience difficulties back at work if they behave differently, because the organization may not understand or support them.

Organization development attempts to tie the power of sensitivity training to the solution of real organizational problems with on-the-job teams. Unfreezing is difficult, and conversion depends heavily on the senior executive's example and the consultant's skill. Internalization and refreezing can be very effective, however.

Effectiveness with OD programs reinforces the general change model but adds some important elaborations:

1. People must want to change because they are dissatisfied with present behavior, because they recognize that it will no longer be appropriate in the near future, or because they agree on how things can be improved over a basically satisfactory present.
2. The senior authority figure involved must present a personal example of willingness to change and to allow subordinates to change. Old relationships must be altered. The change agent is not the organization's chief executive who must have sufficient leeway to act on her or his own.
3. The change process should move from the level of generalized values toward specific operational objectives.
4. Participants should experience better performance and heightened self-esteem from the new patterns of behavior.
5. The new relationships must be supported by the senior authority, team members, and the organization; team members must find the new behavior effective in performance. Verification through experience offers the most potent support for continuation.

Some of the financial and human costs of change could be avoided if managers and engineers grasped the social implications of change—in short, if they thought of the organization as a social and technical system. The introduction of technological change forces readjustments in the social system; individuals find that they have to deal with others who are either new to them or stand in a new relationship to them. These changes in relationships are the major variables in the introduction of change.

Subordinate participation in the change process is generally desirable, but it is not guaranteed to liquidate resistance. A manager's premature and naive invitation to subordinates to decide whether change is necessary can lead to the dilemma of either abdicating responsibility or imposing his or her will. The latter is obviously more desirable, but it may undermine future participatory change. The central point is that managing is a political process—and it is only through organizational politics in the best sense that a change agent can mediate the collision between demands for change and the enormous capacity of institutions to resist such change.

REVIEW QUESTIONS

1. What are the phases in the people-centered approach to change?
2. How can a manager create a felt need for change?
3. What is the unfreezing phase of the change process? How might it be accomplished?
4. What is the "conversion" phase? What are the techniques for achieving it?
5. Why is it necessary for refreezing to occur in the change process?
6. Why do so many people who have been changed revert to their old behavior after the change process?
7. Why are university management development programs strong at unfreezing but weak on refreezing?
8. Why are on-site organization programs weaker on unfreezing but possibly stronger at refreezing?
9. Why is sensitivity training likely to be strong on conversion?
10. What are the objectives of sensitivity training?

11. Why are stranger T-groups likely to be weak on re-freezing?

12. What are the potential dangers in sensitivity training?

13. What is the difference between sensitivity training and organizational development?

14. What are the assumptions of organizational development?

15. Why might organizational development be so effective at refreezing?

16. What is the consultant's role in organizational development?

17. How did the Primacy Life Insurance Company strengthen the management and sales effort in the local branches? What factors were modified?

18. How can change result in undesirable behavioral change and performance deterioration?

19. What are the dangers to a manager in inviting participation?

20. What sequence of events characterizes many successful changes?

21. Why are top management's interest and support so important to change?

Notes and References on Initiating Change

1. For a survey of various approaches to change, see S. R. Michael, Fred Luthans, G. S. Odiorne, W. W. Burke, and S. Hayden, *Techniques of Organizational Change* (New York: McGraw-Hill, 1981). See also, S. R. Michael, "Organizational Change Techniques: Their Present, Their Future," *Organizational Dynamics,* Summer 1982, pp. 67–79.

2. Kurt Lewin, "Group Decision and Social Change," in T. M. Newcomb and E. L. Hartley, eds., *Readings in Social Psychology* (New York: Holt, Rinehart & Winston, 1958). The model is discussed with management development examples in Edgar H. Schein, "Management Development as a Process of Influence," *Industrial Management Review,* May 1961, pp. 59–77, and by Gene W. Dalton, "Influence and Organizational Change," in Dalton and Paul R. Lawrence, with Larry E. Greiner, *Organizational Change and Development* (Homewood, Ill.: Richard D. Irwin, 1970). See also: Larry E. Greiner, "Antecedents of Planned Organizational Change," *Journal of Applied Behavioral Science* 3, no. 1 (1967), pp. 51–86. On the advantage of outside pressure to assist the change agent in pushing change, see N. Tichy, "Agents of Planned Social Change," *Administrative Science Quarterly* 19, no. 2 (1974), pp. 164–82.

3. D. A. Nadler, "Managing Transitions to Uncertain Future States," *Organizational Dynamics,* Summer 1982, pp. 37–45.

4. H. Garfinkel, "Conditions of Successful Degradation Ceremonies," *American Journal of Sociology* 61 (1956), pp. 420–24.

Faith in stressful experience as a change mechanism is illustrated in a variety of programs. One has middle-age executives climb a 10,000-foot mountain on the theory that the experience will toughen them and make them more confident and forceful on the job. "The Way to the Top," *Newsweek,* April 27, 1970, p. 80. Such experiences probably do make a lasting impact. Many people

respect themselves more because they successfully performed hazardous physical activities in the military—like negotiating a 30-foot rope ladder down the side of a rolling transport ship or parachuting from an aircraft. Managers' sedentary lives offer few similar opportunities to prove to themselves that they possess physical courage, but physical courage is simpler than putting one's career on the line by making controversial organizational decisions. It is doubtful that climbing a mountain or riding river rapids on a raft will really be helpful at work.

5. D. Miller and P. H. Friesen, "Momentum and Revolution in Organizational Adaptation, *Academy of Management Journal* 23. no. 4 (1980), pp. 591–614. On the life cycles in organizations, see J. R. Kimberly, R. H. Miles, and associates, *The Organizational Life Cycle: Issues in the Creation,, Transformation and Decline of Organizations,* (San Francisco: Jossey-Bass, 1980).

6. C. C. Manz and H. P. Sims, Jr., "Vicarious Learning: The Influence of Modeling on Organizational Behavior," *Academy of Management Review* 6, no. 1 (1981), pp. 105–13.

7. An observed behavioral model can be especially effective in helping people to overcome fear. J. H. Geer and A. Turtletaub, "Fear Reduction following Observation of a Model," *Journal of Personality and Social Psychology* 6 (1967), pp. 327–31. Prior observation of a tolerant model has also permitted acceptance of higher levels of discomfort. K. D. Craig and H. Neidermayer, "Autonomic Correlates of Pain Thresholds Influenced by Social Modeling," *Journal of Personality and Social Psychology* 29, no. 2 (1974).

8. Experimental-affective training in conflict (actually living it and resolving it in training) is superior to classroom cognitive training or no training. J. Zacker and M. Bard, "Effects of Conflict Management Training on Police Performance," *Journal of Applied Psychology* 58, no. 2 (1973), pp. 202–8. Also see B. King and I. Janis, "Comparison of the Effectiveness of Improvised versus Nonimprovised Role Playing in Producing Opinion Change," *Human Relations* 9 (1955), pp. 177–86.

9. S. Wallace, "How Does Your Exercise Rate?" *The MBA,* July–August 1977, p. 52.

10. For evaluation of various training and development programs, see W. Oberg, "Top Management Assesses University Executive Programs," *Business Topics,* Spring 1963, pp. 7–27; K. R. Andrews, *The Effectiveness of University Management Development Programs* (Boston: Graduate School of Business Administration, Harvard University, 1966); Robert J. House, *Management Development: Design Evaluation and Implementation* (Ann Arbor: University of Michigan Press, 1967), p. 13; and S. J. Carroll, F. T. Paine and G. M. Ivancevich, "The Relative Effectiveness of Alternative Training Methods for Various Training Objectives," *Personnel Psychology,* Fall 1972, pp. 495–509.

John P. Campbell et al., in *Managerial Behavior, Performance, and Effectiveness* (New York: McGraw-Hill, 1970) indicate that companies engage in most training programs on faith; little data is gathered to test the impact on managers or organizations. Another survey concludes that "Education remains the only major profession without the guts to look at itself." Rolf P. Lynton and Udai Pareek, *Training for Development* (Homewood, Ill.: Richard D. Irwin, 1967). C. P. Bowen argues that most formal programs are fads and myths because there is no "ideal" manager model to which people should be trained. The only valid management development in his view is on-the-job training, with opportunities to bear responsibility and make decisions. "Let's Put Realism into Management Development," *Harvard Business Review,* July–August 1973, pp. 80–86. See also W. B. Eddy, "From Training to Organization Change," *Personnel Administration,* January–February 1971, pp. 37–43; and C. E. Watson, "Getting Management Training to Pay Off," *Business Horizons* 17, no. 1 (1974), pp. 51–58.

11. B. I. Oshry, "Cleaning the Air in Human Relations," *Business Horizons* Spring 1966, pp. 35–46; Oshry and R. Harrison, "Transfer from the Here-and-Now to the There-and-Then," *Journal of Applied Behavioral Science* 2, no. 2 (1966), pp. 185–198; R. M. Powell and C. S. Davis, "Do University Executive Development Programs Pay Off?" *Business Horizons* 16, no. 4 (1973), pp. 81–87.

12. Edgar H. Schein, "Forces Which Undermine Management Development," *California Management Review* 5 (1963), pp. 23–34.

13. T. Carron, "Human Relations Training and Attitude Change. A Vector Analysis," *Personnel* 17, no. 4 (1964), pp. 403–24. A study of the impact of a company program in human relations suggested that it did have a positive impact on middle management attitudes and performance, and with a sleeper effect—after 18 months, the changes were greater than after 3 months. See H. H. Hand and J. W. Slocum, Jr. "A Longitudinal Study of the Effect of a Human Relations Training Program on Managerial Effectiveness," *Proceedings, Eastern Academy of Management,* May 1971; and H. H. Hand, M. D. Richards, and J. W. Slocum, Jr., "Organizational Climate and the Effectiveness of a Human Relations Training Program," *Academy of Management Journal* 16, no. 2 (1973), pp. 185–95.

14. Lee G. Bolman, "Laboratory versus Lecture in Training Executives," *Journal of Applied Behavioral Science* 6, no. 3 (1970) pp. 323–36. For descriptions and support of T-groups, see Kenneth D. Benne, "History of T-Group in the Laboratory Setting," in Leland P. Bradford, Jack R. Gibb, and Kenneth D. Benne, eds., *T-Group Theory and Laboratory Method* (New York: John Wiley & Sons, 1964); Chris Argyris, "T-Group for Organizational Effectiveness," *Harvard Business Review,* March–April 1964, pp. 60–74 Edgar H. Schein and Warren G. Bennis, *Personal and Organizational Change through Group Methods* (New York: John Wiley & Sons, 1967); and K. Back, *Beyond Words* (New York: Russell Sage, 1972).

15. Warren G. Bennis describes the implicit goals of laboratory training as incorporating: (1) a spirit of inquiry, (2) expanded interpersonal consciousness, (3) freedom to be oneself, (4) collaborative ability, and (5) conflict resolution through problem solving. "Goals and Meta-goals of Laboratory Training," *NTL Human Relations Training News,* no. 3, 1962.

16. On contradictory evaluation of laboratory training, see Paul C. Buchanan, "Evaluating the Effectiveness of Laboratory Training in Industry," *NTL Explorations in Human Relations* (Washington, D.C.: National Training Labs, 1965); J. P. Campbell and M. D. Dunnette, "Effectiveness of T-Group Experiences in Managerial Training and Development," *Psychological Bulletin* 20, no. 2 (1968), pp. 73–104; Robert J. House, "T-Group Training: Good or Bad?" *Business Horizons* 12, no. 6 (1969), pp. 69–77; Matthew B. Miles, "Changes during and following Laboratory Training. A Clinical Experimental Study," *Journal of Applied Behavioral Science* 1, no. 3 (1965), pp. 215–42; L. A. Gottschalk and E. M. Pattison, "Psychiatric Perspectives on T-Groups and the Laboratory Movement: An

Overview," *American Journal of Psychiatry* 126, no. 6 (1969), pp. 823–29; and Chris Argyris, "Issues in Evaluating Laboratory Education," *Industrial Relations* 8, no. 1 (1968), pp. 28–40.

17. Robert J. House, "Leadership Training: Some Dysfunctional Consequences," *Administrative Science Quarterly* 12, no. 4 (1968), pp. 556–71. A manager who has a task-oriented leadership style that is appropriate to the situation and subordinates may founder if he converts to a more human relations style. See F. E. Fiedler, "The Effects of Leadership Training and Experience: A Contingency Model Interpretation," *Administrative Science Quarterly* 17, no. 4 (1972), pp. 453–70.

18. On the potential danger to the effective manager, see George S. Odiorne, "The Trouble with Sensivity Training," *Training Director's Journal,* October 1963, p. 18; William Gomberg, "Problems in Management Development Programs," *The Personnel Administrator,* September–October 1964, pp. 2–5; and F. I. Steele, "Can T-Group Training Change the Power Structure?" *Personnel Administration,* November 1970. On the supposed dangers of humanistic education to the economic purposes of business managers, see W. P. Chandler III, "A Lot of Learning Is a Dangerous Thing," *Harvard Business Review,* March–April 1972, pp. 122–31.

19. I. D. Yalom and M. A. Lieberman, "A Study of Encounter Group Casualties," *Archives of General Psychiatry,* July 1971. As Chris Argyris has pointed out, in the present state of our culture we may need to be able to hate and to be aggressive, hostile, and nonaccepting. Otherwise, we could be destroyed. *Integrating the Individual and the Organization* (New York: John Wiley & Sons, 1964).

20. A similar process has been termed *transition management.* See L. S. Ackerman, "Transition Management: An In-Depth Look at Managing Complex Change," *Organizational Dynamics,* Summer 1982, pp. 46–66.

21. For descriptions and examples of organizational development, see Warren G. Bennis, *Organizational Development* (Reading, Mass.: Addison-Wesley Publishing, 1969); Robert R. Blake and Jane S. Mouton, *Corporate Excellence through Grid Organizational Development* (Houston: Gulf Publishing, 1968); Wendell French, "Organization Development: Objectives, Assumptions, and Strategies," *California Management Review* 12, no. 2 (1969), pp. 23–54; W. J. Grockett, "Team Building: One Approach to Organizational Development," *Journal of Applied Behavioral Science* 6 (1970), pp. 291–306; E.

F. Huse and M. Beer, "Eclectic Approach to Organizational Development," *Harvard Business Review,* September–October 1971, pp. 103–12; D. L. Kegan, "Organizational Development: Description, Issues and Some Research Results," *Academy of Management Journal* 14, no. 4 (1971), pp. 453–64; Newton Margulies and Anthony P. Raia, *Organizational Development: Values, Process and Technology* (New York: McGraw-Hill, 1972); W. L. French and C. H. Bell, Jr., *Organization Development* (Englewood Cliffs, N.J.: Prentice-Hall, 1973); W. W. Burke, *Current Issues and Strategies in Organizational Development* (New York: Human Sciences Press, 1977); G. H. Varney, *An Organizational Development Approach to Management Development* (Reading: Addison-Wesley Publishing, 1976); E. F. Huse, *Organization Development* (St. Paul: West, 1976); and W. W. Burke, *Organization Development: Principles and Practice* (New York: Columbia University, 1982).

22. B. S. Chakravarthy, "Adaptation: A Promising Metaphor for Strategic Management," *Academy of Management Review* 7, no. 1 (1982), pp. 35–44.

23. Richard Beckhard, *Organization Development: Strategies and Models* (Reading, Mass.: Addison-Wesley Publishing, 1969).

24. Sheldon A. Davis, "An Organic Problem-Solving Method of Organizational Change," *Journal of Applied Behavioral Science* 3, no. 1 (1967), pp. 4–5.

25. For example, a manager's perception of a superior's attitude toward management by objectives is the best predictor of the manager's own view. D. D. White, "Factors Affecting Employee Attitudes toward the Installation of a New Management System," *Academy of Management Journal* 16, no. 4 (1973), pp. 636–46.

26. Edgar H. Schein, *Process Consultation: Its Role in Organizational Development,* (Reading, Mass.: Addison-Wesley, 1969); Gordon L. Lippitt, *Organizational Renewal* (New York: Appleton-Century-Crofts, 1969). Lippitt assigns a central role to a "renewal stimulator" who has four functions: planning leader, information and communication expert, learning specialist, and management consultant. See also F. Steele, *Consulting for Organizational Change* (Amherst: University of Massachusetts, 1975).

27. On union opposition to OD, see M. Scott Myers, "Overcoming Union Opposition to Job Enrichment," *Harvard Business Review,* May–June 1971, pp. 37–49.

28. P. E. Connor, "Critical Inquiry into Some Assumptions and Values Characterizing OD." *Academy of Management Review,* October 1977, pp. 635–44.

29. Robert Tannenbaum and Sheldon A. Davis, "Values, Man, and Organizations," *Industrial Management Review,* Winter 1969, pp. 67–86.

30. The values of many OD practitioners seem so at variance with traditional management views that some feel that business will not support it for long. J. D. Arnold, "Wither O.D. in a Recessionary Economy?" *Training and Development Journal* 28, no. 4 (1974), pp. 3–8. OD consultants have been accused of being politically naive. For a view that they are politically sophisticated, see A. T. Cobb and N. Margulies, "Organizational Development: A Political Perspective," *Academy of Management Review* 6, no. 1 (1981), pp. 49–59.

31. Leonard R. Sayles, "The Change Process in Organizations: An Applied Anthropology Approach," *Human Organization* 21, no. 2 (1961), pp. 62–67; Stanley E. Seashore and David G. Bowers, *Changing the Structure and Functioning of an Organization,* University of Michigan Survey Research Center Monograph No. 33 (Ann Arbor, 1963). Some evidence suggests that large, quantum change is more associated with effective performance than are piecemeal, incremental changes. D. Miller and P. H. Friesen, "Structural Change and Performance: Quantum versus Piecemeal-Incremental Approaches," *Academy of Management Journal* 25, no. 4 (1982), pp. 867–92.

32. Organizational development may concentrate on interpersonal relations at the top because of discretionary control of executive jobs. At lower levels, however, it may have to concentrate on modifying structure and technology. B. O. Saxberg in review of Robert T. Golembiewski, *Renewing Organizations: The Laboratory Approach to Planned Change* (Itasca, Ill.: F. E. Peacock, 1972), in *Personnel Psychology* 26 (1973), p. 409. One study of the persistence of organizational development suggested that it enabled management to face the need for tough structural changes such as elimination of positions more effectively. Robert T. Golembiewski and Robert Munzenrider, "Persistence and Change: A Note on the Long-Term Effects of an Organization Development Program," *Academy of Management Journal* 16, no. 1 (1973), pp. 149–54. For a discussion of the disadvantages of attitudinal versus structural change, see W. Wohlking, "Attitude Change, Behavior Change," *California Management Review* 13, no. 2 (1970), p. 45. Another study argues for structural change by demonstrating that little improvement in government employment of minorities occurred until the federal government gave up exhortation in favor of stiff punishment for noncompliance. D. Hellriegel and L. Short, "Structural Approach to Planned Change: A Study

of Equal Employment Opportunity in the Federal Government," *Proceedings of Eastern Academy of Management,* May 1973.

33. This change is described and analyzed in Jeremiah J. O'Connell, *Managing Organizational Innovation* (Homewood, Ill.: Richard D. Irwin, 1968).

34. J. Sterling Livingston, "Pygmalion in Management," *Harvard Business Review,* July–August 1969, pp. 81–89; D. E. Berlew and D. T. Hall, "The Socialization of Managers: Effects of Expectations on Performance," *Administrative Science Quarterly* 11, no. 2 (1969), p. 208.

35. Larry E. Greiner, "Patterns of Organizational Change," in Gene W. Dalton and Paul R. Lawrence with Larry E. Greiner, *Organizational Change and Development* (Homewood, Ill.: Richard D. Irwin, 1970).

36. M. J. Scurrah, M. Shani and C. Zipfel, "Influence of Internal and External Change Agents in a Simulated Educational Organization," *Administrative Science Quarterly* 16, no. 1 (1971), pp. 113–21. The authors suggest that an external change agent may be more effective than an internal one.

37. Paul R. Lawrence, "How to Deal with Resistance to Change," *Harvard Business Review,* May–June 1954, pp. 49–57. Lawrence also advises the manager not to always expect resistance; an experiment suggests that this can be a self-fulfilling prophecy. A manager who expects no difficulty is apparently less likely to encounter it. A. S. King, "Expectation Effects in Organizational Change," *Administrative Science Quarterly* 19, no. 2 (1974), pp. 221–30.

38. On participation, see Lester Coch and John R. P. French, Jr., "Overcoming Resistance to Change," *Human Relations* 1, no. 4 (1948), pp. 512–32; and Alfred J. Marrow, David G. Bowers, and Stanley E. Seashore, eds., *Management by Participation* (New York: Harper & Row, 1967). A follow-up is reported in Stanley E. Seashore and David G. Bowers, "Durability of Organizational Change," *American Psychologist,* March 1970, pp. 79–93; and A. Lowin, "Participative Decision Making: A Model, Literature Critique and Prescriptions for Research," *Organizational Behavior and Human Performance* 3, no. 1 (1968), p. 68. Routing of questionnaire surveys from the bottom up rather than top down may be a way of generating participation. M. S. Myers and E. D. Weed, Jr., "Behavioral Change Agents: A Case Study," *Management of Personnel Quarterly* 6, no. 3 (1967), pp. 12–19.

39. P. Hesseling and E. E. Konnen, "Culture and Subculture in a Decision-Making Exercise," *Human Relations* 22 (1969), pp. 31–51.

40.   One experiment tested persuasive leadership (the supervisor poses a problem and persuades the group to adopt it) versus participative leadership (the supervisor poses a problem, and the group generates the solution). The latter produced more original ideas, but most supervisors still leaned to the persuasive style because they did not know how to conduct the other one. N. R. F. Maier and M. Sash, "Specific Leadership Behaviors That Promote Problem Solving," *Personnel Psychology* 24 (1971), pp. 35–44. See also A. C. Bartlett and T. A. Kayer, "Toward a Theory of Changing Behavior: An Elaboration on the Role of Influence and Coercion," in A. C. Bartlett and T. A. Kayer, eds., *Changing Organization Behavior* (Englewood, N.J.: Prentice-Hall, 1973).

41.   A participative approach may serve well to generate ideas, but in a complex organization it is often better to take a political or bargaining approach to implementation. J. M. Thomas and W. G. Bennis, eds., *Management of Change and Conflict* (Baltimore: Penguin Books, 1972). Also see Robert H. Guest, *Organizational Change: The Effect of Successful Leadership* (Homewood, Ill.: Richard D. Irwin, 1962); and A. S. Judson, *A Manager's Guide to Making Changes* (New York: John Wiley & Sons, 1966), pp. 109–13.

25

Conflict Potential

The examples of conflict between individuals are legion and familiar: two children fighting over a hill, two managers competing for the same promotion, two executives maneuvering for a larger share of corporate capital, and so on. In every case, each person is striving to possess a scarce resource, which may be a material thing (money) or an immaterial state, such as status, prestige, fame, or power.[1*]

As we saw in Part 3 conflict between individuals and groups occurs when individuals desire to satisfy security, affiliative, or esteem needs through their group, but their associates demand excessive conformity or undesirable behavior. Such conflict may arise from an individual's efforts to promote his or her own interest in making more money by breaking the group's norm on permissible production. Such transgression of the unwritten rules will often result in collective retaliation on the unfortunate offender. It almost seems that there is a "law of interorganizational conflict," in which every group or organization is in partial conflict with every other group with which it deals![2] This is perhaps a little exaggerated, but intergroup conflicts over authority, jurisdiction, and resources are exceedingly common. Staff-line conflicts, interdepartmental fights, labor-management strife, and international warfare provide a few examples.

In this chapter we shall discuss evolving attitudes toward conflict, various forms of conflict, conditions for cooperation or conflict, conflict reinforcement, and techniques for reconciling and managing conflict.

The Commonality of Conflict

Conflict is inevitable, often legitimate, and perhaps even desirable.[3] It does not necessarily indicate organizational breakdown or management failure, as was implied in older management theory and human relations philosophy.[4] Three assumptions underlie recent thinking about conflict.[5]

1. Conflicts are common in organizations because everyone does not agree about their own authority and responsibilities, and all are not equally committed to the same organizational objectives.
2. Some types of conflicts are detrimental and others beneficial for both individual and organizational objectives.
3. The principle of minimizing conflict subscribed to by some managers and social scientists may have some validity for crisis organizations (such as armies) or for routine organizations (such as some manufacturing companies), but it may not be valid for knowledge- and technology-producing organizations, such as those engaged in research and development.

Conflict and tension can be beneficial if they reflect a commitment that promotes challenge, heightened attention, or effort. The emerging thesis is that too little expressed conflict leads to stagnancy, but uncontrolled conflict threatens chaos. Since individuals and organizations have differing abilities to withstand stress, conflict should not be excessive. In short, it is not conflict itself that is dangerous, but rather its mismanagement.[6]

Notes and references will be found at the end of this chapter.

Many recent books and articles about contemporary life have proposed open recognition and rational treatment of conflict. The thrust of much marriage counseling, sensitivity training, psychoanalytical therapy, and management training is not to eliminate conflict but to manage it. It is impossible to determine whether rational handling of conflict is more or less characteristic of real organizations today, but it appears so. Managers report that they now spend 20 percent of their time dealing with conflict and that ability to manage conflict has become more important in the past 10 years.[7] The "organization person" conformity complaint seems less common (among managers, if not among young people) than it once was.[8] Matrix organizations have been designed to foster controlled conflict and provide resolution mechanisms. Some managers even pursue open confrontation in conflict, and such a style may be more effective than forcing conformity or denying differences.[9]

The study of conflict goes by many names in the literature: conflict, social resolution, social negotiations, collective bargaining. Underlying all of these approaches, however, is an emerging commonality: social conflict results from the pursuit of what are perceived to be incompatible goals such that gains to one party occur at the expense of another.[10]

Goals, Activities, and Resources

The potential for conflict (see Figure 25–1) depends on how incompatible the goals are, the extent to which required resources are shared, and the degree of interdependence of task activities.[11] Thus the chances of conflict are small between people who have their own resources and perform entirely different tasks directed toward completely separate goals. Physics professors and cosmetics salespeople seldom conflict because their worlds are totally separate. The potential for conflict is much greater between professors and university deans, or between sales representatives and company credit managers. These pairs draw on common resources, their tasks are interdependent, and they may pursue incompatible objectives (new experimental equipment versus control of university expenditures, and expanded sales versus reduced losses from customer nonpayment).

Competition

Conflict and competition share similarities but have one essential difference (see Figure 25–2). In both cases there is perceived incompatibility between goals; both

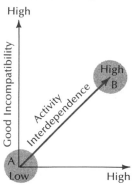

FIGURE 25–1

Potential for Conflict

Space A:
  Low potential for conflict.
Space B:
  High potential for conflict.

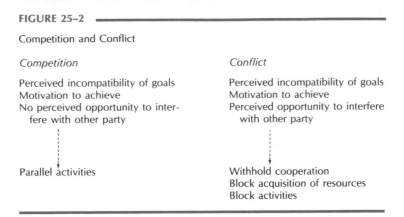

FIGURE 25–2

Competition and Conflict

Competition

Perceived incompatibility of goals
Motivation to achieve
No perceived opportunity to inter-
   fere with other party

Parallel activities

Conflict

Perceived incompatibility of goals
Motivation to achieve
Perceived opportunity to interfere
   with other party

Withhold cooperation
Block acquisition of resources
Block activities

can't win the war or the race. The success of one party comes at the expense of the other. In conflict, however, at least one side perceives an opportunity to interfere with the other's ability to obtain resources or perform activities. Competitors, in contrast, see their activities as quite independent, with no opportunity to interfere with one another.[12] Thus football is conflict, but a ski race in which each competitor races alone is competition. A track race is somewhere in between, but closer to competition than to conflict because most runners adhere to rules that limit interference.

Factors that Reinforce Conflict

Once the potential for conflict exists, certain perceptual, communicational, and personal distortions operate to maintain and escale it as summarized in Figure 25–3.[13]

FIGURE 25–3

Reinforcement of Conflict or Cooperation

Conflict		*Cooperation*
Scarcity ◄─	── Resources ──	─► Sufficiency
Mistrust ◄─	── Attitudes ──	─► Trust
Disagreement ◄─	── Values ──	─► Agreement
Unstable ◄─	── Internal state of parties ──	─► Stable
Rejected ◄─	── Status hierarchy ──	─► Accepted
Stereotypes ◄─	── Perceptions ──	─► Valid

Trust versus Mistrust on Resource Utilization

In the proverbial land of milk and honey, harmony reigns because life's goods are plentiful and available to all. This utopian vision is beguiling; an environment of excess resources reduces interdependence so that every party can obtain what is necessary to accomplish its objective. If someone makes a mistake and wastes resources, the others are not upset or angry because they are unharmed. Unfortunately, real organization life is more contentious. Intellectually, the contending persons may agree that all contribute equally and have equal claim to scarce resources, but emotionally each is likely to believe that his or her concerns are the most important and that any problems originate with others.[14]

These suspicious attitudes are increased if the specific contributions of interdependent parties are not measurable. When objective evaluation is impossible, each tends to blame others for mistakes and waste: production blames maintenance for equipment failures, while maintenance criticizes production for abusing the machinery; sales blames production for late deliveries, while production chastises sales for making impossible promises to customers. Each argues that the other is ignorant of the demands and complexities of one's own operations—which is at least partly true because of their specialized training and differentiated duties. The greater the mutual ignorance, the more unreasonable the demands on one another.[15]

Disagreement versus Common Values

"Variety is the spice of life" may be equally applicable to food and companions, but we sometimes pay for excessive gastronomical spices with growling stomachs and for too many personal alliances with jangled emotions. So it is with conflict between individuals and groups within organizations. The differentiation among the various functions and specialities in organizations leads to different leadership expectations, structural desires, and time perspectives.[16] Groups performing routine tasks may exhibit short-run views and expect close supervision and formalized structure, while craft or creative groups want more participation and informal means for accomplishing long-run tasks. The greater the differentiation in an organization, the greater the potential for conflict.

Unless the parties are aware of their interdependence and agree on the values and objectives of the larger unit of which they are a part (whether that larger unit be a family, company, nation, or human race), conflict will be certain. Instances of inadequate value sharing and competing goals are numerous. Actualization of the individual versus the collectivity is one value conflict that has been and will be fought on many battlefields. At a more mundane business level, salespeople value company responsiveness to customers, while production management desires long production runs for economy; engineers emphasize ingenuity and quality, while financial managers must be concerned about costs; marketing strives for gross income, while the Credit Department endeavors to minimize credit loss; staff values change, while line departments want stability. Thus the basic dilemmas that underlie many interdepartmental differences involve:[17]

Flexibility versus stability.
Criteria for short-run versus long-run performance.
Emphasis on measurable results versus attention to intangibles.
Maximizing organizational goals versus responding to other societal needs.

These value differences will be exacerbated if higher management's reward system emphasizes the separate performance of each department rather than their combined performance.

Internal Instability versus Stability

An individual who is uncertain of desires or in dissonance regarding the priorities among needs and wants will be extremely difficult to work with because he or she will be unpredictable. If you appeal to one need level, the individual shifts to another and resents your interference. A superior may pat a subordinate on the back and voice appreciation for the timely completion of a rush task, but the subordinate with internal conflict may resent the superior's "patronizing" attitude and argue that what he or she wants is a bigger and better task. If the superior responds to good performance only by giving the subordinate more difficult work, however, the subordinate may complain of not being appreciated.

Within interacting and interdependent groups (or nations) similar internal instability can exist, thus making cooperation difficult and conflict likely. It is tough to make peace between groups if either side is experiencing internal conflict about its purpose, structure, and leadership. If you appeal to one leadership faction, the others in the organization may reject your proposal in order to further their own interests. Even dominant leaders will be reluctant to deal with an outside party if their doing so will be denounced by their intragroup rivals as "selling out."[18]

Rejected versus Accepted Status Hierarchy

Disagreements about relative status and authority are numerous and are often manifested in stress generated over work patterns and interactions between the parties—who initiates to whom, who responds. Production managers may think they are just as important, competent, and high status as engineering, and it therefore resent having to accept engineer's initiations of product and process modifications. People who are unable to control a situation will blame those they perceive as being in control.[19]

The conflict between university students and administrators that rocked some campuses in the early 1970s reflected student frustration with situations they couldn't control: war in Vietnam and crowded facilities in school. Since they had no influence in national or school policymaking, they attacked those closest to home who were thought to be in control, that is, college administrators.[20] But of course these educators were not really controlling the factors that were bothering the protesting students. They were just convenient targets of those who were angry (and perhaps rightly so).

Misperceiving the Other Party

We all tend to develop stereotypes that justify conflict. Each side exaggerates the differences that exist between them, a perception that requires only small actual differences to be maintained.[21] This distortion is facilitated by reduced intergroup communication. If forced to interact, each side listens only to its own representatives. Indeed, in the absence of any shared goals, communication tends to reinforce stereotypes, and relations deteriorate further.[22] Unfortunately, one short-run result of forced busing for integration has been the strengthening of biases between blacks and whites rather than the desired growth of understanding. Even in college student groups, the numerically dominant American white males tend to perceive white females as passive nonleaders, black males as troublesome nonconformists, and most foreigners has having lower aspirations.[23] We tend to see what we expect to see. Furthermore, conflicting groups think they understand the other's position when they really do not.[24]

Perceptual distortion thus exaggerates the differences between groups, and the actual overlap that exists is underestimated.[25] For example, unreliable intelligence tests in the past have suggested that the mean intelligence for whites slightly exceeds that for blacks in the United States. We now think that this difference is phony because it reflects different verbal training, schooling, and cultures. Nonetheless, as inaccurate and biased as the old IQ tests have been, the difference between blacks and whites is so narrow that perhaps one third of all blacks tested as superior to the average white.[26] It is doubtful that the "average whites" would accept this even today. They simply would not believe that one third of all the blacks could be smarter than they. Similarly, a difference in sexual mores and behavior between middle-aged adults and today's youth may exist, but it is probably narrower than perceived, with great variation on each side and substantial overlap. A sizable proportion of older people demonstrate more promiscuity than exists among average youth. Nonetheless many, peering across the gap, exaggerate the differences.

Conflict Reinforced by. . . .

- misperceiving the other party: evil stereotypes and exaggerated differences
- misperceiving your own group: good stereotypes and imagined similarities
- personal differences and personality attributes: background, education, age, culture, low self-esteem, dogmatism, authoritarianism, and belligerence

Misperceiving Your Own Group

Stereotypes also extend to one's own group. When in conflict with others, in-group solidarity and cooperation increases, and members tend to naively accept each other as honest, rational, and peace loving. Most even think their group is better than others. In some experiments, *all* groups rated themselves as better than average![27] A "superiority complex" seems to exist. Regardless of what one's group is really like, one can say, "Poor though it may be, my group is at least above average." We do not recognize the selective and self-protective distortion present. Those young people who distrust all authority figures and anyone over 30 sometimes fall prey to exploitation from their age and culture peers, whom they naively perceive as being like themselves and hence good.[28] All too common are reports of rip-offs and physical abuse resulting from hitchhiking, dope buying, and residence sharing with casual acquaintances.

Thus competition and conflict heighten positive identification with one's own group. People close ranks; they become more single-minded. Now they have a clear goal: to win. Even after objective performance measurement in experiments, groups tend toward more favorable subjective evaluation of their own performance and downgrading of others. To them, the numbers can lie.

In general, we homogenize differences within the boundaries of our groups and exaggerate differences across boundaries. We also tend to reverse cause and effect.

We say that the terrible characteristics of the other group justify our hostility and cause the conflict.[29] For example: "The 'gooks' are dirty, lazy, and treacherous, and so we should either kill them or get out," or "Welfare chiselers are shiftless and promiscuous, so they don't deserve help." The social scientist sees the opposite causal direction: conflict leads to distorted perceptions in the interest of justifying hostility.[30] Notice that *any* differences may serve to stimulate hostility; the other side may be too dumb *or* too smart, too flexible (unprincipled) *or* too fixed (stubborn). It is the difference that counts.

Personal Differences

Intergroup conflict occurs even between the most reasonable and secure people, but it can be exacerbated by personal attributes.[31] Differences in background, education, age, and culture lower the probability of collaboration because of their adverse impact on values, knowledge, and communication. This is even more likely if one party is clearly superior in position, pay, or seniority.

Some people seem more predisposed toward conflict. Just which people are so disposed is unclear, and the whole question is distorted by stereotypes and old prejudices. Hard evidence is rare. Nonetheless, it appears that certain personality attributes increase conflict behavior.[32] These include low self-esteem, high dogmatism, and authoritarianism. People who think little of themselves and who fear ambiguity in status, beliefs, or authority seem more likely to seek supremacy and clarity by vanquishing their real or imagery enemies.

The critical attitudinal dimensions determining response to conflict seem to be concern for self and concern for others.[33] Those with high self-concern combined with low concern for others tend to immediately fight and attempt to dominate. In contrast, people with little self-concern combined with high concern for others tend to give up and oblige. These styles for handling interpersonal conflict are summarized in Figure 25–4. Thus it appears that conflict is most effectively handled when one has medium to high concern for *both* self and others.[34]

Some evidence suggests that trusting people are more likely to be belligerent toward those perceived as violating their trust.[35] In comparison with managers in several other nations, Americans exhibit the most trust toward those who appear friendly but are the most belligerent toward provocative others. More suspicious

Reprinted by permission: Tribune Company Syndicate, Inc.

FIGURE 25–4

Styles for Handling Interpersonal Conflict

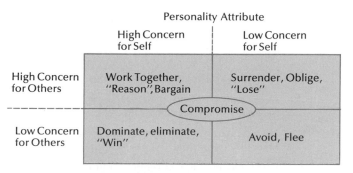

Greek and Spanish managers do not expect as much from others but tend to be more conciliatory toward unfriendly, quarrelsome, and hostile others. Even in the United States, differences seem to exist between managers in different functions: engineering and production more trusting and more belligerent; finance, accounting, marketing, and sales less trusting and less belligerent.

All of this suggests that greater flexibility is likely to decrease conflict, while people with narrower values, beliefs, and behavioral skills will increase it.[36] Locked in their inappropriate styles, they are unable to compromise or collaborate. Total victory or complete withdrawal become the only permissible alternatives to such people—a situation all too common in world history.

SUMMARY

Competition and conflict between and among individuals and groups is common because scarce required resources are shared, task activities are interdependent, and they pursue incompatible goals. Competition tends to become conflict when one party perceives an opportunity to interfere in the other's resource allocation or task performance (especially when no restraining rules exist).

Conflict is perpetuated and reinforced when the parties mistrust the process of resource allocation, disagree about values, are internally unstable, and reject their status relationship. Perhaps worst of all, conflict is aggravated by perceptual, communicational, and judgmental distortions that exaggerate the homogeneity *within* each party and the difference *between* the parties. Each believes that it understands the other but it does not—and the members block out communications not supporting their established bias.

REVIEW QUESTIONS

1. How have views on conflict changed in recent years?

2. Upon what three elements does the potential for conflict depend?

3. What is a state of high potential for conflict? What is a state of low potential?

4. What is similar about conflict and competition? What is different?

5. What organizational conditions contribute to and reinforce conflict?

6. What organizational conditions promote cooperation?

7. How does mistrust of resource allocation affect conflict?

8. How does disagreement about values affect conflict?

9. How does instability in one or both of the parties or groups in conflict affect the relationship?

10. How do parties in conflict tend to misperceive each other? How do they misperceive themselves?

11. What personal factors seem to add to conflict?

12. What basic styles are used in handling interpersonal conflict?

Notes and References on Conflict Potential

1. R. D. Nye, *Conflict among Humans* (New York: Springer 1973); B. Brehmer and K. R. Hammond, "Cognitive Sources of Interpersonal Conflict," *Organizational Behavior and Human Performance,* 10 (1973), pp. 290–313.

2. Anthony Downs, *Inside Bureaucracy* (Boston: Little, Brown 1968). M. Olson argues that interorganizational conflict is so common because "it is theoretically implausible to expect to find a large set of organizations cooperating to take action on behalf of their collective self-interest." *The Logic of Collective Action* (Cambridge, Mass.: Harvard University Press 1965).

3. An early plea to utilize conflict was issued in M. P. Follet, *Dynamic Administration* (New York: Harper & Row, 1940). See also J. Kelly, "Make Conflict Work for You," *Harvard Business Review,* July–August, 1970, pp. 103–13; and H. Assael, "Conservative Role of Interorganizational Conflict," *Administrative Science Quarterly,* December 1969, pp. 573–82.

4. Management theory used to say very little about conflict among managers. One reason for this omission might have been an assumption that managers were basically rational, in contrast to the supposed irrationality of workers. Such a view implied that because of their rationality, managers could clearly see organizational objectives and thus could plan logically. It was assumed that management rationality was sufficient to bring about required cooperation. This assumption was an illusion. T. E. Stephenson, "The Causes of Management Conflict," *California Management Review* 2, no. 2 (1960), pp. 90–97.

Many managers still believe that conflict must be hidden, however, because they consider organizational harmony and personal rationality so important.

> There are few activities more prone to a credibility gap than the way in which executives approach organizational life. A sense of disbelief occurs when managers purport to make decisions in rationalistic terms while most observers and participants know that personalities and politics play a significant if not overriding role.

Abraham Zaleznik, "Power and Politics in Organizational Life," *Harvard Business Review,* May–June 1970, p. 47. See also A. McDonald, "Conflict at the Summit: A Deadly Game," *Harvard Business Review,* March–April, 1972, pp. 59–68.

5. These assumptions are from William M. Evan, "Conflict and Performance in R & D Organizations," *Industrial Management Review* 7, no. 2 (1965), pp. 37–46.

Louis R. Pondy wrote:

> Conflict, like pain, is a signal that the organization is in trouble or on the verge of trouble. An organization or other social system which suppresses conflict, which prohibits the expression of dissent, is depriving itself on the feedback loop necessary for self-regulation and stability.

"Some Cybernetic Models of Conflict in Organizations," in A. R. Negandhi, ed., *Conflict and Power in Complex Organizations: An Interinstitutional Perspective* (Kent, Ohio: Comparative Administration Research Institute, Kent State University, 1972), p. 49.

6. Lewis A. Coser, *The Functions of Social Conflict* (New York: Free Press, 1956).

7. K. W. Thomas and W. H. Schmidt, "A Survey of Managerial Interests with Respect to Conflict," *Academy of Management Journal,* June 1976, pp. 315–18.

8. Lyman W. Porter, "Where Is the Organization Man?" *Harvard Business Review,* November–December 1963, pp. 53–61.

9. Paul R. Lawrence and Jay W. Lorsch, *Organization and Environment* (Boston: Graduate School of Business Administration, Harvard University, 1967).

10. Bernard Berelson and G. A. Steiner, *Human Behavior: An Inventory of Scientific Findings* (New York: Harcourt Brace Jovanovich, 1964), p. 588. The literature of conflict is plagued with a multiplicity of inconsistent, competitive, and conflicting concepts and terms. For an exhaustive review of the different approaches to defining conflict, see C. F. Fink, "Some Conceptual Difficulties in the Theory of Social Conflict," *Journal of Conflict Resolution* 12 (1968), pp. 413–58. On commonality in conflict, the inaugural editorial in the *Journal of Conflict Resolution,* March 1957, p. 2, stated:

> Many of the patterns and processes which characterize it in another. Negotiation and mediation go on in labor disputes as well as international relations. Price wars and domestic quarrels have much the pattern of an arms race. Frustration breeds aggression both in the individual and the state. The jurisdictional problems of labor unions and the territorial disputes of states are not dissimilar. It is not too much to claim that out of the contributions of many fields a general theory of conflict is emerging.

11. S. M. Schmidt and T. A. Kochan, "Conflict: Toward Conceptual Clarity," *Administrative Science Quarterly* 17, no. 3 (1972), pp. 359–70; C. W. Anderson and B. A. Nesvold, "A Skinnerian Analysis of Conflict Behavior," *American Behavioral Scientist* 15, no. 6 (1972), pp. 883–910.

12. V. Aubert, "Competition and Dissensus: Two Types of Conflict," *Journal of Conflict Resolution* 7, no. 1 (1963), pp. 26–42; J. M. Dutton and R. E. Walton, "Interdepartmental Conflict and Cooperation: Two Contrasting Studies," *Human Organization* 25 (1966), pp. 207–20; R. B. Zajonc, "Cooperation, Competition and Conflict," in *Social Psychology: An Experimental Approach* (Belmont, Calif.: Brooks/Cole Publishing, 1967); R. G. Sipes, "War, Sports and Aggression," *American Anthropologist* 75, no. 1 (1973), pp. 64–86; D. J. Cherrington, "Satisfaction in Competitive Conditions," *Organizational Behavior and Human Performance* 10, no. 1 (1973), pp. 47–71.

13. J. A. Seiler, "Diagnosing Interdepartmental Conflict," *Harvard Business Review,* September–October 1963, pp. 121–32; Dutton and Walton, "Interdepartmental Conflict and Cooperation." Pondy describes the preconditions for conflict as "latent conflicts" and analyses three basic types: (1) competition for scarce resources (when the aggregated demands of organization members for resources exceed the available resources of their organization); (2) drives for autonomy (when one group either seeks to exercise control over some activity that another group considers as its own province or seeks to insulate itself from such control); and (3) divergence of subunit goals (when two groups who must cooperate on some joint activity are unable to reach a consensus on concerted action). Louis R. Pondy, "Organizational Conflict: Concepts and Models," *Administrative Science Quarterly* 12, no. 2 (1967), pp. 296–320.

14. D. C. Dearborn and H. A. Simon, "Selective Perception: A Note on the Departmental Identifications of Executives," *Sociometry* 21 (1958), pp. 140–44; Charles Perrow, "Departmental Power and Perspectives in Industrial Firms," in M. N. Zald, *Power in Organizations* (Nashville, Tenn.: Vanderbilt University Press, 1970), pp. 59–89.

15. E. J. Miller, "Technology, Territory and Time," *Human Relations* 12 (1959), pp. 243–72.

16. Lawrence and Lorsch, *Organization and Environment.*

17. H. A. Landsberger, "The Horizontal Dimension in a Bureaucracy," *Administrative Science Quarterly* 6, no. 2 (1961), pp. 298–333.

18. An interesting suggestion from one experiment is that females are more flexible as group representatives than men are. The males tend to take inflexible ideological positions and may be socially trained to this. K. Zechmeister and D. Druckman, "Determinants of Resolving a Conflict of Interest," *Journal of Conflict Resolution* 17, no. 1 (1973), pp. 63–68.

19. M. N. Zald, "Power Balance and Staff Conflict in Correctional Institutions," *Administrative Science Quarterly,* June 1962, pp. 22–49.

20. C. M. Otten, *University Authority and the Student: The Berkeley Experience,* (Berkeley: University of California Press, 1970). For an analysis of such conflict in Germany, see U. Kort-Krieser and P. Schmidt, "Participation and Legitimacy Conflict at West German Universities," *Organizational Studies* 3 no. 4 (1982), pp. 297–319.

21. D. R. Campbell, "Stereotypes and the Perception of Group Differences," *American Psychologist* 22 (1967), pp. 817–29.

22. R. L. Hilgert, "Interaction in an Industrial Plant: A Negative Hypothesis," *Human Organization* 26, no. 4 (1967), pp. 230–34. The detailed report on the pioneering scientific management studies at Western Electric

Hawthorne Works explicitly noted that improvement in face-to-face relations at the first-line supervisory level would do little to dispel industrial conflict. F. J. Roethlisberger and W. J. Dickson, *Management and the Worker* (Cambridge, Mass.: Harvard University Press, 1939).

In many countries anti-American attitudes are positively correlated with U.S. penetration and presence. See C. Tai, E. J. Peterson, and T. R. Gurr, "Internal versus External Sources of Anti-Americanism," *Journal of Conflict Resolution* 17, no. 3 (1973), pp. 455–83; J. W. Burton, *Conflict and Communication* (London: Macmillan, 1969); and A. L. Rich, *Interracial Communication* (New York: Harper & Row, 1974).

23. Ross A. Webber, "Majority and Minority Perceptions and Behavior in Cross-cultural Teams," *Human Relations* 27, no. 9 (1974), pp. 873–90, and R. A. Webber, "Perceptions and Behaviors in Mixed-Sex Work Teams," *Industrial Relations,* May 1976, pp. 121–29. Other experiments suggest that Americans may underestimate the strength of "foreign" others. S. Streuffert and S. I. Sandler, "Perceived Success and Competence of the Opponent on the Laboratory Dien Bien Phu," *Journal of Applied Social Psychology* 3, no. 1 (1973), pp. 84–93.

24. Robert R. Blake and Jane S. Mouton wrote:

Here are two findings stemming from trends toward uniformities in membership behavior associated with protection of group interests which have unusual significance in determining barriers to the resolution of conflict between groups. They suggest that under competitive conditions members of one group perceive that they understand the other's proposal when in fact they do *not*. Inadequate understanding makes it all the more difficult for competing groups to view each other's proposals realistically. Areas they share in common are likely to go unrecognized and in fact be seen as characteristic of one's own group only. Under competitive conditions, areas of true agreement will go undiscovered.

"Reactions to Intergroup Competition under Win-Lose Conditions," *Management Science,* July 1961, p. 252. See also W. B. Pearce, K. R. Stamm, and H. Strentz, "Communication and Polarization during a Campus Strike," *Public Opinion Quarterly* 35 (1971), pp. 228–35.

25. Gordon W. Allport, *The Nature of Prejudice* (Reading, Mass.: Addison-Wesley Publishing, 1954). It is an irony of hierarchical relationships than those on the bottom of the status ladder seem to have a better understanding of those on the top than the reverse. The lowers can role pay the uppers much more effectively. L. W. Doob and W. J. Foltz, "The Belfast Workshop: An Application of Group Techniques to a Destructive Conflict," *Journal of Conflict Resolution* 17, no. 3 (1973), pp. 489–512.

26. Among 71 studies, the percentage of blacks who exceeded the median white intelligence ranged from 0 to 69 percent. A. M. Shuey, *The Testing of Negro Intelligence* (New York: Social Science Press, 1966).

27. Blake and Mouton, "Reactions to Intergroup Competition under Win-Lose Conditions."

28. Rollo May argues that "innocence" is no defense, that the naive and trusting person who is harmed is also guilty. He is guilty of offering himself to people whose true nature he has a responsibility to be aware of. *Power and Innocence* (New York: Norton, 1972).

29. When unjust treatment of another cannot be denied, the *cause* of the unjust treatment can be attributed to sources external to the self, such as "traits" inherent in the exploited group. E. E. Jones and R. E. Nisbett, *The Actor and the Observer: Divergent Perceptions of the Causes of Behavior* (New York: General Learning Press, 1971); W. Ryan, *Blaming the Victim* (New York: Pantheon, 1971).

30. When an aggressor group has harmed another, their members' attitudes toward the victim are more negative than if they had been prevented from hurting the other. The increased negativity seems to follow the infliction. T. P. Cafferty and S. Streuffert, "Conflict and Attitudes toward the Opponent," *Journal of Applied Psychology* 59, no. 1 (1974), pp. 48–53. Dissonance theory suggests that, following the performance of a given behavior, an individual may alter his attitudes to achieve consistency with the behavior he has performed. J. W. Brehm and A. R. Cohen, *Explorations in Cognitive Dissonance* (New York: John Wiley & Sons, 1962).

31. D. Thompson, "Organizational Management of Conflict," *Administrative Science Quarterly* 4 (1960), pp. 389–409.

32. Personality and conflict studies are surveyed in Richard E. Walton and Robert B. McKersie, *A Behavioral Theory of Labor Negotiations* (New York: McGraw-Hill, 1967).

33. M. A. Rahim, "A Measure of Styles of Handling Interpersonal Conflict," *Academy of Management Journal* 26, no. 2 (1983), pp. 368–76. See also R. A. Cosier and T. L. Ruble, "Research on Conflict-Handling Behavior,"

Academy of Management Journal 24 no. 4 (1981), pp. 816–31.

34. The ability of the Japanese to avoid conflict is suggested by the flexibility of the Japanese language. There are 19 ways of saying no. R. T. Pascale and A. G. Athos, *The Art of Japanese Management* (New York: Simon & Schuster, 1981). Americans seem to be less tolerant in ambiguous conflict situations than are the Japanese. J. Sullivan, R. B. Peterson, N. Kameda, and J. Shimada, "The Relationship between Conflict Resolution Approaches and Trust—A Cross-Cultural Study," *Academy of Management Journal* 24 no. 4 (1981), pp. 803–15.

35. L. L. Cummings, D. L. Harnett, and O. J. Stevens, "Risk, Fate, Conciliation and Trust: An International Study of Attitudinal Differences among Executives," *Academy of Management Journal* 14, no. 3 (1971), pp. 285–304. For a survey and bibliography on trust, see "Social and Interpersonal Trust," special issue of *Humanitas* 9 no. 3 (1973).

36. Richard E. Walton and Robert B. McKersie, "Behavioral Dilemmas in Mixed-Motive Decision Making," *Behavioral Science* 11 (1966), pp. 370–84.

26

Managing Conflict

How many times did you "run away from home" when you were young? A child faced with the stress of conflict between self and a justice-dispensing parent, or a strict teacher, or a bigger, tougher classmate, is likely to flee. Some might make it out of the state, but most stop at the town line or the next block.

Flight is probably the most common means of dealing with any conflict.[1]* Such avoidance is usually accompanied by psychological conflict between needs for safety, social esteem, and self-respect, but various rationalizations are advanced to alleviate guilt. We may simply reexamine our "real" desires and "rationally" conclude that overt conflict is not worth whatever we thought we wanted.[2] Or we may convince ourselves that postponing conflict is desirable in order to prepare for the struggle. We sometimes delude ourselves that our objectives are so noble that we had better not run the risk of losing a premature and uneven conflict. Finally, we may feel that conflict avoidance is more mature and reasonable than "childish" argument. Knowing whether these judgments are sincere or self-serving rationalization is extremely difficult, of course. Nevertheless, flight is sometimes an effective and legitimate way to avoid conflict. A manager may not always have this opinion, however.

Assuming that flight is neither possible nor desirable, there are other general mechanisms for handling conflict.[3] Five stand out: dominance, hierarchical decisions, appeal procedures, system restructuring, and bargaining. These approaches to conflict resolution will be discussed in this chapter.

Dominance

The simplest conceivable conflict solution is elimination of the other party—to force opponents to flee and give up the fight or to slay them. The vehicle for this solution is dominance. Dominance can be developed through individuals, coalitions, or majorities.

Individual Dominance

Many creatures settle conflict by individual dominance based on fighting ability or physical strength. (See Figure 26–1.) Thus conflict over territory or prospective mates results in the strongest or most aggressive obtaining their individual desires while simultaneously promoting the survival of the species. Under such circumstances, "the strategy of conflict centers about injuring the other party without simultaneously injuring the self, while inhibiting and defending against retaliatory injury from the opponent."[4] The process is not as bloody as might be expected. Most animals, including humans, replace actual elimination of the losing rival with symbolic injury. Aggression is checked when both parties agree which one is the loser, and the loser follows the rules and withdraws from the conflict. The loser goes elsewhere to compete with less formidable foes. Among some species the loser may remain, but must never again strive for leadership and must demonstrate obeisance to the rival who defeated him or her by symbolic acts of subservience.[5]

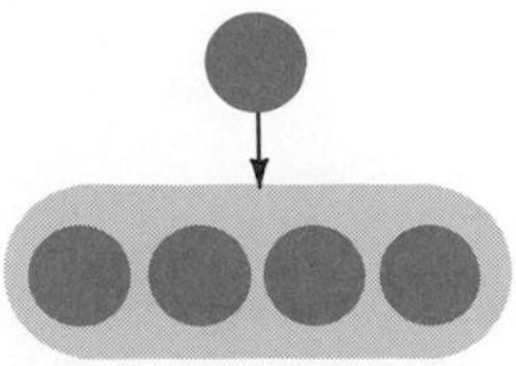

By virtue of formal authority, a manager sometimes can exercise dominance and

FIGURE 26–1

Individual Dominance

---

* Notes and references will be found at the end of this chapter.

dismiss one or more of the conflicting parties. Such a step seems simple and complete. "Fire him" is as tempting a solution to modern executives as "off with his head" was to the Red Queen in Wonderland.[6] Nonetheless, to regard all problems as people problems is too limited. Many conflict situations are not solved by putting a new employee in the position.[7] Marketing specialists and credit analysts tend to fight regardless of whether they are nice guys or SOBs. The conflict rests in the relationship of their jobs. Besides, excessive personnel shifts aggravate stress.

There is no question that judicious personnel selection and transfer are essential managerial techniques. At times a manager may successfully alleviate stress and conflict by shifting and replacing people. Primarily, however, the manager must work with the present subordinates and develop stress-absorbing and conflict-resolving mechanisms.

"This is a recording. You're fired."
From *The Wall Street Journal,* with permission of Cartoon Features Syndicate.

To promote short-run cooperation and to buy time for more fundamental conflict resolution, a manager may assume the burden of conflict and take it away from the subordinates. Thus she may tell competing subordinates that resolution does not rest on their level or her level, but she will represent their interests upward in order to obtain more resources or a different distribution. Meanwhile, the subordinates should drop their fight and get on with the job. Such an approach looks dangerously like buckpassing, but if the leader succeeds he reinforces his influence with his subordinates. A manager should be able to serve as a conflict sponge from time to time by encouraging subordinates to redirect their antagonism from among themselves and onto him.[8] President Harry Truman's observation of being able to stand the heat in the kitchen applies if you want to be a manager. The manager who can maintain calm composure and grace under pressure can give a strong impression of competence and effectiveness.

Coalition Dominance

The prerevolution Russian Bolsheviks' faith in ultimate victory rested less on Marxian inevitability than on a belief that a minority coalition could prevail if it were willing to work harder, longer, and smarter than anyone else. Coalitions of two or more persons are common because they can generate support out of proportion to their numbers. Even the presence of just one other supporter lends substantial strength to an individual's position.[9] No complex organization can function without a coalition that consolidates power around a central figure.[10] Failure to establish an executive coalition in a large organization can lead to slow decision making and even paralysis due to excessive interpersonal conflict. (See Figure 26–2.)

Examination of business career paths suggests that sponsor-protege coalitions are established by the most upwardly mobile people.[11] Mobile young managers are sensitive to what superiors have promotion potential and are effective in attaching themselves to these climbers. The superior is interested in forming a coalition that maximizes the number of others he or she controls. The subordinates strive to form a coalition that will produce the greatest return to them. This will be a group just large enough to win. It will resist the inclusion of excessive members.[12]

Majority Dominance

A manager may endeavor to develop such a majority consensus that the nonconforming minority possesses so little power so as to safely be ignored. (See Figure 26–3.) The minority is expected to withdraw or remain quiet. Historically, the most common device for developing such majority coalitions has been by introducing transcendent objectives. The great leader renders existing conflict irrelevant by defining a new superordinate objective that unites the conflicting parties. This objective should be highly appealing to members of the groups in conflict, and they must recognize that it cannot be attained by the resources and energies of the groups separately.[13] For example, politicians have long united squabbling followers by pointing out a common enemy who would destroy them all unless they fight together (think of George Washington and Europe, Fidel Castro and the United States, Mao Tse-tung and the Soviet Union). Or the leader may articulate the serious internal problems facing everyone, problems of such gravity that chaos will result unless petty dissension is dropped in favor of cooperative behavior (think of Franklin Roosevelt and the Great Depression, Lyndon Johnson and civil rights).

At a more mundane level, a manager can alter the reward system so that contending parties are rewarded for their cooperative performance rather than their individual behavior. For example, rather than rewarding production department managers for performance on their departmental budgets, a plantwide cost index could be tied to a plantwide bonus. The intent is to create an objective to which all parties are

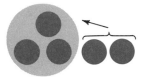

FIGURE 26–2

Coalition Dominance

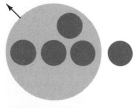

FIGURE 26–3

Majority Dominance

committed and that requires cooperative behavior for achievement. Openness to superordinate objectives and willingness to cooperate depends more on positive motivation than on negative.[14] Fear and distress is less motivating to cooperation than high performance and hoped-for even better results.

Unfortunately, there is a limit to such expansion of objectives. Where the transcendent objective becomes too large and encompasses too many individuals, it loses its motivating force. Each individual feels too small to really affect the whole; each one thinks objective achievement does not significantly reflect his or her personal efforts. Hence, one may give up. The individual worker or even a whole production department may not see an intimate relation between performance and plant bonus. Nonetheless, the fact that this technique of transcendent, unifying objectives is used by demagogues and dictators as well as saints and democrats testifies to its potency as a mechanism for managing conflict.

Hierarchical Decision Making

One of the great innovations was the transfer of conflict management from a dominance basis to hierarchical appeal. For some scholars, the development marks the beginning of civilization.[15]

Appeal to God or Chance

Initially, the shift was more philosophical than physical. The battle went on, but it was assumed that God's might was on the side of the right, that the human combat was just the vehicle for God's will. The efficiency of determining the deity's wishes in less contentious ways was recognized some time ago, and the stars, animal entrails, and tea leaves all have served as communication media. Rationalists consider such appeals superstitious, but this is beside the point. Appeal to even a fictitious god made a major contribution to human advancement through its more efficient conflict management. (See Figure 26–4.)

Appeal to chance also serves the same purpose, even if it is less philosophically and religiously satisfying. A chance event, such as throwing dice or drawing straws, is used to indicate which will dominate. The loser is expected to withdraw actually or symbolically.

Appeal to Positional Authority

The difficulty with a simple appeal to God or Lady Luck is that tremendous faith is necessary for belief that justice is being dispensed. Being of relatively little faith, civilized humans began to look for justice in conflict management through more rational ways. Thus was born the idea of a judge or hierarchical superior who would resolve conflicts. The ancient tale of Solomon and the two competing mothers is the prototypical example. A person in a recognized superior position is to listen to the conflicting parties, then decide who is correct. (See Figure 26–5.)

If the principles of chain of command and unity of command are followed in organizations, any two people in conflict can find the common superior who links

FIGURE 26–4

Appeal to God or Chance

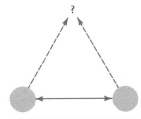

FIGURE 26–5

Appeal to Positional Authority

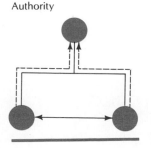

FIGURE 26–6

Common Superior as Conflict Resolver

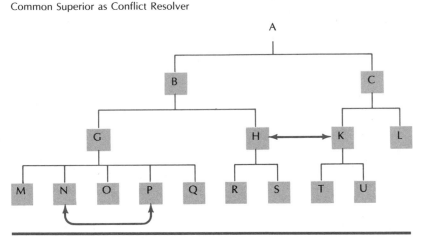

them. The superior can deal with the conflict. Thus in Figure 26–6, if N and P are in disagreement, their common superior G can act as conflict resolver. If H and K are in conflict, their common superior, A, can act as a judge in rendering a just decision and exercising the authority to enforce it.

The judicial system of courts, attorneys, judges, and juries is an elaboration of the basic intention to provide added protection to the defendant and to promote wisdom and justice. The central feature is the same—the provision for difficult decisions through a judicial-bureaucratic-hierarchical structure. Certain persons are designated as having the authority and responsibility to make certain difficult and sometimes unpopular decisions.

With all the attacks today on hierarchical authority systems, it is well to remember the central fact that this system was an enormous step forward in conflict management. No more efficient conflict management mechanism has been developed, and this is probably the greatest contribution of hierarchy.

The hierarchical decision maker still has an important role, but it is shrinking. Optimal performance utilizing this mechanism depends on a happy congruence of authority, knowledge, wisdom, and subordinate respect. When the decision maker cannot understand the issues, or the conflicting parties do not believe he or she does or do not respect the superior's authority, that person's ability to resolve conflict is sharply curtailed. People will not accept the superior's judgment. They will attempt to fight it out without the judge; they will try to eliminate each other like gang leaders contending over turf. Of course, a hierarchical superior can resort to his or her own dominance to force acceptance, but his sharply undermines the efficiency of the system.

The American court system faces this crisis. Simple case overload introduces delays before the conflict mechanism can act, and justice long delayed is not justice. In addition, substantial segments of society do not recognize the nation's laws as

"And don't go off whining to some higher court!"

From *The Wall Street Journal,* with permission of Cartoon Features Syndicate.

their laws and do not respect or recognize either the judge or the jury's decisions. Most organizational managers do not yet face problems of such great magnitude, but their ability to resolve conflict by hierarchical decisions is similarly being eroded by the declining effectiveness of traditional authority.

An additional problem for hierarchical conflict management in organizations is that the neat departmental boxes and lines are breaking down. Boundaries are becoming indistinct, and systems are expanding so that more people who do not have a definite common superior to whom they can appeal are in conflict. Who is the common superior of college alumni and administrators? Of government regulatory agencies and business executives? Of Ralph Nader's "raiders" and company management? Or indeed, of a corporate president and dissenting vice presidents when the board of directors is mainly an inside board? A dramatic increase in unofficial advocacy groups has characterized our society in recent years. Concern for the poor, for minorities, and for the environment has expressed itself in autonomous groups making demands on older, more formal organizations. Such confrontations are increasing, and they are ill-suited to the traditional judicial-bureaucratic mode of conflict management.

Open-Door Appeal

Hierarchical decisions are only as good as the managers are wise and just—and have the time to judge. Unfortunately, optimum conditions do not always prevail, so appeal mechanisms have therefore been developed to supplement the hierarchical process.[16] Employees who think that their problem has not been handled properly by their immediate boss may have an open door to a higher manager. As in Figure 26–7, unhappy employee E may be able to appeal to A, who can make a decision binding on B and E. This is termed an *open-door policy* by many firms that require A at least to listen to the merits of the employee's case.[17]

FIGURE 26–7

Open-Door Appeal

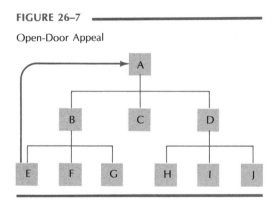

This right of appeal is a fine supplement to hierarchical decisions, but there are problems with it. The higher superior A may be so busy that she or he does not appreciate E's approach. A may even be angry with B for not handling the problem satisfactorily but is still likely to affirm B's influence downward. If A were to override B too frequently, everyone would bypass B. In addition, B may so resent being bypassed by "troublemaker" E that B holds a grudge. For both these reasons, E may conclude that appealing to A runs a grave risk—A would probably only rubber stamp B's judgment anyway.[18]

Appeal to Arbitration

To provide greater impartiality and protection, an independent arbitrator, X, may be engaged to listen to E's appeal, gather information, and render a decision binding on A, B, E, and the organization, as in Figure 26–8.[19] Such a judge can be a trained specialist with the professional reputation to make unbiased decisions.

The assumption is that X will make a better judgment than the common superior because he or she has fewer operational pressures and is less emotionally involved. Appealer E may believe panel X will give the fairest hearing if the panel is composed of a variety of people, including E's peers, H, J, and K. Such panels are common in civil service proceedings in government.

FIGURE 26–8

Appeal to Arbitration

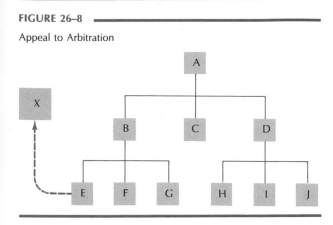

The use of arbitrators is best known in labor-management relations. They handle grievances in a manner that avoids a strike. Under such arrangements, arbitrators are hired in advance under mutual agreement of the two parties. However, an arbitrator doesn't enjoy tenure; one who renders judgments that distress either party is unlikely to be retained for another contract period. Thus even an arbitrator is not totally independent. Still, most arbitrators believe that the only proper way to judge cases is to call them as they see them—without regard to personal consequences.[20]

Many people have advocated an expanded use of arbitration in conflict disputes.[21] It is being used increasingly in professional sports, for example. Nonetheless, most managements rightly fear loss of control if they allow arbitration to become the predominant mode of conflict resolution. It could extend to areas like investment and product design that are generally considered management's central prerogatives. Also, arbitrators tend to emphasize short-run equity and legality in their decisions rather than long-run well-being of the institution or society.[22]

The Ombudsman

The ombudsman is not directly a mechanism for conflict resolution, but because the position stands outside the hierarchical structure, he or she can facilitate communications and ensure that lower levels in the hierarchy can bring their problems up to the top.[23] (See Figure 26–9.) For example, if H thinks that he has not received proper treatment from boss C, he can go directly to the ombudsman O, who will investigate the issue and approach C or even the top executive A, to achieve a solution. Unlike an arbitrator or appeals committee, however, the ombudsman has no authority to make a decision. He or she can merely recommend. Yet the right to ask questions can lead to substantial informal authority for the ombudsman.

The ombudsman's greatest contribution is helping people get information and overcome misunderstanding.[24] People may feel less alienated because someone has expressed individual interest. The ombudsman is unlikely, however, to contribute to the resolution of major conflicts. Since he or she receives a salary from the

FIGURE 26–9

Role of the Ombudsman

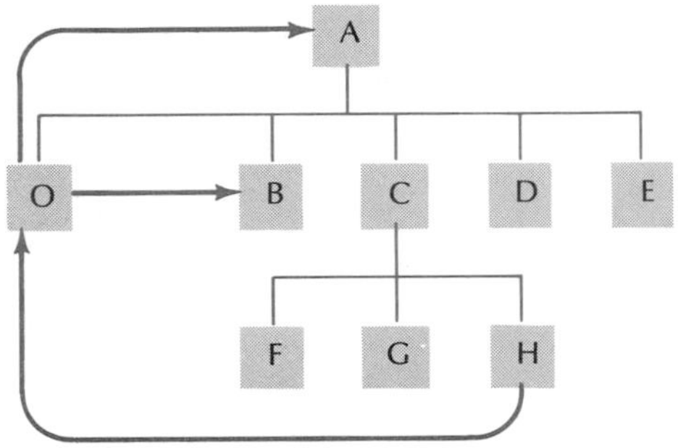

organization and possesses no formal power, A is unlikely to allow the ombudsman to deal with big issues that affect many people.

Use of ombudsmen is still relatively rare, although many governments have instituted such offices. A grieved citizen can appeal to the ombudsman and be assured that someone will consider the problem. However, private organizations have been more reluctant to create such offices because, as with arbitration, managers fear loss of control.

An organization faces a dilemma in appointing an ombudsman. Should it be someone near retirement or a young star? The senior employee will be familiar with the organization and know where to ask questions and may have the wisdom of experience that gains the confidence of people making appeals. The long-term employee, perhaps more loyal to the organization, may not use the position for personal gain. Some newspapers have assigned a very senior editor-writer to control a column used solely to comment on the honesty of the paper's editorial decisions and news coverage. Only an experienced hand could do this well.

In contrast, other organizations have appointed the most promising mid-career manager to the position. They assume that the ombudsman with a reputation of being a comer (someone who might be in command in the future) will be taken more seriously. Thus inquiries would be more likely to be answered.

The Devil's Advocate

To ensure that differences are aired, an organization can designate an individual or group to argue counter to an apparent majority.[25] (See Figure 26–10.) In the canonization proceedings in the Roman Catholic Church, a priest will be assigned to debunk the claims of miracles and thus prove that no supernatural power resides in the candidate for sainthood. Thus the unpopular position is heard. Political and business organizations can institute similar proceedings to ensure that minority views are considered at the top. Individuals or groups are assigned to take the divergent view.

Unfortunately, fulfilling this role can be even more difficult for an insider than it

FIGURE 26–10 ━━━━━━━━━

The Devil's Advocate

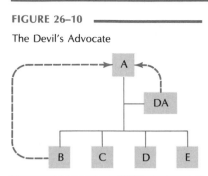

is for an ombudsman. The advocate of an unpopular position can become personally unpopular because of the message he or she bears—even though colleagues know that the advocacy is not a personal view. An independent outsider, a professor or consultant, theoretically requires less courage to tell management what it may not want to hear. Still, even outsiders can be corrupted if they like the money and free lunches that go with playing court jester to executive royalty. Such an advocate may argue, but not *too* forcefully.

System Restructuring

"An ounce of prevention is worth a pound of cure" goes an old aphorism. So it is with conflict. Rather than handle conflict after it occurs, the pattern of work relations might be redesigned to reduce the causes of conflict.[26] People can be rotated, interdependent parties can be separated or linked through a intermediary, and contentious departments might be united under a common superior.[27]

Rotating Personnel

To counter narrow loyalties and misunderstandings due to perceptual distortions, management can periodically rotate people among interdependent groups. In the short run, the newcomer is unlikely to be believed because of mistrust, and the preexisting conflict will probably not be reduced. In the longer run, however, exchanging people can create a favorable background for prevention of future intergroup conflict.[28]

Decoupling with a Buffer

Since much conflict derives from interdependence, a manager can attempt to reduce this by "decoupling" the conflicting parties as illustrated in Figure 26–11. The conflict manager reduces their dependence on common resources or provides ironclad, impersonal allocation rules. Giving each control of its own resources or

FIGURE 26–11

Decoupling with a Buffer

State A: Interdependent

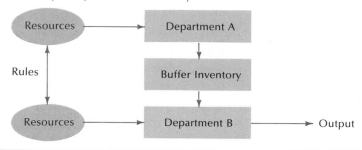

State B: Decoupled by Rules and Inventory

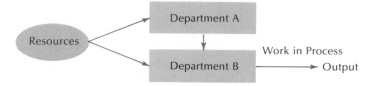

introducing large buffer inventories can be expensive but can reduce interdependence. Thus interdependent state A above may be converted into decoupled state B.

Department A sends its semifinished products into a buffer inventory, which may simply be a big bin. Department B takes goods to be finished from this inventory. Under this system, if department A has problems and falls behind, department B will not be affected because it has the inventory to draw on.

Buffering with a Linking Role

Another form of buffering can be introduced through a "linking" position, such as coordinator or integrator (state C in Figure 26–12). The integrator's role is to

FIGURE 26–12

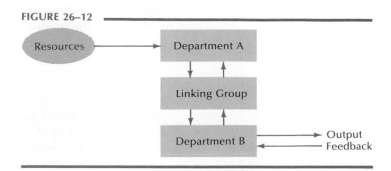

facilitate communication and coordination between interdependent and potentially conflicting departments. The individual carries no substantial authority (other than right of access) but is supposed to detect and manage differences. In the past, this role has usually been a fairly passive and low-status individual, such as an older person whose expertise was outdated. This person was not threatening to any group, and they could vent their antagonisms on him or her without fear of retaliation. It appears, however, that a stronger and more promotable person is desirable in the buffer position, someone who will confront differences rather than papering them over.[29] Examples of linking groups include: field engineers between sales representatives and design engineers; development engineers between research scientists and production managers; order fillers between chefs and waiters; public relations-press representatives between political leaders and the media; and directors of student activities between students and academic administrators.

To play such a role can be extremely stressful. Many go-betweens are caught in the cross fire. The person in this position must be able to absorb substantial flack and withstand great pressure.[30] Or the individual may be the type who will not feel the heat because of insensitivity, guaranteed security, or independent wealth.

Decoupling by Duplication

Decoupling sometimes takes the form of duplicating the facilities of another department upon which one is dependent. Research may develop a small production unit under its control for pilot runs, or a production department may recruit some engineers on its own to reduce its dependence on central engineering. Thus interdependent state A may be converted to decoupled state D in Figure 26–13.

It is tempting for managers to reduce interdependence by introducing duplicate facilities and excess resources or "organizational slack" at various stages. Extra workers, money, and machines can make life easier, but such suboptimization can also harm the whole organization.

Unifying the Work Flow

Much stress and conflict stems from violation of the old organizational principle that authority should equal responsibility. A manager feels upset because he or

FIGURE 26–13

State D: Decoupled by Duplication

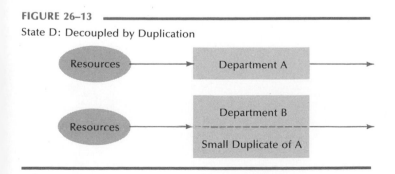

she does not control everything needed to perform the mission. Controlling "everything" is probably impossible, but the system might be restructured into more logical complete work units to bring more control under one hierarchical position, thus decreasing ambiguity. This does increase unit size of course, and additional costs for internal coordination are necessary, but the benefits of defining a hierarchical judge may outweigh the costs. Thus state A may be converted into state E in Figure 26–14.

The difference between decoupling through duplication as in state D and unifying the work flow as in state E is sometimes a matter of judgment and perception. Production feels that developing its own small research or engineering capacity is logically unifying the task, while other groups consider it wasteful slack and illegitimate empire building. The difference is subtle; but as a rule, state D evolves informally, and state E is a formal organizational change. In fact, most unified state Es may just be legitimization of previously existing duplicative state Ds.

FIGURE 26–14

State E: Unified Work Flow

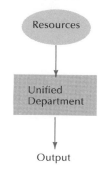

Matrix Organization

Effective managers facilitate conflict recognition and conciliation rather than smoothing it over by denying its reality or forcing solutions by superior power. Such managers recognize that conflict is inevitable if they create a climate in which people express independent ideas rather than just conforming to the prevailing view. What is desired is that this conflict be expressed following certain rules on confrontation.

Within organizations, a matrix structure offers one means for facilitating such confrontation. The most common matrix structure is illustrated in Figure 26–15.

As we noted in Part Six, such a structure is intended to promote flexible use of specialized staff on interdisciplinary programs (e.g., a sophisticated product team

FIGURE 26–15

Organizational Matrix Structure

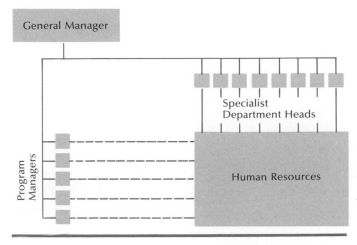

drawing on various scientists and engineers in such fields as electronics, hydraulics, operations research, and metallurgy). It is just as important to note that the matrix defines a battlefield and the combatants. It recognizes the competing interests of program and specialist departments and provides separate managers to stand up for those interests, such as short-run program completion versus long-run specialist career development.[31] The overall executive's major role is to facilitate communication and bargaining, entering into the situation as a hierarchical decision maker only when absolutely necessary.

In research laboratories, interpersonal conflict is negatively associated with performance, while technical conflict (differences of opinion on design, technology, methods, and so on) is positively associated with performance.[32] Emotional, personality-based arguments may hurt organizational effectiveness, and open disagreement and discussion of task differences help. An implied facet of the matrix approach is facilitating technical conflict while bringing interpersonal conflict out into the open where it can be seen and managed.

Of course, there is some role ambiguity for the specialists, since they are in the middle in any potential conflict. But overt conflict may be less debilitating than covert conflict. And if they actively participate in reconciling the conflicts, job satisfaction will be increased in spite of the stress.[33]

Bargaining

Bargaining may be difficult to distinguish from simple dominance. Employers once strove to eliminate unions by firing their leaders and coercing members (some still try this, of course). The crucial difference between dominance and bargaining is interdependence: in dominance, the dominator does not need the loser any longer; in bargaining, both sides recognize their mutual dependence and that they must work together after the conflict.[34] The two parties are aware that each is trying to influence the other and that agreement is a function of the power they bring to the situation and their skill as bargainers.

Bargaining power refers to another person's inducement to agree on your terms. Your bargaining power is my cost of *disagreeing,* on your terms, relative to my cost of *agreeing,* on your terms. Similarly, my bargaining power is your cost of disagreeing, on my terms, relative to your cost of agreeing, on my terms.[35] The

Bargaining

$A \leftrightarrow B$
A possesses great bargaining power and B possesses little when . . .

- A has ability to hurt B by increasing B's cost of disagreement
- A has alternatives and other collaborators which cost less than B
- B has little ability to increase A's cost of disagreement
- B has no alternatives or other collaborators which cost less than A

power may have been bestowed by an external party—such as the power over working conditions given to the manager by his or her corporate directors, or the power to negotiate agreements delegated to elected union officers by the union membership. Or it may be power growing out of the relationship between the two parties—such as the power that management gives, perhaps inadvertently, to any workers (especially to skilled workers) when it hires them and becomes dependent upon them.[36]

Bargaining reflects not a single view but a continuum from hostility to cooperation. The two ends of this continuum are distributive and integrative bargaining.[37]

Distributive Bargaining

Distributive bargaining resembles dominance, but it recognizes that the other party can hurt you and he or she will still be around after this round of conflict. In the short run, the relationship is viewed as a zero-sum game; what either side gains is at the expense of the other. Hence it is bargaining over the pieces to be cut from the pie. The method of resolution is to find the size of slice for each that reflects each side's power and ability to harm the other, without totally disrupting the relationship.[38] Each side attempts to inflate its projected power and willingness to endure injury while endeavoring to discover the other's true minimum position. Confusion, obfuscation, and deception are inherent and necessary. In laboratory experiments in black-white relations, whites were most cooperative when blacks were described beforehand as being "very competitive."[39] The whites were *less* cooperative when the blacks were described as "cooperative." A tough reputation and stance seems to help relations.

In conflict bargaining, the party who doesn't fight tends to elicit exploitative behavior from the other. People tend to walk over "fools" who leave themselves vulnerable. Since strong retaliation tends to escalate conflict, the most cooperation arises when the response is mild retaliation.[40] Bargainers seem to concede more when the other party makes only small initial concessions than when initial concessions are large. Large concessions increase the opponent's expectations.[41] In general, "cautious trust" indicating a willingness to cooperate but also a firmness that prevents others from exploiting their cooperativeness seem to characterize people who work out cooperative relations in competitive games.[42] Finally, effective bargaining requires a certain cool rationality rather than emotional game playing.[43]

Integrative Bargaining

Integrative bargaining is a rare phenomenon. It is not a rejection of conflict because the parties still must look out for their own interests; rather it is a transcendence of conflict, the conversion from bargaining to problem solving. The focus shifts from reducing demands toward expanding the pool of resources, away from how the small pie is to be sliced toward how to bake a larger pie so that both sides can increase their welfare. Ideally, the new satisfactions are bigger than the original demands.

Seventy years ago, scientific management hoped to eliminate worker goldbricking

Distributive Bargaining

- belief that one party's gain is the other's loss
- deception necessary

———————

- honesty essential
- belief that both parties can gain simultaneously

Integrative Bargaining

and destructive conflict.[44] The new industrial engineering techniques were to be used to determine the best way to perform each task. Since the work measurement techniques were supposed to be scientific, labor and management were expected to accept them, thus eliminating argument. Bargaining could then be directed to expanding production and income so that both sides could gain. This denial of the inevitability of class conflict was typically American and idealistic. For the most part, the techniques caught on, but the philosophy was rejected. Perhaps it was too naive to expect rational agreement on distributing limited resources, regardless of how large they are absolutely. Nonetheless, it may not be too much to expect collaborative efforts to improve the pool of resources upon which both sides must draw. Then the basis could shift to distributive bargaining.

Keeping the two approaches separate is a problem, however; the attitudes of distributive bargaining tend to poison the climate for integrative bargaining. In addition, entering a bargaining situation with an integrative perspective can be very dangerous if the other side views it from the distributive side.[45] Integrative bargaining depends on candid disclosure, which reduces the possibility of bluffing, thereby handicapping distributive bargaining and exposing one party to the other's exploitation.

Explicit and Tacit Bargaining

Explicit bargaining occurs when the parties know they are bargaining and have instituted formal procedures for doing so. Their communication lines are open enough to admit that an adversarial situation exists and that they need to talk.

In contrast, tacit bargaining occurs when the parties are not aware of their need to bargain and do not acknowledge their interdependence. Veiled manipulation efforts will occur, but open confrontation is unlikely.

In general, conflict resolution is more promising when bargaining is explicit and integrative rather than tacit and distributive.[46] Figure 26–16 summarizes the four modes of bargaining.

Mediating

A manager may allow and encourage conflicting subordinates to bargain directly.[47] One who does this will have to mediate from time to time. The purpose of a mediator

---

FIGURE 26–16 ━━━━━━━━━━━━

Types of Bargaining Relationships

Qualitative Nature	Mode of Bargaining	
	Tacit	*Explicit*
Integrative	Informal, cooperative bargaining	Formal, cooperative bargaining
Distributive	Informal, competitive bargaining	Formal, competitive bargaining

is not to decide who is right or what is just (an arbitrator or judge does that). Rather, a mediator has these objectives:[48]

> To stop the spiral of conflict by eliminating surrender as a demand and by encouraging each party to acknowledge that they have injured the other (in effect, to grant some justification for the other's hostility to them).
>
> To promote more authentic communications.
>
> If requested, to suggest possible solutions.

Central to conflict resolution is the repair of previous injury and protection against future harm. Conciliation therefore attempts to discontinue conflict without either side demanding or offering surrender. By discovering and communicating the true positions of the parties, the mediator assists them in confronting their real differences and discovering their common problems.[49] As we have seen, the major tragedy in some conflict is that efforts to injure the other party dominate the issues dividing the two. Hence conflict shifts from item to item, philosophy to philosophy, and the original substantive differences may be forgotten. The mediating manager's great contributions can be to return the conflict to the real issues and to articulate the potential damage on all parties if conflict continues.[50] When handling conflict, a mediator should:

> Confront, invite differences.
>
> Listen with understanding rather than evaluation.
>
> Clarify the nature of the issues.
>
> Recognize and accept feelings.
>
> Suggest procedures for resolving differences.
>
> Cope with threats to reasonable agreement.

The mediator also needs synchronization in confrontation; that is, being able to make a judgment that the parties are both ready to confront each other and potentially willing to communicate. Premature confrontation may only promote escalation (a phenomenon known to astute national leaders, who delay summit conferences until the potential for agreement is high). Rejection of one party's overture to talk is viewed as particularly demeaning and as "justifying" strong attack from the rejected party (an event that has characterized many recent conflicts—Israel and Egypt, United States and North Vietnam, Pakistan and India, Iraq and Iran).

The essence of successful mediation is making the warring parties realize that they are dependent on each other and must find an area of common agreement.[51] Such an approach assumes that the issues to be resolved are objective and substantive, not merely reflections of irrational behavior of the contending parties. An objective definition of the problem agreed upon by both sides prior to work on solutions may be the single most important step in resolution. Upon this common definition can sometimes be built a transcendent objective. Substantial laboratory research under conditions in which two parties *apparently* want to maximize their individual incomes indicates that many choices (almost half) are made not to maximize personal income but to decrease the competitor's income.[52] Relative standing seems more important than absolute benefits. If the mediator can stretch the minds of quarreling individuals or groups so they can see how their parochial viewpoints fit into a much larger system, a higher understanding may be developed that integrates seemingly diverse goals. This sense of shared goals is critical.

Internal Organizational Bargaining

Managers increasingly will have to face the anxiety of presiding over conflicts below them as well as participating in bargaining themselves. Some will see bargaining as an improvement over dominance because autonomous individuals can look out for their own interests and manage their own affairs.[53] They are less dependent on a superior to resolve their difficulties. This is probably true, but the problem often is that people new to bargaining attempt to overly dominate the other parties, so that coordination breaks down and the effects of conflict spread. The emphasis tends to be on distributive rather than integrative bargaining. This is the current state in many institutions where the parties have just begun to deal with each other: students and deans, players and coaches, professionals and government bureaucrats, even enlisted personnel and officers. This is similar to the early days of labor-management negotiations before some unions and employers came to recognize the commonality of their problems.

However exasperating collective negotiations are, they represent one of the most important mechanisms of conflict management. At its best, such bargaining signifies recognition and acceptance by the conflicting parties of each other's competing claims on resources within an orderly framework of law and custom. It appears that this mechanism will be expanded to many areas beyond labor and management relations. The activities of most information advocacy groups are initially disruptive because they bring submerged issues to the surface, where inevitably they clash with established institutions and contrary public opinion. For this reason, they often meet with opposition and repression. But as they gain legitimacy and develop support, they will represent another means of resolving conflicts between minority interests and the dominant cultures.

SUMMARY

We have considered various social mechanisms that have been developed for managing conflict in addition to dominance: chance events, hierarchical decisions, appeal procedures, changing role demands, rotating personnel, decoupling, buffering, duplicating, unifying, distributive and integrative bargaining, and mediating.

A manager can play several roles in managing conflict. One might be a judicial-bureaucratic deci-

sion maker (although this aspect may be declining in importance). One might restructure the system by decoupling, buffering, or unifying contending departments. One might introduce superordinate objectives that transcend the conflict or shift it to a higher level, thus unifying the parties. One might even facilitate bargaining by designing an appropriate matrix structure and acting as mediator.

Humans have always been tempted to resort to

simple dominance to handle conflict. Violence and war are not necessarily more common today than in the past, but we can afford them less because the complexity and interdependence of modern life mean that such solutions are not restricted to the people directly involved. Others are drawn in. In the sparsely populated and independent American frontier, two men reconciling their problems via the ubiquitous gun was sad, but it affected few people. Such behavior today threatens chaos. Accordingly, it is of ever-increasing importance that we make alternative conflict management systems work. Unfortunately, these systems also have problems.

It is imperative that we come to see bargaining not as a game to be won or lost but as a problem-solving process; that we develop a new "philosophy of losing" in America—a philosophy that sees exchange in bargaining not as a defeat but as a continuous process of conflict resolution.[54]

We desperately need more effective conflict management. All of our mechanisms face difficulty because of changing patterns of authority and respect, because of the emergence of social action groups promoting change, and just because of the large volume of conflicts to be managed. We need to utilize existing methods more effectively and to develop novel systems.[55] In few areas is human ingenuity more critical, and in none will change be more difficult to achieve.

REVIEW QUESTIONS

1. Why is flight so attractive and common as a means of dealing with conflict?

2. What other general conflict management techniques exist?

3. What is individual dominance as a conflict solution? How does it manage conflict?

4. How can a manager serve as a conflict sponge?

5. What is coalition dominance? How does it manage conflict?

6. What is majority dominance? How does it manage conflict?

7. How can a leader-manager develop majority dominance?

8. What are the limits of transcendent objectives in conflict resolution?

9. How does appeal to God or chance manage conflict?

10. What is judicial management? How does it manage conflict?

11. What is the relation of chain of command, unity of command, and appeal to positional authority?

12. What undermines the effectiveness of judicial management as a conflict management technique?

13. What is an open-door right of appeal?

14. What is arbitration? What are its limitations?

15. What is an ombudsman? How does he or she manage conflict?

16. What is the weakness of an ombudsman for conflict management?

17. What does a Devil's advocate do? Why is it a difficult role?

18. What is system restructuring? How does it manage conflict?

19. What is decoupling as a means of conflict solution? How does it manage conflict?

20. What is buffering with a linking role? How does it manage conflict?

21. How does duplication reduce conflict?

22. How does unifying the work flow reduce conflict?

23. How does a matrix organization relate to conflict?

24. What increases bargaining power? What decreases it?

25. What is the difference between distributive and integrative bargaining?

26. Why is distributive bargaining characterized by obfuscation?

27. What is the danger of attempting to bargain reasonably and in an integrative manner?

28. What does a mediator attempt to do? How does he or she do it?

Notes and References
on Managing Conflict

1. Erich Fromm, *The Anatomy of Human Destructiveness* (New York: Holt, Rinehart & Winston, 1973).

2. J. T. Tedeschi, B. R. Schlenker, and T. V. Bonoma, "Cognitive Dissonance: Private Ratiocination or Public Spectacle?" *American Psychologist* 26 (1971), pp. 685–95.

3. On various modes of resolving conflict, see Louis R. Pondy, "Organizational Conflict: Concepts and Models," *Administrative Science Quarterly* 12, no. 2 (1967), pp. 296–330; R. E. Walton and J. M. Dutton, "The Management of Interdepartmental Conflict: A Model and Review," *Administrative Science Quarterly* 14, no. 1 (1969), pp. 73–84; and M. Deutsch, *The Resolution of Conflict* (New Haven, Conn.: Yale University Press, 1973).

Robert R. Blake and Jane S. Mouton suggest five possible methods of resolving conflict: withdrawal, smoothing, compromise, forcing or win-lose power struggle, and confrontation or problem solving. *The Managerial Grid* (Houston: Gulf Publishing, 1964). The last approach seems to be the most effective and satisfying. R. J. Burke, "Methods of Resolving Interpersonal Conflict," *Personnel Administration* 32 (1969), pp. 48–55.

Business students tend to see withdrawing and compromising as significantly more desirable methods than do experienced managers. In turn, the experienced managers see confronting as significantly more desirable than do business students. See R. J. Burke, "Effects of Organizational Experience on Managerial Attitudes and Beliefs: A Better Press for Managers," *Journal of Business Research* 1, no. 1 (1973), pp. 21–30.

4. Lewis A. Coser, quoted in Ralph Turner, "The Public Perception of Protest," *American Sociological Review* 34 (1969), pp. 815–31.

5. Konrad Lorenz, *On Aggression* (New York: Harcourt Brace Jovanovich, 1966): A. Storr, *Human Aggression* (New York: Atheneum Publishers, 1968). One comparison of business and academic observed that conflict losers are more likely to leave the former but remain in the latter. Because of tenure, the college is more likely to have "walking wounded." Perhaps, but all organizations have individuals who have symbolically withdrawn from conflict. In the United States some people resolve their job-home conflict in favor of the latter by putting in minimal time and energy at work, and there are apathetic older managers performing meaningless tasks below their capacity. In short, we are not too effective in utilizing such losers. (How much easier it is in British politics! One of the prime minister's most comforting powers is the ability to cushion firing by ennobling the victim. A good many peers in the House of Lords are politicians put out to pasture.) J. Bensman, *Money and Sense* (New York: Macmillan, 1967).

6. H. D. Menzies, "The Boardroom at Bendix," *Fortune,* January 11, 1982, pp. 54–62.

7. One study of dismissals concludes that in all cases it was viewed as effective, and any regret was associated with not acting sooner. In no incident was there regret over termination of an employee. Great reluctance to perform this unpleasant task was evident, but never regret once the task was accomplished. J. H. Heizer, "Transfer and Terminations as Staffing Options," *Academy of Management Journal,* March1976, pp. 115–20.

8. President Lyndon Johnson, who was considering Wilbur Cohen as secretary of health, education, and welfare, received a telephone call from someone opposed because he said he thought Cohen looked like he ran a hock shop in Brooklyn, "Well," Johnson reportedly said, "I don't give a _____ what he looks like. He is one of the wisest men in this town and the most loyal. He's going to be Secretary and every anti-Semite in this country can kiss my _____."

9. S. E. Asch, "Effects of Group Pressure upon the Modification and Distortion of Judgements," in Harold

Guetzkow ed., *Groups, Leadership and Men* (Pittsburgh: Carnegie Press, 1951).

10. Abraham Zaleznik, "Power and Politics in Organizational Life," *Harvard Business Review,* May–June 1970, pp. 47–60. Zaleznik suggests that the difficulty of Semon Knudsen at Ford Motor Company in the late 1960s may be related to this. When Knudsen lost the competition for president of General Motors he could have remained, but he withdrew when Henry Ford II offered him the presidency at Ford. Knudsen lasted less than a year, however, apparently because he could not establish personal dominance and was unable to develop a strong coalition with Ford's vice presidents, who seemingly opposed him. Their coalition won. See "The Perils of a President Who is Not a Major Stockholder," *The Wall Street Journal,* September 17, 1969.

11. E. E. Jennings, *The Mobile Manager* (Ann Arbor: Bureau of Industrial Relations, University of Michigan, 1967).

12. S. B. Bacharach and E. J. Lawler, *Power and Politics in Organizations* (San Francisco: Jossey-Bass, 1981).

13. Muzafer Sherif, "Superordinate Goals in the Reduction of Intergroup Conflict," *American Journal of Sociology* 63, no. 4 (1958), pp. 349–56; R. Dynes, "The Absence of Community Conflict in the Early Phases of Natural Disaster," in *Conflict Resolution: Contributions of the Behavioral Sciences,* ed. C. G. Smith (South Bend: University of Notre Dame, 1971); and J. D. Hunger and L. W. Stern, "An Assessment of the Functionality of the Superordinate Goal in Reducing Conflict," *Academy of Management Journal,* December 1976, pp. 591–605.

14. J. R. Schermerhorn, "Openness to Interorganizational Cooperation," *Academy of Management Journal,* June 1976, pp. 225–36.

15. S. Piggott, ed., *The Dawn of Civilization* (New York: McGraw Hill, 1961).

16. On appeal systems and due process, see William M. Evan, "Organization Man and Due Process of Law," *American Sociological Review,* August 1961, pp. 540–47; Evan, "Due Process of Law in a Government and an Industrial Research Organization," *Proceedings of the Academy of Management, 1965,* p. 115; William G. Scott, "Appeal Systems in Organizations," in *The Management of Conflict* (Homewood, Ill.: Richard D. Irwin, 1965), pp. 114–26; and P. Nonet, *Administrative Justice* (New York: Russell Sage, 1969).

17. The Bank of America—one of the world's largest banks, having 77,000 employees—has extensive systems to guarantee student appeal rights. A. W. Clausen is chief executive officer. An Interview with A. W. Clausen, "Listening and Responding to Employee Concerns," *Harvard Business Review,* January–February, 1980, pp. 101–114.

18. In the 1960s a small group of middle-level executives at General Motors reportedly drew up a document calling on the firm to improve its sense of public interest. They tried to obtain supportive signatures from sympathizers in the firm, but with almost no success. Everyone seemed afraid. W. Serrin, "Inside GM and the UAW," *Business and Society/Innovation,* no. 4 (1973), pp. 65–71.

19. R. Coulson, *Business Arbitration—What You Need to Know,* (New York: American Arbitration Association, 1980).

20. The speed at which arbitrators render decisions can save an organization much lost time. L. Josephs, "Arbitrators Keep Tempers Calm and Construction Moving," *The New York Times,* December 20, 1981, p. 2R.

21. Dispute boards are informal bodies used to arbitrate consumer disputes, such as disagreements with an automobile dealer. J. B. Quinn, "Dispute Boards Offer New Way to Settle out of Court," *Philadelphia Inquirer,* November 29, 1980, p. 3B.

22. J. D. Aram and P. F. Salipante, Jr., "An Evaluation of Organizational Due Process in the Resolution of Employee/Employer Conflict," *Academy of Management Review* 6, no. 2 (1981), pp. 197–204.

23. I. Silver, "The Corporate Ombudsman," *Harvard Business Review,* May–June 1967, p. 77.

24. J. O. Freedman, "What Purpose Does an Ombudsman Serve?" *Almanac of the University of Pennsylvania,* May 11, 1976, pp. 4–5.

25. T. T. Herbert and R. W. Estes, "Improving Executive Decisions by Formalizing Dissent: The Corporate Devil's Advocate," *Academy of Management Review,* October 1977, pp. 662–67; J. D. Stanley, "Dissent in Organizations," *Academy of Management Review* 6, no. 1 (1981), pp. 13–19. "The Devil's Advocate," *The Wharton Magazine,* Winter 1981–82, p. 4.

26. Eliott Chapple and Leonard R. Sayles, *The Measure of Management* (New York: Macmillan, 1961).

27. On restructuring, see J. D. Thompson and D. R. Van Houten, chap. 8, "Restructuring Role Networks," in *The Behavioral Sciences: An Interpretation* (Reading, Mass.: Addison-Wesley Publishing, 1970), pp. 143–59.

28. Robert R. Blake and Jane S. Mouton, "Reactions to Intergroup Competition under Win-Lose Conditions," *Management Science,* July 1961, pp. 420–435.

29. Paul R. Lawrence and Jay W. Lorsch, "New Management Job: The Integrator," *Harvard Business Review,* November–December 1967, pp. 142–51.

30. Richard E. Walton, J. M. Dutton, and T. P. Cafferty, "Organizational Context and Interdepartmental Conflict," *Administrative Science Quarterly,* December 1969, pp. 538–55; H. Aldrich, "Organizational Boundaries and Interorganizational Conflict," *Human Relations,* August 1971, pp. 279–93.

31. For an example of managing conflict through matrix organization, see "Teamwork through Conflict," *Business Week,* March 20, 1970, p. 44. Also see A. G. Butler, Jr., "Project Management: A Study in Organizational Conflict," *Academy of Management Journal* 16, no. 1 (1973), pp. 84–101.

32. William M. Evan, "Conflict and Performance in R&D Organizations," *Industrial Management Review* 7, no. 2 (1965), pp. 37–46.

33. Henry L. Tosi, "Organization Stress as a Moderator of the Relationship between Influence and Role Response," *Academy of Management Journal* 14, no. 1 (1971), pp. 7–20.

34. Perhaps the single strongest influence on short-run cooperativeness in competitive-conflict situations is a sense of long-term commitment to the relationship, a feeling that it will remain. E. A. Slusher, K. J. Roering, and G. L. Rose, "The Effects of Commitment to Future Interaction in Single Plays of Three Games," *Behavioral Science* 19 (1974), pp. 119–32.

35. L. Fouraker and S. Siegel, *Bargaining Behavior* (New York: McGraw-Hill, 1963).

36. David Mechanic, "Sources of Power of Lower Participants in Complex Organizations," *Administrative Science Quarterly* 7, no. 3 (1962), pp. 349–64.

37. Richard E. Walton and Robert B. McKersie, *A Behavioral Theory of Labor Negotiations* (New York: McGraw-Hill, 1967). See also, R. B. Peterson and L. Tracy, "Testing a Behavioral Model of Labor Relations," *Industrial Relations,* February 1977, pp. 35–52.

38. The worst conflict is where it actually is a zero-sum situation in which the desired resource or situation cannot be broken up. It is all or nothing, no compromise is possible. K. Zechmeister and D. Druckman, "Determi-

nants of Resolving a Conflict of Interest," *Journal of Conflict Resolution* 17, no. 1 (1963), pp. 63–88. On game theory, see Anatol Rapoport and A. M. Chammah, *Prisoner's Dilemma: A Study of Conflict and Cooperation* (Ann Arbor: University of Michigan Press, 1965), and A. Rapoport, *Two-Person Game Theory: The Essential Ideas* (Ann Arbor: University of Michigan Press, 1966).

39. G. W. Baxter, Jr., "Prejudiced Liberals? Race and Information Effects in a Two-Person Game," *Journal of Conflict Resolution* 17, no. 1 (1973), p. 131.

40. C. L. Gruder and R. L. Duslak, "Elicitation of Cooperation by Retaliatory and Nonretaliatory Strategies in a Mixed-Motive Game," *Journal of Conflict Resolution* 17, no. 1 (1973), pp. 162–74; R. J. Meeker and G. H. Shure, "Pacifist Bargaining Tactics: Some 'Outsider' Influences," *Journal of Conflict Resolution* 15 (1969), pp. 261–69; and R. Miller, "No Play: A Means of Conflict Resolution," *Journal of Personality and Social Psychology* 6, no. 2 (1967), pp. 150–56.

41. G. A. Yukl, "Effects of Situational Variables and Opponent Concessions on a Bargainer's Perception, Aspirations and Concessions," *Journal of Personality and Social Psychology* 29, no. 2 (1974), pp. 227–36; and S. Lindskold, R. Bennett, and M. Wayner, "Retaliation Level as a Foundation for Subsequent Conciliation," *Behavioral Science,* January 1976, pp. 13–20.

42. J. Santa-Barbara and N. B. Epstein, "Conflict Behavior in Clinical Families: Preasymptotic Interactions and Stable Outcomes," *Behavioral Science* 19 (1974), pp. 100–110.

43. F. L. Acuff and M. Villere, "Games Negotiators Play," *Business Horizons,* February 1976, pp. 70–76.

44. Frederick W. Taylor, *The Principles of Scientific Management* (New York: Harper & Row, 1911).

45. S. M. Schmidt and T. A. Kochan, "Interpersonal Relationships: Patterns and Motivations," *Administrative Science Quarterly,* June 1977, pp. 220–33.

46. Samuel B. Bacharach and Edward J. Lawler, *Power and Politics.* See also their *Bargaining: Power, Tactics and Outcomes* (San Francisco: Jossey-Bass, 1981).

47. Neil Chamberlain points out that a manager must also coordinate these bargains:

Because of the number of individuals and groups involved, because of the number of issues concerned of which each has his preferences, because of the requirement that with respect to any issue only one resolution can be made, applying to all affected, and because of the further requirement that the decision on any issue must be consistent and compatible with the decision on all others issues—because of all these conditions it is necessary that there be a coordinator of the bargaining.

A General Theory of Economic Process (New York: Harper, 1955), p. 228.

48. Richard E. Walton, "Third Party Roles in Interdepartmental Conflict," *Industrial Relations* 7, no. 1 (1967), p. 29.

49. G. Levinger, "Kurt Lewin's Approach to Conflict and Its Resolution: A Review with Some Extensions," *Journal of Conflict Resolution* 1, no. 4 (1957), pp. 230–339.

50. Richard E. Walton states that the optimum third-party consultant possesses the following attributes:

1. High professional expertise regarding social process.
2. Low power over prinicipals' future.
3. High control over confrontation setting and processes.
4. Moderate knowledge about principals, issues, and background factors.
5. Neutrality or balance between substantive outcome, personal relations, and conflict resolution methodology.

Although persons in the organization (i.e., peers, supervisors, personnel managers, etc.) may perform third-party functions, an external third party who is consultant to the organization will more likely possess a balance of desirable attributes and thus be a more viable candidate to perform the third-party function. *Interpersonal Peacemaking* (Reading, Mass.: Addison-Wesley Publishing, 1969).

51. H. Henderson, "Toward Managing Social Conflict," *Harvard Business Review,* May–June 1971, pp. 82–90.

52. A. Scodel et al., "Some Descriptive Aspects of Two-person, Non-Zero Sum Games," *Journal of Conflict Resolution* 3 (1959), pp. 114–19. When two parties are in competition where the potential rewards are much greater to one than to the other, they manifest less cooperation than where potential benefits are equal. Concern with relative outcomes, and in particular concern with being surpassed by the other, rather than maximization of own incomes is the primary motivating factor. J. P. Sheposh and P. S. Gallo, Jr., "Asymmetry of Payoff Structure and Cooperative Behavior in the Prisoner's Dilemma Game," *Journal of Conflict Resolution* 17, no. 2 (1973), pp. 321–33.

53. D. W. Ewing, "How to Negotiate with Employee Objectors," *Harvard Business Review* (January–February 1983), pp. 103–110.

54. G. W. Taylor, "Ideas for Social Change," (The Hague: World Academy of Art and Science, 1966).

55. R. Likert and J. G. Likert, *New Ways of Managing Conflict* (New York: McGraw-Hill, 1976).

Discussion Questions and Exercises on Managing Change and Conflict

Discussion Questions

1. Thomas Loundsbury once said, "We must view with profound respect the infinite capacity of the human mind to resist the introduction of useful knowledge." What are the factors influencing the adoption of an innovation?

2. Why is balance between stability and change essential in any organization?

3. As the last exercise in the training program of a large electronics company, a team of programmers, systems engineers, and salespeople are given 48 hours (even over a holiday weekend) to prepare a complete sales proposal. The preparation is extensive and difficult, leaving little time for sleep or relaxation. Why might management impose such an exercise?

4. An old-fashioned, hard-nosed manager might argue that our discussion of change is ridiculous. "The boss is the boss. His job is to decide what change is desirable and to tell subordinates to do it. If they don't respond, the boss should replace them with people who will." What are the pros and cons of such an attitude?

5. An organizational theorist observes that "many times the reward system pays the staff group or the consultant for changes (regardless of necessity), but those in line positions are not in any way rewarded for change and therefore resist it." How does this affect organizations?

6. The large U.S. automobile companies tended to respond to the challenge of small import cars with great difficulty. In the face of rising purchases of foreign cars by Americans, why were the U.S. firms so slow to create new models that were competitive?

7. A study of graduate business schools suggests that curriculum innovation is more likely to occur in the good regional schools rather than the national prestige institutions or in local evening programs. How would you explain this phenomenon?

8. We are often reminded that we live in an age of increasingly rapid change—technological, economic, social, political, and legal. One consequence is that most organizations face an ever-more-dynamic environment. Some organizations appear to be able to adjust relatively more effectively than others by making appropriate changes and innovations. What are some organizational characteristics that are likely to characterize the more adaptable organizations, as compared with those that adapt less well?

9. Why are some organizations characterized by blindness and dishonesty in refusing to confront the necessity for change?

10. Conservative, establishment-type alumni frequently criticize university and college faculties for being too radical and revolutionary. Yet many of their students criticize the same faculty as being too conservative and establishment oriented. Why this apparent contradiction?

11. Many young people call for organizational changes, but almost as many decry organizational and office politics. In its essence, however, change *is* politics. Why this apparent contradiction?

12. What are the advantages of changing organizational behavior by modifying structural factors rather than people?

13. A new college president desires to improve the caliber of teaching at his institution. He can exhort his faculty members to devote more attention to preparing for class and making themselves available to students. But what systemic changes can he initiate to improve education?

14. In the 1980s there appears to be a movement back to more conservative curricula in American high-school and college education. The progressive changes of the 60s and 70s are frequently being rejected or sharply modified. How would you explain this reaction?

15. The production and sales departments in many firms are often at odds. What might be the differences in the views of these two departments?

16. In many businesses, conflict rages between the credit manager and marketing managers. Regardless of personality differences or similarities, people in these positions often fight. Why?

17. "If people would only communicate. . . ." goes a cliché. The assumption is that good communication would overcome most conflict. What are the strengths and weaknesses of this view?

18. What are the advantages of an organization "legitimizing" conflict by dealing with it in an open and rational manner? What are the potential dangers?

19. Why do so many hierarchical organizations deny the presence of internal conflict?

20. President Harry Truman once complained that he could seldom solve any conflict by ordering people to do something. He could only "persuade" them. The president of the United States is supposed to be the most powerful person in the world. Why can't a president just solve conflict by individual dominance or judicial decisions?

21. Conflict between university students and administrators seems to have significantly decreased in the late 70s and 80s in comparison with conditions in the late 60s and early 70s. How would you explain this?

Individual Exercises

1. How do transcendent objectives reduce conflict? Describe a person or situation of which you have knowledge where this technique was utilized.

2. What are the central objectives and techniques of the mediator? Have you ever mediated a conflict (e.g., between family members, school friends, teammates, etc.)? What did you do? Did it work?

3. Describe and analyze a conflict situation in which you were involved. How was the conflict resolved?

4. Sit in a local eating establishment. Observe and plot the flow of work and interactions indicating the points of stress and conflict. What are its causes? Redesign the work flow to reduce conflict.

5. If you were a mediator called to help settle a conflict between students and administrators at your school, what general philosophy and practice would you follow? What would you attempt to do?

6. Describe a successful or unsuccessful change process you have observed or been a part of. Analyze (a) the change agent's behavior, (b) the steps in the change process, and (c) your reasons for thinking the change was successful or unsuccessful.

7. Design a change program for any organization of which you are a member (e.g., school, fraternity, club, team, school). Specify (a) your behavioral and performance objectives, (b) steps in the change process, including the factors you would modify, (c) probable sources of resistance, and (d) mechanisms for monitoring effectiveness.

8. Describe a creative act you have performed. Analyze (a) the steps in the process, (b) the factors in your situation that aided or hindered you, and (c) if and how the act was converted into an innovation or organizational change.

9. Suppose you were an all-powerful, omniscient, and benevolent ruler of your hometown. How would you go about changing the community? Specify (a) your behavioral objectives, (b) sources of resistance, and (c) steps in your change process.

10. Laboratory education (T-groups and sensitivity training) has become a popular but controversial technique for organizational and personal change. Under what conditions would you (a) recommend and (b) oppose their use in an organization?

Managerial Cases and Problems on Managing Change and Conflict

Midwestern University Medical Center (A)*

Midwestern University enjoys a reputation as one of the finest institutions of higher education. It includes a medical school and university hospital complex, which presently ranks among the top medical complexes in research quality and productivity. Its faculty in recent years has published widely in prominent journals and been successful in raising research funds from government and foundation sources. It ranks fourth on the list of medical complexes in terms of such grants. The most outstanding students compete for entry into its education and residency programs.

Seven years ago, when Thomas Simpson, M.D. (age 48) was named Dean of the Medical School (Exhibit 1 summarizes the organization at the time), the situation was different. In his (and others') opinion, the school's reputation was inflated, and the medical complex was falling behind in the rapid pace of innovation in medical research, teaching, and practice. Simpson concluded that substantial changes were required in strategy, organization, policy, and procedures.

At that time, the hospital was in a strong financial position due to high utilization of its capacity and the affluence of many of its patients. Many of the more established and mature physicians maintained dual offices in the hospital and in the wealthier suburbs. When these physicians had their patients admitted to the hospital, a substantial number would directly pay the hospital and their physicians. Patients were generally very pleased with their doctors, who earned incomes up to and beyond $100,000 per year. In addition, patients frequently praised the hospital for its medical care and patient-centered concern. James Schuyler-Jones (age 62), who was executive director

and chief administrator, prided himself on the institution's concern for patients and its ability to maintain close ties with the metropolitan area establishment. He frequently appeared in the newspaper society pages, and the hospital was perhaps the most prestigious charitable occupation for those at the top and those climbing the slopes of the social pyramid. Mr. Schuyler-Jones had fought with several medical school deans in arguing that his hospital existed primarily to care for patients, not to merely provide "guinea pigs" for faculty research or student "trial and error" learning. His personal friendship with the university president and his seniority lent added weight to his influence in the institution.

Most of the physicians who maintained offices at the university hospital had clinical (part-time) appointments at the medical school where they would teach some courses as well as help train interns and residents. For the privilege of practicing private medicine out of the medical complex, physicians would turn over 5 percent of their gross income to the university for overhead support. The complex also employed other physicians, mainly somewhat younger, who engaged in little or no private practice but concentrated on teaching and research. On the average, they were paid approximately $20,000 per year.

In Simpson's view, the weakness of the school's scholarly and scientific prestige lay in insufficient encouragement and support for research. He didn't feel the gray-haired clinical professor-practitioners really kept up with research elsewhere, much less performed any meaningful research themselves. In his opinion, they didn't set a proper example for students and younger faculty. The students were generally good as most medical students are, but Simpson felt many had aspirations limited to developing good bedside manners and that too large a proportion were the offspring of physicians, professionals, executives, and regional gentry.

Dr. Simpson sought to develop a plan that would put

---

* Parts (B) and (C) of this case are contained in the *Instructor's Manual*.

EXHIBIT 1

Partial Organization Chart of Midwestern University

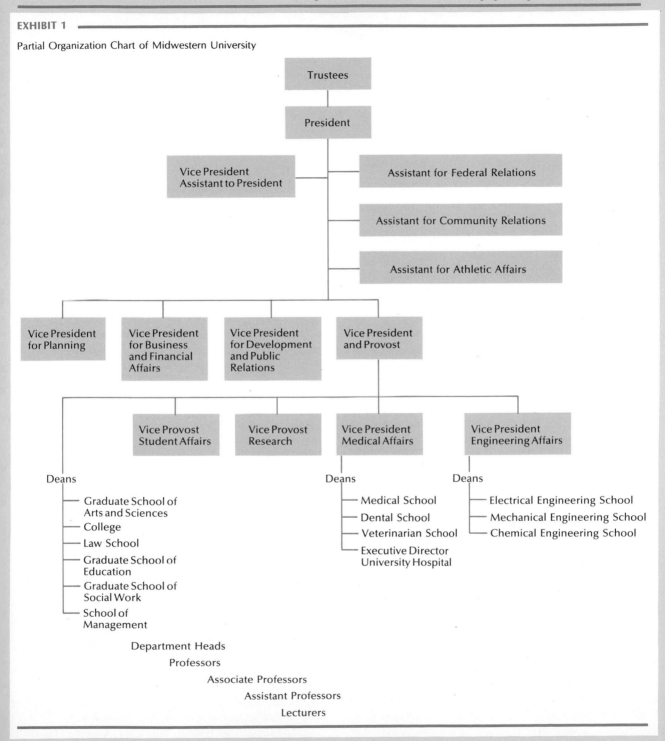

the Midwestern University Medical Complex in the forefront of research and bring scientific and scholarly prestige to the institution.

Questions on Midwestern University Medical Center (A)

1. We know that Dean Simpson succeeded. How do you think he did it? Construct a plausible scenario for the actions he instituted to bring about change.

2. Analyze these actions and the change process. How do they fit the change models discussed?

3. What resistance and conflict do you think he experienced? How do you think he dealt with the conflict?

4. Do you think the successful change created any new problems? What should Dean Simpson be concerned about now?

5. What recommendations would you make to Simpson now?

A Challenge at the Electric Company

The Metropolis Electric Company is an operating utility providing electric and gas service to the Metropolis metropolitan area. The total area served covers 2,400 square miles, with a population of 2 million. The company carries on a continuous expansion and construction program. During a recent five-year period, gross property additions and retirements amounted to $972 million and $98 million, respectively, resulting in an increase of more than 60 percent in utility plant. Capital expenditures for plant additions and improvements to meet the continuing growth in customer needs are expected to approximate $1.6 billion for the next five years. All of this expansion and construction is under the direction of the Engineering Department, which employs approximately 350 graduate engineers and 200 technical personnel. Exhibit 1 is the organization chart for the department, and Exhibit 2 lists the positions levels.

Company headquarters are located in an attractive, modern 15-story building in Metropolis City. The top executives are located on the 14th and 15th floors overlooking the whole river valley. The Engineering Department spreads over the sixth through ninth floors. On the street level is a store run by the Sales Department. Merchandise sold includes fans, refrigerators, freezers, air conditioners, heat pumps, and even radiant electrical heating systems. Sales personnel receive commissions and bonuses for good performance.

Vincent Voight was recently hired as vice president of engineering by the president because of several events over the past few months that led him to conclude that an outsider was needed. To hire an outsider at this level was completely unheard of at Metropolis, where promotions have been overwhelmingly from within. Voight had been a division director of Union Construction, Inc., one of the large international engineering construction firms.

Numerous complaints have been directed at Metropolis by environmentalists, consumer advocates, and even the Gray Panthers (a group promoting the interests of senior citizens). Simple matters, such as ugly transmission towers, have been cited as well as more serious issues of river thermal pollution downstream of ME's cooling towers. And the local newspaper had recently run a critical series on the company that began with a first page picture of ME's Country Club (a club open to *all* employers for a very nominal fee). The paper maintained that electrical rates were high because of such sybaritic luxuries as the country club as well as attractive fringe benefits including five weeks paid vacation per year.

The most serious incident at the company occurred recently at its newly completed nuclear power generating station. One of the two twin units had to be shut down because of a "nuclear accident." No one was killed or injured, and insignificant radiation was released. Nonetheless, the incident brought unwanted publicity to the firm. One of Voight's first tasks was to investigate the matter. He still wasn't sure whether the problem had been caused by operator error, equipment malfunction, or design weakness. When he toured the still-operating sister plant, however, he was struck by the obsolete control center that was only a year old. Process control technology is not Voight's specialty, but he knew that cutting-edge chemical companies use computer-aided on-line control, and ME used servo mechanisms, lights, and bells. When Voight asked his deputy John Tanner about the control center, Tanner said that they had concluded that the control system should be only incrementally advanced over that in the oil and coal fired plants because their operators would not be able to handle anything more complex.

Top management is vitally interested in safety of course but also wants to expand generating capacity to meet needs for lighting, air conditioning, and heating. Concern

EXHIBIT 1

Metropolis Electric Company: Engineering Department

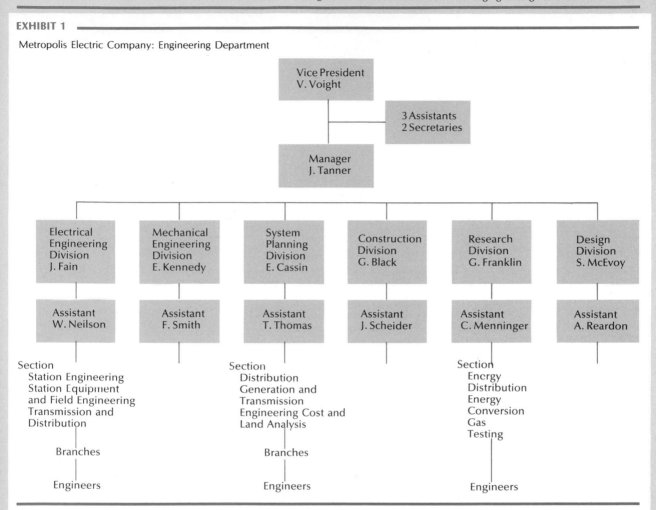

has been expressed that without more capacity the whole system may go dark some January evening when people come home from work and all turn on their lights and heat simultaneously. And the same thing could happen on a hot sultry August night when thousands of air cooling systems are turned on.

Upon walking among the engineers at work at ME, Voight was disturbed to see no computer terminals. The Engineers worked with pencil and paper making calculations with small electronic calculators. Hand sketches were taken to the Design Division where a drafter would draw a finished diagram. Voight asked Jerry Fain, the Head of the Electrical Engineering Division, why he didn't have a computer-aided design system (of course Metropolis had a large computer that was used for billing customers and preparing payroll checks, but not for engineering design).

EXHIBIT 2

Metropolis Electric Company: List of Position Levels in Engineering Department

1. Vice president
2. Department manager
3. Division manager
4. Assistant division manager
5. Section engineer in charge
6. Assistant engineer in charge
7. Branch supervising engineer
8. Senior engineer
9. Engineer
10. Assistant engineer
11. Technicians, drafters, clerks, and other nonprofessional personnel

---

EXHIBIT 3

Metropolis Electric Company: Age and Seniority Distribution of Professionals in Engineering Department

Age			Years with Company		
20–29	21%	(46 returns)	0–4	20%	(43 returns)
30–39	17	(37)	5–9	7	(16)
40–49	32	(71)	10–19	22	(48)
50–59	23	(50)	20–29	36	(86)
60–69	6	(12)	30–39	10	(21)
			40–49	4	(8)

Voight pointed out that designers in advanced electronics firms have computer terminals on their desks. They can call out already designed components from the stored memory, move them around the CRT screen with a "magic pen" into a desired configuration, add new circuits, push a button, and produce a finished drawing.

Fain said he knew about such systems and indeed had tried to hire a systems expert to install such a capability in Electrical Engineering. He had discovered, however, that the going salary for an experienced computer/scientific design person was more than the vice president of engineering earned! Voight's predecessor had argued that ME's vice president of personnel, as well as the president, would not allow them to violate the firm's salary scale.

On his own, Jerry Fain hired a young systems designer to set up the desired capability. Unfortunately, he was not successful—perhaps because he did have the necessary expertise or political skills, or perhaps because he was resented by the younger engineers because he was paid about $5,000 more per year than engineers of similar age and experience. Indeed, even the senior professionals may have resented him because, as Fain observed, "The computer man had long hair down to his shoulders while the older engineers all have crew haircuts!"

Most of the engineers and managers have graduated from local colleges (although those over 50 years of age tend to come from a more national mix of schools, including some of the most prestigious institutions). Both younger and older, however, grew up perceiving the electric company as a most desirable place to work. The age distribution is summarized in Exhibit 3. Turnover has been very low, with many remaining for their entire careers. In short, company management is pleased with the personnel situation in the Engineering Department.

As one of his first steps as vice president, Vince Voight

had a questionnaire administered to all departmental personnel. Results are summarized in Exhibits 4 through 6. Voight is wondering what to do with the survey results in the short run and how to proceed in the longer term. At the moment Voight feels very challenged (if not shocked) by the conditions at the electric company.

EXHIBIT 4

Attitude Survey

Of the following, which three would you consider the most important reasons for working at Metropolis Electric? Relative to other organizations, ME offers (mark three):

Frequency Distribution
of All Answers

31	a.	High pay
154	b.	High security
93	c.	Nice people to work with
7	d.	Low pressures to perform
10	e.	Habit, just never looked elsewhere
0	f.	Rapid promotion
2	g.	Don't think I could find another job
1	h.	High status in community
134	i.	Interesting work
35	j.	Autonomy and freedom on the job; people leave you alone
86	k.	Opportunity to solve interesting problems
33	l.	Opportunity to help people and contribute to society
30	m.	High fringe benefits
5	n.	Opportunity to have substantial control over money and people
17	o.	Other

EXHIBIT 5

Attitude Survey Results

The Marks on the Following Questions Indicate the Average Response to Each Question by People in Each of the Indicated Position and Age Categories

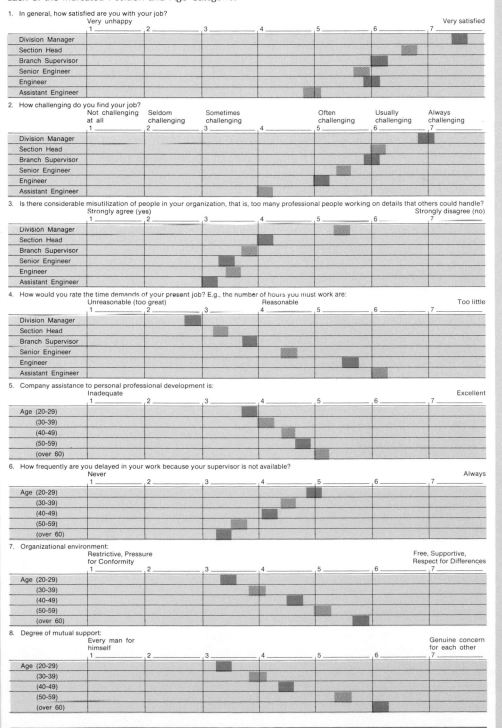

1. In general, how satisfied are you with your job?

2. How challenging do you find your job?

3. Is there considerable misutilization of people in your organization, that is, too many professional people working on details that others could handle?

4. How would you rate the time demands of your present job? E.g., the number of hours you must work are:

5. Company assistance to personal professional development is:

6. How frequently are you delayed in your work because your supervisor is not available?

7. Organizational environment:

8. Degree of mutual support:

EXHIBIT 6

Sample of Question Responses

A. *Sample of responses to question: "What is the most frustrating and dissatisfying aspect of your job?"*

1. Due to heavy work load, one never is able to do a *really good* job on any of numerous assignments. This is frustrating if you take pride in doing good work.
2. Not having time to finish a project to my satisfaction before something more urgent supersedes it.
3. Not enough time; having to abandon one job because another has higher precedence.
4. Lack of time to properly institute new procedures for new equipment.
5. Not being able to follow projects to completion. Receiving inaccurate information from other divisions. Having to pay IEEE dues. No personal benefit is received from being a member. I feel the company should pay this fee and also the PSPE dues. If an individual is willing to be a working member and spend several evenings a year of his own time attending meetings, the fees should be paid.
6. Waiting for action and/or results on my recommendations (not from my direct supervisor but from those above him).
7. The seemingly dead hand of bureaucracy and clerk-mindedness of the system.
8. The small amount of authority given to me. Almost every decision, no matter how small, must be approved at a higher level before it can be acted on.
9. My objection focuses on the mechanism which permits each level of management to modify or compromise my solutions according to their views of the problem. A nontechnical problem has as many solutions as persons attempting to interpret the problem. To get an authorization is unlikely from a probabilistic point of view. Each level reviewing a request has a probability of rejecting it. To get all persons at each level to agree is difficult.
10. Working for a supervisor whom I consider a very poor handler of personnel. He is, however, probably one of the most technically competent men under whom I have served.
11. Having to deal with a supervisor who, in my opinion, is a pathological fault-finder. The long-run net result is a slow destruction of one's confidence and self-esteem. The man is very technically competent but should not be supervising people since he refuses to apply even the most basic principles of human relations. He would make an excellent staff or research engineer but should not be entrusted with the well-being of any subordinates.
12. Taking over work which has been started by others and finding there is no way to tell how the job was being done or how information was obtained.
13. Lack of adequate record keeping by my peers, so that when they are unavailable, one can determine job status or history. Reasons why certain decisions are made are all too often kept only in the minds of those making

them. The successes or mistakes of the past (which I feel are essential to know in the present) are too often forgotten.
14. Poor and inadequate filing systems—spend too much time locating information.
15. Atrocious stenographic service. Not the fault of my present secretary—a very diligent individual. She has too many people to serve and too many extra duties.
16. The total lack of clerical and technician-grade help. Programmers, junior engineers, and keypunching are nonexistent in my area. Projects must stop in order that I take care of work which could be done by someone with much less training. Due to lack of support, projects must be constantly stopped and started so that all get attention.
17. Lack of clerical assitance to retrieve files, Xerox papers, obtain copies of drawings, etc. Limitation of job assignments to those which fit into the scope of my present branch. Inability of construction forces to complete field work because of lack of personnel.

B. *Sample of responses to question: "What company policies or conditions interfere with the performance of your job?"*

1. Upper management becomes too involved with decisions that should be made at the engineering level and approved at the branch head level. Management at the division level and above gets too involved in the details of a project. This increases the time pressure on us and restricts our efforts in carrying out the project.
2. All decisions up the line are based on outguessing of top-level opinion. It seems there is too much effort to look good rather than tell it like it is.
3. Paternalism of M.E.: "The Company is too tolerant of poor performers." "Too much coddling of inept, inefficient employees."
4. Clerical support: totally inadequate. "Also, a poor filing system currently exists—not enough room for personal files."
5. Data processing facilities: Keypunch facilities inadequate. Also, resentment exists over control of the data processing facilities by the financial department.
6. "En masse" promotions: "Nothing I do will help me get promoted."
7. Telephone arrangements are insufficient: not enough telephones per office; annoyance over the use of a single extension number for multistaffed office; M.E. directory needs to be updated.
8. Noise level in the office is annoying: "I need a place where I can go when I concentrate on a difficult problem."
9. Often I feel like I'm not treated like a professional.
10. There's a factory atmosphere here. I feel like I'm constantly being watched (e.g., strict adherence to 8:15–5:00 work hours).

Questions on a Challenge at the Electric Company

1. How would you analyze the state of morale within the Engineering Department? How does age and experience affect the situation?

2. What are the strategic problems for the company? What has apparently caused these problems?

3. What immediate recommendations would you offer the vice president of engineering? What should he do with the questionnaire results? Why?

4. What longer term recommendations would you offer the vice president? Why?

5. What recommendations would you offer the president of Metropolis Electric? Why?

Senator Theodore Kruger's Office (A)*

Theodore Kruger is a U.S. Senator representing a large midwestern state. He is now in his third term, so he is in the middle of the seniority list. Kruger is a conscientious senator and a hard worker. He especially prides himself on being responsive to constituents who call or write him. He believes it is a central responsibility to assist constituents by serving as an ombudsman to the federal government and good politics as well.

During the casewriter's visit to the office, Senator Kruger showed a clipping from a home state, small town newspaper. He had received the clipping that morning from a commercial news auditor who monitors senators' home state papers. The clipping described how the mayor had called a press conference to report that he had heard from Senator Kruger in response to the mayor's complaint about federal regulations on garbage disposal. The senator

EXHIBIT 1

Organization of Senator Kruger's Office (according to Administrative Assistant)

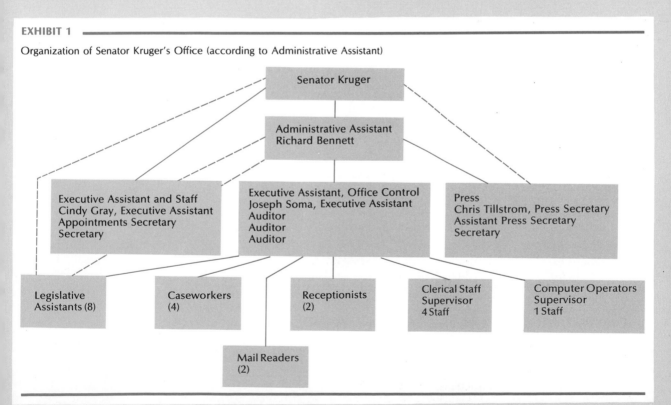

---

* Part (B) of this case is contained in the *Instructor's Manual.*

has expressed support for new regulations. The clipping ended with the mayor's comment that he had not received replies from the other senator nor from the area congressional representative. Kruger was delighted with the clipping and pointed out that in fact he had never seen the mayor's letter, that his staff had answered as they were supposed to, and that his office was organized to facilitate rapid and relevant response.

Senator Kruger's office is composed of 34 people organized as indicated in Exhibit 1. Richard Bennett, administrative assistant, is the chief mananger of the office and devotes substantial time to checking outgoing mail to en-

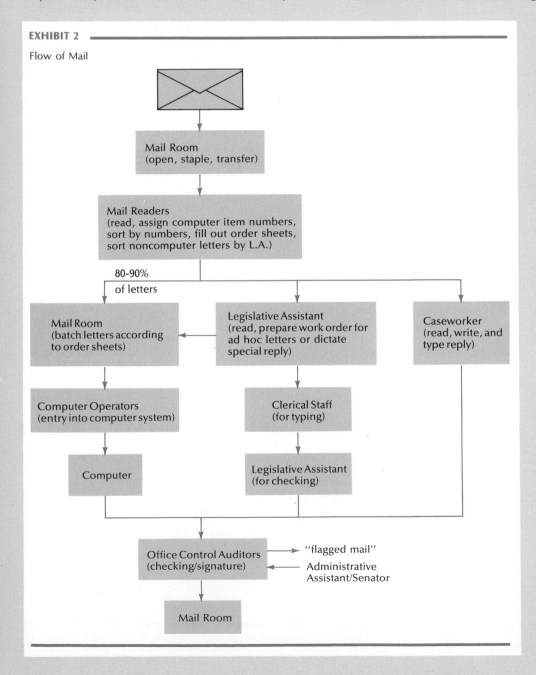

EXHIBIT 2

Flow of Mail

sure that it accurately reflects the senator's views. Bennett told the interviewer a story of how the senator was helped in defeating his predecessor during his first campaign by producing a letter signed with then-senator VanMeter's name—a letter that took a position contrary to his public statements. The former senator argued that he never saw the letter and that an aide had signed his name. The incident severely damaged VanMeter's chances so that Bennett is devoted to seeing that such an event would not occur in this office.

Cindy Gray, executive assistant, is the senator's personal secretary, she works only for the senator and with the appointments secretary, who maintains his busy schedule. They have little communication with the rest of the staff.

Joseph Soma, executive assistant, is a kind of assistant office manager mostly concerned with instituting and maintaining a computerized correspondence system. The volume of letters is so great (5,000–10,000 per week) that it would be impossible to give specific replies by individual drafting and typing. Consequently, the office utilizes a computer system composed of approximately 800 stock paragraphs that are frequently deleted, revised, or newly written to reflect current issues. When a constituent's letter is received, it is opened in the mail room and read by the mail readers. If it is a simple letter that can be answered by a single paragraph, a work order form is completed by a mail reader who indicates the appropriate stock number. If it is a complex letter, it is sent to a legislative assistant or caseworker who must then read the letter, complete the work order with paragraph numbers, or draft a unique response.

The work order contains blanks for the proper salutation ("Dear Mr. Jones," "Dear Henry," or "Dear Hank"), the numbers of the stock paragraphs to be included (e.g., 14, 122, and 433), and the closing ("Yours truly, Senator Theodore Kruger," "Sincerely, Ted Kruger," or "Cordially, Ted"). The work order and original letter go to the Computer Center, where a letter is automatically typed. Exhibit 2 illustrates the flow of mail.

The office Control Group consists of three people who read, approve, or request revisions on all outgoing correspondence after it comes from the Computer Center or office typist. Approximately 80 percent of the outgoing letters are handled through the computer, and 20 percent require individual responses manually typed. The auditors read all outgoing letters to see if they answer the constituent's questions in lay language and with a "warm tone." They indicated to the interviewer that many of the professional staff write too stiffly and in technical jargon. If an auditor doesn't like a letter, she will send it back to the originating staff with a note directing that it be revised. Sensitive mail, especially complex letters, responses to important people and proposals for new computer system stock paragraphs are "flagged" by Control and forwarded to Bennett. Bennett himself samples and reads many letters to check that they are consistent with the senator's expressed views. Responding to mail is only one of the duties of the legislative assistants, but they dislike it most. Their other activities include monitoring senate floor debate, monitoring the status of bills, committee hearings, drafting bills and amendments, advising the senator, and making recommendations on how he should vote.

The caseworkers respond to constituents' specific requests for assistance on such personal matters as lost social security checks, employment possibilities, and veterans'

EXHIBIT 3

Layout of Senator Kruger's Office

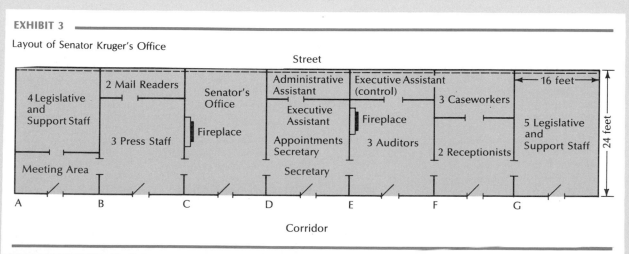

EXHIBIT 4

Data on Staff of Senator Kruger

	Office Control (4)	Press Staff (3)	Case-workers (4)	Legislative Assistants (8)	Support Staff (10)
1. Years working in the Senate	5.3	1.2	6.3	2.0	4.1
2. Years on Senator Kruger's staff	5.3	1.2	5.9	2.0	3.5
3. Age (average)	27	23	32	25	26
4. Education					
High school	1		1		8
College	3	3	3	5	2
Grad school				3	

benefits. Most of their responses are drafted individually and typed manually by themselves. They are also checked by the Control Group.

The support staff consists of various receptionists, secretaries, computer operations, mail readers, mail room personnel, and interns. All of these people are located in a suite of seven rooms in the Russell Senate Office Building as indicated in Exhibit 3 (with the exception of Computer Operations and four clerical staff who are located across the street in a converted apartment building). Other data on the staff is contained in Exhibit 4. Exhibit 5 contains excerpts from a researcher's notebook on questionnaires applied and interviews conducted in the office.

Questions on Senator Kruger's Office

1. What conflicts to you think exist in this office?

2. Analyze the causes of these conflicts.

3. Why are the legislative assistants apparently so dissatisfied?

4. What recommendations would you offer the senator to improve conditions in the office?

5. Where would you locate people in the office suite?

EXHIBIT 5

Excerpts from the Researcher's Notes (based on questionnaires and interviews)

1. This is the only office studied wherein the questionnaire responses indicate that the legislative assistants (LA) feel the least job satisfaction of any group (along with caseworkers) in the office. In most offices, the legislative professionals report the highest satisfaction. Several reasons for this condition may exist:

   a. LAs report the greatest time pressure of any other office personnel (aside from the AA who reports the most of any individual). However, great time pressure on the job doesn't necessarily lead to lower morale (as it doesn't for the AA who also reports the highest job satisfaction of any individual).

   b. LA's questionnaires report greater perception than any other group of inappropriate use of professionals. This is verified by the interviews where they offered comments such as: LA 1: "Too much clerical work! Could and should be done by someone else; takes time from legislative work I could be doing." LA 2: "Many letters could be handled effectively by someone else; they are usually routine." LA 3: "Some letters could be handled by others; they only require someone with reading comprehension."

   c. Some legislative assistants report difficulty in knowing what the senator is thinking on an issue and the basis of his decisions. They feel they have insufficient exposure to the senator, perhaps "three times a month" according to one LA. Another said, "Communications with senator poor; too little access; too long to get answers from him; wouldn't feel comfortable talking to him for a few minutes about an issue; would have to arrange a meeting with AA." A third LA indicated that the senator only gave two briefings a year for staff. And a fourth said, "Too little feedback from senator on work I've initiated; no other staff has as little access to their senator."

   To find out what the senator thinks, LAs may propose a new computer paragraph just to see what feedback they receive. Although the AA is generally perceived as accessible, some LAs are reluctant to go to him because he is so busy that they "don't want to bother him" or because they are "not comfortable in approaching him for help."

   The AA was aware that a weakness of the system at the time of the study was that he didn't see LAs very frequently and that both he and the office manager didn't

EXHIBIT 5 *(continued)*

really follow legislative matters. Apparently, the AA intends to alleviate this situation by adding a senior legislative counsel.

    d. Legislative assistants tend to feel that processing mail is given too high priority to the detriment of more substantive legislative work. Because of the weekly currency report, mail seems to take priority. As one LA said, "Work that won't show up on Mail Report has to take less priority; therefore, inadequate time is spent on legislative research and creative legislation." Some felt this situation exists because "Senator is not an active legislator and therefore no real encouragement to LAs to promote new legislation." And another LA remarked, "Senator unresponsive and unaggressive about introducing new legislation; LAs not forced to be creative."

    e. Some LAs complain about the clerical support, especially, (1) lack of typing support for intraoffice memos and reports, (2) inconsistent and frequent poor typing of manual letters, and (3) that they must personally perform too much clerical work—set up files, maintain, stamping, address labels, and so on.

    f. Finally, LAs complain about poorly defined and communicated office procedures—especially insufficient orientation and training for new legislative assistants; that is, too much "sink or swim!"

2. Substantial stress exists between legislative assistants and the control auditors. More important than the above reasons for low LA morale appears to be the relationship with the auditors.

    a. Most of the LAs resent the control operation. They perceive it as helpful to some extent in catching typo errors, but feel it is carried to extreme when the LAs judgment is questioned on substantive issues.

        LA 1: "Work flow is bogged down rather than helped by them; futile to keep going back and losing the battle with them; control would simply buck it to the office manager who would back up control 100 percent."

        LA 2: "Poor interpersonal relations with auditors.

They don't deal on a personal basis, but use a memo approach. If control people had legislative backgrounds, LA role would be facilitated. Fifty percent of the problem is in personality issues, 50 percent in the control role itself."

        LA 3: Control has added another administrative level. I spend an inordinate time putting together forms for them and doing clerical work. They are not receptive; cannot go to them for help; their solutions to administrative problems are ineffective."

        LA 4: "Their (auditors) attitude is 'picky'; they second guess you after you've spent time considering your response; their judgment is questionable. Work takes additional time. I have to walk to (auditor); she walks back and interrupts me whatever I'm doing; or I have to write memo to control explaining why I'm responding in a particular way."

    b. The concern about sending work through the control staff is echoed by press personnel who do not want their press releases to pass through the control unit.

    c. Legislative assistants don't respect the legislative experience or knowledge of the control staff. There was some feeling that they don't really understand what the LA is trying to do on specific letters: "I don't feel we have the time to answer all letters verbatim so we have to make judgments. I try to think of what the senator and AA would think and about the constituent—what's really bothering him. I may deliberately not want to answer some parts of a letter. I don't think the auditors really understand this, especially since they are not legislative people."

3. The organizational structure of the office is ambiguous with respect to the relationship between legislative assistants and the office manager/control staff.

    a. On their questionnaires, the AA, the office manager, and the auditors *all* perceived the structure in a manner essentially the same as the formal organization in the figure below.

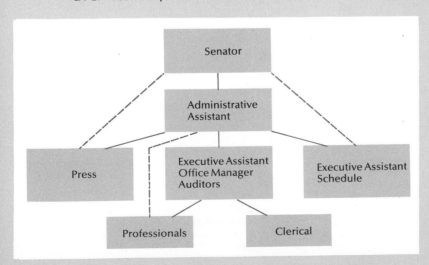

EXHIBIT 5 *(concluded)*

This shows a clear chain of command from senator through AA, office manager, control to legislative staff. It clearly implies that control is in a supervisory relationship to the legislative professionals. The AA stated that at first he envisioned control as a kind of "staff," but now he has used the term "supervisor" to an LA giving an auditor a hard time—supervision in the sense that if there is a difference of opinion, control has the last word.

b. In contrast, not a single legislative assistant perceived the organization as above. Their perception generally put the office manager/control staff to the side as direct superiors only over the clerical staff. LAs saw themselves as reporting directly to the AA with control only in a possible dotted line relationship. All the LAs drew the chart as generally below; half of them included the dot-

ted lines to the control staff; half drew no connection at all.

Clearly, legislative personnel do not see the control unit as being their direct superiors. This probably contributes to their skepticism and resentment about the auditors. The LAs simply do not see them as more educated, more experienced, or hierarchically superior.

c. The control staff seems aware of the skepticism with which they are viewed. Thus, one observed that she doesn't feel they take her procedural memos seriously enough; they don't seem to hold onto them because LAs ask the same questions repeatedly. And another auditor describes the "fuzzy line about supervision; some LAs had to be reminded who was supervising whom!"

As a result, auditors tend to avoid face-to-face discussion with legislative personnel. They discourage LAs and

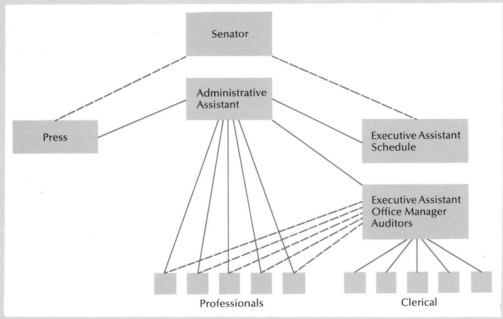

As drawn by legislative assistants.

caseworkers from contacting them before drafting letters, and most of their initiations are via written memos. All in all, however, the control staff feel they have had a beneficial impact on organizational performance; Auditor 1: "LAs not particularly organized; auditors have good work habits and can help to organize the LA; I feel the greatest improvement has been in this area." Auditor 2: "I have seen 100 percent turnabout since control started; office used to be six weeks to two months behind in mail; now we are current every week."

d. In general, the LA's complaints about control are also voiced by caseworkers including criticism of auditors' "nitpicking," "bureaucratic" attitudes, and lack of responsiveness to suggestions of duties among caseworkers.

4. The administrative assistant may be overloaded. His question-

naire response indicates that he experiences the most job demands and time pressure in the office (aside from the senator himself) and is unable or unwilling even to take accumulated vacation. Because he is relatively more insulated from in-office oral communications than some other AAs observed, he spends much time in his office processing mail—more than any other AA observed. Some of it (difficult to determine how much) appears to be minor items that simply don't fit the assignments of others, so the AA does them himself.

The driving motivation for this detailed work seems to be to ensure that the office doesn't make small mistakes that might have substantial political impact.

The AA's day is very fractionated. Discretionary time is divided into very small chunks of only five minutes each before interruptions occur (usually a telephone call).

The Two Nursing Programs

Gargoyle University is one of the world's greatest educational institutions. Over 100 years old, its medical school and university hospital are among the oldest and most respected in the United States. The university includes various undergraduate and graduate programs and schools. A simplified version of its organization is contained in Exhibit 1.

The Hospital School of Nursing.   As the organization chart indicates, Gargoyle contains two units committed to educating registered nurses (R.N.s). The older of the two units is the Gargoyle Hospital School of Nursing, which graduates approximately 75 per year. Most of the R.N.'s in the United States have been trained in such hospital nursing schools. In general, the schools offer three-year programs that accept young people directly from high

school and provide them with an intensive living, learning, and working experience. Students generally live in facilities physically linked to the hospital, so they are closely supervised. Nursing practice and "proper" behavior are considered just as important as theoretical learning.

Attendance at a hospital school of nursing can be a profound socialization experience for the students—mostly young women—who enter to earn their certificates. A young faculty member at GHSN remembers her experience as a student: "My head nurse would personally check our undergarments every morning to ensure that we weren't wearing frilly slips, etc. Everything had to be plain and professional!" Life is not as strictly supervised as it once was, but the level of control is still much higher than in most areas of American life. Exhibit 2 presents the results of a survey of management attitudes among

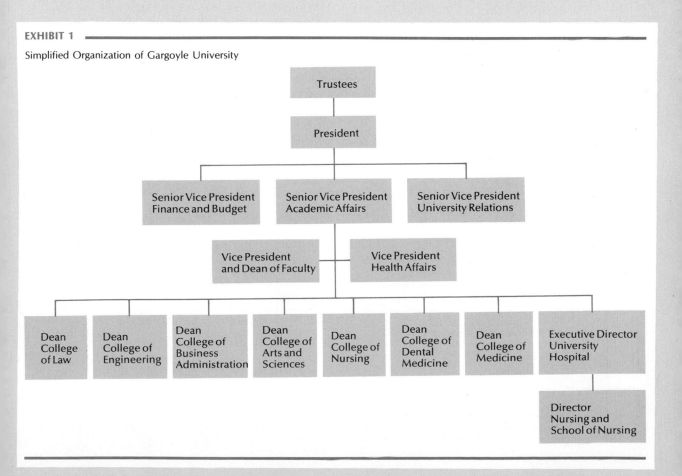

EXHIBIT 1

Simplified Organization of Gargoyle University

nursing supervisors at Gargoyle Hospital. Their responses can be compared with others also sampled.

The Hospital School of Nursing occupies a beautiful new building connected to the Hospital and Medical School. In general, its students come from the local region and are of modest economic backgrounds. For them a hospital school of nursing is attractive because it costs substantially less than a private college.

The College of Nursing.   Gargoyle University also includes a College of Nursing that offers undergraduate and graduate degrees. The four-year undergraduate program leads to a Bachelor of Science in Nursing and prepares the student to qualify for the R.N. certificate. Masters and doctorate programs are also offered. Such underlying disciplines as biology and chemistry receive substantial emphasis in the undergraduate program. These courses along with required traditional liberal arts courses are taught by regular university faculty in the college of arts and sciences.

College of Nursing students do not live in separate dorms, but many live wherever they desire on or off campus. In every respect they are regular university undergrads eligible for sports and extracurricular activities. Their summers are free like those of other students.

The College of Nursing is located on the main university campus in an older building vacated by the engineering school. Its students come from a broad range of states and are charged regular university tuition (more than $6,000 per year, not including room and board).

The faculty of the College of Nursing all have graduate degrees and are generally committed to upgrading the status of the nursing profession. They emphasize the need for nurses to understand basic medical theory in order to reach independent judgments on appropriate care. Substantial research projects have been launched. The new dean of the college observes: "Nursing is the most critical component in solving the health care crisis in the United States. By tradition, they are the most patient oriented of all the health professions. In addition, by proximity and availability, they are best suited to administer the delivery of health care. The nurse of the future will be the central manager of the professionals and technicians attending to patients. We intend to educate self-reliant and assertive young women and men with the scientific, humanistic, and administrative knowledge to meet this future."

EXHIBIT 2

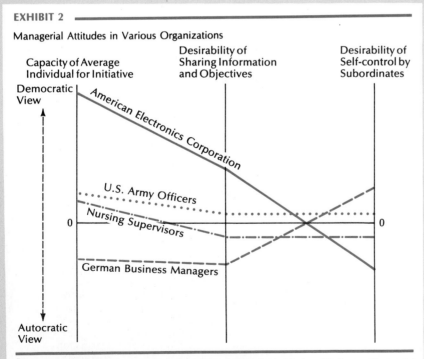

Managerial Attitudes in Various Organizations

Source: Based on data in Mason Haire, Edwin E. Ghiselli, and Lyman W. Porter, *Managerial Thinking* (New York: John Wiley & Sons, 1966). Supplemented with additional data.

Clinical Education and Experience.   Both Gargoyle Hospital School of Nursing and University College of Nursing students receive training on the floors of the hospital. This training is closely integrated into the GHSN program because the students are physically close and available most of the year. (In fact, a few students in the past have complained that they were exploited with regular work because they came free to the hospital). Faculty of the college today, however, complain of inadequate access to the hospital for their students. As one professor observed:

> The Hospital medical and nursing supervisors are very uncooperative. They make it difficult for us to plan a program and are even worse in delivering it. For example, they sent out a notice last August 1 that the planning sessions for the fall clinical work would be held on August 11 and 12. I was on vacation and didn't even hear about the meetings until I returned in September! And then when we complained, they still scheduled the new student hospital orientation sessions for a time when all our freshman college students were in chemistry class. Even when we finally worked out the dates and shifts, too many of our students were cleaning rooms. That's not what we want them to learn over there. It's like dealing with holdovers from the middle ages!

When asked to respond to these comments, the Associate Director of Nursing in charge of the School of Nursing stated:

> Well, our communication could certainly be improved. But it is frustrating when the college faculty are not available. They just seem to disappear in the summer or not answer their phones because they're researching something or other. And I just don't see how we can anticipate all their class conflicts in arranging our programs. We have to care for patients too. At times the college faculty and students do seem like spoiled children. All this agitation to change the state licensing rules to allow only four-year B.S. nurses to earn R.N.s. It seems so mean-spirited to exclude the three-year hospital graduates who care so much for helping patients. I think most nurses oppose the movement to close the three-year programs. I certainly do.

The Medical School and Hospital Physicians.   Several physicians commented on the situation:

> Given a choice, I would pick a three-year hospital program graduate every time. They *know* how to perform nursing; they are more technically competent.

> I can't stand the pro-Feminist views of the Nursing College faculty. Most of them are angry that they didn't go to medical school, and they blame us for that. Their views ruin the attitudes of their students. Many of them just won't take orders. I really wouldn't care if I never have another one in my department.

> I am very impressed with the College Nursing students. They are exceptionally bright (if a little naive). I sometimes get angry because they ask questions when I don't have time to answer. Still, in the long run, I believe medical care will be better off with more of them. But won't there be some explosions with tyrant surgeons!

> I guess I'm a radical on this issue. The present division in medicine between traditional hand-maiden nurses, new nurses-as-professionals, and physicians-as-kings is ridiculous. And now of course we are getting many more female physicians. But most of them are just as authoritarian toward nurses as are their male colleagues. I think we've got to obliterate the distinctions between physician and nurse—perhaps a common educational experience with different departure points."

Complaints have reached the president of the university (including pressure from several members of the trustees). He is considering what might be done.

Questions on the Two Nursing Programs

1. What are the conflicts at Gargoyle University?

2. What are the causes of the conflicts?

3. What possible alternatives are there for managing the situation? What are the advantages and disadvantages of each?

4. What would you recommend to the president of the university? Why?

Part Eight

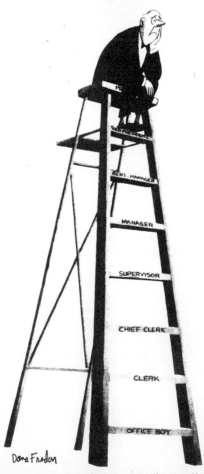

Drawing by Dana Fradon; © 1959, *The New Yorker Magazine*, Inc.

Managerial Careers

27

Personal Growth and Careers

Most people do not have "careers," nor do they expect to. They simply expect to have "jobs."[1]* The difference is a matter of time perspective and a planned direction. For example, future physicians tend to conceive of the career early, during the early teens. Most of them select high school courses and college programs with at least some consideration of their relationship to a medical career 10 to 15 years in the future. In contrast, most restaurant workers and casual laborers never planned for such positions, but merely took whatever work was available. The young physician will probably pursue the practice of medicine until he or she dies; the dishwasher or waiter will probably go on to other jobs and organizations—and even if one stays in the restaurant business as cook or headwaiter, he or she will probably not see it as a coherent career.

Of course, there are exceptions in these views. Some medical students are such mainly because their physician parents expect it, and some young waiters take great pride in their professionalism and aspire to own an outstanding eating establishment in the future. The main point is that career-oriented people have longer time perspectives and a sense of direction.

What of managers? Are they "career" or "job" oriented? Have many of your fellow students planned on a managerial career since their teens? Or are they just looking for anything at which they can earn a living? Most probably have views somewhere between the future physician and the dishwasher. That they are in school studying management suggests concern for future jobs, but few probably planned to study business or public administration very long ago—and most have only a vague sense of the shape of their future careers. In fact, most practicing managers develop a commitment to their careers only after completing their schooling and beginning work.[2]

How you got to where you are is less important than your present and future orientation. The theme of this chapter is that you will be more successful and satisfied if you take a career perspective toward your future—if you understand your own

"No, I'm not a career girl. Are you a career boy?"

From *The Wall Street Journal,* with permission of Cartoon Feature Syndicate.

---

* Notes and references will be found at the end of this chapter.

needs, strengths, and weaknesses, have a rough idea of the kinds of contributions you want to make and the rewards hoped for, and have some views on the types of positions you could fill. These ideas are not to be engraved in stone; they are subject to modification with maturity and experience, but even temporary chalk writing on a portable blackboard can help you achieve meaning and direction.

To assist you in thinking about your careers, this chapter will explore two major topics: personal maturation and changing career concerns. The next chapters will examine the role-stress and career difficulties encountered by many managers.

Conceptions of Maturation

Everyone traverses his or her own more or less rocky road to maturation. No final definition of maturation exists, but we can consider the process from several complementary perspectives.

The Extension of Motivating Needs

From infancy to adulthood, we tend to gradually extend the needs that motivate our behavior.[2] Infants are dominated by physiological drives and needs for safety and security. They are tyrannical and self-centered in their demands that these needs be satisfied, but they are helpless to do anything for themselves. They must come to see the world and their parents as contributing to the satisfaction of their basic needs.[3] When they do so, the world becomes less threatening and uncertain; then new needs emerge. Children discover the enjoyment of love and affiliation with their parents. Soon they experience play and the satisfaction of having playmates include them in their games.

As time passes, the social needs for affiliation and esteem become more powerful. We tend to define ourselves in terms of others' response to us. The child wants to be like others, not out of step—as the child would be by giving in to mother's demand that he or she wear rubbers when no one else in the fourth grade does. Children and adolescents fear being different because they are so unsure of themselves. They are afraid that being different will mean exclusion, and exclusion will mean being nothing. In this period of life, most people are other directed.[4]

Other-directed people are dominated by their social needs. They act in anticipation of how others will react to them after a behavior. In effect, they ask themselves: "What will others think of me? Will I still be part of the in crowd? Will I be liked more or less? Will I have more or less prestige?" (See Figure 27–1.)

As we mature physically, we also mature psychologically. This implies continued movement up the need hierarchy. Sometime in the teens, the individual should begin to realize that one need not be just like others, but has standards, expectations, and wants that are different from those of companions. Most people are a little threatened by this realization, because identifying oneself is a lonely and difficult process. Yet growth demands that the challenge be met and people become inner directed.[5]

Inner-directed people are motivated be ego needs for autonomy, competence, and achievement. They act in anticipation of what they will think of themselves

FIGURE 27–1

Inner-Directed

- Achievement, Creativity
- Competence, Self-Esteem
- Autonomy

Power
- Social Esteem, Prestige
- Affiliation, Love

Security

Other-Directed

after a behavior: "Will I have a sense of freedom? Will I feel competent and proficient? Will I experience the exultation of achievement and creativity? Will I think more of myself, even if the world doesn't agree?"

Whether or not we individually move up the need hierarchy with maturation, changing from being other directed to inner directed, depends mainly on our experience. Most developmental theories hold that it is early experience that counts.[6] Thus the Freudians argue that it is life in the critical development years (before six years of age) that is most influential. The neo-Freudians and others might extend the critical period to 12 or even 20, but all agree that there is some age at which personality development is quite complete, and there is relatively little change thereafter.

Reprinted courtesy Mell Lazarus and Publishers, Hall Syndicate. Copyright, 1973, by Field Enterprises.

The basic hierarchical model of needs suggests that we are born with all of the needs in a latent or potential state. Each higher level need becomes manifest or "felt" upon the relative satisfaction of a lower need. Satisfaction leads to movement up the need hierarchy and more complete maturation. Thus we are not *either* other directed *or* inner directed. We are all potentially both; at an earlier stage more the former; later, more the latter.

Effects of Frustration or Need Satisfaction

Everyone does not move up the hierarchy at the same pace or to the same degree. Some do not advance to new needs for competence, power, or achievement as the lower needs are relatively satisfied. If there is continued, long-lasting deprivation of lower need satisfaction, behavior may continue to be motivated by these lower needs, and the individual will not move on to higher needs.[7] In effect, a person's need structure will be truncated. (See Figure 27–2.) Inability to satisfy, needs for prestige, affiliation, security, and safety—and in some cases even physiological necessities—might mean that future behavior of such a youth would be mainly to satisfy lower level drives, and the needs for self-esteem, competence, and achievement might never become motivating. Aspirations might be permanently low because of these early aversive experiences.

The opposite of lower level need dominance is also possible. A television show dramatically illustrated this with separate interviews of college students and their parents. On a split screen, the two parties were shown responding to similar questions;

FIGURE 27–2

Truncated Need Structure

Esteem,
Affiliation,
Safety, Security,
Physiological

their answers went right by one another. One straight-looking female student described her parents as driven by "home, status, security, and all that. . . . But I don't blame them. After all, they're products of the depression. But that's not my bag."[8] What this sophomore was saying was that she is concerned about self-expression, personal growth, and creation. Perhaps her parents, who appeared to be warm and attractive people, had done their job well. They had created a stable, supportive, loving, respected, and esteemed home life that enabled their daughter to move quickly (and quite effortlessly) up the need hierarchy. Research on leaders of student riots in the 60s supports this thesis.[9] Such leaders tended to come from stable, warm (if overly permissive), liberal, middle-class families.

When lower needs have been satisfied without effort for a long time, they can become undervalued. The upper middle-class youth who has always enjoyed the satisfaction of lower needs may temporarily feel motivated only by higher needs—hence the idealism of some young people who aspire to service, creativity, and achievement but are cynical about the pursuit of lower level needs.[10] Such a condition partly explains the critical view of business careers that characterized college students in the 1960s at some schools. In short, we may now have more young adults with more developed higher needs at a younger age than has ever been true before. Marriage, however, has a way of dramatically lowering an individual's needs, or at least of motivating the person to act on some lower level needs.[11] This is "realism" to middle-age adults and "compromise" to some young people.

Stages of Growth

For many people, movement up the need hierarchy and maturation are not easy. Such growth results from the individual's handling of the various problems and crises encountered. The particular crises are unique to each person, but the general problems we all face are fairly consistent. (See Figure 27–3.) These problems can be described in terms of the seven stages of growth.[12]

Infancy.   The specific problem is that of trust versus mistrust. From and through his or her parents, the child concludes (we hope) that the world is not a hostile or random place and that some people can be trusted.

Young Childhood.   The problems are autonomy versus shame and initiative versus guilt. Again from and through parents (mainly in the conflict over toilet training and freedom to explore the home), the child should learn that she or he is an autonomous person who can and should exercise independence without guilt.

The archtypical event here is not so much the spanking for "messing your pants," but what happens when the infant crawls into the kitchen and pulls out the pots and pans from the lower drawer. If the parents respond with anger and punishment, the young boy or girl is likely to conclude that it is dangerous to exercise initiative in exploration. Of course, a single occasion doesn't settle this, but the pattern is critical.

Childhood and Adolescence.   The problem is industry versus inferiority. Success in exercising initiative tends to be reinforcing; the young person should become energetic and confident in seeking productive activity and challenge.

FIGURE 27–3 ━━━━━━━━━━━━━━

Problems Faced in the Seven Stages of Growth

Approximate Chronological Phase	*Specific Problems*
Old age	Ego integrity versus despair
⇧	
Adulthood and middle age	Generativity versus stagnation
⇧	
Young adulthood	Intimacy versus isolation
⇧	
Adolescence	Identity versus confusion
⇧	
Childhood and adolescence	Industry versus inferiority
⇧	
Young childhood	Autonomy versus shame
⇧	Initiative versus guilt
Infancy	Trust versus mistrust

Source: Erik Ericson, "Identity and the Life Cycle," *Psychological Issues* 1, no. 1 (1959).

The development of achievement need seems to depend on the resolution of this issue. If the child experiences relative success in mastering self-maintenance tasks like tying shoe laces and walking home from school alone, he or she is more likely to later develop a significant need for achievement. Research suggests that this development stems from certain childhood patterns.[13]

Parents' expectations of self-mastery. Too early or too tardy parental expectation are detrimental. If too early, the child's failures tend to be overly frequent and he feels overwhelmed. If too late, the optimal period for discovering the thrill of solving challenging problems is passed.

Parental performance expectations, and dominance. Most research has been done in traditional families of working fathers and at-home mothers, where it appears that the mother's performance expectations are central. If the mother expects little of the child or thinks everything the child does is just wonderful, achievement need development is hindered.

The father's influence is generally less on performance standards than on dominance. Excessive paternal dominance on the young child is perhaps *the* most destructive force on developing achievement need. Parents of a child with high achievement need tend to: (1) expect and encourage high performance, (2) allow the child to make decisions and not give detailed instructions, and (3) reward good performance with hugs and kisses (not gifts, which is more characteristic of parents with less achievement-oriented children).

The dynamic seems to be the same for both sons and daughters, but many parents may expect less from the girl and dominate her more, thus hindering achievement need development. Some suggest that achieving women were earlier treated as "sons" rather than daughters—that is, expectations were high, dominance low, and affectional rewards given for good performance (and probably withheld for poor performance).

Parental Behavior Conducive to Achievement Need Development

- self-mastery expectation at "proper" age
- high performance expectation (especially by mother)
- high performance encouragement (especially by father)
- encouraging child to make decisions
- affectional rewards given for good performance

Parental Behavior
Detrimental to Achievement
Need Development

- too early or too late expectation of self-mastery
- low performance expectation
- lack of encouragement for high performance
- excessive dominance and direction
- affectional rewards not dependent on performance

FIGURE 27–4

Independent

↑
|
|
|
↓

Dependent

FIGURE 27–5

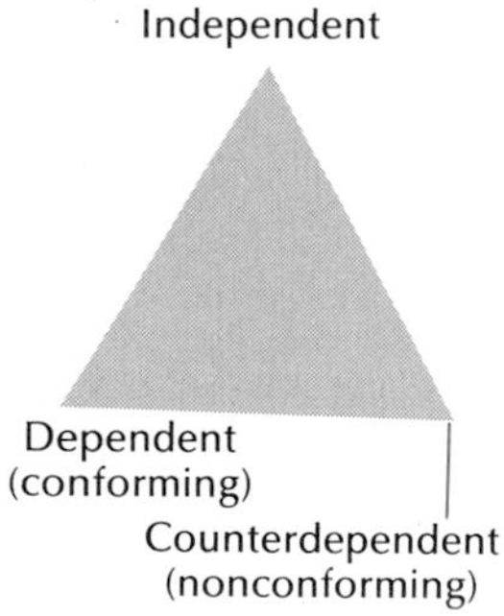

Independent

Dependent
(conforming)

Counterdependent
(nonconforming)

FIGURE 27–6

Interdependence

Dependence

Independence

Counterdependence

Adolescence.   The central issue is the familiar one of identity versus confusion. From examples of elders and personal exploration, young persons should come to know who they are and what they can do.

Young Adulthood.   The problem is intimacy versus isolation. Clarity about self should facilitate entering into close relationships with others.

The identity and intimacy problems are especially evident in attitudes toward authority. We used to view authority maturation as a continuum from being "dependent" to being "independent." The dependent person acts only with respect to how the authority figures want him or her to act. They must always behave as these others want them to. In contrast, the independent acts to satisfy self without regard to what others may think.

This dichotomy is too simple, however. The concept has been modified first to a triangle and now to a diamond.[14] (See Figures 27–4, 27–5, and 27–6.) The third leg on the triangle is a stage intermediate between dependent and independent termed *counterdependence.* The counterdependent person acts in opposition to the desires of authority figures. Note that the dependent person always conforms, and the counterdependent person is always nonconforming—so in effect his or her behavior is as much determined by others as for the dependent person. Such nonconformists may rationalize their behavior in fancy rhetoric about individuality and freedom, but they protest too much. They are every bit as much victims of pressure as is the conformist.

Thus dependent people may do exactly what their parents tell them; counterdependent people will do the opposite of what they are told; and independent people will do what they think will bring the most satisfaction, regardless of whether or not parents like it. This means of course that sometimes independents will behave just like parents and will appear to outsiders to be conforming. In fact, independents sometimes behave similarly to parents but because such behavior is personally satisfying. For example, some young people dislike wearing shoes in conformance to the dictates of parents and store owners. But gradually, after a few accidents and some pain, they reach the conclusion to wear shoes, not because they are conforming but because it makes sense. Therefore, we need to distinguish between conformers, nonconformers, and independents.

The independent is freer, although frequently he or she may behave similarly to group members, when it is appropriate to do so. Such a person sometimes conforms on such trivial matters as dress and courtesy, thus saving energy for more important issues. An elderly radical in flannel suit, white shirt, and regimental striped tie advised a group of college students to wear conservative clothes and short hair because this would leave them freer to *think* differently on important matters.

Independence, however, is not the final stage of maturation according to the diamond model. The fourth corner is interdependence. That is, maturation eventually means that you return to taking others into account when you are deciding how to behave. You consider the impact on those you love and to whom you have extended yourself in intimacy.[15]

Adulthood and Middle Age.   The chronic issue is that of generativity versus stagnation. With maturity and success, the individual faces the problem of maintaining effort and interest. We shall discuss this in the last part of the book when we consider managerial careers.

Old Age.   With declining physical and mental states, the individual struggles to maintain a sense of self-worth and optimism.

In these later stages the overiding issue is anxiety stemming from the motivational dynamism implicit in the need hierarchy. As soon as one need is relatively satisfied, a new one beckons us on. For most, if not all people, the quest is perpetual because satisfaction becomes ever more fugitive as they move up the need hierarchy. Frustration is likely to result from this dynamism, because most people will never completely satisfy every need. At either a low or high level, they will inevitably be denied satisfaction. We will never accomplish or gain all that we desire.

More important than inevitable frustration are the fear and anxiety that precede it. Such anxiety is endemic in people, and managers must frequently deal with it. The bases of our anxieties are multiple. Many philosophers and theologians hold that anxiety stems from our fundamental nature.[16] In contrast to other creatures, we are aware of our possibilities for creative action. Potentially, we can stand outside of our need structure, consider our present position, and be attracted by higher needs. But anxiety often results from this consideration and the possibilities arising from it, for to move up to the next higher need involves danger and the chance of failure in facing the unknown. To be sure, we learn and mature from such confrontation, but facing successive challenges means successive separations, giving up old ways and embracing new ones.

For example, some research suggests that some females with high needs for achievement do not act on this need as much as similarly motivated males do.[17] Such women seem to fear failure (as do many males, of course). Perhaps they unconsciously agree with cultural traditions that females are less competent than males and less likely to succeed. Or perhaps they fear that if they strive too hard, they will lessen the satisfaction of affiliative and security needs. Highly motivated black males may also suffer from this same anxiety about failure.[18] To some extent, however, all humans fear trying because failure might interfere with satisfaction of lower needs. Nonetheless, if mature individuals do not respond to their beckoning needs, they may stagnate and be permanently chained to lower needs, becoming frustrated and embittered.[19] "To venture," wrote Kierkegaard, "is to face anxiety, but not to venture is to lose oneself." Tension between anxiety and opportunity is a central human paradox.[20]

Not all of these "crises" are of equal difficulty for everyone, but they are the general issues with which we all must deal as we move through life.

Changing Career Concerns

Some of these maturation crises have impact on jobs and careers. Thus employees within broad age groups face common problems and opportunities as a function of their developmental stage.[21] Of particular concern are commitment, integrity, and dependence.

Career Phases

Career Phases
- flowering, reestablishing
- potential mid-life crisis
- settling down
- transition period
- provisional adulthood
- pulling up roots

Figure 27–7 lists the common job needs throughout the career cycle. In terms of ages, these can be summarized as follows:

Ages 16–22: Pulling up Roots. For most young people, a central concern in breaking away and establishing independence and autonomy, particularly from parents. They are concerned with proving to themselves that they are competent to make their own way. Consequently, jobs tend to be perceived as immediate vehicles for income and self-support, rather than as introduction to careers.

Ages 22–29: Provisional Adulthood. The formation of intimate relationships is a central concern. These relationships are oriented around other people, especially the opposite sex, but also include the development of ties with organizations and/ or professions. Career success as a goal takes on added value.

Ages 29–32: A Transition Period. Uneasiness about progress tends to be common at this stage. Many worry if they are in the right place, or if they are headed in the desired direction fast enough. Shifting jobs and organizations is common because this group is already becoming aware that personal mobility will begin to decline in the not-distant future.

FIGURE 27–7

Changing Needs throughout the Career Cycle

Stage	*Task Needs*	*Socioemotional Needs*
Early career	1. Develop action skills. 2. Develop a specialty. 3. Develop creativity, innovation. 4. Rotate into new area after three to five years.	1. Support 2. Autonomy 3. Deal with feelings of rivalry competition.
Middle career	1. Develop skills in training and coaching others (younger employees). 2. Training for updating and integrating skills. 3. Develop broader view of work and organization. 4. Job rotation into new job requiring new skills.	1. Opportunity to express feelings about mid-life (anguish, defeat, limited time, restlessness). 2. Reorganize thinking about self (mortality, values, family, work). 3. Reduce self-indulgence and competitiveness. 4. Support and mutual problem solving for coping with mid-career stress.
Late career	1. Shift from power role to one of consultation, guidance, wisdom. 2. Begin to establish self in activities outside the organization (start on part-time basis).	1. Support and counseling to help see integrated life experiences as a platform for others. 2. Acceptance of one's one and only life cycle. 3. Gradual detachment from organization.

From: D. T. Hall, *Careers in Organizations* (Santa Monica, Calif.: Goodyear Publishing, 1976).

Ages 32–39: Settling Down.   For career-oriented, ambitious people, this period is marked by enormous concentration on work, advancement, and creativity. As a consequence, social contacts tend to be reduced as compared with earlier activity. For many, career and family activities leave little additional time for other relationships.

Ages 39–43: Potential Mid-Life Crisis.   At this stage, mobility begins to rapidly decline for most people. They are beginning to recognize that many youthful ambitions will never be fulfilled and that this may be the last time for fruitful evaluation of career progress and change of direction.

Ages 43–50: Reestablishing and Flowering.   Once the critical issues of commitment to a career have been handled satisfactorily, this stage suggests an optimistic stabilization and contentment in relationships. Ambition is not forgotten, but is somehow transcended by many middle-age people. They might still like to be vice president but come to realize that it is not everything in life, that relationships within the organization at their present level can be developed and deepened.

Commitment and Integrity

Many young managers begin to question the fundamental value of their jobs. As one young brand manager from a major food company put it, "I'm a success, I earn over $50,000 per year and get a big kick from seeing the climbing sales chart, but sometimes I wonder if getting 'Colonel Zoom' cereal on every breakfast table is really worth devoting my life to!" (Especially since it was being attacked by nutritional experts as having little food value because it was mainly sugar-coated air.)

This questioning can be difficult for a young manager to understand. After years of apprenticeship, he or she is reaping the rewards of effort: autonomy, discretionary authority, and opportunity to achieve. Job morale is high. But for some this is not enough. They wonder: "Am I really selling out to the organization? Have I forgotten to ask the important question of what I'm contributing to society?" The young manager who concludes that the answers are more affirmative than negative is faced with the dilemma of what to do about it.

Open complaint about the organization's activities may cause others to view the complainer as disloyal, thus hindering present security and future promotability. The organization may suggest to the displeased young manager that she or he keep quiet, work upward, and then change company policy. This is not bad advice, but young managers might find being an executive so satisfying that they forget what it was they wanted to change. Young managers might alleviate their dissonance by changing personal values to agree with the dominant view. This facilitates total commitment to the organization and promotes the certainty that most people desire. Although such a solution may work for the individual (if he or she can still the voice of conscience), it may harm society.

There is no entirely satisfactory solution to this dilemma. If the organization's mission and policy are in violent disagreement with personal values, the best course is resignation and perhaps a new career.[22] But premature departure can also be a cop-out, a flight from difficult moral choices. Those young managers who decide to stay should strive to keep their values alive, to apply them to small matters they control, and to remember the values when they have the power to affect policy.

Attitudes toward commitment are ambivalent. A sense of certainty about career is desired because it simplifies one's life and stills the restlessness about whether one is in the right place. Nonetheless, many young people also fear commitment because it means closing doors and giving up the pleasant illusion that one can still do anything one wants to. Maturity means facing reality and deepening interests. Therefore a central facet of all careers is balancing commitment to the organization with the maintenance of a sense of independence.[23] Pure rebellion, which rejects all organizational values and norms, can end only in departure; pure conformity, which accepts everything, means loss of self. Creative individualism accepts pivotal values and norms but searches for ways to have individual impact.

The occasion for loss of integrity is often a person's first failure. After a history of success in school and work, a young manager with a weak sense of identity can be overwhelmed by destruction of the illusion that he or she cannot fail, is immune to career crisis, and enjoys widespread social support. The current generation of young people may be especially vulnerable in this area because they are the progeny of prosperity. For them success is unclouded with fear of economic deprivation.[24]

Dependence

One aspect of the struggle for maturity is declaring psychological independence of home and parental authority while identifying oneself as an individual. Dependence on others is difficult to handle shortly after successfully establishing one's independence. Thus undergraduate students tend to dislike team projects in which their grades can be lowered by others' mistakes. Nonetheless, total independence is impossible in real organizations. Superiors are dependent on subordinates' performance, subordinates are dependent on their superior's judgment and effective representation, and middle managers are dependent in both directions.

This mutual dependence can provoke anxiety. For example, many junior military officers have suffered from psychosomatic illness because they bear the responsibility for their unit's safety and performance even though they do not have the experience or technical knowledge of senior enlisted personnel. They cannot solve their problems by denying their dependence, but they can reduce them by learning the technical details of subordinates' duties. In the long run, however, young supervisors must recognize interdependence and strive to facilitate subordinate performance while representing their interests upward.

Most young adults are aware of their fear or dislike of being dependent on others, but they are usually not conscious of anxiety about having others dependent on them.[25] As they acquire spouse, family, job status, and community position, they receive increasing demands to give financial, temporal, and emotional support to more and more people and organizations. This sense of others' dependency can be gratifying, but one's time and energy are limited. Independent and self-reliant managers are sometimes disturbed to discover that they feel dominated by the needs of the people dependent on them. If and when the burden becomes too great, they must establish life priorities that balance the demands of family, organization, and community in a way that may fully satisfy none but allows relations to continue with all.[26]

Organizational Careers

Many contemporary structures look like a small pyramid atop a larger one. A college degree or more is needed to gain entry to the bottom rung of the managerial ladder in the upper pyramid. The initial positions are mainly in the wings of the upper pyramid. That is, they are staff professionals in specialized positions where young graduates are not managers in the sense of supervising anyone. Only as they establish and sell themselves do they move laterally or diagonally into the line management. Further movement up the hierarchy should depend on merit and performance.

Primary Skill Transitions

The upper pyramid of contemporary bureaucracies can be visualized as trisectional. (See Figure 27–8.) The primary job requirements in the lower section are technical—understanding equipment, procedures, processes, and techniques.[27] Entry depends on the organization's judgment that you can perform or quickly learn the tasks. Rewards and promotions are based on a combination of seniority and perfor-

FIGURE 27–8

Primary Managerial Skills

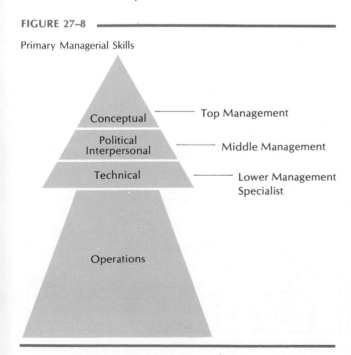

mance in the primarily technical job. Some people will be satisfied with remaining at this technical level, but most graduates probably aspire to advance upward to the middle sector of the upper pyramid at least.

The primary skills in the middle, however, are different—more oriented toward interpersonal, human relations, and politics. To be effective at this level, you need to influence people, to work as a team member, and to build coalitions and cooperation. Of course, technical skills do not become suddenly irrelevant; they are still important, but there is generally a shift in relative weight from technical to political as one moves up to the middle ranks.

This can be a difficult transition for many capable graduates. They find themselves promoted to first-line management precisely because they are the most technically competent. But upon entering management they may become anxious about the interpersonal requirements. The worst course of action for such a person is to ignore leadership requirements and attempt to do all the technical work alone. Unless he or she is an absolute superperson, the load will just be too great to handle. Failure is likely when higher executives conclude that the young-specialist-now-manager does not have promotion potential.

The transition from middle to upper sector shifts emphasis from interpersonal to conceptual skills: ability to think strategically, to perceive the "big picture," to understand how the parts of the organization can be integrated. Of course, political skills (and even technical skills to some extent) are still important, but an additional and rarer attribute is needed to successfully transit to top-level, policymaking levels. A president of the Koppers Company has commented on what it was like as a young engineer making the transition to management: "As an engineer, I was suddenly in a whole new world. In those days, an engineer got exposed to very little. I had had a survey course in business law and economics, but all I remembered about economics was there is decreasing utility in adding more fertilizer to land. I didn't know how to read a profit and loss, or a balance sheet, and here I was 33 years old. I had never done any significant philosophizing."[28]

Vertical Mobility

Most managers who make it to the top move through the three-position sectors. Some of course move faster than others. A study of presidents and executives divided them into three categories: supermobiles, normals, and submobiles.[29] Figure 27–9

Hagar the Horrible by Dik Browne.

FIGURE 27–9

Vertical Mobility of Managers

Level	Super mobiles (years)	Normals (years)	Sub- mobiles (years)
Entrance job (technical)	1–2	2–3	3–4
Development (middle management)	11	14	15
Arrival (executive management)	8	10	17
Time to presidency	21	27	36

Adapted from: E. E. Jennings, *The Mobile Manager* (Ann Arbor: Graduate School of Business Administration, University of Michigan, 1967).

summarizes the times spent in each level. Note that the supermobiles usually spend less than two years in the entrance job and that they change positions about every two years throughout the climb to the top. More common "normals" generally remain in the entrance position less than three years with approximately that interval between position changes. The supermobiles spend some 11 years in middle mangement, and those who make it all the way to the presidency spend approximately eight years in the executive ranks. For normals, it is 14 and 10 years, respectively.

Rate of position moves is apparently an important indicator of progress. If your employer begins leaving you in positions much longer than three years, it may suggest some questioning of your fast-track potential. If the time climbs over five years, it may suggest that you are plateauing.[30]

These frequent position changes are not necessarily, or even usually, intercompany moves. The long-term trend in the United States during the 20th century has been promotion from within. Such a policy varies with industries because some, such as advertising and television, demonstrate higher interfirm movement than the more stable banks and manufacturing concerns—at least after the first few years at work. About 25 percent of the top executives at the latter firms will have worked only for that company since graduation, but the other 75 percent will have had other jobs. Most of these jobs, however, were early in career, mainly in the managers' 20s. By around age 30, most of the climbers had joined the organization in which they made their ascent. As a general rule, mobility under 30 years of age doesn't hurt (unless it is really excessive, suggesting inability to discipline oneself to work); mobility in the 30s can be risky unless it is clearly a promotion in opportunity to exercise autonomy and demonstrate performance (not just for more money); and mobility after 45 is relatively difficult with the exception of organizations needing someone with your experience who is not available internally.

These patterns of vertical mobility may change in the near future. At this time demographic trends are projected to result in a general promotion slowdown. The baby boom generation is moving into the corporate hierarchy, and competition for middle management jobs has increased.[31] Furthermore, the trend toward early retirement has reversed. Executives are more likely to remain on the job longer because they cannot afford to retire; yet the number of candidates for their jobs is great.[32] The combined effect of these trends is likely to block advancement opportuni-

FIGURE 27–10

Achievement Need and
Level in Small Firms

FIGURE 27–11

Achievement Need and
Level in Large Firms

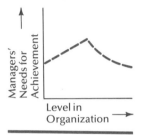

FIGURE 27–12

Perceptions of
Affiliative-Oriented
Manager

Superior's Views

Not Promotable

Affiliative-Oriented
Manager

Undesirable

Subordinates' Views

ties and impact on the motivation and productivity of middle-level managers. The expectation of vertical mobility is likely to be altered.

Personal Needs and Career Transitions

When we discussed leadership back in Chapter 10, we indicated that there was no ideal personality. We are beginning to discover, however, that certain human needs interact differently with one's career at different times and in different positions. For example, many managers possess high needs for achievement. The rigorous self-standards and orientation toward moderately challenging and risky activity leads to behavior that most employers desire and reward. A survey of small, entrepreneurial businesses indicates a direct relationship between achievement need and level: The person at the top has the highest need for achievement.[33] (See Figures 27–10 and 27–11.)

The picture in large organizations may be a little different however. In this setting, achievement need brings promotions only up to a point near the upper portion of middle management. Those who make the transition to the top appear to have somewhat lower achievement needs—still high with respect to most people, but lower than many other managers and professionals. Several interpretations of this finding are possible: (a) that the top executives are older, and achievement need may decline with age and success; (b) that the people at the top got there through connections rather than performance; and (c) that needs other than achievement are central to making a successful transition to an organization's conceptual level. The first two explanations may be partially valid, but (c) appears to be the most promising to explore.

Needs for affiliation, power, and achievement have been examined with reference to managerial success. One study asked superiors and subordinates to rate each manager on desirability and promotability.[34] Primarily affiliation-oriented managers don't work out well. (See Figure 27–12.) There is concensus on this: Subordinates don't like working for them, and superiors don't rate them as promotable. Such managers seem to be dominated by short-run concern for pleasing people and being liked. When talking with a subordinate, they seek a position that will leave both happy. But such a short-range outlook often backfires because of inconsistency and perceived inequity. Tomorrow, the manager may reach a different conclusion on a similar matter with another subordinate who behaves more aggressively. Then yesterday's subordinate may feel cheated.

To be an effective manager requires transcending the present even to see it in the long run as a category of events having general significance. You can't make decisions just to satisfy the present moment and person without anticipating how the decision will affect others in the future.

The predominantly achievement-oriented managers do not fair much better. (See Figure 27–13.) Subordinates tend to see these managers as undesired superiors. Higher executives may accept their performance as acceptable, but not judge them as promotable. The problem seems to be with their political skills, which makes it difficult for them to move out of the technical ranks and up through middle management.

Intensely achievement-oriented people often experience difficulty working with others because of impatience with lower performance standards and their desire for performance results. A test that measures an "Index of Machiavellianism" has been developed to give a rough idea about interpersonal attitudes.[35] Contrary to the test's name, power need is less related to the index than is achievement need. High achievement need people seem to view others as "objects" to be manipulated in the interest of their own accomplishment. Not that the achievement-oriented person dislikes others or even enjoys exercising influence; this is simply irrelevant. What counts is getting those others to behave in the interest of the achievement. Not surprisingly, most subordinates dislike such impersonal and manipulative behavior.

Business students seem to have fairly high indexes of Machiavellianism—higher than most managers (but not as high as business school professors!). Managers have observed that many graduates take two or three years to learn that they must relate to other people as people, not as resources or objects.

Predominantly power-oriented managers seem to be more successful. (See Figure 27–14.) They may be better liked by subordinates and more likely to be promoted by superiors. The reason is not firmly established, but we could surmise that they have different perspectives on time and people. To satisfy one's power need requires insight into other people, who are seen not so much as objects to be manipulated as complex human beings to be influenced. Actual feelings for them may be no warmer than those of the achievement-oriented manager, but the power seeker's political behavior is more sophisticated. Perspectives on events and time is longer run and more directed to the viability of the system. A person with such an orientation is better able to climb through middle management into the conceptual policymaking ranks.

Another researcher has also looked at a variety of executives using stylistic concepts.[36] This approach defines four categories, which we will call: (a) organization person, (b) crafter, (c) jungle fighter, and (d) game player. Figure 27–15 summarizes these categories in parallel to human need orientations.

The organization person is directed toward security and loyalty to the organization. Safety and affiliation needs probably predominate. Such a person is apparently unlikely to climb very high above entry ranks except in very stable and seniority-valuing institutions.

The crafter is concerned mainly about quality task performance. Emphasis is on high standards and timely completion. Needs for competence and achievement appear to be logically linked to this orientation. Such a manager is valued by the organization and promoted early in career but is unlikely to make the transition to the top. Self-centeredness and political insensitivity block higher advance.[37]

Jungle fighters used to climb to the top, but apparently are less likely now to do so. Their power orientation is strong, and influence skills through dominance or manipulation are cultivated. Yet, too open a power orientation is rejected. Because of organizational complexity, as we saw in Chapter 10 on leadership, purely authoritarian styles are of declining effectiveness—especially at top levels.[38]

In this approach, the most successful executive seems to be the game player moderately high in both power and achievement needs who has high standards

FIGURE 27–13

Perceptions of Achievement-Oriented Manager

Superiors' Views
—
Not Promotable above Middle
|
|
↓
Achievement-Oriented Manager
↑
|
|
Undesirable
—
Subordinates' Views

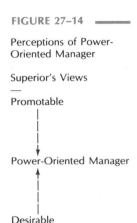

FIGURE 27–14

Perceptions of Power-Oriented Manager

Superior's Views
—
Promotable
|
|
↓
Power-Oriented Manager
↑
|
|
Desirable
—
Subordinates' Views

FIGURE 27–15

Manager's Need and Style Orientation

Manager's Need Orientation	Manager's Style Orientation
Power	Jungle fighter
	Game player
Achievement	Crafter
Affiliation	
Security	Organization person

FIGURE 27–16

Probable Needs of Successful Climbers (gameplayers)

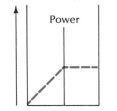

tempered by recognition of political realities.[39] (See Figure 27–16.) Interpersonal skills rest on sufficient technical ability; conceptual thinking visualizes the long run and larger system. Affiliation and status per se are less important—to the point that some observers express concern about their deferred affiliative needs and underexpressed emotions.[40] In explaining why he left a senior executive post at Ford Motor Company eventually to become president at Bell and Howell, Donald Frey catches the game-player orientation:

> I just have to run a *whole* business—it's in here [clutching his abdomen]. In the crudest sense, you could say its a need for power. In an esoteric sense, it's a need for completeness. I'm not happy unless I'm dealing with all the pieces. All through the years, regardless of what function I was performing, I had a desire to find out the broader aspects of what I was doing—to see what the next guy was going to do.[41]

The motivation to succeed in corporate bureaucracies is partially determined by the need to manage or lead others. The desire for advancement, preference for a leadership role, and high career expectations are predictive of future managerial success.[42] These are the individuals who rise to the top and run corporations.

Research at AT&T suggests that this motivation to manage has declined during the past few decades.[43] Young managers do not have the same desire to "climb the corporate ladder" as did the managers in the 1950s. A summary of the preferences and expectations of today's young managers as compared with the young managers in the 1950s is presented below:

Today's young managers have:

- A weaker drive to attain powerful, high-status, and well-paying positions.
- Less optimism about the likelihood of having a challenging job in five years with opportunities to learn and do new things.
- Lower expectations that the organization will make a strong effort to provide all the resources needed to do a good job.
- Lower expectations about having deep friendships with work associates.
- A weaker desire to advance to middle management.

In sum, the current generation of new managers does not want as much, nor do they expect as much as have their predecessors. These trends begin to suggest a shortage of upwardly mobile, capable managers to assume the top management roles in the near future.

SUMMARY

Each person's dominant needs and personality developmemt reflect his or her childhood experiences, cultural background, and life situation. Those who are able to mature and satisfactorily resolve life's crises become motivated by higher level needs. They identify what is important to them, become more open in their interpersonal relationships, and develop deeper interests. From being dominated by existence needs as infants, they move through being other directed and consumed by social needs on to inner-directed growth needs. Nonetheless, they never escape from their pasts nor from lower level needs. The particular need that is motivating at any given time reflects the current situation, with its frustrations and possibilities.

Some of us are more fearful of failure than others, but even mature achievement-oriented persons experience anxiety. As human beings, all of us will be frustrated sometimes as we confront the anxiety that comes from being aware of creative opportunities but afraid of risking failure.

Career concerns change as managers mature and move upward in their organizations. The early objective is mainly to obtain a job that gives independence from parents and facilitates forming relationships with others. In the late 20s to early 30s, for most people concern about commitment and integrity is especially high, and young professionals and managers seek a setting in which to feel comfortable while pursuing a career—a pursuit that is probably strongest during one's 30s and early 40s. Success tends to be accompanied by increasing anxiety about interdependence and decisiveness.

Movement up the professional/managerial ladder means moving through sectors emphasizing different skills: technical at entry level, political in the middle, and conceptual at the top. Supermobiles move rapidly, changing positions about every two years. Normals change positions about every three years.

Predominantly affiliation and achievement-need orientations appear to be detrimental to success in making the climb. The affiliative manager may focus on the short run and being liked to such an extent that subordinates consider him or her as inconsistent and superiors as not promotable. An intensely achievement-oriented manager is likely to manifest interpersonal inadequacies that offend subordinates by treating them impersonally as objects.

Power-oriented managers appear to be more highly rated by both subordinates and superiors. Their political and conceptional skills may be better developed.

Organization people, crafters, and jungle fighters seem to be less successful in climbing to the top than are game players, who have fairly high but balanced needs for achievement and power coupled with lesser need for affiliation. Loyalty and task competence are valued by most institutions but are not sufficient for vertical movement in most. Too naked a power orientation tends to be rejected in favor of the competent achiever and politician who is the game player.

REVIEW QUESTIONS

1. What does being other directed mean?

2. What does being inner directed mean?

3. What is the relationship between experience, maturation, and the need hierarchy?

4. Does everyone move up the need hierarchy? Why or why not?

5. What effect does early frustration have on the need hierarchy?

6. What effect does easy early satisfaction have on the need hierarchy?

7. Why do some people look down on others who are motivated by lower level needs?

8. What are the major problems confronted in the stages of growth?

9. What parental behavior is detrimental to developing a child's achievement need?

10. What parental behavior is conducive to developing a child's achievement need?

11. From dependency, how does the maturing person evolve in terms of attitudes toward authority figures?

12. What does counterdependent mean?

13. What does independent mean?

14. What does interdependent mean?

15. What is the difference between a "job" perspective and a "career" perspective?

16. What are the general career phases from 16–22 to more than 50 years of age?

17. What are the concerns during the phase "16–22: pulling up roots?"

18. What are the concerns during the phase "22–29: provisional adulthood?"

19. What are the concerns during phase "29–32: transition period?"

20. What are the concerns during the phase "32–39: settling down?"

21. What are the concerns during the phase "39–43: potential mid-life crisis?"

22. What are the concerns during the phase "43–50: reestablishing and flowering?"

23. What are the three primary skills in the managerial hierarchy?

24. What are the transitions sometimes difficult across the levels in the managerial hierarchy?

25. What periods of time do managers tend to spend in entrance, developmental, and executive levels?

26. What appears to be the relationship between achievement need and managerial level in small business firms?

27. What appears to be the relationship between achievement need and managerial level in large business firms?

28. How do superiors and subordinates generally perceive the primarily affiliative-oriented manager? Why?

29. How do superiors and subordinates generally perceive the primarily achievement-oriented manager? Why?

30. How do superiors and subordinates generally perceive the primarily power-oriented manager? Why?

31. What appears to motivate the "organization person?" How do they succeed in management? Why?

32. What appears to motivate the "crafter?" How do they succeed in management? Why?

33. What appears to motivate the "jungle fighter?" How do they succeed in management? Why?

34. What appears to motivate the "gameplayer?" How do they succeed in management? Why?

Notes and References on Managerial Careers

1. M. W. McCall and E. E. Lawler III, "High School Students' Perceptions of Work," Academy of Management Journal, March 1976, pp. 17–24. See also J. van Maanen, ed., *Organizational Careers: Some New Perspectives* (New York: John Wiley & Sons, 1977).

2. For a general survey of development, see L. R. Goulet and P. B. Bates, eds., *Life Span Developmental Psychology: Research and Theory* (New York: Academic Press, 1970), and P. B. Bates and K. Warner Schaie, *Life-Span Development Psychology* (New York: Academic Press, 1973).

3. M. Lewis, "The Busy, Purposeful World of a Baby," *Psychology Today,* February 1977, p. 53 ff.

4. David Riesman, with Nathan Glazer and Revel Denny, *The Lonely Crowd* (New Haven, Conn.: Yale University Press, 1950); J. S. Coleman, *The Adolescent Society: The Social Life of the Teenager and Its Impact on Education* (New York: Free Press, 1971).

5. R. G. Simmons, F. Rosenberg and M. Rosenberg, "Disturbance in the Self-Image at Adolescence," *American Sociological Review* 38 (1973), pp. 553–68.

6. On personality, see R. L. Munroe, *Schools of Psychoanalytic Thought* (New York: Holt, Rinehart & Winston, 1955); C. Kuhnholm and H. A. Murray, *Personality* (New York: Alfred A. Knopf, 1956); and W. B. Arndt, Jr., *Theories of Personality* (New York: Macmillan, 1974).

7. Harold J. Leavitt, *Managerial Psychology,* 2d ed. (Chicago: University of Chicago Press, 1964). On the effect of an impoverished environment in infancy, see Ashley Montagu, "Sociogenic Brain Damage," *American Anthropologist* 74, no. 5 (1972), pp. 1045–61.

A few years ago Daniel P. Moynihan, then assistant secretary of labor, issued a report on the role of the family in the urban Negro's situation. Initially the report was warmly received, but later it was rejected and the author was accused of being a racist because he had attributed much of the problem to the fragmented black family. His thesis was that the inability of the black father to support and lead a family had led to a matriarchal society. As the father's role disappears, he suggested, it is filled by a series of male figures. What he was suggesting is that the need hierarchy of some black youths is therefore truncated. *The Negro Family: The Case for National Action* (Washington, D.C.: Office of Policy Planning and Research, U.S. Department of Labor, 1965).

Systematic research, however, has found no significant difference between black students and white students on self-esteem or internal-external control. Deprived backgrounds affect individuals adversely, regardless of race. Poor blacks do develop higher needs with maturation, but society or conditions often limit their opportunity to satisfy these needs through activities acceptable to the white majority. D. W. Edwards, "Blacks versus Whites: When Is Race a Relevant Variable?" *Journal of Personality and Social Psychology* 29, no. 1 (1974), pp. 39–49; G. Lorenz, "Aspirations of Low-Income Blacks and Whites," *American Journal of Sociology* 78, no. 2 (1973), pp. 371–98.

8. See G. Elder, *Children of the Great Depression* (Chicago: University of Chicago Press, 1974).

9. On student attitudes in the 1960s, see R. Flacks, "The Liberated Generation: An Exploration of the Roots of Student Protest," *Journal of Social Issues* 23 (1967), pp. 52–75; K. Kenniston, *Young Radicals: Notes on Com-*

mitted Youth (New York: Harcourt Brace Jovanovich, 1968); and Kenniston, *Youth and Dissent* (New York: Harcourt Brace Jovanovich, 1971).

10. C. Schooler, "Social Antecedents of Adult Psychological Functioning," *American Journal of Sociology* 78, no. 2 (1972), p. 299.

11. P. Cutright, "Income and Family Events: Getting Married," *Journal of Marriage and Family* 32 (1970), pp. 628–37.

12. The stages are based on Erik Erikson, "Identity and the Life Cycle," *Psychological Issues,* vol. 1, no. 1 (1959), and *Childhood and Society* (New York: Norton, 1964). See also, V. L. Bengston, *The Social Psychology of Aging* (Indianapolis, Ind.: Bobbs-Merrill, 1973); G. E. Vaillant, *Adaptation to Life* (Boston: Little, Brown, 1977), and D. J. Levinson, *The Seasons of a Man's Life* (New York: Alfred A. Knopf, 1978).

13. Childhood and achievement need summarized by D. C. McClelland, *The Achieving Society* (New York: Van Nostrand Reinhold, 1961).

14. E. P. Hollander and R. H. Willis, "Some Current Issues in the Psychology of Conformity and Nonconformity," *Psychological Bulletin* 68 (1967), pp. 62–76.

15. In his research on power, McClelland summarizes ego development: stage 1, "It strengthens me" (dependent or oral stage); stage 2, "I strengthen myself" (counterdependent or anal state); stage 3, "I'll have impact on others" (independent or phallic state); and stage 4, "It moves me to do my duty" (interdependent or genital state). *Power: The Inner Experience* (New York: Halsted, 1975). See P. C. Chew, *The Inner World of the Middle-Aged Man* (New York: Macmillan, 1976).

16. During the Renaissance, Pico della Mirandola wrote:

> God said to man, you alone are not bound by any restraint, unless you will adopt it by the will we have given you. I have placed you in the center of the world that you may the easier look about and behold all that it is in it. I created you a creature, neither earthly nor heavenly, so that you could be your own creator and choose whatever form you may choose for yourself.

Quoted in Reinhold Niebuhr, *The Nature and Destiny of Man* (New York: Charles Scribner's Sons, 1949). See also Rollo May, *The Meaning of Anxiety* (New York: Ronald Press, 1950).

A French Philosopher wrote about the pursuit of satisfaction as follows:

> The fact is, perhaps, that with a little bread and water a man ought to be happy, but precisely is not; and if he is not, it is not necessarily because he lacks wisdom, but simply because he is a man.
>
> The owner of a rich estate would still add field to field, rich men would heap up more riches, the husband of a fair wife would have another still fairer, or possibly one less fair would serve, provided only she were fair in some other way.
>
> This incessant pursuit of an ever fugitive satisfaction springs from trouble deep in human nature. . . . The very insatiability of human desires has a positive significance; it means this: that we are attracted by an infinite good.

Etienne Gilson, *The Spirit of Medieval Philosophy* (Paris: J. Vrin, 1932), pp. 270–72. It may be overly optimistic to conclude that infinite good attracts man; a case could be made for just the opposite.

17. On women, achievement need, and fear of success, see E. G. French and G. S. Lesser, "Some Characteristics of the Achievement Need in Women," *Journal of Abnormal and Social Psychology* 68 (1964), pp. 119–28; M. S. Horner, "Femininity and Successful Achievement: A Basic Inconsistency," in Judith Bardwick et al., eds., *Feminine Personality and Conflict* (Belmont Calif.: Brooks/Cole, 1970); and L. Monahan, D. Kuhn, and P. Shaver, "Intrapsychic versus Cultural Explanations of the 'Fear of Success' Motive," *Journal of Personality and Social Psychology* 29, no. 1 (1974), pp. 60–64. A recent review of male and female differences is contained in C. Tavris and C. Offir, *The Longest War: Sex Differences in Perspective* (New York: Harcourt Brace Jovanovich, 1977).

18. On black views, see W. H. Grier and P. M. Cobbs, *Black Rage* (New York: Basic Books, 1968), and R. L. Crain and C. S. Weisman, *Discrimination, Personality and Achievement* (New York: Seminar, 1972).

19. A person who gives up may even become ill because illness conveys a status that may compensate for failure thought to be one's own fault—S. Cole and R. Lejeune, "Illness and the Legitimation of Failure," *American Sociological Review* 37 (1972), pp. 347–56.

20. This tension is captured in Judeo-Christian tradition, which suggests two points about people that bear consideration. The obvious fact is that people are creatures of nature, subject to its vicissitudes, compelled by its necessities, and driven by its impulses. The less obvious view is that people also stand outside of nature, life, their reason, and the world. This conception recognizes unequivocally that one's uniqueness cannot be attributed solely to one's rationality or intelligence. It holds that we are more than just a superintelligent monkey—we are presumably a little less than the angels and a little more than the animals. In this ambivalent position, we are anxious. To overcome this anxiety, theologians suggest that much motivation is a search for a false eternity, an effort to find security in ceaseless activities and material goods. Boundless human wants are a consequence of people's effort to hide their weakness, deny their dependency, and thus quiet their fears.

The suburbanite's consumption desires, the business executive's restless activity, the politician's consuming power drive, and even the hippie's repudiation of society are rooted in the anxious paradox of one's situation. According to this Judeo-Christian view, the more we establish ourselves in affluence, security, power, and glory, the greater the fear of tumbling from our eminence or losing our treasures. Critics maintain that human's material and spiritual ambivalency has made greed the dominant sin in our culture, because modern technology has tempted contemporary people to overestimate the possibility of eliminating their insecurity. For such critics, business has contributed to the temptation to regard physical comforts and security as life's final good and to hope for its attainment to a degree which is beyond human possibility.

In short, people, being both free and bound, both limited and limitless, are anxious. This fear of the indefinite is the inevitable result of the paradox of freedom and determinancy in which we are involved. We are attracted by challenge, excitement, and possibility, but constrained by our needs, weakness, and fear.

21. D. Levinson cited in R. F. Pearse and B. P. Pelzer, *Self-Directed Change for the Mid-Career Manager* (New York: American Management Association, 1975). See D. Levinson, *The Seasons in a Man's Life* (New York: Alfred A. Knopf, 1978).

22. A. Hirschman suggests that economists tend to exaggerate the power of leaving, while political scientists and sociologists underrate it. *Exit, Voice and Loyalty* (Cambridge, Mass.: Harvard University Press, 1970). On new careers, see D. L. Hiestand, *Changing Careers after Thirty-Five* (New York: Columbia University Press, 1971). S. R. Connor and J. S. Fielder recommend that firms pay for the reeducation of unhappy managers, who could then move on to other careers. "Rx for Managerial Shelf Sitters," *Harvard Business Review,* November–December 1973, pp. 113–20.

23. Abraham Zalesnik et al., *Orientation and Conflict in Career* (Boston: Graduate School of Business Administration, Harvard University, 1970). The authors suggest that many people never reconcile this conflict between personal identity and organizational values, yet those in conflict may be more effective than those who are "oriented" toward the organization. See also Edgar H. Schein, "Organizational Socialization and the Profession of Management," in *Organizational Psychology: A Book of Readings,* eds. D. A. Kolb, I. M. Rubin, and J. M. McIntyre (Englewood Cliffs, N.J.: Prentice-Hall, 1971), pp. 1–16.

A. E. Stoess reports a study indicating that managers are relatively more conforming than the general population. "Conformity Behavior of Managers and Their Wives," *Academy of Management Journal* 16, no. 3 (1973), pp. 443–41.

24. E. E. Jennings, *Executive Success: Stresses, Problems and Adjustments* (New York: Appleton-Century-Crofts, 1967), and *The Executive in Crisis* (Lansing: Graduate School of Business Administration, Michigan State University, 1965).

For a detailed discussion of the processes through which linkages develop between employees and organizations, see R. T. Mowday, L. W. Porter, and R. M. Steers, *Employee-Organization Linkages* (New York: Academic Press, 1981).

25. Erich Fromm, *The Art of Loving* (New York: Harper, 1956).

26. J. Steiner, "What Price Success?" *Harvard Business Review,* March–April 1972, pp. 69–74.

27. R. L. Katz, "Skills of an Effective Administrator," *Harvard Business Review,* September–October 1974, pp. 90–102.

28. Fletcher Byrom quoted in *Fortune,* July 1976, p. 184.

29. E. E. Jennings, *The Mobile Manager* (Ann Arbor: Graduate School of Business Administration, University of Michigan, 1967).

For a discussion of the factors that influence managerial career mobility, see J. F. Veiga, "Mobility Influences during Managerial Career Stages," *Academy of Management Journal* 26, no. 1 (1983), pp. 64–85.

30. See E. Roseman, *Confronting Nonpromotability* (New York: American Management Association, 1977).

31. "Americans Change," *Business Week,* February 20, 1978.

32. A. Patton, "The Coming Promotion Slowdown," *Harvard Business Review,* March–April 1981, 46–56.

33. D. C. McClelland, *The Achieving Society* (New York: Van Nostrand Reinhold, 1961).

34. D. C. McClelland and D. H. Burnham, "Power is the Great Motivator," *Harvard Business Review,* March–April 1976, pp. 13–110.

35. One survey indicates that MBA students express more authoritarian and Machiavellian views than practicing managers do, but business school professors are more Machiavellian than either. J. P. Siegel, "Machiavellianism, MBA's and Managers: Leadership Correlates and Socialization Effects," *Academy of Management Journal* 16, no. 3 (1973), pp. 404–11. A similar finding is in R. J. Burke, "Effects of Organizational Experience on Managerial Attitudes and Beliefs: A Better Press for Managers," *Journal of Business Research* 1, no. 1 (1973), pp. 21–30.

36. Michael Maccoby, *The Gamesman* (New York: Simon & Schuster, 1976).

37. T. P. Ference, "The Career Plateau: Facing up to Life at the Middle," *The MBA,* July–August 1977, pp. 21–22; G. Tavernier, "How to Cope with the Middle-Age Crisis," *International Management,* April 1977, p. 24 ff.

38. H. Tosi and H. Sims report that unsuccessful managers tend to be higher in "authoritarianism" than successful ones. "Management Mobility and Turnover: A Longitudinal Study," *Journal of Business Research,* June 1977, pp. 93–108. Among the characteristics of successful executives according to E. E. Ghiselli is orientation toward a restrained democratic leadership. *Explorations in Managerial Talent* (Santa Monica, Calif.: Goodyear Publishing, 1971).

39. A. Hard and C. Erickson, "Organizational Career Development: State of the Practice," *Academy of Management* (36th annual meeting, August 1976).

40. M. Maccoby, "The Corporate Climber Has to Find His Heart," *Fortune,* December 1976, p. 98 ff.

41. A. M. Louis, "Donald Frey Had a Hunger for the Whole Thing," *Fortune,* September 1976, p. 140.

42. D. W. Bray, R. J. Campbell and D. L. Grant, *Formative Years in Business* (New York: John Wiley & Sons, 1974).

43. A. Howard and D. W. Bray, "Today's Young Managers: They Can Do It, But Will They?" *The Wharton Magazine,* Summer 1981.

28

Managerial Role Stress

To paraphrase Shakespeare's words, all the world's a stage and all the men and women are players who are attempting to fulfill the requirements of their various roles. Students may also be sons or daughters, boyfriends or girl friends, athletes, reporters, church members, or citizens. Professors may be teachers, researchers, consultants, wives or husbands, mothers or fathers, community volunteers, or home mechanics. A business executive may also be chairperson of the board of trustees of the local hospital, area chair for college alumni, deacon at church, membership committee member at the country club, and candidate for election to the county board. Some of these roles are more enjoyable than others, but virtually all generate certain stresses and strains. In this chapter we shall examine the concept of role and the stress introduced by lack of fit between individual and role, conflicting or ambiguous role demands, and one-way and unpredictable work flows. Then we shall describe how individuals attempt to alleviate their role stress.

The Concept of Role

Each person in an organization is expected by his or her superiors, peers, subordinates, and others to behave in certain ways (called role demands). These demands are made by the various people with whom the person lives and works—those "role partners" who collectively comprise one's "role set."[1]* However, the individual involved may not perceive his or her role exactly as they do. Said role perception may be correct, or it may reflect wishful thinking, what one would like the role to be. The actual behavior or "role performance" grows out of reconciliation of these differing perceptions. Role effectiveness is determined by the accuracy of the person's

FIGURE 28–1

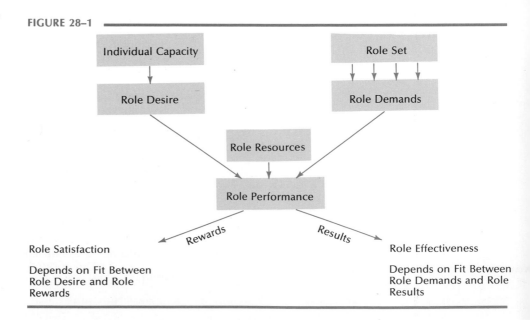

Role Satisfaction

Depends on Fit Between
Role Desire and Role
Rewards

Role Effectiveness

Depends on Fit Between
Role Demands and Role
Results

* Notes and references will be found at the end of this chapter.

understanding of the role demands and how well the behavior meets the role demands, and role satisfaction depends on how closely behavior fits the person's role desire.[2]

Figure 28–1 summarizes these elements and their relationships. Simple as this model is, problems occur at various points, as noted in the section to follow.

Conflict between the Individual and Role Demands

If a person's characteristics and desires are largely unsuited to and incompatible with role demands, he or she is likely to experience frustration leading to low job satisfaction, reduced organizational commitment, and perhaps poor performance.[3] Hence a quiet, passive, contemplative person may heartily dislike the pace and initiative required in a sales position. Or the achievement-oriented hard-driver may have difficulty teaching when student progress is so slow and ambiguous that he or she receives no performance feedback. This is the familiar, if still difficult, problem of fit between person and job.

One way to visualize this problem is to compare personal capacity and role demands as geometric shapes and role performance as the area where they overlap (see Figure 28–2). Conflict between the individual's capacity and role demands may be due to a number of conditions, discussed below.

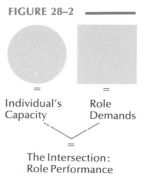

FIGURE 28–2

=   =
Individual's   Role
Capacity   Demands

=
The Intersection:
Role Performance

Misassignment

The individual has been misassigned when the position's demands are mostly outside his or her capacity, as shown by Figure 28–3. Said role performance can be only a small slice of the role's demands. An example is the mythical misassignment of personnel in the military. The civilian truck driver is assigned to the mess hall as cook; the former restaurant chef is ordered to become a radio operator; the former television repairer is sent to the motor pool as a driver, and so on. Actually, the modern Army generally strives to match people and positions.

Inadequate Demand

The problem in Figure 28–4 is inadequate demand when the position's demands are small compared with the incumbent's capacity. This is the familiar stereotype of the narrowly defined and programmed blue-collar production job. Many young college graduates (especially females) also find their first jobs do not challenge them. Research on the strikingly low morale among engineers indicates that this condition is widespread.[4] Many organizations have graduate engineers performing activities that do not draw on their abilities and could be better performed by lesser educated technicians. Overeducation for American jobs is exceedingly common—so common that at each hierarchical level, those individuals with less education may have higher morale and have just as effective performance as those at the same level with greater education.[5]

FIGURE 28–3

Misassignment

Role Demands

Individual

FIGURE 28–4

Inadequate Demand

Individual

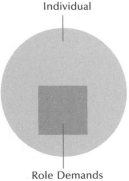

Role Demands

Demand Overload

In the demand overload condition illustrated in Figure 28–5, the position is much larger than the incumbent. The person is performing to maximum capacity but cannot meet all the role demands. The popular Peter Principle maintains that everyone eventually faces this state.[6] Supposedly, we all rise to the level of our incompetence until we reach the job where role demands are just too large for us. The popularity of the concept suggests that it has some validity, but most of us probably use the "principle" to explain our superiors' problems—not our own. The major weakness in the idea is that it ignores the possibility of growth, for expanding demands can challenge the incumbent to grow. Harry Truman rose to the level of his incompetence, but then he seemed to develop into a competent (some say even outstanding) president.[7] Somewhere there is a job that is bigger than virtually all of us, but it is not necessarily in our hierarchy, and we do not necessarily reach it.

Matching Demand

The almost perfect match of individual capacity and role demands pictured in Figure 28–6 is not necessarily a static fit. Where a person's role demands are slightly larger than his or her capacity, the challenge of self-growth may be optimal.[8] The individual has the feeling of moderate, invigorating stress that motivates development, in contrast to an overwhelming challenge that discourages effort. An incumbent whose capacities are slightly larger than the position demands will probably attempt to expand the role. Creativity, innovation, and empire building may be actively pursued in this situation.

The above conditions are common and fairly easy to imagine but are difficult to predict. The problem is that role demands and individual attributes are not defined in similar terms, and both are difficult to measure very accurately.[9]

FIGURE 28–5

Demand Overload

Role Demands

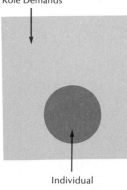

Individual

ENCLOSURES

Drawing by Joseph Farris; reprinted by permission of the Chicago Tribune—New York News Syndicate, Inc.

Ambiguity or Incompatibility in Role Demands

The dual role of Dr. Jekyll and Mr. Hyde in Robert Louis Stevenson's tale is an actor's dream. It is a challenge to portray the dual facets of one person's character, but in the horror story the facets occur sequentially, not simultaneously. Unfortunately, some people in organizations are under simultaneously conflicting demands from one person, multiple people, and several roles.[10]

Contradictory Demands from One Person

Even if only one person is making demands, as in Figure 28–7, the individual can confront inconsistency and contradiction. The demands may call for simultaneous behavior patterns that are impossible to combine. Mother expected little David to keep clean, straighten his room, study his school work, practice the piano, play with his friends, and complete household chores, all between 4:00 and 5:00 P.M.

Similar problems exist at work. Colleges frequently hire graduate students as dormitory advisers, who are expected to simultaneously live with undergraduates and be a friend and adviser to them, be a communications link to the administration, and be an enforcer of university regulations. However, it is difficult to be both friend and police officer. Being too conscientious in the latter role can destroy the former. Similarly, in industry some industrial engineers are expected to be advisers to line managers at the same time they monitor production performance and set standards and budgets.[11] But advising and monitoring are tough to combine because people are unlikely to discuss their real inadequacies with anyone who evaluates them. The managers may not necessarily lie, but they sometimes hide the truth. This is the same reason teenagers do not confide in their parents; they consult friends instead because talking truthfully to parents might destroy the ideal image that they want mother and father to hold of them.

As we saw in Part Three, "Planning and Controlling," the control system can be a source of great stress.[12] Evaluation by competing criteria is especially frustrating—faster production *and* fewer rejects; stable prices *and* greater market share; or higher quality *and* less cost.

Conflicting Demands from Different People

All members of a person's role set (especially one's superior) depend in some way upon one's performance; they are rewarded by it or they require it in order to perform their own tasks. Because they have a stake in the performance, they develop various expectations about one's behavior. Unfortunately, these several expectations do not always agree, so the role set imposes conflicting demands suggested by Figure 28–8. The harried incumbent is compelled to demonstrate contradictory or inconsistent behavior. For example, university professors experience substantial role conflict. They are expected to teach, and pressure is increasing from students and administrators to do a better job; they are also expected to do research and to publish. In recent years, they also have been expected to assist in the solution of local and national social problems.

The classic business example of role conflict has been production supervisors,

FIGURE 28–6

Matching
Role Demands

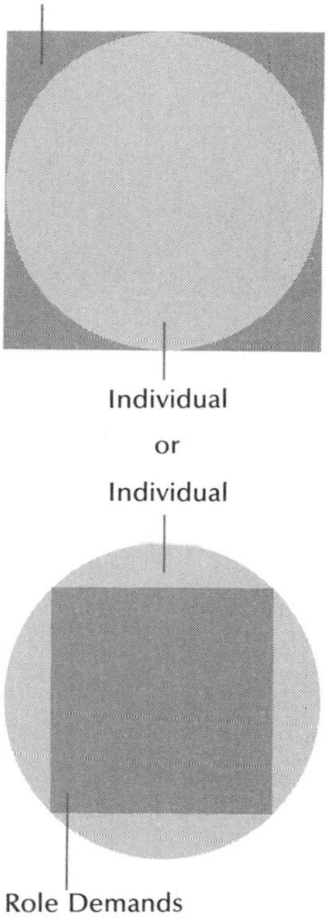

Individual

or

Individual

Role Demands

FIGURE 28–7

Contradictory
Demands

FIGURE 28–8

Conflicting Demands

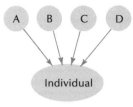

FIGURE 28–9

Conflicting Roles and Demands

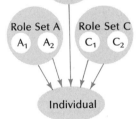

FIGURE 28–10

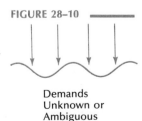

described as a "people in the middle" and "victims of doubletalk."[13] These supervisors are caught between the declaration of superiors that they are members of management, the power residing in staff "advisers" who tell them what to do, and the pressures of former working companions who control much of their social satisfactions.

Managers occupying boundary positions, such as marketing managers who have extensive contacts with outsiders, work under role conflict.[14] Some of their customers' expectations on delivery time, product quality, and credit terms may be inconsistent with company policies.[15] Nevertheless, corporate executives still expect the manager to complete.

Division general managers in large corporations occupy rewarding but stressful positions.[16] They must maintain three-way relationships—upward to corporate staff, laterally to other divisions, and downward to subordinates. Unfortunately, responding to one of these can undermine another. For instance, a middle manager who obediently follows orders from headquarters may thereby weaken authority over subordinates, who perceive the manager as a mouthpiece. Pushing the subordinates' interests too strongly, however, may lead the superiors to conclude that the manager has no overall perspective or, even worse, is disloyal. Adding to the ambiguity is the fact that responsibility almost always exceeds authority. The middle manager is responsible for the performance of the division and the profits achieved, but sometimes corporate staff sets policies that she or he thinks are incorrect and that hinder the achievement of objectives.

Conflicting Roles and Demands from Different People

In the complex theater of modern life, most people play not to one audience but to several, and they play several roles almost at the same time, as in Figure 28–9. Unfortunately, the expectations of one role can conflict with those of another. For example, married men and women often suffer from conflicting expectations about separate roles: their spouse's expectations about devotion to the family and their employers' demand for commitment to the job.[17] The working parent may want to be both a good, attentive father or mother *and* an ambitious, mobile employee, but there is neither energy nor time to live up to both competing desires fully.

American managers may also experience conflict between competing ideologies of success and equality.[18] Success is often associated with attainment of higher status. But equality is also a strong American value, so managers are expected to strive to differentiate themselves from their subordinates and peers and, at the same time, to consider them as equal. The result is the strange (to foreigners) custom of American superiors and subordinates calling each other by their first names.

Unknown or Ambiguous Demands

Perhaps the most stressful situation is shown in Figure 28–10 when individuals do not know what is expected of them.[19] Students dislike teachers who give no feedback on performance so that grades seem like they were drawn from a hat. And managers complain when they cannot determine the criteria by which superiors are evaluating their performance.

All promotions carry some ambiguity stress, for the promoted manager must give up the comforting known for the sometimes threatening unknown.[20] Managers must acclimate themselves to new demands and learn new behaviors to perform their roles. To add to the difficulty, some of their old friends and peers may now be subordinates on whom the managers must depend for information and assistance. As the managers move upward in status, pay, and power, they unexpectedly find themselves in increasingly dependent and ambiguous positions.

The problem of knowing who to play to and how to evaluate performance is widespread. Research on the early careers of young managers suggests that the central problems are ignorance or misunderstanding of the precise standards used to evaluate performance (i.e., ignorance of real role demands) and insensitivity to the actual power structure in the organization (i.e., confusion about the role set).[21]

The Response to Role Stress

The most debilitating response to role stress paradoxically is the most passive. The unfortunate person can respond by simply accepting the ambiguity and endeavoring to overcome it by working harder to meet everyone's expectations. Some great men and women may be all things to all people, but most cannot be. Trying to meet all demands can have a markedly adverse impact on satisfaction and even on mental or physical health.[22] Therefore individuals caught in the middle of role conflict may attempt to alleviate their stress by resigning, modifying demands, changing desires, withdrawing, responding to power and authority, or compartmentalization.

Resign

Total withdrawal by formally resigning is the most radical device for eliminating demands and alleviating stress.[23] It is tempting because it appears easy to drop out of school, quit a job, resign from a community position, or even flee from an incompatible spouse. But its simplicity is misleading, for no one can live in a vacuum. Complete escape from role demands is an impossibility short of hermitism, insanity, or death. People who habitually run from stress have a way of repeatedly finding themselves in similar stressful situations. Certainly resignation is a valid step for courageous people, but only when other devices will not work.

Responses to Role Stress
- meet all demands
- reject or resign
- modify demands
- change desires
- selective withdrawal
- respond to power
- respond to authority
- compartmentalize demands

MOMMA by Mell Lazarus. Courtesy of Mell Lazarus and Field Newspaper Syndicate.

Modify Demands

The most active and healthiest response to role stress and frustration is to attempt to modify the demands of others by confronting and bargaining with the role set.[24] The misassigned individual could apply for a transfer; the underchallenged could request more interesting work; the overwhelmed could demand a relaxation of the pressure. Similarly, the person experiencing role conflict could inform the superiors that they should coordinate or simplify their expectations. The college dormitory adviser could ask to be relieved of his or her police duties; the professor could request evaluation as a teacher *or* researcher, but not both; the supervisor could ask for a transfer to a department where he or she is not supervising friends; the division general manager could ask central corporate staff to rescind undesired policies; and spouses could agree to change their expectations of each other.

Unfortunately for the person experiencing stress, however, the people imposing the undesired demands may be unwilling to modify them. Whether their reasons for refusal are valid or not is quite irrelevant if they believe in them. Consequently, requesting change requires some courage, and to push too hard can be foolish. An individual who initiates a talk with his or her spouse about changing their marriage relationship can deeply offend the other party. An organizational superior will probably listen to a subordinate who respectfully requests a change, and no retaliation will result. The boss may not make the change, however. And if the subordinate becomes too insistent, the superior may feel angry and threatened, so much so that the superior may punish the person who rocks the boat.

An astute manager will fight to change role demands, but not always. For example, a division general manager should oppose the most crippling central policies, but continual fighting can totally expend his or her influence upward and destroy credibility. Like an army general, battle only on the most favorable grounds.

Change Desires

An unpleasant result of role stress is the conflict generated among one's various needs. You may desire security but also want love. The latter, however, means exposing yourself to another, who then could hurt you. Or you desire social prestige and self-esteem, but in some situations the former may require sacrifice of the latter. The dissonance of the ambitious person who seeks fame, finds it, and then bemoans lack of privacy is well known.

Most of us desire fulfillment and consistency. We want to satisfy a variety of needs simultaneously, and we attempt to maintain consistency in our behavior. Critical of hypocrites who say one thing and behave contradictorily, we want other's perceptions and judgments about ourselves to be consistent with our own.[25] If a professor who believes he is a good teacher hears that his students consider him a bore, to restore equilibrium he will probably either (1) reorganize and upgrade his notes and seek guidance to improve his teaching or (2) reject the student's assessment by pointing out their immaturity and lack of knowledge. Either might succeed in eliminating his dissonance and restoring his sense of well-being.[26]

An individual caught in conflicting desires and demands might respond by changing what she can change—and this is more likely to be her desires. The person can conclude that autonomy is not that important to her, or that she really didn't want a promotion anyway. For example: "I wouldn't want that guy's job for all the money in the world. How does he stand it?" or "I'm glad I didn't get that promotion I asked for. I sure would've missed all my pals in this section."

Such redefinition of desires may be either a game to fool oneself out of frustration or a mature decision that clarifies one's personal identity. An ambitious manager whose route upward is blocked may tell himself that, after all, leisure and family are more important. Whether he *really* means it will depend upon the actual satisfaction he derives later on. If the ambition still drives him, he may find himself uneasy and awkward with his family, sometimes even resentful because they symbolize his lost opportunity.[27]

Selective Withdrawal

A person under stress may temporarily withdraw when stress builds up.[28] For example: "Every time we get a rush job, he gets one of those headaches and has to go home." Or, an individual may informally ignore some of the conflicting demands and avoid the persons imposing them. The dormitory adviser might avoid all communication with school administrators and quietly stop enforcing regulations. The professor may simplify the situation by teaching as little as possible and literally hiding from students. The aim of withdrawal is to reduce and simplify role demands. A naval officer's comments are typical:

> The Executive Officer's job was to check on my performance. I never liked having to respond to him. . . . I soon decided that to maintain my equilibrium I should avoid interaction with him if at all possible. I made it a habit to spend prolonged periods of time down in the hot engine rooms where he was unlikely to follow—and I never went for coffee in the ward room.

Rather than totally ignoring a person, it is possible to compromise by responding only to exceptionally important demands. Thus the competitive elements of conflicting demands can be played down. The dormitory adviser might take action against *major* rule violations only and ignore the more numerous minor ones. The newly promoted supervisor might apply pressure on former working buddies only when a crisis arises or when higher management is physically present. Otherwise, the supervisor adheres to the group's informal code.

Respond to Power

Perhaps the easiest and most pragmatic response to conflicting demands from various people is to minimize pain; that is, to give priority to the person who can reward or punish the most. The question asked is who has the most power to satisfy or frustrate your needs.[29] In the organization this is likely to be some superior.

The problem with this criterion is that it is not always easy to determine who really has the most power. And even if this is possible, responding only to that person can still hurt because others may also possess power that can be used in retaliation for ignoring their demands. Finally, such a self-centered rule will adversely affect relations with the respondent's lateral associates and subordinates. They may believe that they have been sold out.

Even the boss may not be entirely satisfied if giving him or her priority means the role is not performed well. One study indicates that the lowest rated supervisors conformed the most to direct superiors, but higher rated managers ignored demands that interfered with performance.[30] They get the job done, and this is what most superiors value.

Respond to Authority

Similar but a little different from responding to power is giving priority to the demands that are judged most legitimate. The question asked is, Who has the most right to the results of your role performance?[31] Power and authority may reside in the same superior, but not always. A powerful vice president might bypass your department head to order you to concentrate on Project Baker, while your direct boss wants Project Able completed first. The most legitimate demand is probably the department head's, but the vice president has more power.

The conflict between power and authority can be particularly acute where powerful figures want the individual to exploit others or to violate the law. Some unfortunate managers may see their careers blocked unless an undeserving subordinate is wrongfully fired, a competitor illegally spied upon, or a pollution statute broken. A morally

"I don't sit around worrying when something goes wrong. I just quickly panic!"

From *The Wall Street Journal,* with permission of Cartoon Features Syndicate.

sensitive person may know what is right in such (we hope) rare circumstances, but the choice will still be unpleasant either way.

Compartmentalize Demands

The person under stress can develop arbitrary personal rules that separate demands and are followed even when they are not appropriate to the unique situation.[32] For example, a professor might sequence response to demands. She might devote Tuesdays and Thursdays wholly to classes and students, Mondays and Wednesdays to research and writing, Fridays to community service or pursuit of extra income. Note that the intent of such arbitrary rules is to simplify the professor's life. She does not have to decide what to do with each demand; she just fits it into a category.

Similarly, an executive might allot three nights a week to his family, regardless of job demands, and never depart from this pattern. Or he may unquestioningly work late when the superior demands it, regardless of his son's basketball game. The advantage of such impersonal rules is that one does not have to analyze the specific situation before applying the prescription.

A Broader View of Stress at Work

Stress has become a common part of our day-to-day work lives. Almost any aspect of the work environment is capable of producing stress.[33] All stress is not bad. Moderate levels of stress serve a useful purpose, but highly stressful situations have negative personal and organizational consequences. Individual differences (e.g., tolerance of ambiguity and need for achievement) help to determine the reaction.to a stressful situation.

Stress can be viewed as a condition of poor fit between the individual and the work environment.[34] It is likely that either excessive demands are being made or individuals are not equipped to handle a particular situation.

Much of the research on the effects of job stress has focused upon dramatic events in the work place (e.g., being fired, retirement), but the minor and more freuqent daily events are just as important. These minor events are irritating, frustrating, and distressing incidents that can be referred to as hassles.[35] Hassles trigger unpleasant emotions, which have an adverse effect on health and well-being. Although major stress events do have long-term effects, in the short term, hassles seem to have a much stronger impact on mental and physical health.

The Effects of Stress

The effects of stress are numerous and largely dependent upon individual characteristics. Some may be positive (e.g., increased motivation and drive), but most often the effects are negative. Over time these effects may become disruptive, dysfunctional, and even dangerous. The possible consequences of stress can be grouped into the following areas:[36]

Subjective Effects. Frustration, irritability, boredom, apathy, anxiety, depression, fatigue, aggression, nervousness, guilt, and loneliness.

FIGURE 28–11

The Major Causes of Work-Related Stress

Factors	Examples
Job	Work overload
	Role conflict and
	ambiguity
	Responsibility for people
	Career goal discrepancy
Work group	Lack of cohesiveness
	Status incongruence
	Group dissatisfaction
	Intragroup conflict
Organizational	Climate
	Technology
	Management styles
	Organizational design
	Control systems
Physical environment	Light
	Noise
	Temperature
	Vibration and motion
	Polluted air

Adapted from J. M. Ivancevich and M. T. Matteson, *Stress and Work: A Managerial Perspective* (Glenview, Ill.,: Scott, Foresman, 1980), p. 44.

Behavioral Effects.   Excitability, nervous laughter, emotional outbursts, excessive eating or loss of appetite, excessive drinking or smoking, accident proneness, impaired speech, restlessness, trembling, and impulsive behavior.

Cognitive Effects.   Hypersensitivity to criticism, mental blocks, forgetfulness, inability to concentrate, and inability to make decisions.

Physiological Effects.   Increased heart rate, dryness of the mouth, difficult in breathing, increased blood pressure, dilation of the pupils, hot and cold spells, and numbness or tingling in the limbs.

Organizational Effects.   High accident rates, poor organizational climate, job dissatisfaction, absenteeism, turnover, and lower productivity.

Major Sources of Stress

Job stress has been linked to numerous factors. There are literally dozens of possible causes, but the major areas seem to be job, work groups, and organizational characteristics. The most common sources of stress are identified in Figures 28–11 and 28–12.

FIGURE 28–12

Common Job Situations Promoting Stress

Interunit conflict
Technical problems
Efficiency problems
Role frustration
Staff shortages
Short Lead times
Too many meetings

Source: S. Parasuraman and J. A. Alutto, "An Examination of the Organizational Antecedents of Stressors at Work," *Academy of Management Journal* 24, no. 1 (1981), pp. 48–67.

Individual Approaches to Stress Management

The coping strategies listed below are individually initiated. That is, the individual employee can do much to control (or at least minimize the negative effects) the amount of stress in his or her work life.[37]

Set Priorities.   Group your work units into three categories: essential, important, and trivial. Forget about doing the trivial tasks if possible. Be satisfied with a less than perfect job if the alternative is not getting the job done at all. Learn to say no when asked to do something that overloads you. Delegate or hire others to perform some of your tasks.

Organize Your Time.   Good time management will do much to reduce the amount of stress in your life. Identify the time wasters. Figure out your most productive time of the day—perform your essential tasks then. Schedule your tasks carefully, allowing time for unexpected delays.

Develop Consistent Living Habits.   Try to eat, sleep, and exercise at about the same time every day. Fatigue reduces your body's ability to cope with stress.

Learn Relaxation and Meditation Techniques.   Take time to contemplate—redirect your mental processes away from your daily concerns. Relaxation techniques may be as simple as listening to music, watching a sunset, praying, deep breathing, or taking a walk. More sophisticated techniques introduced for stress management include transcendental meditation (TM), the relaxation response, or yoga.

Exercise.   Proper exercise is a positive force in mental as well as physical health. Exercise is an effective stress-management tool, since it enhances your energy and has a distinct relaxing effect. Those who exercise regularly report reduced tension, greater mental energy, and improved feelings of self-worth.

Organizational Approaches to Stress Management

The organization has two broad responsibilities in relation to stress management.[38] First, develop individuals so that they can diagnose and handle their own stress. Second, create an environment in which they are able to do so. The broad strategies for fulfilling these responsibilities are discussed below.

Organizational Design and Structure.   Clarify policies regarding transfers and promotions; change the reward system; alter the patterns of communication; decentralize; clarify the performance evaluation system; modify selection and placement policies.

Training and Development.   Provide career planning workshops, career counseling services, role analysis and clarification, obsolescence prevention programs, retirement preparation workshops.

Job Redesign.   Increase participation; clarify role expectations; develop effective leader behaviors in managers; reduce overload; provide opportunities to better utilize skills, initiate goal-setting practices.

Stress Reduction Services.   Provide facilities for physical exercise, stress management workshops, a health testing facility, biofeedback facilities.

SUMMARY

All members of organizations are subject to role demands, which they must reconcile with their individual capacities and role desires. The effectiveness of role performance reflects the fit between behavior and demands, and role satisfaction stems from closeness between behavior and role desires.

Role frustration and stress are generated by: (1) misassignment, so that demands and individual capacity do not overlap; (2) inadequate demands, so that the individual is not challenged; (3) demand overload, so that he or she cannot respond to all demands; (4) contradictory demands from one person; (5) conflicting demands from different people; (6) conflicting roles and demands from different people; (7) unknown or ambiguous demands; and (8) one-way work relationships.

Persons experiencing role stress endeavor to alleviate the condition by a variety of devices: (1) resigning, (2) modifying demands, (3) changing role desires, (4) selectively ignoring conflicting demands, (5) giving priority to most legitimate demands, (6) giving priority to demands from the most powerful figures, and (7) compartmentalizing and scheduling demands sequentially.

Work-related stress is prevalent in the manager's work life. The negative effects of stress on the job are numerous and can be organized into five different areas: subjective, behavioral, cognitive, physiological, and organizational. The major causes of stress can be traced to job, work group, and organizational characteristics. Individuals can do much to reduce the negative effects of stress. In addition, organizations can work to minimize stress for their employees.

REVIEW QUESTIONS

1. What are role demands? Where do they come from?
2. What is role performance? What affects it?
3. What is role effectiveness? What affects it?
4. What is role satisfaction? What affects it?
5. What is misassignment of an individual?
6. What is inadequate demand on an individual?
7. What is demand overload on an individual?
8. What is matching demand?
9. What are contradictory role demands? Why are they stressful?
10. What are conflicting role demands? What causes them?

11. What are conflicting roles? What causes this situation?

12. What are ambiguous demands?

13. What are the various responses possible to role stress?

14. How can an individual attempt to modify role demands?

15. How can an individual alleviate role stress by modifying his or her role desires?

16. What is selective withdrawal as a response to role stress?

17. What is responding to power as a response to role stress?

18. What is response to authority as a response to role stress?

19. What is compartmentalization of demands as a response to role stress?

20. What are the major effects of work-related stress?

21. What are the primary causes of stress?

22. Identify several common job situations that might promote stress in the individual.

23. How can the individual cope with or reduce the effects of stress in the work place?

24. What techniques can organizations introduce to help employees manage stress?

Notes and References on Managerial Role Stress

1. Robert K. Merton, *Social Theory and Social Structure,* rev. ed. (New York: Free Press, 1957).

2. The accuracy of the subordinate's perceptions of what a superior expects of him/her and the extent to which the subordinate complies to those expectations are significantly related to job satisfaction expressed by the subordinate and his/her performance evaluated by the superior. C. N. Greene, "Relationships among Role Accuracy, Compliance, Performance Evaluation, and Satisfaction within Managerial Dyads," *Academy of Management Journal* 15, no. 2 (1972), pp. 205–15. See also J. W. Getzels and J. W. Guba, "Role, Role Conflict and Effectiveness: An Empiric Study," *American Sociological Review,* April 1954, pp. 164–75.
H. Nix and F. Bates define conflict between role demands and individual personality as "role inadequacy." "Role frustration" is defined as conflict between role demands and recurrent situational factors (crises, war, economic depressions) that make it impossible to respond to role demands. "Occupational Role Stress Model," in *The Social Dimensions of Work,* ed. C. D. Bryant (Englewood Cliffs, N.J.: Prentice-Hall, 1972).

3. Role conflict and role ambiguity create job stress, which is associated with low job satisfaction and feelings of threat and anxiety. Nonetheless, job stress is not always associated with lower effectiveness. Some people can perform effectively for substantial periods of time while quite dissatisfied. See Henry L. Tosi, "Organization Stress as a Moderator of the Relationship between Influence and Role Response," *Academy of Management Journal* 14, no. 1 (1971), pp. 7–20. L. G. Hrebiniak and J. A. Alutto indicate that absence of role tension and greater seniority are positively related to organizational commitment (as are being male instead of female and being married instead of single). "Personal and Role-Related Factors in the Development of Organizational Commitment," *Administrative Science Quarterly* 17, no. 4 (1972), pp. 555. On the relationship between role and personality, see D. J. Levinson, "Role, Personality and Social Structure in the Organizational Setting," *Journal of Abnormal and Social Psychology* 58 (1959), pp. 170–80.

4. R. Ritti, *The Engineer in the Industrial Corporation* (New York: Columbia University Press, 1971); and W. Imberman, "As the Engineer Sees His Problems," *Conference Board Record* April 1976, pp. 30–34.

5. Ivar Berg, *Education and Jobs: The Great Training Robbery* (New York: Praeger, 1970).

6. Laurence J. Peter and Raymond Hull, *The Peter Principle* (New York: Morrow, 1969).

7. Clinton Rossiter, *The American Presidency,* rev. ed. (New York: Harcourt Brace Jovanovich, 1960).

8. H. K. Downey, D. Hellriegel, and J. W. Slocum, Jr., "Congruence between Individual Needs, Organizational Climate, Job Satisfaction and Performance," *Academy of Management Journal,* March 1975, pp. 149–54; H. Selye, "On the Real Benefits of Eustress," *Psychology Today,* March 1978, pp. 60 ff.

9. Despite their popularity, tests of intelligence, aptitude, and personality have only limited value in predicting the fit between manager and job. See J. P. Campbell, M. Dunnette, E. Lawler, and K. Weick, *Managerial Behavior, Performance and Effectiveness* (New York: McGraw-Hill, 1970).

10. For many examples of role conflict, see George Ritzer, *Man and His Work: Conflict and Change* (New York: Appleton-Century-Crofts, 1972).

11. Ross A. Webber, "Innovation and Conflict in Industrial Engineering," *The Journal of Industrial Engineering,* May 1967, p. 13.

12. W. R. Scott et al., "Organizational Evaluation and Authority," *Administrative Science Quarterly* 12, no. 1 (1967), pp. 93–117; W. E. Turcotte, "Control Systems, Performance and Satisfaction," *Administrative Science Quarterly* 19, no. 1 (1974), pp. 60–73.

13. B. Gardner and W. F. Whyte, "The Man in the

Middle: Position and Problems of the Foreman," *Applied Anthropology* 4, no. 2 (1945), entire issue; F. J. Roethlisberger, "The Foreman: Master and Victim of Doubletalk," *Harvard Business Review,* May 1945, pp. 283–98.

14. R. L. Kahn. et al., *Organizational Stress* (New York: John Wiley & Sons, 1964).

15. Salespeople express greater job satisfaction when they have control over credit, delivery, and price. H. O. Pruden and R. M. Reese, "Inter-organization Role-Set Relations and the Performance and Satisfaction of Industrial Salesmen," *Administrative Science Quarterly* 17, no. 4 (1972), p. 601. Stockbrokers have especially knotty role conflicts. On various overlapping occasions, they are a broker for an investor, a dealer for themselves, an investment adviser, an underwriter, and even a corporate director. The conflict between being a fiduciary agent and a salesperson is especially risky. W. M. Evan and E. G. Levin, "Status-Set and Role-Set Conflicts of the Stockbroker," *Social Forces* 45, no. 1 (1966), pp. 73–85.

16. H. E. R. Uyterhoeven, "General Managers in the Middle," *Harvard Business Review,* March–April 1972, pp. 75–85.

17. D. T. Hall and F. E. Gordon, "Career Choices of Married Women: Effects on Conflict, Role Behavior and Satisfaction," *Journal of Applied Psychology* 58, no. 1 (1973), pp. 42–48. This study found that home-oriented women who did only housework or volunteer work experienced the least role conflict; women working part time experienced the most and in general were less satisfied than full-time workers. Also see S. R. Orden and N. M. Bradburn, "Working Wives and Marriage Happiness," *The American Journal of Sociology* 74 (1969), pp. 392–407; S. Algrist and E. Almquist, *Careers and Contingencies: How College Women Struggle with Gender* (Port Washington, N.Y.: Kennikat, 1975); and M. M. Ferree, "The Confused American Housewife," *Psychology Today,* September 1976, pp. 76 ff.

On the job, there is no doubt that women are discriminated against, especially on promotions. Nonetheless, men are also discriminated against when they make personal requests to meet family duties, requests that are routinely granted to women. See B. Rosen and T. H. Jerdee, "Influence of Sex Role Stereotypes on Personnel Decisions," *Journal of Applied Psychology* 59, no. 1 (1974), pp. 9–14; and Rosen and Jerdee, "The Influence of Sex Role Stereotypes on Evaluations of Male and Female Supervisory Behavior," *Journal of Applied Psychology* 57, no. 1 (1973), pp. 44–48; E. J. Walker, " 'Till Business Do Us Part?" *Harvard Business Review,* January–February 1976),

pp. 94–101. See also E. W. Jones, Jr., "What It's Like to be a Black Manager," *Harvard Business Review,* July–August 1973, pp. 108–116.

18. M. Seeman, "Role Conflict and Ambivalence in Leadership," *American Sociological Review,* August 1953, pp. 373–80.

19. J. M. Ivancevich and J. H. Donnelly, Jr., "A Study of Role Clarity and Need for Clarity," *Academy of Management Journal* 17, no. 1 (1974), pp. 28–36. Not all individuals are similarly upset by role ambiguity, however. Certain personality types like neurotics, introverts, and rigid people find it difficult to operate under role conflict. Flexible, extroverted, and nonneurotic people, in contrast, sometimes favor ambiguous situations because they have more freedom to maneuver. R. J. House, J. R. Rizzo, and S. I. Lirtzman, "Organizational Stress and Inflexibility," paper presented at joint meeting of the Institute of Management Sciences and Operations Research Society, San Francisco, May 1968. See also D. W. Organ and C. N. Greene, "The Perceived Purposefulness of Job Behavior," *Academy of Management Journal* 17, no. 1 (1974), pp. 69–78.

20. Harry Levinson, "Easing the Pain of Personal Loss," *Harvard Business Review,* September–October 1972, pp. 80–88.

21. W. R. Dill, T. L. Hilton, and W. R. Reitman, *The New Managers* (Englewood Cliffs, N.J.: Prentice-Hall, 1962).

22. S. M. Sales and J. House, "Job Dissatisfaction as a Possible Risk Factor in Coronary Heart Disease," *Journal of Chronic Diseases,* May 1971, pp. 861–73; H. J. Montoye et al., "Serum Uric Acid Concentrations among Business Executives with Observations on Other Coronary Heart Disease Risk Factors," *Annals of Internal Medicine,* May 1967, pp. 838–50.

23. T. W. Johnson and George Graen, "Organizational Assimilation and Role Rejection," *Organizational Behavior and Human Performance* 10 (1973), pp. 72–87.

24. D. T. Hall, "A Model of Coping with Role Conflict: The Role Behavior of College Educated Women," *Administrative Science Quarterly* 17, no. 4 (1972), no. 471–86.

25. The theory of cognitive dissonance describes and predicts people's rationalizing behavior. Dissonance occurs whenever a person simultaneously holds two inconsistent cognitions (ideas, beliefs, opinions). The inconsistency is so uncomfortable that people strive to reduce the conflict in the easiest way possible. See Leon Festinger, *A Theory of Cognitive Dissonance* (Palo Alto, Calif.: Stanford University Press, 1957); and P. G. Zimbardo, *The Cognitive Control of Motivation* (Glenview, Ill.: Scott, Foresman, 1968). For a popular description of rationalization, see E. Aronson, "The Rationalizing Animal," *Psychology Today,* May 1973, p. 46. See also D. S. Holmes and B. Kent Houston, "Effectiveness of Situation Redefinition and Affective Isolation in Coping with Stress," *Journal of Personality and Social Psychology* 29, no. 2 (1974), pp. 212–18.

26.   D. G. Hampton, C. E. Summer, and R. A. Webber, *Organizational Behavior and the Practice of Management,* 2d ed. (Glenview, Ill.: Scott, Foresman, 1973). Consider what happens when a smoker is confronted with evidence that smoking causes cancer. The smoker will become motivated to change either his/her attitudes about smoking or behavior. And as anyone who has tried to quit smoking knows, the former alternative is easier. The smoker may decide that the studies are lousy. He/she may point to friends who smoke and are still alive. He/she may conclude that filters trap all the cancer-producing materials, or may argue that a short and happy life with cigarettes is better than a long and miserable life without them. People will ignore danger to avoid dissonance.

27.   J. Steiner, "What Price Success?" *Harvard Business Review,* March–April 1972, pp. 69–74; B. B. Wolman, *Victims of Success: Emotional Problems of Executives* (New York: Quadrangle Books, 1973).

28.   H. Benson, "Your Innate Asset for Combating Stress," *Harvard Business Review,* (July–August 1974, pp. 49–60; K. E. Weick, "The Management of Stress," *The MBA,* October 1975, pp. 37–40; W. W. Suojanen and D. R. Hudson, "Coping with Stress and Addictive Work Behavior," *Atlanta Economic Review,* March–April 1977, pp. 4–9; and R. K. Peters and H. Benson, "Time out from Tension," *Harvard Business Review,* January–February 1978, pp. 119–24.

29.   The person who always responds to power has been described as "expedient oriented." N. Gross, A. W. McEachern, and W. S. Mason, "Role Conflict and Its Resolutions," in *Readings in Social Psychology,* ed. E. E. Maccoby et al. (New York: Holt, Rinehart & Winston, 1958).

30.   R. G. Simmons, "The Role Conflict of the First-Line Supervisor: An Experimental Study," *The American Journal of Sociology,* January 1968, pp. 482–95.

31.   The person who always responds to legitimate authority has been described as "morally oriented." Gross, McEachern, and Mason, "Role Conflict and Its Resolutions."

32.   O. G. Brim calls these rules "meta-prescriptions." O. G. Brim and S. Wheeler, *Socialization after Childhood* (New York: John Wiley & Sons, 1966). Military chaplains occupy positions caught in conflict between military and religious ideologies. In one study, more than half of them denied there was a conflict. They behaved by religious standards when performing religious duties and by military standards when performing organizational duties, such as being a member of a court martial. They denied the relevance of rank in their relations with soldiers, asking to be called by name rather than rank. But they also maintained that they could not operate effectively as chaplains without holding officer rank. W. W. Burchard, "Role Conflicts of Military Chaplains," *American Sociological Review,* October 1954, pp. 528–35.

33.   J. E. McGrath, "Stress and Behavior in Organizations," in M. D. Dunnette, ed., *Handbook of Industrial and Organizational Psychology* (Skokie, Ill.: Rand McNally, 1976).

34.   J. R. P. French, "Job Demands and Worker Health," paper presented at the 84th Annual Convention of the American Psychological Association, September 1976.

35.   R. S. Lazarus, "Little Hassles Can Be Hazardous to Health," *Psychology Today,* July 1981, pp. 58–62.

36.   T. Cox, *Stress* (Baltimore: University Park Press, 1978).

The conclusions of one of the most comprehensive studies of job stress are reported in J. R. P. French, R. D. Caplan, and R. V. Harrison, *The Mechanisms of Job Stress and Strain* (New York: John Wiley & Sons, 1982).

37.   See J. M. Ivancevich and M. T. Matteson, *Stress and Work: A Managerial Perspective* (Glenview, Ill.: Scott, Foresman, 1980); K. Albrecht, *Stress and the Manager* (Englewood Cliffs, N.J.: Prentice-Hall, 1979); A. P. Brief, R. S. Schuler, and M. Van Sell, *Managing Job Stress* (Boston: Little, Brown, 1982).

38.   C. L. Cooper and J. Marshall, *Understanding Executive Stress* (New York: PBI Books, 1977).

29

Career Problems of Young Managers

The central idea of this book has been managerial leadership. We critically need knowledgeable and courageous young people to strive for power in the organizations that compose our society. Your education can furnish some of the necessary knowledge, but you must supply the courage.

Since expected problems can be easier to handle than unexpected ones, this final chapter examines some of the difficulties commonly experienced by young specialists and managers. No one should be so unlucky as to confront them all, but forewarned is forearmed. We shall conclude the chapter with some advice on career management.

Early Dissatisfaction

The early years on a first permanent job can be difficult. When the college graduate's job expectations exceed reality, the resultant feelings of underutilization can result in early departure.[1]* This condition can be due to the young person, organizational policy, or incompetent first supervisors.

Conflicting Expectations of Individual and Organization

Causes of Early
Dissatisfaction
● unrealistic expectations
● insufficient challenge
● not treated as unique
● incompetent first supervisor
● lack of visibility and exposure
● insensitivity to politics
● personal passivity

Business school graduates are often trained with case studies to think like managers and to find solutions to top-level executive problems. If they enjoy this perspective, they may expect real work to be similar and assume their actual authority will equal the synthetic authority accorded in class exercises. Such authority takes years to achieve, however, and graduates frequently experience difficulty in adapting to the changed time horizons that accompany the transition from school to work. Many students have been accustomed to almost immediate gratification and to short time spans—this semester, next academic year, a few years to graduation. During student years the passage of time and status changes are clearly signaled by changes in routine and frequent vacations. A permanent job is different. The time horizon is much longer, fewer events mark the passing of time, and a full year must go by before a short vacation.[2] Not surprisingly, some young employees attempt to perpetuate the school perspective by changing jobs frequently and taking off on unofficial vacations. However understandable this behavior, older managers perceive it as immature.

Older managers may be at fault because they do not provide young specialists and managers with sufficient challenge. Large organizations tend to treat newly employed graduates as identical and to assign them to boring tasks that could be performed by people with less education. Management argues that young people's expectations are unrealistic and that they must prove themselves before being assigned to more important jobs.[3] But many young people detest being treated as average or as a member of a category. They want to be considered unique, if not special, because the youth culture stresses the individual.[4] Corporate culture, however, emphasizes efficiency in handling large numbers of people identically until individuals have demonstrated their uniqueness. Paradoxically, management's attitudes and policies may promote the very "immature behavior" that is given as

---

* Notes and references will be found at the end of this chapter.

the reason for their establishment. Patience and understanding are needed on both sides.

Beginning professional and managerial positions in smaller businesses are reported to be more challenging and satisfying than similar posts in large firms. Small companies cannot afford to train young graduates on unproductive jobs, so they put them to work on important tasks immediately. Before you conclude that you should work for a smaller organization, you should realize that situations change. Five to 10 years into careers, the views reverse. Middle managers in large organizations report that their jobs are more challenging and rewarding than those of people on the same level in small firms, who may suffer from frustration and pressure for conformity. In the large organizations, middle-level jobs apparently carry more autonomy and authority than do similar level positions in small firms, where top management can dominate everything.[5]

Part of the difficulty stems from overemphasis on educational credentials. For some organizations, a high school diploma is required to be hired at all. Not only are those unfortunate enough not to possess the credentials arbitrarily excluded regardless of individual ability, but the skills of the more educated are widely underutilized. Boredom and resentment may set in so that a paradox results: At all levels, employees with more education tend to have lower morale and to perform no better than those with less education working at the same level.[6] (See Figure 29–1.) In fact, several studies indicate that people with less education outperform co-workers with more education.

Education may lead to higher (some say inflated) expectations of intrinsic job challenge and satisfaction.[7] Consequently, when jobs do not draw on the skills people

FIGURE 29–1

Education and Morale

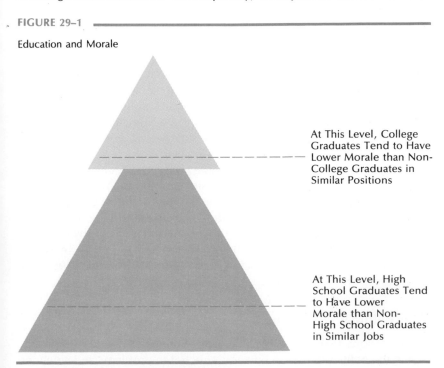

At This Level, College Graduates Tend to Have Lower Morale than Non-College Graduates in Similar Positions

At This Level, High School Graduates Tend to Have Lower Morale than Non-High School Graduates in Similar Jobs

think they possess, or when they believe they are being used below their status, disappointment and anger are likely. Employees may psychologically withdraw from the job, so that morale and perhaps even performance decline. These results do not argue for abolishing college (after all, college may be helpful in living a better life, even if it doesn't get you a better job). Rather, the situation suggests that companies should eliminate arbitrary and unrealistic requirements for educational credentials in favor of evaluating individual skills and abilities. All custodians don't need to be high school graduates, as some blue chip corporations require. Similarly, all department heads need not be college graduates, nor need vice presidents be holders of masters' degrees. Finally, we should recognize that greater education cannot carry an automatic guarantee of a more interesting and rewarding job.

Incompetent First Supervisor

A first boss plays a disproportionate role in a young person's career.[8] The impact of an incompetent first supervisor can be especially unfortunate because the early experience tends to be perpetuated in a kind of self-fulfilling prophecy. A superior who does not expect much of young subordinates fails to challenge them, and many of them will not perform well.[9] Even worse, incompetent supervisors who do not set high standards for themselves cause almost everyone's performance to deteriorate.[10] The word spreads that other managers do not want people from their groups, and the young person who works for such a supervisor can be stuck in a dead end.

Ambitious young specialists and managers want visibility and exposure—opportunity to show higher level executives how well they can perform and to learn to understand executive problems and objectives. A fearful intermediate supervisor can block such opportunity by relaying all communications herself and not allowing subordinates to see higher levels. Handling a report to your immediate boss with no opportunity to argue in its favor and never hearing what happens to it can be very disturbing (especially if you discover later that your name on the cover was replaced by your superior's). Organizations should institute policies to ensure that young employees enjoy the opportunity to communicate with and be evaluated by several higher executives, not just their immediate supervisors. And young managers should fight for the right to present reports personally.

Resignation may be the best answer to an untenable position under an incompetent supervisor, but short of this step, understanding the situation may allow an individual to set higher personal standards than the boss does. He or she may be able to perform better than others in a demoralized department; even performing only slightly better may bring the attention of other executives who are not blind to the difficulty of performing well in the department. The organization would of course be better off if young graduates were assigned mainly to the best supervisors, and many firms do this.

Insensitivity to Political Environment

All human organizations are political. For an organization to be effective, its managers must engage in the politics by which power is directed to problems and solutions are implemented. Unfortunately, many young managers are insensitive to or resentful of the political aspects of organizations.[11] This hurts them personally because they become passive about their careers, and it hurts the organization because it hinders the development of power coalitions, which are necessary for effective results.

Managers who rapidly climb hierarchies tend to be protégés of successful higher executives.[12] These sponsor-protégé linkages move together because their members come to respect and trust each other. They personalize organizational life and make it more predictable. A manager who has a problem prefers to consult a friend, not just an anonymous occupant of a bureaucratic position. Unfortunately, the criteria for inclusion in the group are often arbitrary and undemocratic—devoted to old-school ties and "proper" religion, race, or sex—but they are important nonetheless.

The importance of political relationships to the organization is that they form the power coalitions necessary to make and implement decisions.[13] Very few organizations are autocratically ruled by an omnipotent single person; even fewer are pure democracies in which the majority dominates. Most require a skillful minority coalition able to lead the majority through competent argument and common action. Without strong coalitions, power remains fractionated, actions are divisive, and the organization drifts willy-nilly.

A common complaint about recent business school graduates is that they overemphasize analytical tools and rational decision making, to the detriment of human understanding.[14] In spite of their desire to be treated as unique individuals, they treat others as objects to be manipulated. Thus they apparently are more Machiavellian in their managerial attitudes and more willing to use coercion than are practicing managers. As one corporation vice president puts it, "It takes us a couple of years to show our business school graduates than an organization is composed of people with whom they must develop personal relationships."

Insensitivity and Passivity . . .
- to political environment and need for coalitions
- to what is expected and real authority
- to tension between older and younger managers

Personal Passivity

The young managers who are insensitive to the political environment are frequently also characterized by personal passivity and inadequate probing of the world around them.[15] Such people fear what they may discover about themselves; or they assume that virtue guarantees reward, and their good intentions are enough to make everyone think they are doing a fine job.

FIGURE 29–2

Clarifying Delegation

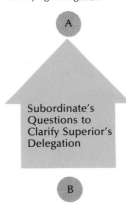

Subordinate's Questions to Clarify Superior's Delegation

When accepting a delegated task, it is important that a subordinate clarify the nature of the delegation, as indicated in Figure 29–2. The subordinate (B) must try to determine precisely what action the superior (A) expects (B) to take:

1. After I look into the problem, should I give you all the facts so that you can decide?
2. Should I let you know the alternatives available, with the advantages and disadvantages of each, so you can decide which to select?
3. Should I recommend a course of action for your approval?
4. Should I select the alternative, let you know what I intend to do, and wait for your approval?
5. Should I take action, let you know what I did, and keep you informed of results?
6. Should I take action and communicate with you only if it is unsuccessful?

Passivity sometimes springs from a feeling of helplessness, that the organization has so many confining rules and traditions that you can't be different. To behave differently than those others might be dangerous because "one simply doesn't do that." Of course, organizations demand substantial conformity, but some management observers suggest that many binding chains are of our own forging—and that many organizations would accept and reward initiative.[16] Thus, a young assistant manager in a department store was told by everyone that he wouldn't be allowed to sell used jeans. Their affluent clientale would supposedly be offended and store management angered. But he did, and no one was. His initiative was very successful, and he was widely praised.

It is always easier to drift with the times and hope things will work out for the best, but this is not a recipe fro managerial success. The paradox is that it may be the most promising young staff specialists who find it easiest to drift. To be in demand is a mark of status, and being busy gives a feeling of importance. Consequently, a talented young person might allow himself or herself to be dominated by others' desires, to become overcommitted to a narrow specialty, and to remain in a staff position too long. If you think of the organization as a cone, the staff tends to be on the outer surface, and line management is closer to the central power axis (see Figure 29–3).[17] A 30-year-old staff member may decide because of the lower pay not to accept a lower line position that is farther away from the top but has a more direct route to it. Young managers should take time to explore and probe the organization environment and to understand people's attitudes, develop relationships, and clarify their own positions.

FIGURE 29–3

An Organization's Power Axis

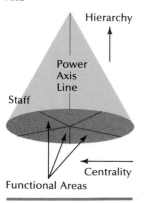

Hierarchy

Power Axis Line

Staff

Centrality

Functional Areas

Ignorance of Real Evaluative Criteria

A central rule for managerial success is "Please your boss." Unfortunately, what pleases the boss is not always clear, and insensitive and passive young managers may not know the real criteria by which their performance is being evaluated. Business is often less structured and more ambiguous than the authoritarian stereotype that many young people bring with them. Of course, managers highly value good performance as measured by profits, sales, productivity, and so on. Subordinates who occupy positions in which results can be easily measured in these terms tend to report greater satisfaction and autonomy in their jobs than those in posts in which performance cannot be evaluated quantitatively.[18] People in positions subject only to subjective performance evaluation tend to be less satisfied and to feel greater pressure for conformity in dress, thought, and action. In the absence of other criteria, they may be measured by how closely they fit the superior's prejudices rather than by their actual results.

Most people are biased by their own success or failures in making judgments. We like others to be like ourselves, especially *successful* others, because they verify our own correctness. Superiors tend to rate more highly those subordinates who are like them in appearance and managerial style.[19] Hence hair length, speech habits, and clothes do affect how personnel are evaluated. Some organizations see mustaches and mod clothing as signs of immaturity and radicalism, but others perceive them as showing creativity and vitality.

The same is true of evaluation on the basis of managerial style. Since the predominant style has been authoritarian, many superiors value subordinate managers more highly if they demonstrate authoritarian leadership. Even in the absence of corroborating hard performance data, authoritarian managers may be more highly rated than those who are participative or abdicative. One study indicated that a "permissive" manager whose division had good performance and much higher morale was rated as not being promotable, but a parallel authoritarian division manager with equal performance and lower morale was cited for excellent potential.[20]

A difficult situation results when a manager wants to utilize a less directive style that is ill-suited to the superior's expectation. A boss who is a hard-driving authoritarian manager may expect good subordinate managers to behave in a similar way. By asking frequent questions and demanding reports, the boss makes it difficult for the subordinate to be anything but authoritarian (see Figure 29–4). A courageous, tough, and independent middle manager can serve as a buffer between his or her superior and subordinates. By absorbing the pressure coming from above and not passing it on immediately to subordinates, the manager allows them enough autonomy to proceed in a participative manner. Such leadership requires demonstrable success in order to survive.

FIGURE 29–4

Pressure for Authoritarian Style

When A Is Very Authoritarian toward B . . .

It Is Very Difficult for B to Be Other than Authoritarian toward C.

Tension between Older and Younger Managers

Tension between older and younger professionals and managers is very common. It may be exacerbated by individual personalities, but basically it stems from differences in life and career stages. A recent graduate understandably relies on what he or she knows best—academic knowledge from school. The graduate is at least somewhat familiar with statistics, psychology, and economics, and they can be very valuable. Unfortunately, they can also hinder working relationships with older managers. Armed with an arsenal of analytical techniques, the graduate looks for problems to which they can be applied; but frequently the problems the textbook has solved are not the important ones. Worse yet, talking to older personnel in the arcane vocabulary of *stochastic variables, break-even points,* and *self-actualizing opportunities* can be very threatening to them. Older personnel to whom such terms are unfamiliar may believe they are being manipulated.

In some cultures older persons are automatically respected for age and assumed wisdom, but in the United States the young often respond to older people's skepticism with thinly veiled contempt. Because an older manager does not know the new techniques, the young specialist or manager erroneously infers that he or she is incompetent or unimportant. This can be a career-crippling mistake, because organizational contribution and influence have little to do with technical knowledge. An offended older executive can oppose the younger one's future advancement.

A young person should recognize that some older managers will see him or her as a threat (although the managers will deny it even to themselves). The threat is related not to position but to obsolescence and serves as a reminder of human mortality.[21] Tension can arise even when the older person personally likes the younger one. Young specialists should endeavor to manifest respect for older managers, to frame their vocabularies appropriately, and to avoid condescension. As the young people come to recognize the importance of political influence and intuitive judgments, they can develop the vertical coalitions helpful to both older and younger managers.

Conflict between Specialists and Generalists

One of the most common manifestations of intergroup conflict within business organizations is between staff specialists and line generalists.[22] The expanded and still growing role of staff is one of the salient aspects of modern organizations because technological sophistication growing out of physical and behavioral science has demanded more and more specialists.[23] Fitting these new people into organizations is not always easy, however.

Territorial Encroachment

Some line managers may fear that specialists will infringe on their jobs and diminish their power and status. The structural evolution of many organizations suggests expansion of specialist influence, often at the expense of line authority and autonomy. As we noted in Part Six, two of the most time-honored management principles are disappearing: (1) unity of command (one should have only one boss) and (2) authority must equal responsibility. These long-standing organizational postulates derive from common sense. If a person is receiving conflicting orders from more than one superior, what should she or he do first? How should priorities be assigned? Similarly, how can a manager be held responsible for performance without having the tools or managerial power to perform the necessary duties?

The growth of specialization, sophistication, and complexity in modern organizations has made it virtually impossible to respect these old principles. The aeronautical engineering group leader responsible for developing an airframe is dependent upon access to a wind tunnel controlled by a testing manager over whom the group leader has no authority. It would be much too expensive for the group leader to have a separate tunnel, nor does he have the necessary expertise to operate it. A production manager is responsible for the productivity of her department, but she is dependent upon planning specialists, industrial and mechanical engineers, and

Conflict between
Generalists and Specialists
- territorial encroachment
- incompatible styles
- conflicting loyalties
- interaction pattern
- separation of knowledge and authority
- change versus stability

industrial relations personnel over whom she has no authority. Although the manager presumably receives no orders from these staff people, she does receive "suggestions," "schedules," and "procedures." Under these conditions, conflict is not rare.

Incompatible Styles

Stress in line and staff relations also grows out of age and social differences. The younger, more educated, and better dressed staff specialist frequently is disliked and distrusted by older production managers who came up via what they perceive as a harder route. To make matters worse, the ambitious specialist sometimes betrays condescension toward the generalist whom he or she sees as less able and less promotable. Of course, many specialists are only putting on an act, attempting to appear more confident and influential than they really are. To support this image, they sometimes project an aura of infallibility, which hinders an open and free exchange of communications with their line associates. Insecurity about their real status and contributions leads many specialists into elaborate charades. At all organizational levels, staff personnel tend to feel greater anxiety and dissatisfaction than line managers do at comparable levels.[24]

These stressful relations between line and staff were first analyzed 30 years ago.[25] Their adverse impact on organizational life may have declined in the intervening years, but much still remains. The specialists' hair may be longer, their clothes more stylish, their expertise more legitimate, but gaps are still common between specialists and generalists because their education and experience may train them to think differently. Engineering school may develop analytical ability and decrease creativity, and liberal arts may do just the opposite. Differing work experiences seem to have a similar result.[26] Consequently, different education and job experience can lead to divergent thought patterns that hinder cooperation. The generalist may still think that the specialist is too theoretical, too impractical, or too narrow.

It is difficult to reconcile needs for differentiation and for integration in organizations. To deal with complexity, management has resorted to specialization and specialists who have diverse cognitive and emotional orientations.[27] Such people frequently experience trouble in communicating and cooperating. Yet, for the organization to act as a unity, there must be collaboration or integration among the various departments. Thus management faces a problem: Long-run performance requires substantial integration, but efforts to generate collaboration often produce short-run conflict.[28] It is often easier to allow specialization or differentiation to dominate over integration, with the result that the generalist is squeezed between competing specialists.

Conflicting Loyalties

When two interdependent parties must cooperate, divided loyalties always exist. This is not unique to generalist-specialist relations, but it is a problem. Orientation toward a discipline or function rather than loyalty to the organization sometimes characterizes professionals and staff specialists.[29] The researcher feels himself to be a chemist first and a member of Du Pont second, whereas a production manager is first and foremost concerned with producing nylon and making a profit for the company. Not surprisingly, the "cosmopolitan" professional tends to be more critical of the firm than does the "local" manager.[30]

Interaction Patterns

The traditional theory of staff implies that the adviser will respond to inquiries from the generalist. Early in his or her career, however, the specialist learns that sufficient calls do not automatically come in—and that not being busy is a mark of not being in demand and of low status. Accordingly, the ambitious staff specialist begins to look around for places to "offer" advice. The specialist begins to initiate communications to line management. Advice that has not been requested, however, is often resented.

Separation of Knowledge and Authority

For the line managers, this proliferation of staff advisers and specialists means that they no longer have complete control over their own operations. They personally may not have the knowledge necessary to manage their departments. Thus a growing gap between knowledge and authority has emerged, paralleling the gap between ownership and control, which took managerial control away from stockholders as they multiplied and transferred power to professional management.[31] Generalists realize that they are dependent on the specialist, who is frequently a staff specialist lower on the organizational hierarchy. Line managers may possess the formal authority to make decisions, but if all they can do is sign the proposals submitted by staff specialists, who is really in control? One of the burdens of Lyndon B. Johnson's presidency (and indeed any presidency) is that he felt himself short of the required knowledge to judge who was correct among his various advisers. In areas in which he had little expertise, he had the power to decide, but only among the alternatives proposed by specialists who had the knowledge (but whose advice was sometimes contradictory, thus throwing into question their actual knowledge and competence).[32]

The trained and specialized professional may resent performance evaluation by a generalist manager whom he or she considers to be professionally incompetent.[33] The professional expects to be evaluated and rewarded by fellow professionals, but in hierarchical organizations these functions reside with management.

Change versus Stability

Many managers fear change and see the staff specialist as embodying threats to present stability. The manager struggles to maintain equilibrium, while the specialist endeavors to demonstrate ability and creativity. Usually this leads to a change proposal. Most managers are not categorically opposed to change; the problem is that sometimes they see no need for the specialist's proposed modification. There is no felt need on their part. In short, the specialist often sees problems needing correction when the managing generalist sees none or sees different problems.

Loyalty Dilemmas

Loyalty is a popular but vague concept that is subject to both praise and scorn. There is little doubt that most people in authority highly value subordinates' loyalty.[34] Some of the various concepts of loyalty that superiors expect of subordinates are: (1) obey me; (2) work hard; (3) be successful, whatever it takes; (4) protect me, and don't let me look bad; and (5) tell me the truth. All of these concepts are partially valid and contribute to organizational effectiveness. Unfortunately, all can also be distorted, to the detriment of the individual and the organization.

Loyalty Dilemmas—Is Loyalty . . .
- obedience?
- effort?
- success?
- protection?
- honesty

Loyalty as Obedience

A superior can equate a subordinates' loyalty with doing what they are told. All managers have a right to expect obedience, but excessive emphasis on it enshrines the "yes man" philosophy as an organizational principle. It is understandable that a subordinate's willful disobedience would be construed as disloyalty, but equating loyalty and obedience assumes that authoritarian management is the only valid style, while it ignores the possibility that loyalty may sometimes reside in *not* doing what the boss has ordered because disaster could follow.[35]

"I never met a 'yes man' I didn't like."

From *The Wall Street Journal,* with permission of Cartoon Features Syndicate.

Loyalty as Effort

Young managers are rightly expected to work hard in the interest of the organization. Executives are skeptical of the intentions of young people who make a minimal commitment to their work. Yet when effort and hours worked are equated with loyalty, people will tend to put in excessive hours without real effort or contribution. Consider the comments of some young managers in the home office of an insurance company:

> The officers are the first here in the morning and the last to leave at night; they are always here Saturdays and many Sundays.
>
> They set the pace and, at least implicitly, it is the pace we must accept and follow.
>
> If you want to get ahead, this is the pattern you must accept.
>
> Contribution tends to be judged in terms of time spent in the office, not things accomplished.
>
> If you want to get ahead, you come in on Saturdays regardless of whether it is necessary or not. The cafeteria and offices are sometimes filled with people who just feel they can't afford not to come in on Saturday.

Thus behavior can become a game to convince others of loyalty, even when it contributes nothing to organizational effectiveness.

Loyalty as Success

The superiors can see loyalty as synonymous with reliability and successful performance whatever it takes (and don't bother them if it entails shady things they shouldn't know about). It is reasonable to expect honest effort, but this version of loyalty is difficult because it adds a moral criterion to the judgment of competence. Not all young managers who miss deadlines are disloyal; the task may simply be impossible within legal or ethical limits. A superior who judges all people and performance from such a loyalty perspective will discourage honest communication and encourage illicit managerial practice to achieve the success he or she demands.

Loyalty as Protection

The superiors expect subordinates to protect them and the organization from ridicule and adverse evaluation by others. Subordinates who follow their superior's instructions to the exact letter *are* disloyal if they do not exercise common sense to fill in obvious gaps. This version of loyalty has particular relevance where the superior is a generalist and the subordinates are specialists who know more than he or she does in their areas of expertise. In return for subordinate concern and protection, the superior implicitly promises to look out for their personal and political interests.

This loyalty concept sometimes includes an injunction to subordinates never to disagree with the superior in public when the boss's boss or outsiders are present. This makes sense, but it can become exaggerated when a sharp distinction is made between "us" to whom loyalty is due and "them" to whom it is not. The efforts

agree that economic self-interest is a good criterion for ethical decisions at the individual level. Most people see no connection between "ethical" and "economic" or "self-interest."

Ethics as Law

When asked about kids buying pornographic magazines, a publisher and purveyor of "adult" reading material responded: "What's the matter, don't you like to look at pictures of naked pretty girls and boys? I keep within the law. My magazines aren't meant for kids, but I can't keep them from buying them. That's the government's problem."

For this businessman, law is the criterion for decision making. If society thinks what he is doing is unethical, it is government's responsibility to legislate against it. In the absence of prohibition, he does what is allowed. Certainly, managers have responsibility as citizens to obey the law.[43] The young marketing managers in the electrical equipment industry who secretly met to fix prices and allocate markets violated the law, and in their case the law was relatively clear.[44]

Most people think that adherence to law is a necessary but insufficient basis for ethics. Behaving legally so you will not be punished is merely being prudent, not ethical. Law imposes demands from outside, while ethics should come from inside.[45] Besides, if law constituted the only behavior limits, government and law enforcement would swell to overwhelming proportions. Big Brother would be everywhere, and freedom to do either wrong or right would disappear.

Ethics as Religion

If governmental law is not sufficient, is there a higher law? A business executive suggests that there should be no problem of knowing what is proper: "If a man follows the Gospel he can't go wrong. Too many managers have let basic religious truth out of their sight. That's our trouble."

Most religions maintain that there are universal moral principles that should guide human behavior.[46] In almost all times and places, thou shalt not lie, steal, or murder, for example. Advertisements that deceive customers and industrial espionage to discover competitors' secrets are clearly proscribed by religious principles. Nonetheless, only a minority of managers think such principles are the basic ethical criteria for their managerial decisions. The problem is that moral principles are often abstract and difficult to apply to specific cases.[47] To be sure, intentional lying is clearly wrong, but most business executives sincerely believe they must hide information and distort public communications as protection against competitors or unions. And stealing is wrong, but padding expense accounts or "borrowing" company tools does not seem so immoral when the employer knows and seemingly condones it (perhaps they are a form of supplemental compensation). Catholic theology holds that every employer has an obligation to pay at least a living wage, but determining exactly what this is is subject to debate. Perhaps it is unrealistic to expect a guide to conduct developed in the Middle East 2,000 years ago to have direct relevance to the complex conditions modern managers face.[48]

Pragmatists argue that religious teachings and the Golden Rule are not meant to apply to competitive business and that management is more akin to a poker game than to the religious life.[49] If obfuscation and deception are part of the game and everyone knows it, then they are not sinful. Finally, many people subscribe to no religious beliefs and resent believers' attempts to impose their tenets on everyone. Clearly, religion as an ethical guide is helpful and good, but only to some people some of the time.

Ethics as Common Behavior

"But everyone does it" has long been a popular justification for behavior. Realists argue that if the majority engages in a certain activity it must be OK, regardless of what the authorities say. The young manager could base judgments upon the characteristic behavior of a boss, an organization, or an entire industry, not on universal rules (see Figure 29–6). Thus the garment sales representative argues that it is impossible to follow the computer industry's prohibition against booze and sex as selling aids. The garment industry accepts such inducements; buyers expect them; and one cannot compete without them. Similarly, managers in fiercely competitive industries argue that they cannot be as open about costs and policies as a monopoly, such as telephone communications, can be.

Every young manager will experience the pressure of others' behavior as a determinant of his or her own. This results in a paradox: Most agree that others' behavior is not the best criterion for individual decisions, but they still maintain that their superior's behavior is the major reason they behave unethically. It is the top that sets the ethical tone in most organizations; this is one of the gravest obligations of high-level executives. Their behavior will be emulated and converted into institutionalized custom by lower level managers.[50]

A young people caught in such an unhappy situation pursue one of several courses: They adjust their personal beliefs and stay happily; they stay but have guilty consciences (perhaps to change things when they gain power), or they depart.

FIGURE 29–6 ━━━━━━━━━━━

What Influences a Manager to Make
Unethical Decisions?

- Behavior of Superiors
- Climate of Industry
- Behavior of Peers
- Lack of Company Policy
- Personal Financial Needs

Least
Influence

Source: R. Baumhart, *Ethics in Business* (New York: Holt, Rinehart & Winston, 1968).

Ethics as Impact on People

Upon being asked about unethical managers, a former president of General Electric observed that they are not the problem: "What we must fear is the honest business-man who doesn't know what he is doing." Most companies that have polluted the air and despoiled the land did so out of ignorance, not immorality. Knowledge may assist managers in making decisions based upon what is best for the greatest number of people.

This is what schools of business administration and management have striven for—to make management a profession whose primary concern is social contribution, not narrow self-interest.[51] By teaching prospective managers how business, economy, society, and environment interact, they hope their graduates will take the broader picture into account when making decisions. No intelligent executive in the last quarter of the 20th century can really believe that air and water are free goods to be used as he or she unilaterally deems most profitable for the firm. Even if the firm does not pay for them, the executive's education should have shown that society does.

No doubt ignorance has occasioned much apparently unethical behavior, and greater professional knowledge should be of great benefit to all. But unfortunately, professionals who have taken the Hippocratic Oath or sworn allegiance to the Consti-tution cheat clients, defraud the public, and rape the environment. It is naive to expect that education alone is a sufficient guide for ethical behavior. Besides, what contributes most to the greatest number of people may mean exploitation of the few or the breaking of laws. Some executives have violated various business laws in order to protect the jobs of employees on the grounds that no one is hurt by colluding with a competitor, but many would be out of work and collecting unemploy-ment compensation if pure competition existed.

Guarding against Cynicism

No single ethical criterion is sufficient. Young managers striving to be ethical should do more than depend on economic self-interest, more than obey the law, more than observe their religious principles, more than follow their superior, and more than obtain the greatest good for the most people. They will have to filter all these through their subjective judgment of what is right. In making these judgments, the managers must guard against cynicism.

Most people attribute comparatively poorer motivation and more unethical behav-ior to others than to themselves. Young people today seem to be very cynical about business ethics and managers. They tend to believe that practicing managers engage in more unethical behavior than *they* would and more than the managers themselves think they do. Thus students attribute such activities as padding expense accounts, illegal use of inside tips, stealing of trade secrets, and immoral cooperation to manag-ers to a greater extent than the managers anonymously report they use these practices. Research suggests that the younger the person, the greater the cynicism about manag-ers; the older the managers, however, the greater the optimism about others (see Figure 29–7).[52] Whether this reflects time or the times is unknown. If people become

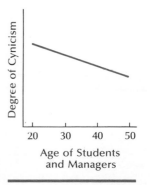

FIGURE 29–7

Relation of Cynicism to Age of Managers

*"I'm looking for an
honest man, not an honest kid!"*

Drawing by Weber; © 1964, The New Yorker Magazine, Inc.

less cynical as they become older and see that everyone is not as unethical as they thought, today's young people might become less cynical as they climb their organizational ladders. Whether today's cynicism is actually justified because older managers forget what it is like at lower levels or delude themselves about actual practice is not known.

Because cynicism encourages unethical behavior on the grounds that "I'd be a fool not to if everyone else is," it can be self-fulfilling prophecy. It is more likely, however, that a young manager who believes everyone "does it" will discover that they do not do so. The young manager who indulges in such behavior may find the result to be a ruined career.

Problems of Minority Managers

Blacks and white females face all the career problems that we have discussed: transitions, vertical mobility, Machiavellianism, early frustration, passivity, uncertainty, and so on. Indeed, they may even suffer from increased burdens of these common problems because to even reach management, they are probably more intensely motivated and hence at even greater risk of slighting the human and political aspects of organizations. In addition, they confront other difficulties unique to their minority status.

Entry

The first difficulty is simply gaining entry, or more appropriately, even thinking about preparing for managerial careers.[53] Women are now flocking to undergraduate and graduate management programs, but it is a relatively recent development. In the past, women seeking careers were usually oriented to traditional female occupations, such as teaching and nursing. Female management graduates are still largely at the technical and lower middle-management levels. Nonetheless, a 1975 survey of female subscribers to the newsletter *Executive Woman* indicates an average age of 38 and average salary of $25,930 per year with the top over $100,000.[54] That average salary is probably $35,000 today.

Black enrollment, aside from predominantly black colleges, has apparently not greatly climbed in business and management. Many bright young blacks are skeptical about business careers and see more promise in other professions. Nonetheless, admissions officers at the prestige MBA programs are aggressively recruiting talented black graduates, and young black MBAs are among the most sought-after people in America. Only time will suggest how high and how far they will go.

Problems of Minority Managers
- gaining entry
- dead-end positions
- political isolation
- overdependence on sponsor
- rejection by subordinates
- burden of being a symbol

Dead-End Positions

All too often an effective young minority manager is rewarded with a "promotion" away from the organization's power axis into a post directly related to minority status. Hence, a good female market analyst may be appointed supervisor of the support staff (mainly clerical) with a nice wage increase (but not as great as her male colleague promoted to supervisor of an analyst group). Or a young black sales representative is appointed manager of black merchandising. This could be a central position depending on the firm's products, but often the company sees marketing to the black community as low status. Once in an auxiliary or peripheral position, moving back to more central activities can be very difficult. One can become dead-ended.

Note that these are not strictly token jobs without content.[55] They are necessary activities, but not ones traditionally on the route to the top. In commenting on his firm's efforts to integrate women into the hierarchy, one corporation personnel manager observed that it went well while the central personnel department was watching. But after five or six years, personnel became more concerned with newer entrants, and the earlier women began to get sidetracked.

Political Isolation

We have repeatedly stated the importance of a social matrix in organizational life: independence is much easier with some support; creativity is facilitated with resonant colleagues; and promotions are assisted by vertical coalitions. While males are sometimes reluctant to accept minority members into their informal networks so essential to personal effectiveness. They may fear that the solo woman will destroy group cohesiveness by sparking sexual competition among the males.[56] She may be accepted only if she accepts low status and expected female passivity. Or the black male may be rejected because of feared interference with white camaraderie if he is "culturally" different.

An enticing, but dangerous, way of handling this isolation is to slavishly conform to all formal rules and informal traditions.[57] By becoming a super organization person the minority member hopes to be accepted. And he or she may well be, but such passive behavior will only validate higher judgment that the minority persons are unsuited to more responsible positions.

Overdependence on Sponsor

Sponsors are important and sometimes difficult for minority members to find. For this reason, some minority managers (and, of course, some majority members as well) become too dependent on a single more senior person.[58] To avoid endangering the relationship, they may become too accepting, too uncritical. Some superiors complain especially about female protégés who are reluctant to ask questions or to point out their superior's mistakes. One study of this problem suggests women in the business world make too much of the simple routine action of going to see a superior about a problem.[59] They tend to think the boss is busy with other more important matters or feel they lack the ability to cope competently with a superior in his or her office. Specific topics avoided include asking for a pay raise, requesting a promotion, correcting a superior who is wrong, challenging a decision, and selling a new idea. Of course, many young men also suffer from similar reluctance.

Consequently, female subordinates may work diligently on incorrectly understood problems, or their superiors may believe there is insufficient loyalty upward. Most discussion of protégé-sponsor relations suggest that one must outgrow the sponsor (and indeed several in a lifetime) and declare one's independence—but only after having developed relationship with other higher level people.

Rejection of Minority Superior

Although the attitude is probably declining, many white males still feel very uncomfortable working for a minority superior. Remember that upwardly mobile managers are a little surprised to confront increased dependence as they move upward. The stress can be even greater for minority managers who recognize how easily disloyal subordinates can wreck their careers. Males may feel threatened by female superiors because of unresolved childhood conflicts with Mom and her authority.[60] And even whites who consider themselves liberals may be surprised by their resentment of a black boss who is necessarily tough in saying no.

Some minority superiors try to reduce the tension by identifying downward and striving to become one of the gang. This may ease personal strain but can be a recipe for managerial disaster. The superior can lose credibility downward and influence upward as his or her own boss becomes less responsive.

Burden of Being a Symbol

Minority managers who have fought the good fight and performed better than their white male contemporaries in order to stay even may weary of their role as minority symbol. Thus they may come to mature decisions that they really don't want to be a vice president or head of the finance department, that department head in personnel is more satisfying even if less central. As we have seen, white males experience difficulty in judging whether they are truthful to self or just rationalizing failure. It is even harder for minority managers who worry whether or not they are selling out, copping out, or have been coopted by accepting a well-paying and personally satisfying, but fringe position.

Advice on Career Management

Advising young people on how to manage their careers is a risky proposition. It depends upon the individual's objectives and definition of success: Climbing to the top? Maintaining integrity? Keeping job and home separate? Happiness? These goals are not all mutually exclusive, but they can be competitive.[61]

For those whose objectives include climbing to higher managerial ranks, the following suggestions have been offered by a variety of sources.[62]

Suggestions for Minority Managers

No simple answers exist for all problems. Advice tends to sound naive and glib, but here are some suggestions:

1. Fight for high visibility, power axis positions, especially in mid career. Don't accept lateral transfers or diagonal "promotions" away from the power axis. And don't accept positions where your particular sex or race is an asset.

2. Conform to the cultural style in appropriate ways: control your language, wear conservative clothes, learn to play golf or tennis, talk about stock prices or what ever is necessary to encourage the group to feel comfortable around you. This may appear to be sacrificing one's personal style or integrity, but such superficial conformity may make you less threatening, thus freeing you to be more independent and initiating on important issues.

A black consultant to black managers observes:

> The basic problem facing many minority group applicants is attitudinal. That is, they have a chip on their shoulder. We counsel the individual, try to make him think. If a guy has a chip on his shoulder it can affect the whole work environment and defeat the purpose of bringing the guy in in the first place. There's no place in industry for militant attitudes. . . . There's a lot of distrust and skepticism about business in the black community. But a man is judged by his ability. He can achieve and be black. We have to operate within the system until we control the system. Then we can set our own groundrules.[63]

In the post-World War II period, males from various white ethnic groups have made enormous progress in climbing organizational ladders displacing earlier males. Most made it by learning to behave like traditional white, Anglo-Saxon, Protestant

Suggestions for Minority Managers
- strive for visibility and power axis
- attempt to "fit in" with culture; strive for independence on important issues
- initiate upward
- utilize contacts
- expand upon technical skills

culture—controlled emotions, cool communications, and prudent rationally. Thus history suggests that aspiring black and female managers should learn this executive culture. Nonetheless, some black and female reformers decry this loss of distinctness. They criticize the black who becomes an "oreo" (after the cookie with chocolate pastry exterior and white sugar interior, black appearance around white values) or the woman who behaves as cold and unfeeling as the coldest male. Some feminists want us to reform organizational society and make it more feminine, more caring, and supportive. It is even suggested that women can feminize managerial jobs and thereby make them even more effective than a male could.[64] The weight of experience would suggest, however, that promotional success is more likely to go to those who act more in accord with traditional executive culture.

3. Remember that sponsor-superiors may be flattered by obedience and faithfulness, but that the good ones even more desire assistance and protection. Therefore, be active in initiating reports, advice, criticism, and warnings. This is best done on a confidential in-writing or one-on-one basis. Use your token visibility as an opportunity to impress your superiors that you have the ability to do other things. And don't feel apologetic or guilty about whatever extra vertical links your race or sex give you. It is just one compensating factor against other blocking factors.

4. Move beyond technical expert power. Minority managers probably have moved ahead faster in areas where their technical expertise could be clearly demonstrated, hence converted into expert power. Engineering, science, and computers have been areas in which the relatively few females experience less difficulty in managing men—the women managers can show they know more. But managerial success eventually brings you to levels where technical expertise must be supplemented by general business knowledge and interpersonal competence. Early supplemental training in broader topics and interpersonal skills can be helpful preparation, but more important is an awareness that one's abilities must be expanded.

Suggestions for All Young Managers

Suggestions for All Young Managers

- clarify objective and subjective performance criteria
- strive for visibility and exposure
- develop sponsor-protege relations
- train replacement, be prepared to move
- move for power and responsibility, not pay
- continuously assess personal strengths and weaknesses
- don't be confined by job descriptions
- learn to live with ambiguity and dependence
- do not become excessively cynical

1. Remember that good performance that pleases your superiors is the basic foundation of success, but recognize that not all good performance is easily measured. Determine the real criteria by which you are being evaluated, and be rigorously honest in evaluating your own performance against these criteria.

2. Manage your career; be active in influencing decisions that will be taken about you, because pure effort is not necessarily rewarded.

3. Strive for positions that have high visibility and exposure where you stand out as a hero, and be observed by higher officials. Check to see that the organization has a formal system of keeping track of young people. Remember that high-risk line jobs tend to offer more visibility than such staff positions as corporate planning or personnel, but visibility also can sometimes be achieved by off-job community activities.

4. Develop relations with a mobile senior executive who can be your sponsor. Become a complementary crucial subordinate with different skills than your superior.

5. Learn your job as quickly as possible, and train a replacement so you can be available to move and broaden your background in different functions.

6. Nominate yourself for other positions; modesty is not necessarily a virtue.

However, change jobs for more power and influence, not primarily status or pay. The latter could be a substitute for real opportunity to make things happen.

7. Before taking a position, rigorously assess your strengths and weaknesses, what you like and don't like. Don't accept a promotion if it draws on your weaknesses and entails mainly activities that you don't like.

8. Leave at your convenience, but on good terms without parting criticism of the organization. Do not stay under an immobile superior who is not promoted in three to five years.

9. Do not be trapped by formal, narrow job descriptions. Move outside them, and probe the limits of your influence.

10. Accept the ideas that responsibility will always somewhat exceed authority and that organizational politics are inevitable. Establish alliances and fight necessary battles, limiting upward ones to very important issues.

11. Get out of management if you cannot stand being dependent on others and having them dependent on you.

12. Recognize that you will face ethical dilemmas no matter how moral you try to be. No evidence exists that unethical managers are more successful than ethical ones, but it may well be that those who move faster are less socially conscious.[65] Therefore, from time to time you must examine your personal values and question how much you will sacrifice for the organization.

13. Do not automatically accept all the tales of managerial perversity you hear. Attributing others' success to unethical behavior is often an excuse for one's own personal inadequacies. Most of all, do not commit an act you know to be wrong in the hope that your superior will see it as loyalty and reward you for it. Some will, but they may also sacrifice you when the organization is criticized.

SUMMARY

Frustration and dissatisfaction in young graduates' early careers is widespread because of several factors. Their job expectations are unrealistic; they find it difficult to change from school's short-range time perspectives to work's long-range view; employers assign them boring tasks that do not challenge them; or they begin under an incompetent first supervisor. As a result, turnover from first positions is substantial.

Many young specialists and managers are insensitive to the organization's political aspects, so that they needlessly offend older managers and fail to develop the alliances necessary to concentrate power on important issues. To compound their problems, some are passive in not asking questions to clarify what is expected of them and to determine what authority they possess. They let their careers drift under the control of others without even knowing the real criteria by which superiors evaluate their performance.

Loyalty presents one of the most difficult dilemmas for many young managers; everyone values it, but its meaning varies. For some superiors, loyalty is subordinates doing exactly what they are told. For some, it is subordinate success, whatever the means. For still others, it is subordinates who keep the executives and the organization from looking bad. Finally, for a few it is subordinates who communicate honestly what is going on. All of these conceptions of loyalty are partially valid; an organization should value obedience, effectiveness, effort, reliability, and honesty, but all can distort behavior if carried to excess.

Personal anxiety about integrity and commitment occurs when young managers are faced with ethical dilemmas. Although they should be guided by personal feelings, this is extremely subjective, and ethics should be examined in the light of other criteria: economic self-interest, regulations and laws, religious principles, others' customary behavior, and impact on people. All of these can be helpful in making decisions, but none alone is always sufficient. In reaching decisions, the manager must be wary of cynicism that assumes the worst in everyone else. It can lead to improper and inappropriate behavior.

The career advice offered includes admonitions to perform well, be active in managing your career, strive for visibility and exposure, develop relations with senior sponsors, learn quickly and train a subordinate, nominate yourself for new positions, rigorously assess your strengths and weaknesses, don't be trapped by narrow job descriptions, recognize that organizational politics are inevitable, and be prepared for ethical dilemmas.

Make no mistake about it, you will encounter career problems and dilemmas. Even if you now maintain that you are not so ambitious that you cannot afford to be ethical, you may well feel differently when an ethical choice could limit your future. It is much easier to be courageous and ethical in abstract terms than in concrete ones. What is right and ethical is not always clear in practice.

Since much supposedly unethical behavior stems from ignorance and not malevolence, future managers must accept the professional obligation of keeping current or managerial techniques and social problems. You will have the responsibility of knowing how your organizational activities affect others, immediately and eventually. Ignorance of the primary and secondary consequences of unsafe products and dangerous technology is morally unacceptable.

Increased government regulation of managerial activities is probable because society cannot depend entirely on the good intentions of business executives (nor anyone else). The strength of our tradition is the institution of procedures, safeguards, and countervailing forces to limit the few in the interest of the many. But we delude ourselves if we think that governmental legislation is the answer. If we want to preserve a relatively free, private enterprise system, we must have honest and knowledgeable managers. The alternative is tyranny.

REVIEW QUESTIONS

1. What are the causes of "early frustration and dissatisfaction" among young managers?

2. What expectations of recent graduates sometimes conflict with organizational expectations?

3. How does an incompetent first supervisor affect young graduates' careers?

4. What are visibility and exposure, and why are they desirable to ambitious young managers?

5. What are young managers sometimes insensitive and passive about?

6. What are sponsor-protégé linkages, and why do they develop?

7. Why are political coalitions important to organizations?

8. How can young managers clarify what their superior delegates to them?

9. In what ways is a staff position not always desirable for a young specialist-manager?

10. What is difficult about a position where performance can be evaluated only by subjective criteria?

11. How do superiors tend to evaluate subordinates in such positions.

12. Why is tension between older and younger managers common?

13. Why is conflict between specialists and generalists common in organizations?

14. What is territorial encroachment between specialists and generalists?

15. What are the incompatible styles of specialists and generalists?

16. How do conflicting loyalties contribute to conflict?

17. How does the separation of knowledge and authority contribute to conflict?

18. How do orientations toward change and stability contribute to conflict?

19. What is valid about "obedience" as loyalty? What is dangerous about it?

20. What is valid about "effort" as loyalty? What is dangerous about it?

21. What is valid about "success" as loyalty? What is dangerous about it?

22. What is valid about "protection" as loyalty? What is dangerous about it?

23. What is valid about "honesty" as loyalty? What is dangerous about it?

24. What are the sources of "personal anxiety" which plague young managers as time passes?

25. Why is "dependence" often difficult to experience?

26. What are the various criteria for determining the "ethicalness" of managerial decisions?

27. What is helpful about ethics as "economic self-interest?" What is its weakness?

28. What is helpful about ethics as "law?" What is its weakness?

29. What is helpful about ethics as "religious principles?" What is its weakness?

30. What is helpful about ethics as "common behavior?" What is its weakness?

31. What factors influence managers to make unethical decisions?

32. What is helpful about "professionalization" and ethics as "impact on people?" What are their weaknesses?

33. What are the particular problems of young minority managers?

34. What are dead-end positions?

35. How do young minority managers sometimes become politically isolated?

36. How do some young minority managers become overly dependent on a single sponsor? How does this affect their behavior?

37. What suggestions are advanced to assist young minority managers in dealing with their particular career problems?

38. What suggestions are advanced to assist all young managers in dealing with career problems?

Notes and References on Career Problems of Young Managers

1. Over 50 percent of all M.B.A.'s leave their first employer within five years. J. A. DePasquale and R. A. Lange, "Job-Hopping and the MBA," *Harvard Business Review,* November–December 1971, p. 4 ff. See also J. A. DePasquale, *The Young Executive: A Summary of the Career Paths of Young Executives in Business* (New York: MBA Enterprises Inc., 1970), and G. F. Farris, "A Predictive Study of Turnover," *Personnel Psychology* 24 (1971), pp. 311–28.

When a graduate joins an organization, a "psychological contract" is forged between individual and organization. If the organization does not live up to the individual's perception of the contract, he/she feels offended and leaves. Unfortunately, the specific terms of this implied contract are seldom discussed. J. P. Kotter, "The Psychological Contract: Managing the Joining-up Process," *California Management Review* 15, no. 3 (1973), pp. 91–99.

The means of coping with a new job can be considered from both a career perspective and a stress perspective. For a detailed description of how employees deal with the uncertainty and challenges presented by a new job, see D. C. Feldman and J. M. Brett, "Coping with New Jobs: A Comparative Study of New Hires and Job Changers," *Academy of Management Journal* 26, no. 2 (1983), pp. 258–72.

2. For an interesting discussion of work role transitions, see N. Nicholson, "A Theory of Work Role Transitions," *Administrative Science Quarterly,* June 1984, pp. 172–91. Edward E. Lawler argues that the worker's expectation of immediate gratification means that management should shorten periods between evaluations and award frequent small raises rather than yearly ones. "Compensating the New Life-Style Worker," *Personnel* 48, no. 3 (1971), pp. 19–25. See also T. F. Stroh, *Managing the New Generation in Business* (New York: McGraw-Hill, 1971).

3. In general, the younger the managers, the *higher* the level they expect to reach in their careers. Thus virtually all are disappointed at some time. M. L. Moore, E. Miller, and J. Fossum, "Predictors of Managerial Career Expectations," *Journal of Applied Psychology* 59, no. 1 (1974), pp. 90–92.

Some executives are highly skeptical of M.B.A.s in particular. Here is a portion of a letter written to the editors of *Columbia Journal of World Business* 3 no. 3 (1968), p. 5:

> I can't agree completely with Mr. (T. Vincent) Learson's statement (January–February 1968) that the salvation of the business world is the "scientifically trained mind that comes from the ranks of the graduate schools." I have found many of these people have no concept of the value of a dollar. They are theorists only and for the most part have no desire to learn the basic fundamentals of the business they are engaged in, but rather consider themselves above finding out the basic principles of the business by experience. They want everyone to hand them experience on a velvet pillow and are too concerned with taking over the presidency of an organization six months after they enter an organization. I do believe the scientifically trained graduate student does have his place in industry, but . . .

4. A. G. Athos, "Is the Corporation Next to Fall?" *Harvard Business Review,* January–February 1970, pp. 49–60. For more on characteristics and expectations of young managers and specialists, see Judson Gooding, "The Accelerated Generation Moves into Management," *Fortune,* March 1971, p. 101 ff.; and L. B. Ward and A. G. Athos, *Student Expectations of Corporate Life* (Boston: Graduate School of Business Administration, Harvard University, 1972).

5. Lyman W. Porter, "Where Is the Organization Man?" *Harvard Business Review,* November–December 1963, pp. 53–61.

For a detailed description of the nature of a career in general management, see J. P. Kotter, *The General Managers* (New York: The Free Press, 1982).

6. I. Berg, *Education and Jobs: The Great Training Robbery* (New York: Praeger Publishers, 1970); M. E. Gordon and R. D. Arvey, "The Relationship between Education and Satisfaction with Job Content," *Academy of Management Journal,* December 1975, pp. 888–92.

K. J. Arrow suggests that higher education may not contribute any productive skill to the student, but it does differentiate for the benefit of employers. "Higher Education as a Filter," *Journal of Public Economics* 2, no. 3 (1973), pp. 193–216. See also B. Jacobson and J. M. Kendrick, "Education and Mobility: From Achievement to Ascription," *American Sociological Review,* 38 (1973), pp. 439–60.

The educational attainment of workers will probably advance rapidly in the next 20 years. D. F. Johnston, "Education of Workers: Projections to 1990," *Monthly Labor Review* 96, no. 11 (1973), pp. 22–31.

7. J. W. McGuire summarizes the impact of education on organizations as follows:

1. The ratio of salaried to wage employees may be expected to increase steadily.
2. Personnel, educational, and developmental departments within the enterprise are going to expand and play a more important role.
3. The tendency toward "professionalism" in business will become more important.
4. Increased demands for independence and competence will be associated with professionalism.
5. In order to attract and hold educated workers, it will be necessary for companies to create task forces to work on interesting and stimulating projects.
6. Old concepts of the line organization will be increasingly revised to take advantage of knowledge most efficiently.
7. Organizational communications will become a problem of growing significance.
8. Adaptability lags will have to be shortened.
9. The tasks of top management will be substantially altered.

"Knowledge: The Basic Business Commodity," *Business Horizons* 12, no. 3 (1969), pp. 31–38.

8. J. A. Livingston, "Pygmalion in Management," *Harvard Business Review,* July–August 1969, pp. 81–89.

9. D. E. Berlew and D. T. Hall, "The Socialization of Managers: Effects of Expectations on Performance," *Administrative Science Quarterly* 11, no. 2 (1966), pp. 207–23.

10. In general, the more stringent a superior's personal standards, the higher subordinate performance will be. The superior's personal standards also seem to exert more influence on subordinate performance than their own personal standards do. The best performance is achieved where both superior and subordinates have high persoanl standards. John P. Campbell et al., *Managerial Behavior, Performance and Effectiveness* (New York: McGraw-Hill, 1970), pp. 447–51.

As J. Hall puts it, "The needs and quality of motivation characterizing a manager's subordinates may say more about the manager than about his subordinates." "To Achieve or Not: The Manager's Choice," *California Management Review,* Summer 1976, pp. 5–18.

11. For some case studies of sensitive and insensitive young managers, see W. R. Dill, T. L. Hilton, and W. R. Reitman, *The New Managers* (Englewood Cliffs, N.J.: Prentice-Hall, 1962); R. R. Ritti and G. R. Funkhouser, *The Ropes to Skip and the Ropes to Know* (Columbus: Grid, 1977).

12. E. E. Jennings, *The Mobile Manager: A Study of the New Generation of Top Executives* (Ann Arbor: Graduate School of Business Administration, University of Michigan, 1967); J. G. Bensahel, "Let your Protégé Make His Own Way," *International Management,* May 1977, pp. 44–46.

On helping one's boss to succeed, see A. Pleninger, *How to Survive and Market Yourself in Management* (New York: American Management Association, 1977).

13. On the importance of power, R. N. McMurray wrote:

The most important and unyielding necessity of organizational life is not better communications, human relations or employee participation, but power. . . .

Without power there can be no authority; without authority there can be no discipline; without discipline there can be difficulty in maintaining order, system and productivity. An executive without power is, therefore, all too often a figurehead—or worse, headless. . . .

If the executive owns the business, that fact may ensure his power. If he does not, and sometimes even when he does, his power must be acquired and held by means which are essentially political.

"Power and the Ambitious Executive," *Harvard Business Review,* November–December 1973, p. 140.

14. J. S. Livingston, "Myth of the Well-Educated Manager," *Harvard Business Review,* January–February 1971, pp. 79–88. In general, Livingston argues that there is no relation between managerial success and school performance and that schools do not develop important attributes. Lyndall Urwick maintains that "wisdom" is the neglected attribute. "What Have the Universities Done for Business Management?" *Management of Personnel Quarterly,* Summer 1967, pp. 35–40.

15. D. Moment and D. Fisher, "Managerial Career Development and the Generational Confrontation," *California Management Review* 15, no. 3 (1973), pp. 46–55.

16. D. Moment and D. Fisher, *Autonomy in Organizational Life* (Cambridge, Mass.: Schenkman, 1975).

17. E. H. Schein, "The Individual, the Organization and the Career: A Conceptual Scheme," in D. A. Kolb, I. M. Rubin, and J. M. McIntyre, *Organizational Psychology: A Book of Readings* (Englewood Cliffs, N.J.: Prentice-Hall, 1971), pp. 302–16.

In the 1970s both personnel managers and controllers we apparently becoming more central. "The Controller: Inflation Gives Him More Clout with Management," *Business Week,* August 15, 1977, p. 84 ff. "Personnel: A New Route to the Top," *International Business,* May 1977, p. 24 ff.

18. Lyman W. Porter, "Where Is the Organization Man?" *Harvard Business Review,* November–December 1963, pp. 53–61.

19. John P. Campbell et al., *Managerial Behavior, Performance and Effectiveness* (New York: McGraw-Hill, 1970), pp. 447–51. On how to dress, see J. T. Molloy, *Dress for Success* (New York: McKay, 1976), and Molloy, *Women's Dress for Success* (New York: Follet, 1977).

20. The study compared three regional managers of different styles—"authoritarian," "permissive," and "recessive" (laissez-faire). Objective measurements indicated no difference in regional performance, but higher management consistently rated the authoritarian as most effective and promotable. J. H. Mullen, *Personality and Productivity in Management* (New York: Columbia University Press, 1966).

21. Harry Levinson, "On Being a Middle-Aged Manager," *Harvard Business Review,* July–August 1969, pp. 51–60.

22. J. A. Belasco and J. A. Arlutto, "Line and Staff Conflicts: Some Empirical Insights," *Academy of Management Journal* 12, no. 1 (1969), pp. 469–77.

23. S. Melman, *Dynamic Factors in Industrial Productivity* (Oxford: Blackwell, 1956).

24. Porter, "Where Is the Organization Man?" Another survey of organizational stress attributed much of the problem to the dominance of the physical sciences, which created a need for specialists; and the growth of large-scale organizations, which generated greater interdependence among members. R. L. Kahn et al., *Organizational Stress* (New York: John Wiley & Sons, 1964).

25. Melville Dalton, "Conflicts between Staff and Line Managerial Officers," *American Sociological Review,* June 1950, pp. 342–51. Also see Dalton, *Men Who Manage* (New York: John Wiley & Sons, 1959) and E. Rhenman et al., *Conflict and Corporation in Business* (New York: John Wiley & Sons, 1970).

26. R. H. Doktor, "Some Cognitive Implications of Academic and Professional Training," *Experimental Publication System of the American Psychological Association,* Issue No. 7, Manuscript 266–126, 1970.

27. Paul R. Lawrence and Jay W. Lorsch, *Organization and Environment.* (Boston: Graduate School of Business Administration, Harvard University, 1967). R. G. Corwin found that greater organizational differentiation in public schools is associated with conflict between teachers and administrators. "Patterns of Organization Conflict," *Administrative Science Quarterly* 14 (1969), pp. 507–19.

28. Gideon Sjorberg, "Contradictory Functional Requirements and Social Systems," *Journal of Conflict Resolution* 4 (1960), pp. 198–208.

29. Amitai Etzioni states that there appears to be a basic incompatibility between expert orientation and bureaucratic orientation. "Authority Structure and Organizational Effectiveness," *Administrative Science Quarterly* 4 (1959), pp. 43–67. R. W. Scott wrote: ". . . the profession and the bureaucracy rest on fundamentally different principles of organization, and these divergent principles generate conflict between professionals and their employers in certain specific areas." "Professionals in Bureaucracies: Areas of Conflict," in *Professionals,* ed. H. M. Vollmer and D. L. Mills (Englewood Cliffs, N.J.: Prentice-Hall, 1966). Also see J. E. Sorensen and T. L. Sorensen, "The Conflict of Professionals in Bureaucratic Organizations," *Administrative Science Quarterly* 19, no. 1 (1974), pp. 98–106.

30. On the difference between "cosmopolitan" professionals oriented toward the profession and "locals" giving primary allegiance to the organization, see A. W. Gouldner, "Cosmopolitans and Locals: Toward an Analysis of Latent Social Roles," *Administrative Science Quarterly* 2, no. 3 (1957), pp. 281–306, and P. K. Berger and A. J. Grimes, "Cosmopolitan-Local: A Factor Analysis of the Construct," *Administrative Science Quarterly* 18, no. 2 (1973), pp. 223–35.

31. V. Thompson, *Modern Organization* (New York: Alfred A. Knopf, 1963). On the gap between owners and management, see A. A. Berle, *The Twentieth-Century Capitalist Revolution* (New York: Harcourt Brace, Jovanovich, 1954).

32. Lyndon B. Johnson, *The Vantage Point: Perspective of the Presidency* (New York: Holt, Rinehart & Winston, 1971).

33. On professional-organizational conflicts, see G. Ritzen, *Man and His Work: Conflict and Change* (New York: Appleton-Century-Crofts, 1972).

34. J. A. Pearce III, "An Assessment of Supervisors, Organizational Loyalty," *MSU Business Topics,* Summer 1977, pp. 50–56. On declining loyalty, see A. Patton, "The Boom in Executive Self-Interest," *Business Week,* May 24, 1976, p. 16 ff.

35. That *not* obeying may be loyalty is demonstrated by D. Wise in *The Politics of Lying* (New York: Random House, 1973). Newton Minow, who was appointed head of the Federal Communications Commission by President John F. Kennedy, is quoted as saying that in April 1962, after a story that was highly critical of the president was broadcast on the NBC "Huntley-Brinkley Report," Kennedy called Minow. As Minow recalls the conversation, it went like this:

JFK: Did you see that goddamn thing on Huntley-Brinkley?

MINOW: Yes.

JFK: I thought they were supposed to be our friends. I want you to do something about that.

Minow says he did not do anything, but he called a Kennedy aide the next morning and asked him to tell the president he was lucky to have an FCC chairman who does not do what the president tells him to.

36. For a disturbing example of the retribution heaped on a manager who reported his firm's shortcomings to the press, see K. Vandivier, "The Aircraft Brake Scandal," *Harper's Magazine,* April 1972, pp. 45–52.

37. A. O. Hirschman, *Exit, Voice and Loyalty* (Cambridge, Mass.: Harvard University Press, 1970); E. Weisband and T. M. Franck, *Resignation in Protest* (New York: Grossman/Viking, 1975).

38. See S. H. Miller, "The Tangle of Ethics," *Harvard Business Review,* January–February 1960, pp. 59–62; J. W. Towle, ed., *Ethics and Standards in American Business* (Boston: Houghton Mifflin, 1964); T. M. Garrett, *Business Ethics* (New York: Appleton-Century-Crofts, 1966); and C. C. Walton, *Ethos and the Executive* (Englewood Cliffs, N.J.: Prentice-Hall, 1969).

39. G. F. F. Lombard, "Relativism in Organizations," *Harvard Business Review,* March–April 1971, pp. 55–65; J. F. Fletcher, *Situation Ethics* (Philadelphia: Westminster Press, 1966); J. F. Fletcher, *Moral Responsibility: Situation Ethics at Work* (Philadelphia: Westminster Press, 1967).

40. M. S. Baram, "Trade Secrets: What Price Loyalty," *Harvard Business Review,* November–December 1968, pp. 66–74. For "horror stories" of managers who supposedly put profits over ethics, see F. J. Cook, *The Corrupted Land* (New York: Macmillan, 1966) and R. L. Heilbroner et al., *In the Name Of Profit* (Garden City, N.Y.: Doubleday Publishing, 1972).

41. M. Freedman, *Capitalism and Freedom* (Chicago: University of Chicago Press, 1962). A. Z. Carr argues that it is dangerous to a manager's career to act purely upon personal beliefs, but one can help one's organization by showing how unethical policies actually harm economic performance. "Can an Executive Afford a Conscience?" *Harvard Business Review,* July–August 1970, pp. 58–64. Thus, Carr is both pessimistic and optimistic—pessimistic that only economics guides business behavior, but optimistic that many dilemmas may be converted to economic terms where economics and public interest correspond. That good ethics is good economics and good business is argued by G. Gilman, "The Ethical Dimension in American Management," *California Management Review* 7, no. 1 (1964), pp. 45–52.

42. John K. Galbraith, *The New Industrial State* (Boston: Houghton Mifflin, 1967).

43. A. Chayes, "The Modern Corporation and the Rules of Law," in E. S. Mason, ed., *The Corporation in Modern Society* (Cambridge, Mass.: Harvard University Press, 1959), p. 25 ff.

44. C. C. Walton and F. W. Cleveland, Jr., *Corporations on Trial: The Electrical Cases* (Belmont, Calif.: Wadsworth, 1967).

45. A former chairman of the Chase Manhattan Bank wrote about ethical problems as follows:

Government's response to the problem, characteristically, has been that "there oughta be a law." In the first session of this Congress, more than 20,000 bills and resolutions were introduced, 20 percent more than in the first session of the previous Congress. The same approach has been in evidence on the state and local levels.

The objective seems to be to hold together our fractured moral structure by wrapping it in endless layers of new laws—a kind of LSD trip by legislation. Yet it should be clear by now, even to busy lawmakers, that the great lesson to be learned from our attempts to legislate morality is that it can't be done. For morality must come from the heart and the conscience of each individual.

George Champion, "Our Moral Deficit," *The MBA,* October 1968, p. 39.

46. H. L. Johnson, "Can the Businessman Apply Christianity?" *Harvard Business Review,* September–October 1957, pp. 68–76; J. W. Clark, *Religion and the Moral Standards of American Businessmen* (Cincinnati: South-Western Publishing, 1966).

47. T. F. McMahon, "Moral Responsibility and Business Management," *Social Forces,* December 1963, pp. 5–17.

48. See *Fortune* editorial in response to Pope Paul's encyclical "On the Development of Peoples," May 1967, p. 115. The editors argue that the Church's view would hinder growth and harm the underdeveloped nations more than a few unethical companies do.

49. A. Z. Carr, "Is Business Bluffing Ethical?" *Harvard Business Review,* January–February 1968, pp. 143–53. In a similar vein, T. Levitt argues that advertising is like art: it is not reality but illusion, and everyone knows it. Therefore, some distortion is acceptable. "The Morality of Advertising," *Harvard Business Review,* July–August 1970, pp. 84–92.

50. On the difficulties of managers who are confronted with accepting questionable conduct by their superiors, see J. J. Fendrock, "Crisis in Conscience at Quasar," *Harvard Business Review,* March–April 1968, pp. 112–20. For reader response to the situation, see J. J. Fendrock, "Sequel to Quasar Stellar," *Harvard Business Review,* September–October 1968, pp. 14–22; 98 percent said it was wrong to keep quiet, but 64 percent admitted they would be tempted to do so.

51. K. R. Andrews, "Toward Professionalism in Business Management," *Harvard Business Review,* March–April 1969, pp. 49–60. Some are skeptical about whether business schools really affect the ethics of their graduates. An executive observes, "They tend to get the notion up at Harvard that some things are more important than profits. But that doesn't affect them when they come here. They're not really contaminated. They're typical, intelligent, ambitious, greedy, grafting, ordinary American males." Quoted in S. Klaw, "Harvard's Degree in the Higher Materialism," *Esquire,* October 1965, p. 103.

Edgar H. Schein argues that educational institutions tend to accept the values of the enterprises they prepare students for. "The Problems of Moral Education for the Business Manager," *Industrial Management Review* 8, no. 1 (1966), pp. 3–14.

52. Our research suggests the following:

Business executives averaging age 45 think approximately 30 percent of all other executives behave more unethically than they do.

Young managers averaging age 33 think approximately 40 percent would be more unethical.

M.B.A. students averaging age 25 think approximately 70 percent would be more unethical.

Undergraduate students averaging age 19 think almost 100 percent of executives would be more unethical than they.

53. V. E. Schein, "Think Manager—Think Male," *Atlanta Economic Review,* March–April 1976, pp. 21–24.

54. *Executive Woman,* April 1975, p. 5.

55. R. M. Kanter, "Tokenism: Opportunity or Trap?" *The MBA,* January 1978, pp. 15 ff. See also R. M. Kanter, *Men and Women of the Corporation* (New York: Basic Books, 1977); M. Hennig and A. Jardim. *The Managerial Woman* (Garden City, N.Y.: Anchor Books, 1977).

56. C. Woman and H. Frank, "The Solo Woman in a Professional Peer Group," *American Journal of Orthopsychiatry,* January 1975, pp. 164–171.

57. R. A. Webber, "Perceptions and Behaviors in Mixed Sex Work Teams," *Industrial Relations,* May 1976, pp. 121–29.

58. G. Sheehy, "The Mentor Connection: The Secret Link in the Successful Woman's Life," *New York,* April 5, 1976, pp. 33–39; J. Thompson, "Patrons, Rabbis, Mentors—Whatever You Call Them, Women Need Them Too," *The MBA,* February 1976, pp. 26 ff.

59. C. C. Vance, *Boss Pschology: Help Your Boss Make You a Success* (New York: McGraw-Hill, 1976).

60. "How Men Adjust to a Female Boss," *Business Week,* September 5, 1977.

61. On different career perspectives, see H. O. Prudent, "The Upward Mobile, Indifferent and Ambivalent Typology of Managers," *Academy of Management Journal* 16, no. 3 (1973), pp. 454–64.

For a detailed description of how individuals make career decisions, see W. L. Mihal, P. A. Sore, and T. E. Comte, "A Process Model of Individual Career Decision Making," *Academy of Management Review* 9, no. 1 (1984), pp. 95–103.

62. Career advice is summarized in E. E. Jennings, *Routes to The Executive Suite* (New York: McGraw-Hill, 1971).

63. P. H. Bensen, "Tips on Being Black and Successful," *Philadelphia Bulletin,* October 4, 1973, p. 42.

64. Caroline Bird, *Everything a Woman Needs to Know to Get Paid What She's Worth* (New York: McKay, 1973), and *Enterprising Women* (New York: Norton, 1976). See also B. L. Harragan, *Games Mother Never Taught You* (New York: Rawson Associates, 1977).

65. B. M. Bass and L. D. Eldridge, "Accelerated Managers' Objectives in Twelve Countries," *Industrial Relations* 12, no. 2 (1973), pp. 158–70.

Discussion Questions and Exercises on Managerial Careers

Discussion Questions

1. Concerned about the high incidence of mononucleosis, shingles, and Vincent's disease (trench mouth) among shipboard ensigns and junior lieutenants, naval physicians and psychologists investigated. Their conclusion was that most of the cases were psychosomatic—related to the stress and strain in the junior officers' positions. What might be the causes of such difficulty?

2. In his book *Managerial Behavior,* L. R. Sayles describes how staff specialists attempt to modify their relationships to line managers—from service to advisory to auditing to controlling. Why might staff personnel attempt to change their relationships in this manner?

3. Thomas Jefferson once described the presidency of the United States as "a splendid misery." To a lesser extent, this can be said of many high executive posts. Why?

4. The eminent anthropologist Margaret Mead has commented that a central cause of the problems of teenagers and young adults in the United States is that in our society their adoption of adult life roles is postponed. What are the role conflicts and ambiguities of these years?

5. A study by S. Talacchi reported that employee morale and job satisfaction tend to be lower in larger organizations than in small ones. As corporations grow larger, he reports, there is a significant decrease in satisfaction with the company, supervision, fellow employees, and the job. Other studies also report higher rates of absenteeism and turnover in larger organizations. In contrast, a study by Lyman Porter indicates that managers in larger organizations see their positions as more rewarding and satisfying than

those in small organizations. They say that they have more freedom and autonomy (and less need for conformity) than managers say they experience in small firms. How would you explain these findings?

6. Supervisors in the printing industry are members of management who have usually been promoted from the ranks, yet most are still members of their respective trade unions. What problems exist for such supervisors?

7. Often, the basis for selecting a sales manager out of the sales staff is performance as a salesperson. Why might picking a highly effective and highly achievement-oriented salesperson for the job of sales manager be a mistake?

8. Critics of modern business (and especially critics of banks, insurance companies, and brokerage firms) have complained about management's "irrationality" in hiring and promoting executives on the basis of coming from the "correct" social background, attendance at "prestige" colleges, and wearing "conservative" clothes. What are the advantages and disadvantages of such criteria?

9. One observer of modern business has written: "The so-called private business corporation owned by many individual stockholders is in effect a private government with officials who are only loosely responsible to the owners. They are even less responsible to the citizens of the government—the employees. In spite of management's appeal to rational decision making and scientific organization, its fundamental internal administration is authoritarian. The business organization especially implies more of Genghis Khan than Thomas Jefferson. This centralized authority is not justified and must be replaced

by a more democratic system whereby employees at all levels have guarantees about due process and representation." How would you agree or disagree with this position?

10. Read some of the literature on organizational democracy, particularly as practiced in Europe, and discuss (a) the form and practice, (b) advantages for the organization and people, and (c) disadvantages for the organization and people. Would it work in the United States?

11. In beginning the search for a new administrator, a group of faculty members said that they did not want anybody who "enjoyed exercising power." What do you think of their attitude? Why is the need for power so widely distrusted and condemned, when in fact many people have it?

12. In what ways do many young business school graduates contribute to their own problems in organizations?

13. Some minority managers maintain that they are happy in what appear to be dead-end positions, but they feel guilty about being happy. How would you explain this?

14. What would be the advantages of making management a profession, such as medicine or law—that is, with mandatory educational requirements, ethical oaths, and self-policing? What might be the disadvantages?

15. Research suggests high-level executives from more modest socioeconomic backgrounds tend to suffer from a higher incidence of psychosomatic illness than do executives from more privileged backgrounds. How would you explain this?

16. Speaking to a college class, a retiring director of corporate management development cited two factors as most important when considering employment in an organization: (a) that the organization have "institutionalized" visibility/exposure, and (b) that the student should feel comfortable with the organization's style and values. What do you think of this advice? Discuss.

17. Some research suggests that actual behavior may be more ethical at higher executive levels than at lower managerial levels. How would you explain this.

18. Although no reliable research data exists, anecdotal evidence suggests that ambitious young male managers are less effective than older males in supervising female subordinates. Presumably the older males are less sympathetic to the feminist movement, so how would you explain this?

19. The so-called index of Machiavellianism is a measure of a person's tendency to see others as objects to be manipulated without respect for their integrity as individuals or recognition of their shared humanity. Research suggests that business school professors and students tend to rate higher on this index than do practicing managers. How would you explain this? What problems might the difference in attitudes create?

20. Recent sociological research suggests that in the United States virtually every Catholic ethnic group has now passed all Protestant groups in average salary (e.g., Irish-American Catholics earn higher salaries than do Episcopal Anglo-Saxon Americans, etc.). This appears to be a recent phenomenon. How would you explain it?

21. Discuss why middle-aged people today seem to feel that teenagers and young adults are much more mature than they were at the same ages. Do you agree or disagree?

22. Perhaps the most group-oriented phase of life is the early teen years. For example, the decision to smoke is influenced more by peers than by parents' words or behavior. Discuss why.

23. Some managers have compared being loyal to a work unit or organization with being a player on a sports team. The loyal subordinate knows how to play "team ball." What are some of the characteristics of this type of loyalty?

24. In the 1960s and early 1970s, many college students took a critical view of business careers. This trend reversed in the late 1970s and the 1980s. Entrance to business schools became keenly competitive. What factors contributed to this change?

Individual Exercises

1. Have you ever been in a situation in which you experienced stress from conflicting role demands (e.g., in your roles as son or daughter, friend, church member, etc.)? Discuss why and what you did.

2. Describe and analyze a person whom you have observed experiencing role ambiguity or conflict. What did the person do? Did it work?

3. Plot the flow in university or college registration. Where are the points of stress for students? For administators or secretaries? For faculty? Recommend changes to reduce stress and conflict.

4. Drawing on the career stages described, by memory or interview discuss what a parent or grandparent was doing at each phase. How did he or she handle each transition?

5. Using the vertical scales for needs for affiliation, achievement, and power, estimate your own possible need strengths. What do your estimates suggest about the kinds of positions you would perform well in?

6. How does your current education relate to the three skill levels in management: technical, political, and conceptual? How could these skills be better developed?

7. If you were president of an organization, what kind of loyalty would you desire from your managerial subordinates? Why? What risks would you run?

8. Interview two young managers, preferably recent graduates of your school. Have them talk about their job successes and difficulties. Analyze their comments.

9. Draw up a list of five principles that might guide you in guiding your own career. Why did you select your particular list?

Managerial Cases and Problems on Managerial Careers

Edwin Mesko and Elizabeth Sternberg

Edwin Mesko. Ed was the seventh and youngest child of Gertrude and Peter Mesko. He was born and grew up in a small Western Pennsylvania mining town whose residents primarily worked in the region's coal mines. The town was deteriorating badly and had been since the end of World War II brought the decline in demand for coal. Peter Mesko had managed to work off and on, but it was a hard life.

Mesko distrusted both the mine owners and the union organizers, so he tried to work nonunion mines. Peter was very cynical about business managers and union officials who wore ties and jackets while sitting around drinking coffee and exchanging money under the table (or so he suspected).

The pay and conditions have dramatically improved in recent years, but Peter was too old really to benefit, and by then Edwin had long since left home to join the Navy.

Peter Mesko didn't have a shorter fuse to his temper than most people, but his youngest child had a way of lighting it more frequently. At home and at school, Edwin was always getting into trouble—nothing major, but every once in a while he would refuse to take directions. And Peter Mesko expected obedience to his words—or else! Sometimes his son would fight back, but usually Ed would retreat into his own world of blocks, trucks, and eventually building model airplanes and ships.

Although he had never seen an oceangoing ship, at age 17 Ed left home to join the Navy as a seaman apprentice. A bit frightened to leave home, he nonetheless enjoyed his basic training at the Great Lakes Training Station. He even found the discipline looser than at home. Ed liked his petty officer, but did receive some demerit points for making some derogative remarks under his breath about the lieutenant in charge of his division.

Ed did surprisingly well on the mathmatics aptitude test, so he was assigned to a gunnery specialty as a fire controlman (as in gunfire pointing, not fighting fires). He was eventually assigned to a warship, where his job was to maintain and operate a radar system that controlled a bank of antiaircraft rockets. Ed took great pride in his ability to keep his equipment in operating shape, and he enjoyed the comradeship of his fellow seaman at sea and in port. Because of his hard work and competence, Ed's supervisors generally left him alone, even overlooking his usually sloppy appearance and occasional overdrinking while on liberty off the ship. At age 25, Ed found himself one of the youngest first class petty officers in the Navy (see Exhibit 1 for naval ranks).

EXHIBIT 1 ━━━━━━━━━━━━━━━━━━━━━━━━━━

United States Navy Ranks

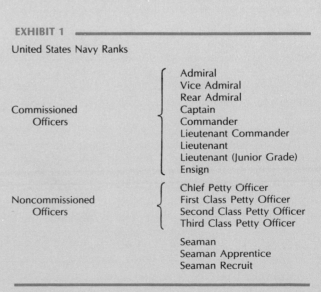

Commissioned Officers	Admiral
	Vice Admiral
	Rear Admiral
	Captain
	Commander
	Lieutenant Commander
	Lieutenant
	Lieutenant (Junior Grade)
	Ensign
Noncommissioned Officers	Chief Petty Officer
	First Class Petty Officer
	Second Class Petty Officer
	Third Class Petty Officer
	Seaman
	Seaman Apprentice
	Seaman Recruit

Ed even received a letter of commendation from the ship's commanding officer for an act of extraordinary coolness and courage. While the ship was engaged in a highline transfer at sea (e.g., exchanging personnel and mail with another ship while underway), an expected wave forced the two ships apart. Unfortunately this pulled taut the line between the ships, and the line was wrapped around a sailor's hand. The hand was almost entirely pulled off right in front of the officers on the bridge. One fainted, and the horrified commanding officer even vomited. While others were frozen in fear, Ed almost instantly climbed up to the screaming sailor and cut him loose.

Impressed with Mesko's technical skill and personal courage, the commanding officer directed the gunnery officer to talk to Ed about attending officer candidate school where in three months he could earn his commission as an ensign. The gunnery officer, Lieutenant Henderson, was a graduate of the U.S. Naval Academy and a career officer. In talking to Mesko, Henderson emphasized the honor that the Commanding Officer had done Ed in advancing the opportunity. He praised the status, prestige, and potential power to command that goes with being a commissioned officer (along with more money, nicer uniforms, and more private living quarters). Henderson was surprised when Mesko didn't immediately reply affirmatively but indicated that he wasn't sure and would have to think about it.

Elizabeth Sternberg.   Liz had always admired her parents. Of course, she argued with them from time to time, but she loved to be home, to cook and sew, and to help with her younger brothers and sisters. To her parents Liz was a model child. She never did especially well in school but never received an F, either. School social life was more important than studies to Elizabeth. Yet she was a little shy, more a group follower than a leader. Although she dated frequently, most of the boys seemed too immature for her.

Liz never planned to go to college. Her real dream was to get married and have children. However, at age 17 this seemed far off, and after high-school graduation she expected to look for a job—but not for about six months. The summer and autumn went very slowly. Many of her friends left the neighborhood; some of the boys joined the military, some traveled, others went off to college. Liz missed the excitement of the crowded halls and active conversation of high school. Finally, in November she took a clerical job in the regional office of a large insurance company.

From the beginning, Liz fitted right in. She did what she was told, was polite and willing. She thought the work was fine, but she really enjoyed the beautiful new office, so clean and neat. Even more, she liked the girl friends she made, the fun of chatting and planning bridal and baby showers. Liz found herself taking a more active role in planning these affairs than she had ever done in school.

It was her social sensitivity that prompted Liz to drop a note into the suggestion box. The office had been arranged in long straight rows and columns, all rather forbidding looking. Liz suggested that the setup be modified to several semicircles. This would facilitate communicating with the group leader located in the middle and between cooperating desks. It would also create a sense of belonging. Management subsequently introduced the arrangement, and everyone was pleased.

As time passed, Liz Sternberg's Prince Charming never appeared, so she continued working. She perfected her typing, shorthand, and telephone style so much that she received several merit raises. She was even assigned a position as office claims agent and became the first women to handle routine policyholder claims over the telephone. She was flattered by the promotion, but the job did make it more difficult to keep up with her friends in the office. Nonetheless, she enjoyed talking with policyholders, who also liked to deal with her. Everyone thought she was doing an outstanding job.

Shortly after Liz's 25th birthday last year, her mother died. At first Liz wanted to quit her job to take care of the family, but her father said it wasn't necessary and that she had her own life to live.

Last week the regional vice president called Liz into his office, praised her, and offered her a promotion to assistant office manager in charge of hiring and training all clerical employees. The position includes a private office and a salary that exceeds her father's. Liz is in a terrible quandry. She doesn't want to accept the promotion and she is considering quitting the firm.

Questions on Edwin Mesko and Elizabeth Sternberg

1. Why did Ed not immediately accept the offer to attend officer candidate school?

2. What advice would you give Ed? Why?

3. What advice would you give Ed's commanding officer? Why?

4. What did Liz want from work?

5. Why was she successful at the insurance office?

6. What is her problem with regard to the promotion? What, do you think, causes her to feel as she does?

7. What advice would you offer Liz?

8. What advice would you offer the vice president.

9. Compare and contrast Elizabeth and Edwin and the situations they confronted.

Grover Lestin (A)*

Grover Lestin is a 34-year-old banker in a large, northeastern city bank. He has come a long way from a poverty-stricken town in Virginia. At age 17 Grover left home and joined the army. He spent almost three years in the army, mainly in a variety of European posts. While in the service he completed his high school equivalency and even a couple of college correspondence courses. He liked the military and was nominated for staff sergeant shortly before he was discharged.

Upon leaving the army Grover attended Tidewater State College, a predominately black college, where he majored in business administration. He worked hard, performed well, and graduated in the top 5 percent of his class. Unfortunately, the job opportunities weren't very good, and Grover decided to apply for an army commission. He was subsequently commissioned a second lieutenant and embarked on a successful military career of eight years, leading to promotions up to captain and including a Bronze Star and Purple Heart for action in Vietnam.

Four years ago, Grover decided to leave the military and try the civilian world again. He enjoyed the army but felt that job opportunities for educated blacks had significantly improved in recent years. Besides, he had three young children to support, and he wanted to earn more money.

Grover resigned his commission and accepted a position with the Reliable Trust Company in Northeastern City. He was the first black professional ever hired by this medium-size bank, and he was to initiate a new bank activity—loans to minority enterprises who in the past had not been eligible for loans through the regular procedures.

After a two-month training program, Grover was appointed an assistant treasurer (AT) and given the title of manager of minority enterprise credit. He was assigned a modest office and a secretary who also worked for a regular loan officer. Grover was a little older than the

others at his level, but his salary seemed fair at $16,000, and he was enthusiastic.

Grover's immediate superior, Frank Swain, assistant vice president of credit, was not enthusiastic about lower credit standards for minority applicants. However, President Alfred Robbins put his weight behind the effort, and Grover was given substantial autonomy in making loans below $25,000. Indeed, the bank's advertising emphasized its awareness of its social responsibility and featured Grover on many television commercials.

During the past four years, Grover has enjoyed good relations with the bank's president. Many times Robbins has directly called him about specific problems with minority enterprises and has even solicited advice on personnel policies questions concerning black clerical employees. Several times Grover was invited to accompany the president on speaking engagements. In total, Grover has probably spent more time with the president than anyone except the senior vice presidents. And last year, his title was upgraded to assistant vice president, with a salary of $21,000.

All of this has been heavy stuff to Grover, and he feels a great sense of satisfaction (and some anxiety) when he considers how far he has come from the Virginia farm. He and his family live in a predominately white suburb, where his kids walk to school and his wife drives to the supermarket.

Nonetheless, Grover has become increasingly unhappy with his situation. He enjoys his job and autonomy, but believes that his limited responsibility curtails his ability to contribute. Last year when his title was upgraded, he requested an increase in his loan authorization authority to a level more equal to that of equally experienced regular loan officers. Frank Swain said he would look into it, but then he was transferred to the Trust Department. His replacement, Andrew Widder, has put off Grover's request because "changes are necessary in this operation—we're losing too much money."

Grover is beginning to think he has spent enough time in minority loans. He would like to transfer into the regular Loan Department or into trust or investments, where he can learn more about the banking business and prepare

---

* Part (B) of this case is contained in the *Instructor's Manual.*

EXHIBIT 1

Partial Organization Chart of Reliable Trust Company

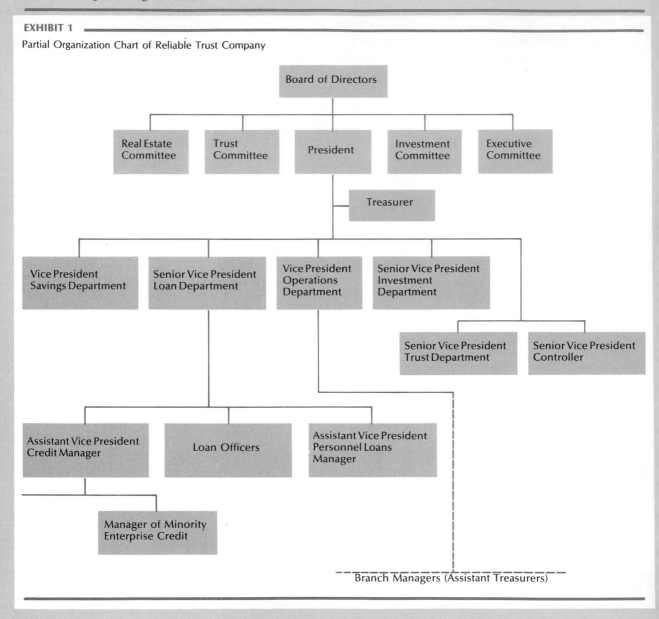

himself for future promotions. Grover has been especially upset by the fact that he has not been invited to the weekly informal training conferences conducted by the senior vice president of loans where large and interesting loans are discussed. Grover has requested a transfer through Widder, but so far nothing has happened. Recently, Grover has been experiencing severe headaches, which his physician says are psychosomatic.

Questions on Grover Lestin (A)

1. What kind of a person is Grover Lestin? How would you describe him?

2. What is Grover's problem? Why is he upset?

3. How has Grover contributed to his situation?

4. What advice would you give Grover? Why? What risk is involved?

Two Women at Trustworthy Trust

Trustworthy Trust Company is a large, multiservice bank headquartered in a metropolitan area. Its assets rank it in the top 50 banking institutions in the United States. Its main office is an imposing granite structure in the center of the financial district. The physical setting fairly reeks of stability and conservatism. Yet it has been aggressive in opening branches and courting customers. A simplified organizational chart is presented in Exhibit 1.

Judith Greene.   Judith Greene is the vice president for administration of the International Division of Trustworthy. She joined the division as a junior analyst 12 years ago right after she graduated from Eastern College with the B.S. in economics. She was one of the first women analysts at the bank and has been a hard worker and fast learner. These attributes have always characterized her from childhood, when as a single child she helped her father with the bookkeeping in his dental practice. They spent many evenings discussing sports and investments rather than dental medicine (conversation from which her mother has felt rather excluded) so Judith more naturally gravitated to economics rather than to a health care field. One of her proudest moments came in college, when her father gave her $5,000 to invest (but not spend!) in any way she desired. She still has that initial capital, which has grown considerably.

Judith has mixed feelings about her early years as an analyst. A lot of the work was boring because the tasks were routine and feedback inadequate. At times she felt like a nameless, faceless automaton, but she enjoyed the bank as an institution and initiated opportunities both inside and outside the division to talk about investments. She was very active in several professional banking and investment societies. She got along well with most of the staff, including the support personnel. (Apparently, part of the reason for this was that she did much of her own typing, something that she saw not as a status issue but as a pragmatic opportunity. Her reports would frequently be submitted while her peers were still waiting to get their's back from the typing pool.)

Judith believes that she did a better job than most analysts, but she frankly states that her break and promotion to area supervisor occurred rather fortuitously. Judith's husband, a manager for a local industrial firm, had graduated from the prestigious old Ivy University. At an alumni dance he introduced her to Marshall Wilde, with whom Mr. Greene had done business. Wilde was at that time senior vice president in the Corporation Loan Division of Trustworhty Trust. Shortly thereafter, Wilde was named executive vice president and head of the International Division. Wilde was a dynamic, flexible person interested in

EXHIBIT 1

Simplified Organization of Trustworthy Trust Company

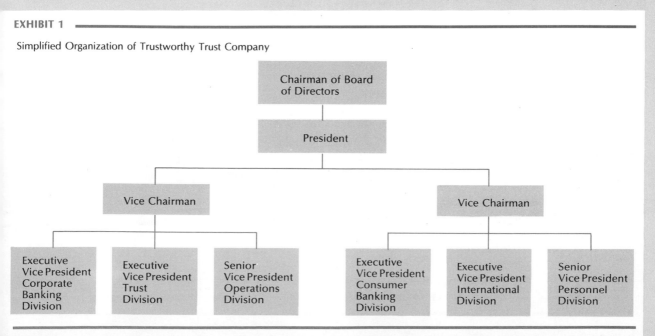

improving opportunities for minorities. Since Judith clearly had the requisite skills and performance, she was subsequently promoted to area supervisor. Although a little younger than the other supervisors, she had accepted the promotion without hesitation. Judith performed well as an area supervisor and grained insight from a number of informal conversations with Wilde.

The International Division is the smallest of the bank's five major units, but it is headed by an executive vice president, like the others. The division's structure is illustrated in Exhibit 2. The International Division is charged with maintaining correspondent relations with foreign banks, exchanging different currencies, and assisting its large corporate customers in raising funds and conducting business in foreign countries. The division annually hires four or five MBAs with special skills and experience (usually a foreign language and knowledge of a particular country). However, the executive vice president, is presently considering whether or not to hire more people right out of college rather than after graduate school. New professional employees are assigned to the analyst pool, where they write reports requested by various officers. Much of their data is gathered from the bank's extensive library,

and some from a local university. Frequently they write to foreign embassies and governments. Sometimes they request division officers to gather information on their trips. The analysts are located in a common work area called the bull pen. It is crowded, warm, and a little shabby.

After 18 months to two years, a junior analyst is normally promoted to senior analyst. This means that he or she handles more difficult assignments, but work location and process are unchanged.

The first substantial promotion comes after three to four years, when a senior analyst could become a junior officer and area supervisor. In this position the junior officer would be in charge of four or five analysts specializing in a specific country (such as France) or an area (such as Central America). The area supervisor makes decisions on relatively small transactions and consults with appropriate senior officers on major matters. Once or twice a year, a junior officer makes a three-to-five day business trip to his or her geographical area of responsibility. These trips are anticipated with much interest and excitement. The junior officers' offices are located in private rooms opening into the bull pen area. Except for the lack of windows in some, they are pleasant though small.

EXHIBIT 2

Trustworthy Trust Company: Organization of International Division

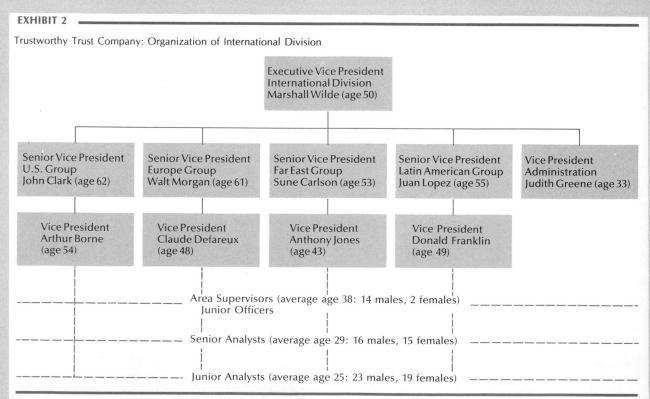

The division's senior vice presidents and vice presidents (also called senior officers) are the critical decision makers. Their offices are located in another area opening to the public elevators. The reception space and offices can only be described as impressive and luxurious—all done in co-lonial decor and Williamsburg green and with wall-to-wall carpeting. Each officer has a spacious private office and secretaries' work areas are located just outside each office door. Exhibit 3 gives the layout of the International Division.

EXHIBIT 3

Trustworthy Trust Company: Layout of International Division

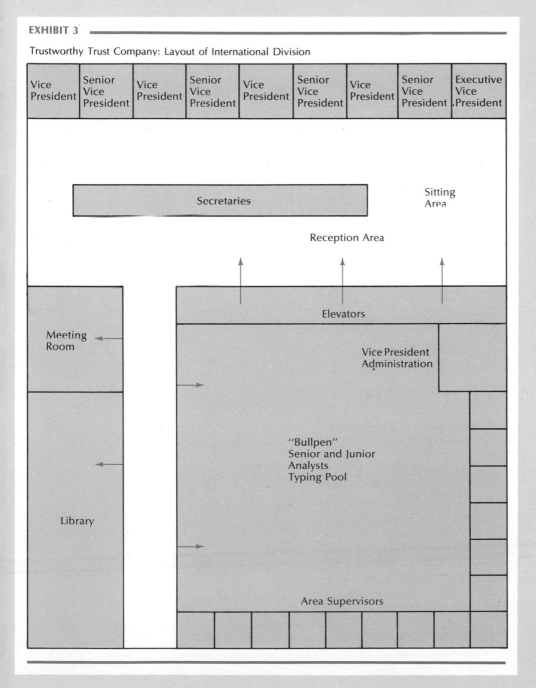

EXHIBIT 4

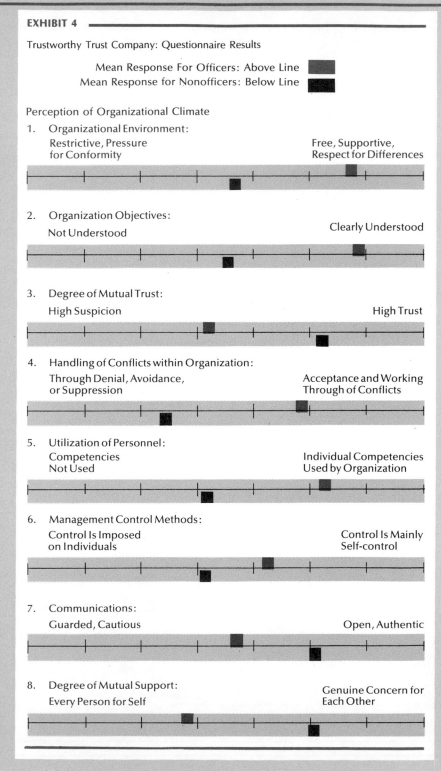

Trustworthy Trust Company: Questionnaire Results

Mean Response For Officers: Above Line

Mean Response for Nonofficers: Below Line

Perception of Organizational Climate

1. Organizational Environment:
    Restrictive, Pressure   Free, Supportive,
    for Conformity   Respect for Differences

2. Organization Objectives:
    Not Understood   Clearly Understood

3. Degree of Mutual Trust:
    High Suspicion   High Trust

4. Handling of Conflicts within Organization:
    Through Denial, Avoidance,   Acceptance and Working
    or Suppression   Through of Conflicts

5. Utilization of Personnel:
    Competencies   Individual Competencies
    Not Used   Used by Organization

6. Management Control Methods:
    Control Is Imposed   Control Is Mainly
    on Individuals   Self-control

7. Communications:
    Guarded, Cautious   Open, Authentic

8. Degree of Mutual Support:
    Every Person for Self   Genuine Concern for
                                              Each Other

EXHIBIT 4 *(concluded)*

Job Attitudes

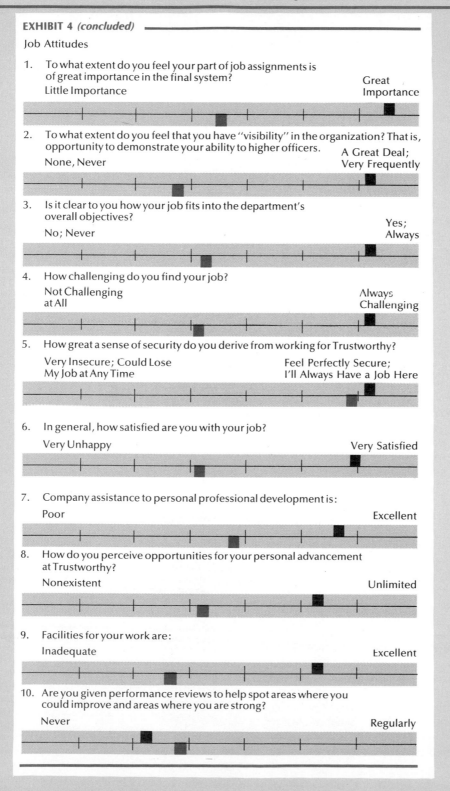

1. To what extent do you feel your part of job assignments is of great importance in the final system?

    Little Importance   Great Importance

2. To what extent do you feel that you have "visibility" in the organization? That is, opportunity to demonstrate your ability to higher officers.

    None, Never   A Great Deal; Very Frequently

3. Is it clear to you how your job fits into the department's overall objectives?

    No; Never   Yes; Always

4. How challenging do you find your job?

    Not Challenging at All   Always Challenging

5. How great a sense of security do you derive from working for Trustworthy?

    Very Insecure; Could Lose My Job at Any Time   Feel Perfectly Secure; I'll Always Have a Job Here

6. In general, how satisfied are you with your job?

    Very Unhappy   Very Satisfied

7. Company assistance to personal professional development is:

    Poor   Excellent

8. How do you perceive opportunities for your personal advancement at Trustworthy?

    Nonexistent   Unlimited

9. Facilities for your work are:

    Inadequate   Excellent

10. Are you given performance reviews to help spot areas where you could improve and areas where you are strong?

    Never   Regularly

The senior officers specialize by areas and travel frequently. Either the senior vice president or the vice president for each area is expected to be in headquarters, but actually both are often gone on trips. About half of their time is spent traveling. They frequently complain about the onerous burden of these trips.

The Trustworthy Trust Company is a successful institution, and the International Division enjoys a high reputation. Nonetheless, the executive vice president has been concerned about the younger employees. More than half of them leave the bank after 18 to 30 months. Most join smaller banks; some get married and have children; and some just drop out, throw their watches away, and move around. Exit interviews produce complaints about being bored, the lousy working conditions, the crisis atmosphere, being hemmed in and not knowing what's going on or what happens to their reports. A consultant was called in and administered a questionnaire to all divisional professionals and managers. The results are summarized in Exhibits 4 and 5. No significant differences between male and female responses were evident within any position category.

In addition, the consultant conducted some training sessions for the senior officers, which covered such topics as human needs, the meaning of work, motivation, and the generation gap. Unfortunately, several of the senior vice presidents and vice presidents did not attend all the meetings. Some who did attend took strong exception to the consultant's view on people's needs for autonomy, competence, and achievement. A couple of senior officers seemed to sleep through the sessions.

Wilde has now promoted Judith to the newly created position of vice president of administration. He has not given an explicit job description for the new position, but he sees it as dealing with the apparently low morale among analysts and the poor administration of support staff activities. Judith appears to be very enthusiastic and optimistic about the opportunities in the new post.

Heather Campbell. In additon to his position as Executive Vice President-International Division, for the past six months, Marshall Wilde has served as vice chair of the board of directors of the Trustworthy Bank. As vice chair, he oversees several divisions (including International). One of those divisions is Personnel. Wilde has been very disappointed with Atkins Lawrence, the vice president of personnel. Wilde disliked Lawrence personally and disapproved of his passivity. Personnel just wasn't respected in the bank, and Lawrence was dismissed (as Wilde put it privately) for being "an immaculately suited

---

EXHIBIT 5

Comments by Analysts

Sample of answers to question: "What Is the Most Dissatisfying Aspect of Your Job?"

1. The detail work involved and the constant phone calls from branches for foreign exchange rates. These jobs could be done by a clerk.
2. Being involved with clerical work, such as typing and being taken for granted.
3. Lack of knowledge as to where my job will lead.
4. The close-mined, narrowness of most of senior management that leads to pettiness, lack of communication, and the lack of a more democratic environment.
5. Lack of contact with people outside the bank. Lack of physical activity.
6. Lack of experience causes me to waste too much time.
7. Lack of sufficient time for free thinking.
8. The physical working conditions are intolerable in that there is too little space, no privacy, and a very high noise level.
9. The remuneration—the salary structure is such that it presents an unoptimistic future. If one would desire to stay, you would be passing up a great deal of financial reward. In order to financially succeed in banking, one must transfer to another bank to receive financial remuneration.

Sample of answers to question: "What Is the Most Satisfying Aspect of Work?"

1. Learning something new every day and the mental challenge that is intellectually stimulating.
2. The opportunity to pursue a field of great interest to me in a personal and flexible manner. The ability to interact in the decision-making process on a high level.
3. High degree of responsibility and independence to perform assignments which have to be supervised at every turn.
4. To do my own thinking and have others rely on my judgment.
5. The actual dealing aspect of the job. Being able to be of real assistance to customers by giving them accurate information and proper guidance.
6. When a given project is completed and done well which in turn receives recognition. Helping customers with problems.
7. Customer satisfaction.
8. The international aspect—keeping apprised of the political and economic situation in other countries, working with other languages. Second, learning something about finance and accounting. Third, the sources of information available—the department library, our training sessions, seminars outside the bank, etc.
9. Those few brief moments of loveliness when one is totally responsible for one's actions. . . . Those few brief moments of group interaction where people take an idea and move ahead with it, rather than get bogged down by personality considerations, biases, or insecurities in new prospectives.

---

social snob and intellectual lightweight." About the only thing Lawrence had done well was to maintain links with the prestige colleges from which Trustworthy usually recruited young analysts.

Wilde recently announced the appointment of Dr. Heather Campbell as vice president of personnel. Following is the text of the bulletin from Wilde announcing her appointment:

OFFICIAL STAFF APPOINTMENT

I am pleased to announce the appointment of Heather Campbell as Vice President in charge of our Personnel Division.

At the present time, Dr. Campbell is head of Heather Campbell Associates, a consulting firm dealing primarily with personnel matters and specializing in affirmative action.

From 1961 until 1974, she was chief psychologist and research director for Attitude Survey Corporation in Boston, where her responsibilities included motivational and attitudinal studies and the development of training programs for the firm's corporate and institutional clients.

Dr. Campbell is a graduate of Radcliffe College and holds a master's degree as well as a Ph.D in Social Psychology from Columbia University. She has lectured widely and written on such subjects as personnel administration, education and training, affirmative action, and corporate responsibility.

Dr. Campbell will join us at the end of the month. Under her leadership, our Personnel Division expects to give first priority to improving the use of our human resources. She will give special attention to such functions as recruiting and selection of personnel, education and training programs, counseling and grievance procedures, career planning, staff communications, and affirmative action.

Shortly before she began her new post, Campbell described her intentions:

For the past eight years, I've been running my own consulting firm because my children needed me and I wanted the flexibility of setting my own hours. Now, however, I'm ready to assume direction of the personnel function in a major institution. And I'm excited about the possibilities. My objectives will be roughly as follows: (1) To establish my personal control over the personnel function by evaluating all activities and key personnel. I understand many of the people are rather weak. A number of replacements will probably be necessary. (2) To demonstrate to the bank that the Personnel Division has importance and clout. Too many Divisions have been ignoring Personnel and going their own way on recruiting and training. (3) To improve the opportunities for women and minorities. My appointment can be a symbolic communication to certain bank officers that their blatant discrimination must be ended.

In his new office as Executive Director of the Metropolitan Y.M.C.A., Atkins Lawrence commented on the problems Campbell will face:

I'm sure Dr. Campbell is a competent person, but she had better not be too ambitious. Trustworthy is a conservative organization—and is correct in being so. It was built by tending to the investment needs of the old families of this city. This go-go New York banking will alienate those people. We, excuse me, the bank needs distinguished appearing men who inspire confidence. Experience is the best teacher in banking, so there are no short cuts to instantly make men (or women for that matter) into competent bankers.

And banking needs independent go-getters. You just can't impose a lot of central rules on everyone without hurting performance. I was never offended when a hard-charging department head hired his own people or set up his own training. My job was to provide help when needed. Besides, the president would never have backed me up if I had complained. Well, I wish Campbell luck. She'll need it. As for me, I'm really enjoying this new position. It gives me the opportunity to help some wonderful young people.

Questions on Two Women at Trustworthy Trust

1. What are the motivational problems in the International Division? What are the causes?

2. What problems may Judith Greene confront in her new position as vice president for administration in the International Division? Why?

3. What recommendations would you offer Greene?

4. What problems may Heather Campbell confront in her new position as vice president of Personnel Division for the bank? Why?

5. What recommendations would you offer Campbell?

6. What recommendations would you offer Vice Chair and Executive Vice President Marshall Wilde?

Case Index

Organization Index

Name Index

A

Abbey, A., 528
Abeggleu, J. C., 13
Acheson, D., 152, 159
Achison, T., 254, 257
Ackerman, L. S., 554
Ackoff, R. L., 279, 281
Acton, L., 55
Acuff, F. L., 594
Adam, 58
Adams, J. S., 104, 173
Adams, T. F. M., 173
Adizes, I., 448
Adler, A., 45
Adorno, T. W., 225
Aiken, M., 445, 526, 527
Ajiferuke, M., 250
Akers, R. L., 52
Albanese, R., 205, 509
Albrecht, K., 656
Aldag, R., 446
Alderfer, C. P., 53, 54
Alderson, W., 280
Aldia, O., 223
Aldrich, H., 445, 446, 594
Alexander, C. N., 141
Alexander, T., 279, 525
Alexander the Great, 195
Alger, H., 381, 383
Algrist, S., 655
Allen, L. A., 426
Allen, S. A., III, 447
Allison, G. T., 159
Allport, G. W., 569
Almquist, E., 655
Alpander, G. G., 250
Alutto, J. A., 650, 654, 684
Alvares, K., 248
Anatol, K. W. E., 205
Andele, V., 204

Anderson, C., 280
Anderson, C. W., 568
Anderson, H. H., 525
Anderson, L. R., 158
Anderson, T. R., 401
Anderson, W., 308, 310
Andrews, F. M., 526
Andrews, K. R., 279, 304, 553, 686
Ansbacher, H. L., 54
Ansbacher, R. R., 54
Ansher, M., 281, 446
Anslow, A., 115
Ansoff, H. O., 159, 281
Anthony, R. N., 320
Appelbaum, R. L., 205
Aram, J. D., 593
Arendt, H., 204
Argyle, M., 142
Argyris, C., 30, 108, 343, 553, 554
Armbruster, F. E., 108
Arndt, W. B., Jr., 635
Arnold, J. D., 555
Aronoff, C., 14
Aronson, E., 656
Arpan, J., 249
Arrow, K. J., 682
Arvey, R. D., 108, 203, 682
As, D., 250
Asch, S. E., 592
Ashby, W. R., 320, 426
Ashour, A. S., 248
Assael, H., 567
Athanassides, G. C., 482
Athos, A. G., 570, 682
Atkins, B., 343
Atkinson, J. W., 104, 203
Aubert, V., 568
Aufhauser, R. K., 204

B

Bacherach, S. B., 526, 593, 594
Back, K., 142, 553
Baker, J. C., 76
Bales, R. F., 160, 173
Bandura, A., 52
Baram, M. S., 685
Bard, M., 552
Bardwick, J., 636
Barnard, C. I., 52, 104, 204, 403, 426
Barrett, G. V., 249
Barrett, M. E., 344
Bartlett, A. C., 556
Bartol, K. M., 228
Barton, R., 358
Bass, B. M., 249, 687
Bassett, G. A., 358
Bates, F. L., 445, 654
Bates, P. B., 635
Batten, J. D., 358
Bauer, R. A., 304
Baumhart, R., 670, 672
Bavelas, A., 247, 445
Baxter, G. W., Jr., 594
Beak, J., 528
Beatty, R. W., 228
Beck, A. C., 358
Becker, H. S., 30
Beckhard, R., 457, 554
Bedeian, A. G., 31, 320
Beer, M., 359, 554
Beer, S., 159
Behling, O., 73, 203
Belasco, J. A., 684
Bell, C. H., Jr., 554
Bell, G. D., 402
Bem, D. J., 158
Bendix, R., 204, 250, 402, 403
Benedict, R., 30, 56
Bengston, V. L., 636

Subject Index

This book has been set CAP, in 10 and 9 point Optima, leaded 2 points. Part numbers are 60 point Optima Bold and part titles are 30 point Optima Bold. Chapter numbers are 48 point Optima Bold and chapter titles are 24 point Optima Bold. The size of the type page is 39 by 48 picas.

Management

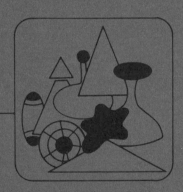